# Living Sociologically

# Living Sociologically
## CONCEPTS AND CONNECTIONS

### SECOND EDITION

Ronald N. Jacobs

Eleanor Townsley

OXFORD
UNIVERSITY PRESS

# OXFORD
## UNIVERSITY PRESS

Oxford University Press is a department of the University of Oxford.
It furthers the University's objective of excellence in research, scholarship,
and education by publishing worldwide. Oxford is a registered trade mark
of Oxford University Press in the UK and in certain other countries.

Published in the United States of America by Oxford University Press
198 Madison Avenue, New York, NY 10016, United States of America.

© 2026, 2022, 2020 by Oxford University Press

For titles covered by Section 112 of the US Higher Education Opportunity Act, please visit www.oup.com/us/he for the latest information about pricing and alternate formats.

All rights reserved. No part of this publication may be reproduced, stored
in a retrieval system, transmitted, used for text and data mining, or used
for training artificial intelligence, in any form or by any means, without
the prior permission in writing of Oxford University Press, or as expressly
permitted by law, by license or under terms agreed with the appropriate
reprographics rights organization. Inquiries concerning reproduction
outside the scope of the above should be sent to the Rights Department,
Oxford University Press, at the address above.

You must not circulate this work in any other form
and you must impose this same condition on any acquirer

Library of Congress Control Number: 2024925876

ISBN 978-0-19-775543-3

Printed and bound in Marquis, Canada

# Brief Contents

Preface  xix

## PART I  THE BASICS  1

1  What Is Sociology?  3
2  American Sociology: Theory and Methods  27

## PART II  STRUCTURE AND CONTROL  67

3  Culture  69
4  Socialization, Social Interaction, and Group Life  105
5  Deviance, Crime, and Punishment  137

## PART III  DIFFERENCE AND INEQUALITY  171

6  Inequality, Mobility, and Social Change  173
7  Race, Ethnicity, and Immigration  209
8  Gender, Sexuality, and the Body  255

## PART IV  INSTITUTIONS AND ISSUES  293

9  Marriage, Family, and the Law  295
10  Science, Religion, and Knowing  329
11  Education, Work, and Recreation  373
12  Health, Illness, and Medicine  413
13  Politics, Economy, and Social Movements  449
14  Media and Technology  489

## PART V  CHANGE, ISSUES, AND THE FUTURE  523

15  Climate Change and Sustainability  525

Glossary  560
References  575
Credits  631
Index  635

# Contents

Preface xix

## PART I  THE BASICS  1

### CHAPTER 1  What Is Sociology?  3

**What Is Sociology?**  5
⬅ CAREERS: Opportunities for Sociology Majors  6
   The Sociological Imagination  7
   The Discipline of Sociology  8
   Sociology and Everyday Knowledge  10

**Levels of Analysis**  11
   Microsociology  12
   Macrosociology  14
   Institutional Perspectives  15

**Thinking Relationally: The Paired Concepts**  16
   Solidarity and Conflict  16
   Power and Resistance  17
   Inequality and Privilege  18
   Global and Local  19
   Structure and Contingency  20

**Why Sociology?**  21

### CHAPTER 2  American Sociology: Theory and Methods  27

**Thinking Like a Sociologist**  28
   Critical Questions and the Sociological Imagination  28
⬅ METHODS AND INTERPRETATION: Measuring the Effect of Education on Earnings  29

**Sociology: Theory and Contexts**  30
⬅ CAREERS: The Importance of Theory  31
   Classical Sociology  31
   The European Canon  33

Sociology in America 38
Moving Away from Grand Theories 41
Theories about Difference 41
The Cultural Turn 43
Global Context 43
Sociology Today 44

## Social Research: Purpose and Process 44
Social Research and Ethics 45
Research Methods and Critical Literacy 47
Data and Measurement 49
Variables, Data Collection, and Causal Relationships 51
Common Strategies for Sociological Research 54
Basic, Applied, and Public Sociology 57
◄ CASE STUDY: Understanding COVID-19 59

## PAIRED CONCEPTS 37
■ INEQUALITY AND PRIVILEGE: Forgotten Founders in Sociology 37
■ POWER AND RESISTANCE: Protecting Human Subjects in Social Research 46
■ GLOBAL AND LOCAL: Citizen Science: Using Local Data to Understand Global Patterns 48
■ SOLIDARITY AND CONFLICT: Race, Difference, and the Politics of Medical Research 56
■ STRUCTURE AND CONTINGENCY: The Baby Einstein Phenomenon 58

# PART II  STRUCTURE AND CONTROL  67

### CHAPTER 3  Culture  69

## How Do Sociologists Study Culture? 70
What Is Culture? 70
Ideal Culture and Material Culture 72
◄ METHODS AND INTERPRETATION: How to Measure What People Think 72

## Culture and Power 77
Cultural Power 77
Recognizing and Resisting Cultural Power 83

## Types of Culture in Today's World 86
Global Culture 86
Dominant Cultures and Subcultures 89
Popular Culture, Commercial Culture, and High Culture 93
▶ CAREERS: Working in the Creative Industries 95
▶ CASE STUDY: Protesting the National Anthem 99

## PAIRED CONCEPTS 82
■ STRUCTURE AND CONTINGENCY: *The Protocols of the Elders of Zion* 82
■ GLOBAL AND LOCAL: The History of Manga 90
■ SOLIDARITY AND CONFLICT: Music and Social Protest 92
■ POWER AND RESISTANCE: Fanfiction 97
■ INEQUALITY AND PRIVILEGE: Who Goes to the Museum and the Opera? 98

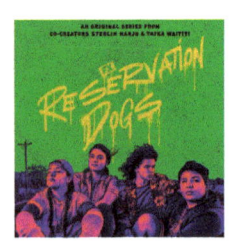

# CHAPTER 4  Socialization, Social Interaction, and Group Life 105

## Socialization and Selfhood 106
Nature and Nurture 106
The Social Self 107
Agents of Socialization 109
Adult Socialization 112

## Interaction and the Social Construction of Reality 116
Status and Role 116
▶ METHODS AND INTERPRETATION: Life-Course Research on Socialization 117
Performance and the Social Self 119
Social Interaction in a Digital Age 120

## Group Life 122
Group Size 122
Primary Groups and Secondary Groups 123
Reference Groups 125
Bureaucracy in Group Life 126
Social Networks in Group Life 129

- CAREERS: Getting a Job: The Strength of Weak Ties  129
- CASE STUDY: Becoming "The Rock"  131

### PAIRED CONCEPTS  115
- INEQUALITY AND PRIVILEGE: Different Styles of Parenting  115
- STRUCTURE AND CONTINGENCY: What Is the Meaning of Fair Play? The 2012 Olympic Badminton Controversy  118
- POWER AND RESISTANCE: Challenging Gender Norms during the 2022 Iranian Protests  121
- SOLIDARITY AND CONFLICT: The Stanford Prison Experiment  124
- GLOBAL AND LOCAL: Bureaucracy in Singapore  127

## CHAPTER 5  Deviance, Crime, and Punishment  137

### Deviance  138
Why Does Deviance Exist?  140
The Social Construction of Deviance  145

### Crime  150
- CAREERS: The Criminal Justice Field  151
Categories of Crime  152
- METHODS AND INTERPRETATION: Measuring the Crime Rate  154
Policing Crime  156
Surveillance  160

### Punishment  160
Punishment as a Public Display of Morality  161
Punishment and Treatment  162
Incarceration  162
- CASE STUDY: Why Are Crime Stories So Popular?  166

### PAIRED CONCEPTS  139
- STRUCTURE AND CONTINGENCY: Is Chewing Gum Deviant?  139
- SOLIDARITY AND CONFLICT: The Moral Panic over Hoarding  141
- POWER AND RESISTANCE: What's Wrong with Graffiti?  144
- GLOBAL AND LOCAL: The Global Drug Trade  157
- INEQUALITY AND PRIVILEGE: Punishment and Plea-Bargaining  163

## PART III  DIFFERENCE AND INEQUALITY  171

### CHAPTER 6  Inequality, Mobility, and Social Change  173

**What Is Inequality?**  175
  Is Inequality Natural or Social?  175
  Is Inequality Good or Bad?  175
  Inequality and Stratification  177

**Types of Stratification**  177
  Caste Systems  178
  Class Systems  180
  Status Systems  181
  Party Systems: Inequality through Meritocracy  182

**A Portrait of Stratification Today**  184
  Stratification in the United States  184
  Global Stratification  189

**Social Mobility**  192
  Social Factors Associated with Mobility  193
  ⬅ METHODS AND INTERPRETATION: Measuring Status Attainment and Social Mobility  194
  Structural Mobility  196
  ⬅ CAREERS: Social Mobility and Career Planning  197

**Social Change and the Attempt to Create More Equality**  198
  Social Policy  199
  Social Conflict  201
  ⬅ CASE STUDY: *The Bachelor*: Crystallizing Stratification on TV  202

**PAIRED CONCEPTS**  179
  ▪ POWER AND RESISTANCE: Ending Apartheid in South Africa  179
  ▪ INEQUALITY AND PRIVILEGE: Marketing to the Super-Rich  183
  ▪ GLOBAL AND LOCAL: Wealthy Chinese Students at Elite US Schools  191
  ▪ STRUCTURE AND CONTINGENCY: Creating Social Security  199
  ▪ SOLIDARITY AND CONFLICT: A Short History of the Workers' Strike in the United States  200

## CHAPTER 7  Race, Ethnicity, and Immigration  209

### The Social Construction of Race  211
Race and Biology  211
The Changing Understanding of Race over Time  212
Race and Ethnicity  214

### Racial and Ethnic Groups in the United States  214
METHODS AND INTERPRETATION: Defining and Measuring Race in Official Government Data  216
Native American People  217
White People  219
Black or African American People  220
Hispanic or Latino People  223
Asian American People  226

### Race, Privilege, and Inequality  227
The Privileges of Being in the Majority Group  228
Racial Discrimination and Segregation  229
Consequences of Discrimination  231
Racial Conflict  232

### Multiculturalism and Diversity  236
Multiculturalism (Movement and Policy)  236
Multiracial and Multiethnic Identities  237
CAREERS: Multiculturalism in the Workplace  238

### Immigration  239
Trends in Immigration  240
What Causes Immigration?  241
Immigrant Communities  242

### The Politics of Immigration  245
Laws about Citizenship and Immigration  245
Anti-Immigrant Movements  246
CASE STUDY: Intersecting Identities  248

### PAIRED CONCEPTS  219
STRUCTURE AND CONTINGENCY: The Growth and Success of Native American Casinos  219
SOLIDARITY AND CONFLICT: W. E. B. Du Bois, Booker T. Washington, and the Struggle to Define Black Politics  222

xii CONTENTS

■ GLOBAL AND LOCAL: Latino Computer Engineers from Colombia and Puerto Rico 225
■ INEQUALITY AND PRIVILEGE: How Irish Americans Became White 229
■ POWER AND RESISTANCE: Black Lives Matter 235

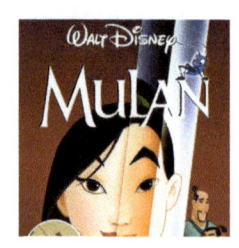

## CHAPTER 8  Gender, Sexuality, and the Body 255

### Sex, Gender, and the Body 256
Gender Socialization and Gender Performance 258
Gender Stereotypes 260
➡ CAREERS: Women, Men, and Social Networks 262
➡ METHODS AND INTERPRETATION: Gender Bias in Social Research 262

### Gender and Power 264
Masculinity and Femininity and the Gender Order 265
Divisions of Labor 268
Workplace Harassment and Sexual Exclusions in Work and Public Spaces 272
Challenging Patriarchy and the History of the Women's Movement 275

### Sexuality and the Body 278
The Marketing of Romance 278
Heteronormativity 281
Queer Identities beyond the Closet 283
➡ CASE STUDY: Gender Intersections at McDonald's 285

### PAIRED CONCEPTS 259
■ STRUCTURE AND CONTINGENCY: Classifying Intersex Babies 259
■ INEQUALITY AND PRIVILEGE: Men in Pink-Collar Work 273
■ SOLIDARITY AND CONFLICT: Feminist Politics 277
■ GLOBAL AND LOCAL: Sex Work 280
■ POWER AND RESISTANCE: Stonewall 284

# PART IV  INSTITUTIONS AND ISSUES 293

## CHAPTER 9  Marriage, Family, and the Law 295

### Family and Society 296
Family, Kinship, and Society 297

◀ CAREERS: **Marriage and Family Therapists** 300
Marriage and Family as Social Institutions 301
◀ METHODS AND INTERPRETATION: **The Debate about Birth Order Effects** 302

### Changes in Marriage and Family 305
Traditional Families and Nuclear Families 305
Divorce 307
Single-Parent Families 309
Delay and Decline of Marriage 311
Boomerang Kids and Sandwich Parents 314
Transnational Families 315

### Challenging Family Forms 318
Feminist Challenges to the Family 318
Blended Families 319
Multiracial Families 320
Lesbian and Gay Families 321
◀ CASE STUDY: **Family Names** 324

### PAIRED CONCEPTS 303
■ INEQUALITY AND PRIVILEGE: **Legal Biases in Favor of Marriage** 303
■ SOLIDARITY AND CONFLICT: **Disagreements over Parenting Styles** 308
■ STRUCTURE AND CONTINGENCY: **"Bird-Nesting" as a Co-Parenting Strategy after Divorce** 313
■ GLOBAL AND LOCAL: **Korean "Wild Geese" Families** 316
■ POWER AND RESISTANCE: *Loving v. Virginia* 322

## CHAPTER 10  Science, Religion, and Knowing 329

### Religion and Science as Ways of Knowing the World 331
Religious Cosmologies 332
Scientific Cosmologies 333

### Religion as a Social Institution 336
◀ METHODS AND INTERPRETATION: **Measuring Religious Commitment** 337
Elements of Religious Institutions 338
The Major Religions and Their Global Impact 340

### Modern Society and Secularism 347
The Secularization Thesis 348
The Persistence of Religion 350
Religion and Politics 352

### Science as a Social Institution 356
◀ CAREERS: Women's Careers in STEM 357
The Sociology of Science 358
Science and Technology Studies 361

### The Crisis of Knowing, and the Importance of Belief 363
Epistemological Doubts 363
Can Science and Religion Coexist? 364
◀ CASE STUDY: Debating Evolution in Public Schools 365

### PAIRED CONCEPTS 334
■ POWER AND RESISTANCE: Galileo, Darwin, and the Church 334
■ GLOBAL AND LOCAL: Catholicism in Africa 345
■ SOLIDARITY AND CONFLICT: Religious Proselytizing 353
■ INEQUALITY AND PRIVILEGE: Science and the Matthew Effect 359
■ STRUCTURE AND CONTINGENCY: The Invention of Velcro 362

## CHAPTER 11   Education, Work, and Recreation 373

### What Is Education for? 375
Literacy, Socialization, Citizenship, and Job Training 375
Social Sorting, Social Reproduction, and Social Mobility 380
Childcare and Employment 381

### Going to School 382
Types of Schools 382
Teaching, Learning, and Assessment 387
◀ METHODS AND INTERPRETATION: Measuring Learning Outcomes and Teaching Effectiveness 392
Making Friends and Building Networks 394

### Work, Jobs, and Satisfaction 398
Power, Privilege, and Inequality in the Workplace 399
The Sociology of Job Satisfaction 400

⬅ CAREERS: The Uberization of the Economy  405
⬅ CASE STUDY: What Kind of Education Do People Need in Today's Economy?  407

## PAIRED CONCEPTS  389

- SOLIDARITY AND CONFLICT: The Fight over Campus Speech Codes  389
- GLOBAL AND LOCAL: The Spread of Singapore Math  393
- INEQUALITY AND PRIVILEGE: How Elite Students Get Elite Jobs  397
- POWER AND RESISTANCE: The #MeToo Movement  401
- STRUCTURE AND CONTINGENCY: How Indoor Cycling Became a Multi-Billion-Dollar Industry  404

## CHAPTER 12  Health, Illness, and Medicine  413

### Health  415
Geography, Class, Race, Gender, Age, and Other Differences  415
Genetics  416
Environment  417
⬅ METHODS AND INTERPRETATION: Race-Based Medicine  418
An Intersectional Understanding of Health Disparities  419

### Illness  421
Experiencing Illness Differently  422
Being a Patient  423
Medicalization  428

### Medicine  430
Public Health  431
Medical Institutions  433
Social Responses to Sickness and Illness  434
⬅ CAREERS: Sociology and Medicine  435
Access to Health Care  440
⬅ CASE STUDY: Genetic Testing  442

## PAIRED CONCEPTS  420

- INEQUALITY AND PRIVILEGE: How Inequality Shapes Our Final Years  420
- POWER AND RESISTANCE: Stigma and Size  427
- SOLIDARITY AND CONFLICT: Disruptive Behavior in Medical Settings  436
- GLOBAL AND LOCAL: Does Modern Society Make You Sick?  437
- STRUCTURE AND CONTINGENCY: Waiting for an Organ Transplant  439

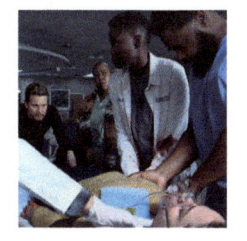

## CHAPTER 13  Politics, Economy, and Social Movements  449

### Politics as the Struggle for Influence  451
Power, Authority, and Hegemony  452

### Politics and Democracy  454
Systems of Representation  456
Representing the People  458

### Politics and the Economy  461
Political Economy  462
The Power Elite  462
Geopolitics, Colonialism, and International Trade  464

### Historical Changes in the Economy  466
The Transition to Capitalism  467
Post-Industrialism and the Changing Nature of the Economy  469
**METHODS AND INTERPRETATION:** Measuring the Unemployment Rate  470
Economic Crisis and Insecurity in an Age of Globalization  471

### Social Change  472
Challenging the Powerful  473
**CAREERS:** Sociology and Politics  475
Organizing and Mobilizing for Change  475
Getting Noticed  478
Movement Success  480
**CASE STUDY:** The Strange History of the US Electoral College  482

### PAIRED CONCEPTS  454
■ POWER AND RESISTANCE: Public Protests in Tunisia  454
■ INEQUALITY AND PRIVILEGE: Who Gets Elected to the US Senate?  456
■ SOLIDARITY AND CONFLICT: Push Polls and the Politics of Division  459
■ STRUCTURE AND CONTINGENCY: Haiti and the French Revolution  465
■ GLOBAL AND LOCAL: The Creation of Greenpeace  476

## CHAPTER 14   Media and Technology   489

### Technology and Society   491
Salvation or Apocalypse: Competing Frameworks for Understanding Technology   491
The Paradox of Convenience   492

### Economic Dimensions of Media and Technology   495
Wealth   495
Inequality   496
Jobs   499
↠ CAREERS: New Job Titles in the Age of Artificial Intelligence   500

### Media, Technology, and Politics   502
Media and Agenda-Setting   503
Economic Distortions of the Media Agenda   504
↠ METHODS AND INTERPRETATION: Does Concentration of Media Ownership Matter?   505
Filter Bubbles, Algorithms, and Social Polarization   506
Voice and Engagement among Marginalized Groups   508

### Media, Technology, and Social Relationships   511
Benefits of Mediated Relationships   511
Social Harms of Mediated Relationships   513
↠ CASE STUDY: The Rise and Fall of FTX   516

### PAIRED CONCEPTS   493
■ STRUCTURE AND CONTINGENCY: Doomsday Scenarios for Artificial Intelligence   493
■ INEQUALITY AND PRIVILEGE: What Happens When Google Moves into Town   497
■ POWER AND RESISTANCE: The Battle over Privacy   507
■ GLOBAL AND LOCAL: BTS Army: Global Fandoms and National Elections   509
■ SOLIDARITY AND CONFLICT: Social Media and Cancel Culture   514

# PART V CHANGE, ISSUES, AND THE FUTURE 523

## CHAPTER 15 Climate Change and Sustainability 525

### Climate Change and the "Risk Society" 527
The Unequal Distribution of Environmental Risk 528

### Structural Factors Contributing to Environmental Risk 531
Demography and Population Growth 532
Urbanization 533
METHODS AND INTERPRETATION: How to Measure Urban Sprawl 535
Industrialization, Global Capitalism, and the Treadmill of Production 536

### Controlling the Narrative: Denial and Expertise 538
Culture, the Media, and Socialization 540
Science and Religion 541

### Profit, Politics, and the Environment 542
Renewable Energy 543
Corporate Social Responsibility 543
CAREERS: Job Prospects in the Green Economy 545

### Sustainability: Promise and Responsibility 546
Making Wastefulness Deviant 547
The Free-Rider Problem 551
CASE STUDY: The Destruction of the Amazon 553

### PAIRED CONCEPTS 530
- STRUCTURE AND CONTINGENCY: COVID-19 and Air Pollution 530
- INEQUALITY AND PRIVILEGE: Contaminated Water in Flint, Michigan 538
- POWER AND RESISTANCE: The Dakota Access Pipeline Protests 544
- SOLIDARITY AND CONFLICT: The Battle for Yellowstone 548
- GLOBAL AND LOCAL: The Causes and Consequences of Transboundary Water Pollution 552

Glossary 560
References 575
Credits 631
Index 635

# Preface

## Why Did We Write This Book?

Our students already live sociologically. They are drawn to topics of urgent sociological concern—race, class, gender, family, popular culture, health, and crime—by a need to understand the forces that shape their world, as well as a desire to change that world for the better. Yet they do not always find it easy to connect sociological concepts with real-world applications. Helping students make that connection is what we have sought to do with *Living Sociologically: Concepts and Connections*, Second Edition. The task was made more urgent by the extraordinary events of 2020, and the aftermath of those events that unfolded as we created the second version. Alongside our students—metaphorically, as we all became remote teachers and learners—we witnessed and sought to make sense of the protests and uprisings after the murder of George Floyd; the economic devastation and medical challenges of COVID-19; and the fear, misinformation, and rage leading up to (and falling out from) the 2020 US presidential election. Sociology gives us both structure and vocabulary to analyze these events—to search together for not just meaning but resolution.

Students naturally want to know how the study of sociology can inform their career and professional choices. Throughout this textbook, we illustrate not only the ways in which sociologists live their profession but also the rich and surprising ways in which sociological theories inform parenting and romantic relationships, political commitments, economic decisions, cultural expressions, and religious beliefs. Living sociologically is not only interesting—it's *useful*. Sociology provides not only big ideas to understand social life but also concrete tools for acting in the world with purpose and meaning. Sociology helps connect the individual level with the system level, revealing a layer of reality that is not always immediately obvious. We wrote *Living Sociologically* because we wanted a teaching resource that was grounded in the sociological tradition but also offered a more contemporary and practical approach to the discipline. By the end of the Introduction to Sociology course, our hope is that students will be critical rather than cynical, empirically committed rather than scientifically or politically dogmatic, and attuned to social relationships as well as individual stories.

# Relational Thinking

*Living Sociologically* offers a new formula to help students develop the relational thinking that is at the core of the sociological project. Five paired concepts structure the book and appear in every chapter, through extended case studies, compelling box features, and active learning exercises. The paired concepts aim to sensitize students to the idea that social things *always exist in relationship to other things*.

- *Inequality* does not exist without *privilege* that accrues to those who benefit from the disadvantage of other people. How particular relationships between inequality and privilege are organized through institutions, cultural norms, and patterns of behavior is a sociological question.
- *Structure* is inextricably linked to *contingency*. Critical sociological thinking means staying alert to unexpected contingencies that might disrupt the main social pattern.
- All *global* things occur in *local* contexts. Thinking across levels of scale is a fundamental sociological competence.
- There is no "us" without "them"; or, to put it sociologically, there is no *solidarity* that does not contain the possibility of *conflict* with those beyond the group boundary.
- Every act of *power* contains possibilities for *resistance* and social change when people say no and choose to follow another path of action.

We offer the paired concepts to help students get started with sociological thinking. But relational thinking does not stop there. Examples multiply quickly, and students are good at identifying them. All categorical identities, for example, exist in relation to other identities. In fact, they presume them. The category "women" presumes "men," binary gender identities presume more fluid nonbinary gender identities, Black presumes white, racial presumes multiracial, dominated presumes dominant, wealthy presumes poor. None of these categories is essential or necessary; rather, they are historically developed social institutions. *Living Sociologically* fosters a practical, comparative, critical awareness that social arrangements have a history, are made by people, and could be organized differently.

To illustrate this change, in this second edition we follow the new AP style for race categories in public writing. The AP now capitalizes "Black" as it conveys "an essential and shared sense of history, identity, and community among people who identify as Black" (Associated Press 2020). They use lower case for "white," as the category is less distinct. The AP states: "capitalizing the term white, as is done by white supremacists, risks subtly conveying legitimacy to such beliefs."

## Intersectionality and Critical Social Literacies

Social relationships intersect in multiple and complex ways. More than ever before, students today recognize that they are positioned in overlapping relationships of privilege, solidarity, and power—relationships that are structured locally and globally. Thinking in relational terms helps students not only think intersectionally but also link their individual experiences to the operation of multiple systems of oppression. *Living Sociologically* offers abundant opportunity for practice in thinking intersectionally.

While the paired concepts help students see the hidden aspects and complicated contexts of otherwise familiar social structures, scientific thinking and social research methods help them engage with these more complex realities. We want our students to become critical consumers and users of social information, and we want them to appreciate the power and potential of sociological research. The paired concepts work together with practical skills that use diverse data in different media to help students think critically. Throughout the book we provide active learning exercises connected to the paired concepts, affording students the opportunity to practice the habits of mind and concrete skills required to find good information. At the end of each chapter, we offer additional exercises for students to practice their data and media skills. As part of the book's digital resources package, we provide *Media+Data Literacies* exercises in which students further practice these skills and assess their own learning in a low-stakes environment. Instructors could also use these exercises as jumping-off points for class discussions or group activities.

## Teaching with *Living Sociologically*

*Living Sociologically* combines what is useful from our experiences at a variety of institutions. We distill usable, high-quality, reliable teaching and learning resources for instructors and students alike. Our approach is designed for multiple settings: flexible enough that instructors in hybrid, in-person, or online classrooms will find it useful; rich enough that instructors with different interests can rely on it for detailed support when teaching the wider field; and inviting enough that students can follow exercises on their own if they desire. The second edition, which we crafted as we (like others) adapted to teaching and learning under the extraordinary constraints of COVID-19, is especially sensitive to the need for flexibility.

*Living Sociologically* moves toward a new narrative for the Introduction to Sociology course that takes the best of new innovations in pedagogy and updates the standard formula. We include enough recognizable content to align with standard learning objectives, while offering new features that distinguish our book from other introductory sociology texts:

- a narrative that explains the changes that have taken place in sociological theory since the 1960s
- an extended analysis of culture that considers new approaches in cultural sociology, including work on codes, narratives, mass media, social networks, and the public sphere
- an extended focus on the range of research techniques contemporary sociologists use, including observation/ethnography, interpretive methods (textual analysis and cultural analysis), open-ended interviewing, survey research, historical-comparative methods, experimental methods, and computational approaches that rely on large-language models and other sources of "big data"
- a commitment to drawing connections between sociological subfields and anchoring them in specific real-world social processes
- an active learning approach that offers tools to students and instructors to succeed in their work.

### A Contemporary, Applied, and Inclusive Introduction

The traditional model of three major theoretical perspectives followed by many introductory sociology textbooks relies on the Anglo-European history of sociology to describe the field. This is an important story, but we believe it needs to be placed in critical historical context. Today, most sociologists are also interested in "theories of the middle range" that are concerned with understanding concrete social practices, specific social contexts, and particular social outcomes.

Our aim is to present the foundational curriculum in sociology to all the students in our increasingly diverse classrooms. We introduce the history and core ideas of the classical canon, we present extended criticisms of the canon, and we place these critiques in the context of broader currents in the academic field.

Last, as instructors who teach Introduction to Sociology every semester know, a unified social science does not exist. Moreover, there are important intersections between sociology, anthropology, economics, geography, psychology, history, literary studies, gender studies, and ethnic studies; and students are trying to figure them out. We believe the foundational curriculum in sociology should help students to navigate these boundaries between fields and to distinguish sociology from its closest colleagues and competitors. *Living Sociologically* contextualizes sociology within the story of the emergence of the social sciences and by identifying similarities and differences between social science disciplines. This interdisciplinary sensibility is woven through the text as we point to connections to other academic projects as well as applied settings for sociological research.

## Chapter Structure

Every chapter of *Living Sociologically* has a specific focus and contains the following elements:

- An **opening vignette** that begins the chapter. In Chapter 1, "What Is Sociology?," we open with the decision by Simone Biles to give up her spot on the US Olympic gymnastics team and ask how a sociological perspective can help us understand it. This is used as a foundation to ask questions about sports, national pride, race, media, and celebrity. It also helps us introduce the five paired concepts. Similarly, in Chapter 13, "Politics, Economy, and Social Movements," the chapter opens with a discussion of the extraordinarily charged US presidential elections of 2016 and 2020. This is used as a foundation to discuss other social movements and the institutional landscape of global and national power today. We explicitly link the case to the five paired concepts that organize the narrative of the textbook.

- **Examples of classic and contemporary research**, anchored in the discussion of a specific empirical focus. For example, in Chapter 1, "What Is Sociology?," we consider examples of the sociological imagination in published research and discuss classic works by Peter H. Rossi on homelessness and by William Julius Wilson on race and class in the inner city. In Chapter 7, "Race, Ethnicity, and Immigration," we consider E. Digby Baltzell's *The Protestant Establishment* on the institutionalization of the WASP establishment, Noel Ignatiev's book *How the Irish Became White*, and Christina Mora's *Making Hispanics*.

- Box features that illustrate the five **paired concepts**. In Chapter 2, "American Sociology: Theories and Methods," we discuss in "Global and Local" the role of citizen scientists in collecting data to support the development of scientific knowledge. In Chapter 3, "Culture," we examine "Inequality and Privilege" through the lens of taxpayer support for cultural institutions. In Chapter 6, "Inequality, Mobility, and Social Change," we describe the development of Social Security to understand "Structure and Contingency." In Chapter 8, "Gender, Sexuality, and the Body," we discuss "Power and Resistance" in the context of the Stonewall uprising and LGBTQ activism. And in Chapter 14, "Media and Technology," the emergence of cancel culture is highlighted as an example of "Solidarity and Conflict."

- **Career boxes** in each chapter encourage students to explore the relevance of sociological study to many different career fields. For example, in Chapter 4, "Socialization, Social Interaction, and Group Life," we discuss the sociological research on getting a job, focusing on Granovetter's famous research on the strength of weak ties. Chapter 7,

"Race, Ethnicity, and Immigration," discusses career opportunities designed to help companies develop multicultural policies in the workplace.

- **Methods and Interpretation boxes** provide an opportunity to approach sociological questions with the critical thinking and research skills of a sociologist. For example, in Chapter 11, "Education, Work, and Recreation," we discuss different strategies for measuring learning outcomes and teaching effectiveness. Chapter 15, "Climate Change and Sustainability," discusses different techniques for measuring urban sprawl.
- **Case studies** at the end of each chapter apply the five paired concepts as analytical tools to understand a cultural, political, or social phenomenon relevant to the chapter's key themes. For example, in Chapter 3, "Culture," we analyze the social ritual of standing for the national anthem at sports events in the United States through all five of the paired concepts. In Chapter 12, "Health, Illness, and Medicine," we discuss the rise of commercial genetic testing as it influences understanding of health. In each case, the paired concepts encourage students to use their sociological imagination to engage with complexity and contradiction.
- **Review sections** at the end of each chapter revisit the chapter's learning goals and provide lists of key terms, review questions, further readings, and suggestions for further exploration.
- **Practical activities** at the end of chapters encourage students to use their sociological imagination, develop their media and data literacy, and discuss compelling questions and issues.

## Changes in the Second Edition

Instructors who used the first edition of *Living Sociologically* will find many similarities in the structure and organization of the new edition. At the same time, we have extensively revised and updated every chapter. We have updated all the statistics and also added new research studies, so that the new edition will accurately represent the discipline of sociology in its contemporary form. We have carefully reviewed every example, every vignette, and every box feature, replacing those that were outdated. In some instances, we have added significant new material that was missing from the previous edition, particularly in specific areas that represent new fields of interest for students, or new areas of empirical scholarship for sociologists, or both.

The most visible changes can be seen in revisions to the Table of Contents. Chapter 2, "American Sociology: Theory and Methods," provides an integrated discussion of sociological theory and methods, to introduce students to the core theoretical concepts and research strategies that contemporary sociologists use in their scholarly activities. Chapter 7, "Race, Ethnicity, and Immigration," now includes an extended discussion of immigration trends, immigrant communities, and the cultural and political impact of immigration in the United States and elsewhere. Chapter 13, "Politics, Economy, and Social Movements," has been reorganized to focus more closely on how political and economic power are related to each other. Introducing the perspective of political economy to students, the chapter now focuses extensively on how political and economic elites create alliances to maintain their control over society. Chapter 13 also devotes significant attention to how colonialism shapes the global distribution of wealth and power, how the global economy influences international political alliances and conflicts, and how historical changes in the economy reorganize power and privilege at local and global levels. Chapter 15, "Climate Change and Sustainability," adds a new section on the structural factors that contribute to environmental risk; this includes a discussion of how population, urbanization, industrialization, and global capitalism have each created challenges for ecological sustainability.

Chapter 14 is a new chapter that explores the role that media and technology play in contemporary social life. Technology is a central feature of our students' lives today, and a chapter on technology and society is one that is certain to engage them and to demonstrate the usefulness of the sociological imagination. The chapter begins with a discussion of different sociological theories that help to explain why technology is so often met with a mix of excitement, anxiety, and ambivalence. Next, the chapter explores the economic impacts of media and technology, with a specific focus on how technology influences jobs, wealth creation, and economic inequality. From there we turn to the world of politics, discussing how news media shape the agenda of public discussion, how social media increase polarization, and how marginalized groups use new media technologies both to build social solidarity and also to increase their voice in the larger public sphere. We end with a discussion of mediated social relationships, focusing on how these technologies impact our attention, our ability to concentrate, and our general mental health.

Specific changes for each chapter are described below:

Chapter 1: We have updated the discussion on how to count the unhoused population, and we have updated the discussion of sociological research on race, crime, and job applications. In our introduction of the five paired concepts, we have expanded the discussion of structure and contingency.

Chapter 2: We have combined and streamlined the introduction of theory and methods (Chapters 2 and 3 from the first edition) into a single chapter, "American Sociology: Theory and Methods." We updated the active learning prompts for the box features on Inequality and Privilege ("Forgotten Founders in Sociology") and Power and Resistance ("Protecting Human Subjects in Social Research"). The chapter also includes more contemporary examples of scholars doing public sociology, including short profiles of Matthew Desmond and Alondra Nelson. In the box feature on Methods and Interpretation, statistics have been updated for the effects of education on earnings.

Chapter 3: We updated the active learning prompts for the box features on Structure and Contingency ("The Protocols of the Elders of Zion"), Solidarity and Conflict ("Music and Social Protest"), and Careers ("Working in the Creative Industries"). We expanded the discussion of the World Values Survey to include some of the methodological criticisms that have been made of that research project. There is a new box feature on Methods and Interpretation, focusing on recent developments in sociology for measuring what people think. Statistics for global sales of manga have been updated.

Chapter 4: We updated the chapter-opening vignette, focusing on the recent television series *Reservation Dogs*. We updated the active learning prompts for the box features on Solidarity and Conflict ("The Stanford Prison Experiment"), Global and Local ("Bureaucracy in Singapore"), and Methods and Interpretation ("Life-Course Research on Socialization"). The new box feature on Power and Resistance explores the 2022 protests in Iran that challenged the law requiring women to wear the *hijab* in public places. The box feature on Methods and Interpretation has been expanded to include a discussion of some of the newer ways that sociologists conceptualize and measure the socialization process. Statistics on media consumption by children have been updated. The new end-of-chapter case study describes the socialization and biography of Dwayne Johnson, exploring how he became the Hollywood celebrity known as "The Rock."

Chapter 5: We updated the active learning prompts for the box features on Power and Resistance ("What's Wrong with Graffiti?"), Global and Local ("The Global Drug Trade"), and Methods and Interpretation ("Measuring the Crime Rate"). Statistics have been updated for the violent crime rate, property crime rate, incarceration rate, breakdown of hate crime incidents, and breakdown of arrest data by type of arrest and by race. The chapter also pays more attention to the history of racial profiling, tracing the practice back to the periods of slavery and Jim Crow.

Chapter 6: We updated the active learning prompts for the box features on Power and Resistance ("Ending Apartheid in South Africa"), Inequality and Privilege ("Marketing to the Super-Rich"), Structure and Contingency ("Creating Social Security"), and Solidarity and Conflict ("A Short History of the Workers' Strike in the United States"). The box feature on Global and Local has been updated to include the most recent data on the number of Chinese students enrolled in US universities. Statistics have been updated for income and wealth levels for different social classes. US tax rates have been updated to reflect the most recent threshold levels for the highest tax bracket.

Chapter 7: The discussion of immigration, which was in Chapter 15 in the first edition, now appears in Chapter 7. We updated the active learning prompts for the box features on Global and Local ("Latino Computer Engineers in Colombia and Puerto Rico"), Inequality and Privilege ("How Irish Americans Became White"), Power and Resistance ("Black Lives Matter"), and Methods and Interpretation ("Defining and Measuring Race in Official Government Data"). We updated the census data on the racial and ethnic composition of the US population. Statistics have been updated for the number of people who self-identify as Native Americans, the national origins of the US Latino population, the demographic profile of the Asian-American population, the number of people who self-identify as multiracial, the size of the global refugee population, and the economic value of remittances.

Chapter 8: We updated the active learning prompts for the box features on Structure and Contingency ("Classifying Intersex Babies"), Inequality and Privilege ("Men in Pink Collar Work"), and Global and Local ("Sex Work"). There is an expanded discussion of gender role expectations, parenthood, and the wage gap. The discussion of feminist politics has been expanded to include the 2022 Supreme Court decision overturning *Roe v. Wade*, the legislation protecting women's right to reproductive freedom. The Methods and Interpretation box ("Gender Bias in Social Research") has been expanded to include a discussion of recent studies documenting bias in science laboratories and artificial intelligence algorithms. Statistics have been updated for the gender composition of the US Congress, and women's and men's labor participation rates.

Chapter 9: We updated the active learning prompts for the box feature on Structure and Contingency ("'Bird-Nesting' as a Co-Parenting Strategy after Divorce"). Statistics have been updated for the percentage of children living with single parents, marriage rates and trends, trends in multiracial families, and public opinion data on attitudes toward gay marriage.

Chapter 10: In the section on secularization and the persistence of religion, we have expanded the discussion that shows how government support of religion has actually been increasing in many parts of the world over the last twenty years. Statistics have been updated for global spending on scientific research, population sizes for the different world religions, trends in secularization, trends in government support of religion, and women's employment in STEM occupations.

Chapter 11: In order to maintain a more consistent focus on education, work, and job satisfaction, we moved the section "Historical Changes to the Economy" to Chapter 13. We also added a more extended discussion of homeschooling, including a discussion of the stresses associated with homeschooling during the COVID-19 pandemic. The section "Schools in a Digital Age" now includes a more extended discussion of the challenges associated with remote learning during the COVID lockdowns. The section "Power, Privilege, and Inequality in the Workplace" now includes a discussion of how the shift to remote work during and after COVID reinforced existing social inequalities. We expanded the discussion of the growing power employers have over workers, pointing to the decline of union membership, the erosion of wages for workers without a college degree, and the growing threat of automation. The section "The Sociology of Job Satisfaction" has also been expanded, with more information about structural patterns and trends related to job satisfaction, as well as an extended discussion of the "great resignation" of 2021–2022 and the changing meanings about work that were associated with it. We have updated the active learning prompts for the box features on Power and Resistance ("The #MeToo Movement") and Structure and Contingency ("How Indoor Cycling Became a Multi-Billion-Dollar Industry"). In the box feature on Solidarity and Conflict ("The Fight Over Campus Speech Codes"), we updated the discussion by giving examples drawn from 2022 about university speeches that were canceled or disrupted by student protests. Statistics have been updated for student internships, employer attitudes about the preparedness of college graduates, global literacy trends, the percentage of children worldwide who go to school, the number of people employed by schools in the US, the number of homeschooled students in the US, the results from the PISA international school assessment, and wage trends in the "gig economy."

Chapter 12: The section "Experiencing Illness Differently" now begins with a discussion of the 2019 book by Celeste Watkins-Hayes, *Remaking a Life: How Women Living with HIV/AIDS Confront Inequality*. The section "Being a Patient" includes a longer discussion of chronic illness, particularly for people who are over the age of 65. The section "Access to Health Care" includes a discussion of US policy changes that were enacted during the Biden Administration. We updated the active learning prompts for the box features on Inequality and Privilege ("How Inequality Shapes Our Final Years"), Power and Resistance ("Stigma and Size"), Solidarity and Conflict ("Disruptive Behavior in Medical Settings"), Global and Local ("Does Modern Society Make You Sick?"), Structure and Contingency ("Waiting for an Organ Transplant"), and Methods and Interpretation ("Race-Based Medicine"). Statistics have been updated for global rankings of health care performance.

Chapter 13: This chapter has been extensively reorganized, focusing more closely on how political and economic power are related to each other. This includes a new section, "Politics and the Economy." The section begins by introducing the perspective of political economy, which is a major source of influence in the disciplines of economics, political science, and sociology. The section then outlines the two main areas where the political economy perspective has inspired sociological research: (1) the study of the power elite, and (2) the study of geopolitics, colonialism, and international trade. The chapter includes two additional learning goals that reflect this new focus on political economy. We have also moved the section "Historical Changes in the Economy" (which was in Chapter 14 in the first edition) into this chapter, to show how historical changes in the economy reorganize power and privilege at local and global levels. There is a new Power and Resistance box, focusing on the 2010 political protests in Tunisia, and a new Structure and Contingency box, which focuses on the influence the Haitian slave revolt had on the French Revolution. We updated the active learning prompt for the box feature on Solidarity and Conflict ("Push Polls and the Politics of Division"). There is a new Methods and Interpretation box about measuring the unemployment rate. Statistics have been updated for the demographic composition and median net worth of the US Senate, the amount spent by political lobbyists in the US, and the number of US states that have signed on to the National Popular Vote Interstate Compact.

Chapter 14: This is a new chapter on media and technology. It begins with a chapter-opening vignette about the artificial intelligence chatbot ChatGPT. A theoretical discussion emphasizes how technological conveniences are often associated with a loss of freedom, and how new technologies tend to get discussed in terms of competing narratives of salvation and apocalypse. Next, the chapter explores the economic impacts of media and technology, with a specific focus on how technology influences jobs, wealth creation, and economic inequality. We discuss how technology has led to a greater concentration of wealth, an increase in segregation, a proliferation of precarious jobs, an increase in digital surveillance technologies in the workplace, and a growing reliance on automation and artificial intelligence technologies. From there, the chapter turns to the exploration of media, technology, and politics. This includes a discussion of media agenda-setting and the economic forces that influence the media agenda (which were located in Chapter 13 in the first edition), as well as new discussions of (1) the ways that computer algorithms are encouraging political echo chambers and social polarization, (2) the sources of resistance that are challenging the power of algorithms, and (3) the ways that marginalized groups are using new media technologies to build strategies of political resistance. The chapter ends with a new section on mediated social relationships, focusing on how these technologies impact our attention, our ability to concentrate, and our general mental health. The chapter-ending case study explores the rise and fall of the cryptocurrency company FTX and its leader, Sam Bankman-Fried. A new box feature on careers explores new job titles in the age of artificial intelligence. A new Power and Resistance box examines the different actions that governments, nonprofit groups, and social movements have taken to protect privacy and to resist the growing power of technology companies. A new Inequality and Privilege box describes how Mountain View, California (the location for Google's headquarters), became unaffordable for low- and middle-income residents. A new Structure and Contingency box examines some of the different "doomsday scenarios" for artificial intelligence. A new Solidarity and Conflict box explores the emergence and the growth of cancel culture. A new local and global box describes how K-pop fans have intervened in different political campaigns around the world.

Chapter 15: This chapter adds a new section on three structural factors that have contributed to environmental risk: (1) demography and population growth, (2) urbanization, and (3) industrialization and global capitalism. The discussion of demography and urbanization were in Chapter 15 in the first edition, but they have been rewritten with a focus on challenges for ecological sustainability. The discussion of industrialization and global capitalism includes an expanded description of the treadmill of production, as well as a new discussion of why poorer nations are forced into ecologically damaging economic policies that concentrate on resource extraction. In the section "The Uneven Distribution of Environmental Risk," there is an expanded discussion of concentrated disadvantage, including an examination of the massive resettlements out of poorer regions that are likely to occur as a result of environmental crisis. The discussion of global climate agreements has been expanded to include developments that have occurred since 2020, including the signing of the Glasgow Climate Pact in 2021. There is a new Methods and Interpretation box about how to measure urban sprawl. The chapter-ending case study on the destruction of the Amazon has been extended to include developments that have occurred since the end of the Bolsonaro regime in Brazil.

## Teaching and Learning Support

Oxford University Press offers students a variety of digital solutions that:

- Engage your students in the required reading
- Make assigned content available on the first day of class
- Provide the required resources available at the lowest cost possible

**Inclusive Access**: Your institution may already have an Inclusive Access (IA) program in place in which students pay for their course materials through their course registration.

Rather than relying on individual student purchases, with inclusive access, digital products are delivered directly to students through their LMS (learning management system) at the most affordable price. Our partnerships with major higher education bookstore retailers and e-learning delivery leaders make it possible for students to easily and quickly access affordable content on the first day of class.

**With Inclusive Access, you can:**

- Provide students with course material on **Day One**
- Make course material **more affordable**—students **save as much as 70 percent**
- **Increase engagement** with immersive, engaging digital content
- **Enjoy academic freedom**—virtually any content can be adopted for use in Inclusive Access
- **Improve student success and retention** with analytical tools and insights

For more information, please visit https://pages.oup.com/he/us/oup-inclusiveaccess

**Direct-to-Student purchasing**:

Students can purchase their course materials directly from OUP at the lowest retail price available. Please visit https://global.oup.com/ushe and search for "Living Sociologically."

# Digital Learning Tools

## Oxford Learning Link

Oxford Learning Link delivers a wealth of engaging digital learning tools and resources to help both instructors and students get the most out of *Living Sociologically: Concepts and Connections*, Second Edition.

Students can access self-study resources and instructors can view instructor resources at **oup.com/he/jacobs-townsley-2e**

**Instructors:** This title can be integrated directly into learning management systems. To find out more about integration, or if you have any questions about the course content, please contact your OUP representative at (800) 280–0280 or http://learninglink.oup.com/support

## Enhanced e-book

Included in Oxford Learning Link, Oxford's enhanced e-book combines high-quality text content with a rich assortment of integrated multimedia and practice questions to deliver a more engaging and interactive learning experience.

The enhanced e-book version of *Living Sociologically: Concepts and Connections*, Second Edition is available via RedShelf, VitalSource, and other leading higher education e-book vendors.

Oxford Learning Link for *Living Sociologically: Concepts and Connections*, Second Edition includes the following resources.

*Instructor Resources:*

- **Instructor's Resource Manual**—A robust and innovative manual that includes chapter summaries, learning goals and objectives, lecture outlines/chapter overviews, key terms and definitions, review questions with discussion, essay, critical response prompts, and multimedia question prompts.
- **Essay Questions**
- **Test Bank**—The test bank that accompanies this text is designed for both novice and advanced users. Instructors can create and edit questions, as well as upload the file into various learning management systems (LMS).
- **PowerPoint-Based Lecture Slides**

*Student Resources:*

- **Enhanced E-Book**—The enhanced e-book provides students with a versatile, accessible, online version of the textbook, with *digital resources* integrated throughout.

- **Video Clips with Assignable Quizzes**—Brief, engaging videos related to the paired concepts, with assignable quizzes that capture students' understanding and application of key concepts
- **Pop Culture Guide**—A valuable guide to media (movies, TV shows, podcasts) that can be used to demonstrate sociological ideas or concepts, organized by chapter. These come from multiple sources and include suggestions for clips as well as full-length features. Each suggested clip includes the concept being represented, the time stamp (if relevant), as well as the streaming service where the media can be accessed.
- **Paired Concepts Playlists**—These curated Spotify playlists are paired with key sociological concepts to help students connect sociological content and ideas with their everyday lives.
- **Check Your Understanding Questions**—Show/Hide multiple choice comprehension questions at the end of all e-book sections.
- **Chapter Quizzes**—The chapter quizzes consist of around 20 multiple choice questions per chapter aimed to test chapter content understanding.
- **In the News Quiz**—A resource for both instructors and students that provides current news articles on a regular basis throughout each teaching term, along with low-stakes assessments that ensure student engagement and encourage students to connect the article to what they are learning in their course. These articles are selected specifically to relate to a particular sociological idea or concept and are designed to demonstrate to students the sociological relevance of everyday events.
- **Data Literacy Exercises**—Developed by Ron Jacobs and Eleanor Townsley and edited by Randolph Hohle are innovative, interactive exercises that help students build their data skills and assess their learning in a low-stakes environment. These exercises push students to critically analyze photos, charts, and graphs in an effort to highlight how easily information can be manipulated or misinterpreted. They can be assigned to students or used as jumping-off points for class discussions or group activities.
- **Connections to MCAT Content**—In 2015, the MCAT (Medical College Admission Test) was revised to include a section on the social and behavioral sciences, which includes questions about sociological concepts and ideas. This correlation guide indicates where information about those questions can be found in *Living Sociologically* to serve as a helpful study guide for pre-med students enrolled in this course.
- **Flashcards**

# Acknowledgments

The authors would like to thank the reviewers who provided substantive, helpful, and critical feedback throughout the development and after publication of the first and second editions of this text:

*Alabama*
Matt Cousineau, Auburn University
Paige Vaughn, Spring Hill College
Angela Ware, Auburn University

*Arizona*
Celeste Atkins, Cochise College

*Arkansas*
Rebecca Barrett-Fox, Arkansas State University
Linda Brady, Arkansas State University
Jason Ulsperger, Arkansas Tech University

*California*
Terri Anderson, University of California–Los Angeles
Jean Beaman, University of California–Santa Barbara
Eileen Ie, East Los Angeles College
Minu Mathur, College of San Mateo
Shaneel Pratap, Evergreen Valley College
Darby Southgate, Los Angeles Valley College

*Colorado*
Michael Briscoe, Colorado State University, Pueblo
Ting Jiang, Metropolitan State University of Denver

*Connecticut*
Erika Del Villar, University of Connecticut
Eric Mielants, Fairfield University

*District of Columbia*
Sarah Stiles, Georgetown University

*Florida*
Stephen Lippmann, Miami University
Richard Tardanico, Florida International University
Phillip Wiseley, Florida South Western State College

*Georgia*
Elaina Behounek, Middle Georgia State University
Tricia Noone, Georgia Southern University
Laura Simon, Mercer University

*Idaho*
Kyle Fields, Boise State University

*Illinois*
Tennille Allen, Lewis University
Gregory Goalwin, Aurora University
Matthew Green, College of DuPage

*Indiana*
Rachel Einwohner, Purdue University
Amy Hemphill, Ivy Tech Community College of Indiana
Carmon Hicks, Ivy Tech Community College of Indiana
Yanming Kuang, Indiana University
Stephanie Medley-Rath, Indiana University–Kokomo
Melinda Messineo, Ball State University
Carla Pfeffer, Purdue University North Central
Kody Steffy, Indiana University

*Kansas*
Pelgy Vaz, Fort Hays State University

*Kentucky*
Andrea Deal, Madisonville Community College

*Louisiana*
Christobel Asiedu, Louisiana Tech University
Jaita Talukdar, Loyola University New Orleans

*Massachusetts*
Walter F. Carroll, Bridgewater State University
Linda McCarthy, Greenfield Community College

*Michigan*
Inna Mirzoyan, Wayne State University
Sarah Prior, Michigan State University

*Minnesota*
Bridget Conlon, St. Cloud State University
Ronald Ferguson, Ridgewater College
Elizabeth Scheel-Keita, St. Cloud State University
Krishna Roka, Winona State University
Jason Torkelson, University of Minnesota-Duluth
Wayne T. Whitmore, Inver Hills Community College

*Mississippi*
Heather-Ann Layth, Mississippi State University
Earnestine Lee, Alcorn State University

Diane Lindley, University of Mississippi
Jessica Omoregie, University of Mississippi

*Missouri*
George Carson, Ozarks Technical Community College
Kamel Ghozzi, University of Central Missouri
Joachim Kibirige, Missouri Western State University
Aurelian Mauxion, Columbia College

*Nebraska*
Ron Carter, Northeast Community College

*Nevada*
Marynia Giren-Navarro, Truckee Meadows Community College

*New Jersey*
Edward Avery-Natale, Mercer County Community College
Sanford "Sandy" Shevack, Montclair State University
Patricia Stott, Kean University
Richard A. Zdan, Rider University

*New York*
Francisco Gonzalez Camelo, Borough of Manhattan Community College
Marc (Jung-Whan) De Jong, Fashion Institute of Technology
Randolph Hohle, The State University of New York at Fredonia
Andrew Horvitz, The State University of New York at New Paltz
Katie Kikendall, John Jay College of Criminal Justice
Andrew Lindner, Skidmore College
Madeleine Novich, Manhattan College
Kristin Shorette, The State University of New York, Stony Brook
Justin Thompson, Herkimer College
Elizabeth A. Wissinger, Borough of Manhattan Community College

*North Carolina*
Anne Hastings, University of North Carolina–Chapel Hill
Andrew Jacobs, East Carolina University
Jennifer L. O'Neill, East Carolina University

*Ohio*
Keith Durkin, Ohio Northern University
Amy Grau, Shawnee State University
Alexandra Herron, Ohio University

*Oklahoma*
Travis Lowe, University of Tulsa
LiErin Probasco, Oklahoma City Community College

*Pennsylvania*
Kaci Griffin, Temple University
Jess Klein, Robert Morris University
Teelyn Mauney, St. Francis University
Molly Monahan Lang, Penn State Erie, The Behrend College
Julie Raulli, Wilson College
Alecea Standlee, Gettysburg College

*South Carolina*
Julia M. Arroyo, College of Charleston
Andrew Mannheimer, Clemson University

*South Dakota*
Kristi Brownfield, Northern State University
Pamela Monaghan-Geernaert, Northern State University

*Tennessee*
Jessica Dalton-Carriger, Roane State Community College
Kelly James, Christian Brothers University
Laurie E. Woods, Vanderbilt University

*Texas*
Janet Armitage, St. Mary's University
Jennifer Lara Fagen, Lamar University
Dorothy Kalanzi, University of Texas at Arlington
Pamela Neumann, Texas A&M International University
Christopher Pieper, Baylor University
Helen Potts, University of North Texas
Michael Ramirez, Texas A&M University–Corpus Christi
Allison Ray, Texas Woman's University
Arthur Sakamoto, Texas A&M University
Terri Schrantz, Tarrant County College
Dawn Tawwater, Austin Community College

*Virginia*
Tom Linneman, College of William & Mary
Ashley Lumpkin, John Tyler Community College
Christa Moore, University of Virginia–Wise
Rachel Sparkman, Virginia Commonwealth University
Allison Wisecup, Radford University

*Wisconsin*
David Barry, University of Wisconsin, Stevens Point
Sheena Finnegan, Wisconsin Lutheran College

Matthew Sargent, Madison Area Technical College
Eighteen anonymous reviewers

The authors and OUP also sincerely thank the scholars and instructors who created and adapted the high-quality resources that accompany this text:

Rebecca Barrett-Fox, Kansas State University
Ian Callahan, The State University of New York at Albany
Lindsey Elliott, The State University of New York at Albany
Randolph Hohle, The State University of New York at Fredonia
Andrew Horvitz, The State University of New York at New Paltz
Andrew Mannheimer, Clemson University

Finally, we would like to thank the team at Oxford University Press, especially Sherith Pankratz and Meg Botteon. Special thanks also to Content Development Editor Maeve O'Brien, designer Michele Laseau, production editor Keith Faivre, and copy editor Tara Tovell.

## About the Authors

**Ronald N. Jacobs** (PhD, UCLA) is professor of sociology at the University at Albany, State University of New York. He is coeditor of the *Oxford Handbook of Cultural Sociology* (2012), coauthor of *Cultural Sociology* (Blackwell, 2012), coauthor (with Eleanor Townsley) of *The Space of Opinion: Media Intellectuals and the Public Sphere* (OUP, 2011), and author of *Race, Media, and the Crisis of Civil Society: From Watts to Rodney King* (Cambridge, 2000), as well as author of numerous journal articles and book chapters. He is cofounder and coeditor of the *American Journal of Cultural Sociology*, and he has served on the editorial boards for *Sociological Theory*, *International Journal of Sociology and Social Policy*, *Qualitative Sociology*, *Sociological Forum*, and *American Journal of Sociology*. In addition to teaching an introductory sociology course, he regularly teaches courses on sociological theory, mass media, and the sociology of culture.

**Eleanor Townsley** (PhD, UCLA) is the Andrew W. Mellon Professor of Sociology and the director of the curriculum to career program, Nexus, at Mount Holyoke College. She is coauthor (with Ron Jacobs) of *The Space of Opinion: Media Intellectuals and the Public Sphere* (OUP, 2011) and coauthor of *Making Capitalism without Capitalists: The New Ruling Elites in Eastern Europe* (Verso, 1998), as well as author of numerous journal articles, book chapters, and book reviews. She has served on the editorial boards for *Sociological Theory* and the *American Journal of Cultural Sociology*. She regularly teaches Introduction to Sociology as well as courses on media, organizations, inequality, the public sphere, and research methods. She is the recipient of two teaching awards and was named one of Princeton Review's "300 Best Professors" in 2012.

Both authors are dedicated teachers. With the exception of her time as a dean, Townsley has taught Introduction to Sociology every semester for the last 20 years, while Jacobs continues to offer Introduction to Sociology to classes with enrollments of over 400 students a semester. Both have taught at a variety of colleges and universities in different parts of the United States: Santa Monica Community College, UCLA, SUNY Albany, Rice University, the University of Pennsylvania, and Mount Holyoke College.

# PART I
# THE BASICS

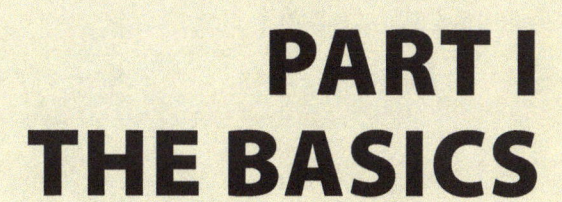

**1** What Is Sociology?

**2** American Sociology: Theory and Methods

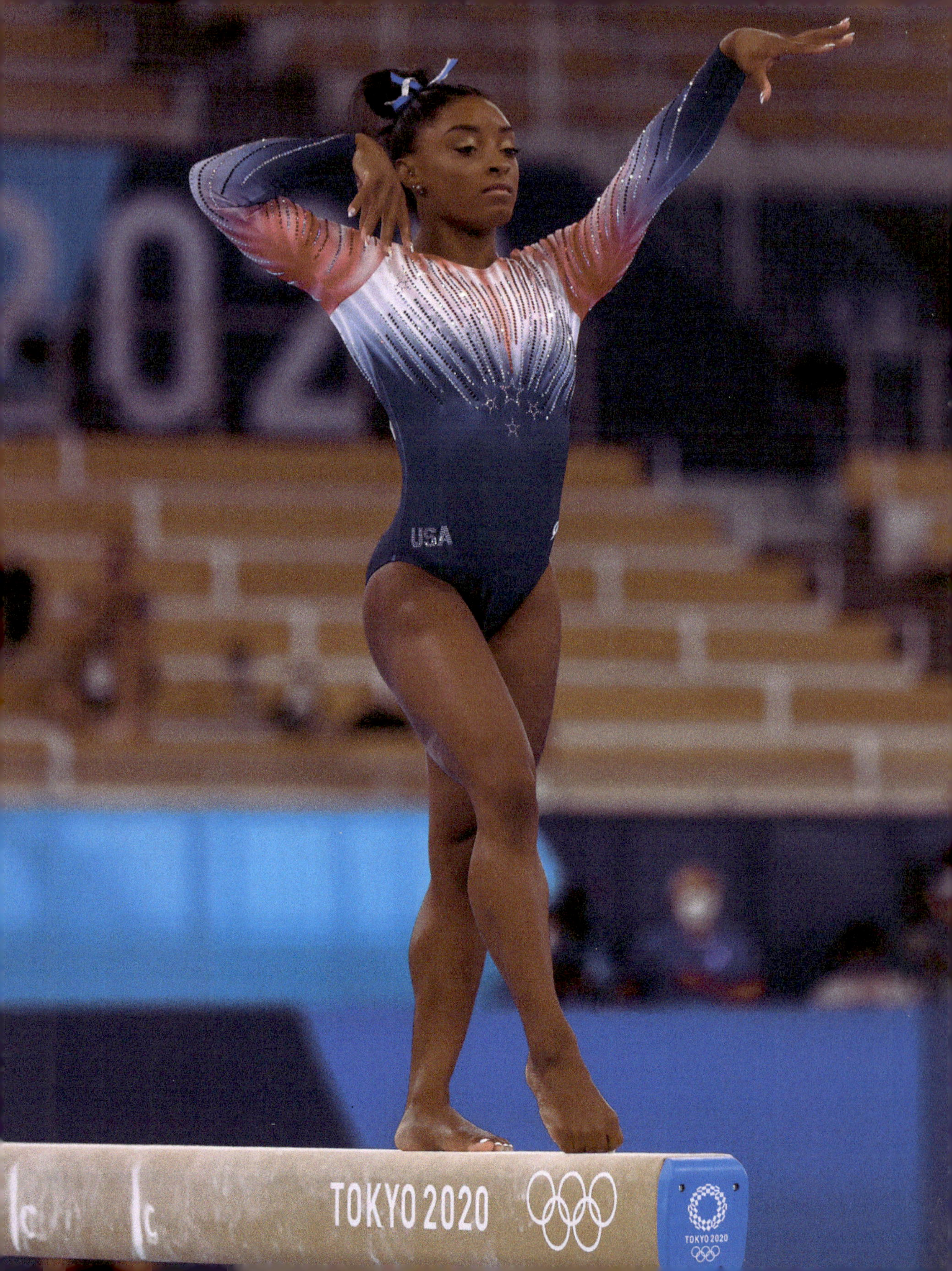
USA
TOKYO 2020
TOKYO 2020

# What Is Sociology?

On July 27, 2021, during the final of the team all-around competition at the Tokyo Olympics, Simone Biles gave up her spot on the USA gymnastics team. Biles was the most highly decorated gymnast and one of the most famous athletes at the Olympics. She had won one bronze and four gold medals at the 2016 Olympics, and her 23 world championships were the most in gymnastics history. Heavily favored to win at least four gold medals at the Tokyo Olympics, Biles cited her mental health as the reason for giving up her spot in the all-around team competition. After the team competition, she withdrew from the first four individual event finals where she was scheduled to compete. Biles returned on August 3 for her final event competition, where she won a bronze medal in the balance beam.

Controversy swirled around Biles's decision to withdraw from the Olympics. People who disagreed with her decision argued that Biles was disrespecting the Olympics, that she was a bad role model, and that she was just making excuses for a poor performance. The conservative commentator Charlie Kirk called Biles a sociopath and a national disgrace. But most of the public response she received was much more supportive. Opinion polls revealed that two-thirds of adults in the US supported Biles's decision to withdraw from the competition. Her sponsors all issued public statements of support, with Visa describing her decision as "incredibly brave" and Nabisco calling her "an inspiration to us all." In July 2022, Biles was awarded the US Presidential Medal of Freedom, with President Joe Biden calling her "a trailblazer and a role model."

**Simone Biles at the Tokyo Olympics 2020**

### Chapter Outline

**1.1 WHAT IS SOCIOLOGY? 5**
*The Sociological Imagination 7*
*The Discipline of Sociology 8*
*Sociology and Everyday Knowledge 10*

**1.2 LEVELS OF ANALYSIS 11**
*Microsociology 12*
*Macrosociology 14*
*Institutional Perspectives 15*

**1.3 THINKING RELATIONALLY: THE PAIRED CONCEPTS 16**
*Solidarity and Conflict 16*
*Power and Resistance 17*
*Inequality and Privilege 18*
*Global and Local 19*
*Structure and Contingency 20*

**1.4 WHY SOCIOLOGY? 21**

The support that Simone Biles received was part of a larger movement to recognize mental health issues in sports. Several months before the Tokyo Olympics the professional tennis player Naomi Osaka had withdrawn from the French Open, citing mental health issues. The US track and field sprinter Noah Lyles announced in 2020 that he was taking antidepressants, and that he wanted to help remove the stigma associated with mental health–related drug treatments. The Olympic gold medalist Linsay Vonn was open about her challenges with depression throughout her professional skiing career. Former Olympian Michael Phelps has become a major advocate for mental health issues in sports, releasing a documentary about the issue that was broadcast by HBO in 2020. In all these instances, the athletes have maintained the support of their sponsors as well as most of the public.

Questions about mental health and sports are interesting because they raise difficult questions about important social issues. Are sports merely another form of entertainment or a vehicle for expressing opinions about social causes and social issues? What moves professional athletes to put their careers at risk by making statements they know will be controversial? Why do we care about the social views of athletes, and why do we expect them to be role models? As we return to this case periodically throughout this chapter, we will find that factors such as race, class, gender and sexuality, inequality, privilege, work, globalization, and national identity all played a role in how the controversies unfolded and how they were publicly understood.

Sociology asks you to see the social world as complex and interconnected. Understanding this complexity is required for success in the workplaces and communities of our globalized world. Today, sociology majors build successful careers in law, medicine, education, social work, the arts, public service, and business. Sociology is a useful field of study because it enables people to perceive the relationship between individuals and society through application of systematic methods for studying people. These scientific and cultural methods, and the knowledge they generate, are invaluable for navigating the world.

This chapter introduces the academic discipline of sociology. It points out how sociological knowledge is different from the everyday knowledge that we all learn by living in the world. It draws on examples from different social institutions to highlight different sociological ideas. Last, it introduces basic concepts that you can use to understand your own life and the world around you. These paired concepts are put to work throughout this book and form the basic toolkit you can use to build your sociological imagination.

> **LEARNING GOALS**
>
> **1.1** Define the sociological imagination.
> **1.2** Understand that there are different levels of social things: for example, individuals, relationships, and institutions.
> **1.3** Apply the paired concepts of sociology to the worlds of work, politics, and other domains of social life.
> **1.4** Describe how sociologists pursue sociology as a way to secure human freedom and social justice.

## 1.1 What Is Sociology?

**LG 1.1 Define the sociological imagination.**

Sociology is typically defined as the study of society, but this general definition does not get us very far. Not only does it *not* tell us what society is; some people go so far as to argue that society does not even exist! Margaret Thatcher, the former prime minister of the United Kingdom (1979–1990), famously said, "There is no such thing as society." She meant that some people blamed society for their problems rather than taking responsibility for their own lives. But if Thatcher was wrong about this—and most sociologists would argue that she was—then we need to be able to define "society" more precisely.

We can begin our inquiry by looking at what early sociologists studied. French sociologist Émile Durkheim (1858–1917), for example, defined sociology as a scientific discipline devoted to the discovery of social facts (Durkheim [1893] 2014). He argued that these facts described a level of reality, external to individuals, that influences their lives. For Max Weber (1864–1920), cofounder of the German Sociological Association, the goal of sociology was to understand social actions. He wanted to understand how people share meanings and act together. For W.E.B. DuBois (1868–1963), who was the most important American sociologist of the early-twentieth century, sociology was the scientific study of the scope and the causes of human action. DuBois shared Durkheim's and Weber's goal of a sociology that would contribute scientific knowledge about the social world, but he also emphasized the different ways that people could use sociological knowledge to enact effective social reform. For Albion Small (1854–1926), who created the first American sociology department at the University of Chicago, sociology was the science of social relationships. Small saw that while our individual lives are patterned by the organization of group life, they are also capable of change. All four of these figures were committed to collecting facts about social actions and social relationships so that they could explain why they occurred the way they did and not in other ways.

Other influential sociologists have emphasized the useful resources sociology offers that people can use in their everyday lives. C. Wright Mills (1916–1962), for example, promised that sociology could help us to understand the problems we face, by showing how personal troubles are often connected to larger social issues. Zygmunt Bauman (1925–2017) believed that sociology should help us understand the hopes, desires, and worries of other people. This understanding is important, he thought, because it is the foundation for making positive social connections and living peacefully with others. Pierre Bourdieu (1930–2002) argued that sociology is a "martial art." He meant that sociology is a method for defending ourselves in the face of powerful, dominating social forces. Patricia Hill Collins (1948–) has argued that sociology should help to shed light on the knowledges and experiences of historically marginalized social groups, as a way to help combat social injustice. For these four sociologists, sociology is an intellectual perspective that promotes social understanding, human empowerment, and freedom.

## CAREERS

### Opportunities for Sociology Majors

Sociology is useful because it teaches critical thinking about social relationships and social systems. Sociology helps us see how individual and group behavior is influenced by the patterns of group life and how individuals can shape wider social systems. Sociologists use theoretical logic and data to analyze social problems and social puzzles. Sociological ideas and methods also help us imagine new ways to organize our social world.

Examples of prominent sociology majors include former first lady Michelle Obama; actors Dan Aykroyd and Nina Dobrev; politicians such as Shirley Chisholm and Maxine Waters; and writers, journalists, and poets including Saul Bellow, Mitch Albom, Shelby Steele, and Linton Kwesi Johnson. Graduates of sociology programs include judges like Richard Barajas, retired chief justice of the Texas Supreme Court, as well as athletes and philanthropists like retired basketball player Alonzo Mourning. Business leaders who majored in sociology include Christopher Connor, executive chair of Sherwin-Williams; Brad Anderson, former CEO and vice chair of consumer electronics for Best Buy; and Alexis Herman, CEO of New Ventures and the former US secretary of labor.

#### ACTIVE LEARNING

**Find out:** Ask a family member, a teacher, or someone else who is in the workforce what kind of skills and abilities they think employers are looking for. Ask them what kinds of skills and abilities make people successful in their lives.

If we put these claims together, we see that sociology is composed of three basic elements:

1. Sociology is interested in social facts, social actions, and social relationships. It looks at how individual actions are shaped by larger patterns that structure people's social lives.
2. Sociology is based on systematic research. Sociologists collect facts about the social world and are interested in explaining why things happen the way they do and not otherwise.
3. Sociology hopes to provide people with a deeper understanding about the world around them so that they can empower themselves and try to make the world a better place.

## The Sociological Imagination

The moral perspective shared by DuBois, Bourdieu, Collins, and others asserts that sociology should be a force for good. It holds that sociology should help us to recognize and challenge structures of domination and inequality; encourage greater understanding, tolerance, and empathy for different points of view; enable us to recognize that larger social forces shape our successes and failures; and prompt us to think critically about how the world around us came to be organized the way it is.

For Mills, this kind of thinking defines the **sociological imagination**. "The sociological imagination," Mills (2000: 6) wrote, "enables us to grasp history and biography and the relation between the two in society." Mills wanted us to connect our own private troubles to larger public issues. To do that, we need to understand not only how our society is organized but also how it is different both from other societies in the past and from other places in the present. Mills argued that we need to understand why certain types of people tend to be successful in our society, asking how successful people are selected and in what ways the characteristics of successful people change over time. Mills believed that sociologists were in the best position to provide good answers to these questions.

In *The Truly Disadvantaged* (1987), William Julius Wilson offers a powerful example of the sociological imagination. Wilson's book explores the reasons for poverty in Black inner-city neighborhoods in the 1980s, despite the efforts of social welfare programs of the 1960s and 1970s to help people and despite the victories of the 1960s Civil Rights Movement that helped to overturn racial discrimination in housing and other public policies. At the time Wilson was doing the research for *The Truly Disadvantaged*, influential social critics argued that government welfare programs had created a "culture of poverty." These critics argued that this culture encouraged people living in poverty to depend on welfare and discouraged them from working harder

**Sociological imagination**
The ability to see the connections between individual lives and wider social structures and the way they affect each other.

*If you change where you stand, you can change your perspective.*

to improve their lives. By the late 1980s, politicians were using these arguments about the "culture of poverty" to propose policies that would dramatically reduce social welfare, to help people to "escape" what President Ronald Reagan called "the spider's web of dependency" on government.

Wilson's book was an important intervention in the debate about race and welfare because it used the sociological imagination to tell a more complicated story about what was happening in poor inner-city neighborhoods. Wilson's research showed that manufacturing and other low-skill jobs had left the cities, only to be replaced by service jobs that required more education. Women, who were entering the labor market in greater numbers, competed successfully with men for these service jobs. These factors made it much harder for the low-skilled and poorly educated men living in the inner city to find work. In addition, Black middle-class families were taking advantage of antidiscrimination housing laws to leave the inner city. As they did so, community institutions such as churches and schools were weakened. Young children living in the inner city had access to fewer positive role models, while teenagers were cut off from the kinds of informal social contacts that could help them get jobs. In other words, many of the problems that young Black men faced in the inner city were not of their own making. Rather, Wilson demonstrated, they were the result of deeper structural changes in race, class, and gender relations.

Sociologists often use the idea of the sociological imagination to explain why what they do is important. Mills and the sociological imagination are featured in every sociological textbook written in the United States, and books like *The Truly Disadvantaged* are held up as examples of the kind of deep, systematic sociological research that needs to be part of the public conversation about important social issues.

## The Discipline of Sociology

As one of the main social science disciplines in the university, sociology has always been committed to the idea that systematic and scientific research is the best way to understand the social world. Early proponents of sociology were attracted to the prospect of developing a science of society. While most of the early sociologists were trained in other disciplines, such as philosophy, law, and theology, they embraced sociology because they believed that it offered a more scientific way of understanding the social world.

The goals of a scientific sociology are based on two ideas: (1) if we want to understand a social issue, it is important to get the facts right and (2) it is often quite difficult to get the facts right. What facts you collect depends on how you define the issue. For example, if we want to understand and respond effectively to the problem of homelessness, we need to define the problem. We need to know:

- how many people there are who are unhoused
- what kinds of people are more likely to become homeless
- what homelessness is and how homelessness has changed over time
- how effective different social policies are at reducing homelessness

This information can be difficult to collect.

Social scientists do not have a definite answer to the question, "How many unhoused people are there?" People move in and out of periods of homelessness, making it hard to define them as "homeless" or "not homeless." The most common strategy for counting the homeless population is to count the people who are either in the streets or in homeless shelters, even though most experts agree that this strategy results in undercounts (Shlay and Rossi 1992). It misses people who are living temporarily with friends and family but who are likely to be homeless soon. It misses people who managed to scrape up enough money to stay in a motel for a day or two. And it misses people sleeping in their cars, at temporary

**Counting the number of people who are unhoused in New York City**
Workers from the Robin Hood Foundation, an organization that helps people living in poverty, speak to an unhoused person as they take part in a survey of the homeless population on the streets of New York. Hundreds of people fanned out across the city to conduct the survey just after midnight on February 9, 2016.

campsites, in abandoned buildings, and other places that researchers have a hard time locating.

Social scientists have used different strategies to try to overcome these measurement difficulties. Rossi (1989a) combined a count of the shelter population with a systematic nighttime survey of the street population in Chicago. After interviewing both groups, Rossi used the results of the interviews to make a more informed estimate of the total homeless population in the city.

Knowing the exact number of unhoused people helps to inform important questions, such as what causes homelessness or what the experience of homelessness is like. For example, Rossi (1989b) used the monthly Current Population Survey (conducted by the US Census Bureau) to identify the number of extremely poor single people, arguing that this population was at the highest risk of becoming homeless. More recent research has tried to identify people who are living in poverty and have precarious housing situations, arguing that this is a population at great risk of becoming homeless (Link et al. 1995; Smith and Castañeda-Tinoco 2019). This focus on at-risk populations has produced a shift in the things being measured. For example, instead of trying to measure the precise number of unhoused people, research now focuses on the factors that increase the risk of homelessness (Jencks 1995; Snow and Anderson 1993), the ways that an individual's life chances are impacted by periods of homelessness (Burt et al. 2001), and the coping strategies that unhoused people use to get by and to maintain respect (Dordick 1997; Duneier 2000; Gowan 2010). It has also anchored recent research that points beyond individuals to structural factors that shape homelessness, such as the availability of rental housing (Colburn and Aldern 2022). It may be impossible to get a perfectly exact count of the homeless population, but knowing more about the behaviors of the unhoused and the precariously-housed can help researchers to develop better estimates and improve the accuracy of existing measurements (Roncarati et al. 2021).

As we will discuss in Chapter 2, sociologists use many different strategies to collect accurate and useful information about the social world. This focus on **research methods** is one of the defining features of social science, and it is central to the practice of sociology.

## Sociology and Everyday Knowledge

Social-scientific knowledge is different from ordinary, everyday knowledge about the world. In most of social life, people tend to look for information that reinforces the beliefs they already have. This tendency to look for information that reinforces personal beliefs is known as **confirmation bias**. Confirmation bias often leads to more polarized social attitudes. As an antidote

**Research methods** Strategies to collect accurate and useful information about the world.

**Confirmation bias** The tendency to look for information that reinforces prior beliefs; occurs when research is biased to confirm the researcher's preexisting beliefs or hypotheses.

to confirmation bias, sociology and the other social science disciplines are an important part of your education.

While the discipline of sociology is part of the social sciences, it is also distinct from the other social science disciplines: psychology, economics, political science, and history. The main difference is that sociologists want to understand how different social things are related to one another, and (as we shall see in the next section) sociologists combine different levels of analysis to achieve that understanding. While psychologists focus primarily on individuals and small groups, sociologists want to see how larger social forces influence groups. While economists and political scientists focus on a single sphere of social life, like the economy or the political system, sociologists are interested in the relationships of different social institutions to one another. While sharing the historian's interest in the past, sociologists are more interested in comparing different historical outcomes to develop general explanations about why things occurred the way they did. As we discuss in Chapter 2, sociology aims to develop a science of society itself.

## 1.2 Levels of Analysis

**LG** **1.2** Understand that there are different levels of social things: for example, individuals, relationships, and institutions.

Sociologists think about social issues in terms of historical trends and structural patterns. Instead of relying on their own personal observations and opinions, they collect data systematically in order to identify patterns that were not obvious at the outset. They are also interested in combining different **levels of analysis** in their research.

Sociologists commonly define three levels of analysis. Microsociology is the level of individuals and small group interaction. Macrosociology is the level of large-scale structural patterns and historical trends, including the workings of the economic, political, and cultural systems. In between microsociology and macrosociology is the intermediate or **institutional level of analysis**. This is the level of analysis of specific institutions and social relationships.

For example, when sociologists study divorce they are interested in the specific decisions that people make to stay married or get divorced, but they are also interested in how divorce rates are connected to larger social patterns. To use the language of the sociological imagination, while getting divorced is a "private trouble," the overall divorce *rate* is a "public issue."

The decision to file for divorce is shaped by the relationship between individuals, which can be understood and analyzed at the microsociological level of analysis. But the challenge of marriage is often magnified by

**Level of analysis**
The size or scale of the objects sociologists study.

**Institutional level of analysis**
The intermediate level of analysis, between microsociology and macrosociology, of specific institutions and social relationships.

macrosociological factors. For example, there may be a lack of high-paying jobs in the city where the married couple lives because of a shift in jobs to other parts of the country or the world. At the institutional level, an individual's choice to stay married or get divorced will be shaped by the general social belief that people should get married, as well as by government tax policies that encourage and reward marriage. To study divorce and other social issues, sociologists will look for patterns and measure outcomes at every level of analysis and ask, "How do causes at one level affect causes at another?"

## Microsociology

**Microsociology** examines the everyday interactions of individuals and small groups. It emphasizes the things that we have to do to coordinate our actions with the people around us to establish what sociologists call "a shared definition of the situation." Microsociology focuses on the rules that we follow in social situations, as well as the strategies we use to bend those rules to our advantage.

Take rules of the road in the United States as an example. Two drivers approach a four-way stop sign. Even though there is no way of knowing, each driver acts as if the other person knows the rules of the situation. The person who arrives first has the right of way. If both people arrive at the same time, the person on the right has the right of way. But there are other strategies that drivers use to navigate the interaction. Some drivers will "stop short," making it appear that they arrived at the intersection first even though they may not have done so. Other drivers will be excessively polite, always waving the other person through in any instance where there is a question about who arrived first. Different rules might apply depending on the weather, the geographical location, the time of day, or one driver's assessment of the other driver's intentions. As we can see, even the ordinary activities of our lives are highly choreographed, requiring both social interpretation and cooperation from others around us.

The idea that social life is choreographed suggests that we are all actors on a stage, performing roles and responding to the performances of those around us. We have a clear sense of how we want to present ourselves, and we use a variety of "props" to signal that presentation to others. At the same time, we acknowledge other people's signals by adopting supporting roles that reinforce their self-presentations. If the performances are coordinated effectively and nobody's performance is challenged, then there is no problem. According to Erving Goffman (1922–1982), this kind of "impression management" is one of the most important features of social life.

Microsociology can help us see how individuals and groups collaborate with each other to create a "shared definition of the situation," as well as how everyday social interactions recreate patterns of inequality. One example is

**Microsociology**
The analysis of individuals and small group interaction.

research showing that even though science teachers in middle schools are committed to treating all their students equally, they actually spend significantly more time with the male students than the female students in their classrooms (Shumow and Schmidt 2013; Watson 2022). To take another example, despite laws against racial discrimination in hiring for jobs, microsociological research shows that Black applicants receive a callback or a job offer about half as often as equally qualified white applicants; in fact, Black applicants with no criminal record receive a callback for a job about as often as a white applicant with a felony conviction (Pager 2007b; Pager, Western, and Bonikowski 2009). There have been no significant changes in hiring discrimination against Black applicants in the US over the last 25 years (Quillian et al 2017). Additional research has found that there are statistically significant levels of discrimination against every non-white group in every country in Europe and North America (Quillian et al. 2019). All these examples show how larger patterns of inequality are reproduced in the everyday interactions of individuals and small groups.

Microsociology can also help us ask better questions about the case we introduced at the beginning of the chapter. When Simone Biles withdrew from the team competition during the Olympics, she stayed at the venue to support her teammates. The entire USA team was distressed by her unexpected decision, and they were worried about Biles, but they needed to follow the script and pretend like everything was fine. Competing teams were also surprised by Biles's withdrawal, as she had been expected to be one of the top competitors, but they too needed to follow their carefully choreographed warmup and performance protocols, to try to give the impression that everything was "business as usual." The television commentators had to make quick decisions about when to talk about the competition and when to talk about Biles, taking their cues from other commentators and trying to maintain a professional broadcast even

**Simone Biles and her teammates together during competition**
Simone Biles supports her teammates before they compete without her at the 2020 Tokyo Olympics.

though the script had clearly changed, and they were forced to improvise. Fans in the stands had to make a decision about where to place their focus—should they watch the competition, or should they watch Biles? In making this decision they took their cues from the other fans around them. Fans watching at home had to make the same kinds of decisions as they watched the competition together with other friends and communicated with other fans on social media.

## Macrosociology

**Macrosociology**
The analysis of large-scale structural patterns and historical trends, including the workings of the economic, political, and cultural systems.

While microsociology examines the everyday activities of individuals and small groups, **macrosociology** explores how large-scale historical trends and structural patterns influence social life. This is why the sociological imagination tells us to look at the relationship between biography and history. The choices we make in our lives matter, but they are structured by the society into which we are born as well as by our own position in that society.

Macrosociologists examine population patterns, differences in wealth and resources, and the organization of political and economic systems. They also investigate power differences that are organized along the lines of race, gender, and class; legacies of military conquest, colonization, and resistance; and religion and other cultural belief systems.

Macrosociological and microsociological perspectives complement each other, resulting in a more complete understanding of sociological life. If microsociological perspectives approach social life as if we are all actors on a stage, macrosociological perspectives show us how the stage we act upon was built in the first place. For example, a macrosociological perspective helps to explain why social protest by athletes attracts so much attention, particularly around matters of race. Professional sports are big business, and athletes are worshipped by their fans. In many countries, in fact, sports are treated as a national religion so that when people cheer for their team they are actually cheering for their country and the values it represents (Dayan and Katz 1992). At the same time, sport has a complicated racial history in the United States. The racial integration of professional sports leagues was an important part of the historical

**Honoring a history of athletes' protest against racism**
Tommie Smith, left, and John Carlos pose for a photo at San Jose State University campus on October 17, 2018. The statue honors their iconic, black-gloved protest celebrating the 50th anniversary of their medal ceremonies at the 1968 Olympic Games in Mexico City.

fight for racial justice in America. Black athletes have been among the most famous celebrities in the country since the 1960s, even though many of them grew up in impoverished, racially segregated communities. For many Americans, the success of these athletes is a "rags to riches" story that is part of the American Dream, and they get upset when successful athletes do not seem to be sufficiently appreciative of the good fortune they have had. However, the intersection of biography and history can make athletes (especially athletes of color) feel a responsibility to use their fame to speak against social injustice. In the same way, while athletes are not mental health professionals, many of them feel a responsibility to publicize issues related to mental health, and to challenge a historical culture of athletics that emphasizes toughness and that discourages athletes from showing vulnerability. Using your sociological imagination can help you to better understand these competing expectations and to ask good critical questions about public controversies when they develop.

## Institutional Perspectives

Social life is patterned and predictable because it is organized into institutions. An **institution** is an established system of symbolic meanings, rules and strategies that defines how people are related to each other and how they should act in a given social situation. Sociologists use the term in two ways: to refer to the coordinated activities of many different kinds of organizations in a particular domain (the overall social organization of religion, the family, or the economy) and to refer to specific organizations within a domain that follow and contribute to wider institutional logics. The family is a social institution; your family is an organization.

**Institution**
An established system of symbolic meanings, rules and strategies that defines how people are related to each other and how they should act in a given social situation.

Institutions act as gatekeepers by controlling access to important social resources. Some institutions give out formal credentials, such as a school diploma, a driver's license, or a board certification to practice a profession. To earn a credential, you have to take the right classes, learn proper behaviors, and pass tests demonstrating that you understand the meanings and know the rules associated with the credentialed role. By defining different expectations for different types of people, institutional gatekeeping reproduces social privileges and disadvantages. For example, because mothers have historically been expected to be the primary caregivers in the family, mothers (and women in general) have often been devalued by gatekeepers in other institutions such as schools and the workplace (Epstein and Goode 1971). Institutional gatekeeping also helps wealthier and better-educated parents pass their advantages on to their children because institutional gatekeepers tend to recognize and reward privilege. Annette Lareau's study *Unequal Childhoods* (2011) analyzes differences between middle-class and working-class parenting styles. She shows that, unlike working-class parents, middle-class parents encourage their children to communicate with adults, to ask questions, and to share their opinions. These children grow up expecting teachers, doctors, and other adults to take them seriously and to treat them like present or future equals. These children are rewarded by these gatekeepers for the styles of interaction their parents taught them because schools and workplaces tend to value this kind of assertiveness. And they are supported by the assertive behavior of their privileged parents, who use their professional expertise, their social status, and their powerful social networks to challenge the authority of teachers and school administrators (Lareau, Weininger and Cox 2018). In these examples, we can see microsociological, macrosociological, and institutional factors combining to produce specific social outcomes.

## 1.3 Thinking Relationally: The Paired Concepts

**LG 1.3 Apply the paired concepts of sociology to the worlds of work, politics, and other domains of social life.**

Our social world is complex. We cannot separate out each of the demands and projects with which we are involved or try to understand them in isolation. Instead, the choices we make in one part of our lives have a cascading effect on the rest of our lives. This is why sociologists focus on the relationships among different social forces.

To think relationally is to avoid thinking about any *single* social force as if it exists in isolation. We don't live in a carefully controlled laboratory where we can isolate a single social factor to measure its impact. In real life, we respond to everything at once. Thinking relationally can help you to move through the world more effectively. To help you to begin thinking relationally, we offer you five sets of paired concepts. These paired concepts include many of the key terms that sociologists have developed for thinking about the social world. They will also help you distinguish how a sociological approach is different from other approaches in the social sciences. Finally, the paired concepts will provide you with useful tools for thinking about how to live in the modern world. The paired concepts are there to remind you that social forces do not exist in isolation but instead exist in relationship to other social forces.

### Solidarity and Conflict

Sociologists understand society as a kind of social fabric that connects us to each other. People want this fabric to be woven tightly enough that it comforts and supports them but not so tightly that it feels constricting. As we move around the social world, we identify with some groups but not with others. We make judgments about good and bad, appropriate and inappropriate, sacred and profane—and we know that others are making the same kinds of judgments.

When people make moral judgments between in-groups and out-groups, they create categories of "us" and "them." **Solidarity** is the sense of belonging and connection that we have to a particular group. It is the sense of "us" feeling connected together. Solidarity is one of the most powerful social forces because the feelings of connection, belonging, and community encourage us to cooperate with others and to act for the greater good. But solidarity also produces **conflict** because it always produces a "them." We can only feel connected to a group by drawing boundaries around it, and these boundaries only work by defining those outside the group who are both different from us and not connected to us.

The relationship between solidarity and conflict can range from the mundane to the very serious. On a larger scale, the concept of national identity can encourage a people to think their own national group is superior to other national groups. On a smaller scale, you might face issues of solidarity and conflict when you try to integrate a new romantic partner into a long-standing friendship group. Old friends may not like your new partner, who may feel threatened by the solidarity between old friends. The point is that solidarity and conflict are deeply interconnected, and the relationship between solidarity and conflict produces some of the most powerful social forces in our lives.

**Solidarity** The sense of belonging and the connection that we have to a particular group.

**Conflict** Disagreement, opposition, and separation between individuals or groups.

### Power and Resistance

Sociologists understand **power** as a social relationship in which one individual or group is able to influence the conduct of other individuals or groups (Scott 2006: 127). In its most direct form, power operates by physical force or by the threat of force. Usually, though, power operates in other ways. You may follow an order because you believe that the person giving it has a legitimate right to do so, like when you agree to pay your monthly phone bill. You may follow somebody's suggestion because they manage to convince you that they have a good solution to a common problem. You may act without much thought at all, either because it is something you have done many times before or because everyone around you is doing the same thing. You may be strongly attracted to a particular person and willing to do virtually anything they ask you. Each of these relationships involves an exercise in power.

**Resistance** is the other side of power. The exercise of power always produces resistance. People resent being forced to do things. They dislike feeling trapped. They do not like to feel powerless. They question whether the people ordering them to do something really have the right or the authority to do

**Power** A social relationship in which one individual or group is able to influence the conduct of other individuals or groups either directly through force or indirectly through authority, persuasion, or cultural expectation; the ability of individuals or groups to get what they want, even against the resistance of others who are participating in the same action.

**Resistance** Opposition to the exercise of power.

so. They get angry when they disagree with decisions made by elected politicians. Their leaders disappoint them, and they grow more cynical and distrustful of people in positions of power.

The complicated relationship between power and resistance plays itself out in small-scale interactions, social institutions, and larger social structures. It is organized very much like a complex game because each "move" by one player will influence the next move by the other, and the different moves are not equally available to all players. For example, the use of force is mainly reserved for police, military forces, and other agents of government. When other people use force, they are met with considerable social criticism and may even attract the attention of law enforcement. Many uses of power require both money and resources, which are distributed unequally throughout society. It is generally easier for privileged people to exercise power. At the same time, because the exercise of power produces its own resistance, these privileges are frequently challenged. For all these reasons, the relationship between power and resistance is a primary research interest of sociology.

### Inequality and Privilege

**Inequality** The unequal distribution of social goods such as money, power, status, and social resources.

**Inequality** refers to the uneven distribution of social resources. Inequality exists in all societies and for virtually every resource that people care about, including income, wealth, education, food, health care, and access to power. Patterns of social inequality map key social divisions, including race, ethnicity, gender, age, social class, and geography. They also reflect past patterns of power and resistance, including colonization and decolonization, slavery and abolition.

Sociologists analyze how inequality is organized across time and place since a key dimension of addressing inequality is to understand how it is created and sustained. Sociologists study inequality in single societies such as the United States, they compare how inequality is organized in different societies, they look at global inequality, and they track changes in inequality over time.

**Social protest following the *Dobbs* decision that overturned *Roe v. Wade***
This decision by the US Supreme Court ended the legal right to abortion in the United States in 2022.

Inequality creates the social conditions for **privilege** because of the advantages that flow to people at the top of the hierarchy. People with privilege have more resources and are able to segregate themselves from the less fortunate. In the United States and elsewhere, privileged people live in different neighborhoods, send their children to different schools, belong to different clubs, and work different jobs. Because they live almost completely different lives, surrounded by other people just like them, the well-off do not always consider how inequality makes their privileges possible. Sociological research helps show how inequality and privilege are inextricably related to each other, locally, globally, and historically.

**Privilege** The greater resources possessed by some individuals and groups compared to others.

## Global and Local

Social life on our planet is increasingly global. Because of this interconnectedness, the COVID-19 pandemic has touched every corner of the Earth. Corporations that we work for, and whose products we purchase, have a global reach. Financial turmoil in one country influences financial markets an ocean away. People everywhere watch the same movies and TV programs, play the same video games, and communicate with strangers over social media. The number of global migrants continues to increase as political conflict and climate change make regions of the world increasingly uninhabitable. Sociologists refer to this international integration of social life and increasing global interconnection as **globalization**.

**Globalization** A concept that refers to the growing social, economic, cultural, and political interdependence of the world's people.

**Local** The specific particular settings of everyday life, including face-to-face relationships.

Despite increased globalization, we still live much of our lives in specific **local** places. Although we might email and text friends from around the world, for most of us the majority of our communication is with people who live near us or work with us. The COVID-19 pandemic and the experience of quarantine continue to reshape our sense of what is "local." Sociologists emphasize that the local and the global do not exist in isolation but are related to each other.

**Privilege and inequality**
While most privileged people can insulate themselves from people living in poverty by residing in different neighborhoods and attending different schools, in these luxury buildings in São Paulo, Brazil, residents can see the Paraisópolis favela from the swimming pools on their balconies.

## Structure and Contingency

While social life is patterned in important ways, the patterns do not control us completely. As we move through the world, we are continuously reading and interpreting social cues. We plan our actions, trying to predict their outcomes. We improvise, we try new things, and we play with new identities. We may know the rules and the social conventions, but we do not always follow them. There is contingency, or openness, in action—outcomes are not completely determined by the regular patterns in social life that sociologists call **social structures**.

**Social structures**
The seen and unseen regular, organized patterns of social life.

As we discussed in the previous section, patterns or structures that sociologists study include population patterns, political and economic structures, cultural belief systems, and power differences that are organized along the lines of race, gender, and class, among other social differences. These structures are created and re-created at all three levels of analysis—microsociologically, macrosociologically, and institutionally. People re-create social structures such as stereotypes when they cross the street to avoid people they perceive as threatening. They re-create structures such as employment and migration patterns when they move to a new city or a new country in search of work. They re-create structures of status inequality when they treat doctors and judges with more respect than nurses and secretaries. They re-create structures of gender inequality when they hand restaurant bills to men rather than women and when they refuse to acknowledge someone's preferred pronouns. These structures are so deeply ingrained in our social environment that we hardly notice them.

**Contingency**
Openness in social life produced by human choices and actions.

However, the fact that social structures have to be reproduced in our everyday actions means that they are connected to the openness of social life. **Contingency** refers to this openness and to the fact that a given outcome is never guaranteed, despite the likelihood that things will happen in a specific way. For example, while it is expected that someone will shake your hand if you extend it to them in greeting, there is never a guarantee that this will happen—especially as rules of social contact adapt to the need for social distancing. While you are waiting patiently in line to buy a ticket, there is always the possibility that someone will cut in front of you. There is also contingency connected to institutional and macrosociological structures. A severe economic downturn can cause a massive increase in homelessness. International trade can be disrupted by a pandemic, and important news can be preempted by a catastrophic natural disaster. These unexpected and unanticipated events are a regular occurrence in social life, and they help to explain why most organizations develop elaborate contingency plans. And yet, as the events of 2020 demonstrated, no matter how much planning they do, it is impossible to predict exactly what is going to happen.

When people act differently from expectations, they challenge social structures. One of the things that happens during times of great social change is that people are more likely to challenge existing structures and to create new ones (Swidler 1986). Sociologists work to make people aware of social structures so that they can make a more conscious decision about which structures to reproduce and which ones to challenge. And sociologists also try to think about the role of contingency in their social research. No matter how much they know about social structures, they remain attentive to the ways that the contingent actions of individuals and groups can challenge and disrupt social structures and social outcomes.

**Structure and contingency**
Economic downturn, ill health, family dysfunction, and natural disaster are all events that can affect people's ability to find shelter. The lack of social resources and social care for people affected by such contingencies results in homelessness, with people sleeping on the sidewalk in very cold weather.

These five paired concepts are connected to each other in important ways, and thinking about them together can help you understand the complex and dynamic nature of social life. For example, the relationship between "us" and "them" is connected to the exercise of power and resistance and to the organization of inequality and privilege. The intermingling of the global and the local helps us to see social structures, to try out new things, to form different kinds of groups. When groups form into social movements that challenge the powerful, their actions highlight the contingency of social action and the possibility of challenging social structures.

## 1.4 Why Sociology?

**LG 1.4 Describe how sociologists pursue sociology as a way to secure human freedom and social justice.**

Why sociology? There are many reasons to pursue a sociological life, but two literacy skills acquired by a study of sociology are especially important. First, sociology teaches a literacy of concepts. By developing a grasp of key sociological concepts and theories, you will be better able to identify how different social forces are connected in real life. Second, sociology teaches data and information literacy, by developing a range of research methods that help you think critically and creatively about how to get the facts right when asking social questions. Both are important skills valued by employers. They are also important for developing a deeper understanding about the world in which you live.

This is the larger promise of sociology: that it will inform the pursuit of human freedom and social justice. How? The goal is not to tell people what to think but rather to help us all think more clearly and comprehensively about our shared social life. In the highly individualized societies that we live in today, this collective level of thinking is often missing or underdeveloped. By thinking about interactional norms, social scripts, organizational routines, and broader institutional principles, a sociological imagination can help us see the face of the "other" outside our own narrow circle, while illuminating our own complex positions in social relationships of solidarity, privilege, and power. Practically, sociologists do research on behalf of social movements, governments, nonprofit organizations, and businesses that help people make more informed decisions and think carefully about the social impact of their choices. Sociologists also create theories that help us think imaginatively about our shared social future. In short, sociology enables us to consider the human face of social action and identify our own capacities to defend—or transform—social life.

## LEARNING GOALS REVISITED

**1.1 Define the sociological imagination.**

- The sociological imagination is the ability to connect "biography with history"—that is, to connect our individual life story with the historical and cultural patterns of the society in which we live.

- The sociological imagination shows us how individual choices might be affected by wider social forces and social change.

- The sociological imagination shows that people can resist larger social forces by acting in ways that change or challenge the social structure or by forming social movements for social change.

**1.2 Understand that there are different levels of social things: for example, individuals, relationships, and institutions.**

- Early sociologists defined sociology as a new science of social facts, social action, and social relationships. They identified a special social domain that was different than the level of individuals alone.
- Sociologists identify different levels of analysis and different levels of scale in research: microsociological, macrosociological, and institutional.
- Sociologists are interested in how causes at one level affect causes and outcomes at other levels.
- Sociology is distinct from the other social sciences because it is committed to multiple research methods to study the intersections between different dimensions of social life. Sociological research strategies are designed to eliminate or reduce confirmation bias.

**1.3 Apply the paired concepts of sociology to the worlds of work, politics, and other domains of social life.**

- Sociologists are found in many different careers, including law, medicine, education, social work, the arts, public service, business, and more.
- Social-scientific knowledge is different from ordinary, everyday knowledge about the world because it self-consciously uses systematic strategies to collect accurate and useful information.

**1.4 Describe how sociologists pursue sociology as a way to secure human freedom and social justice.**

- Sociology teaches a literacy of concepts and a literacy of data and information. Both of these literacies involve concrete skills that are of interest to employers in many fields.
- Sociological research strategies are designed to eliminate or reduce bias, particularly confirmation bias, where people are more likely to think something is true because it confirms prior beliefs.
- Sociology is a perspective on social life that promotes understanding, human connection, empowerment, and freedom.
- Sociologists understand humans as individuals with free will who make judgments about good and bad, right and wrong. Sometimes people will choose to support the social structures, and other times they will act to change them.

## Key Terms

Confirmation bias 10
Conflict 17
Contingency 20
Globalization 19
Inequality 18
Institution 15
Institutional level of analysis 11
Level of analysis 11
Local 19
Macrosociology 14

Microsociology 12
Power 17
Privilege 19
Research methods 10
Resistance 17
Social structures 20
Sociological imagination 7
Solidarity 17

## Review Questions

1. What is sociology? Describe the three basic elements of sociology.
2. What is the sociological imagination? Give an example of a research study that exemplifies the sociological imagination.
3. Why do sociologists believe that systematic and scientific research is the best way to understand the social world?
4. How is sociology different from other social sciences, such as psychology or economics?
5. What is microsociology? Give an example of a microsociological approach to understanding the world.
6. What is macrosociology? Give an example of a macrosociological approach to understanding the world.
7. What is an institution? How do institutions shape our lives? Give an example of an institutional understanding of the world.
8. Why do sociologists insist that we think about the social world relationally?
9. How are solidarity and conflict connected? Give an example of how solidarity produces conflict.
10. What is power? Why does the exercise of power always produce resistance? Give an example of resistance.
11. What is inequality? How does inequality help to produce privilege?
12. What is globalization? Give an example of how the global and the local are connected to each other.
13. Give an example of how people recreate social structures in their everyday lives.
14. What is contingency? How is contingency related to social structure? Give an example of contingency in action.

## Explore

### RECOMMENDED READINGS

Bauman, Zygmunt. 2008. *The Art of Life*. Malden, MA: Polity Press.

Bourdieu, Pierre. 2010. *Sociology Is a Martial Art: Political Writings by Pierre Bourdieu*. New York: New Press.

Goffman, Erving. 1959. *The Presentation of Self in Everyday Life*. New York: Anchor.

Mills, C. Wright. [1959] 2000. *Sociological Imagination*. New York: Oxford University Press.

Wilson, William Julius. 1987. *The Truly Disadvantaged*. Chicago: University of Chicago Press.

### ACTIVITIES

- *Use your sociological imagination*: Are you a member of any kind of social group? Make a list of the ones you belong to. How many are there? Rank your list of groups in different ways, for example, by size or how strongly you feel connected to them. What are other groups that are different from but related to your group? Compare your findings with your classmates'.

- *Media+Data Literacies*: Are there any celebrities (politicians, actors, or musicians) whom you follow regularly? Explain why you find them persuasive. Where do you get information about celebrities? Using your sociological imagination, can you identify "gatekeepers" who might have shaped your opinions?

- *Discuss*: Why do you think you are in college right now when other people are not? Are there social reasons? What are they?

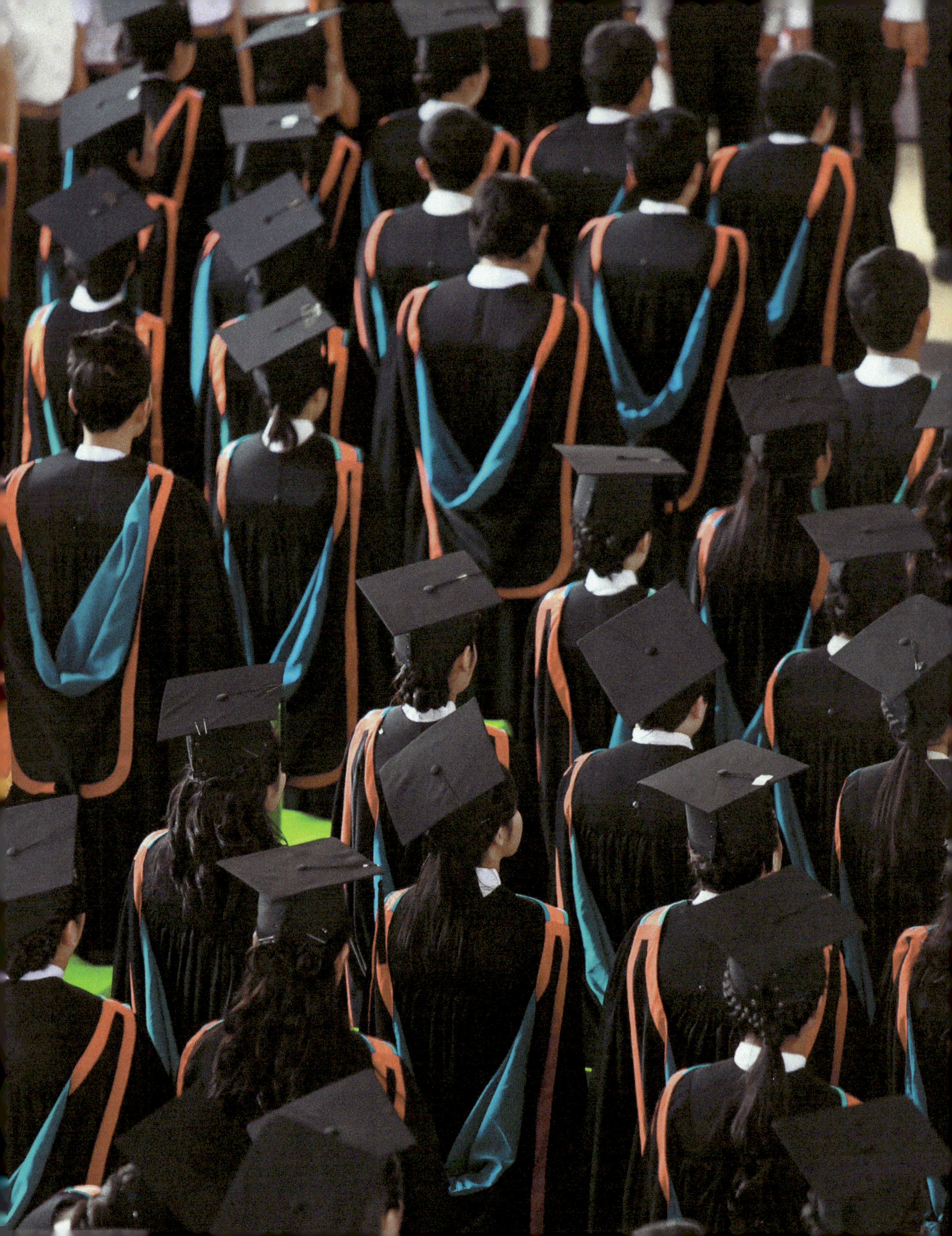

# American Sociology
## *Theory and Methods*

Are you already a sociologist? American sociologist Charles Lemert thinks you are, because you use ideas about the social world to navigate your life. This might be called common sense. For example, you might share the widely held view that college education is linked to increased income. But why? What is the source of your understanding?

The difference between common sense and sociology is that sociologists use specific theories and methods to ask critical questions about social life (Lemert 2008). In this case, sociologists ask questions about how education works to produce differences in income. What is it about college education exactly that leads to higher average incomes among college graduates compared to nongraduates: Is it the content of specific classes, the prestige of the particular institution, or the cultural knowledge learned at college that is important? Do the habits and mannerisms of educated people help college graduates navigate job interviews by signaling that they are the "right kind of people" for the job? Perhaps these are questions you will pursue in your own career as a teacher, a lawyer, a doctor, a politician, or . . . a sociologist?

**Graduation**
In today's global economy, a college degree is required for entry to many workplaces.

### Chapter Outline

**2.1 THINKING LIKE A SOCIOLOGIST 28**

*Critical Questions and the Sociological Imagination 28*

**2.2 SOCIOLOGY: THEORY AND CONTEXTS 30**

*Classical Sociology 31*
*The European Canon 33*
*Sociology in America 38*
*Moving Away from Grand Theories 41*
*Theories about Difference 41*
*The Cultural Turn 43*
*Global Context 43*
*Sociology Today 44*

**2.3 SOCIAL RESEARCH: PURPOSE AND PROCESS 44**

*Social Research and Ethics 45*
*Research Methods and Critical Literacy 47*
*Data and Measurement 49*
*Variables, Data Collection, and Causal Relationships 51*
*Common Strategies for Sociological Research 54*
*Basic, Applied, and Public Sociology 57*

**CASE STUDY: UNDERSTANDING COVID-19 59**

> **LEARNING GOALS**
>
> **2.1** Understand that sociology developed as a way to explain social patterns and social change and is one of a family of social science disciplines located within the liberal arts.
>
> **2.2** Identify core theoretical concepts in the discipline.
>
> **2.3** Define the major elements of the research process and describe a range of sociological research techniques.

# 2.1 Thinking Like a Sociologist

**LG 2.1** Understand that sociology developed as a way to explain social patterns and social change and is one of a family of social science disciplines located within the liberal arts.

Sociological theories can refine our common-sense image of the world, by challenging us to think differently about things we believe we already know. For example, it is true that people with a college education usually do have higher incomes. But this is not only because people learn job-specific skills in college. College is also about status and credentials. For most of the 20th century, college attendance was a sign of privilege and a way to access prestigious social networks. In the 1960s, US government programs were established to expand college enrollment in an effort to reduce social inequality.

However, this was not a perfect solution for reducing inequality because, as sociological research on education shows, the people who are most likely to do well in college are those whose parents are well educated, have good jobs, or both (Blau and Duncan 1967; Bourdieu and Passeron 1979, 1990; Lareau 2011; also see Yosso 2005). By comparing children's success in the labor market relative to their parents and by looking at the operation of classrooms and schools, sociological researchers have documented how these institutions reproduce the privileges of inherited wealth, status, and opportunity. Sociological theories about inequality and privilege can help us better understand what might seem to be a common-sense relationship between college education and income. By asking critical questions, these theories encourage us to see the social world in new ways.

### Critical Questions and the Sociological Imagination

A critical question relies on reason, theory, prior knowledge, and new evidence to reflect upon social actions. Critical questions allow for more nuanced and complicated answers. Sociologists who ask critical questions reject the idea that a given social outcome was inevitable. Instead, they seek to explain why something happened the way it did—and not otherwise. At their best, critical questions help us imagine new social possibilities.

## METHODS AND INTERPRETATION

## Measuring the Effect of Education on Earnings

The US Census Bureau and the Department of Labor collect national data showing that education has an enormous impact on earnings for most of the US population. They report that "education levels had more effect on earnings over a 40-year span in the workforce than any other demographic factor, such as gender, race and Hispanic origin" (Julian and Kominski 2011). Figure 2.1 shows that in 2023, the median weekly earnings for workers with a bachelor's degree ($1.493) were more than 60 percent higher than earnings for workers with only a high school diploma ($899) and more than twice the median weekly earnings of people with less than a high school diploma ($708).

There are exceptions to the general pattern of relationship between education and earnings. Some well-known people never attended college or dropped out, including Facebook founder Mark Zuckerberg, Microsoft founder Bill Gates, and Apple founder Steve Jobs. While these individuals are comparatively rare, they show how chance, contingency, and choice can play a role in individual life outcomes. In the language of sociology, these exceptions show that people's lives are not entirely shaped by social structures.

**Unemployment rate (%)** | **Median usual weekly earnings ($)**

| Educational attainment | Unemployment rate (%) | Median weekly earnings ($) |
|---|---|---|
| Doctoral degree | 1.6 | 2,109 |
| Professional degree | 1.2 | 2,206 |
| Master's degree | 2.0 | 1,737 |
| Bachelor's degree | 2.2 | 1,493 |
| Associate's degree | 2.7 | 1,058 |
| Some college, no degree | 3.3 | 992 |
| High school diploma | 3.9 | 899 |
| Less than a high school diploma | 5.6 | 708 |

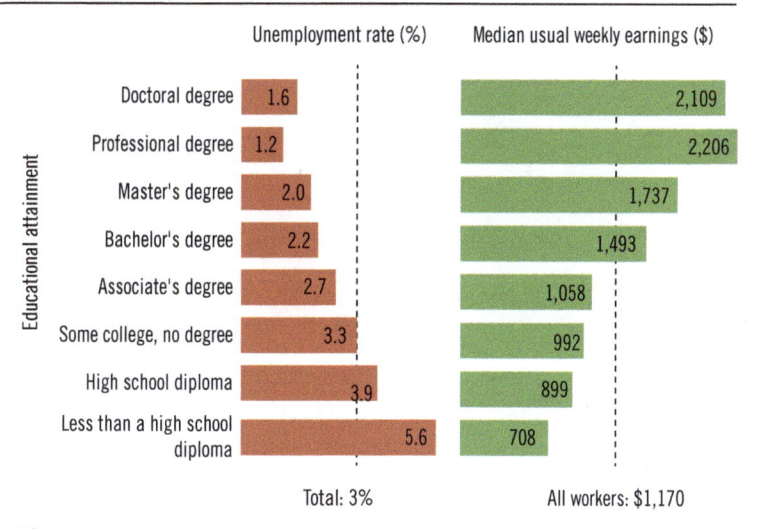

Total: 3% | All workers: $1,170

**Figure 2.1** Unemployment rates and earnings by educational attainment, 2023.
Note: Data are for persons age 25 and over. Earnings are for full-time wage and salary workers.
Source: US Bureau of Labor Statistics, Current Population Survey.

### ACTIVE LEARNING

**Discuss:** Ask your parents or another adult why they think college is important for career success. Be sure to ask what it is exactly about education that pays off for most people.

---

Cultivating the ability to ask a critical question is fundamental to what C. Wright Mills (1916–1962) called the sociological imagination. As we discussed in Chapter 1, the sociological imagination is the ability to see the connections between individual lives and wider social structures.

The sociological imagination implies that where you stand determines what you can see. This imaginative ability to move outside of yourself, using your mind to view yourself as part of a wider social scene, is a mental capability called **reflexivity**, and it is central to social theory.

**Reflexivity** The imaginative ability to move outside of yourself in order to understand yourself as part of a wider social scene.

**C. Wright Mills**

The sociological imagination is based on reflexivity. It acknowledges that our perceptions are limited by our social positions. Our views are shaped by the time and place and bodies where we live and the experiences that we have. These experiences are further shaped by the groups, families, and other institutions to which we belong. By asking critical questions about ourselves and our social world, sociology can help us extend our perceptions. The promise of the sociological imagination is that we will be able to see a much wider picture, tell much better stories, and take much more effective social action.

This chapter introduces the theories and core concepts of the sociological tradition. It also highlights voices that were once left out of the history of social thought before describing the contributions of contemporary critics of sociological theory. The second part of the chapter introduces research methods that enable sociologists to analyze critical questions in applied contexts. Doing sociology requires both kinds of literacies: a literacy of theoretical concepts and a critical understanding of research methods.

## 2.2 Sociology: Theory and Contexts

**LG 2.2** Identify core theoretical concepts in the discipline.

The French philosopher Auguste Comte (1798–1857) was one of the first sociologists. He was interested in how different types of scientific knowledge were connected to each other. Comte identified six "fundamental sciences": mathematics, astronomy, physics, chemistry, biology, and sociology. Of these six, Comte believed that sociology was destined to become the most important, because social phenomena were the most complex. Comte wanted sociology to integrate all the other sciences into a single theory of social phenomena, which people could use to create a new and better society.

This ambitious agenda for sociological theory was influential for a long time. In fact, many sociologists in the 19th century believed that **social science** would eventually replace religion as the major intellectual force organizing in the world. They looked to sociology to develop a science of society itself, by establishing a master theory that could explain social phenomena.

**Social sciences**
The disciplines that use systematic scientific and cultural methods to study the social world, as distinct from the natural and physical worlds.

> **CAREERS**
>
> ### The Importance of Theory
>
> Career advisors often emphasize the importance of acquiring specific technical skills. Fortunately, the study of sociology will teach you many such skills.
>
> Today's workplace also requires people who have general theoretical skills since creative and flexible thinking is crucial to solving social challenges, such as the challenges created by the COVID-19 pandemic. National employer surveys find that problem solving, critical thinking, and communication skills are among the top qualities employers are looking for in candidates (National Association of Colleges and Employers 2024). Business magazines like *Forbes* assert that the most important career skill is critical thinking (Casserly 2012), and in his best-selling book *The World Is Flat*, Thomas Friedman argued that the "special sauce" that creates innovation in today's world is the ability to integrate technical skills with a broad-based liberal arts education in art, music, literature, and popular culture (Friedman 2005). A knowledge of theory is what helps people integrate these different kinds of knowledge and come up with innovative solutions to critical problems.
>
> #### ACTIVE LEARNING
>
> **Find out:** Go to your library or your library's online resources and find a dictionary such as the *Oxford English Dictionary*. Look up the word "theory." Where does the word come from? What are some of its different meanings and uses?

Émile Durkheim (1858–1917), one of the founders of sociology in France, believed strongly in this vision of sociology as the most important of the social sciences. Durkheim wanted sociologists to study **social facts**, which are the forces external to the individual that influence how people act, think, or feel (Durkheim [1895] 2014). Social facts are different from biological facts or psychological facts because they exist outside of the individual's body or conscience. Durkheim also wanted to develop a single theory to understand and explain these social facts. The same kind of grand vision motivated the work of Talcott Parsons (1902–1979), an American sociologist who led Harvard University's Department of Social Relations in the middle of the 20th century. Parsons worked to create a single theory for all the social sciences that could help support a democratic society. This pursuit of a single theory that could explain all social phenomena fell out of favor during the 1960s and 1970s, and was replaced by the idea that different disciplines should collaborate to solve the problems of the day.

**Social facts** Facts about the collective nature of social life that have their own patterns and dynamics beyond the individual level.

## Classical Sociology

Early sociologists sought to explain big changes in society, such as the Industrial Revolution. Beginning around 1760 in England, the Industrial Revolution had spread throughout Europe and North America by 1850 and reorganized almost every part of social life. Where once goods were made by

**Urbanization**
A social process in which the population shifts from the country into cities and where most people start to live in cities rather than rural areas.

hand at home, now goods were mass-produced in factories using machines. Scientific improvements in health and medicine extended life, food became more plentiful, and life expectancy increased. The logic of marriage and families adapted to meet the needs of factory production. The Industrial Revolution also led to **urbanization** as cities grew rapidly to accommodate people moving from the countryside to cities to work in factories. At the same time, social inequality and crime increased, and professional police forces were created to control disorder and to act as a deterrent against theft and violence. Industrialization and urbanization were also linked to **globalization**, which connected human action across different regions and continents (Held 1999). Taken together, industrialization, globalization, and urbanization changed the way that people interacted with each other. Sociologists of the time believed that they could help describe and explain these momentous social changes.

The second change was the spread of modern democracy, understood as the rule of the people. The American Revolution (1776) and the French Revolution (1789) replaced the rule of kings with the rule of the people and ushered in the era of the nation-state. In a nation-state, a government has control over a defined territory; the people who live in that territory are citizens of the nation, united by a common identity, a common history, and a strong sense of social connection (Mann 1993). The most powerful industrialized nations also engaged in **colonialism**, which extended Western influence and control around much of the world.

**The new industrial landscape**
This 19th-century engraving by Durand-Brager of Vivian's copper foundry in Swansea, Wales, depicts the pollution from open-pit mines and smoke from foundries that transformed the landscape.

**Industrial division of labor**
This 19th-century watercolor by I. F. Bonhomme shows women and children working in the coal-sifting room at the Blanzy mine, Saone-et-Loire, France. Women and children were among the first factory workers.

**Machine technology**
The Industrial Revolution witnessed a rapid pace of technological invention in new factories. This steam hammer was erected in James Nasmyth's foundry near Manchester, England, in 1832. Today's factories can be cleaner, but they are still based on industrial technology.

**The patriotism of the colonies**
Instead of resisting British colonial government, the colonized were asked to fight on behalf of the British Empire. In this 1917 postcard, a British and an Indian soldier pose next to the Red Ensign, an extension of British nationalism in a flag symbolizing Britain's overseas possessions.

European nations justified their conquests by claiming they were bringing modern benefits to "less civilized" societies, and they developed pseudoscientific arguments about the supposed superiority of the "European race" to justify their enslavement and exploitation of colonized peoples (Smedley 1993).

## The European Canon

Early sociological theorists struggled to describe and explain these changes, among them Karl Marx (1818–1883) and Max Weber (1864–1920) in Germany and Émile Durkheim in France. Their combined work helped create the **canon** for sociological scholarship.

**KARL MARX.** Marx saw economic conflict as the central social fact determining every society, shaping social relationships between masters and slaves, landowners and peasants, factory owners and workers. In modern Western societies he described this fundamental economic conflict in terms of private property, or capital. **Capitalism** is a system that transforms the means of material life—food, clothing, shelter—into objects to be bought and sold in markets. A small class of capitalist owners controls all the land, finance,

**Globalization**
A concept that refers to the growing social, economic, cultural, and political interdependence of the world's people.

**Colonialism**
A global stratification system in which powerful nations used their military strength to take political control over other territories and exploit them economically.

factories, and machinery of production. Everyone else is destined to be a worker with no choice but to labor for capitalists for low wages under bad conditions. Instead of producing for their own purposes, Marx argues that capitalism strips workers of their humanity and creates **alienation**—a condition where humans have no meaningful connection to their work or to each other. According to this view, all government, justice, cultural, and religious institutions are organized to support the rule of capitalists; and thus, the workers often fail to realize their own exploitation, a situation that Marx called "false consciousness." The key for overcoming this situation was the creation of a revolutionary class consciousness among the workers.

Marx was one of the most influential intellectuals of the 19th century. His 1848 *Communist Manifesto* (which he published with Friedrich Engels) argued that economic inequality is a permanent feature of capitalist society and that the economic interests of powerful corporations and a few extremely wealthy individuals shape the law and culture. Many sociologists have also been inspired by Marx's goal of using social science to improve the lives of the less fortunate. For example, the project of public sociology is a commitment to using sociological ideas in wider public conversations and struggles for social justice both in the United States and around the globe.

**MAX WEBER.** Unlike Marx, Weber believed that science needed to be separate from politics. Weber was also interested in the role of modern bureaucratic organizations in social life. In a modern **bureaucracy**, organizations are run according to formal rules and regulations rather than personal ties, traditions, or customs. Weber argued that all institutions in modern society—governments, militaries, corporations, and even cultural and religious organizations—were organized as bureaucracies.

Weber saw the rise of bureaucracy as part of the process of **rationalization**, in which all social relationships become more

**Karl Marx**

**Canon** The set of thinkers and ideas that serves as a standard point of reference for a scholarly or artistic tradition.

**Mass worker action. The Manchester General Strike, 1926**
The *Illustrated London News* captures the size and organization of the Manchester General Strike on May 15, 1926. Depicted here is the Great Procession of Corporation Tramwaymen starting from Albert Square and led by their band.

Max Weber

Émile Durkheim

organized, standardized, and predictable. This was central to the rise of capitalism. Weber warned that a rationalized world can be a tedious and dehumanizing place in which to live and work. Weber was concerned that rationalization has led to a **disenchantment** in modern life, in which people blindly follow bureaucratic rules without any sense of passion or ultimate purpose.

**ÉMILE DURKHEIM.** The third key classical sociologist was Émile Durkheim. Like Marx and Weber, Durkheim was interested in the way that changes in the division of labor were shaping social life in industrial societies. Where Durkheim differed was in his focus on solidarity, which refers to the social ties that bind people together.

In *The Division of Labor in Society* ([1893] 2014), Durkheim examined how solidarity was changing in industrializing, urbanizing nation-states such as France. In pre-industrial, agricultural, and smaller societies, people were tied to each other through a strong sense of similarity, which Durkheim called **mechanical solidarity**. As a result, they tended to think the same way as everyone else, and they could assume that everyone in their society shared the same values and beliefs. In contrast, in modern industrialized societies people have different jobs and different experiences but are connected through their dependence on other people's specialized expertise. For example, we are connected to our doctor and our postal delivery person, even if we do not know much about them personally. Durkheim called this **organic solidarity**.

**Capitalism** An economic system based on the private ownership of property, including the means of material life such as food, clothing, and shelter, in which the production of goods and services is controlled by private individuals and companies, and prices are set by markets.

**Alienation** A condition in which humans have no meaningful connection to their work or to each other.

**Bureaucracy** An organizational form with a clearly defined hierarchy where roles are based on rational, predictable, written rules and procedures to govern every aspect of the organization and produce standardized, systematic, and efficient outcomes.

**Rationalization** A major dynamic of modernity in which social relationships become more predictable, standardized, systematic, and efficient.

**Disenchantment** The condition of rationalized bureaucratic societies characterized by the growing importance of skepticism and the decline of belief as a source of social action.

**Solidarity in prayer, September 23, 2001**
People pray holding American flags during a prayer service at Yankee Stadium for the victims of the World Trade Center terrorist attacks in New York in 2001.

**Division of labor** A central principle for organizing the productive work in society that sorts different people into different work roles to ensure the production and reproduction of human life. This includes the separation of work and life into different, more specialized parts.

**Mechanical solidarity** A system of social ties that produces social cohesion on the basis of similar work and life in less complex divisions of labor.

**Organic solidarity** A system of social ties that produces social cohesion based on differences in a complex division of labor.

Durkheim believed that, while organic solidarity encouraged greater individuality and tolerance, it also could lead to people feeling isolated and disconnected, a situation he referred to as **anomie**. Durkheim wanted sociologists to identify alternative sources of social connection that would promote solidarity. For example, Durkheim thought that national identity and national symbols could create a sort of common consciousness among the members of a nation-state and that, as such, the nation could be an important source of social solidarity that was similar to the mechanical solidarity of older societies (Durkheim [1893] 2014; Smith 2004). Durkheim believed that **collective representations**—the images we have of our own social groups like the nation but also ethnicity, race, and religion—produce social solidarity.

It is true that the classical sociological theories of Marx, Weber, and Durkheim are limited by a distinctly 19th-century European point of view. Marx did not comprehend the complexity of occupational and technical change, and he underestimated the power of nation-states, ethnicities, and religious identities to shape individual lives and world history (Guibernau 2020). Weber underestimated the ability of religious traditions to adapt and thrive despite the onslaughts of secular life (Weidner 2014). Durkheim's references to "primitive" societies have been criticized for being Eurocentric and simplistic (Go 2017). Neither Marx, Weber, nor Durkheim developed an adequate theory of race, gender, or colonialism (Go 2016).

It remains the case, however, that Marx, Weber, and Durkheim serve as a common frame of reference in sociology and enjoy a privileged status (Alexander 1987: 11). New theoretical movements in sociology often develop through arguments about the classical theorists, by reinterpreting what one or more of the classical theorists "really meant." This is just as true in the United States as it is in Europe, despite the fact that American sociology has its own distinctive history.

## PAIRED CONCEPTS

## Inequality and Privilege

### Forgotten Founders in Sociology

Ibn Khaldun is considered one of the premier philosophers of the Arab world. His scholarly output contains fundamental conceptual work in what we would recognize as the social sciences, specifically anthropology, economics, and sociology (Dhaouadi 1990; Gates 1967; Haddad 1977). Khaldun wrote prolifically on many topics, including six volumes of general sociology (Khaldûn 2004). Centuries before Émile Durkheim wrote about solidarity, Khaldun invented the term *'asabiyyah* to refer to the social cohesion among humans arising from group life.

There is evidence that 19th-century thinkers were aware of Khaldun's work but omitted reference to him and other non-European traditions in their theorizing. This is an example of how the classical sociological canon is Eurocentric in its exclusion of non-European voices and references.

The 19th-century English writer Harriet Martineau argued that the study of society must include key political and religious as well as social institutions. Martineau wrote about political economy, taxation, the poor laws, travel, women's rights and education, and the abolition of slavery. In 1834 she travelled widely in America, observing its morals and manners. On her return to England, she published *Society in America* (1837). Her book about research methods, *How to Observe Morals and Manners* (1838), and her introduction and translation of sociological ideas in Auguste Comte's *Cours de Philosophie Positive* (1853), are particularly important.

Despite her influence and popularity during her lifetime, Martineau's ideas were excluded when sociology was institutionalized as an academic discipline in the late 19th century. Historians like Michael Hill argue that this reflects the pervasive gender inequality of the early institutions of the discipline. Today, however, Martineau is considered to be one of the founders of the field of sociology (Giddens and Griffiths 2006; Hill 2002). A similar story can be told about Jane Addams, who was the first American woman to receive the Nobel Peace Prize and who is today recognized as one of the founders of sociology in the US. Despite the fact that her research had a significant impact and was well known among the sociology faculty at the University of Chicago, her influence was almost entirely erased in the historical accounts of American sociology that were written throughout the twentieth century (Deegan 1990).

W. E. B. Du Bois was an American sociologist and civil rights activist. He was the first Black person to earn a doctorate at Harvard University, and he was a professor of history, sociology, and economics at Atlanta University. A prolific author and editor, Du Bois had a long and distinguished career, writing landmark studies on Black culture, communities, and politics. These include *The Philadelphia Negro* (1899); *The Souls of Black Folk* (1903); his influential chapter, "The Talented Tenth," in *The Negro Problem* (1903), which made a case for education and collective racial uplift; and *Black Reconstruction in America* (1935), which chronicled the continuing oppression and inequality that followed the emancipation of enslaved people in the United States. Later in his career, he became a pan-Africanist and published

**Ibn Khaldun**

**PAIRED CONCEPTS CONTINUED**

**Harriet Martineau**

**W. E. B. Du Bois**

many works on Africa, including *The World and Africa* (1947). Du Bois is also recognized as a foundational theorist of colonialism (Go 2016).

Although Du Bois was the founder of the first school of scientific sociology in the United States (Morris 2015: 1) and his academic career almost precisely spans the formation and development of the discipline of sociology, his scholarly voice and output were disconnected from influential institutions in the discipline until recently. The context of this exclusion was the deep racial segregation of US society during his lifetime and explicit exclusion by his privileged white peers in sociology. The exclusion of DuBois is a key example of the way white privilege worked to preserve some voices in the new discipline of sociology rather than others. It is only since 2000 that American textbooks have regularly included Du Bois in the sociological canon.

**ACTIVE LEARNING**

**Find out:** Look at the textbook from another introductory course you are taking, and find the section where they describe the history of the discipline. What are the social characteristics of the people who are described as the "founders" of that discipline? Are there any biases that you can identify? Are these biases acknowledged?

**Anomie** The condition of feeling isolated and disconnected in the absence of rich social connection.

**Collective representations** Pictures, images, or narratives that describe the social group and are held in common.

## Sociology in America

American sociology began to gain a distinct identity when the University of Chicago created a department of sociology—the first in the world—in 1892.

**THE CHICAGO SCHOOL AND AMERICAN SOCIOLOGY.** Chicago sociologists were interested in immigration, urbanization, and crime. They used the city of Chicago as a social laboratory to study social change in industrial society. Using a special kind of method—ethnography based on participant observation—Chicago sociologists painted a detailed portrait of early 20th century American life (Deegan 2007).

The Chicago School of sociology is especially well known for developing a theory of the social self. Charles Horton Cooley (1864–1929) offered an early version of this theory called the "looking glass self." Cooley ([1922] 2012: 152) emphasized how society serves as a mirror people use to develop a self-concept as they reflect on how others see them. People react to their sense of others' social perceptions, often in ways that meet social expectations. George Herbert Mead (1863–1931) developed a more complex theory of the social self, with his distinction between the "I" and the "me." For Mead, the "I" is the prior, pre-social part of the self. The "me" is a socialized version of the self (Mead 1967). By the middle of the 20th century, the Chicago School's focus on the social self was developed as the theory of symbolic interactionism, described in the following section.

**CONFLICT, CONSENSUS, AND SYMBOLIC INTERACTION.** Following World War II (1939–1945), sociologists in the United States converged on three general models for thinking about society: consensus theory, conflict theory, and symbolic interactionism. **Consensus theory** (also referred to as structural functionalism) was associated with the work of Talcott Parsons, who tried to develop an ambitious general theory of society that could be used by all the social sciences. Drawing on the European theories of Max Weber, Émile Durkheim, and Sigmund Freud, Parsons argued that modern American society was a *functional equilibrium*, a social system where things like money, political power, social influence, and cultural values tended to balance out so that no single type of social resource could dominate society. Parsons also argued that all societies were converging toward a single modern form, in which each part of the social system became autonomous and self-organizing, designed to fulfill a specific function with maximum efficiency.

Parsons's critics argued that the theory of functional equilibrium was insensitive to human domination, suffering, conflict, and inequality. These critics argued instead that the world's most powerful nations were imposing capitalism on the rest of the world. Critics also argued that Parsons's theory could not explain social change. **Conflict theory** developed out of these criticisms. Associated with the sociologists C. Wright Mills and Ralf Dahrendorf (1929–2009), conflict theory focused on power inequalities and domination. Instead of a functional equilibrium between different parts of society, conflict theorists emphasized that social structures were designed to reinforce the unequal distribution of power and resources.

The tradition of **symbolic interactionism** emerged from the work of Chicago School sociologist Herbert Blumer (1900–1987). Blumer defined

**Consensus theory**
Consensus theorists focus on social equilibrium, which is the way that different parts of society work together to produce social cohesion.

**Conflict theory**
Conflict theorists argue that social structures and social systems emerge out of the conflicts between different groups.

**Symbolic interactionism**
A perspective associated with the Chicago School of sociology that argues that people develop a social self through interaction with others.

three basic propositions that inform symbolic interactionism: (1) individuals act based on the meanings they have about the world, (2) those meanings develop through the social interactions they have with other people, (3) those meanings continue to develop and change as the individual interprets the social interactions and experiences they have (Blumer 1968; Morrione 1988; Shibutani 1988). While conflict and consensus theory emphasized the ways that structures shape actions, symbolic interactionism emphasized the ways that actions shape structures.

Symbolic interaction could both reproduce social structures and be a key to social change. Erving Goffman (1922–1982) argued that people deliberately collaborate to maintain social order through interaction. His masterwork, *The Presentation of Self in Everyday Life* (1959), uses a theatrical metaphor to explain how social encounters are scripted like plays. In this view, people are like actors who know how to perform in social life because social interactions are organized around scripts. While Goffman's work has been used to explain how and why people follow social scripts and maintain social order, the idea that social life is scripted has also been used as a critical tool for challenging oppressive social rules. Interactional theorists like Goffman provide tools for thinking about both conflict and consensus in social life.

By the middle of the 20th century, a standoff between consensus theory, conflict theory, and symbolic interactionism dominated American sociology. The resulting three-fold model braided together sociological traditions from Europe and America. It balanced a focus on inequality with the study of social values, and it linked the analysis of large-scale social structures with smaller scenes, psychological theories, and interactional settings. Framing all sociological theory in terms of conflict, consensus, and symbolic interactionism was an extremely successful conceptual move: the three-fold model appears in nearly every general sociology textbook today.

**SOCIOLOGICAL THEORY TODAY.** Central as it is to the history of sociology, the three-fold model is inadequate for understanding the work of contemporary sociologists. Instead, it is best understood as a way to think about a particular moment in sociology's history.

By the second half of the 20th century, the economic structure of Western industrial societies was becoming globalized. Women, members of the LGBTQ community, and individuals from other historically marginalized groups began to claim civil rights. Wars of liberation were waged to overthrow European colonial powers. Global migration also began to accelerate. The rapid circulation of technology and cultural ideas connected people in new ways over greater distances (Appadurai 1996). With the development of the internet and social networks, traditional links between politics, economics, and culture dissolved. Sociologists wanted to understand and explain these changes, what Zygmunt Bauman (1925–2017) described as "the growing conviction that change is the only permanence, and uncertainty the only certainty" (2000: 82).

Facing this situation of permanent uncertainty, sociologists turned to different kinds of theories to understand the social world. They moved away from grand theories that attempted to explain everything toward more specific and concrete "theories of the middle range." Sociologists began to pay more attention to issues of identity, difference, and exclusion and the ways in which sociological theories tended to privilege certain voices at the expense of others. Sociologists also adopted a more cultural perspective, examining the ways in which interpretation informs social life. Finally, sociologists considered more seriously the global dimensions of contemporary life.

**Figure 2.2** Diagram of theories of the middle range

## Moving Away from Grand Theories

Contemporary sociologists are interested in what Robert Merton (1968) called **theories of the middle range**, which focus on particular social practices and outcomes. Mid-range theories encourage sociologists to move away from abstract ideas about "society in general" toward issues and problems that can be studied empirically (Figure 2.2).

**Theories of the middle range** Theories that focus on particular institutions and practices rather than an overarching theory of society.

## Theories about Difference

Contemporary sociologists have paid more attention to how sociology has ignored theoretical works written by women, racial minorities, and people living outside Europe or North America. This disregard is especially problematic since sociology has long been a discipline that studies gender and family structures, racial and ethnic relations, immigration, and class difference. Feminists, post-colonial theorists, queer theorists, and theorists of intersectionality have criticized these exclusions for reproducing inequality and encouraging a limited view of the social world.

**Feminism** A theoretical critique and historical series of social movements that proposed women as equal to men and argued that women should be treated as equals in major social institutions.

**Feminism** began with the idea that women have political, economic, and social rights equal to men. It is an intellectual movement that extends well beyond sociology, influencing almost every type of academic scholarship. Feminist sociologists uncover how assumptions about gender differences continue to encourage the exclusion or marginalization of women in scholarship and social life (Stacey and Thorne 1985).

**Kimberlé Williams Crenshaw**

**Critical race theory** A theory that first developed in critical legal studies to show the ways that the law reinforced racial injustice and domination.

**Intersectionality** A perspective that identifies the multiple, intersecting, and situational nature of the categories that shape people's identities and experiences.

**Post-colonial theory** A critical perspective that argues that the ways we see globalization, power, and economic systems in the modern world are all shaped by the conquest and subordination of the world's peoples by Western European powers dating from the 15th and 16th centuries.

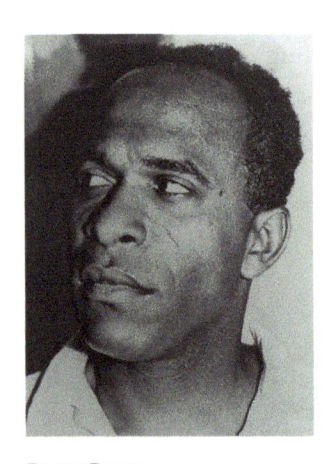

**Frantz Fanon**

**Critical race theory** begins from the idea that race is a social construct connected to violent histories of oppression, social conflict, political organization, and cultural classification (Crenshaw 2016; Crenshaw et al. 1996). Omi and Winant (1994: 52) argue that the history of conflict over race creates a "racial common sense" in society, which connects racial stereotypes with institutionalized patterns of social inequality to create a racial formation. Racial stereotypes and inequalities are often written into the law, in a way that guarantees the subordination of racial minorities (Brooks 1994; Crenshaw 2016; Crenshaw et al. 1996).

**Intersectionality** is a way of thinking about the multiple, intersecting, and situational nature of the categories that shape people's identities. Initially developed by legal scholar and civil rights advocate Kimberlé Williams Crenshaw (1989), the intersectional perspective argues against the common sense that people have a single dominant identity. In sociology, intersectionality provides a lens through which to study power in a more complex way, taking into account multiple social categories such as race, class, gender, age, ethnicity, nativity, language, and disability (Collins 1990; Hankivsky 2014).

**Post-colonial theory** is a critical response to global European conquest, which began in the 15th and 16th centuries and accelerated with the creation of nation-states. Post-colonial theory focuses on the politics of knowledge (Bhambra 2009) and identifies the challenge of thinking beyond the history of racial difference and racial hierarchy that came with Western conquest. Post-colonial theorists like Edward Said (1935–2003) and Frantz Fanon (1925–1961) criticized the way that European theories about modern society privileged the distinction between (modern) Western societies and (traditional) non-Western ones. This distinction made it easier for Western nations to justify their actions through the belief that they were bringing civilization instead of suffering and exploitation to non-Western societies.

**Queer theory** offers a critical perspective that identifies the logic of homophobia and heterosexism in social practice and social institutions and shows how that logic works to maintain social order. Queer theorists like Judith Butler (1956–) and Steven Seidman (1948–) criticize binary thinking and the idea that anything is normal. They analyze the ways that societies reinforce assumptions about heterosexual desire, and seek to punish those who challenge or who do not accept these assumptions.

Sociologists and students today reflect on the exclusions present in any given theory and interrogate how expert social knowledge can work to exclude and marginalize people. Sociologists are also more likely to orient to a variety of different theories to understand specific social questions.

**Edward Said**

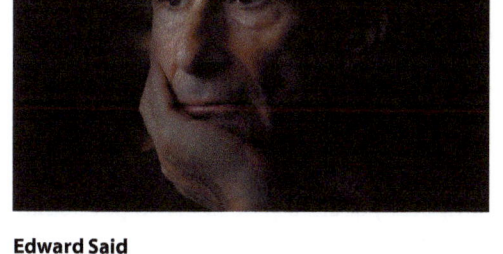

**Judith Butler**

## The Cultural Turn

The **cultural turn** in sociology emerged in the 1970s and became a significant influence in the 1990s. The cultural turn was a return to the **Thomas theorem**, one of the earliest theoretical statements of American sociology, which argues that the way people interpret a situation has real consequences for how they act. In other words, if we want to understand social life, we need to pay attention to the stories that people tell about themselves and the world around them. Similar to symbolic interactionists, cultural sociologists study the meanings that people use to understand their lives as well as the ways that meanings circulate in collective memories, mass media, public rituals, and everyday objects. For example, while the American flag is a globally recognized symbol, it is also subject to conflict over what it really means. Is the American flag a symbol of freedom or of global power? Today, there is a growing recognition that cultural issues are important for all sociological research (Hall, Grindstaff, and Lo 2010: 3) and that these kinds of cultural conflicts are just as important as political or economic conflicts.

## Global Context

"Globalization" refers to the growing interdependence of the world's people. As we discuss in Chapter 3, the economic, political, and cultural dimensions of globalization are major forces in social life. The rapid onset and spread of the novel coronavirus that causes COVID-19 also illuminates the global interdependence of humanity.

Sociologists recognize that there are many important global actors in modern society beyond territorially distinct nation-states (Beck 2005, 2006). Multinational corporations orient to a global market that is beyond the control of any single country. New immigrant communities maintain a simultaneous involvement in their nation of origin as well as their nation of

**Queer theory**
A critical perspective that criticizes binary thinking and identifies how the logic of homophobia and heterosexism in social practice and social institutions works to maintain social order.

**Cultural turn**
An interdisciplinary movement in sociology and other disciplines that emphasizes the collective cultural dimension of social life.

**Thomas theorem**
The proposition that the way people interpret a situation has real consequences for how they act.

choice (Faist 2000; Faist and Özveren 2004). Millions of stateless people and refugees fall between the boundaries of nation-states (Gatrell 2013). Global civil-society organizations promote human rights and pursue global environmental actions. Sociologists draw our attention to the "excluded others" of contemporary society, reminding us that the misfortunes of displaced, poor, and oppressed peoples are directly related to and a side effect of the modern societies in which we live (Bauman 2004).

## Sociology Today

Contemporary sociologists use theory to ask critical questions about 21st-century social life. Some contemporary sociologists focus on particular institutions, historical events, and cultural structures. Some focus on race, gender, sexuality, and how these interact to produce different systems of hierarchy and social inequality. Other sociologists turn their attention to global power and post-colonial resistance. Many sociologists combine different theoretical resources to analyze a particular problem or imagine a new kind of social relationship. All sociologists draw on the history of sociological thinking to do their work. They also use a wide range of social research methods.

> **Logic** Valid reasoning.
>
> **Empirical evidence** Fact-based information about the social or natural world.
>
> **Beliefs** All the things we think are true, even in the absence of evidence or proof; ideas about the world that come through divine revelation or received tradition.

## 2.3 Social Research: Purpose and Process

**LG 2.3** Define the major elements of the research process and describe a range of sociological research techniques.

> **Opinions** Ideas about the world that stem from common values or experience.
>
> **Falsifiability** The idea that scientific statements define what condition or evidence would prove them wrong.
>
> **Social research** The systematic investigation of some aspect of the social world, which aims to contribute to our general understanding of society.

Our society values a culture of evidence based on rules of logic and the scientific method. Learning about the process of social research is important to develop the critical information and scientific skills we need as citizens, consumers, and workers.

Scientific statements are based on research which is systematic, logical, and empirical. Researchers are systematic when they make every effort to locate previous research about their topic, evaluate what kind of new information they will need to answer their questions, and consider what information they may not be able to find. Researchers use **logic** to figure out if their explanation is the best one. In addition to being systematic and logical, scientific researchers are especially interested in **empirical evidence**, or fact-based information, that might prove their explanation wrong.

The idea that scientific statements can be proven to be false is fundamental to science (Popper 2005). This is why scientific statements are different from **beliefs**, which may come through divine revelation or received tradition, or from **opinions**, which may stem from common values or experience.

While opinions and beliefs are a very important part of society, they are not subject to the same standard as scientific statements. **Falsifiability** requires scientists to conduct a systematic search for a falsifying logic or evidence that could prove that a scientific statement is wrong.

Researchers across disciplines and industries share a commitment to the scientific ideal, defined by falsifiability. While social science research is also committed to the ideals of the scientific community, social researchers face several challenges that other scientific researchers do not.

## Social Research and Ethics

Sociology is a social science that generates sociological knowledge through systematic **social research.** Social research is conducted by social scientists, who work in universities, government agencies, and private companies and who follow scientific method.

Scientific studies are based on the model of the **controlled experiment**, in which a researcher controls the conditions of some outcome of interest and studies it systematically to isolate the causal logic that produces the observed effects. For example, if a botanist wants to know how light affects plant growth, they would divide a set of plants into groups and control how much light each group receives. They can then compare the plants receiving different amounts of light. Controlled experiments are not as common in social science as they are in natural science research because there are widely shared legal and ethical rules about experimenting on people. Unlike the botanist, who can run the risk that a plant might die in an experiment, social scientists must be far more careful of the consequences of their research.

**Ethics** in social research is a commitment to ensure that no harm is caused to individuals or groups in the conduct of research. It is based on an approach to critical reasoning about moral questions. For example, researchers will ask, does the potential social good of this study outweigh the potential harm to participants? Researchers who work with human subjects must first get their research approved by an **institutional review board** (IRB). IRBs protect human subjects from harm and support good research. **Informed consent**, which is monitored by IRBs, means that researchers must tell people they are being studied and provide enough information about the study so that they can make an informed and voluntary decision about participating.

Finally, social science—like all scientific knowledge—is systematically reviewed, evaluated, and tested by a community of experts. All scientists believe in the importance of **peer review**. Before they can publish their work or get funding for their research, scientific proposals and research findings are evaluated by experts in the field. This evaluation is usually anonymous;

**Controlled experiment** Scientific method that systematically controls the factors that affect some outcome of interest to isolate the causal logic that produces the observed effects.

**Ethics** Critical reasoning about moral questions. Ethical research weighs the benefits of research against possible harm to human subjects of research.

**Institutional review board** A governing group that evaluates proposed research with the goal of protecting human subjects from physical or psychological harm.

**Informed consent** The idea that people must consent to being studied and that researchers must give their subjects enough information about the study so that they can make a truly voluntary decision about whether or not to participate.

**Peer review** The process of review of proposed research or publication by the community of scientific experts in a profession or scientific field.

## PAIRED CONCEPTS: Power and Resistance

### Protecting Human Subjects in Social Research

Studying other people creates relationships of power between researchers and those studied. This is the reasoning behind policies that protect vulnerable human subjects such as children, prisoners, or medical patients.

There are many shocking historical cases of ethical breaches by researchers where people have been hurt or even killed. These include the medical experiments on Jewish prisoners conducted in Nazi concentration camps during World War II and the clinical experiments conducted by the US Public Health Service between 1932 and 1952 on the campus of the Tuskegee Institute in Alabama, where Black men were denied medical treatment even after it was clear that penicillin could effectively treat their illness (Centers for Disease Control and Prevention 2013). Both these cases resulted in the formulation of laws to protect the human subjects of social research. After World War II, the Nuremberg Code was part of a new international expression of human rights to define the respect and dignity owed to all human beings. In the United States, the federal Office for Human Research Protections was established to prevent the ethical breaches of the Tuskegee experiments from ever happening again (Office for Human Research Protections 1978).

Public controversies erupt when social research does not protect human subjects. For example, in June 2014 it was revealed that Facebook had been conducting a secret experiment: manipulating the news feeds of nearly seventy thousand users to see if this would affect their emotions (Goel 2014). Only a month later, the same thing happened with the online dating site OKCupid, when it was discovered that the website was secretly manipulating the algorithm it used to match potential partners (Wood 2014). Both cases resulted in bad publicity for the companies, which were accused of violating the ethical standards of social research.

**Ethical breaches in science**
The Tuskegee experiments stand as one of the worst ethical breaches in the history of modern science, as scientists withheld medicine from sick patients for the purposes of research.

**ACTIVE LEARNING**

**Discuss:** What do you know about the Tuskegee experiment? Did you learn about it in high school? When was the study terminated, and why?

---

the reviewers' identities are kept private and so are the identities of the people whose work they are evaluating.

The goal of a good peer review process is to ensure the credibility and validity of scientific work and to protect the scientific process from political influence or the agendas of powerful social actors in government, religion, or business.

## Research Methods and Critical Literacy

Evaluating the production of scientific knowledge is an important critical literacy because it can help you navigate a world full of data and complex analysis. Sociologists use many different types of data and evidence in their research, and all of them are collected with the goal of producing good scientific knowledge about social things.

A particular challenge for all researchers is **confirmation bias**, which exists when a researcher's methods or interpretations produce findings that confirm the researcher's preexisting beliefs, experiences, or social interests. By committing to a collective, systematic, scientific research process and through using insights from our shared theoretical tradition, we try to sensitize ourselves to confirmation bias. In the process, we use our sociological imaginations to extend and enhance our ability to see the social world. In the remainder of the chapter, we discuss the research process and describe some of the main strategies sociologists use to do social research.

The goal of social research is to make a contribution to scientific knowledge. Most sociologists begin with a research question: What causes some children to succeed in school while others fail? Why do some countries have higher homicide rates than others? How have beliefs about motherhood and childrearing changed in the last 50 years? The next step is to find out what other researchers have written about the topic. For some topics, there will be competing theories about a particular social phenomenon, and new research can introduce new evidence to shed light on which theory offers a better explanation. Another way to make a research contribution is to ask new or different types of questions about a particular social phenomenon. The paired concepts that appear throughout this book are useful for making this kind of research contribution. If most researchers are focused on inequality, for example, it might be helpful to study privilege. If most researchers studying a topic are focused on structure, maybe you should study contingency. This is

**March for science**
Citizens marched in Portland, Oregon, on April 14, 2018, to defend scientific standards for research. Does science need to be defended? Does this mean that scientific knowledge is no longer dominant and unquestioned?

**Confirmation bias** The tendency to look for information that reinforces prior beliefs; occurs when research is biased to confirm the researcher's preexisting beliefs or hypotheses.

> **PAIRED CONCEPTS**
>
> ## Global and Local
>
> ### Citizen Science: Using Local Data to Understand Global Patterns
>
> Citizen science is scientific research conducted by amateur scientists or community members. Recent examples include data collected by bird watchers and butterfly counters, citizen oceanographers who track marine debris, and community conservationists who tally roadkill to assess the impact of traffic on wildlife (Vercayie and Herremans 2015).
>
> With mobile phones in nearly everyone's pocket, citizen observers can contribute a wide range of local data to build up a picture of global patterns. At the same time, crowdsourcing scientific data can create new social challenges. For example, a British organization called Speedwatch relies on community volunteers to "monitor the speeds of vehicles using speed detection devices" and then report those observations to police. In this case, citizens contribute to police surveillance of motorists.
>
> Social researchers have also expressed concern about the rise of crowdsourced data collection online. Anonymous researchers who perform a small piece of an overall task for very little pay are neither acknowledged nor compensated for the results of their work (Brown 2015). Other critics raise the specter of experimentation on online subjects without obtaining consent or thinking about protecting human subjects (Goel 2014; Wood 2014).
>
> **Citizen science**
> In an example of citizen science, volunteers in Costa Rica assist with a project that aims to protect sea turtles.
>
> > **ACTIVE LEARNING**
> > **Discuss:** In the context of the COVID-19 pandemic, should public health authorities have used contact tracing applications on social media to gather citizen-generated health information by showing who individuals had been in physical contact with and who was at risk of spreading the disease? What are the benefits of this approach? What are the drawbacks? Are there ethical concerns?

the approach Robert Sampson and his colleagues took in their pathbreaking research on the causes of delinquency. When virtually no researchers were asking about solidarity but were focused on conflict in poor communities, Sampson showed that the level of violence in a community was connected to levels of trust and cooperative social action (Sampson, Raudenbusch, and Earls 1997). When most researchers were examining the structural factors that led children to become delinquents and adults to become criminals, Sampson asked whether there might be turning points (such as getting married or joining the military) that could help set a person on a different path (Sampson and Laub 1995).

Sociological research presents special challenges because it is hard to understand the lives of the people we are studying without comparing them to our own lives. This creates a basic challenge of interpretation. Are we using our lives to understand their society, or are we using their lives to understand our own society? It is often difficult to disentangle these two goals.

A second challenge is that people often change their behavior in response to social research in a broader process called **institutional reflexivity**. Institutional reflexivity makes it harder to replicate important research findings because people change their behavior after being exposed to those findings. For example, research in the sociology of education shows that teachers generally pay more attention to boys than girls (Sadker and Sadker 1995). But this finding has been integrated into teacher training programs, and many teachers now consciously try to be more equitable in the way they treat boys and girls. To the extent that they succeed, future research on gender and education may not be able to find the same levels of difference in the attention boys and girls receive from their teachers. The earlier findings were not "wrong." Rather, the newer research reflected the fact that teachers had absorbed the lessons of the older research and changed the way they taught.

**The effects of studying people**
When education research revealed that teachers more often call on boys than girls in classrooms, many teachers self-consciously attempted to moderate their behavior and be aware of the gender dynamics of classroom discussions.

**Institutional reflexivity** The phenomenon where people change their behavior in response to social research.

**Sociological research methods** All the different strategies sociologists use to collect, measure, and analyze data.

**Quantitative methods** Sociological research methods that collect numerical data that can be analyzed using statistical techniques.

## Data and Measurement

Sociologists use many different kinds of data as evidence for arguments. There are established standards about the best way to collect, measure, and analyze each type of data.

**Sociological research methods** are all the different strategies that sociologists use to collect, measure, and analyze the data they collect. **Quantitative methods** are used for numerical data that can be analyzed using statistical techniques. Quantitative methods offer powerful approaches to complex questions. In an era when humans and computers are generating an enormous amount of digital information, quantitative methods can help us explore large social phenomena.

Statistical techniques also allow social researchers to mimic the powerful logic of the controlled experiment. Using statistics, quantitative sociologists can hold some factors constant while examining how variation in other factors affects the outcome. Once they have identified important relationships between different social factors, they can also use statistical theory to determine how likely it is for those relationships to have occurred by chance. A statistical model can approximate a change in social condition to discover causal relationships.

Quantitative methods are useful for numerical data, and some social things are more numerical than others (Table 2.1). How much money someone earns, for example, is a numerical question. Money can be counted. In the language of statistical measurement, money is a **linear** or **continuous** variable because it is numerical. By contrast, your sex is less inherently numerical. To be sure, sociological researchers assign numbers to sex categories in statistical models, traditionally coding men "1" and women "2" so that groups can be compared. From a mathematical point of view, however, you cannot perform calculations on these numbers in the same way you can

**Linear or continuous variable** A measure of inherently numerical phenomena that can be counted, divided, and multiplied, such as money or time.

### TABLE 2.1 Levels of measurement

| COMPLEXITY ↑ | | | |
|---|---|---|---|
| The interval between categories is known (interval), and zero is a true value (interval ratio). | You can perform higher mathematical operations on variables when the interval between categories is mathematically precise and where zero is a true value. | Continuous and interval ratio[1] | Income in dollars can run from $0 to $1,000,000 and more. Income can also be negative. Age begins at zero and increases in numerically precise units. |
| Categories are ranked higher or lower, but the distance between categories has no precise numerical value. | You can count occurrences in each category and make comparative statements about higher and lower. | Ordinal (ranked) | Social class<br>1. Upper class<br>2. Middle class<br>3. Working class<br>Opinion about desirability of a new tax<br>1. In favor<br>2. Neutral<br>3. Against |
| Categories are labels, not numerical values. | You can count occurrences in each category. | Nominal (categorical) | Mortality status<br>1. Alive<br>2. Dead<br>Sex<br>1. Male<br>2. Female |

Note: Levels of measurement determine what kind of statistical methods can be used to analyze data. Increasing numerical precision allows for more complex statistical analysis.

[1] The difference between interval variables and interval-ratio variables is rarely an issue in social science research. The difference rests on the idea that there is an "absolute value" denoted by numbers measured in increments from true zero. Interval-ratio variables include distance, age, time, and weight. With interval variables, there are equal intervals between numbers, but there is no true zero. Variables include calendar years and IQ.

manipulate numbers representing money. For example, you cannot take a meaningful average of sex. Other researchers have raised questions about the social consequences of using only two categories for sex, when a substantial population does not identify with either category. Whatever the case, it remains true that, unlike money, a numerical measure of sex in a statistical model is assigned simply so that statistical software can recognize the data. The numbers have no inherent numerical meaning. This is true for many social categories, including race and ethnicity, where there is no immediately obvious numerical meaning for the numbers we use to describe groups. In statistical language, we call these **categorical** or **nominal variables**.

In between continuous and nominal measures are **ordinal variables**. Ordinal variables are used when it is clear there is some order to categories—there is more or less of some quality—but it is unclear what the precise distances are between the categories; consequently, there are limits to the statistical manipulation of the numbers associated with the category. An example of an ordinal variable is social class. Social researchers distinguish between the upper class, the middle class, and the lower class, assigning them values like 1, 2, and 3. While it seems intuitive that there is a rank order in these categories, it is far less clear what the precise numerical distance is between categories, and it is also likely that those distances may vary over time.

Sociologists recognize that not all information can be meaningfully converted into numbers, and they use **qualitative methods** to examine this kind of information.. We use qualitative methods when we want an in-depth examination of a specific social process or a specific social outcome. Given this interest in depth, qualitative researchers typically study smaller groups of people or organizations than quantitative researchers. Sociologists who use qualitative methods talk to people, observe their actions, and try to interpret what they hear and observe. Most qualitative researchers agree with the argument that Max Weber made about sociological research methods: if we want to understand why something happened, we need to try to understand it from the perspective of the people who were involved in the action.

## Variables, Data Collection, and Causal Relationships

Regardless of whether you use a qualitative or quantitative approach, before you can analyze your data and draw conclusions, there are basic questions about your data that you will need to answer: What are your variables? How good are your measurements? What is the causal relationship between your variables?

**WHAT ARE YOUR VARIABLES?** A **variable** is a quantity that changes, or varies, in a population. Social scientists distinguish between a **dependent variable** (the outcome to be explained) and an **independent variable**

---

**Categorical or nominal variable** A variable that measures phenomena that are not inherently numerical, such as gender, race, or ethnicity. In this case the numerical code assigned to a quality is more a name than a number.

**Ordinal variable** A measure of categorical order, such as more and less, where the distances between categories are not numerically precise.

**Qualitative methods** Sociological research methods that collect nonnumerical information, such as interview transcripts or images.

**Variable** A quantity that changes, or varies, in a research population.

**Dependent variable** The outcome to be explained in a research study; the researcher wants to identify what produces the effects on the dependent variable.

**Independent variable** The factor that produces a change in the dependent variable.

**Operationalization** The process of defining measures for a sociological study.

**Validity** When data accurately measure the phenomenon under study.

**Reliability** The consistent measurement of the object over units in a population or over repeated samples.

**Research population** The entire universe of individuals or objects in a study.

**Sample** A selection from a research population for the purposes of research.

**Convenience sample** A sample collected from a research population on the basis of convenience or easy access.

**Random sample** A selection from a research population based on a random mechanism, such as a dice roll, a flipped coin, or a random number generator.

**Representative sample** A selection from a research population that contains all the features of the wider population from which it is drawn.

(the thing they think causes a change in the dependent variable or produces the outcome). For example, in Sampson's research about what causes juveniles to become delinquents, the dependent variable was delinquent behavior. The independent variables were social factors such as community trust that made delinquency more or less likely.

You also need to plan how to **operationalize** your variables. Most of the things sociologists are interested in studying are too big to measure directly. We may be interested in delinquency, health, or trust; but we need to find specific ways to measure them. For example, we might collect data on juvenile arrests as an indicator of delinquency in a neighborhood. We might use blood pressure as a general indicator of public health or ask people whether they agree with the statement that "most people can be trusted" to capture levels of trust in society. The things that we measure "stand in" for the more general things we are interested in studying. When we operationalize our variables in this way, we turn them into things that can be measured.

**ARE YOUR MEASUREMENTS RELIABLE AND VALID?** **Validity** refers to whether our data actually measure what we think they measure. For example, do standardized tests like the SAT really measure academic ability, or do they measure something else, like family income? How valid are such tests? **Reliability** refers to the consistent measurement of the object being measured. If you took a standardized test three times and your score increased each time, does this really mean that you have genuinely learned more—or that you've simply improved at test-taking? Is a standardized test a reliable measure of learning? By asking questions about the measurements we use, we can speak more confidently about the strengths and weaknesses of our research.

Another measurement concern is the relationship between a research sample and the larger **research population**. The research population is all the members of the group we are interested in studying. The research population can consist of people (e.g., the population of a city, the population of at-risk youth), but it can also consist of other types of social objects (e.g., Twitter posts, social protests, food). Sometimes it is possible to collect data on the entire research population of interest, but it is usually impractical because of size or cost. In these situations, we need to collect data from part of the population, which is our **sample**.

There are different ways of selecting samples. If you are a student, you might decide to interview people on campus. This is called a **convenience sample**. Convenience samples are, well, convenient; but your findings might be biased because your sample only includes people you know or who all attend the same university.

A **random sample** is a preferred approach. In a random sample, every member of the research population has an equal chance of being selected by chance. This means the sample is likely to be **representative** of the research population at large and mirror its central characteristics. Random samples are more likely to be valid and reliable and less likely to be biased because they provide a strong basis for making a logical connection between what is discovered in the sample and what is really going on in the larger population.

In cases where a random sample is hard to collect, sociologists use other types of nonrepresentative samples. In a **snowball sample**, the researcher begins with a few people who agree to participate in the research and then asks those people to recommend other people they think would be willing to participate. Snowball sampling is effective when studying sensitive issues or vulnerable populations. A second strategy is a **theoretical sample**, where decisions about data collection change after the initial data have been collected, based on what is theoretically important (Glaser 1978). A third strategy is **case study research**, where a researcher selects a small number of cases that offer special insight into a particular social process.

**Snowball sample** A selection from a research population taken by asking the first few research subjects to identify and recommend others for study.

**Theoretical sample** A selection from a research population that focuses on a sample as research progresses and where the sampling strategy changes after the initial data have been collected, based on what is theoretically important.

**Case study research** Research that relies on a small number of cases that offer special insight into a particular social process and are studied in depth, typically using comparative methods.

## WHAT IS THE HYPOTHESIZED CAUSAL RELATIONSHIP BETWEEN YOUR VARIABLES?

A **hypothesis** is a specific statement about the causal relationship between variables. More than a hunch or a guess, a scientific hypothesis is a statement that is falsifiable, which means that your data can prove it wrong.

Just because two variables appear to be related does not mean that one factor is a **cause** of the other. This is a case of confusing **correlation**, which is when two variables share a pattern, for **causation**, which is when two variables share a pattern because one variable produces the pattern in the other. For example, there is a very strong statistical correlation between the consumption of margarine in the United States and the divorce rate in Maine (Figure 2.3). But it would be ridiculous to claim that this correlation is a causal relationship because there is no theoretical basis for believing that one of the variables actually produces a change in the other.

|   | 2000 | 2001 | 2002 | 2003 | 2004 | 2005 | 2006 | 2007 | 2008 | 2009 |
|---|---|---|---|---|---|---|---|---|---|---|
| Divorce rate in Maine Divorces per 1,000 people (US Census) | 5 | 4.7 | 4.6 | 4.4 | 4.3 | 4.1 | 4.2 | 4.2 | 4.2 | 4.1 |
| Per capita consumption of margarine (US) Pounds (USDA) | 8.2 | 7 | 6.5 | 5.3 | 5.2 | 4 | 4.6 | 4.5 | 4.2 | 3.7 |

Correlation: 0.992558

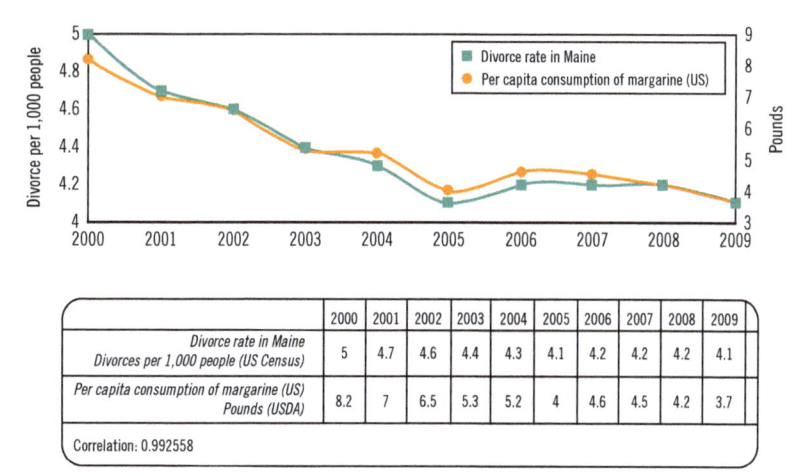

**Figure 2.3** Divorce rate in Maine correlates with per capita consumption of margarine (US)
Source: US Census; USDA.

**Hypothesis** A specific statement about the causal relationship between variables that is falsifiable, which means it is a statement that can be proved wrong on the basis of empirical evidence.

**Cause** Something that produces an outcome. Technically, a cause is where a first event is understood to produce a material effect on a second event.

**Correlation** An observed statistical dependence between two variables, but it does not mean the variables are *causally* related.

**Causation** A phenomenon that occurs when two variables share a pattern because one variable produces the pattern in the other.

**Surveys** A sociological research method that asks a series of defined questions to collect data from a large sample of the research population.

**In-depth interviews** A sociological research method that uses extended, open-ended questions to collect data.

**ANALYZING YOUR DATA AND DRAWING CONCLUSIONS.** Once data have been collected and analyzed, sociologists draw conclusions from their analysis. Most sociologists situate their findings in the context of previous research and specify what extra insight or factual understanding the new research adds. As we outline in the next section, there are different strategies for collecting and analyzing social data and several different audiences for sociological research.

## Common Strategies for Sociological Research

Most sociological research can be divided into three types of activities: talking to people, observing social settings, and examining publicly available data. For each of these activities, sociologists have developed quantitative and qualitative methods, different ways to collect data, and different approaches to explaining their findings.

**TALKING TO PEOPLE: SURVEY ANALYSIS, INTERVIEWS, AND FOCUS GROUPS.** When sociologists want to know why people act a certain way or what they think about a particular social issue, they ask them questions. Sociologists conduct **surveys**, where they ask defined questions to a large sample of the population. They do **in-depth interviews**, where they ask extended, probing, and open-ended questions to a smaller sample of people. And they conduct **focus groups**, where they gather groups of people together and facilitate a discussion about a particular social issue.

Survey research is a good research tool for asking specific questions of large numbers of people. Surveys can rely on random sampling strategies to create representative samples. As a result, researchers can **generalize** their findings from the data analysis to the larger population in a way that is both valid and reliable. But survey researchers also face constraints. They have to decide in advance what questions they are going to ask, and they also have to decide what the possible answers will be. Survey researchers do not have a lot of flexibility to ask more probing questions, and survey researchers struggle with low response rates.

Extended interviews are particularly useful for asking open-ended questions and when talking with vulnerable populations who may be more difficult to locate or less inclined to talk with a stranger on the phone. Extended interviews usually take more time and energy to complete than surveys, and they are more likely to use nonrandom samples. With a focus group, the researcher recruits people into the study and then leads them in a group discussion about a particular social issue. Focus groups allow the sociologist to see how people interact with each other and how collective opinions develop within a natural setting.

**OBSERVATION: ETHNOGRAPHY AND EXPERIMENTS.** What individuals say can be informative, but sometimes what people say is not a good indicator of how they behave (Jerolmack and Khan 2014). This is why sociologists also observe how people act in social life. The two most commonly used strategies for observing social action are ethnography and experiments.

**Ethnography** is research based on **participant-observation**, where researchers go into the field and participate in the everyday lives of the people they are studying. Rather than trying to isolate different variables, ethnographers try to capture social life in all of its detail and complexity. By immersing themselves in a social setting for a long period of time, ethnographers can capture the interaction between structure and contingency. Because ethnographers focus intensively on a single case, however, it is more difficult for them to isolate specific social processes or to generalize from their findings. To draw general arguments, they will either compare their findings with similar cases from other research or consider how their findings either support or challenge other social theories (Burawoy 1998).

Another way to observe social action is to conduct an **experiment** by controlling the conditions of observation to isolate the effects of different factors on some outcome of interest. In one interesting **field experiment**, pairs of matched resumes were sent out to US employers, with half of the resumes listing a leadership position in a gay campus organization and the other half listing a leadership position in a campus political organization (Tilcsik 2011). The study revealed that the applicants with the gay campus organization listed on their resume were less likely to be invited to interview, with the levels of discrimination being higher in companies located in Florida and Texas than in California and New York.

**ANALYSIS OF PUBLICLY AVAILABLE DATA SOURCES.** In many types of sociological research, it is not possible to talk to people or to observe their behavior directly. This is the case for **comparative-historical** sociologists, who study events that took place in the past. For example, in his study of slavery, Orlando Patterson compared how slavery was organized in 66 different societies throughout the world over a period of nearly two thousand years (Patterson 1982).

To do comparative-historical research, sociologists rely on data from the past, such as historical archives and official records like census data, bank transactions and other commercial records, newspaper reports, and legal documents. They read autobiographies, diaries, and letters written by the people they are studying.

One advantage of using publicly available data is a lower likelihood of **reactivity**, a situation where the researcher affects the social phenomenon being studied. A possible drawback, however, is that we depend on what other people thought was important enough to collect, store, and share in

**Focus groups** A sociological research method that gathers groups of people together for discussion of a common question or a particular social issue to collect data.

**Generalize** To make the argument that the finding from a particular sample of people or a single research study applies to a wider research population.

**Ethnography** A sociological research method based on participant-observation in the field where researchers try to capture social life in all of its detail and complexity.

**Participant-observation** A research method of observing people in social settings by participating in those social settings with them.

**Experiments** A sociological research method that controls the conditions of observation with the goal of isolating the effects of different factors on some outcome of interest.

**Field experiments** Research using experimental methods in natural settings outside of the laboratory.

**Comparative-historical methods** A set of research methods that uses comparison of events and processes in the past to understand the development and operation of social things.

archives and public records. This is a **selection effect**, which means that the information we have is shaped by the way it was selected.

With the rise of the internet and the rapid expansion of social media, sociologists are also beginning to analyze **big data**, which are data produced by our technological ability to capture the behavior of humans (and machines and others) over huge populations and time spans. For example, while social scientists used to organize small focus groups to see how people discussed social issues, they now have access to billions of social media posts as well as responses to those posts. While in the past they might have compared the representation of colonized populations in a few dozen novels, they can now

---

**PAIRED CONCEPTS**

## Solidarity and Conflict

### Race, Difference, and the Politics of Medical Research

For most of the 20th century, medical researchers did not account for differences in gender or race when recruiting research subjects; instead, most of their studies used white men. Doctors assumed that they could take the findings from that research and generalize them for the entire population. This began to change in the 1980s.

As Steven Epstein shows in *Inclusion: The Politics of Difference in Medical Research* (2007), health advocacy groups and civil rights leaders began complaining about the underrepresentation of women, racial minorities, and youth in clinical medical studies. After attracting public attention to this problem, these advocacy groups convinced health industry insiders and influential politicians to join their cause. The US Congress passed a law in 1993 mandating that clinical medical research must include underrepresented groups, and it must study medical differences based on gender, race, ethnicity, and age. Medical journal guidelines and medical school curricula also changed to reflect these social concerns.

The idea that social categories were relevant for medical research came not from the medical community but rather from the worlds of politics and social movements. Epstein shows how there was a gradual "categorical alignment" between social and medical research; medical researchers did not develop their own set of categories, but instead they used the categories of race, gender, and ethnicity that were being used in the US Census.

In demanding changes in the design of medical research, advocacy groups and politicians promoted greater equality and social justice in health outcomes. As Epstein demonstrates, however, these efforts had limits. By focusing on a small list of group identities that were deemed to be relevant politically, other factors were overlooked. The result is that medical research has not been very effective at identifying the full range of factors that lead to differences in health and health care. By focusing on racial, ethnic, and gender categories, it becomes harder to see how differences in wealth, power, and other social factors contribute to health disparities. There is also a danger of biological essentialism, in which people come to believe that differences in health are based on biological differences rather than social factors.

**ACTIVE LEARNING**

**Find out:** Use Google Scholar to search "gender bias in medical research" or "race bias in medical research." What do experts say today about the inclusion of race and gender in medical research? What other social factors do these experts say should be included in future medical studies?

compare these kinds of representations for thousands of different novels. This is made possible because most information is now stored digitally, and because they have developed new research techniques that rely on computers to help with the analysis of these large amounts of data.

This resource presents opportunities for sociologists, who are beginning to develop new techniques for collecting and measuring culture using big data and automated text analysis. Sociologists can now use automated text-extraction programs and automated text-classification programs to assign values to variables—or code—their data (Bail 2014). As exciting new research directions expand, it remains important to think critically about the origins and limitations of the data and to consider ethical concerns about protecting privacy and guaranteeing informed consent when analyzing any data.

### Basic, Applied, and Public Sociology

Sociology, like most scientific disciplines, distinguishes between basic and applied research. With **basic research**, the goal is to advance our knowledge of the world, by developing theories and testing them with empirical evidence. The primary audience for basic research is other scientists. Basic research is usually published in academic journals and books and funded by universities, government agencies, or large science-focused nonprofits. Much of the work that sociologists do is basic research.

The goal of **applied research** is to use empirical social science to solve practical problems in society. People who do applied sociology work for private businesses, government agencies, or nonprofit organizations or they are self-employed as research consultants. The primary audience for applied research is the client who pays for expertise, and the primary type of writing in applied sociology is the research report for their client. There are many good jobs in applied research for people who have a graduate degree in sociology.

The goal of **public sociology** is to bring sociological knowledge to public debates about important social issues. With public sociology, the primary audience consists of the general public, as well as journalists and media organizations who set the agenda for public debate. The classroom is also an important place where public sociology happens, given the tens of thousands of undergraduate students who take sociology courses each year (Burawoy 2005).

There are many well-known examples of people doing public sociology today. Matthew Desmond has written several best-selling books about poverty, and he writes regular opinion columns for leading news organizations. Pepper Schwartz, who has appeared on many talk shows, is a relationship expert for the reality television show "Married at First Sight." Alondra Nelson served as the director for the White House Office of Science and

**Reactivity** A situation where the researcher has an effect on the behavior and the responses of the interview subject.

**Selection effect** The bias produced in data by the way the data are chosen or selected.

**Big data** A term for the large amount of data produced by our technological ability to study large data sets that have been recorded and stored in digital formats.

**Basic research** Research with the goal of advancing our fundamental knowledge and understanding of the world.

**Applied research** Research with the goal of solving practical problems in society.

**Public sociology** A commitment to bringing sociological knowledge to a general public audience and participating in wider public conversations and struggles for social justice.

## PAIRED CONCEPTS: Structure and Contingency

### The Baby Einstein Phenomenon

Institutional reflexivity does not only happen when individuals are exposed to social research. Businesses can also get involved, trying to expose people to research findings and then selling a product that is connected to those findings.

The story of Baby Einstein begins with a 1993 study which showed that listening to Mozart improved the spatial reasoning ability of college students and that music training improved the nonverbal cognitive ability of three-year-old children (Rauscher, Shaw, and Ky 1993; Rauscher et al. 1994). Described as the "Mozart effect," the research was reported widely in the media (Campbell 1997, 2000), which overstated the findings and claimed that the research demonstrated that listening to classical music makes you smarter.

Amid all this hype about the Mozart effect, a former teacher and mother created a video called *Baby Einstein* in 1997. Playing classical music in the background, the video showed children playing with educational toys, interspersed with images of numbers and words. The video was a huge commercial success, and at its peak the Baby Einstein brand was worth nearly $400 million.

At the same time, some researchers argued that the Mozart effect did not really exist and that parents were being misled by false advertising. Not only did the videos have no demonstrable effect on children's intelligence, they asserted, but the extra time spent in front of the television was bad for child development. In 2007, public health researchers published a study showing that toddlers did not get any intellectual benefit from watching educational media and that infants who watched these videos actually scored lower on language development tests (Zimmerman, Christakis, and Meltzoff 2007). The American Academy of Pediatrics reminded parents that infants and toddlers should be discouraged from watching television. Groups filed complaints with the Federal Trade Commission, and the Baby Einstein Company responded by removing many of the claims it had been making in its advertisements. Baby Einstein videos were no longer produced after 2009, and public belief and interest in the Mozart effect faded rapidly after that.

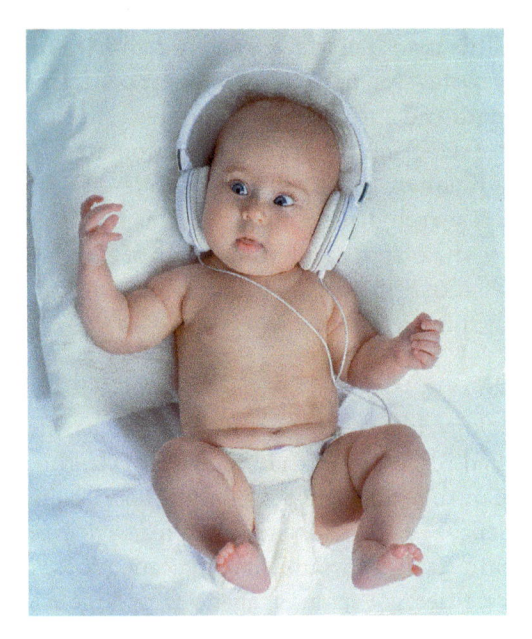

**Intelligent babies?**
The Baby Einstein phenomenon argued that scientific research proved that babies who listened to classical music would be more intelligent. Why do you think so many parents found this credible?

### ACTIVE LEARNING

**Find out:** Did you watch educational videos as a child? Did they make research claims or cite any research studies? Do your parents or others remember those claims? Can you discover if those research studies actually say what the videos claim they say?

Technology Policy, and she is a frequent guest on television news programs and public affairs podcasts. Mitchell Duneier taught an online version of his introductory sociology course to more than forty thousand students in 2012, but then very publicly stopped teaching the course because of his concerns about state funding for public universities.

In reality, the boundaries between basic research, applied research, and public sociology shift over time. Regardless of what type of sociology you choose to do, considering the kinds of research questions described in this chapter—as well as the ethical implications of different approaches—will help you do more effective social research. It will help you evaluate other sociological research you confront, in your studies as well as in everyday life. And it will help you sharpen your data and information literacy skills.

**Alondra Nelson**
A well-known public sociologist, Alondra Nelson studies science, race, and technology. She speaks widely in the media and has served as a policy advisor on science and technology for local, state, and federal governments.

### CASE STUDY

## Understanding COVID-19

Sociological theory and research help us explain the world, and the five paired concepts that frame this book provide tools to analyze different dimensions of social life. We conclude this chapter by applying the paired concepts to analyze the coronavirus crisis and the multiple overlapping crises associated with it.

The COVID-19 pandemic is a public health crisis of such severity and rapid onset that for well over a year it overwhelmed the ability of human infrastructure to manage illness and disease. At the time of this writing, more than 776 million people have been infected worldwide, and over seven million have died—and the numbers continue to rise. Despite repeated scientific and public health warnings of the risk of a pandemic like COVID-19 (Fan, Jamison, and Summers 2018), the devastation level of the pandemic is shocking. The world was not prepared for a public health crisis of this magnitude or for its myriad economic, political, and cultural consequences.

To be sure, humans balance the risks of multiple *contingencies* against commitments to existing

### CASE STUDY CONTINUED

social structures. Preparing for the contingencies of a pandemic is a complicated process involving a high degree of judgment. Hospitals and other care facilities are *structured* based on informed predictions about the numbers of patients they see in a day or a week. Hospitals may have extra resources in place for times when there is more than average intake, but they don't want to leave too many resources idle: medicines that aren't used go bad, and equipment that isn't used may not work when needed. The pandemic created an enormous spike in demand for resources that was not, and perhaps could not, be planned for.

In the face of enormous resource pressure, the public health response to the pandemic has been fundamentally sociological. Initially, the primary goal was to shape social behavior to avoid spreading the virus. Everyone was dependent on the behavior of others, and they needed to trust that people would do everything possible to avoid infecting others by engaging in social distancing, wearing masks, and practicing good hygiene. In short, there was a need for social *solidarity*, defined as the sense of connection that we feel with other people.

When António Guterres, secretary-general of the United Nations, asserted that the pandemic was "above all, a human crisis that calls for solidarity," he wanted people to feel connected on a *global* scale. Sadly, however, this has not been a universal response. More *local* solidarities, like the family, neighborhood, and nation, can create *conflict* as well as solidarity. For example, some individuals and nations responded to the pandemic by hoarding groceries, food, and medical resources at the expense of other individuals and nations.

That said, we have seen that higher levels of solidarity produced good collective outcomes in the pandemic too. In high-solidarity contexts where people trusted each other, individuals tended to follow public health recommendations about social distancing. In New Zealand, Denmark, and Vietnam, for example, there has been overwhelming public compliance with government *power* to define the public health response. People have followed social distancing advisories closely, and these countries have been less impacted by COVID-19. In countries like Italy, where the public was not initially compliant; Sweden, which did not mandate lockdowns; and the United States, where social distancing and economic shutdowns were met with active *resistance*, social protests, and public non-compliance, both the frequency of infection and death rates have been far higher (Johns Hopkins University Coronavirus Resource Center 2020).

Finally, the COVID-19 crisis has shown clearly that the risks of contracting the virus and of dying from it are linked to preexisting intersecting *inequalities* associated with race, income, and age. People who are poor and of color and others who live in spatially segregated communities are less able to practice social distancing. They are more likely to live in denser housing, and they may not have the opportunity to work remotely. People with fewer resources are also more likely to work in delivery, service, custodial, and health occupations, where they are more likely to be exposed to the virus. Sociological research shows clearly that in the United States there is a concentration of disadvantage where the poorest and most racially segregated communities suffer the most from environmental risk (Muller, Sampson and Winter 2018), and this has been borne out in COVID-19 statistics (Yancy 2020).

Wealthier, educated, and more powerful people have been able to practice social distancing. *Privilege* enabled them to stock up on supplies and minimize their exposure to the virus by working remotely from their homes. Privileged people also have better access to medical care. Finally, privileged people are less likely to suffer from the preexisting conditions that predict worse health outcomes if they contract the virus.

## LEARNING GOALS REVISITED

**2.1 Understand that sociology developed as a way to explain social patterns and social change and is one of a family of social science disciplines located within the liberal arts.**

- Social thinkers like Marx, Weber, and Durkheim, as well as thinkers from the "forgotten canon" like Harriet Martineau and W. E. B. Du Bois, invented theories to explain social changes occurring in the modern era. They developed a sociological way of thinking about social life as an interacting system of political, economic, and cultural relationships.
- Sociology insists on the relational quality of social life. Much good social analysis occurs at the rich disciplinary boundaries with other social science fields.

**2.2 Identify core theoretical concepts in the discipline.**

- Marx identified the economic system of capitalism as the most important feature of modern societies. Weber analyzed rationalization as the driving force of institutional and cultural change. Durkheim studied social facts and focused on the way group organization, such as the division of labor and collective representations, made social life possible. The Chicago School thinkers, who founded symbolic interactionism, identified the stable patterns of interactional settings in modern cities and institutions as a critical part of social life.
- Consensus theorists like Talcott Parsons emphasized the stability of social systems, while conflict theorists like C. Wright Mills analyzed the role of conflict in social change. Symbolic interactionists like Herbert Blumer analyzed how social meanings and social interaction play a part in both social equilibrium and social change.
- In the first half of the 20th century, the European legacy, along with the symbolic interactionist tradition developed at the University of Chicago, were synthesized into the three-fold model of American sociology. This model began to unravel in the 1960s and 1970s with critics from within the discipline arguing for mid-range theory. Critics within and outside the discipline also pointed to the limitations of the white, male, European perspective of the field. With the cultural turn, and the rising need to address global concerns, a new global sociology was established.
- Many voices were excluded from early sociological institutions, particularly women's voices but also scholars from non-European backgrounds. Today, some previously silenced voices have been recovered by historians, and new critical voices have entered the discipline, including feminists, critical race

theorists, post-colonial theorists, queer theorists, and theorists of disability and intersectionality.

**2.3 Define the major elements of the research process and describe a range of sociological research techniques.**

- Sociology uses the research methods and techniques of scientific research. Sociology is committed to logical, empirical research. Sociologists test empirical hypotheses using systematically collected data.

- Sociology shares the ethical commitment of scientific research to prevent and avoid harm to human subjects. Sociologists submit their research to peer review by the wider scientific community. There is a very high standard for any kind of experimental design for studying living human subjects.

- The major elements of the research process are (1) define a research question, and explore the history of research on the topic; (2) define the variables; (3) operationalize variables by specifying valid, reliable measures; (4) state a hypothesis about the expected causal relationship between variables; (5) collect the data; (6) analyze the data; and (7) draw conclusions. Sociologists use a range of research techniques. These include asking people questions, participant-observation methods, comparative-historical methods, case studies, and analysis of publicly available data.

- Basic research in sociology advances knowledge and understanding about the world by developing theories and testing them with empirical evidence. Its primary audience is other scientists.

- Applied research in sociology is used to address practical questions and to solve practical problems in society. The primary audience for applied research is the client who pays for their expertise.

- The goal of public sociology is to bring sociological knowledge to a general audience. With public sociology, the primary audience consists of the general public, as well as journalists and media organizations who set the agenda for public debate. Public sociology is published in the mass media but also includes the sociology classroom.

## Key Terms

Alienation 34
Anomie 36
Applied research 57
Basic research 57
Beliefs 44
Big data 56
Bureaucracy 34
Canon 33
Capitalism 33
Case study research 53
Categorical or nominal variable 51
Causation 53
Cause 53
Collective representations 36

Colonialism 32
Comparative-historical methods 55
Confirmation bias 47
Conflict theory 39
Consensus theory 39
Controlled experiment 45
Convenience sample 52
Correlation 53
Critical race theory 42
Cultural turn 43
Dependent variable 51
Disenchantment 35
Division of labor 35
Empirical evidence 44
Ethics 45
Ethnography 55
Experiments 55
Falsifiability 45
Feminism 41
Field experiments 55
Focus groups 54
Generalize 54
Globalization 32
Hypothesis 53
Independent variable 51
In-depth interviews 54
Informed consent 45
Institutional reflexivity 49
Institutional review board 45
Intersectionality 42
Linear or continuous variable 50
Logic 44
Mechanical solidarity 35
Operationalization 52
Opinions 44
Ordinal variable 51
Organic solidarity 35
Participant-observation 55
Peer review 45

Post-colonial theory 42
Public sociology 57
Qualitative methods 51
Quantitative methods 49
Queer theory 42
Random sample 52
Rationalization 34
Reactivity 55
Reflexivity 29
Reliability 52
Representative sample 53
Research population 52
Sample 52
Selection effect 56
Snowball sample 53
Social facts 31
Social research 45
Social sciences 30
Sociological research methods 49
Surveys 54
Symbolic interactionism 39
Theoretical sample 53
Theories of the middle range 41
Thomas theorem 43
Urbanization 32
Validity 52
Variable 51

## Review Questions

1. What is the sociological imagination, and how is it connected to reflexivity?

2. What is the sociological canon? Who are the major figures in the canon? What is the forgotten canon, and what does it tell us about inequality and privilege?

3. What conditions were the early sociological theorists trying to explain? How is that similar to or different from today?

4. What is the three-fold model of sociology? How are conflict, consensus, and symbolic interactionist perspectives different? Identify three critiques of the three-fold model of sociology.
5. What other disciplines are close to sociology in the modern academic field?
6. What is scientific about sociology? How is social science different from natural science?
7. How is scientific research systematic, logical, and empirical?
8. How are scientific statements different from beliefs or opinions?
9. What is the difference between correlation and causation?
10. Are random samples better than other kinds of samples? Why?
11. What is the difference between a survey question and an open-ended question, and when would you use each?

## Explore

**RECOMMENDED READINGS**

Abbott, Andrew. 2001. *Chaos of the Disciplines*. Chicago: University of Chicago Press.

Deegan, Mary Jo. 2007. "The Chicago School of Ethnography." In *Handbook of Ethnography*, eds. Paul Atkinson, Amanda Coffey, Sarah Delmont, John Lofland, and Lyn Lofland (pp. 11–25). Newbury Park, CA: Sage.

Luker, Kristin. 2008. *Salsa Dancing into the Social Sciences: Research in an Age of Info-Glut*. Cambridge, MA: Harvard University Press.

Madoo Lengermann, Patricia, and Jill Niebrugge-Brantley. 1998. *The Women Founders: Sociology and Social Theory, 1830–1930. A Text with Readings*. New York: McGraw-Hill.

Mills, C. Wright. [1959] 2000. *Sociological Imagination*. New York: Oxford University Press.

Morris, Aldon. 2015. *The Scholar Denied: W. E. B. Du Bois and the Birth of Modern Sociology*. Los Angeles: University of California Press.

Said, Edward W. 1994. *Culture and Imperialism*. New York: Vintage Books.

Seidman, Steven. 2013. *Contested Knowledge: Social Theory Today*, 5th ed. New York: Wiley-Blackwell.

Spradley, James. 1979. *The Ethnographic Interview*. New York: Harcourt Brace Jovanovich.

Weber, Max. 1946. "Science as a Vocation." In *From Max Weber: Essays in Sociology* (pp. 129–156). New York: Oxford University Press.

**ACTIVITIES**

- *Use your sociological imagination*: If you were interested in the relationship between education and earnings and wanted to study it, in what different ways could you operationalize the variables "education" and "earnings"?
- *Media+Data Literacies*: Google the names of the major social theorists and

forgotten theorists from this chapter. How many results are returned for each? Are there differences by gender or race?

- *Discuss*: Should there have been additional penalties for Facebook or OKCupid when it was found they manipulated their customers to research emotional behavior? Why or why not? What sort of sanction might be effective?

# PART II
# STRUCTURE AND CONTROL

**3** Culture

**4** Socialization, Social Interaction, and Group Life

**5** Deviance, Crime, and Punishment

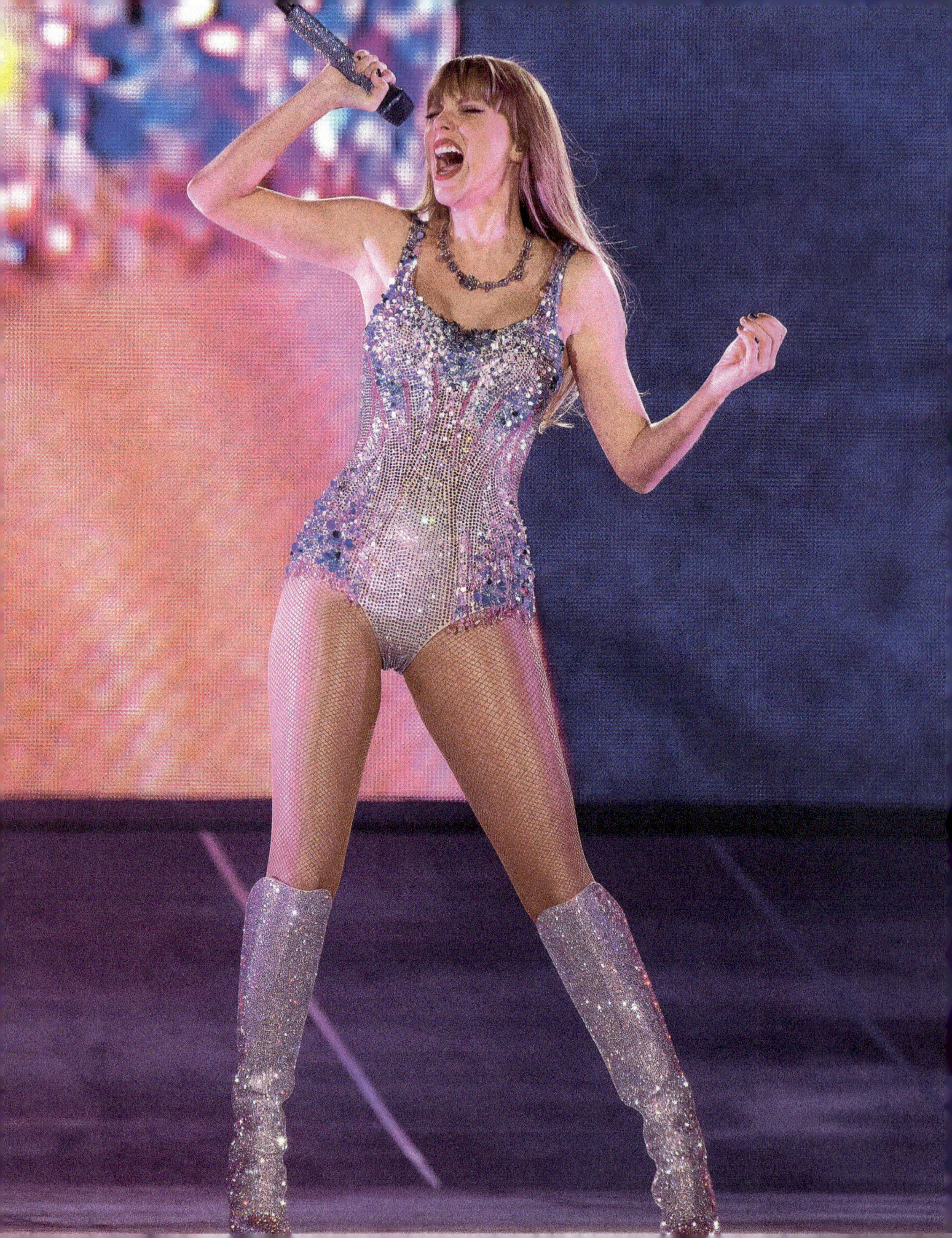

# 3

# Culture

It is not unusual for parents to dislike the cultural activity of teenagers. Music is an especially potent way for teenagers to bond with their friends while expressing their difference from their parents. The conflict over culture also works in the other direction. Teenagers do not always want to share their lifestyles and hobbies with their parents. Consider Facebook, which was launched in 2004 as a social network for college students. Initially limited to Harvard undergraduates, within two years it had become absolutely central to the social life of high school and college students. As of July 2023, Facebook reported 3.03 billion monthly active users.

Yet many of the students who drove the early success of social media came to believe that their parents were ruining Facebook. A 2013 Pew Research Center study found that teenagers were tired of Facebook, and they were more interested in new social media platforms that their parents had not yet discovered. As one college student commented, "Yeah, that's why we go on Twitter and Instagram [instead of Facebook]. My Mom doesn't have that" (Soper 2013; Madden et al. 2013). User data reflects these changes. Of the 1.6 billion monthly active users of Instagram, only 15 percent are older than 45 years old (Statista 2024).

Why do adults care so much about their children's hobbies? Why do high school and college students cringe when their parents start listening to the same music or using the same social media that they do? Why do teenagers and their parents both try

**Chapter Outline**

**3.1 HOW DO SOCIOLOGISTS STUDY CULTURE? 70**

*What Is Culture? 70*
*Ideal Culture and Material Culture 72*

**3.2 CULTURE AND POWER 77**

*Cultural Power 77*
*Recognizing and Resisting Cultural Power 83*

**3.3 TYPES OF CULTURE IN TODAY'S WORLD 86**

*Global Culture 86*
*Dominant Cultures and Subcultures 89*
*Popular Culture, Commercial Culture, and High Culture 93*

**CASE STUDY: PROTESTING THE NATIONAL ANTHEM 99**

**Taylor Swift**

to cultivate a lifestyle that expresses their true identity? Last, what can these lifestyle choices and conflicts tell us about the society in which we live?

In this chapter we consider the important role that culture plays in social life. We begin by discussing how sociologists define culture and how they study it. We discuss how people use culture in everyday life, then consider the relationship between culture and power. Last, we consider the many different types of culture.

## LEARNING GOALS

**3.1** Define culture, identify the difference between material and ideal culture, and understand that meanings are made in a cultural context.

**3.2** Identify the connection between culture and power: identify ideologies, stereotypes, cultural hierarchies, and cultural resistance.

**3.3** Distinguish different types of culture.

# 3.1 How Do Sociologists Study Culture?

**LG 3.1** Define culture, identify the difference between material and ideal culture, and understand that meanings are made in a cultural context.

**Beliefs** All the things we think are true, even in the absence of evidence or proof; ideas about the world that come through divine revelation or received tradition.

**Culture** The entire set of beliefs, knowledge, practices, and material objects that are meaningful to a group of people and shared from generation to generation.

Most sociologists agree that culture is a basic dimension of social life and important to include in their sociological research. But what is culture? Is it the **beliefs** and values inside our heads? Our everyday habits and customs? What we see in the museum? What we post on Instagram? Is there anything that is *not* culture? Raymond Williams (1921–1988) defined culture as "a whole way of life," meaning that the web of culture was so wide that it included virtually everything in society (Williams 1983). Because culture is everywhere, figuring out how to study it can be a real challenge.

### What Is Culture?

**Culture** is the set of beliefs, knowledge, practices, and material objects that are meaningful to a group of people and shared from generation to generation. While "culture" can refer to objects like a book, a house, or a work of music, it can also refer to cultural practices, such as reading, designing a house, or singing the national anthem at a football game. When we study culture, we are studying how people make their lives meaningful, how they share those meanings, and how they use those shared meanings to do things collectively.

Culture is something members of a society learn. While many scientists believe that we have an innate biological ability to learn language and culture (Chomsky 2006), we still have to learn the specific culture into which we are born. As we live our lives, we gradually learn the shared meanings that connect us to our family, friends, and larger society. This ongoing process of learning the social meanings of our culture is known as **socialization** (Chapter 4).

The shared meanings of culture can change depending on which people are sharing them and how they are using them. Even the meanings of words and phrases can change, if groups start using them for different purposes.

**HOW DOES CULTURE DEVELOP?.** Cultural meanings develop in relationships. Language provides the basic model for how this works, and it has provided the framework for how many sociologists think about culture. From linguistics, we know that words get their meaning through their relationship to other words (Saussure 1998). One of the most basic relationships is similarity and difference. We know the meaning of something because it is similar to or different from something else. Building on these basic relationships, the meaning of words can derive from the larger sequence of words and the social context in which they are used. The **symbolic meaning** of a word can be shaped by its relationship with other cultural images, emotions, meanings, and associations. For example, while the word "red" identifies a particular color worldwide, its symbolic meaning changes depending on the cultural context. In Japan, red symbolizes happiness, whereas in South Africa it is the color associated with mourning.

**PATTERN AND VARIATION.** Over time, cultural patterns develop by placing beliefs, practices, and cultural objects into groups of similar things and groups of different things. These groupings develop into **classification systems**, which create increasingly complex identifications of similarity and difference. As people become more fully immersed in a given culture, they become more sophisticated in the kinds of classifications they can identify. Most of us can recognize the difference between basic kinds of music—classical versus pop, rock versus hip-hop, and so on. But for true experts, their "insider status" is based on their ability to identify and classify distinctions that other people cannot hear (Bennett et al. 2009). The distinctions are already there, in the system of cultural classification; but only the true insiders can see them and make them visible for the rest of us.

Priscilla Parkhust Ferguson shows how cultural patterns of similarity and difference develop over time in her book *Word of Mouth: What We Talk about When We Talk about Food* (2014). She argues that how we talk about food is just as meaningful as what we choose to eat or how we choose to eat it. This new language about food, Ferguson argues, tells us a lot about who we are

**Socialization** All of the different ways that we learn about our society's beliefs, values, and expected behaviors; the ongoing process of learning the social meanings of a culture.

**Symbolic meaning** The broader cultural content of a cultural object, idea or, event, which is based on the other images, emotions, meanings, and associations that come from the larger culture.

**Classification systems** Elaborate and nuanced identifications of similarity and difference based on cultural patterns that develop over time when people place beliefs, practices, and cultural objects into groups of similar things and groups of different things.

and how our cultural identities are changing. To be sure, there is still a value to eating traditional American food on the Fourth of July or at Thanksgiving, but there are now also critical, global, and more environmentally and health-conscious standards of consumption.

### Ideal Culture and Material Culture

While cultural patterns allow groups to share meanings and to do things with other people, they do not completely determine shared meanings. Culture itself is always changing because individuals and groups are constantly trying to distinguish themselves by using culture in new ways. The ways that shared meanings change over time can provide important evidence about how people in a society understand themselves and the world around them.

One way to think about the many different types of culture is to distinguish between ideal culture and material culture. **Ideal culture** refers to all the social meanings that exist in nonmaterial form. This includes language, values, beliefs, and norms. **Material culture** refers to all the cultural objects that are produced by a social group or a society. Material culture includes objects that we find around us, such as furniture, clothes, toys, and cars. Most shared meanings include elements of both material and ideal culture.

**Ideal culture** All the social meanings that exist in nonmaterial form, such as beliefs, values, expectations, and language.

**Material culture** All the cultural objects that are produced by a social group or a society.

## METHODS AND INTERPRETATION

### How to Measure What People Think

One of the challenges with measuring culture is that a lot of it exists inside the minds of people—things like our values, our beliefs, our definition of the situation, and so forth. We can ask people what they are thinking, but how do we know that this is an accurate representation of what they are *actually* thinking? How can we be sure that they are being honest with us? How can we be sure that they really understand their own thoughts and intentions? How do we deal with the fact that people often say one thing and then act completely differently? In their book *Measuring Culture* (Mohr et al. 2020), a group of sociologists set out to answer these questions, and to develop guidelines for how to measure the culture that exists inside our heads.

Sociologists who want to understand culture have to do more than just ask people what they are thinking. This is because (a) much of our thinking is not conscious, and (b) our conscious thoughts are rarely expressed in our heads as single attitudes or belief statements. Summarizing the research in cognitive science and applying it to cultural sociology, Stephen Vaisey (2009) argued that people think through two different cognitive processes. Deliberative cognition is slow, conscious, and often characterized by a lot of reflection. This is how we usually imagine the process of thinking. But there is also non-deliberative cognition, which is fast, unconscious, and implicit. Vaisey argues that sociologists need different methods to measure these two different forms of thinking.

Sociologists have many techniques for measuring deliberative cognition. We can use extended interviews, asking people questions and then asking additional probing questions to get them to think more deeply about what they are telling us. We can organize focus groups, where people engage in extended discussions with one another

### METHODS AND INTERPRETATION CONTINUED

about a topic of mutual interest. We can ask people to spend some time writing reflections about their experiences, or we can rely on diaries or letters they have already produced. We can even rely on survey research, asking them about their preferences, their beliefs, and how strongly they hold those beliefs.

There are different strategies for measuring non-deliberative cognition. One option is to give people forced-choice survey questions under tight time pressure, to try to simulate the kinds of "gut reactions" that are closer to non-deliberative processes (Vaisey 2009). Another approach is to use the implicit association test, which social psychologists developed to measure implicit biases that people have (Mohr et al. 2020). A third strategy is to measure the amount of time it takes people to evaluate different statements, based on the idea that answers that take a lot of time are deliberative and those that are answered more quickly are non-deliberative. A fourth strategy is to increase the "cognitive load" for research subjects—for example, asking them to remember an eight-digit number while answering questions—in order to make it harder for them to access their deliberative cognition (Miles 2015). The basic idea behind all these strategies is that researchers need to be more creative in developing a variety of different "indirect research techniques" that can allow them to measure non-deliberative cognition (Mohr et al. 2020).

Once sociologists have developed better techniques for measuring non-deliberative cognition, the next challenge is to design techniques to explore how non-deliberative and deliberative cognition interact with one another to produce "thinking" (Mohr et al. 2020). Sociologists are interested in identifying the conditions and the mechanisms that allow deliberative cognition to override non-deliberative cognition. They want to know more about how these complicated cognitive processes get transformed into key stories we tell about ourselves and the world around us, and how those key stories structure deliberative and non-deliberative cognition. They still want to know more about the connection between thoughts and actions. And they want to know how the thoughts in a person's head are influenced by the larger public culture, particularly in an era when that public culture is increasingly digitized and always available to us through media technologies (Chapter 14).

#### ACTIVE LEARNING

**Discuss:** Of the strategies for measuring non-deliberative cognition described above, which one do you think would be the most useful and insightful? What do you think are the advantages and disadvantages of this measurement technique?

**IDEAL CULTURE: LANGUAGE, VALUES, BELIEFS, AND NORMS.** Ideal culture is based on language, which is the way that people in a society communicate with one another. Linguistics, the study of language, documents how language is organized, the rules for its use, expectations about what words mean, and how different words are related to one another. In fact, linguists have argued that reality is literally unthinkable outside the categories and rules of language.

Language is one of the most powerful ways for a society to store culture and to transmit shared meanings from one generation to the next. Most societies take pride in their language or languages, and they take significant steps to preserve its heritage and purity. However, languages can be suppressed through colonization or other forms of ethnic violence. For example, most indigenous languages in North America are endangered or extinct (Gordon 2005).

**Values** General social ideas about what is right and wrong, good and bad, desirable and undesirable, important and unimportant.

**Traditional values** Widely held social beliefs that emphasize the importance of traditional religion, family, national pride, and obedience to authority.

**Secular-rational values** Widely held social beliefs that emphasize the importance of individualism, science, and critique.

**Survival values** Widely held social beliefs that emphasize the importance of economic and physical security.

**Self-expression values** Widely held social beliefs that emphasize the importance of tolerance, political participation, personal happiness, and environmental protection.

Language shapes how we express ourselves and how we make ourselves understood to others. When new words enter the language, they signal important social changes and important new meanings that bind people together. When the word "bureaucracy" (from the French word *bureau*, which means both "desk" and "office") first entered the English language in the late 18th century, its arrival reflected the growing importance to society of officials and administrators. Today, words such as "clickbait," "hashtag," and "influencer" reflect the influence of social media in everyday life.

Some words in a language help define a society's **values**, which identify the basic standards that people use to define what is important, desirable, right, and morally good. Values point to a society's ideals. They help us think about what it means to live a good life.

Sociologists have long compared the values of different countries. One of the earliest sociological studies, Alexis de Tocqueville's (1805–1859) *Democracy in America* ([1835, 1840] 2003) compared French and American values in the 19th century. Tocqueville found that Americans had a distinct set of values, which emphasized individualism, hard work, economic success, and religious and political freedom.

More recently, social scientists have argued that there are two important dimensions that explain most of the value differences in the world: the difference between traditional and secular-rational values and the difference between survival and self-expression values (Inglehart and Welzel 2005). In the first dimension, **traditional values** emphasize religion, family, national pride, and obedience to authority, while **secular-rational values** place less importance on family and religion and more importance on individualism, science, and critique. In the second dimension, **survival values** emphasize economic and physical security, while **self-expression values** place more importance on tolerance, political participation, personal happiness, and environmental protection. The United States is characterized by self-expression values and traditional values, while European countries such as Denmark and Sweden combine self-expression values and secular-rational values. China combines secular-rational values and survival values, whereas Pakistan and Morocco combine traditional values and survival values. The survey research that is used to make these comparisons is updated approximately every five years, and the most recent wave of data collection was completed in 2020. While this research project has been very influential among social scientists, it has also faced criticism. Some researchers argue that the model presents an over-simplified understanding of national culture (Flanagan and Lee 2003). Others point out that the project started out as a study of a small number of European democracies, and that its measurements are much more effective of capturing the cultural dynamics in those places than in other nations that are a lot different from those European democracies (Aleman and Woods 2016).

Ideal culture also includes beliefs, which are all the things we think are true, even in the absence of evidence or proof. We cannot "prove" that God exists or that there is such a thing as a "just war," and yet people hold strong beliefs about these and other fundamental social issues. As Émile Durkheim pointed out, beliefs are primarily social and come from the groups to which we belong.

Social differences between groups and societies are often expressed as differences in belief. Within societies, significant social conflicts often develop between groups that maintain different beliefs about important social issues. In recent years, major social conflicts have divided Americans based on their beliefs about abortion, gay marriage, sex education, racial justice, and globalization and immigration policy. Some sociologists have argued that there is a profound **culture war** in America, based on fundamental differences in belief (e.g., Hunter 1991; Ellison and Musick 1993). Survey researchers have documented agreement about some shared values in America over time (Hunter and Wolfe 2006; Demerath and Yang 1997; Snow and Fingerhut 2019) but in a context of chronic political polarization (Snow and Fingerhut 2019; Dimock and Wike 2020) . Despite the intensely polarized 2020 and 2024 presidential elections, most voters also think that the US president should address the concerns of all citizens (Dimock and Wike 2020).

**Culture war** A profound, society-threatening conflict over values.

Between societies, conflicts over beliefs can create deep divisions. While global conflicts are often influenced by differences in wealth and power, they are also based on basic differences in belief. In such conflicts, there is no evidence or data that can resolve the dispute. The shared beliefs unite each side together in solidarity, just as they heighten the conflict with those who have different beliefs.

Ideal culture is also expressed in **norms**, which are the common set of expectations about how people should behave in any specific situation. Norms, which are necessary for people to coordinate their activities, are learned through the process of socialization and enforced through social interaction. While norms point to overarching social values, they are not universal rules of behavior. Norms are particular to time and place and connected to specific societies and specific cultures. What we consider to be polite, considerate, or "normal" behavior comes from wider cultural ideas as they are lived in particular settings.

**Norms** Shared expectations, specific to time and place, about how people should act in any particular situation.

Sociologists distinguish many different kinds of norms. There are social distance norms that specify how close or distant someone can be with another and that vary widely depending on the status and identity of the individuals involved. Indeed, the COVID-19 pandemic has seen new social distance norms develop rapidly, with as yet unknown consequences for public life. There are also new expectations about when people are expected to wear masks, shake hands, or even leave their house. Other norms govern behaviors of people of different ages or different sexes in a wide variety of situations.

**Folkways** Common-sense and fairly unserious norms.

**Mores** Norms that define serious expectations about behavior that invoke central values.

**Sanctions** Actions that punish people when they do not act in a way that accords with norms.

An important distinction is between folkways and mores. **Folkways** are common-sense behavioral expectations, such as turning off the faucet after washing our hands or throwing out trash after eating. **Mores** are more serious expectations about behavior that reflect central values. For example, in US culture, while adultery is not against the law, it is considered a serious breach of social norms. Misgendering someone by using the wrong pronoun can also be considered a serious breach of norms.

All norms are socially enforced through **sanctions**, which reward people when they act in the expected way and punish them when they do not. Many of these punishments are formal sanctions, which are written down in specific rules that describe both the expected behavior and the consequences for violating the rules. But many norms are enforced by informal sanctions, where other people give us feedback about our behavior. Most norms about politeness and rudeness are enforced by informal sanctions (Smith, Phillips, and King 2010). For example, if you cut in front of somebody in line, they may confront you or shake their head in disapproval. Over time, as people experience these formal and informal sanctions, they come to internalize the culture. We begin to police ourselves, and we feel guilty or wrong when we violate social norms.

**MATERIAL CULTURE.** Culture also shapes the meanings we attach to the objects we interact with in our social lives. Even ordinary objects that may not necessarily capture our interest contain social meaning. Consider the toaster. In the United States and other English-speaking countries, the toaster is associated with breakfast. The toaster is also connected to the ideas of progress and convenience because toasters arrived in the early 20th century, just as the bread slicer was invented and US home kitchens were wired for electricity (Molotch 2005).

**The meanings associated with toasters**
The toaster is one of the most common kitchen appliances found in the home. It is generally associated with breakfast.

It can be difficult to separate material culture from ideal culture because cultural objects always have symbolic meanings. We have already discussed how this works for a variety of cultural objects, such as music, social media, clothes, kitchen appliances, and food. But it is also true for paintings, buildings, furniture, pictures, flags, and religious objects. These objects help us understand ourselves and the world around us (Woodward 2012: 671).

As we discuss later in the section on global culture, the production, distribution, and consumption of cultural objects form one of the biggest parts of the global economy. Enormous industries are devoted to making objects that we want to buy, while others are devoted to advertising these objects to us and suggesting what they should mean in our lives.

## 3.2 Culture and Power

**LG 3.2** Identify the connection between culture and power: identify ideologies, stereotypes, cultural hierarchies, and cultural resistance.

Because culture is such an important part of social life, it is connected to all of the paired concepts we introduced at the beginning of this book. Shared meanings are possible because they are organized into common patterns and relationships, but these meanings are always changing due to the different ways that people combine cultural objects and symbolic meanings. Cultural objects circulate globally, but their actual meanings often vary depending on the local context in which they are being used. Culture brings people together, but it is also a source of inequality as well as privilege. Shared values are a source of solidarity, but disagreement over values produces conflict.

### Cultural Power

On August 18, 2023, President Joe Biden welcomed South Korean President Yoon Suk Yeol and Japanese Prime Minister Fumio Kishida to a summit at Camp David, a Maryland country retreat built for US presidents in 1938. Camp David has a lot of historical significance, having been used to host some of the most important meetings between US presidents and foreign leaders. Underscoring this significance, Japanese prime minister Kishida noted, "Here at Camp David, numerous historical meetings have taken place and it is a huge honor to have printed a fresh page in its history with this meeting." As Biden said during the joint press conference held during the summit, "I can think of no more fitting location to begin the next era of cooperation—a place that has long symbolized the power of new beginnings and new possibilities." In fact, this was the first stand-alone summit that had ever taken place between the three countries.

World leaders who can stage these kinds of public events and command media attention have a special kind of cultural power because they control the means of symbolic production (Alexander 2006). Their access to resources (such as formal political and military power) means they can stage events for the sole purpose of getting media publicity. Importantly, they use these events to put forward interpretations of the world that they hope will become shared meanings in the larger society (Boorstin 1961; Dayan and Katz 1992). In this case, the summit was intended to underline the growing cooperation between Japan and South Korea, and the intention of the three countries to create a strong alliance that would counter the influence of China in the East Asian region. This intention was reflected in media reports and op-ed columns about the summit, which noted that the summit sent a clear message to China and had the potential to create a more effective pan-Pacific partnership, undoing some of the lingering tensions that were

August 18, 2023, President Joe Biden welcomed South Korean president Yoon Suk Yeol and Japanese prime minister Fumio Kishida to a summit at Camp David, a Maryland country retreat built for US presidents in 1938.

the result of Japan's 1910 colonization of Korea.

In an increasingly sophisticated social media environment, however, there is no guarantee that the meanings of a staged public event will go unchallenged. Chinese and North Korean leaders criticized the summit, arguing that it would destabilize the region rather than bringing peace and security (Madhani et al., 2023). In the US, conservative radio and television commentators claimed that Biden's performance at the press conferences showed that he was old, confused, and ineffective as a leader. Conservative social media sites criticized the summit for prioritizing global affairs over national interests, and stated that instead of putting "America First" it put "America Last." While it is true that privileged, powerful people have more resources to advance their agendas than others do, in a world of social media they are not always able to fully control the message.

**Ideology** A system of shared meaning that is used to justify existing relationships of power and privilege.

**IDEOLOGY. Ideology** is any system of shared meaning that is used to justify existing relationships of power and privilege. In other words, ideology is culture in the service of power (Thompson 1991). The concept of ideology was first introduced in sociology by Karl Marx (Chapter 2), who argued that the dominant class used culture to get people to believe things about the world that were against their true interests. Marx argued that ideology distorted people's beliefs and prevented them from recognizing what they needed to do to improve their lives. Sociologists influenced by Marx's theory of ideology were particularly critical of religious beliefs and ideas about national patriotism because these ideas made it harder for people to see how they were being exploited in their everyday lives (Adorno et al. 1950).

Ideology operates in two different ways. First, it works through misdirection. By focusing attention on issues that will not have any impact on people's material well-being, ideology creates cultural conflicts between groups that have the same economic interests and that should be allies with one another. In the late 19th and early 20th centuries, for example, business owners used antiimmigrant and racial ideologies to encourage conflicts between white, immigrant, and Black workers, as a strategy for weakening labor unions (Lieberson 1980). In recent years, many social scientists have argued, political parties in the United States have used controversial issues such as abortion, illegal immigration, and gay marriage to distract voters' attention and to make it harder for them to form alliances based on shared economic interest (Gitlin 1995; Frank 2004). Analysts observing the 2016 and 2020 US presidential elections, for example, observed that many poor and working-class Americans opted to vote for Donald Trump (a wealthy, white New York businessman) because he represented an alternative to a cosmopolitan vision for a diverse, secular, more globally integrated American society.

Sociologist Arlie Hochschild (2018) conducted ethnographic interviews with people who eventually voted for Donald Trump in 2016. Hochschild argues that these voters felt the loss of the American Dream. They wanted to return to an earlier version of America in which good jobs, home ownership, global power, Christian heterosexual marriage and family, and white dominance (or at least an end to what they saw as political correctness around race and gender) prevailed. This is why they chose a candidate who apparently empathized with their loss (Hochschild 2018).

This is the second way ideology works, by making certain beliefs seem like "common sense" so that they cannot be challenged easily. For example, the ideology of the American Dream encourages people to believe that their successes and failures are entirely of their own making and to see social policies in terms of individual stories of fairness and luck. This makes it harder for people to perceive that their life chances are shaped by structural forces beyond their control, such as systemic racism, population movements due to war or climate change, or economic restructuring resulting from automation, international competition, or the behavior of financial markets (Messner and Rosenfeld 2007). If people accept these ideologies, it changes the way they think about themselves and can limit the decisions they make. In other words, ideologies make it harder for people to develop their sociological imagination.

**Stereotypes** A form of ideology that encourages people to believe in the natural superiority or inferiority of different groups of people.

**STEREOTYPES. Stereotypes** are a form of ideology that encourages people to believe in the natural superiority or inferiority of different groups of people. Throughout history, stereotypes have been used to reinforce and justify systems of inequality, particularly those

**The American Dream**
Buying a home is associated with living the "American Dream." In recent years, severe economic downturns have challenged that idea.

that discriminate against marginalized and under-represented groups. In the United States, for example, women were not allowed to vote until 1920 because of stereotypes claiming they were too delicate and emotional to participate in politics. The African slave trade was frequently justified by racial stereotypes suggesting that people of African descent were uncivilized and lacked the natural intelligence to take care of themselves. Many of these stereotypes persist today as informal systems of prejudice, long after the legal systems of discrimination have been eliminated. (We discuss racial and gender stereotypes in more detail in Chapters 7 and 8.)

As systems of cultural power, stereotypes get distributed by people who have an interest in using them to reinforce their own advantages over other groups in society. Those who successfully propagate stereotypes are able to do so because they have access to the **means of symbolic production**, the organized social resources for creating, producing, and distributing communications. These resources include education, literacy, museums, and libraries, as well as the media. When stereotypes become instruments of cultural power, they result in both formal laws and informal sanctions used to single out specific groups for unfair treatment. Criticizing stereotypes and challenging prejudiced beliefs are ways we can use culture creatively to resist cultural power when we think it is illegitimate or wrong.

**Means of symbolic production** The organized social resources for creating, producing, and distributing communications.

**CULTURAL POWER, KNOWLEDGE, AND SELF-CONTROL.** While stereotypes are used to discriminate against specific groups, there is another kind of cultural power based on knowledge and self-discipline. This kind of cultural power was first analyzed by the French philosopher Michel Foucault (1926–1984), who produced pioneering historical research about madness, punishment, and sexuality. For Foucault, power operates by producing and organizing systems of knowledge about people's activities. These knowledge systems, or **discourses**, define what we count as true and normal and what kinds of meanings we attach to people who are "not normal."

**Discourses** Organized systems of knowledge and power that define what meanings we count as true and normal and what kinds of meanings we attach to people who are "not normal."

Discourses produce cultural power by defining who needs to be watched, how they are to be watched, and how they are to be disciplined. Discourse also produces cultural power by encouraging us to watch over ourselves, to be always on the lookout for signs that there is something wrong with us, and to turn to specific sources of knowledge and guidance to cure ourselves of any problems or weaknesses we identify within ourselves.

Foucault argued that the discourses of surveillance and rehabilitation have made self-control more important than ever. In the prisons, schools, and mental hospitals that he studied, Foucault saw that surveillance was replacing violence as the main form of power. Because people knew that they were always being watched, they learned to control their own behaviors to stay out of trouble. Today, systems of surveillance have spread throughout society, and people have learned to accept them as a normal part of life.

We know there are cameras watching us in stores and in public streets, and we know that everything we do on the internet can be traced and recorded (Ericson and Haggerty 2006). Public safety campaigns, such as the "If You See Something, Say Something" anti-terrorism campaign spearheaded by the New York Metropolitan Transportation Authority and later adopted nationwide by the Department of Homeland Security, remind us that the people around us are also watching (Doyle, Lippert, and Lyon 2012). We accept this as part of the cost of living in the modern world, and we learn to carefully monitor our own behavior so as not to arouse suspicion. In the process of accepting these shared meanings about the world, we exercise power over ourselves on behalf of these larger cultural systems.

The second cultural change Foucault identified was the discourse of rehabilitation, or the influence of therapy and self-help as forms of self-discipline. His research on madness shows how prisoners became objects of treatment: they were not just dangerous people who needed to be locked up; they were people with pathologies who could be treated and rehabilitated (Foucault 1988). Tracing the history by which madness was gradually redefined as a mental illness that could be treated by pharmaceuticals, psychology, and other therapies, Foucault shows how this language of rehabilitation and therapy gradually spread throughout society. Today, people read self-help books, use self-help apps, and see therapists to try to identify and resolve pathological and self-destructive tendencies (Giddens 1991). They search for drugs and other kinds of cures that can help treat these destructive tendencies (Conrad 2007). They make themselves into objects of study, and they turn themselves into projects of rehabilitation and redemption.

**Cultural hierarchies** Socially organized inequality based on ideas about what counts as "good" or worthwhile culture.

**CULTURAL HIERARCHIES AND CULTURAL POWER.** Cultural power is also exercised in **cultural hierarchies** that enforce particular ideas about what counts as "good" or worthwhile culture. The examples we introduced at the beginning of the chapter demonstrate the exercise of power in one kind of cultural hierarchy, music. When adults try to enforce cultural hierarchies, they are attempting to impose a set of shared meanings about how people should be spending their time and what their tastes should be.

Sociological researchers examine how people use conflicts over culture to try to enforce their own cultural tastes and preferences on an entire society. Politicians frequently attack the arts and culture during elections as a way of appealing to voters and mobilizing constituencies who might not otherwise vote for them (Kidd 2010). Conflicts over culture tend to increase when a large number of immigrants move into a community, threatening the

**Surveillance** Discourses of surveillance encourage people to watch over others and to expect that they are being watched too.

**PAIRED CONCEPTS**

# Structure and Contingency

## The Protocols of the Elders of Zion

*The Protocols of the Elders of Zion* is the most infamous example of anti-Semitism published during the 20th century. First circulated in Russia in the late 19th and early 20th centuries, the *Protocols* was a central part of a 1905 propaganda campaign in which more than 2,500 Russian Jews were targeted and killed. The *Protocols* later became an important part of Nazi propaganda in Germany and was used as historical evidence to justify Nazi persecution of the Jews. In the United States, the wealthy industrialist Henry Ford paid for the printing of 500,000 copies of the book in the 1920s.

*The Protocols of the Elders of Zion* was produced through a series of contingencies that included both plagiarism and fabrication. Beginning as a political satire written in 1864 by the French writer Maurice Joly, it was plagiarized by a German anti-Semitic writer, Herman Goedsche, who changed the plot about a conversation between two political thinkers into a story about a mythical Jewish conspiracy. This German text was then rewritten as a fabricated eyewitness account of a supposedly real meeting that had taken place, renamed *The Protocols of the Elders of Zion*, and printed as a pamphlet in 1897. The pamphlet was translated from French into Russian in 1903 and then circulated more widely in 1905, when Russian officials decided to release it as part of their anti-Jewish propaganda campaign. At this point, the pamphlet took on a new life, and it spread throughout the world. The writer of the document claimed to have witnessed a secret meeting in which Jewish leaders made plans for world domination. Despite the fact that the meeting had never happened, the book drew on existing stereotypes about Jews and a supposed international Jewish plot to control the world.

The truth about the *Protocols* was first noticed by Irish journalist Philip Graves, who wrote a series of newspaper articles in 1921 documenting the plagiarism and the forgery. In the same year, the American journalist Herman Bernstein published a book documenting the hoax. Despite this, in Germany the *Protocols* continued to be taught in schools as a work of history well into the 1930s, and the pamphlet continues to fuel conspiracy theories about international Jewish conspiracies to this day. The Southern Poverty Law Center (2004) reports that the *Protocols* was available at Walmart as recently as 2004. In most of the world, however, the *Protocols* is now recognized for what it is: a work of anti-Semitic propaganda, which stole the structure of a fictional story and modified it for sinister purposes. At the same time the basic structure of the story continues to circulate, further fueling anti-Semitic movements around the world.

**Henry Ford**
American icon and car manufacturer Henry Ford helped to finance the distribution of anti-Semitic literature in the United States.

### ACTIVE LEARNING

**Discuss:** Can you think of another conspiracy theory that is circulating today? What is the basic structure of the story? How is it similar to the story told in the *Protocols*? How is it different? What elements of structure and contingency do you think help to explain why people believe this particular conspiracy theory?

lifestyle and tastes of the residents who already live there (Gusfield 1963; Tepper 2011). Wealthier and more privileged people regularly use their own tastes and cultural preferences as a way of excluding people with different social backgrounds, who are made to feel inferior because their cultural preferences get criticized for being tasteless and uncivilized (Bourdieu 1984). We explore this relationship between cultural preferences and social class in more detail in Chapter 6.

## Recognizing and Resisting Cultural Power

As we have emphasized throughout this book, attempts to exercise power always meet resistance. Where cultural power is concerned, we need to recognize that people are never completely brainwashed by the shared meanings of culture. As the sociologist Harold Garfinkel (1967) pointed out, social actors are not "cultural dopes." They do not blindly follow rules, and they do not mindlessly accept the shared meanings of culture. People often recognize when cultural power is being used against them. They develop strategies for resisting that power, and they have the ability to take control of the cultural meanings they use in their social lives.

**ACTIVE AUDIENCES.** As we know from earlier discussions of structure and contingency, the fact that our social life is patterned and organized into structures does not mean that those structures completely control us. Culture may provide shared meanings that we use to interpret the world and to do things with other people, but this does not mean that we accept those shared meanings uncritically or without modification. People are active, skillful interpreters of the world. They have the ability to recognize and resist cultural power.

The British sociologist Stuart Hall (1932–2014) talked about cultural power and resistance in terms of two stages of meaning, which

**Cultural tastes**
Our cultural tastes and preferences give signals about the kinds of people we think we are and the types of culture we think are valuable.

**Culture jamming**
Culture jamming is a strategy of criticizing corporate advertising, to try to get people to think more critically about the cultural products that surround them. This antismoking ad campaign, sponsored by the California Department of Health Services, is an especially vivid example of culture jamming.

**Encoding** The process through which people with power try to create forms of material and ideal culture that encourage cultural consumers to adopt specific shared meanings.

**Decoding** The process in which cultural messages are interpreted by specific people.

he referred to as encoding and decoding. During **encoding**, people with power try to create forms of material and ideal culture that encourage us to adopt specific shared meanings. In the example of the Camp David summit with Korean and Japanese leaders, President Biden positions the US between the Korean president and the Japanese prime minister, as the three men stand side by side on an equal footing with each other. Biden and his administration sought to encode the central, mediating position of the United States and its role as a stabilizing influence in East Asia that could offset the power of China. But the success of these encoded meanings depends on the process of **decoding**, which refers to how the cultural messages are interpreted by specific people.

People do not always accept the encoded meaning of a cultural message. If they distrust or dislike the person delivering the message, they are more likely to reject the intended meaning. The Camp David summit, for example, was criticized by Chinese and North Korean leaders for heightening tensions between neighbors. Ideologies are only successful when people decode the messages similarly to the way they were encoded. In these kinds of situations, where people recognize and reject encoded meanings, it is harder to exercise cultural power.

**CULTURAL CRITICS.** Cultural and institutional resources are available to help people challenge and resist cultural power. As we discuss in Chapter 13, social movements work to challenge and criticize official cultural messages and suggest alternative ways to think about social issues. The sociological imagination can teach us to recognize unstated assumptions, to evaluate arguments based on logic and evidence, and to move through the world with both a healthy skepticism and a creative attitude about how things could be different. Critical thinking about culture can also be part of the discussion in institutions like churches, social clubs, reading groups, and community organizations, while artists, writers, musicians, and other cultural producers have engaged with and amplified social protest and social movement resistance.

Expert cultural critics have become important figures in modern democratic society (Alexander 2006). From music and art to fashion and politics, critical cultural experts help us evaluate cultural objects and cultural performances. They help us decode the intended meaning of the encoded message, and they show us the techniques or tricks that are used to try to get us to accept that encoded message.

Other critics call attention to the ways media shape the public conversation. Some media critics engage in culture jamming, where they deliberately invert or undermine the intended messages of mainstream media. All these critics help us develop our ability to decode the meanings of our culture. They encourage us to be skeptical of people who have cultural power, and they help us see how ideological messages get encoded with intended meanings. In doing so, they can help us resist cultural power.

**MULTICULTURALISM AND THE CONTEMPORARY WORLD.** Cultural power can be easier to exercise in societies where people have limited exposure to other cultures and where they are intolerant of people who have different social and cultural backgrounds. Stereotypes are reinforced through **ethnocentrism**, which occurs when people assume that their society is superior to others and when they use their own cultural standards to judge outsiders. Ethnocentrism and stereotypes exist in all societies, and they are often challenged by critics and social movements. When ethnocentrism is not challenged, it can lead to **xenophobia**, which is the fear and hatred of strangers who have a different cultural background. History is full of tragic examples where cultural power was used to fuel ethnocentrism and xenophobia. Ethnocentrism and xenophobia encourage racism, violence, disrespect, and even genocide.

Social scientists recognize the dangers of ethnocentrism, and to counter those dangers, many of them have argued in favor of cultural relativism and multiculturalism. **Cultural relativism** is the idea that we should not try to evaluate other cultures according to our own standards; instead, we should try to understand those other cultures and engage them on their own terms as we relate to them from a very particular position in our own culture. The principle of cultural relativism was developed by anthropologists in the early 20th century, and it has become a basic principle guiding research in the social sciences, including sociology.

Since the 1960s, many critics and social movements have used the principle of cultural relativism to argue in favor of social policies based on **multiculturalism**. A society committed to multiculturalism celebrates and protects the different cultural practices and traditions of all its people, and officially recognizes the existence of different groups and identities. Arguments about multiculturalism and cultural relativism have helped challenge stereotypes and overturn laws that singled out specific groups and treated them unfairly. Arguments about multiculturalism have also helped change immigration laws in many countries (Chapter 7).

**Ethnocentrism** A bias that occurs when people assume that their society is superior to others and when they use their own cultural standards to judge outsiders.

**Xenophobia** Fear and hatred of strangers who have a different cultural background.

**Cultural relativism** The idea that all meaning is relative to time and place.

**Multiculturalism** A culturally pluralistic society's official recognition of the existence of different cultural groups and identities, and its development of policies promoting cultural diversity.

**Multicultural worlds**
The Dragon Boat Festival, a traditional Chinese occasion, is celebrated by many people in cities around the world. Here, dragon boat racers compete in New York City.

While multiculturalism promotes social tolerance and cultural relativism, it has not eliminated ethnocentrism or xenophobia. In fact, where multiculturalism has been successful, its advocates have encountered backlash and resistance. Using the language of a "culture war," these critics try to convince people that the fight against cultural relativism is a battle for the soul of their society. Throughout Europe and North America, these criticisms have helped reduce public support for official multicultural policies (Joppke 2004; Bloemraad and Wright 2014). At the same time that opponents of multiculturalism worry about the negative effects that immigrants will have on the safety and prosperity of their societies, however, there are also large segments of the population that seek to welcome and support immigrants.

## 3.3 Types of Culture in Today's World

**LG 3.3 Distinguish different types of culture.**

There are many different kinds of culture in the world today. Some people live lives very similar to the lives their parents and grandparents lived, while others embrace an emerging global culture and pursue constant change. There is also cultural traffic between groups that once had little contact, a process in which cultural elements are shared, adopted, critiqued, and transformed. Different types of culture are not necessarily mutually exclusive. Many people engage in traditional, modern, and global cultures as they live complex and rich cultural lives.

### Global Culture

**Globalization**
A concept that refers to the growing social, economic, cultural, and political interdependence of the world's people.

**Globalization** is the process of international integration in many domains affecting cultural, economic, and political relationships. It is made possible by advances in transportation, telecommunications, media, and information technology. **Global culture** is a product of globalization and refers to beliefs, knowledge, practices, and material objects that are shared all around the world. A good example of global culture is global material culture, where billions of people worldwide have access to the same fashion, cuisine, music, film, literature, television, and social media. These shared material objects along with the information and ideas that circulate globally create the possibility of shared meanings and relationships.

Some cultural objects began in small, local enterprises and have now become global brands. McDonald's was created in 1940 as a single restaurant in California, but today it is a global chain with more than 35,000 restaurants in 120 different countries. Coca-Cola began as a medicinal drink sold by an Atlanta pharmacist in 1886, but today it is the most recognizable drink in the world, available in every country except for Cuba and North Korea. These and similar corporations have global strategies for design, production, marketing, and distribution. They create and market their products to be consumed by the world.

While companies like Coca-Cola and McDonald's can manufacture identical products that they distribute globally, the people who create global culture often adapt their product for specific local markets. McDonald's sells its French fries and Big Macs everywhere, but in India it also sells the McSpicy Paneer, a cheese-based burger that caters to the large vegetarian population. When Disney began building a new theme park in Shanghai in 2012, it created new cartoon characters and programs specifically geared for the Chinese market. In these instances, global culture is created through a combination of global and local influences.

A major concern about global culture is **cultural imperialism**, which happens when a small number of countries dominates the market for culture and destroys smaller local cultures. Historically, American companies have been the most successful at creating global culture,

**Global culture** Beliefs, knowledge, practices, and material objects that are shared all around the world.

**Cultural imperialism** A process that occurs when a small number of countries dominate the market for culture and destroy smaller, local cultures.

**McDonald's is global**
McDonald's is a global business with a global brand. In what ways does this McDonald's restaurant in Bangkok, Thailand, look both similar to and different from McDonald's restaurants in the United States?

and the concern about cultural imperialism is often expressed as a concern about American cultural power. The media critic Herbert Schiller (1991: 34) once described American television as a "cultural bomb," eradicating local cultures and replacing them with American sitcoms and cartoons. Even when products are adapted to fit local cultural needs, like the case of the McSpicy Paneer, there is a concern that the American company is displacing the local tradition, especially when profits flow back to the corporate headquarters located in the United States.

While concerns about global culture are important, other research shows that there are limits to cultural imperialism. People around the world may recognize and desire global brands, but they still have strong preferences for locally produced culture (Bekhuis et al. 2014; Nielsen 2016; Tunstall 2007: 449). Cultural imperialism is also limited in many countries by cultural policies that privilege local and national media (Borkum 2016; Carrington 2013; Yang 2011).

Globalization also influences nonmaterial culture because it has made it easier for languages, values, beliefs, and norms to circulate around the world. Research by the sociologist John Meyer has identified the existence of a **world society** that shares cultural norms about progress, science, democracy, human rights, environmental protection, and a host of other basic values (Meyer 2010). World society theorists argue that these basic values are recognized by governments around the world and are reinforced by international bodies such as the United Nations. The values of world culture are also expressed in national constitutions, national parks services, national education and science policies, and national professional associations, which express the same basic principles in most places in the world (Benavot et al. 1991; Baker and Letendre 2005; Drori et al. 2003; Frank and Meyer 2007; Meyer et al. 1997; Meyer 2010).

Individuals, groups, and governments can criticize or reject the norms and values of world culture, but when they do this there is a good chance they will face formal or informal sanctions from the global community and resistance internally from citizens with access to world culture (Beck 2006). Powerful nongovernmental organizations such as Greenpeace, Oxfam, Doctors Without Borders, and the Red Cross and Red Crescent publicize violations of world culture and push for sanctions against offending groups and governments.

Although critics argue that the idea of a world society is just another form of cultural imperialism, in which the values of the West are imposed on the rest of the world (Carney, Rappleye, and Silova, 2012), evidence suggests that the existence of a world society with shared cultural norms does not mean that all people share the same values or even that they follow all the same norms. Public opinion surveys show that there is uneven global

**World society**
The view that there is a common global culture consisting of shared norms about progress, science, democracy, human rights, and environmental protection.

support for the values of world culture (Welzel and Inglehart 2009). For example, while there is strong global support for the principle of democracy, support for women's rights and sexual freedom is weaker in many parts of the world. There is also a concern that the values of world society do not have much influence on how people behave (Baiocchi 2012).

Despite anxieties about cultural imperialism and an emergent global culture, the forces of cultural diversity are very strong in world society. People resist global culture, they criticize it, and they create cultural policies designed to protect local culture. They change the meanings of global culture by using it in unexpected ways and by combining it with their own local tastes and fashions. They maintain pride in their cultural heritage, and they celebrate the cultural traditions of others. As we discuss in the following sections, the creators of material culture frequently draw on these sources of cultural diversity in their attempts to create something new and different.

## Dominant Cultures and Subcultures

For any given society, there is one common culture that everybody recognizes and shares. It is for this reason that we can talk about French culture, American culture, or even global culture. But within this shared culture, there are many smaller cultures that influence how we understand the world. We each belong to many different groups, and each of those groups is held together by its own culture. These groups are not all equal, though. Some groups are more organized and have more power, money, and influence than others. In the world of culture, these differences often show up as conflicts between dominant cultures and subcultures.

The **dominant culture** consists of the ideas, values, beliefs, norms, and material culture of society's most powerful groups. Because dominant groups control the means of symbolic production, they are able to make sure that their culture circulates prominently throughout the society. We learn about the dominant culture from schools, the media, museums, national monuments, national holidays, and our interactions with business and government.

The dominant culture is an ideology because it makes it appear that the culture of the dominant group is in fact identical to the culture of the entire society. Historically, in the United States, the dominant culture has been the culture of white, educated, wealthy, heterosexual men who are involved in business and professional life. The dominant culture does not eliminate other cultures, but it treats them as smaller, more distinctive, and only connected to specific groups within society. We learn about women's history, Black literature, and reggae music; but when we learn about these forms of cultural expression, they are identified with specific subgroups of society.

**Dominant culture** The ideas, values, beliefs, norms, and material culture of society's most powerful groups.

**PAIRED CONCEPTS**

## Global and Local

### The History of Manga

Although Japanese comic art, or manga, predates the 20th century, its modern form came about as a result of Japan's defeat in World War II, when comic books were brought into the country by American soldiers. Younger Japanese citizens were influenced by the superhero themes and nationalistic viewpoints of the American comic books and by the desire of Japanese artists and intellectuals to revive prewar cultural forms. These influences melded and produced something entirely new.

The atomic age—the period following the detonation of the first nuclear bomb in 1945—itself was a significant influence on manga, specifically the work of Osamu Tezuka, known for his *Mighty Atom*. His work was based on Western cinematic approaches to character interaction. Manga has also been the inspiration for anime, which are animated cartoons based upon the manga drawing style. *Mighty Atom* was adapted for television under the title *Astro Boy* in Japan, and there have been several English-language versions, feature films, video game adaptations, and re-releases of the manga in Japanese and English. Manga is a good example of cultural traffic because it originated in Japan, was influenced by contact with the United States and Europe, and then returned to these places through English- and other-language adaptations.

Manga stories aimed at boys (*shōnen manga*) tended to focus on stereotypical boys' interests, such as science fiction, action, and sports (although, interestingly, the superhero genre did not dominate, as it did in American comics). Girls' stories were more domestic and humorous in nature (*shōjo manga*). Although mid-century manga artists tended to be men, by the 1960s, audience demand for manga grew and more female artists entered the genre.

Although the right-to-left reading style of the Japanese language has become a challenge for translations into languages that read left-to-right, this has not prevented manga from becoming popular in markets outside of Japan. In 2022, for example, annual manga sales in Japan were about $5 billion, but total global sales of manga were more than $12 billion, including $246 million in the US and $417 million in France (Aoki 2023). Artists outside of Asia have picked up the drawing style, and "Amerimanga" (original English-language work) has proliferated. Today, animation throughout the world shows clear traces of the manga influence.

**Manga**
A popular global cultural form, manga has origins in pre-20th-century Japanese culture.

**ACTIVE LEARNING**

**Find out:** Ask three of your friends what their favorite film, television show, or book is. How many are global? How many are local? How can you tell? Who produces and distributes the cultural object? Are they local or global organizations?

By contrast, the cultural expressions of the dominant group do not get marked in a similar way. They are just "American culture."

**Subcultures** are the ideas, values, beliefs, norms, and material culture of all the nondominant groups in a society. A subculture's members set themselves apart as being somehow distinctive and different from the mainstream culture of the society and attach considerable importance to their common identity as members of a distinctive group. Their shared culture allows them to easily identify other members of the group, through the use of their subcultural language, style, and set of norms.

**Skateboard subculture**
Keegan Palmer performs in the Men's Skateboard Park during X Games in Ventura, California, on July 22, 2023.

Because subcultures emphasize their uniqueness and difference from the mainstream society, they are often marginalized by mainstream society. But some subcultures, such as hip-hop and comics, can also become major influences on the larger culture. Subcultures are also important sources of social criticism. Subcultural groups like skateboarders and graffiti artists ask important questions about who controls public space (Beal 1995; Snyder 2009). The 1960s hippie subculture and the 1970s punk subculture strongly rejected the dominant values of the time, encouraging their members to reject materialism and to be deeply suspicious of governments and corporations (Brake 2013).

When subcultures become part of the larger popular culture, there is a risk that they might lose their critical edge. Advertisers and others working in popular-culture industries recognize that subcultural styles are important sources of new fashion, and they market those subcultural styles to the larger society. We no longer recognize that the leather jacket originated as part of the biker subculture of the 1950s or that deliberately torn T-shirts came from the punk subculture of the 1970s. They have become fashion items to be consumed.

**Subcultures** The ideas, values, beliefs, norms, and material culture of all the non-dominant groups in the society.

## PAIRED CONCEPTS: Solidarity and Conflict

## Music and Social Protest

Music can be a powerful way to build solidarity, and virtually every country in the world has a national anthem that is played or sung at public events. But music can also provide a place for expressing social criticism, bringing together groups of people who participate in social movements and subcultures that are critical of the dominant culture.

The music of activism and social protest has a long history. In the United States, leaders of the abolitionist movement developed their own culture of protest music, which they used to popularize antislavery sentiment during the 1830s and 1840s. Singing was an important part of abolitionist meetings, and abolitionist songbooks allowed dispersed groups to sing the same songs. The Hutchinson Family Singers, a popular group of entertainers who performed throughout New England during the 1840s, helped popularize these songs and spread the abolitionist message throughout the region (Gac 2007).

As Eyerman and Jamison (1998) show in their book *Music and Social Movements*, music continued to be used as an expression of social protest throughout the 20th century. In the 1920s, the leaders of the American labor movement distributed songbooks for their members to use during meetings and demonstrations. In the 1950s and 1960s, the folk singer Pete Seeger's version of "We Shall Overcome" became the anthem of the Civil Rights Movement. The 1969 Woodstock Music Festival became one of the most famous events associated with the 1960s hippie subculture, and the musicians who performed there translated the movement's social criticisms into popular songs that united a generation of students who were trying to change the world. Reggae music was a powerful force responsible for the global spread of the Rastafarian movement, which criticized racism and Western colonialism while preaching the importance of pan-African unity (Murrell 1998).

More recently, hip-hop music has continued this focus on social criticism in music. The genre of "conscious rap" first appeared in the early 1980s, with the release of Grandmaster Flash's "The Message," a social commentary on race and the challenges of contemporary urban life. By the late 1980s conscious rap had become an important critical voice in the Black community. Chuck D, the leader of the group Public Enemy, declared in 1989 that conscious rap had become the "Black CNN." Today, the tradition of social criticism continues in conscious rap, with artists such as Mos Def, Immortal Technique, Common, and Talib Kweli. Like the folk music and reggae artists who preceded them, conscious rappers help spread the sociological imagination in the larger world of popular culture, by identifying social problems and giving a name to feelings of alienation and unhappiness (Eyerman and Jamison 1998: 138).

**Talib Kweli**
Talib Kweli is a social critic who works in the hip-hop genre. Conscious hip-hop identifies social problems and expresses cultural feelings of alienation while also creating shared identity and solidarity among listeners.

### ACTIVE LEARNING

**Reflect:** Are there any songs you listen to that contain themes of protest or social criticism? What social criticism is the song making? For this particular artist, how many of their different songs contain these kinds of themes?

## Popular Culture, Commercial Culture, and High Culture

Before the modern era, most communities produced their own culture. They made their own art and music, created their own games, organized their own festivals and folk dances, and made their own clothes. Literacy as well as imperial and monarchical history were imparted to elite children, and elite schools and universities exposed only a tiny number of students (almost exclusively male) to "masterpieces" of literature, music, and art.

The world of culture began to change rapidly during the 19th century. Improvements in education and the spread of literacy meant that more people could read. Advances in transportation and printing technologies made it possible to mass-produce and distribute books, newspapers, and other forms of writing. Beginning in Europe, new markets developed to cater to the tastes of ordinary people through **popular culture**, or objects of material culture that were being industrially produced and distributed for the masses.

As the market for popular culture grew, new products, formats, and technologies revolutionized how people communicated and entertained themselves. Radio was invented in 1895, and the motion picture was invented in 1896. Commercial television arrived in the 1940s. The first commercial internet browser was released in 1994. Apple introduced the iPhone in 2007, and by 2012 there were more than one billion smartphones in use around the world. Popular culture has become a **commodity**, or a product that exists to be bought and sold. These commodities are controlled by large and increasingly multinational corporations.

As the creative industries have grown, **commercial culture** has pushed aside other forms of popular culture in many parts of the world. Rather than making our own clothes, we buy our clothes online or at the mall. Instead of playing instruments or singing

**Popular culture** Objects of material culture industrially produced and distributed for the masses.

**Commodity** An object that is bought and sold in a market. Commodity production is a system of producing goods and services to be bought and sold on markets.

**Commercial culture** Cultural commodities that exist to be bought and sold.

**Commercial culture**
Disney is a premier global commercial cultural brand. It makes enormous profits not only from films but also from promotional products and gear associated with their content. The Disney Flagship Store in Shanghai, China, opened in May 2015, is the largest retail space operated by Disney in the world, with what Disney calls five thousand square feet of "immersive shopping experiences."

ourselves, we stream music on our mobile devices. Instead of imaginatively telling a story to our children, we let them watch a Disney video. For many sociologists, the growth of commercial culture is a problem because it teaches us to equate culture with consumption (Pugh 2009; Schor 2004; Bookman 2016).

Two concerns about commercial culture studied by sociologists are the concentration of ownership and gatekeeping. The concentration of ownership means that only a few large companies control the majority of commercial culture. These companies act as **cultural gatekeepers**, which means that they decide what kind of popular culture will be available to everyone. We depend on the gatekeepers to make sure that there is enough variety in popular culture, that different groups and perspectives are represented, and that all groups and perspectives are treated fairly. But these gatekeepers are not primarily interested in cultural diversity or combating stereotypes. Their primary concern, as corporations, is to make money for their shareholders.

There is also resistance to the power of commercial culture. Many people seek out alternative sources of popular culture, which are not controlled by the large cultural industries. New media technologies such as online streaming make it easier for individuals and small companies to distribute popular culture. In fact, a strong anticorporate movement promoting "Do-It-Yourself," or DIY, culture has been building since the 1990s (Hartley 1999). DIY culture emerged from subcultural movements such as punk music, rave dance parties, and environmental and anticonsumerist social movements. Today, though, DIY culture is much more closely connected to mainstream popular culture because of the popularity of social media. The boundary between use and content creation is now so blurry that we can say that those who post on YouTube, TikTok, or Instagram are all content creators.

We can also find criticism of commercial culture in public debates. Wherever there has been a commercial market for popular culture, there have been critics condemning it for lacking in positive qualities. These critics argue that culture should do more than merely entertain us. It should also serve the public interest through educating and exposing us to art, literature, and other forms of high culture. This could be analyzed as a way of trying to impose cultural hierarchies that defend traditional values. Whatever your thinking, it is clear that conflict over cultural values is an important element in social life that is linked to social position, ideas about right and wrong, and power and resistance in a complex global world.

When people criticize popular culture and argue that society deserves better than what is provided by commercial culture, they usually point to art,

**Cultural gatekeepers**
Decision-makers who control access to or influence what kind of culture is available to an audience.

## CAREERS

### Working in the Creative Industries

Jobs in film, music, broadcasting, publishing, gaming, social media, architecture, fashion, design, advertising, marketing, and web content can be especially rewarding, even in today's challenging economy. These kinds of jobs are often grouped together under the label "creative industries" because what they share in common is the creation of cultural content.

There are many different kinds of jobs in the creative industries (Hesmondhalgh 2019). Primary creative personnel create most of the actual content; they include musicians, writers, directors, artists, and designers. There are many more people who want to do this kind of work than there are available jobs. This means that except for a few stars, most primary creative personnel are underemployed and underpaid. In contrast to primary creators, technical workers such as sound engineers, copy editors, camera operators, web designers, and low-end software operators have more job security but less creative independence. Their job is to help bring the visions of creative personnel to life. In both cases, possessing a critical sense of social interaction and social context is important for creating cultural content.

On the business side, creative managers include book and magazine editors, film producers, and agents, who help connect primary creative personnel with the owners and executives who run businesses. Here, sociology's emphasis on research skills, organizations, and group dynamics is very useful. This is also true for marketing personnel, who help sell creative content by promoting it to audiences. Jobs in marketing include publicity, advertising, and market research. Marketing has become the fastest-growing part of the creative industries. Many creative personnel end up working in marketing—writing advertising copy, updating online materials, acting in commercials, and creating music for those commercials.

Last, owners and executives oversee the strategic and economic side of the creative enterprise. Although they set the general goals for the company, they mostly stay out of the creative process. In small companies, the owners will also often double as creative managers, working directly with creative personnel. As it does for other business occupations, sociology provides key social insights into the day-to-day running of creative companies.

Governments around the world now recognize that the creative industries are an important and growing part of the global economy, and they are developing specific policies to promote the growth of the creative economy. Jobs in the public sector that focus on the creative industries are also expanding. Higher-education institutions are tracking these shifts, and programs focused on the creative industries are emerging at universities around the world.

**Working in the creative industries**
A wide range of creative workers operate behind the scenes on this film set in Malibu, California. There are many opportunities in creative industries for people with backgrounds in sociology.

### ACTIVE LEARNING

**Discuss:** Do you follow any content creators on YouTube, Instagram, or another social media site? Compared to the description of work in the creative industries above, how do you think creative work is different on social media sites? How is it similar?

**High culture** All the cultural products that are held in the highest esteem by a society's intellectuals and elites.

great literature, and other forms of **high culture** as examples of the kind of culture they prefer. High culture refers to all of the cultural products that are held in the highest esteem by a society's intellectuals and elites. Typical examples of high culture include art museums and galleries, great literature and poetry, classical music and opera, ballet, theater, and modern dance.

High culture is produced and organized differently from commercial culture. With commercial culture, success is associated with sales and revenue. For high culture, however, the primary interest is the production and preservation of "great works." Governments set up national funding agencies like the National Endowment for the Arts (NEA) in the United States, the Arts & Culture Trust in South Africa, and the Ministry of Culture in India to support, promote, and preserve high culture. Wealthy philanthropists set up nonprofit foundations to do the same thing. Instead of looking at sales, people in the world of high culture spend most of their time focusing on the decisions of these funding agencies as well as the reviews of cultural experts (Ostrower 2004; Shrum 1996).

**Cultural capital** Education, cultural knowledge, and cultural consumption that signals privilege to others; the knowledge and consumption of culturally valued things. Higher levels of cultural capital are associated with success in school.

The French sociologist Pierre Bourdieu (1930–2002) defined **cultural capital** as the knowledge and consumption of culturally valued things. He showed that people use their tastes and their cultural knowledge to create social advantages for themselves and their family as well as to exclude others. Possessing education credentials, knowing the right clothes to wear, or knowing what knives and forks to use at a formal social occasion are all forms of cultural capital. When cultural capital is tied to economic consumption, it reinforces the privilege of elites and the exclusion of those without cultural capital. All social groups use their cultural knowledge and taste to build social solidarity and to identify insiders and outsiders. But what is distinctive about cultural capital is that it is a way for elites to display their cultural knowledge and to distance themselves from lower social classes.

Like all culture, the world of high culture is dynamic and complex. Meanings about high culture develop into relatively stable patterns, by organizing the world of material culture into separate groups of similar and different things. But these meanings are always changing too, because of the different ways that people use and share material culture. Furthermore, while high culture is connected to the exercise of power and the reproduction of inequality, people have the ability to recognize and resist the cultural hierarchies and the meanings about art that are presented to them. As they develop their sociological imagination, they learn to recognize when high culture is being used as a tool for cultural power, and they can decide for themselves how they want to use and share the many different kinds of culture that are available to them. In fact, there is good evidence that,

> **PAIRED CONCEPTS**
>
> ## Power and Resistance

### Fanfiction

The contemporary idea of fanfiction, or "fic," emerged in the 1960s with individuals—mostly women—writing stories about characters from *Star Trek*, often about Captain Kirk and Mr. Spock (Jamison 2013). These were compiled in collections called "fanzines," which were sold at science fiction conventions. Fic writers were free to explore sexuality, plot, and character development that the television shows themselves never could. With the emergence of the internet, fanfiction became much easier to distribute to a wider audience.

There is a complicated and sometimes volatile relationship between fic writers and the original authors or creators. In 2000 Anne Rice, author of the *Vampire Chronicles* series, criticized fic writers for infringing copyright, causing all stories about her characters to be removed from the fanfiction.net online archive. But it is difficult to prevent such content from being published on the internet. Since then, fanfiction has flourished, and the distinction between original content and fanfiction has become blurrier. The blockbuster trilogy *Fifty Shades of Grey*, for example, was originally published as a work of fanfiction, inspired by the *Twilight* book series (Bertrand 2015). There are a number of recently published young adult fiction novels that started out as *Star Wars* fanfiction, including *The Hurricane Wars* (2023), *We'd Know by Then* (2022), and *For Love and Bylines* (2022).

Fanfiction is a large and diverse community, including many writers who challenge assumptions and stereotypes about sexuality that circulate within cultural industries. For example, "slash" fanfiction (so named for the slash in character pairings, such as "Kirk/Spock") explores sexual romantic relationships between same-sex protagonists from popular movies and television programs. Popular slash fiction has explored the relationships between Harry Potter and Draco Malfoy, Luke Skywalker and Han Solo, Sherlock Holmes and Dr. Watson, Captain Kirk and Mr. Spock, Xena and Gabrielle, and many others.

In the process, fic writers respond to what they see as the pervasive practice of "queerbaiting" in popular culture, which happens when movies and television programs add sexual tension between two same-sex protagonists in order to appeal to the LGBTQ audience, without ever intending to explore the development of the sexual relationship.

In this way, fic might be understood as a form of culture jamming—a form of cultural and political resistance that seeks to subvert the dominant messages of a powerful commercial culture.

**Fifty Shades of Grey**
*Fifty Shades of Grey* originated as fanfiction inspired by the *Twilight* book series and later became a best-selling trilogy and a blockbuster film series. From left to right, US filmmaker James Foley, British writer E. L. James, US actress and cast member Dakota Johnson, and Irish actor and cast member Jamie Dornan on the red carpet in Spain, February 2017.

> **ACTIVE LEARNING**
>
> **Find out:** Find an online example of culture jamming. What does the text seek to reveal or poke fun at? Does the author employ any ideas about power and resistance?

among the privileged, younger generations are less likely than their parents to limit themselves to the world of high culture. Instead, they are "cultural omnivores" (Peterson 1992; Hazir 2018). They consume everything, as part of an attempt to curate their own distinctive and authentic combination of high and commercial culture.

## PAIRED CONCEPTS: Inequality and Privilege

### Who Goes to the Museum and the Opera?

In the United States, support for museums and the performing arts comes from three primary sources (National Endowment for the Arts 2012). Approximately 40 percent of arts revenue comes from paying audience members in the form of ticket sales and subscriptions. A second form of arts funding, about 7 percent, comes in the form of direct government subsidies from the NEA and other state, local, and regional arts agencies. The third source of funding—about half of all arts funding—comes from tax-deductible gifts from individuals, corporations, and philanthropic foundations. While the COVID-19 pandemic has shifted philanthropic giving toward urgent needs laid bare by the pandemic itself, and even wealthy organizations are challenged to stay financially afloat, it remains the case that arts philanthropy continues to be a crucial support for high-culture institutions. The rationale for the tax deductions for arts donations, as with all charitable giving, is that they encourage people to support causes that improve society.

While many of the groups that receive tax deductions do so because they donate to organizations that serve poor and vulnerable populations, this is not as obvious in the case of arts funding. Organizations exist that are committed to building audiences for the arts, but it remains the case that audiences for the arts in the United States have more education, a higher income, and a higher occupational status than the population as a whole (National Endowment for the Arts 2015). Minority groups are underrepresented in audiences for the arts. Audiences for the performing arts (dance, classical music, and opera) are even more privileged than museum audiences. In effect, public support for the arts subsidizes the cultural tastes of the most privileged part of society.

Why don't the arts attract a more diverse audience? One reason has to do with how parents socialize their children to value certain kinds of culture, as Pierre Bourdieu's research on cultural capital showed. Rates of arts attendance are significantly higher for people who took art lessons and art appreciation classes when they were children; attendance is also significantly higher for people whose parents took them to museums and the performing arts when they were growing up (Schuster 1991). In the United States, public funding cuts combine with decisions by some elementary schools to stop offering arts education in favor of a focus on reading and math skills (Fang 2013; Mahnken 2017). These changes mean the audience for the arts is likely to become even more privileged in the future.

#### ACTIVE LEARNING

**Discuss:** Do you think it would be better to eliminate public funding for the arts or to increase public funding for arts appreciation in elementary schools? What are the advantages and disadvantages of each approach for different groups of people?

**High culture**
High culture is art held in high esteem by elites. This gallery in the Metropolitan Museum of Art in New York features European oil paintings that are several hundred years old. Would you want to hang these in your home? Why or why not?

## CASE STUDY

# Protesting the National Anthem

Culture refers to the meanings we create, share, and understand in the world. We can analyze how culture works by using the five paired concepts to analyze a central social ritual in America as a case study: standing for the singing of the national anthem, the "Star-Spangled Banner," before sports events. This ritual occurs at nearly every professional and amateur sports event that occurs in the United States and has done so since a military band played it in 1918 during the seventh-inning stretch at a Red Sox game (Cyphers and Trex 2011).

Seen through the lens of the five paired concepts, the cultural practice of singing the national anthem at sporting events is one that creates *solidarity* by making group members feel connected to their team, their school, and the nation. At the same time, it is linked to a history of *conflict*, or war, and of conquering an enemy. These metaphors are shared with sporting competition. The use of a military song at sports events can also be seen as an exercise of cultural *power* that reinforces the idea of the nation as it also reinforces the idea that a particular sports event and the solidarity it invokes are legitimate and important. Those who *resist* the ritual by failing to stand or challenging the sacred meaning of the song itself are sanctioned. When NFL player Colin Kaepernick knelt in public during the anthem in 2016 to protest

### CASE STUDY CONTINUED

police brutality, he was condemned by many in the media, and he was essentially blackballed by the league.

The joint singing of the song also highlights the *privilege* of American cultural power in a global world. The initial singing of the "Star-Spangled Banner" at that 1918 Red Sox game, for example, took place against a global backdrop of World War I and in a domestic context of massive industrial unrest, which included the bombing of the Chicago Federal Building that was initially blamed on the International Workers of the World, a radical labor organization that protested economic *inequality* in the United States and around the globe. The singing of the song, as well as the solidarity and power it generates, have both global and local dimensions. As a war song, the "Star-Spangled Banner" places the image of the embattled nation at the center of public sporting events on an almost daily basis. As Cyphers and Trex wrote in *ESPN Magazine*, "The anthem is a show, and a show of force. Every year, the Pentagon approves several hundred requests for military flyovers. . . . At lesser events, even at the high school level, a color guard is often on hand with the flag as the anthem is played. A game without the anthem is likely one that doesn't matter much" (Cyphers and Trex 2011). Singing the anthem is a *local* expression of national solidarity that reminds participants of their belonging to a powerful military nation with *global* power. The flag itself references an international system of nations and flags. In fact, for other countries, national anthems are typically played only at international sporting events.

Finally, the ritual itself is also highly socially *structured* by norms as it invokes the central values of the American nation. People are asked to stand for the national anthem. Nearly everyone stands. People place hands on their hearts, turn to face the flag, and maintain a respectful expression on their face. Some audience members salute. As with any ritual, however, there is always a possibility of *contingency* and the possibility that the event will not unfold in the expected way. When people disrupt or resist a ritual, they can create a different social meaning and a different social pattern. Colin Kaepernick did this when he knelt in protest—a form of protest that has been repeated at sporting events around the nation. In another example, Goshen College in Indiana made headlines in 2011 with its decision to sing "America the Beautiful" instead of the militaristic "Star-Spangled Banner" because it is a better fit with the college's pacifist Mennonite tradition.

Cultural moments like singing the anthem at sporting events are important moments in social life. They tell us much about how social interaction is structured and reveal fundamental dynamics of group life. As Chapter 4 will show, the five paired concepts offer a way to understand both the way culture works to shape individuals and the operation of groups.

## LEARNING GOALS REVISITED

**3.1** Define culture, identify the difference between material and ideal culture, and understand that meanings are made in a cultural context.

- Culture is the entire set of beliefs, knowledge, practices, and material objects that are meaningful to a group of people and shared from generation to generation.

- Culture can refer both to material objects like a book, house, or work of music and to the actions and words of people doing things to share meaning by reading, designing a house, or

singing the national anthem with others at a sporting event.
- Words, ideas, and cultural objects get their meaning through relationships to other words, ideas, and cultural objects.
- Symbolic meanings are shaped by the association of a word, idea, or cultural object with other cultural images, emotions, meanings, and associations.
- There are symbolic meanings for all types of culture, not just for language.
- Cultural relativism is the idea that cultural meanings are relative to time and place (i.e., context). Social scientists taking a position of cultural relativism assert that we should not try to evaluate other cultures according to our own standards. Instead, we should try to understand those other cultures and engage them on their own terms as we relate to them from a very particular position in our own culture.

**3.2 Identify the connection between culture and power: identify ideologies, stereotypes, cultural hierarchies, and cultural resistance.**

- Cultural hierarchies define some cultural objects, people, institutions, and meanings as good and others as bad or not good.
- Different people contend over the meanings of different cultural things, arguing about what is good or appropriate. For example, parents and children often disagree about the value of cultural things, from music to video games.
- Ideology is a system of shared meaning that is used to justify existing relationships of power and privilege. Ideology is culture in the service of power.
- Ideology misdirects attention away from power and creates an idea that the way things are is common sense and therefore right.
- Stereotypes are a form of ideology that asserts the superior value of one group of people, institutions, or objects over others. They are linked to racism, ethnocentrism, and xenophobia. Stereotypes are often conveyed and reinforced through literature, films, and music.
- Cultural hierarchies are a form of organized cultural power in which some groups are able to define the dominant culture, which is often understood as common sense.
- In modern societies, one important form of cultural power is exercised through self-policing and physical and psychological therapies where individuals evaluate and alter themselves to meet cultural norms.
- Cultural power is met in many cases by the cultural resistance of individuals, critics, and organized social movements. Existing cultural meanings are powerful, but they can be and have been changed.

**3.3 Distinguish different types of culture.**

- Material culture refers to cultural objects.
- Ideal culture refers to ideas, actions, and meanings.

- Global culture is a product of globalization and refers to the beliefs, knowledge, practices, and material objects that are shared all around the world.
- Local culture intersects with global culture to interpret and alter the meanings of words, ideas, and cultural objects. Global brands like McDonald's or Disney produce local versions of their successful formulas to cater to the local tastes of consumers.
- The dominant culture consists of the ideas, values, beliefs, norms, and material culture of society's most powerful groups.
- Subcultures are the ideas, values, beliefs, norms, and material cultures of all the nondominant groups in the society.
- Popular culture refers to objects of material culture industrially produced and distributed for the masses.
- Commercial culture refers to cultural commodities that exist to be bought and sold. These commodities are controlled by large and increasingly multinational corporations.
- High culture refers to all of the cultural products that are held in the highest esteem by a society's intellectuals and elites.

## Key Terms

Beliefs 70
Classification systems 71
Commercial culture 93
Commodity 93
Cultural capital 96
Cultural gatekeepers 94
Cultural hierarchies 81
Cultural imperialism 87
Cultural relativism 85
Culture 70
Culture war 75
Decoding 84
Discourses 80
Dominant culture 89
Encoding 84
Ethnocentrism 85
Folkways 76
Global culture 87
Globalization 86
High culture 96
Ideal culture 72
Ideology 78
Material culture 72
Means of symbolic production 80
Mores 76
Multiculturalism 85
Norms 75
Popular culture 93
Sanctions 76
Secular-rational values 74
Self-expression values 74
Socialization 71
Stereotypes 79
Subcultures 91
Survival values 74
Symbolic meaning 71
Traditional values 74
Values 74
World Society 88
Xenophobia 85

## Review Questions

1. What is the difference between material and ideal culture?
2. List three different kinds of culture, and provide an example of each.

3. How does dominant culture work as an ideology? Give an example.

4. How does a stereotype about a social group work as a moral standard? Give an example.

5. How is global culture different from local culture?

6. What is a discourse of power, and how does it encourage our self-control?

## Explore

**RECOMMENDED READINGS**

Alexander, Jeffrey C. 2003. *The Meanings of Social Life: A Cultural Sociology*. New York: Oxford University Press.

Back, Les, Andy Bennett, Laura Desfor Edles, Margaret Gibson, David Inglis, Ron Jacobs, and Ian Woodward. 2012. *Cultural Sociology: An Introduction*. New York: Wiley-Blackwell.

Bourdieu, Pierre. 1984. *Distinction: A Social Critique of the Judgement of Taste*. Cambridge, MA: Harvard University Press.

Hebdige, Dick. 1979. *Subculture: The Meaning of Style*. New York: Routledge.

Mukerji, Chandra, and Michael Schudson. 1991. *Rethinking Popular Culture: Contemporary Perspectives in Cultural Studies*. Los Angeles: University of California Press.

Smith, Philip, and Alexander Riley. 2008. *Cultural Theory: An Introduction*, 2nd ed. New York: Wiley-Blackwell.

**ACTIVITIES**

- *Use your sociological imagination*: Cultural capital is knowledge and consumption of socially valued things. Do you have cultural capital? What is it? Have you ever felt excluded by another person's cultural capital? How did that work?

- *Media+Data Literacies*: Go to the reference section in your library and find a dictionary that gives historical information on words. Look up the words "culture" and "individual." How have they changed over time? Do you have any theories about why they changed?

- *Discuss*: McDonald's in Australia serves the Aussie Burger with an egg, bacon, and pickled beetroot on it. In India, McDonald's makes the vegetarian McSpicy Paneer. Do you think these are examples of cultural imperialism? Are they the same in both cases? Why or why not?

AN ORIGINAL SERIES FROM
CO-CREATORS STERLIN HARJO & TAIKA WAITITI

# RESERVATION DOGS

# 4

# Socialization, Social Interaction, and Group Life

The 2021 television series *Reservation Dogs* follows the coming-of-age of four Native American teenagers growing up in a small Oklahoma town in the Muscogee Nation. Elora, Bear, Cheese, and Willie Jack grieve the death of one of their best friends, they plan to travel to California, they deal with family responsibilities, and they interact with the elders in their community. Historical flashbacks show scenes from when the community elders were growing up, and offer insight into the experience of growing up and going to school in a Native American community. Critics and audiences have praised the show, which is the first television series to feature all Indigenous writers and directors, as one of the most interesting and authentic coming-of-age stories to appear on television in many years.

In literature, the coming-of-age story has always been popular. Classics like *Jane Eyre*, *Great Expectations*, *The Adventures of Huckleberry Finn*, *The Catcher in the Rye*, and *To Kill a Mockingbird* are about young people learning how to live in society. Just like in *Reservation Dogs*, the characters in these stories struggle to navigate different kinds of social groups, social settings, and social institutions. They face moral dilemmas, they make mistakes, and through these mistakes they become more mature.

**Chapter Outline**

**4.1 SOCIALIZATION AND SELFHOOD 106**

*Nature and Nurture 106*
*The Social Self 107*
*Agents of Socialization 109*
*Adult Socialization 112*

**4.2 INTERACTION AND THE SOCIAL CONSTRUCTION OF REALITY 116**

*Status and Role 116*
*Performance and the Social Self 119*
*Social Interaction in a Digital Age 120*

**4.3 GROUP LIFE 122**

*Group Size 122*
*Primary Groups and Secondary Groups 123*
*Reference Groups 125*
*Bureaucracy in Group Life 126*
*Social Networks in Group Life 129*

**CASE STUDY: BECOMING "THE ROCK" 131**

**Reservation Dogs**
Coming-of-age stories are important because they capture something universal and important about being human: growing up.

In this chapter, we discuss how the social self develops, and we consider the different agents of socialization that help bring this about. We examine the relationship between socialization and social interaction, and we explore how the socialization process changes over the course of our lives. Finally, we look at the different ways that group dynamics influence social life, considering informal groups as well as large, formal organizations.

## LEARNING GOALS

**4.1** Define socialization, and identify the primary agents of socialization that operate over the life course.

**4.2** Understand the difference between a status and a role, and describe how interactional performances sustain the social self.

**4.3** Define groups, and distinguish different kinds of groups.

# 4.1 Socialization and Selfhood

**LG 4.1** Define socialization, and identify the primary agents of socialization that operate over the life course.

**Socialization** All of the different ways that we learn about our society's beliefs, values, and expected behaviors; the ongoing process of learning the social meanings of a culture.

In sociology, the process of growing up and learning how to live in society is called socialization. **Socialization** refers to all of the different ways that we learn about our society's culture: its beliefs, values, and expected behaviors. Socialization begins when we are infants, and it continues throughout our lives. Socialization happens when we are with our family and our friends, when we are watching television or using social media, and when we are at school or at work. It is an interactive process because we are helping to socialize others at the same time that we are being socialized ourselves.

### Nature and Nurture

When we speak of the roles of "nature" and "nurture" in determining the outcomes for an individual's life, we are making a distinction between biology (nature) and the social environment (nurture). Take height, for example. While your height is influenced by your genetics (nature), it also depends on the quality of your nutrition and health care (nurture) (Grasgruber et al. 2014). The consequences of being short or tall are related more to our social environment than our genes. In most contemporary societies, taller people are more likely to be seen as attractive, more likely to have positive interactions with other people, and more likely to have higher self-esteem (Freese 2008). These consequences are connected to the social meanings placed on height, rather than the biological nature of height itself.

Nature and nurture also interact when we respond to stressful events in our lives. Our genetic makeup influences whether we react to stress positively or negatively. Some people are naturally more resilient and resourceful in the way they deal with problems, while others have a tendency to become withdrawn or depressed (Ising and Holsboer 2006; Villada et al. 2014). But the frequency with which people experience stressful events is connected mainly to their social environment. People who live in poverty, for example, face extremely stressful events on a regular basis, testing their ability to respond to stress much more often than people who live with privilege.

Regardless of biological makeup, people who are socially isolated have a much more difficult time functioning effectively in society. Children who are too isolated have problems with short-term memory and language development and are more likely to develop learning disorders, emotional problems, issues with aggression, and social withdrawal (Rubin and Ross 1982; Almeida et al. 2021). Adults who are socially isolated have worse physical and mental health, and they tend to die younger than people who have stronger social attachments to family, friends, and community (Cornwell and Waite 2009). Genetics has some impact on how we respond to these situations of social isolation, but it is the experience of social isolation itself that is the most powerful factor that limits our ability to develop our social selves.

## The Social Self

As social beings, we begin very early in life to learn the values and the culture of our society. We learn to imagine how others are feeling before we act, we consider how others might respond to our actions, and we engage in processes of reflection and self-assessment. We feel guilt, shame, or pride based on our interactions with others. We try out different personalities or even pretend to be something we are not. We worry that we are wasting our lives or failing to fulfill our true potential. In short, we have a social self.

**THE LOOKING-GLASS SELF.** Charles Horton Cooley (1864–1929) developed one of the earliest theories of the social self, which he referred to as the **looking-glass self**. Cooley argued that the self is shaped by the social interactions we have and the interpretations we make of those interactions. When we interact with other people, we imagine what they are thinking about us and wonder if they are judging us. On the basis of this imagined judgment, we have an emotional response. In this way, society serves as a mirror—a looking glass—we use to develop our sense of self throughout our lives.

**Looking-glass self** A concept that describes how we develop a social self based on how we think other people perceive us.

**Play stage** A stage of social development when children around three years old begin to engage in role-playing games.

**Game stage** A stage of social development when children are around seven years old and begin to make friends, learn to pick games that other people want to play, and learn how to avoid or to quickly resolve arguments that arise when a game is being played.

**Generalized other** The rules of society that the child internalizes through the process of socialization.

**MIND, SELF, AND SOCIETY.** Our social self becomes more complicated as we grow older. George Herbert Mead (1863–1931) observed that once children enter the **play stage** of development, at around three years old, they begin to develop a social self by engaging in role-playing games, imagining themselves as other people.

By seven years old, children enter the **game stage** of development. For young children, learning how to play games is a crucial skill for making friends (Frankel 1996), and may be a protective factor against later mental health difficulties (Zhao and Gibson 2022). Children learn how to choose games that other people want to play. They learn how to solve problems and respond to arguments. They can only do this, Mead argued, if they can take the perspective of the **generalized other**, which means that they think about how they appear to "society in general." In other words, when children play games, they are learning the expectations of their social group, seeing themselves from the viewpoint of the typical child, reflecting upon who they are in relationship to the world around them, and beginning to make decisions about the kinds of people they want to become.

Sigmund Freud (1856–1939) also wrote about the internal dialogue between mind, self, and society. Freud's theory of the social self proposed that there were three interconnected parts of the mind: ego, superego, and id. The **id** is an unconscious part of the mind, which seeks immediate pleasure and gratification. The **superego**, by contrast, is the moral part of our mind, which acts as our conscience. Similar to the generalized other, the superego is our internalized image of society, with its rules for behavior. Within our mind, the superego acts to suppress any urges by the id that are considered wrong or socially unacceptable, by making us feel guilt. The superego is what tells you not to take candy from a baby.

In between the id and the superego, Freud argued, is the **ego**. The ego tries to strike a balance between the urges of the id and the morality of the superego in order to determine the most practical

**Early childhood**
Playing games is an important part of early childhood socialization.

course of action for a given situation. The ego allows us to delay gratification when that is in our long-term interests, and it provides us with important defense mechanisms that prevent the superego from allowing us to feel so much guilt that we endanger ourselves.

**CULTURE, NORMALIZATION, AND THE SELF.** Mead and Freud both viewed socialization as a force of social control. Our internalized image of society's rules and expectations encourages us to act in appropriate ways and makes us feel guilty when we do not do so. The generalized other that we carry inside our head is there to remind us what behavior is expected of us. Our superego disciplines our instinctual urges and makes us want to be "normal" members of society.

As we discussed in Chapter 3, the social construction of normal and pathological behavior is a form of cultural power. We feel guilty when we act in ways that are considered not to be normal. We read self-help books and seek out therapists to help us identify our pathological tendencies. We are encouraged to believe that these pathological tendencies are holding us back in our lives and causing us unhappiness. Michel Foucault described this as **normalization** (1995), which refers to the way that discourses about the normal and the pathological identify the kinds of behaviors that will attract special attention, as well as the forms of rehabilitation that deal with people who are deemed to be "not normal."

**Id** The unconscious part of the mind, which seeks immediate pleasure and gratification.

**Superego** The moral part of the mind, which acts as the conscience.

**Ego** The part of the mind that balances the demands of the id and the superego to determine the most practical course of action for an individual in any given situation.

**Normalization** The process through which social standards of normal behavior are used to judge people and to reform those who are determined not to be normal.

## Agents of Socialization

**Agents of socialization** are the people, groups, and organizations that teach us about society's beliefs, values, and expected behaviors. Sociologists have identified five important agents of socialization: family, school, peer groups, media, and the workplace.

**FAMILY.** The family is our first social group. It is where we establish our first social and emotional bonds. It is where we learn how to communicate and

**Families**
Families are primary agents of socialization, in early childhood and throughout the life cycle.

**Agents of socialization** The people, groups, and organizations that most powerfully affect human socialization. The five primary agents of socialization are family, school, peer groups, media, and the workplace.

how to interact with other people. It is where we first learn about the rules of appropriate social behavior, and it is where we begin to learn the shared beliefs and values of our culture. The bonds we form with our parents and siblings are particularly strong, and they leave a deep imprint on our social self.

For the first five years of our lives, we spend most of our time with our family. As we discuss in Chapters 8 and 9, these early years provide important moments of gender socialization, when we learn about the different social expectations that exist for women and men. The family also begins to socialize children about the values and expectations of the larger society, and different parenting styles reflect cultural differences. In countries such as China and Japan, children are taught about the importance of obedience and cooperation, and parents tend to maintain stricter control over their children's behavior (Jordan and Graham 2015). By comparison, in countries such as the United States and Australia, children are taught more about the importance of individuality, personal happiness, and self-expression.

**SCHOOL AND PEER GROUPS.** School is a new social environment for children, who quickly have to learn the rules, expectations, and culture of their school. Along with subject areas and instructional goals, schools also have a **hidden curriculum**. This consists of the rules of behavior children need to learn to function effectively in the school and the larger society (Giroux and Purpel 1983; Anyon 2006). The hidden curriculum is really about socialization.

**Hidden curriculum** The rules of behavior students need to learn to function effectively in the school and the larger society.

What kind of socialization do children get at school? They learn how to be on time, how to listen to an authority figure, and how to ask questions without being disruptive. They learn how to work hard, when they are supposed to compete with their classmates, and when they are supposed to cooperate. They learn what kinds of behaviors are rewarded and what kinds are punished.

**Peer groups** Groups of people of similar age who share the same kinds of interests.

School-age children also spend more time with **peer groups**, which consist of people of a similar age who share the same kinds of interests. Peer groups become an important agent of socialization throughout the school-age years. Many adolescents and teenagers spend more time with their peer groups than they do with their families (Larson and Richards 1991; Brown and Larson 2009). Peer groups help us form a social self that is separate from our parents.

**Peer pressure** Peer groups encourage adolescents and teens to engage in behaviors that they would not perform if their parents were watching.

As we discussed in Chapter 3, peer group subcultures develop their own set of values and expected behaviors that can create conflicts between parents and their children. Many parents worry about **peer pressure**, which occurs when peer groups encourage adolescents to engage in behaviors that they would not do if their parents were watching. Peer pressure has been linked to risky social behavior such as underage drinking, drug use, and shoplifting (Lewis and Lewis 1984; Laurson and Veenstra 2021). Peer pressure is also a big factor in early sexual activity, gossip, and bullying (Fried 1998).

Sociological research shows that the peer groups that form in school tend to be homogeneous, composed of individuals who are similar in race, gender, and social class (Shrum, Creek, and Hunter 1988; Leszcezensky and Pink 2019). Because peer group identities form by drawing boundaries between different groups, the similarity within peer groups has the effect of intensifying social differences. In her book *"Why Are All the Black Kids Sitting Together in the Cafeteria?" and Other Conversations about Race* (2017), Beverly Tatum argues that these peer groups provide an important opportunity for students to establish and affirm their group identity. For minority students, peer groups allow them to secure a racial identity that is free of the negative racial stereotypes that circulate in the media and the larger society. For more privileged students, the peer groups they form help them develop and learn subtle ways of signaling their privilege to others (Khan 2012).

**Peer groups**
Peer group interactions are an important part of the school experience. Did your peer group look like this stock image? How was it similar or different?

**MEDIA.** School-age children are voracious media consumers. The most recent data from Common Sense Media show that entertainment media use is more than 5.5 hours per day for

**Digital natives**
Very young children use media and media technologies with ease.

children aged 8–12, and more than 8.5 hours per day for teenagers (Rideout et al. 2022). This combines time spent watching traditional and time-shifted television as well as time on a game console, computer, or another multimedia device. Importantly, their parents also report spending between eight and nine hours per day consuming entertainment media. During the COVID-19 pandemic lockdowns, the time spent consuming media increased even further as school and work switched to remote modalities and in-person socializing switched to digital media interactions.

Like peer groups, media help us form a social self that is separate from our parents, and media can be a source of conflict between parents and children. Many parents and educators are concerned that media encourage children to embrace a more materialistic lifestyle (Schor 2004; Behal and Soni 2018). Others are concerned that media expose children to inappropriate levels of sexual imagery and promote sexist and degrading beliefs about women (Corsaro 2005: 276). There is also concern about media violence and the possible effects that this exposure has on children's behavior (Anderson and Bushman 2018; Barker and Petley 2001).

Most sociological research shows that media exposure cannot completely change our values and behaviors because media are only one agent of socialization among many. But media are always there. Living with the media, Gitlin (2001: 5) argues, is one of the main things that humans do.

## Adult Socialization

**Generation** A group of individuals who are of a similar age and are marked by the same historical events that take place during their youth.

According to the sociologist Karl Mannheim (1893–1947), youth is a time when generations form. Mannheim (1952) defined a **generation** as a group of individuals who are a similar age, who get swept up by the same historical events that take place during their youth. In the United States, for example, the "millennial" generation is composed of those Americans born between 1981 and 1996 (Strauss and Howe 2000). Millennials, both as individuals and collectively, are likely to consider the attacks of September 11, 2001, as an event that defines their generation. For Generation Z—those born between 1997 and 2012—the most significant generation-defining event has been COVID-19.

**Total institutions** Institutions like prisons, nursing homes, or the military that control every aspect of their members' lives.

While generational identity is formed during our teenage years, the process of socialization continues to shape us throughout our adult lives. As we grow up, the agents of socialization act on us differently. Some adults live in **total institutions**, such as prisons, nursing homes, or the military, which control every aspect of their lives. For others, the workplace becomes a major agent of socialization. Family socialization changes, too, as people become parents and begin to raise children. Many adults experience significant disruption during their lives, and as they grow old and retire, they have to learn to adjust to a society that treats them differently. As people adjust their lives in response to these new circumstances, they adjust their attitudes and behaviors accordingly. This is a transition that sociologists call **resocialization**.

**WORKPLACE.** As we finish school and begin our careers, the workplace becomes an important agent of socialization. Every profession has informal rules and expected behaviors that can only be learned on the job, and as people spend more time working in a particular profession or career, they begin to internalize the values of the workplace. Police officers become more distrustful of the public at large (Crank 2004). Investment bankers value short-term risk-taking (Ho 2009). Doctors value expertise (Freidson 1988; Stivers and Timmermans 2020). These values are learned and reinforced on the job, as part of workplace socialization.

**Work**
For many adults, experiences in the workplace have a significant impact on the development of the social self.

**Resocialization**
The process through which we adjust our lives, attitudes, and behaviors in response to new circumstances.

Because social status is linked closely with occupational prestige, our experiences in the workplace have a significant impact on the development of our social self. People who are successful in their jobs benefit from the material advantages of job success. On the other hand, people who experience unemployment face disruption in their lives, and they also have to deal with the stigma that is associated with not working.

**DIVORCE, UNEMPLOYMENT, AND DISRUPTION.** Adult resocialization happens most intensely during disruption, such as unemployment and divorce. When people lose their jobs, they may be forced to give up their home and move to a neighborhood with fewer advantages. They are more likely to lose contact with their friends and peer groups. They get sick more often and may lose their health insurance just when they have the greatest need of it. Unemployment places great stress on families as well and often leads to divorce.

Divorce also usually requires resocialization. While divorce creates emotional and social difficulties for children (Wallerstein 1991), it also creates challenges for the adult couple who are separating. When couples marry, they rearrange their entire social worlds, sharing the same family and friends, and they value their identity as a spouse (Vaughan 1990; Haggerty et al. 2023). When the marriage ends, individuals have to redefine all of those relationships, establish new social routines, and create a new identity as a single person. At least one of the partners will have to find a new place to live, and often both partners will do so. There are also economic consequences as women who get divorced usually end up poorer than they would have been if the marriage had lasted (Peterson 1996; de Vaus et al. 2017).

In fact, any significant disruption—whether positive or negative—during our adult years will be associated with resocialization. Resocialization is a common part of adult development.

**RETIREMENT AND OLD AGE.** For most people, the final period of resocialization comes with retirement and old age. This phase of life is much longer than it used to be because people are living longer. In the United States today, the average age of retirement is 65 for men and 62 for women (Tretina 2022). On the other hand, for a person who is 65 years old in the United States today, the average life expectancy is 82 for men and 85 for women (Copeland 2014).

For most people, aging and retirement create challenges for the social self. Those who spent more than half their lives working often get depressed if they cannot find a new identity away from work (Schlossberg 2009). Aging also poses a challenge for people whose sense of self is attached to their role as a parent. By the time most people reach retirement age, their children are grown, and they may have to readjust to the role of being a grandparent. Media are not much help either. Despite the fact that half of the viewers of television are at least 54 years old, most media celebrate youth and offer few positive images of older people.

Retirement also creates financial challenges that demand adjustments in our social routines. Many older workers are pushed

**Retirement**
Retirement is a major source of resocialization for most adults.

**PAIRED CONCEPTS**

## Inequality and Privilege

### Different Styles of Parenting

The COVID-19 pandemic has created enormous challenges for parents. With widespread quarantines, children have spent significant time learning at home, and many parents have been working from home. Everyone has had a harder time accessing their peer groups as adults and children have been encouraged to sharply limit their social interactions with people not already living in their household. Parents and children are spending more time together than they are used to spending, and how they have responded to these challenges is shaped in important ways by inequality and privilege.

Family socialization varies depending on the social class background of the parents. Working-class and professional parents socialize their children according to different sets of values and expectations (Lareau 2003). Working-class and poor parents tend to be less involved with their children's activities, they are less likely to include their children in adult socializing, and they give their children a lot of unstructured free time to play. This choice is not entirely voluntary as these parents often work long hours and do not have the money to pay for organized social activities. Many of these parents have jobs where they have had to leave the house to work during the pandemic, leaving their children at home alone for long stretches of time.

In contrast, professional parents have a parenting style that Annette Lareau calls "concerted cultivation." They enroll their children in multiple organized activities, invest considerable time and money to ensure that their children are exposed to educational enrichment activities, and direct their children toward activities that will look good on a college application.

Lareau also found that professional parents communicate with their children in a different way than working-class parents. Using the style of concerted cultivation, professional parents encourage their children to communicate with adults, ask questions, and share their opinions. They socialize their children to be assertive and to expect to be taken seriously in the adult world. This socialization pays off later in life when children begin school and later when they enter the workplace.

**Concerted cultivation**
Concerted cultivation is a parenting style fostering middle-class culture. More privileged parents pay for private music lessons and a range of athletic and academic experiences for their children in the hope that it will pay off in their social development and success. Think about the extracurricular activities you had access to in high school. Why do you think schools and parents supported them?

**ACTIVE LEARNING**

**Find out:** Interview someone who is a parent and not in your sociology class. Ask them about their views on parenting. Do they think children should be in multiple extra activities outside of school? Ask the reason why. How much time do they think parents should be spending to support the extracurricular activities of their children? Applying Lareau's ideas of concerted cultivation and natural growth, what kind of parenting strategy would you say this person has?

out of their jobs earlier than they would like, due to pervasive age discrimination in the workplace (Roscigno et al. 2007). The vast majority of Americans fail to save enough money during their working lives to maintain their standard of living after they retire (Ghilarducci 2008). This often means selling their house and moving to a different community, traveling less, and reducing consumption.

Aging brings other challenges as well. Illness and the loss of mobility make people less confident in public spaces, and they often respond by spending less time outside of the house. The death of friends means that the peer groups of older people often get smaller. With the death of a spouse, many people find themselves living alone for the first time in decades. Whereas the elderly once moved in with relatives when they could no longer care for themselves, today they are more likely to move into total institutions such as nursing homes. As they lose their independence, the elderly struggle to maintain the social interactions and the connections that had once helped nourish and reproduce their social selves.

## 4.2 Interaction and the Social Construction of Reality

**LG 4.2** Understand the difference between a status and a role, and describe how interactional performances sustain the social self.

We are socialized and create a social self through all the social interactions that occur over the course of our lives. Collectively, these social interactions create the social reality to which the social self belongs. There are common patterns to this process that help create shared beliefs and expectations. While these social patterns can be very stable, people also sometimes struggle over shared meanings with different beliefs about what is right and wrong, appropriate and inappropriate.

**Status** A specific social position that an individual occupies in the social structure.

**Ascribed status** A status assigned to people by society, which is not chosen and which cannot be changed easily.

**Achieved status** A status that can be earned through action.

### Status and Role

Interaction with other people provides us with important clues about our different statuses and roles. **Status** refers to a specific social position that an individual has relative to other people. Sociologists distinguish between **ascribed status** and **achieved status**. An ascribed status is something that is assigned to us by society, which we do not choose and which we often cannot change. Important examples of ascribed status include race, gender, family origin, and age. Achieved status is something that we earn through our own actions. Achieved statuses include things like our jobs and hobbies.

Our status often changes as we move through the life course, like when we transition from being a child to a parent. Other statuses remain mostly

## METHODS AND INTERPRETATION

## Life-Course Research on Socialization

The *Up* series of films, produced by ITV and the British Broadcasting Corporation (BBC), was one of the most famous television documentary projects ever made. The first installment of the series, *Seven Up!*, was released in 1964. The director of the documentary followed the lives of 14 seven-year-old children, who were selected to represent a variety of social backgrounds in England. The goal of the series was to catch up with the children every seven years, and to see how their lives developed. Almost all of the children have agreed to continue participating in the project. The latest installment, *63 Up*, was released in 2019.

The *Up* series does a remarkable job of showing the power of socialization. Already at age seven, the children from wealthy families have plans to attend elite prep schools and universities. The children of privileged parents ended up living mostly privileged lives, while the children of working-class parents mostly ended up living working-class lives. The influences of religion, race, and gender socialization were already apparent in the seven-year-olds, and they continued to exert a powerful influence. But the disruptions that took place in their adult lives also had a significant impact on the development of their social selves. Divorce was a particularly powerful event in the lives of the adult characters, but the series also shows the influence of unemployment, homelessness, and illness. Influenced by the *Up* series, similar documentary projects have been undertaken in more than 10 different countries.

While the *Up* series is a powerful demonstration of socialization through the life course, sociologists have criticized certain features of the documentary series. As Mitchell Duneier has pointed out, the director asked leading questions to some of the subjects in the films, and he makes claims about their life-course trajectories that cannot be supported by the data (Duneier 2000). The director of the series has agreed with these criticisms, admitting that the assumptions he made about social background and life outcomes did not always turn out to be correct (Apted 2009).

Social scientists have also conducted research that examines socialization over the life course (Kuo et al. 2019; Vaillant 2012). Among sociologists, the most famous life-course study is probably Glen Elder's *Children of the Great Depression* (Elder 1998). In this study, Elder follows 167 people in Oakland, California, who were born in 1920–21, and then another group of children born in 1928–29. Beginning his research when they were in elementary school, Elder follows them through the 1960s, to see how the Great Depression of the 1930s influenced their lives. While the economic crisis was a major factor for all of his research subjects, Elder found that people were more resilient if they went to college, if they had a stable marriage, or if they entered the military.

Some sociologists have moved away from life-course research on socialization, focusing more attention on the ways in which individuals resist, oppose, negotiate, and creatively modify the messages they are receiving about how they are supposed to act in society (Guhin et al. 2021). Other sociologists are using different concepts in their research, even as they continue to study the role that socialization plays over the life course. There is also a growing recognition that previous research on socialization focused too much on childhood, and that a focus on adulthood can allow for greater attention to how people creatively incorporate new experiences into existing scripts about the self and society (Lutfey and Mortimer 2003). Despite these challenges and criticisms, however, the concept of socialization continues to have a wide recognizability within sociology as well as within other social science fields, and there is every reason to believe that life-course research on socialization processes will continue (Guhin et al. 2021).

### ACTIVE LEARNING

**Discuss:** Watch *Seven Up!*, the first film in the *Up* series. Do you think the focus on social class background as a determinant of future life trajectory is convincing? What other aspects of these individuals' social lives will be important for their future life-course trajectories?

**PAIRED CONCEPTS**

## Structure and Contingency

### What Is the Meaning of Fair Play? The 2012 Olympic Badminton Controversy

During the 2012 London Olympics, a scandal erupted when four of the teams in the badminton competition appeared to deliberately lose their matches during early-round play. Like many Olympic sports, badminton uses a round-robin format in which the results from early matches are used to determine seeding for later matches. In principle, teams should want to win their matches so that they will have a higher seed and get to play weaker opponents during the "knockout" rounds that advance teams into the semifinals and the finals. But sometimes teams make different strategic decisions.

In the badminton matches that caused the scandal, the teams from China, South Korea, and Indonesia had already qualified for the knockout round and decided that they would be in a better position if they lost their matches. The players were making errors on basic shots, and no rallies lasted more than four shots during one of the matches. There was an obvious lack of effort by the competitors. Fans booed during both matches, and the referees interrupted play several times to issue warnings to the competitors. A disciplinary committee disqualified the teams the next day, charging them with violating the spirit of fair play. British and American journalists praised the decision, arguing that fans had paid good money to watch the matches and the play of the competitors demeaned the sport as well as the Olympic spirit.

Not everyone accepted this social construction of reality. All four teams protested their disqualification. The Chinese players said they were just trying to preserve energy for the next round. The South Korean players said they were responding to China's actions and trying to increase the odds of having two South Korean teams advance into the final match. The Indonesian players said they thought they would have a better chance of advancing to the final if they didn't have to play the Chinese team in the knockout round.

**The 2012 Olympic badminton controversy**
An official talks to women's-doubles pairs from South Korea and China after they allegedly made deliberate mistakes to lose the match in order to avoid meeting another team from their own country in the next round.

All of these players rejected the idea that they were violating the spirit of fair play. Their goal was to win the entire Olympic competition, and they had made a strategic decision that they thought would improve their chances. Sports experts noted that athletes often preserve their energy in the early rounds to make sure they are fully prepared for the later rounds, and they questioned whether these badminton matches were really any different. Furthermore, China and South Korea were trying to increase the chances of having an all-Chinese or an all-Korean final. Were their decisions based on bad sportsmanship or patriotism?

**ACTIVE LEARNING**

**Discuss:** Socialization is a part of the social construction of reality because it teaches us "what everybody knows" and provides a "cultural common sense." Whose common sense do you think should have prevailed in the Olympic badminton scandal of 2012? Why?

the same, such as our family of origin. At any given time we will have many different statuses.

Statuses can also change between interactional contexts. Elijah Anderson's classic study *The Code of the Street* (1999) documented how inner-city youth in Philadelphia switched between what they called "decent" and "street" behavior to adapt to different role expectations on the street, at home, and at school. Anderson called this behavior of adapting to different role expectations in different interactional contexts **code-switching**.

A **role** is the expected behaviors that are associated with each status. Roles emerge in social interaction as people decide which statuses are the most relevant for the situation. But role expectations are not always straightforward. There can be **role strain**, which occurs when the different expected behaviors associated with a status are in tension with one another. Parents feel role strain frequently as they balance love for their children with the need to establish and enforce rules their children need to follow. There can also be **role conflict**, which happens when there are competing expectations coming from different statuses. A working parent experiences role conflict when the expected behaviors associated with the workplace come into conflict with the expected behaviors of a parent.

**Role conflict**
Because people occupy multiple statuses, they often experience role conflict. A common conflict is between work and parenting roles.

## Performance and the Social Self

As the sociologist Erving Goffman (1922–1982) observed, we are all actors on the stage of social life. Our statuses define specific roles for us to play in different situations, and we have to perform those roles in a way that is true to our social selves. At the same time, we are always giving other people clues about the roles they are supposed to be playing, and we provide them in-the-moment information about whether they are playing those roles effectively or not. Goffman described the **dramaturgical theory** of society, which refers to social life as a series of theatrical performances (Goffman 1959).

Goffman argued that people want to convey a particular image of themselves in their interactions with others. To do this effectively, they prepare for their social interactions the same way an actor would prepare for a performance. They practice the role they expect to play. They select their costume

**Code-switching** Adapting behavior to meet different role expectations across interactional contexts.

**Role** The set of expected behaviors associated with a particular status.

**Role strain** Occurs when the different expected behaviors associated with a status are in tension with one another, individuals experience strain trying to meet expectations.

**Role conflict** Occurs when there are competing expectations coming from different statuses and role expectations clash, individuals become conflicted.

**Dramaturgical theory** A theory of society developed by Erving Goffman that refers to social life as a series of theatrical performances.

carefully so that it will convey the right image. They pay careful attention to the cues they get from others, to see if their performance is succeeding. They improvise when their performance takes an unexpected turn.

Goffman made an important distinction between front-stage and back-stage actions in the presentation of self. The front stage is where our social interactions take place. As actors in social life, we are always aware of the fact that we are being watched when we interact with others. We notice the setting where the interaction takes place, and we do everything we can to present ourselves in a particular way. But there is also action and preparation that take place backstage, where we can step out of character and prepare for our front-stage performance without fear of ruining our presentation of self.

As a theatrical performance, our presentation of self needs the cooperation of others to be successful. Most of the time, people go along with our presentation of self because they don't want to embarrass us or because they know that they also rely on others to go along with their own presentations of self. But there is no guarantee that our performances will succeed, as people might misinterpret or deliberately reject our performances.

## Social Interaction in a Digital Age

During the social quarantines, the remote instruction, and the remote work that defined social life in 2020, many people came to appreciate the differences between life on the screen and interactions that take place "in real life." Even before the global COVID-19 pandemic, the amount of time people spent using media technologies to interact with each other had increased dramatically over the previous 20 years. According to the Pew Research Center, 92 percent of teenagers go online daily, and 24 percent say that they are online "almost constantly" (Lenhart 2015). Social media networks have a major impact on socialization and group life.

Many of us have experienced the effects that digital media have on social interactions. As soon as class ends, most students (and teachers) immediately reach for their phones to check their email, text messages, and other social media. Internet forums allow us to interact with other people in complete anonymity and to try on different personas.

In her book *Life on the Screen: Identity in the Age of the Internet* (1997), the sociologist Sherry Turkle examined how the internet was changing how people thought about their identities. In fact, Turkle argues, our virtual identities can play an important therapeutic role because they encourage us to see that we can be many different selves. This was the main point of Goffman's dramaturgical theory: we are always playing a role in social interaction. We are always performing.

More recently, Turkle has argued that our interactions in the digital world might be damaging our ability to form meaningful social relationships.

> **PAIRED CONCEPTS**
>
> ## Power and Resistance
>
> ### Challenging Gender Norms during the 2022 Iranian Protests
>
> Since the 1979 Islamic Revolution, women in Iran have been required to wear the *hijab* in public places. A law passed in 1983 dictates that those women who disobey it can be imprisoned for up to sixty days, fined, or sentenced to as many as 74 lashes. A study that examined enforcement of this law found that between 2003 and 2007 about 30,000 women were arrested for violating it, and about 460,000 women were issued warnings by the police (Loft 2023). Police began enforcing the law even more strictly after 2021, despite the fact that a public opinion survey in Iran suggests that at least half of the population does not want the government to be enforcing it (Loft 2023: 9).
>
> Recent years have seen an increase in protests in Iran, with repeated protests being mounted against food prices and fuel prices. The typical government response has been to use violence against protesters, to arrest many of them, and to shut down the internet. It was in this context of heightened social protest that Mahsa Amini, a 22-year-old Iranian Kurdish woman, was arrested in September 2022 for failing to wear the *hijab* in public. Amini died three days later while in police custody. Mass protests ensued, and continued for more than 100 days.
>
> Though the government employed its usual response—violence, arrests, and shutting down the internet—they could not stop the protests. Women, students, workers, and members of historically marginalized ethnic groups joined together and rallied around the slogan "women, life, freedom" (Loft 2023: 17). The UN Human Rights Council denounced the government response to the protests. The Iranian government blamed the US and the UK for organizing the protests, increased its use of violence against protesters, and actually strengthened its laws requiring women to wear the *hijab* in public. Despite these coercive practices, however, many women continue to defy the law, and continue to fight for changes in beliefs and practices about the place of women in Iranian society (Far 2023).
>
> **ACTIVE LEARNING**
>
> See if you can find any photographs or video from the Iranian protests of 2022. Using Goffman's dramaturgical theory of social interaction, see if you can describe how the protests are being choreographed, and what kinds of messages are being emphasized.

Turkle calls this the "Goldilocks effect" of social media (Turkle 2011). We want to have social relationships, but only on our terms. We turn to technology when we are lonely, but too often this technology prevents us from making real connections, from having real conversations, and from developing the skills of empathy and compassion that are the cornerstone of meaningful social connections (Turkle 2015).

Others are worried that social media encourage us to be less tolerant in our social interactions. In his book *# Republic* (2018), Cass Sunstein argues that social media encourage social polarization by allowing people to be exposed only to things that interest them and to people who agree with them. As these like-minded people interact, they encourage each other to develop more extreme versions of the positions they already hold.

The extreme polarization experienced on social media during the 2016, 2020, and 2024 US presidential elections provides good evidence that Sunstein's fears were well founded. Sophisticated computer algorithms now analyze users' media browsing patterns, suggesting and selecting new information that is similar to things they have looked at before and creating "filter bubbles" within which they see only information that confirms their pre-existing biases (Pariser 2011). Because these computer algorithms do not distinguish between high-quality and low-quality information, political actors (domestic as well as foreign) have been able to take advantage of social media to spread propaganda, manipulate public opinion, and sow division and discord (Jacobs 2020; Golebiewski and Boyd 2019).

## 4.3 Group Life

**LG 4.3** Define groups, and distinguish different kinds of groups.

Most of our social interaction takes place in groups, and social learning occurs in groups. Some of these groups consist of people we know very well, while others consist of casual acquaintances, and still others are made up of people who have never met each other. Groups can be loosely organized and informally regulated, or they can be complex, formal organizations with official rules and procedures. Taken together, the groups we belong to affect who we become and what opportunities we have in our lives.

**Dyad** A group of two people with one relationship.

**Group size**
Group dynamics get a lot more complicated as soon as there are three people.

### Group Size

The number of people in a group has a major influence on the behavior of its members, independent of any other characteristics of the group. For instance, a **dyad** (a group of two people) is fundamentally different than any other kind of group. The sociologist Georg Simmel (1858–1918) argued that a dyad is the most unstable kind of group because the withdrawal of even one person will destroy its existence. Dyads are intensely personal because there is no way to shift responsibility or attention onto a third person. The romantic couple is the classic example of the dyad.

As soon as a group becomes a **triad**, consisting of three people, group dynamics become more complicated. Triads have more stability because when two of its members have a conflict they can appeal to the third person to help resolve the situation. Triads also develop more complicated power dynamics than dyads. One of the members can deliberately create conflicts between the other two, or alliances can form, where two of the members agree to isolate the third. For children, an important part of their socialization involves learning how to navigate the power dynamics that exist in triads and larger groups.

As groups get larger, they become more complex. The number of possible relationships in a group increases exponentially with the addition of each new person. There are also more opportunities for conflicts to develop.

**Triad** A group of three people with three relationships.

## Primary Groups and Secondary Groups

The first groups we belong to are small groups, such as our family, close friends, and peer groups. Because of how important they are for socialization and for the development of the looking-glass self, Cooley referred to these kinds of groups as **primary groups**. For most of us, spending time with our primary groups is a valuable end in itself, with no ulterior motive.

The larger and more impersonal groups we belong to are known as **secondary groups**. A secondary group is usually organized around a specific activity or interest, and the expectation is that we will only interact with other members of such groups when we are engaged in that activity. As a result, the interactions we have in secondary relationships are more impersonal than the ones we have in our primary groups.

The larger size and the more limited scope of interactions give secondary groups a distinctive quality. On the one hand, their relative anonymity gives us the freedom to participate on our own terms. We can

**Primary groups** Small groups typically based in face-to-face interaction that foster strong feelings of belonging.

**Secondary groups** Large, impersonal groups usually organized around a specific activity or interest.

**Secondary groups**
Secondary groups are often organized around a common activity like work or sports, with the expectation that you interact with members of that group only when doing that activity.

## PAIRED CONCEPTS: Solidarity and Conflict

### The Stanford Prison Experiment

The Stanford Prison Experiment was conducted in 1971 by Stanford psychology professor Philip Zimbardo. Funded by the US Office of Naval Research, the goal of the study was to learn about how conflicts develop between military guards and prisoners. Specifically, the researchers wanted to know whether abusive behavior was caused by the social setting of the prison or the inherent personality characteristics of the guards.

In the study, 24 male students were randomly assigned the role of prisoner or guard and placed in a makeshift prison. The prison simulation was designed to last two weeks. Guards worked for eight-hour shifts and were allowed to go home when they were not on duty. Prisoners had to remain in the prison during the entire period of the study. Prisoners were given identification numbers, and they were only allowed to refer to themselves or to other prisoners by using these numbers.

Trouble began on the second day of the experiment, when some of the prisoners began to taunt the guards, refusing to follow instructions or come out of their cells. In order to force compliance, guards attacked the prisoners with fire extinguishers. From this point forward, guards used physical and psychological harassment in order to maintain control. Guards became increasingly sadistic, and prisoners exhibited signs of extreme stress. The experiment was ended after six days.

Today, the Stanford Prison Experiment is considered an ethically flawed study because it neither adequately protected its research subjects nor did enough to ensure informed consent. But the experiment showed how social settings that create in-groups and out-groups also produce solidarity and conflict. The prisoners and the guards in the study internalized their roles, bonding with other members of their group and quickly growing to dislike the members of the other group. The research study also showed how in-group and out-group conflicts are shaped by differences in power. Guards had all the power and were able to morally distance themselves from their actions by dehumanizing the prisoners.

While the Stanford Prison Experiment was an artificially created research study with serious design flaws (Blum 2018), similar dynamics have developed in real-world prison contexts. When Amnesty International publicized the physical and psychological abuse of war prisoners committed by US soldiers at the Abu Ghraib prison in Iraq in 2003, Zimbardo argued that the social factors that led his research subjects to act like sadistic prison guards were the same ones that led the military guards to act the way they did (Zimbardo 2007).

**The Stanford Prison Experiment**
Commemorative plaque marking the site of the Stanford Prison Experiment.

### ACTIVE LEARNING

**Think about it:** Do you think it would be possible to design a study similar to the Stanford Prison Experiment today, without violating research ethics guidelines? What would you need to change to the research design?

show up when we want, and if we decide we no longer want to be in the group, it is much easier to leave.

But these freedoms come with their own costs. While large secondary groups have many members who are participating on their own terms, they also need leaders who are willing to carry the burden of organization. In fact, large groups almost always make formal status distinctions between the leaders of the group and everyone else. In addition, people often experience large groups as being more complex, inefficient, and inflexible than they need to be. This is particularly the case with bureaucratic organizations, which we discuss at the end of this chapter.

## Reference Groups

Any group that helps us figure out where we fit in society is called a **reference group**. Reference groups include groups where we are members as well as those where we are not. A reference group gives us standards we can use to measure ourselves. In our family, it is common to make comparisons with our siblings, our cousins, and even our parents. We measure ourselves against their achievements, and we get clues about the kinds of achievements and interests that are valued in the group. But there may also be groups we aspire to join, such as an athletic team, a sorority or fraternity, a community group, or a professional organization. We may also use the behaviors or attitudes of a reference group we do not like (and to which we would not want to belong) as negative standards to avoid in our own lives.

**Reference group** A group that people use to help define how they fit in society by providing standards to measure themselves.

**IN-GROUPS AND OUT-GROUPS.** An **in-group** is a positive reference group. We feel a strong bond of solidarity with the other people in the group, whether we have met them or not. We feel pride in the accomplishments of the group, and our membership gives us feelings of security and pride. On the other hand, an **out-group** is a reference group toward which we have a negative connection. We look down on members of out-groups, and we try to avoid them.

**In-group** A reference group that a person is connected to in a positive way and feels bonded to, whether or not they know people in the group personally.

**Out-group** A reference group toward which a person has a negative connection.

Social inequality influences how in-groups and out-groups form. Dominant in-groups define what counts as normal and desirable in society, often by identifying specific out-groups as abnormal or undesirable. The members of those stigmatized out-groups get treated as less valuable and are often subjected to humiliating social interactions that injure their self-respect (Margalit 1996). Historically, racial, ethnic, religious, and sexual minorities have been targeted as stigmatized out-groups. Other stigmatized out-groups who have suffered humiliation and exclusion include people with physical and mental disabilities (Goffman 1963), the homeless (Phelan et al. 1997), refugee groups (Bauman 2003), and people who are obese (Saguy 2014).

## Bureaucracy in Group Life

Groups can be organized in different ways with different consequences for group life. A **bureaucracy** is an organized group with a clearly defined hierarchy, specific rules and procedures that govern every aspect of group life, and official documentation of everything considered important. Leadership in a bureaucracy follows a clear organizational structure and hierarchy of managers and workers.

Bureaucracies have many advantages for group life. They define statuses and role expectations clearly, and by sorting jobs into departments based on specific tasks, workers are placed into groups of people who have similar knowledge, skills, and resources. This enables people to do their work within the bureaucratic organization efficiently, and it helps them develop greater expertise in their role. In addition, most bureaucracies are organized in a similar way. This makes it easier when people change jobs or interact with an organization for the first time. Bureaucracies also minimize favoritism and arbitrary exercises of power because they tend to treat everyone according to the same rules and procedures. Max Weber argued that bureaucracy was particularly suited for organizing the large-scale complex societies emerging all over the world (Weber 1946).

Despite bureaucracy's many advantages, some of its features have unintended consequences that can undermine an organization's effectiveness. Bureaucracy's rules and regulations may minimize favoritism, but they also make the organization more impersonal and alienating. The specific tasks that are defined in bureaucratic jobs may encourage efficiency and expertise, but they also make many of these jobs monotonous and repetitive. This can create a crisis of motivation for workers.

Not only are bureaucracies seen as impersonal, alienating, and unnecessarily complicated, but these characteristics are also what make them seem inflexible and resistant to change. In recent years, people have begun to create different kinds of work environments, with start-up

**Bureaucracy**
An organized group with a clearly defined hierarchy that relies on specific written rules and procedures to govern every aspect of the organization.

**Bureaucracy in group life**
These clerks in a government office in Malawi, Africa, organize their activities methodically, by dividing work into distinct tasks and keeping detailed, color-coded records, shown on the shelves behind the workers. The bureaucratic social form defines what is appropriate behavior in this work setting, which is to sit separately and process forms.

## PAIRED CONCEPTS

## Global and Local

### Bureaucracy in Singapore

While most bureaucracies are organized in a similar way, each specific organization will also have its own peculiarities. As people develop their own patterns of interaction and their own strategies for getting things done together, small differences accumulate that distinguish one organization from another (Eliasoph and Lo 2012). Sociologists talk about this in terms of **organizational culture**, which refers to the distinctive beliefs and patterns of behavior that develop within any organization.

Differences in national cultures also shape bureaucratic organizations. For example, a Chinese MBA student going to a networking event in the United States knows that American business culture values assertiveness and self-promotion. Historically, these behaviors have conflicted with Chinese national culture, which values the group over the individual, encourages deference to authority, and tries to avoid conflicts (Hsu 1981). While Chinese business culture has adapted to some of the norms of American business, it is also the case that Americans and others are adapting themselves to Chinese business organizations and their cultures.

Singapore provides an example of an Asian country that adapted to the organizational culture of Western-style bureaucracies. Singapore achieved independence from England in 1963 and separated from Malaysia in 1965 to become an independent state. Singapore is a multiethnic nation. Seventy-four percent of the population consists of Chinese Singaporeans, but there are significant minorities of Malaysians, Indians, and Eurasians. Singapore has four official languages—Mandarin, English, Malay, and Tamil—which reflect the main ethnic groups as well as the nation's history as a British colony. Singapore has quickly become one of the wealthiest places in the world, with a very high standard of living, one of the best school systems, and excellent medical care. The World Bank consistently ranks it as one of the best places in the world to do business, and it is considered to have the most efficient bureaucracy in Asia (Reuters India 2009).

**Singapore business district**
Singapore is one of the most bureaucratic and one of the wealthiest nations in the world. Its organizational culture emphasizes courtesy and the welfare of the group over the individual.

Singapore's bureaucracies have developed in distinctive ways that are connected to its national culture and history (Quah 2010). Relying on values that privileged the group and the nation over the individual, Singapore established a system where government bureaucracies had most of the control over the economy. Government salaries were set higher than in the private sector, which attracted the most talented Singaporean citizens into government bureaucracies (Bell 2015).

Singapore's legal system punishes inconsiderate behavior, and its culture encourages people to be more thoughtful of others. Jaywalkers in Singapore can be arrested, and failing to flush a public toilet can incur a hefty fine. Punishments such as these may seem overly harsh when viewed from a Western perspective, but they also make it easier for Singapore to combat the moral indifference that plagues bureaucracies in so many other countries. Indeed, Singapore has been more successful at reducing bureaucratic corruption than any other country in Asia.

Finally, by putting the interests of society ahead of those of the individual, Singapore has fostered a public-spirited culture that helps reduce the impersonality and the alienating tendencies that often come with living in a highly bureaucratic society. This is reflected

**PAIRED CONCEPTS CONTINUED**

in Singapore's system of public housing. More than 80 percent of the population lives in large public housing estates that are designed to reinforce a sense of community. Housing estates are designed to promote social interaction and social support, with schools, stores, hospitals, parks, recreation areas, and public transportation stations all located within the estates.

**ACTIVE LEARNING**

**Find out:** Look up the World Bank's ranking of the best places in the world to do business. How do the top countries compare to the US in terms of differences in national culture and differences in bureaucracy?

**Organizational culture** The distinctive beliefs and patterns of behavior that develop within an organization.

**Moral indifference** Occurs when we distance ourselves from the consequences of our actions for others.

companies and decentralized networks of collaboration as alternatives. People and organizations who had to rapidly adjust to working from home during the pandemic have realized that flexibility in everything from the hours people work to the clothes they wear while working confers benefits in terms of productivity and cost savings.

A significant problem with bureaucracy is that its focus on following rules and procedures makes it less likely that people will consider the consequences of their actions. This is a key feature of bureaucracy, which insists that decisions get made according to specific rules and "without regards to persons" (Weber 1946: 215). But the unintended consequence of this impersonal decision-making is that it encourages **moral indifference**, which happens when we distance ourselves from the consequences of our actions. In a bureaucracy, we treat people as categories, and we treat every situation in terms of the appropriate rule that is supposed to apply. This is not a situation that encourages us to care about the well-being of others.

In Silicon Valley, the home of technology giants such as Apple and Google, bureaucracy has come to be seen as the enemy of success and innovation. In place of an

**Against bureaucratic cultures**
In the tech industry, bureaucracy has come to be seen as the enemy of success and innovation. Many of today's tech companies try to design their offices in a way that they believe will encourage innovation and creativity.

older bureaucratic model, these companies are creating more decentralized networks, in order to encourage collaboration and to allow people to try out new solutions to problems and take greater responsibility for their actions.

## Social Networks in Group Life

A **social network** is a set of connections that link individuals to one another. Today, when we think of social networks, we usually think of social media. But the study of social networks predates the internet. In fact, Simmel's discussion of dyads and triads was arguably the first study of network structure and the social relationships they enable.

**Social network**
A group organized through social ties between individuals that works through the connections that link individuals to one another.

### CAREERS

#### Getting a Job: The Strength of Weak Ties

If you are trying to get a job, it always helps to be related to the boss. This is an example of a strong network tie. But strong ties embedded within dense networks are not the only resources that are useful. In fact, in one of the most frequently cited research studies in sociology, Mark Granovetter found that weak ties are particularly helpful in securing a job.

In his book *Getting a Job: A Study of Contacts and Careers* (1995), Granovetter found that people relied mainly on their social contacts to get information about professional job opportunities, rather than using more formal resources such as job postings or employment agencies. Most social contacts came from family or work. Surprisingly, the social contacts that people saw the most frequently were not the ones who provided the most useful information. Rather, the most helpful contacts were the people they saw occasionally (more than once a year but less than twice a week). People they saw once a year or less were more useful social contacts than people they saw every week (Granovetter 1973: 1371).

How can these weak ties be so useful? The answer is that the weaker and more indirect ties in our network travel in different circles than we do. Because of this, they have access to information we do not have. By comparison, our close friends and relatives are much less likely to bring us new information. They have strong direct ties with our other close friends and family members. In this kind of dense network, shared information is fully contained within the network. Strong ties can still be important career resources but only by linking us with their friends, the friends of their friends, and so forth. In fact, Granovetter (1973: 1372) found that chance encounters with friends of friends often yielded surprising new information that people used to get a new job. Weak ties are an important source of useful new information, and they are what make social networks so powerful (Miller 2016; Grant 2014). But it is important not to generalize too much from these findings. Recent research has revealed how gender interacts with networks and careers; structural exclusion blocks women from many powerful networks, and women have demonstrated more reluctance to instrumentalize social contacts (Greguletz, Diehl, and Kreutzer 2018).

#### ACTIVE LEARNING

**Find out:** Who is central in your social network? How do you know? Can you tell by looking at your Instagram or LinkedIn account or your phone? Do you have a lot of weak ties? Do you maintain them? How?

**Network centrality** A network position that has many individual direct ties with many people in the network, or someone who is highly influential in a network.

**Social capital** Group ties and network attachments that people have and the sense of trust and security that they get from their group memberships and network attachments; the relationships and experience of social connection and cooperation people have with each other that allow them to act together.

A network is held together by social ties between individuals. These ties can vary in intensity, from strong to weak. We have strong ties with our family and friends, and we generally have weaker ties with our neighbors, classmates, and coworkers. Each network will have its own structure, depending on how the different social ties are organized. Some individuals may occupy a position of **network centrality**, which means that they have direct ties with a lot of people in the network, while others may be only indirectly connected to a few people.

The world of social media is a world of networks. How do these online social networks influence the rest of our social lives? According to the Pew Research Center, people who use social networking sites have more close ties and are less likely to be socially isolated than the average American (Pew Research Center 2018). Facebook users are more politically engaged than the average American. Facebook also makes it possible for people to revive and maintain the distant, weak, and indirect ties that are so useful in the job market. Overall, the internet appears to help build **social capital**, which refers to the group ties and network attachments people have and the sense of trust and security that they get from their group memberships and network attachments. But there are limits to these apparent benefits. People who rely less on social media as a news source exhibit higher levels of political knowledge (David, Pascual, and Torres 2019). And during the COVID lockdowns, the people who experienced less loneliness were the ones who were having more face-to-face interactions and more interactions with very close ties (Kovacs, Caplan, and King 2021).

The online media and digital technology that organize many of today's social networks are not equally available to everyone. The poorest people in our society are less likely to have internet access. As social networks increasingly use social media to communicate and maintain their social ties, vulnerable populations become more socially isolated. Expensive data plans and high-speed internet connections that are required to use these newer media technologies create a serious risk that the media-augmented social networks will end up reproducing inequality and privilege.

## CASE STUDY

# Becoming "The Rock"

Dwayne Johnson, also known as "The Rock," is one of the most recognizable celebrities and one of the highest-paid actors in Hollywood today. Using the five paired concepts to explore his biography, we consider what Johnson's story tells us about socialization and group life.

Dwayne Johnson was born in Hayward California, though he also spent time growing up in North Carolina, Connecticut, Hawaii, Tennessee, Pennsylvania, and New Zealand. Both of his parents had biographies that were shaped in important ways by *power* and *resistance*. His father, born in Nova Scotia, was descended from Black loyalists who came to that Canadian province after escaping slavery in the US during the Revolutionary War. His mother was from Samoa, a group of islands in the South Pacific that was shaped by American colonization after coming under US control in the late-1800s. While Samoa is an important naval outpost for the US military, Samoans have no voting rights in the US. In fact, Samoa is the only inhabited territory of the US where citizenship is not granted at birth.

In high school Johnson gravitated toward a peer group that spent their time getting into fights, forging checks, and committing petty theft. By age 17 he had been arrested several times, and there was nothing in his path of socialization that predicted the person he would become. But the patterned *structure* of socialization can be altered by the *contingency* of new events. For Johnson, this contingency came from the high school football coach, who recruited him to join the team, initiating a period of personal growth, transformation, and resocialization focused around athletic achievement and ambition. As a result of his new ambition and his athletic successes, Johnson was recruited to play football at the University of Miami, where he hoped to become a professional football player. These dreams were met with disappointment; Johnson was not drafted into the National Football League and he was cut from the Calgary Stampeders before the end of his first season in the Canadian Football League. From this disappointment emerged his next career path, which was professional wrestling.

Johnson's decision to become a professional wrestler was shaped by his family background. Even though his family did not have a lot of money when he was growing up, they had an extensive background in professional wrestling. His father and maternal grandfather were both professional wrestlers, and his maternal grandmother was an influential wrestling promoter. Dwayne Johnson's father, Rocky, helped him to get his first contract with the World Wrestling Federation (WWF), coaching him and helping to guide his career in its early ears. While there was a lot of *inequality* that shaped Johnson's early life, in the specialized world of professional wrestling he benefited from the *privilege* of his family's contacts.

Dwayne Johnson built his career in professional wrestling by developing the persona of "The Rock." He initially used the name Rocky Maivia, combining the ring names of his father and grandfather. He then decided to adapt his character to become more of a villain. Refusing to acknowledge the name Rocky Maivia, he began referring to himself in the third person as "The Rock." The Rock was a trash-talker who insulted the audience, the promoters, and other wrestlers. As he feuded continuously with almost everyone, he found that this type of *conflict* was increasing his fan support. Fans developed strong *solidarity* either for The Rock or against The Rock, and television ratings continued to increase as The Rock became the biggest star performer for the WWF.

Dwayne Johnson was able to use the star power he developed as The Rock to transition into a wildly successful acting career, focusing on action-adventure films as well as comedies.

### CASE STUDY CONTINUED

He wrote a bestselling autobiography, founded his own entertainment production company, and became a co-owner of a professional football team in the XFL. As of 2023 he had more than 390 million followers on Instagram, and he has become one of the most recognizable and influential *global* celebrities. At the same time, he has continued to maintain strong connections to his family's *local* roots. In 2004 the Samoan head of state bestowed on him the noble title *Seiuli*, recognizing that he is a descendant of Samoan chiefs. He gained Canadian citizenship in 2009, maintaining the connection to his father's heritage. And he has donated more than $1 million to the University of Miami football program, emphasizing how important that period of his life was to his later development.

## LEARNING GOALS REVISITED

**4.1** Define socialization, and identify the primary agents of socialization that operate over the life course.

- Socialization refers to the ways that we learn about our society's beliefs, values, and expected behaviors as we grow up.
- There are five primary agents of socialization: family, school, peer groups, media, and the workplace. Each operates with varying degrees of influence over the life course.

**4.2** Understand the difference between a status and a role, and describe how interactional performances sustain the social self.

- A status is a specific social position, and a role is a set of expected behaviors associated with that status. An individual *occupies* a status and *plays* a role.
- People perform their social self in social interaction and construct social life in the same process. In interaction, individuals display their own statuses and cultural understandings, engage with the statuses and cultural understandings of others, and co-construct social meanings and social life.
- Group life cannot exist without social interaction and the accomplishment and performance of our social selves.

**4.3** Define groups, and distinguish different kinds of groups.

- Groups are collections of individuals and vary in size from very small two-person dyads to millions of people.
- Primary groups are small groups based on face-to-face interaction, while secondary groups are larger, more

impersonal, and usually organized around a specific activity or interest.

- A reference group is any group that people use to help define how they fit in society by providing standards we can use to measure ourselves.
- An in-group is a reference group that a person is connected to in a positive way and feels bonded to, while an out-group is a reference group toward which a person has a negative connection.
- A bureaucracy is an organized group with a clearly defined hierarchy that relies on specific written rules and procedures to govern every aspect of the organization.
- A social network is a group organized through social ties between individuals and that works through the connections that link individuals to one another. Networks are more decentralized than bureaucracies and tend to have flatter authority structures.

## Key Terms

Achieved status 116
Agents of socialization 109
Ascribed status 116
Bureaucracy 126
Code-switching 119
Dramaturgical theory 119
Dyad 122
Ego 108
Game stage 108
Generalized other 108
Generation 112
Hidden curriculum 110
Id 108
In-group 125
Looking-glass self 107
Moral indifference 128
Network centrality 130
Normalization 109
Organizational culture 127
Out-group 125
Peer groups 110
Peer pressure 110
Play stage 108
Primary groups 123
Reference group 125
Resocialization 113
Role 119
Role conflict 119
Role strain 119
Secondary groups 123
Social capital 130
Social network 129
Socialization 106
Status 116
Superego 108
Total institutions 112
Triad 123

## Review Questions

1. What is the difference between a role and a status?
2. Compare and contrast the difference between bureaucracy and a network as a form of group life.
3. In what ways can bureaucracies foster moral indifference?

4. Why did Simmel think dyads were less stable than triads?
5. How might parents suffer from role strain or role conflict?
6. When is an in-group a reference group?
7. Briefly describe Erving Goffman's dramaturgical theory of society.
8. What is the difference between an ascribed and an achieved status?
9. Does college have a hidden curriculum? What is it?
10. What is the generalized other, and why is it important?
11. What is the relationship between the looking-glass self and the social self?
12. What is the superego, and how is it related to the ego?
13. What is resocialization, and when does it happen?

## Explore

### RECOMMENDED READINGS

Freud, Sigmund. [1930] 2010. *Civilization and Its Discontents*. New York: W. W. Norton.

Gitlin, Todd. 2007. *Media Unlimited: How the Torrent of Images and Sounds Overwhelms Our Lives*, rev. ed. New York: Picador.

Grazian, David. 2008. *On the Make: The Hustle of Urban Nightlife*. Chicago: University of Chicago Press.

Herbert Mead, George. 1967. *Mind, Self and Society*. Chicago: University of Chicago Press.

Illouz, Eva. 2008. *Saving the Modern Soul: Therapy, Emotions and the Culture of Self-Help*. Berkeley: University of California Press.

Lareau, Annette. 2011. *Unequal Childhoods: Class, Race, and Family Life*, 2nd ed. with an update a decade later. Berkeley: University of California Press.

Tatum, Beverly. 2003. *"Why Are All the Black Kids Sitting Together in the Cafeteria?" and Other Conversations about Race*. New York: Basic Books.

Turkle, Sherry. 1995. *Life on the Screen: Identity in the Age of the Internet*. New York: Simon & Schuster.

Turkle, Sherry. 2011. *Alone Together: Why We Expect More from Technology and Less from Each Other*. New York: Basic Books.

### ACTIVITIES

- *Use your sociological imagination*: What do you think the similarities and differences are between the process in which you were socialized and those of people in your parents' generation?

- *Media+Data Literacies*: How do people who did not grow up with personal computers, the internet, or smart phones learn how to use them?

- *Discuss*: In what ways can bureaucracies foster moral indifference? Do you think social networks also foster moral indifference? Why or why not?

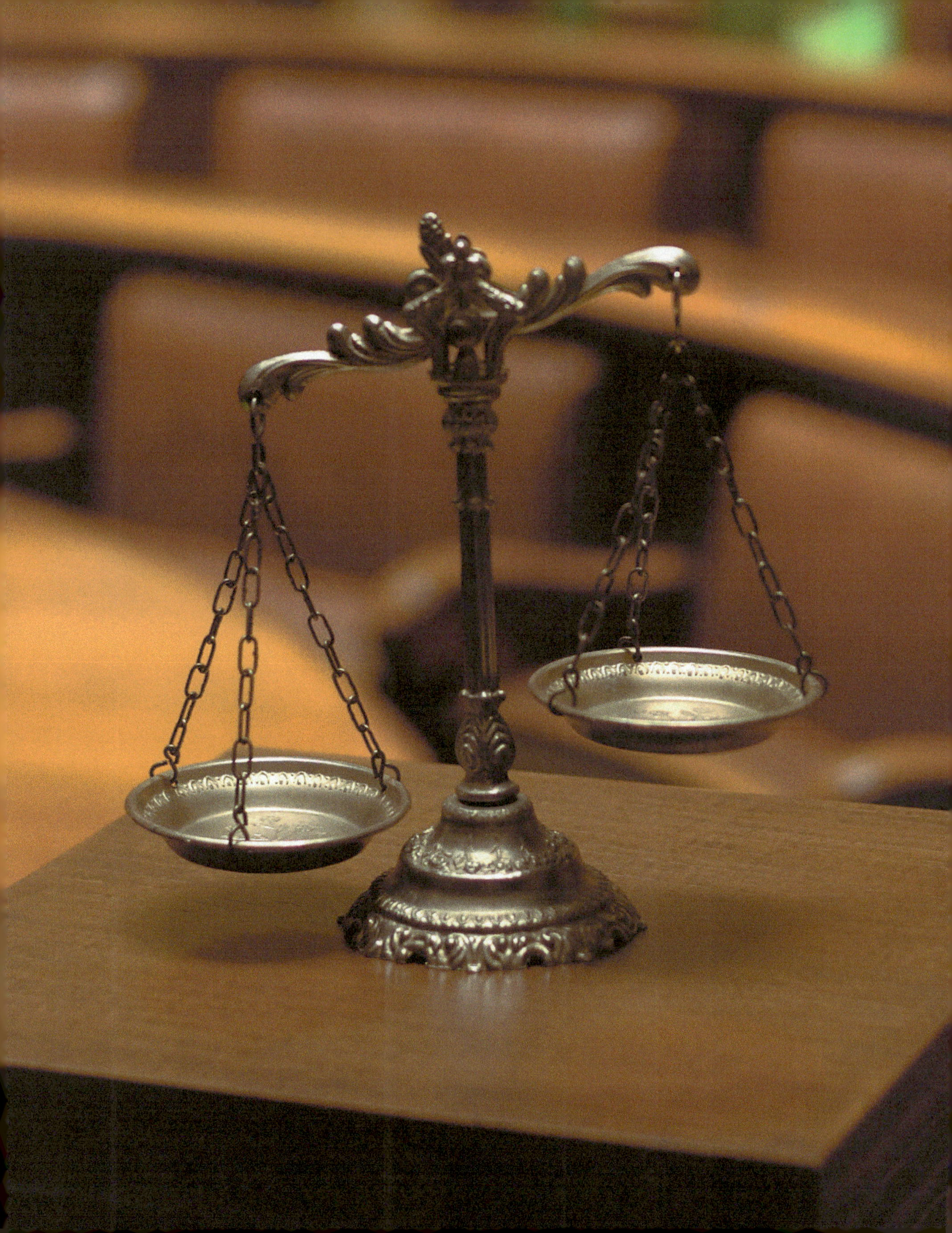

# 5

# Deviance, Crime, and Punishment

In 2012, a woman in Beverly, Massachusetts was sentenced to serve six months in prison for providing alcohol to teenagers during a party at her house. It was the first time in the state that somebody had received a jail sentence for violating the "social host law" in a case where a fatality was not involved. When the sentence was announced, the district attorney explained that the case "sends a clear message to adults who think they can control a gathering of underage drinkers or that by providing young people with a place to drink that they are keeping them safe" (Arsenault 2012).

The district attorney claimed that the laws regulating underage drinking were clear and that they were necessary to protect children, but the truth is a little more complicated. Most states, including Massachusetts, allow parents to serve wine to their children during religious ceremonies. Other countries, which have more relaxed laws about underage drinking, have less of a problem with adolescent binge drinking than the United States does. In fact, a 2004 study in the *Journal of Adolescent Health* found that children whose parents introduced drinking to them at home were significantly less likely to develop problems with binge drinking and alcoholism (Foley et al. 2004).

Why are Americans more worried than people in other parts of the world about underage drinking? Why is underage drinking

### Chapter Outline

**5.1 DEVIANCE 138**

Why Does Deviance Exist? 140
The Social Construction of Deviance 145

**5.2 CRIME 150**

Categories of Crime 152
Policing Crime 156
Surveillance 160

**5.3 PUNISHMENT 160**

Punishment as a Public Display of Morality 161
Punishment and Treatment 162
Incarceration 162

**CASE STUDY: WHY ARE CRIME STORIES SO POPULAR? 166**

**Scales of justice**
A metaphor of balance and fairness, the scales of justice convey the application of law, regardless of privilege or favor. Do you think the scales are a fitting image to describe justice? Why or why not?

## Chapter 5  DEVIANCE, CRIME, AND PUNISHMENT

**Deviance** Any behavior that is outside social boundaries for what counts as normal and acceptable.

**Crime** Deviant behavior that is defined and regulated by law.

viewed as a social problem, while adult drinking is viewed by many people as normal? How do people decide what counts as "normal drinking" and what counts as "problem drinking"? How do societies respond to drinking problems? Do they rely on criminal prosecution, education, treatment, or social pressure? Are these social responses standardized, or do they vary depending on social factors such as race, class, age, and gender? This chapter explores how some actions get defined as normal, while others are seen as dangerous. We begin with a discussion of **deviance**, which consists of any behavior that is outside social boundaries for what counts as normal and acceptable. We then explore **crime**, which is deviant behavior that is defined and regulated by law. Finally, we explore the different ways that crime is punished.

## LEARNING GOALS

**5.1**  Define deviance, and understand the social functions of deviance.
**5.2**  Distinguish different categories of crime and the challenges of measuring crime.
**5.3**  Define different approaches to punishment, and analyze their effectiveness.

## 5.1 Deviance

**LG 5.1** Define deviance, and understand the social functions of deviance.

The boundaries that distinguish normal behavior from deviant behavior are socially constructed. They are shaped by our culture, learned during our ongoing socialization, and reinforced in our everyday interactions. It is usually easy to tell when we do something that other people think is deviant. They may give us a stern look, stand back from us, or say something to us. If they think our deviance is serious enough, they may even call the police.

What counts as deviant behavior depends on the social context. Things that are considered deviant in some places or at some times are considered normal in others. Prior to the COVID-19 pandemic, visitors to Japan were surprised to see people wearing surgical masks in public places; in fact, in Japan it was considered to be very inconsiderate not to wear a mask if you were sick. In Virginia, by comparison, it was illegal to wear a mask in public; and if you did want to wear a surgical mask, you had to carry a doctor's note that explained why it was necessary. Following the worldwide spread of the novel coronavirus in 2020, norms around mask-wearing changed dramatically, and masks are commonly worn in an attempt to slow the spread of

**PAIRED CONCEPTS**

## Structure and Contingency

### Is Chewing Gum Deviant?

The mass production of chewing gum began in the 1860s, when the then president of Mexico, Antonio López de Santa Anna, brought a substance called chicle with him on a trip to New York. Santa Anna used the chicle, derived from the sap of a tree, as a chewing gum.

While many adults in Mexico chewed chicle, public gum-chewing by adults had been viewed as a deviant act in 16th-century Aztec society where the practice originated. The Aztecs thought that men who chewed chicle in public were effeminate and that women who did this were sexually promiscuous (Matthews 2009). Most Aztec adults did chew chicle in private, but they avoided doing so publicly so that they would not be labeled as deviants.

Thomas Adams, an American inventor who was working with Santa Anna, did not know about the social meanings that Aztecs attached to public gum-chewing. In fact, Adams was primarily interested in chicle as a rubber substitute that could be used for tires. When this failed, he used it to create a chewing gum product. His Chiclets chewing gum proved to be very popular with American consumers. Adams soon partnered with William Wrigley and helped to create the Wrigley gum empire.

Americans at first thought that chewing gum was a woman's activity, but Wrigley aggressively marketed his product to men. Wrigley organized the first ever nationwide direct-marketing campaign in 1915, mailing sticks of gum to every address listed in the US phone book. By the 1920s, the average American was chewing more than one hundred pieces of gum per year. Wrigley also gave free gum to US soldiers during World War I, using this marketing strategy to associate his product with masculinity and national patriotism. The "gum-chewing soldier" became a global ambassador for the product, and in much of Europe the practice of chewing gum came to be associated with American culture.

But gum-chewing continued to be considered a deviant activity in certain places. In France, gum-chewing has often been viewed alongside Hollywood films and comic books as an uncivilized feature of American

**The context of chewing gum**
Barack Obama chews nicotine gum as a way to control the urge to smoke. Do you think his gum chewing breaches social expectations? Is it an important breach?

culture that any self-respecting French citizen would want to avoid (Kuisel 1996). In Singapore, the government passed a law in 1992 that banned the use, distribution, and sale of chewing gum. People caught selling gum in Singapore face fines of up to $100,000 and prison sentences of up to two years. The law against gum is presented as evidence of Singapore's commitment to efficiency and cleanliness.

Sometimes, gum-chewing is only seen as a deviant activity in specific contexts. In 2014, President Obama was criticized throughout China for chewing gum during the Asia Pacific Economic Cooperation Summit in Beijing. As a former cigarette smoker, Obama often chewed Nicorette gum as a way to control his smoking urges. But the Chinese press criticized Obama's behavior as disrespectful toward Chinese leaders and inappropriate for a formal political event. Obama was criticized for the same behavior during a 2014 visit to France and a 2015 visit to India.

**ACTIVE LEARNING**

**Find out:** Are there times and places that chewing gum is inappropriate? List two such times or places. Compare your list to those of your classmates. Can you see any patterns?

**Mask shaming**
At the height of the COVID-19 pandemic, people who refused to wear masks in public were frequently confronted for their deviant and inconsiderate behavior.

the virus. In fact, people who refuse to wear masks can be subjected to public mask shaming and even attacked for placing others at risk (Ryan 2020).

The boundary that distinguishes the normal from the deviant often changes over time. When Harvard University opened in 1642, breakfast consisted of bread and beer; today, this same breakfast would be a violation of the university's alcohol policy and is now a deviant act. Things also change in the opposite direction, from deviant to normal. In the early 20th century, women who went to the beach in the United States were expected to wear long one-piece garments as well as stockings, and if they did not do so, they ran the risk of being arrested. These laws and social norms no longer exist, and today women's swimwear is an $8 billion global industry.

## Why Does Deviance Exist?

Despite social efforts to combat and control deviance, sociologists argue that societies *need* deviance. The presence of deviance helps to reinforce the boundaries between acceptable and unacceptable behavior, and in the process it sets the standard for what is normal. Deviance is an important part of our ongoing socialization and an important source of social change. Many innovative and revolutionary figures in history were considered to be highly deviant and even dangerous in their own times.

In our everyday socialization, deviance helps us draw boundaries. Parents, schools, peers, and media tell us what they expect of us; but they also highlight examples of behavior that is "over the line." The line is always moving as social norms change and behaviors that used to be punished begin to pass unnoticed. There is a **zone of permitted variation** around the rules, and it is in this zone that much experimentation and change can occur.

While it is natural for us to test these boundaries in order for us to know the limits, we are still expected to develop enough self-control so that we will avoid getting into trouble. According to **social control theory**, people who have strong social bonds and attachments in their community are less likely to engage in deviant behavior. In his book *Causes of Delinquency*, Travis

**Zone of permitted variation** A social space around a boundary where rules can be contested.

**Social control theory** A theory that people who have strong social bonds and attachments in their community are less likely to engage in deviant behavior.

**PAIRED CONCEPTS**

## Solidarity and Conflict

### The Moral Panic over Hoarding

Sociologist and criminologist Stanley Cohen defines a **moral panic** as a situation in which a "condition, episode, a person or group of persons emerges to become defined as a threat to societal values and interests" (Cohen 2002: 1). According to Cohen, moral panics have a number of common features, and they develop in a similar way. First, there is an event that captures public attention and gets defined as a serious threat to society. The sense of danger increases when "moral crusaders" enter the scene and begin to demonize the offenders and stoke the sense of outrage. Moral crusaders are important because they manufacture a feeling of public danger that is out of proportion to the actual threat (Hall et al. 1978). This encourages media to sensationalize the story. Politicians and law enforcement further help to define the threat and to suggest solutions. The public follows along closely, swept up in the excitement and drama. Interest in the episode eventually subsides but not before reinforcing specific cultural values and marking the limits of social tolerance.

Hoarding during a pandemic is a good example of a social problem that entered the public consciousness as moral panic in 2020. To be sure, hoarding has been recognized as a psychological disorder since 2013, and it reportedly affects 1 in 14 Americans (Mathews 2020; Birchall and Cronkwright 2020). The widespread panic buying and individual hoarding that occurred in the early days and weeks of the COVID-19 pandemic were interpreted as a predictable response to the pandemic crisis and to the lockdowns and stay-at-home orders that were put into effect. Moral sensibilities were far more outraged by those seeking to profit from the pandemic. This is when hoarding became a public threat.

A moral panic over hoarding began after reports in March 2020 that unscrupulous entrepreneurs were purchasing and stockpiling medical supplies like hand sanitizer and face masks and then reselling these items at inflated prices. In one example, the *New York Times* reported that Matt Colvin and his brother Noah amassed supplies of hand sanitizer and antibacterial wipes by purchasing all the supplies they could find in Tennessee and Kentucky from big box stores as well as small country stores (Nicas 2020a). They began to acquire these supplies after the first death from coronavirus in the United States was announced on March 1, 2020.

As the pandemic deepened and the death rate climbed, regulators, customers, and politicians began to redefine resellers like the Colvins as unethical price gougers and as threats to the public good. The *New York Times* reported an angry social response online, including hate mail and death threats. The article also quoted one nurse as saying to the brothers, "'You're being selfish, hoarding resources for your own personal gain." By mid-March, Amazon released a statement saying, "Price gouging is a clear violation of our policies, unethical, and in some areas, illegal . . . [I]n addition to terminating these third party accounts, we welcome the opportunity to work directly with states attorneys general to prosecute bad actors." As a state investigation of price gouging by the Colvins began, the brothers opted to donate their stockpile of sanitizer and other supplies to a local church to distribute to people in need in Tennessee (Nicas 2020b). The state also saw one-third of the reserve of hand sanitizer distributed in Kentucky.

By mid-April, journalists reported, the case against the Colvin brothers was closed, although similar stories about fraud and price gouging were reported in California and Georgia (Vigdor 2020a; Fazio 2020). The Colvins had avoided prosecution and a fine, but they would not be permitted to recoup the money they had spent on their sanitizer stockpile. The brothers had expressed public remorse, and the *New York Times* quoted Tennessee attorney general Herbert H. Slatery III, who stated, "Disrupting necessary supplies during an unprecedented pandemic is a serious offense. . . . It became clear during our investigation that the Colvins realized this, and their prompt cooperation and donation led to an outcome that actually benefited some consumers" (Vigdor 2020b).

**PAIRED CONCEPTS CONTINUED**

**Hoarding**
Early in the COVID-19 pandemic in the United States, shoppers depleted shelves of basics such as toilet paper and hand sanitizer. Their hoarding behavior meant that many others found it difficult to purchase necessities.

The article went on to cite a Tennessee price-gouging law against charging unreasonable prices for essential goods during a disaster, and reported on President Trump's executive order to investigate and prosecute cases of price gouging and hoarding during the pandemic.

The moral panic over hoarding as a public threat slowly subsided during the summer of 2020 as regulators and producers of supplies began to manage demand for their products. Newspaper coverage of hoarding turned to how food producers and other suppliers were managing the surge in demand for shelf-stable supplies during the third coronavirus surge as the United States entered the holiday season in fall 2020 (Querolo and Patton 2020).

**ACTIVE LEARNING**

**Discuss:** Who benefits from the creation of a moral panic? In the given example of hoarding during a pandemic, who and what were the threats to the public? Who were the villains in the story? Who were the heroes?

---

**Moral panic**
A situation in which a "condition, episode, a person or group of persons emerges to become defined as a threat to societal values and interests" (Cohen 2002: 1).

Hirschi argued that people who have strong bonds with their parents and their schools were much more likely to follow the rules because they would not want to jeopardize those relationships by engaging in deviant behavior (Hirschi 1969). In other words, Hirschi argued, it is not enough simply to know the rules. We also have to care about how breaking the rules will damage our relationships with other people. Too much deviant behavior can be an indicator that people do not have strong enough attachments to society.

Deviance can also serve to bring people together. As Durkheim argued, deviant acts arouse strong collective feelings among the people who believe that important social norms are being violated. This shared collective indignation creates social solidarity (Durkheim [1893] 2014). When people hear news about identity theft, cyberbullying, or drug use, their concern is not only for themselves or their families. They worry about where their society is headed. In COVID times, they discuss the issue of toilet paper hoarding with their friends, neighbors, and casual acquaintances. People may even attend a community meeting or join a civic group to try to deal with a perceived social threat. All of this serves to reinforce their bond with the larger society.

**DEVIANCE AND SOCIAL CHANGE.** Many of history's great innovators and revolutionaries were viewed as deviant people in their own societies. As a child, the Nobel Prize–winning physicist Albert Einstein was constantly getting in trouble with his teachers, who thought he was lazy and irresponsible. The civil rights leader Martin Luther King Jr. was targeted for years by the FBI, branded as a communist by southern politicians, and ultimately assassinated.

The link between deviance and innovation is not surprising. Innovation happens when people think differently, push boundaries, and try things that are neither normal nor expected. This does not mean that all deviance leads to constructive innovation. If somebody cuts in front of you in line, this does not make them a revolutionary; they may just be an inconsiderate jerk. But if everybody followed the rules, societies would never change. Some rule-breaking behavior ends up making society function more effectively.

In order to explain how deviance can lead to changes that improve society, Durkheim turned to the theory of evolution. Plants and animals are constantly mutating; over time a species adopts the changes that help them to survive better. The same thing happens in society, where other individuals and groups adopt innovative deviance. The challenge is that we can usually only recognize innovative deviance after the fact. If society were able to eliminate all deviant behavior, it would not only be eliminating the inconsiderate behavior of unpleasant people. It would also be eliminating the future Einsteins and Kings.

**Deviance and social change: The 1963 March on Washington**
Law enforcement officials targeted Martin Luther King Jr. as a criminal, but his social protests received broad social support and they are now remembered as positive acts of social change and social justice in the civil rights movement. Here, King marches with colleagues on August 28, 1963.

**DEVIANT SUBCULTURES.** People who push boundaries and break rules may feel threatened by the negative attention they receive, but they can also receive social support and encouragement if they are part of a **deviant subculture**. As we discussed in Chapter 3, members of a subculture set themselves apart as being different from the larger mainstream culture of the society. Because subcultures emphasize their differences from the larger society, it is not surprising that many of their behaviors get labeled as deviant. However, deviant subcultures can also be trend-setters and sources of social innovation.

According to sociologist Claude Fischer (1975), deviant subcultures spread with the growth of cities. Because cities have more diverse populations,

**Deviant subculture** A group of people who set themselves apart as being different from the larger mainstream culture of the society.

## PAIRED CONCEPTS: Power and Resistance

### What's Wrong with Graffiti?

Graffiti refers to unauthorized writings or drawings that appear in public places. While archaeologists have found examples of graffiti in the ruins from ancient Greece, modern forms of graffiti emerged in the 1960s, as a form of illicit street art displayed in urban areas (Snyder 2009).

In New York, graffiti became part of a subcultural art scene. It developed into a form of cultural and political expression where outsider artists (i.e., people who were not recognized as artists by museums and galleries) could gain recognition. Modern graffiti took three main forms: tags, which are the artist's signature; throw-ups, which consist of two-color outlined text; and pieces, which are more ambitious multicolor murals. Graffiti artists competed with each other to place their work in the most visible places, such as subway cars, train tunnels, bridges, and freeway overpasses. Some of the most highly regarded graffiti artists became famous, and the subcultural movement spread to cities around the world.

But graffiti was considered vandalism by law enforcement authorities, who perceived that criminals were defacing property they did not own. By 1980, police departments around the country began to crack down on graffiti writers (Austin 2001). In 1995 the mayor of New York City created a task force to stamp out graffiti, arguing that the presence of graffiti caused more crime. Between 1995 and 2005, the Anti-Graffiti Task Force has made more than 2,800 arrests in New York City.

But the attempt to control and eliminate graffiti has met with resistance. Graffiti artists continue to do their work, despite arrests and despite repeated instances where the authorities paint over their work. The art community has also challenged the assertion that graffiti is equivalent to vandalism. Instead, they argue, graffiti is a legitimate form of artistic expression, worthy of being shown in museums and art galleries. Graffiti artists have benefited from this artistic credibility, and many of them have translated this credibility into successful careers as professional artists and designers. In some cities, the local government has even decided to encourage graffiti artists instead of prosecuting them. In Melbourne, Australia, for example, there are approved outdoor locations throughout the city where graffiti is both allowed and encouraged. Aiming to become the street art capital of the world, Melbourne sees graffiti as an important part of the tourist economy. These images of respectability challenge the earlier attempts to define graffiti as a deviant subculture and a problem to be eliminated.

**Art or vandalism?**
This wall mural in Flushing, New York, celebrating neighborhood diversity, is clearly a work of art. There are different interpretations of graffiti. Do you think all graffiti is art?

### ACTIVE LEARNING

**Think about it:** While most cities have laws against graffiti, this type of art is also widely available for sale, in art galleries as well as through online art websites. Can you think of other examples of activities that are defined by law as illegal but that are also widely available for sale and are part of contemporary culture?

their inhabitants are more likely to find unconventional and innovative subcultures than they would in smaller, more homogenous towns. These subcultures allow individuals to create community that is deliberately set apart from "normal" society. It is for this reason that artists, intellectuals, students, political dissidents, and other experimental communities have tended to congregate in cities. Deviant subcultures still feel social pressure to conform, but they have more social supports to resist these pressures. At the same time, ironically, creative urban subcultures contribute to the hipster vibe that so often leads to gentrification of urban neighborhoods, making it progressively harder for the subcultural participants to afford to live in the community (Moss, McIntosh, and Prasiuk 2023).

Deviant subcultures embrace their difference from the larger society, and they help people resist the strong social pressures to conform. In some cases, as we saw with the example of graffiti, they actively challenge the idea that they are engaging in deviant behavior, by offering new interpretations about what they are doing (e.g., graffiti is not vandalism but art). Today, social media make it easier than ever to create and sustain deviant subcultures that challenge social conformity.

**Yakuza boss with his champion fighting dog**
The yakuza is a Japanese crime syndicate whose subculture includes elaborate social rituals that define group life. This includes dog fighting, which has deep roots in yakuza culture.

Not all deviant subcultures are committed to innovation or to expanding the boundaries of what is considered "normal." The Italian mafia, the Japanese yakuza, the Chinese triads, and other crime syndicates around the world have elaborate initiation ceremonies and strict codes of conduct that bond their members together and help them to coordinate their activities. The same is true of hate groups such as the Ku Klux Klan and the Aryan Brotherhood. These groups are also deviant subcultures.

## The Social Construction of Deviance

Normal and deviant behaviors are both socially constructed. There is quite a lot of cultural variation, and things that are considered deviant in some places are treated as normal in other places. Specific individuals and organizations have more power than others to label things as deviant. And different societies use different strategies to deal with deviance, such as punishment, banishment, education, treatment, and medical intervention.

**The Moulin Rouge Bar and Sex Shop, Amsterdam**
Compared to most other countries, the Netherlands has a relatively high tolerance for deviance and has a well-developed and legal red-light district.

### DEVIANCE AND CULTURAL VARIATION.

The identification of deviance depends on the social context. Even within the same society, the definition of the normal and the deviant is always changing. While the definition of deviance varies from one society to another, there are some general historical and cross-cultural patterns that we can identify.

Most societies make distinctions between "everyday deviance" and more serious behaviors. Serious threats like violent crime spark the kind of collective indignation that produces moral panics. But a typical encounter with deviance is more likely to make us annoyed than afraid (Smith, Philips, and King 2010). Somebody bumps into us in the crowd, talks too loudly, uses inappropriate language, or cuts in front of us in line. We may give them a disapproving stare, but we don't call the police or alert the media. We get annoyed about the social boundaries that are being violated, but we get over it.

While deviance exists in all societies, there are still differences in how much behavior a given society will define as deviant, as well as the amount of tolerance there will be for deviant behavior. In a study of 33 nations, Gelfand et al. (2011) found patterned differences between "tight" and "loose" societies. In tight societies, such as India, Malaysia, and Singapore, there are rigid social norms and a low tolerance for deviant behavior. In contrast, loose societies, such as Brazil, Israel, and the Netherlands, have flexible social norms and a high tolerance for deviant actions.

Large-scale historical changes also influence the social construction of deviance. For example, the rise of democracy (Chapter 13) encouraged people to emphasize the importance of individual rights and freedoms and to view actions that violated individual rights as deserving of criticism and punishment. The point is that what is considered deviant changes across time and place. This is an example of cultural relativism (Chapter 3).

### THE POWER TO CALL THINGS DEVIANT.

During our childhood and adolescent socialization, our families and schools have the power to define behavior as either normal or deviant. Schools teach a hidden curriculum that consists of all the different rules of behavior we need to learn to function effectively in the school and the larger society (Giroux and Purpel 1983). The hidden curriculum teaches us that there are consequences for being late, for being disrespectful, and for not doing work that is assigned to us (Chapter 4). These understandings of normal and deviant behavior are intended to help us become successful in our adult lives, and they are similar to the social expectations that we will find in the workplace.

Mass media and social media also have considerable power to label things as deviant. It often appears that the media are obsessed with crime, violence, and other forms of deviance. Nearly one-quarter of all local news stories are about crime and deviance (Graber 1980; Lotz 1991; see Heath and Gilbert 1996 for a review). Media present a limited and distorted view of crime and deviance, focusing on certain kinds of behaviors and offenders while ignoring others. There is a disproportionate emphasis on violent behavior, despite the fact that the vast majority of crime and deviance does not involve violence (Reiner, Livingstone, and Allen 2003). Black men in the city are overrepresented by the media as offenders and underrepresented as victims (Gilliam and Iyengar 2000; Weiss and Chermak 1998; Yanich 2016).

Media representations of crime also point to the role that ideology plays in the social construction of deviance. The behavior of poor and powerless people is much more likely to be called deviant than the behavior of privileged people. In fact, depending on the social context and the people involved, the exact same behavior can be treated as normal for one person but deviant for another. People hardly notice a man dressed in work clothes having a beer after work in an outdoor cafe. But a homeless person drinking the same beer on a park bench one hundred feet away will get treated as a panhandler and a vagrant and risks arrest for drinking in public (Satran 2013).

**Media effects**
Media coverage often portrays a world of random victimization, in which everybody is at risk. Media have enormous power to label things as deviant and shape public understandings of social issues.

**Primary deviance** A deviant act or behavior that does not result in the person adopting an identity as a deviant person.

**Secondary deviance** A deviant act or behavior that occurs when a person has taken on the role of the deviant person.

**Labeling theory** A theory that people become deviant when they are labeled as deviant people.

**Stigma** A form of dishonor, discredit, or shame associated with illness or deviance; a spoiled identity.

**DEVIANCE AND SOCIAL STIGMA.** While we all engage in deviant behavior at different times in our lives, not all of us become deviant people. Many acts of deviance go almost completely unnoticed, with little or no impact on the person engaging in the deviant behavior. Pedestrians will often cross the street illegally if there are no cars on the road, but this does not make them more likely to commit future acts of deviance. As many as 75 percent of college students admit to having cheated at some point during school, but they rationalize it as normal behavior that all students do at some point (Shrader, Kaufmann, and Ravenscroft 2006; Burgason, Sefiha and Briggs 2019). These isolated behaviors are called **primary deviance** because they do not result in the person adopting an identity as a deviant person. Primary deviance is not a strong predictor of future rule-breaking behavior. On the other hand, if the person is breaking the rules because they have taken on the role of the deviant person, sociologists refer to this behavior as **secondary deviance**. Secondary deviance does increase the chances that a person will participate in subsequent (and often more serious) forms of rule-breaking behavior (Lemert 1967; Liberman, Kirk and Kim 2014).

In seeking the causes of secondary deviance, sociologists emphasize the role of social factors. According to Howard Becker, secondary deviance is created by social groups, who focus on the rule-breaking behavior of particular people and then label those people as outsiders who need to be controlled (Becker 1963). This is the central insight of **labeling theory**, which argues that people become deviant because they are labeled as deviant people. In other words, society not only focuses on problematic behavior like dishonesty, theft, and rudeness; it also identifies problematic people, who get labeled as liars, thieves, and jerks. If everybody around you labels you as a jerk, you start thinking about yourself as a jerk, and you embrace the behavior associated with that identity.

Once the deviant label has been successfully applied to a person, the label becomes a **stigma**, or a spoiled identity that the person so labeled has to manage in their everyday lives. According to Erving Goffman (1963), people who have been stigmatized as deviants spend considerable energy trying to manage their spoiled identity. They are aware that discovery of their stigma can be dangerous in many social situations because it is likely to mean that they are treated worse than "normal" people.

For people who are arrested and sent to prison, the mark of a criminal record is a stigma that shapes the rest of their lives. The stigma of being in prison creates strong feelings of shame and anger, for the people who go to jail as well as for their families (Hagan and Dinovitzer 1999). Employers are much less likely to hire an ex-prisoner than a job applicant who has similar job skills and credentials but no criminal record (Holzer 1996; Graffam, Shinkfield and Hardcastle 2008). This places even greater stress on ex-prisoners and their families, leading to significantly higher rates of divorce for families where the husband has gone to prison (Western and McLanahan 2000). There is also a racial dimension, with the stigma of prison being worse for Black men than it is for other ex-prisoners (Pager 2003).

Stigma is not only an issue for criminals and violent offenders. Despite public opinion surveys that find greater public tolerance of divorce now than in the past, research by Gerstel (1987) finds that divorced men and women still find themselves being excluded and devalued in many social settings. Many report that married couples stop inviting them to parties and tend to avoid them in informal social settings. Others dread having to tell their friends that the marriage has ended, and they find themselves retreating from the social groups where they used to spend their time. Over time, many find themselves gravitating toward other people who have been divorced, who understand what they are going through and who can share similar stories.

**THE MEDICALIZATION OF DEVIANCE.** Another response to deviance is to deal with it as a form of illness that should be treated by medical professionals. As we discuss in Chapter 12, medicalization means that many challenges people face get defined as illnesses that require medication, surgery, or some other kind of medical intervention (Conrad 2007). For example, people who are disorganized, chronically late, and having trouble concentrating are now diagnosed with adult attention deficit disorder and prescribed a combination of behavioral and drug therapies. Increasingly, people turn to doctors, therapists, and the pharmaceutical industry to try to improve themselves or at least to become more "normal."

In their book *Deviance and Medicalization*, Peter Conrad and Joseph Schneider show how the process of medicalization began as an attempt by the medical establishment to treat deviance and to rehabilitate deviant individuals (Conrad and Schneider 1992). Madness was redefined as mental illness in the early 19th century, and by 1900 psychiatry had developed as the science of mental disease. In the United States, the National Institute of Mental Health was established in 1949. Alcoholism began to be redefined as an illness in the 1940s and opiate addiction, in the 1960s. Mental disorders stemming from child abuse were defined during the 1960s and 1970s.

Because our beliefs about deviance are socially constructed and often change over time, the medicalization of deviance carries significant risks. When society becomes more tolerant of behaviors that were once considered deviant, the medical interventions that were originally intended to "cure" people are revealed as unnecessary and cruel actions that destroyed peoples' lives. In fact, as Conrad (2007) shows, this was the experience that gay people suffered for decades. Homosexuality was deeply stigmatized by psychiatrists in 1952, when it was listed as a sociopathic personality disturbance in the

*Diagnostic and Statistical Manual of Mental Disorders* (DSM). Throughout the 1950s and 1960s, medical professionals used a variety of different behavioral therapies to try to "cure" gay people. In the 1970s, though, gay activists began to challenge psychiatrists about this diagnosis of homosexuality, and by 1987 the classification of homosexuality as a disorder was removed from the DSM. By this time, unfortunately, thousands of individuals had been subjected to dangerous and unnecessary medical interventions. In fact, even today many gay, lesbian, and transgender people continue to be subjected to medical and behavioral interventions seeking to "cure" their behavior, despite the fact that the changes to the DSM were made nearly forty years ago.

## 5.2 Crime

**LG 5.2** Distinguish different categories of crime and the challenges of measuring crime.

**Laws** Attempts by governments to establish formal systems of rules about how people are allowed to behave, as well as a system of punishments for when they break those rules.

**Criminal justice system** All the government agencies that are charged with finding and punishing people who break the law.

**Civil law** Law that deals with disputes between individuals and organizations. Most legal cases are civil cases.

Crime is a special category of deviant behavior, which is defined and regulated by law. **Laws** are attempts by governments to establish a formal system of rules about how people are allowed to behave, as well as a system of punishments for when they break those rules. The **criminal justice system** consists of all the government agencies that are charged with finding and punishing people who break the law. This includes the legislators who make the laws, the courts that determine if a person is guilty of committing a crime, and the correctional authorities who are responsible for punishing the guilty offenders.

Not all law-breaking behavior is defined as crime. The majority of legal cases are regulated by **civil law**, which is law that deals with disputes between individuals and organizations. Civil cases are filed by private parties rather than by the government. They still take place in the courts, but instead of focusing on punishing the wrongdoer, civil cases are concerned with restitution, which usually comes in the form of financial compensation paid to the aggrieved party. Examples of civil cases include things like property disputes, custody proceedings, and medical malpractice suits. As Emile Durkheim pointed out in *The Division of Labor in Society* ([1893] 2014), civil cases are much more common than criminal cases in modern society.

While civil cases are more common, it is the criminal cases that get the most public attention. The goal of a criminal case is to punish the offending person, to make a strong public display that will discourage others from engaging in the same kind of behavior, and to reassure the public that the most serious forms of deviance will not be tolerated. As we have seen, media coverage of criminal cases can produce the kind of public outrage and indignation that is often associated with moral panics.

## CAREERS

### The Criminal Justice Field

Careers in the criminal justice field have always been one of the most popular destinations for undergraduates who major in sociology, and there is evidence that this interest is increasing (Senter et al. 2015). A survey of sociology majors found that 7.7 percent of them planned to pursue careers in criminal justice after they graduated (Spalter-Roth et al. 2006: 33). An additional 11 percent plan to go to law school, where many of them will pursue careers as prosecuting attorneys and defense attorneys.

The job of police officer is one of the most common in criminal justice. Key duties of police officers include patrolling, traffic control, assisting with fire and medical emergencies, investigating accidents and crime scenes, testifying in court hearings, and participating in public safety awareness campaigns. Jobs for police officers are relatively plentiful in communities nationwide.

Many sociology graduates who concentrate in criminal justice take jobs as probation officers, parole officers, and correctional treatment specialists. Correctional treatment specialists work with prisoners to develop rehabilitation and treatment plans. They develop educational and training plans to improve job skills, and they determine whether any mental health counseling or drug treatment is necessary. They make recommendations about release, and they develop rehabilitation and treatment plans that will continue after the prisoner is released. Parole officers work with prisoners after they have been released, to increase the likelihood that they will have a successful return to society. They meet regularly with the ex-prisoners and their families, they provide counseling, and they ensure that the conditions of release are being followed. Probation officers also supervise people who have been placed on probation instead of being sent to prison. They meet regularly with the offenders, making sure that they are meeting the conditions of their probation, that they are not a danger to their community, and that they are progressing in their rehabilitation and treatment.

Sociology majors also pursue research-based careers in criminal justice. They work as crime analysts in local police departments, as social scientists in state departments of criminal justice services, and as research analysts in federal departments such as the FBI and the Department of Justice. These jobs require strong quantitative research skills and typically graduate-level training in sociology.

For sociology majors who go to law school, there are many opportunities to practice criminal law. Criminal defense attorneys represent their defendants in criminal courts at the federal, state, and local levels. They can work for private law firms, or they can work for the state, as public defenders. Prosecuting attorneys work for the government, trying to secure convictions against people charged with committing crimes. For both prosecuting and defense attorneys, their work involves collecting police reports, interviewing witnesses, examining the crime scene, looking for additional evidence, performing legal research, and preparing for court trials.

Finally, there are roles in organizations advocating for prisoners and their families both within and outside the formal system of criminal justice. They include jobs as social workers, researchers, lawyers, and policy-makers. Organizations such as the Sentencing Project, the American Civil Liberties Union, the Equal Justice Initiative, and the Prison Activist Resource Center are all committed to providing legal and social resources for prisoners and their families. They also are involved in thinking about alternative models, such as restorative justice models, that avoid the negative consequences and stigma of the current system of incarceration.

#### ACTIVE LEARNING

**Find out:** Go to the library or look online and find two entry-level job ads for a career in the criminal justice field. What are the duties and responsibilities needed for the jobs? What characteristics or qualities would recommend you as a good candidate for these jobs?

## Categories of Crime

From 1930 to 2020, the FBI summarized crime statistics for the United States in the Uniform Crime Reports (UCR). UCR data come from law enforcement agencies around the country and are divided into Part I offenses and Part II offenses (Table 5.1).

Part I offenses are considered to be the most serious crimes that occur regularly and that are likely to be reported by the police. Homicide, aggravated assault, forcible rape, and robbery (i.e., stealing something by using force or the threat of violence) are defined as **violent crime**. Burglary (entering a home or business to commit theft), motor vehicle theft, larceny (other forms of theft), and arson are defined as **property crime**.

Property crime is much more common than violent crime. As Table 5.1 shows, the violent crime rate peaked in 1991 and has been gradually declining since then. The property crime rate peaked in 1980 and has been declining consistently since 1991. According to Richard Rosenfeld, the declining crime rate was sudden, unexpected, and significant; by the year 2000, in fact, the homicide and burglary rates had fallen to a lower level than at any time since the 1960s (Rosenfeld 2002: 25).

There are several factors that help to explain why the crime rate has fallen since the 1990s:

- The aging population meant that after 1980 there were fewer young people. This was an important factor because older people are less likely to commit serious crimes (Rosenfeld 2002: 27).
- Economic growth during the 1990s helped to reduce unemployment and gave people better opportunities for finding legal work (Rosenfeld 2002: 30).
- The market for drugs began to shrink after 1990 (particularly the market for crack cocaine), which led to a reduction in firearm violence in the inner cities (Rosenfeld 2002: 28–29).
- Changes in police practices—such as targeted policing of high-crime areas and the use of DNA evidence—have led to more effective crime prevention (Telep and Weisburd 2012).
- A massive increase in the size of the prison population (Levitt 2004).

While most social science research and public attention focus on Part I offenses, the UCR also collected data for crimes that are considered to be less serious and are defined as Part II offenses. Part II offenses include the following categories: simple assault (i.e., where no weapon is used), forgery and counterfeiting, fraud, embezzlement, buying or receiving stolen property, vandalism, illegal possession of a weapon, prostitution, sex offenses, drug abuse violations, gambling, driving under the influence, violation of liquor laws, drunkenness,

**Violent crime**
Defined by the Uniform Crime Reporting Program as homicide, aggravated assault, rape, and robbery.

**Property crime**
Defined by the Uniform Crime Reporting Program as burglary (entering a home or business to commit theft), motor vehicle theft, larceny (other forms of theft), and arson.

**TABLE 5.1** Crime rates, per 100,000 Inhabitants, 1994–2019

| YEAR | VIOLENT CRIME RATE | PROPERTY CRIME RATE |
| --- | --- | --- |
| 1994 | 713.6 | 4,660.2 |
| 1995 | 684.5 | 4,590.5 |
| 1996 | 636.6 | 4,451.0 |
| 1997 | 611.0 | 4,316.3 |
| 1998 | 567.6 | 4,052.5 |
| 1999 | 523.0 | 3,743.6 |
| 2000 | 506.5 | 3,618.3 |
| 2001[1] | 504.5 | 3,658.1 |
| 2002 | 494.4 | 3,630.6 |
| 2003 | 475.8 | 3,591.2 |
| 2004 | 463.2 | 3,514.1 |
| 2005 | 469.0 | 3,431.5 |
| 2006 | 479.3 | 3,346.6 |
| 2007 | 471.8 | 3,276.4 |
| 2008 | 458.6 | 3,214.6 |
| 2009 | 431.9 | 3,041.3 |
| 2010 | 404.5 | 2,945.9 |
| 2011 | 387.1 | 2,905.4 |
| 2012 | 387.8 | 2,868.0 |
| 2013 | 367.9 | 2,730.7 |
| 2014 | 361.6 | 2733.6 |
| 2015 | 373.7 | 2574.1 |
| 2016 | 386.6 | 2500.5 |
| 2017 | 383.8 | 2451.6 |
| 2018 | 370.4 | 2209.8 |
| 2019 | 366.7 | 2109.9 |

[1] The murder and non-negligent homicides that occurred as a result of the events of September 11, 2001, are not included in this table.

Source: FBI: UCR 2020.

Note: From 2021 forward summary homicide data is based on the National Incident-Based Reporting System (NIBRS). Along with the National Crime Victimization Survey (NCVS) will be used to provide a fuller picture of violent crime in the United States. (Morgan and Thompson 2022). See also the Federal Bureau of Investigation Crime Data Explorer.

disorderly conduct, vagrancy, and loitering. Data for Part II offenses only include those cases where arrests are actually made, which presents an inaccurate and distorted picture of how often those crimes are committed. In fact, social scientists have criticized all of the UCR data for presenting an inaccurate

## METHODS AND INTERPRETATION

# Measuring the Crime Rate

In the United States the **crime rate** is defined as the number of criminal offenses that are committed per 100,000 people 18 years or older in the population. The violent crime rate and the property crime rate have both declined since the 1990s. In 2020, the violent crime rate was 398.5 offenses per 100,000 population, and the property crime rate was estimated at 1958.2 offenses per 100,000 population. Crime rates are not uniform, and some places have higher crime rates than others. Memphis, Tennessee, had a violent crime rate of 1358 per 100,000 population in 2020, but in Irvine, California, the violent crime rate was only 32 per 100,000 population.

The crime rate is not a perfect measurement, because it does not measure all the crimes that actually take place. Crimes like murder, aggravated assault, auto theft, and arson are more likely to be reported and investigated by the police, while crimes like buying stolen property, vandalism, and gambling are much less likely to be reported or investigated. International comparisons are nearly impossible to make, because the police in different countries have different levels of resources and community trust. In Mexico, for example, it has been estimated that fewer than 25 percent of crimes are reported to the police (Edmonds-Poli and Shirk 2012). Even within the same country, the quality of the crime data that is collected can vary. Some cities do a better job of identifying crime than others, and some cities enjoy more trust among their citizens than others. These differences influence the quality of crime data. It is important to realize that all crime rates are estimates.

In the United States, the Department of Justice has historically used two strategies to estimate the crime rate. The first was the UCR Summary Reporting Program (phased out in 2021). Data for the UCR came from nearly eighteen thousand city, county, state, tribal, federal, and university law enforcement agencies, which voluntarily reported data on crimes that were brought to their attention. The FBI examined the reports that came in, looking for large deviations that might indicate errors. Beginning in 1988, the UCR began converting to a National Incident-Based Reporting System (NIBRS), in an effort to standardize the data collection effort and to collect more information about each incident. The NIBRS system reported a far wider range of crimes and included data on hate crimes and a wider range of detail on each crime incident.

Recognizing that not all criminal offenses were reported or entered into the UCR, the Bureau of Justice Statistics also began the National Criminal Victimization Survey (NCVS) in 1973. The survey continues to be conducted twice yearly, using a nationally representative sample of forty-three thousand households. Households stay in the sample for three years. The survey collects data on all the crime that the household experienced, regardless of whether the incident was reported to the police. In addition to the information about the victims, the offenders, and the crimes that were committed, the survey also covers questions about the experience victims had with the criminal justice system, the self-protective measures that the household uses, and the reasons that victims give for reporting or not reporting a crime. This allows researchers to estimate the proportion of each crime type that is reported to the police. It also allows researchers to track changing public attitudes toward crime and the police.

### ACTIVE LEARNING

**Find out:** Go to the Federal Bureau of Investigation's Crime Data Explorer site and look at rates of violent crime over time. Do you notice any patterns? Can you compare your local level of crime with national rates?

and distorted measure of the crime rate because they only include those criminal cases that the police know about and decide to investigate and therefore only capture a proportion of all crime (Anderson 2015: 23–25).

Another category of crime is **hate crime**, which refers to violence and intimidation against people because of their race, ethnicity, national origin, religion, gender identity, sexual orientation, or disability. Attempts to prevent and punish hate crimes began as early as 1871 in the United States, with the passage of the Ku Klux Klan Act that was designed to fight white supremacy organizations after the end of the American Civil War. The 1968 Civil Rights Act also contained provisions designed to prevent hate crimes by making it illegal to hurt or intimidate someone on the basis of their race, religion, or national origin. Protections for sexual orientation and disability were added in the 1980s. The Hate Crimes Statistics Act was passed in 1989, which required the Department of Justice to collect and publish data on hate crimes. In 1994, two additional hate crime laws were passed: the Violence against Women Act, which authorized special police units and prosecutors focused on gender-related hate crimes, and the Hate Crimes Sentencing Enhancement Act, which authorized harsher sentences for hate crimes compared with other violent crimes (Grattet and Jenness 2001).

The most recent data from the FBI show that there were 11,447 single-bias hate crimes reported in 2023, which affected 13,857 victims. In addition, there were 415 multiple-bias incidents that involved 559 victims. As Table 5.2 shows, the top three bias categories were race (52.5 percent), religion (22.5 percent), and sexual orientation (18.4 percent).

The final category of crime we will discuss is **white-collar crime**, which refers to financially motivated nonviolent crime, usually committed

**Crime rate** Calculated in the United States as the number of criminal offenses committed per 100,000 people in the population.

**Hate crime** Acts of violence and intimidation against people because of their race, ethnicity, national origin, religion, gender identity, sexual orientation, or disability.

**White-collar crime** Financially motivated, nonviolent crime, usually committed by business professionals in the course of doing their jobs.

**TABLE 5.2 Breakdown of Hate Crime: Bias Motivation Categoies for Vicitms of Single-Bias Incidents 2023**

| BIAS MOTIVATION | PERCENTAGE |
|---|---|
| Race/ethnicity/ancestry | 52.5% |
| Religion | 22.5% |
| Sexual orientation | 18.4% |
| Gender Identity | 4.1% |
| Disability | 1.6% |
| Gender | .09% |
| **Total** | 100% (11,447) |

Note: There were 415 multiple-bias incidents that involved 559 victims.
Source: FBI: UCR 2024.

by business professionals in the course of doing their jobs. Examples include accountants who embezzle money from their employer, financial advisors who steal money from their clients, and government workers who accept bribes.

White-collar crime may be nonviolent, but it causes enormous damage. In the United States, scholars estimate that one in every four households has been victimized by white-collar crime, with total financial losses of between $300 and $600 billion every year (Kane and Wall 2005; Wall-Parker 2019). While the average loss in a case of street robbery is about $1,000, the average loss in a case of embezzlement is $1 million (Payne 2011: 48). Single cases of white-collar crime can have a national and even a global economic impact. In one of the most infamous cases, when Bernard Madoff's fraudulent investment firm collapsed in 2008, the financial damages he caused were estimated at between $10 billion and $20 billion. Madoff's victims included banks, hospitals, universities, and charities around the world.

Today, new categories of white-collar crime are emerging, as an increasing proportion of economic transactions are coordinated through computer networks. **Cybercrime**, or crime conducted using computer networks, is today worth about $400 billion per year. "Phishing" attackers target more than one hundred thousand internet users every day, tricking people into giving away valuable personal information to criminals masquerading as friends, employers, government agencies, or other trustworthy groups. Another new type of computer fraud is ATM skimming, in which a small card-reading device is attached to an ATM machine in order to steal bank account information. These types of fraud often lead to **identity theft**, in which people use stolen personal and financial information to assume a person's identity in order to obtain credit and other financial advantages in that person's name. More than 25 million Americans were victims of identity theft in 2016, according to a report by the US Department of Justice (Harrell, 2019).

## Policing Crime

In modern societies, the **police** enforce the law, prevent crime, pursue and bring to justice people who break the law, and maintain social order. As an agent of the state, the police are one of the only groups in society (along with the military) that is authorized to use physical force or violence to achieve its objectives (Terpstra 2011). This places considerable moral responsibility on police officers, who are licensed to use coercion against citizens and to intrude on the private lives of others (Waddington 2002).

In order for someone to be labeled as a criminal, they first have to be pursued and apprehended by the police. Police are constantly making decisions about what crimes are worth pursuing, where crime is most likely to occur, when they should make an arrest, and when they should give a warning to people they find breaking the law (Rumbaut and Bittner 1979).

**Cybercrime** Crime conducted using computer networks.

**Identity theft** The use of stolen personal and financial information to assume a person's identity in order to obtain credit and other financial advantages in that person's name.

**Police** A group of people authorized to enforce the law, prevent crime, pursue and bring to justice people who break the law and maintain social order.

> **PAIRED CONCEPTS**
>
> ## Global and Local
>
> ### The Global Drug Trade
>
> While most police departments are organized at the local, state, or national level, crime does not always respect these boundaries. The illegal drug trade is a form of global crime which thrives despite the efforts of police forces around the world. The economic size of the illegal drug trade is difficult to assess but the most recent official estimates suggest that the global drug trade is a $300 billion industry, with most of the revenue coming from the sale of cannabis, cocaine, and opiates (United Nations 2020). North America accounts for 44 percent of all drug sales, followed by Europe (33 percent) and Asia (11 percent). In North America, per capita expenditure on illegal drugs is more than $300 per year.
>
> In a study of the heroin and cocaine trade, Peter Reuter found that there is a complicated global network linking production, distribution, and sales (Reuter 2009). Most of the production takes place in poor countries. Myanmar and Afghanistan produce 80 percent of the world's supply of opium. Bolivia, Colombia, and Peru produce all of the cocaine, with Colombia responsible for nearly two-thirds of all production.
>
> In his research, Reuter found that the actual producers and refiners of the drugs receive 2 percent or less of the revenues. The majority of the earnings go to a very large number of low-level retailers selling the drugs in wealthy countries located in North America and Europe. The largest fortunes are made by a small number of global cartels, who control the distribution of the drugs and supply the retailers located in wealthy nations.
>
> The global distribution networks have used a variety of strategies to avoid the efforts taken by local and national authorities to stop the flow of drugs. Drug cartels have come to exploit transnational immigrant networks as a way to coordinate their smuggling activities and to help avoid detection (Reuter 2009: 17). The ability to speak a non-native language makes it more difficult for local police to use wiretaps and helps the smuggling networks to avoid detection. The use of family networks makes it easier to identify and trust new recruits; references from family members already in the organization are more trustworthy, and the cartel can easily identify family members in the sending country they can hold hostage if the new recruit decides to steal money or drugs from the cartel. In other words, the global distribution networks rely on the existence of local networks connecting sending and receiving countries.
>
> **ACTIVE LEARNING:**
>
> **Think about it:** If drugs were to be decriminalized in the US, do you think that this would increase revenues that go to the producers and refiners of the drugs living in poor countries, or would the revenue just get transferred to US government agencies? Do you think that decriminalization would impact the global drug cartels?

Police also have to decide how they will divide up their time among their various responsibilities (Wilson 1968). After all, police provide many other services to the community in the course of their day.

Since the 1990s, the way that police set their priorities has been shaped by the **broken windows theory** of deviance. First described in a 1982 article by George Kelling and James Q. Wilson, the broken windows theory argues that ignoring small crimes and minor violations creates a spiral of increasing deviance and more serious criminality. In other words, if people

**Broken windows theory** A theory of policing that states that ignoring small crimes and minor violations creates a spiral of increasing deviance and more serious criminality.

see broken windows and graffiti in their neighborhood, they will assume that nobody cares about the community and that the neighborhood is unsafe. This becomes a self-fulfilling prophecy. If people stay off the streets, believing them to be unsafe, the streets will actually become more dangerous. The decreased levels of informal social control allow more serious crime to move into the neighborhood (Kelling and Wilson 1982).

Influenced by the broken windows theory, police began to focus on preventing less serious crime, as a way of creating a sense of social order and preventing more serious crime from developing. New York City adopted a "zero-tolerance" policy to policing in the 1990s, aggressively patrolling against graffiti, vandalism, begging, drunkenness, and disorderly behavior. Misdemeanor arrests increased by 70 percent, and more serious crime decreased. Police departments around the nation took notice and shifted their policing practices to try to follow New York City's success. While social scientists dispute how much of the crime reduction could be attributed to the new police practices, the general consensus is that they had a statistically significant impact (Messner et al. 2007).

Because police have so much discretion in their work, the decisions they make about where to look for crime and when to make arrests are hugely consequential. Often, these decisions reinforce existing relationships of privilege and inequality. Of particular concern is **racial profiling**, which refers to the police practice of targeting an individual because of their race or ethnicity. This is part of a more general process in which people are targeted by police and civilians for humiliating and harsh treatment because of their perceived race, ethnicity, national origin, or religion. Sociological research has shown that police are much more likely to treat people as potential criminals when they are patrolling in poor and minority communities, and they are much more likely to make arrests in those neighborhoods (Tomaskovic-Devey and Warren 2009). Police have long used race as an indicator of suspicion, targeting minorities for questioning and arrest (Kennedy 1997). In fact, racial profiling was a central part of policing for much of US history, used to control Black people during the period of slavery and

**Racial profiling**
A process in which people are targeted by police and civilians for humiliating and harsh treatment because of their perceived race, ethnicity, national origin, or religion.

**Broken windows theory**
The broken windows theory of policing assumes that smaller crimes like broken windows lead to more serious crimes. This theory resulted in more intensive policing in poorer communities and communities of color.

then used to reinforce racial segregation after the end of the US Civil War (Seigel 2017).

Today, Black people are overrepresented among those who are arrested, as annual data from the Department of Justice indicates. Though Black people were 13.6 percent of the US population in 2020, they made up 26.1 percent of all arrests. Particularly noteworthy is the disproportionate Black share of the arrests for drug violations (25 percent), disorderly conduct (29 percent), vagrancy (28 percent), and curfew and loitering violations (25 percent). Such arrests suggest how the broken windows theory of deviance has led to the targeting of Black communities.

Race influences police practices even more in routine traffic stops and encounters with pedestrians. A study of the New York Police Department found that 85 percent of all New Yorkers who were stopped and frisked between 2005 and 2008 were Black (Center for Constitutional Rights 2009). In the nation as a whole, research shows that Black drivers are more than twice as likely as white drivers to be arrested during a traffic stop, and they are nearly three times as likely to be subjected to a police search during a traffic stop (Durose, Smith, and Langan 2005). This phenomenon, which is sometimes referred to as "driving while Black," leads to fear, anger, humiliation, and distrust of police by many in the Black community (Harris 1999).

Racial bias in routine traffic stops is now well understood and well documented. The Pew Foundation reported in 2020, for example, that both Black and white Americans think "Black people are treated less fairly than whites in dealing with the police and by the criminal justice system as a whole." They also found that Black adults are about "five times as likely as whites to say they have been unfairly stopped by police because of their race or ethnicity." In this context, some states have begun to routinely audit data about traffic stops as a way to identify and prevent racial profiling. The results are uneven. In one well-documented case in Connecticut, for example, *The Connecticut Mirror* (2023) reported charges that Connecticut State Police troopers "falsified tens of thousands of traffic stop records submitted to the state's racial profiling data reporting program, potentially skewing the numbers to reflect more infractions for white drivers and fewer for Black and Hispanic motorists." This scandal indicates that despite an effort to stem police targeting of Black and Hispanic motorists, the practice continues.

In his book *Race, Crime, and the Law*, Randall Kennedy (1997) argues that racial targeting by the police ends up making Black communities more dangerous. The unwanted attention creates resentment and distrust by Black people toward the police. This leaves Black communities more isolated and more vulnerable to criminal victimization. There are also attendant health impacts for community members of racism and violence (National Academies of Sciences, Engineering, and Medicine, 2017).

## Surveillance

**Surveillance**
The practice of monitoring other people's activities, often by using video and other media technologies.

**Surveillance** refers to the practice of using technology to monitor people's activities. Popular culture tends to represent surveillance as a threat to society, portraying it as part of a dystopian future world in which citizens have every aspect of their lives monitored by the government.

Ideas about surveillance also come from historical writings about crime and deviance. Writing about prison design in the 1700s, the philosopher Jeremy Bentham described a "Panopticon," in which a single guard positioned in a tower could view inside every jail cell and monitor the activities of all the prisoners at all times. Prisoners would not be able to see into the guard's tower, but they would be aware that at any given moment they might be being watched. Because they could never know whether they were being watched, they would have to act as if they were being watched. As a result, Bentham argued, prisoners would end up policing themselves.

According to Michel Foucault, Bentham's ideas about the Panopticon created a new form of power in modern society, based on the principle of surveillance. We know that we are being watched, but we cannot see the people who are watching us, nor can we know when they are watching us. As a result, we have to act at all times as if we are being watched. Not surprisingly, Foucault argued, the principle of the Panopticon has been extended from prison design to many other spheres of life, such as work and education. Eventually, with the spread of closed-circuit cameras, the surveillance model of the Panopticon appeared in public spaces such as streets, airports, train stations, and shopping malls.

Research by sociologists and criminologists has found that the use of surveillance technologies is not a very good way to reduce crime. The place where video surveillance seems to be most effective is in parking lots, as a way of deterring vehicle theft (Welsh and Farrington 2009). Besides this specific use, though, studies in the United States and England have found consistently that the use of video surveillance does not have a statistically significant impact on crime (Welsh and Farrington 2009). A review of the National Security Agency's surveillance program found that it was not an essential tool for preventing terrorist attacks (Swire 2015).

## 5.3 Punishment

**Punishment**
A social response to deviance that controls both deviant behavior and the offender and that aims to protect the social group and its social standards.

**LG 5.3** Define different approaches to punishment, and analyze their effectiveness.

**Punishment** is a social response to deviance that controls the deviant behavior and the offender and that aims to protect the social group and its social standards. There is a social pressure to punish people who get labeled as deviant and even stronger pressure to punish people who are accused of committing a crime. But there is a lot of variation in how people get punished and what people think they are accomplishing when they punish deviants and criminal offenders.

## Punishment as a Public Display of Morality

For much of history, punishment was both a violent and a public event. Public executions were common well into the 19th century, and they were popular events attended by entire families (Smith 2008: 37–38). In France, the guillotine was used as the official form of public execution until 1939. Public executions by hanging lasted until 1939 in the United States.

According to Émile Durkheim ([1893] 2014), violent and public forms of punishment are a way for a community to express moral outrage toward acts that offend collective social values. By making the punishment public, the community is able to reinforce its moral beliefs in a way that also reaffirms the social solidarity that holds them together. Durkheim argued that this form of punishment would become less common in modern society because the type of organic solidarity that holds people together is based more on trust and interdependence between individuals than on similarity of life and shared experience. In modern, diverse societies, people no longer rely on their similarities or assume that they share all beliefs and values. In this situation, Durkheim argued, maintaining trust and interdependence requires a form of punishment that is more like conflict resolution, where the goal is restitution for the aggrieved party rather than the public punishment of the offending party.

Public forms of punishment became less common throughout the 19th and 20th centuries, as Durkheim predicted. Many people found public executions to be cruel and uncivilized, and they campaigned for a system of punishment that granted more

**The public hanging of Rainey Bethea, August 14, 1936, in Owensboro, Kentucky**
Punishment is a public display of morality. A huge crowd of over 15,000 people gathered to witness the public hanging of 26-year-old Rainey Bethea, a Black man found guilty of the rape and murder of a White woman, in 1936. Public outrage over the execution made Bethea's death the last public hanging by legal authorities in the United States.

dignity and respect toward criminals (Spierenberg 1984). Fearful that the crowds that attended public executions were unpredictable and often violent, government authorities decided that it would be safer and more effective to punish prisoners in private (Foucault 1995).

## Punishment and Treatment

**Rehabilitation**
An approach to punishment that seeks to improve the offenders and restore them to society.

Influenced by the medicalization of deviance, **rehabilitation** became an important part of punishment during the 20th century. Incarcerated people were encouraged to develop job skills and to work with medical professionals to resolve any psychological issues that might prevent a successful reintegration into society. People who were convicted of crimes often received sentences that mandated treatment for things like substance abuse, personality disorders, and impulse-control problems. The goal was to help them successfully re-enter society and to reduce the likelihood they would engage in future criminal behavior, or **criminal recidivism**.

**Criminal recidivism**
The likelihood that an incarcerated person will engage in future criminal behavior.

The goal of rehabilitation led many criminal justice systems to develop alternative systems of punishment. In the United States, the National Probation Act of 1925 allowed courts to sentence criminal offenders to probation instead of sending them to prison. A person who is placed on probation agrees to be subject to supervision by a probation officer and to follow the conditions of probation that are set by the court. Typical conditions include community service, regular meetings with the probation officer, periodic drug testing, avoiding certain people and places, and appearing in court during requested times. Violation of the conditions of probation can increase the probation time, result in fines, and in some cases result in probation being revoked and the person being sent to jail.

**Parole** A process through which prisoners who appear to have reformed themselves can earn an early release from their prison sentence.

Parole is another form of punishment that was designed to encourage rehabilitation. With **parole**, prisoners who appear to have reformed themselves can earn an early release from their prison sentence. Prisoners who earn parole have a period of probation after they are released, where they have to meet regularly with a parole officer and demonstrate that they are fully rehabilitated.

## Incarceration

**Incarceration**
A form of punishment in which the offender is confined in prison.

**Incarceration** is a form of punishment in which the offender is confined in prison. The modern prison developed during the 19th century, when an international prison reform movement proposed new standards in which prisoners would each be housed in a separate cell, receive healthy food and living conditions, and be watched over by professional guards (Smith 2008: 61–69). The prison reform movement was connected to the rehabilitation model and focused on education, vocational training, and psychiatric treatment.

**PAIRED CONCEPTS**

## Inequality and Privilege

### Punishment and Plea-Bargaining

Fewer than 10 percent of all criminal cases ever go to trial. Instead, they get resolved through **plea-bargaining**, in which the defendant pleads guilty to a lesser charge that has been negotiated by the prosecuting and defense attorneys (Devers 2011). In the United States, plea-bargaining has been the dominant form of resolving criminal cases since the 19th century (Fisher 2003). Plea-bargaining is an advantage for the criminal justice system because it reduces costs (Savitsky 2012). Plea-bargaining also benefits the prosecuting and defense attorneys because both parties to a plea-bargain count the outcome as a victory (Alschuler 1968, 1975). Prosecutors record a conviction, and defense attorneys can claim a lesser penalty than the defendant was charged with in the first place.

There are three kinds of criticisms that legal scholars and social scientists have made about plea-bargains (Alkon 2014). First, the plea-bargaining system is too coercive. Defendants are pressured to accept plea deals by police, by prosecutors, and even by their own attorneys, in a way that weakens their right to a fair trial. Second, plea-bargains largely eliminate the moral component of crime and punishment. For the accused, the plea bargain becomes a cynical game about getting the best deal, rather than an opportunity to make a confession of guilt or to fight for justice. For victims, the plea-bargain denies their opportunity to testify about how they were wronged and the opportunity to witness the sentencing and punishment of the offender.

The third (and most common) criticism of plea-bargaining is that it reinforces social inequality. The vast majority of poor defendants rely on court-appointed lawyers. These lawyers have huge caseloads and usually do not have enough time to consult with their clients in a meaningful way or to develop a defense strategy. Instead, they take the first plea deal that is offered to them, which is usually a worse deal than plea offers that are made to wealthier clients who have higher-priced attorneys representing them (Alkon 2014).

There is also an important racial dimension to plea-bargains. For example, in a study of misdemeanor marijuana arrests, researchers found that Black defendants were less likely to receive reduced-charge offers and more likely to receive plea-bargain offers that included jail time (Kutateladze, Tymas, and Crowley 2014). For defendants who had no prior record, Blacks and Latinos were less likely than White defendants to have felony charges against them dropped during the plea-bargaining process (Schmitt 1991). These structural differences lead to the disproportionate and unequal incarceration of racial minorities, in a way that dramatically increases social inequality. This is especially concerning given the massive increase in plea-bargaining over time and the fact that over 90 percent of criminal cases never go to trial (Clarke 2013).

**ACTIVE LEARNING**

**Think about it:** Do you think plea-bargaining is fair? Why? What would you do if you were charged with a crime with a very long sentence and were offered a plea-bargain that included a shorter amount of time in jail? How would you make the decision? Who would you talk to?

**Plea-bargaining**
A process in which a defendant pleads guilty to a lesser charge that has been negotiated by the prosecuting and defense attorneys

During the 1970s, the rehabilitation model of punishment was the subject of criticism by politicians as well as social scientists, who claimed that rehabilitation does not reduce criminal recidivism, that it weakens the deterrent effect of punishment, and that it ignores the structural causes of crime such as poverty and inequality (Sundt 2002). Many criminal justice systems

**TABLE 5.3** Incarceration Rate per 100,000 National Population, Selected Countries, 2023

| | |
|---|---|
| Australia | 167 |
| China | 119 |
| Canada | 104 |
| South Korea | 105 |
| France | 119 |
| Germany | 70 |
| Sweden | 73 |
| Japan | 37 |
| United States of America | 629 |

abandoned rehabilitation. The US Congress abolished parole in 1984, emphasizing instead longer and less flexible prison sentences (Clear 1994).

The end of parole and the emphasis on longer prison sentences has caused a significant increase in the prison population in the United States. In 1978, there were 294,400 prisoners in federal and state prisons in the United States; by 2009, this number had increased by a factor of five to 1,555,600 (Carson and Golinelli 2013). Today, the US prison population is more than 2 million, which is the largest in the world. The United States has a prison population rate of 629 prisoners per 100,000 of national population (Table 5.3), which is more than seven times higher than other countries in North America, Europe, and Asia.

Despite the fact that the violent crime rate has been decreasing since the 1990s, the incarceration rate increased because of new "tough on crime" policies that led to more prison sentences for nonviolent drug-related crimes (Tonry 1995). These new policies had the biggest impact in poor, minority communities, where police are much more likely to make arrests for drug violations (Pager 2003). In fact, police arrest Black people for drug violations at twice the rate they arrest whites, despite the fact that the rate of drug use is the same for the two groups and despite the fact that whites are actually more likely than Blacks to sell drugs (Rothwell 2014).

Most sociologists who have studied the growing prison rate agree that it has had a particularly hard impact on Black men (Pager 2003; Western 2006). Among Black men born since the late 1970s, nearly 25 percent had gone to prison by their mid-30s; among those who never completed high school, nearly 70 percent ended up in prison. This has had a devastating impact on Black urban communities. Prisons are usually located far away from urban Black neighborhoods, making it difficult for families to stay connected. There is also a significant financial strain since more than half the fathers in prison had been the primary source of income in their households (Western and

Petit 2005). As Bruce Western has shown, the growth of the prison population has been an important factor contributing to rising inequality between Blacks and whites in the United States (Western 2006, 2018).

The system of punishment and the rapid growth of the prison population sets the United States apart from the rest of the world. The United States is the only Western country in the world that still uses capital punishment, or the death penalty (Garland 2010). The United States is much more likely to treat juvenile offenders as adults, and it is much more likely to imprison them (Tonry 2007). Prison sentences are much longer in the United States than they are in Europe. Unlike in Europe, prisoners in the United States are not allowed to vote while they are in prison (except in Vermont and Maine), and they are prohibited from certain types of jobs once they are released (Manza and Uggen 2006).

The US system of mass incarceration is also extremely expensive. Each new prison cell costs between $25,000 and $100,000 to build, depending on the inmate security level (Gottschalk 2007). Many experts and policy-makers question whether this is a good financial investment, and they fear that the cost of incarceration is taking money away from schools, hospitals, and other important social services (King and Mauer 2002). The onset of the COVID-19 pandemic also highlighted how prison conditions that make social distancing impossible intensify risks of infection for prisoners and guards. In a few jurisdictions, some prisoners were released in an effort to slow the pandemic, and efforts were made in some states to prevent the rapid movement of people in and out of jail for minor offenses (Prison Policy Initiative 2020). Pointing to countries like Germany and Finland, which have enacted policies to reduce their incarceration rate, a growing "decarceration" movement is campaigning for new criminal justice policies to reduce the number of prisoners in the United States (Tonry 2014).

Critics have described the US system of mass incarceration as the **prison–industrial complex**. Coined by the intellectual and activist Angela Davis in 1997 and subsequently elaborated by a range of prison reformers and social scientists, the prison–industrial complex is understood as a profit-making system that uses prison labor and prisons to support a wide array of economic activities from private prisons to corporations that rely on prison labor to construction companies that build new prisons to the food service industry that feeds the enormous prison population (Harcourt 2012). Theorists of the prison–industrial complex observe that the massively disproportionate incarceration of Black men in the contemporary United States parallels the earlier slavery system in this country (Pelaez 2008; Friedmann 2012; Childs 2015). Prison labor is poorly paid and can be dangerous, a fact highlighted by the use of prisoners to fight wildfires in California (Funes 2019). Calls for prison reform, decarceration, and police and prison abolition have been made as part of the wider civil rights mobilization associated with the Black Lives Matter movement.

**Prison–industrial complex** A profit-making system that uses prison labor and prisons to support a wide array of economic activities.

## CASE STUDY

# Why Are Crime Stories So Popular?

Crime and deviance—and the social control responses to them—define moral boundaries. To explore this idea, we conclude the chapter with a brief examination of a particular kind of crime story, the "police procedural." Originating in the 19th century, these gritty crime dramas developed alongside mystery and detective fiction genres. As their name suggests, procedurals focus on investigative police procedure. They typically highlight teamwork among investigators to solve a crime, usually a violent murder or rape, which is laid out for the audience in grisly, realistic detail (Hausladen 2000: 18).

Today, police procedurals make up a substantial slice of network television programming. Several well-known police procedurals are also *global* franchises. This means they adapt the basic format to different places around the world to connect to local audiences. *Law & Order*, for example, ran from 1990 to 2010. There were five American spinoffs: *Law & Order: Special Victims Unit* (1999–), *Law & Order: Criminal Intent* (2001–2011), *Law & Order: Trial by Jury* (2005–2006), *Conviction* (2006), and *Law & Order: LA* (2010–2011). In addition, there were two *Law & Order* shows set in Moscow, Russia (adaptations of *Special Victims Unit* and *Criminal Intent*), and a version of *Criminal Intent* set in Paris called *Paris enquêtes criminelles*. Finally, *Law & Order: UK* (2009–2014) offered a British take on *Law & Order* with more of a focus on forensics. Clearly, the contemporary police procedural holds very wide appeal.

Fascination with crime stories is not a new phenomenon. Historians emphasize that "stories of crime and punishment play a central role in the storytelling matrix of most cultures" (Turnbull 2014). Such stories are powerful because they distinguish right from wrong and separate the good guys from the bad guys. Police procedurals are like other crime stories because they invoke *solidarity* among those on the side of good—the police, responsible citizens, and innocent community members—and this is in fundamental *conflict* with those who are portrayed as evil, namely the criminals who hurt others and violate the community.

Viewers of police procedurals are invited to take the perspective of the police officer who brings criminals to justice. A unifying theme of these stories is that the law protects the social good regardless of social status. In some stories, the criminals are portrayed as poor, violent, and/or dangerous. There are often racial, ethnic, and/or nationalist dynamics that reveal relationships of *inequality* in wider society. Urban gangs that are Black or Latinx, for example, or crime families associated with Italian, Chinese, or Russian immigrants are staples of the genre. The role of the police in these stories is either to justify, enforce, or overcome these racial–ethnic dynamics in the name of the social good. In other stories, where the criminal is *privileged* because they are wealthy, educated, powerful, or white, the narrative emphasizes that no one is beyond the law. Criminals who believe they are superior to the police or who think they are above social rules of the community inevitably discover that they are no match for the relentless, systematic process of police investigation. In contrast to both kinds of criminals, the police protagonist in the story is invariably depicted as a citizen-hero doing good in a complex world. They are good guys who represent the best interests of society.

Importantly, police procedurals are also important stories about the legitimate exercise of lawful *power*. Criminals are bad because they transgress fundamental social boundaries—and the police procedural can be used to question or reflect on those boundaries. As it has developed historically, the police procedural has complicated questions of right and wrong. In episodes about corrupt police, for example, a more nuanced analysis is offered where *resisting* authority might be a legitimate course of action, as long as justice is done in the end (Riordan 2018). In the well-known storyline where some police officers (or lawyers or politicians) are identified as criminals, the story's conflict is resolved when they are brought to justice. As a recent review suggests, the "detectives at the heart of the best procedurals believe that they are the last best hope for justice in a compromised world" (Riordan 2018).

Police procedurals also rely on a narrative tension between *structure* and *contingency*, especially in their focus on investigating every detail of the crime. In police procedurals, even the most brilliant criminals cannot control every contingency. They are inevitably foiled by an unknown witness who sees them or by the DNA evidence that places them at the scene. They might be brought down by their own emotional weakness or by the brilliant police officer who makes connections between the details of multiple cases to identify the perpetrator. At the same time, police procedurals also rely on the idea of a structured, understandable world and the belief that the tenacious, detail-oriented investigation by the police will identify the criminal and solve the crime. This tension between structure and contingency is a central part of the appeal of criminal investigation.

Importantly, police procedurals tell fictional stories. They close the moral breach created by terrible crime. In the real world, the story is very different. Not only are crimes under-reported, but the majority of crimes that are reported to police are never solved. According to FBI data, in 2023 (the year for which data are most recently available) only about 41 percent of violent crimes were solved (and fewer than 12 percent of property crimes were solved). Whatever the case, there is no doubt that the moral drama captured by the police procedural holds a wide social fascination because it defines the boundary of the deviant—separating right from wrong, good from bad, sacred from profane.

## LEARNING GOALS REVISITED

**5.1 Define deviance, and understand the social functions of deviance.**

- Deviance is any behavior that is outside social boundaries for what counts as normal and acceptable by a social group.
- Deviance helps social groups define and reinforce the boundaries of normal and acceptable behavior because it is the occasion when social standards are defined and articulated.
- What is considered normal behavior is socially constructed and varies across time and place.
- People who are defined as deviants are often stigmatized in a way that has consequences for their life outcomes. Once they are labeled as a deviant, this may influence them to engage in additional deviant behaviors or to join a deviant subculture.
- For some individuals and groups stigma and deviance can be empowering, serving as a source of collective resistance to power.
- Some deviance is defined medically, and whether or not it is subject to criminal sanction is a matter of social context and social judgment.

**5.2 Distinguish different categories of crime and the challenges of measuring crime.**

- Crime is deviance that is defined and punishable by law.
- The criminal justice system consists of all the government agencies that are charged with finding and punishing people who break the law.
- There are different types of crimes. Violent crimes such as homicide,

aggravated assault, forcible rape, and robbery and serious property crimes such as burglary, motor vehicle theft, larceny, and arson are measured in the Uniform Crime Reports that were published by the FBI until 2020, and are considered to be the most serious offenses. Part II offenses are considered less serious and include simple assault (where no weapon is used), forgery and counterfeiting, fraud, embezzlement, buying or receiving stolen property, vandalism, illegal possession of a weapon, prostitution, sex offenses, drug abuse violations, gambling, driving under the influence, violation of liquor laws, drunkenness, disorderly conduct, vagrancy, and loitering.

- Other categories of crime include hate crimes such as gay-bashing, white-collar crimes like insurance fraud or embezzlement, and cybercrimes such as identity theft.
- Even the best crime data have serious drawbacks: much crime is never reported; statistics are typically based on successful arrests and/or prosecutions, which means that those cases that do not result in arrest are not counted; and violent crimes are more likely to be reported, while property or white-collar crimes are much less likely to be reported.
- Crime data are also limited by well-documented biases, and especially racial biases, in the definition of crime, the policing of crime, and the social control response to crime.

**5.3** Define different approaches to punishment, and analyze their effectiveness.

- Over the last 200 years, modern societies have shifted from public and sometimes gruesome punishment of criminal offenders to more private punishments and later a focus on rehabilitation of offenders in the hope that they can re-enter society and refrain from engaging in criminal behavior.
- Civil law, which deals with disputes between individuals and organizations, is aimed at restitution of harm and as far as possible repairing a relationship or contract that has been broken. Criminal law is different because its focus is the punishment of the wrongdoer and the protection of the community and community values.

## Key Terms

Broken windows theory 157
Civil law 150
Crime 138
Crime rate 154
Criminal justice system 150
Criminal recidivism 162
Cybercrime 156
Deviance 138
Deviant subculture 143
Hate crime 155
Identity theft 156
Incarceration 162
Labeling theory 148
Laws 150
Moral panic 141
Parole 162

Plea-bargaining 156
Police 156
Primary deviance 148
Prison–industrial complex 156
Property crime 152
Punishment 160
Racial profiling 158
Rehabilitation 162
Secondary deviance 148
Social control theory 140
Stigma 148
Surveillance 160
Violent crime 152
White-collar crime 155
Zone of permitted variation 140

## REVIEW QUESTIONS

1. What is recidivism?
2. What is the difference between crime and deviance?
3. What is the prison–industrial complex?
4. Can cybercrime be white-collar crime? Can you think of an example?
5. What is the difference between primary and secondary deviance? Are they connected?
6. Explain how labeling theory works to define criminal behavior. Do you think labeling people has effects in other parts of life too, like the family or classrooms?
7. How is crime related to social norms and values?
8. Why is it difficult to measure crime?
9. Does crime serve any social function?
10. Why do societies punish offenders? Does it work?
11. How do policing and incarceration serve to reinforce racial inequality?

## EXPLORE

### RECOMMENDED READINGS

Becker, Howard S. [1953] 2015. *Becoming a Marihuana User.* Chicago: University of Chicago Press.

Davis, Angela. 2001. *The Prison Industrial Complex.* Audio CD. AK Press.

Durkheim, Emile. [1893] 2014. *The Division of Labour in Society.* New York: Free Press.

Kennedy, Randall. 1997. *Race, Crime, and the Law.* New York: Random House.

Smith, Philip. 2008. *Punishment and Culture.* Chicago: University of Chicago Press.

### ACTIVITIES

- *Use your sociological imagination*: Members of which groups are more likely to be arrested for illegal drug use in the United States? How can you find out?

- *Media+Data Literacies*: Go online to discover the crime rate statistics for your county. Use search terms such as "Your county [enter the name of your county] crime rates." Are you surprised at the finding? Why or why not?

- *Discuss*: Minor acts of deviance are very common. Have you ever committed an act of deviance? Have you ever seen someone else commit an act of deviance? Was it punished?

# PART III
# DIFFERENCE AND INEQUALITY

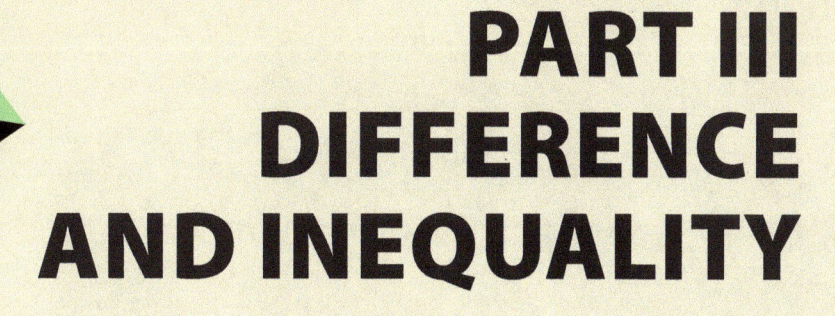

**6** Inequality, Mobility, and Social Change

**7** Race, Ethnicity, and Immigration

**8** Gender, Sexuality, and the Body

A FUTURE TO BELIEVE IN

BERNIESANDERS.COM

# Inequality, Mobility, and Social Change

In May 2023, Vermont senator Bernie Sanders made news headlines when he argued in an interview that the US government should tax 100 percent of all income over $999 million. Sanders has been a consistent critic of extreme wealth and extreme inequality. In his book *It's OK to be Angry About Capitalism*, Sanders (2023) argued that billionaires should not be allowed to exist. In 2019, he proposed an "ultra-wealth tax," which would start with a 1 percent tax on net worth over $32 million and progressively increase up to an 8 percent tax on wealth over $10 billion. Another proposal was to impose additional taxes on corporations that had excessively large gaps between the compensation paid to their executives and their typical workers. Sanders argued that the revenue generated by these proposals would allow the government to provide all its citizens with free health care, free college, free universal childcare, expanded financial support for the elderly, expanded benefits for military veterans, and more affordable housing.

Sanders had already organized several successful political campaigns around the theme of inequality. In 2016 he announced that he was running for the nomination of the Democratic Party to become president of the United States, claiming that that he was motivated to enter the race because of the "obscene level of wealth and income inequality" that he saw in the country. Nearly winning

**Bernie Sanders, 2016 US presidential campaign**
The choice of young Democratic voters in 2016 and an early contender for the Democratic nomination in 2020, Bernie Sanders made the problem of inequality the centerpiece of his campaign.

## Chapter Outline

**6.1 WHAT IS INEQUALITY? 175**

*Is Inequality Natural or Social? 175*
*Is Inequality Good or Bad? 175*
*Inequality and Stratification 177*

**6.2 TYPES OF STRATIFICATION 177**

*Caste Systems 178*
*Class Systems 180*
*Status Systems 181*
*Party Systems: Inequality through Meritocracy 182*

**6.3 A PORTRAIT OF STRATIFICATION TODAY 184**

*Stratification in the United States 184*
*Global Stratification 189*

**6.4 SOCIAL MOBILITY 192**

*Social Factors Associated with Mobility 193*
*Structural Mobility 196*

**6.5 SOCIAL CHANGE AND THE ATTEMPT TO CREATE MORE EQUALITY 198**

*Social Policy 199*
*Social Conflict 201*

**CASE STUDY:** *THE BACHELOR*: **CRYSTALLIZING STRATIFICATION ON TV 202**

his party's nomination in 2016 and then campaigning again (unsuccessfully) for the Democratic Party nomination in 2020, Sanders ensured that inequality was a central issue in both presidential elections. His consistent focus on extreme wealth and inequality has continued to influence public opinion and public policy. A 2023 opinion poll found that nearly two-thirds of Americans supported tax increases for wealthy individuals and large corporations (Oliphant 2023). In 2024, finance ministers from Brazil, Germany, South Africa, and Spain proposed a 2 percent tax on every billionaire in the world, with the money raised from the tax to be used to support global antipoverty programs (Elliott 2024). President Joe Biden included a billionaires tax in his 2023 and 2024 US federal budget proposals.

Why does the topic of inequality provoke so much public interest and attention, especially in the current moment? How do ordinary people think about inequality? With whom do they compare themselves? What strategies do they use to try to improve their circumstances, and how confident are they in their ability to do so?

**Inequality** The unequal distribution of social goods such as money, power, status, and social resources.

This chapter explores social inequality and social mobility. **Inequality** refers to the unequal distribution of social goods such as money, power, and status. We begin by considering theories about inequality, and we discuss how patterns of inequality get organized into systems of stratification. We compare different stratification systems, and we describe how inequality is organized in today's world. Next, we turn to mobility, which refers to a change in a person's social status or a movement to a different place in the stratification system. We compare ways of thinking about mobility, and we discuss the social factors that contribute to increasing mobility. Finally, we consider how groups of people respond to inequality by creating movements for social change and demanding more effective social policies.

## LEARNING GOALS

**6.1** Understand stratification as the way sociologists think about social inequality.

**6.2** Distinguish types of stratification.

**6.3** Develop an understanding of broad patterns of stratification in the United States and globally.

**6.4** Comprehend the concept of mobility, and distinguish different kinds of mobility, such as structural mobility and intergenerational mobility.

**6.5** Consider factors that affect mobility and the stratification system, such as education, family background, disability, and racial and gender differences, as well as social policy and social conflict.

## 6.1 What Is Inequality?

**LG 6.1** Understand stratification as the way sociologists think about social inequality.

Like most things in the social world, inequality is based on relationships and comparisons. For most people, the way they think about inequality is based on more than how much income they earn, what kind of house they live in, or how many televisions they own. In addition to these factors, people are making frequent comparisons with the people around them, particularly with the people who serve as their reference groups.

### Is Inequality Natural or Social?

Philosophers and social theorists have long debated the causes of inequality. Some thinkers emphasize the natural differences in strength, intelligence, age, beauty, and technical skill that can lead to inequalities. The Greek philosopher Aristotle (384–322 BCE), for example, argued that good governments and good societies were those in which the naturally gifted were able to develop the virtue to lead their inferiors without exploiting them.

But most theories of inequality emphasize social causes. For the French philosopher Jean-Jacques Rousseau (1712–1778), the existence of social relationships leads to social comparisons and ultimately to the desire for personal gain and advantages. We want to have higher status than other people, and we become jealous of those who have more prestige or wealth than we do. People may use their power and wealth to pursue their own private interests instead of the public good. These social causes of inequality, Rousseau argued, were more important than any natural differences in ability that may exist.

Karl Marx (1818–1883) also emphasized the social causes of inequality. As soon as people begin to cooperate and divide up necessary labor, he argued, inequality and exploitation will follow. The interests of those who control the work are in direct conflict with the interests of the workers under their control. As the dominant class, those who control the means of production organize society to their benefit. They invent ways to maximize their own profit and to exploit workers. For Marx, the history of society is the history of increasing inequality and exploitation.

### Is Inequality Good or Bad?

Marx and Rousseau each saw inequality as a social problem to be solved, through either better social policies, social movements to mobilize popular support for more social equality, or social conflicts.

There is abundant evidence for the negative effects of inequality. At the individual level, inequalities in income are associated with

**Protests in Paris, May 2023**
A protestor in Paris kicks a tear gas canister during a demonstration against pension reform on Boulevard Voltaire on Monday, May 1, 2023. The public response to Macron's pension reform spilled into the streets of Paris as more than half a million people marched across France to challenge a law raising the retirement age.

**Categorical inequality** The inequality between social categories or social groups.

**Relative deprivation** A form of inequality between groups where people believe they are being treated unequally in comparison to another group they view as similar to themselves.

**Davis–Moore theory of inequality** The theory that some level of inequality is necessary to motivate people to do the most difficult and important jobs in a society.

differences in health, educational attainment, and family stability (Neckerman and Torche 2007). Inequality also harms social development and the collective good. Inequality between groups, which Charles Tilly calls **categorical inequality**, is associated with an increase in political violence (Tilly 1999). **Relative deprivation** is another form of inequality between groups. It happens when people believe they are being treated unequally in comparison to another group they view as similar to themselves. Sociological research shows that increases in relative deprivation lead to higher levels of crime (Lea and Young 1984; Webber 2021) and that for many people relative deprivation has a bigger impact on a person's quality of life than their objective circumstances (Firebaugh and Tach 2012). At the collective level, cross-national research shows that high income inequality in a society is associated with negative health and wellness outcomes, such as higher rates of infant mortality, mental illness, drug use, and vulnerability to infectious diseases. In other indicators, higher inequality is also associated with higher incarceration rates and homicide rates (Wilkinson and Pickett 2009).

But inequality is not always viewed as a negative. Though the Scottish philosopher Adam Smith (1723–1790) was concerned that extreme levels of inequality encouraged people to worship the rich and to scorn the poor, he thought that normal levels of inequality were unimportant as long as everyone in the society could satisfy their basic needs. Furthermore, Smith argued that normal levels of inequality encouraged people to work harder, leading to greater levels of innovation and economic productivity that benefit all. Many sociologists in the 1950s, like Kingsley Davis (1908–1997) and Wilbert E. Moore (1914–1987), held a similar view of inequality. The **Davis–Moore theory** argues that some level of inequality is necessary to motivate people to do the most difficult and important jobs in a society (Davis and Moore 1945).

In economics, **marginal productivity theory** argues that inequality is a way of rewarding people who make a greater contribution to society, encouraging them to work hard and use their talents. According to these arguments, giving bigger rewards to the most productive and the most talented people benefits everyone.

Sociologists today are critical of the Davis–Moore and marginal productivity theories because these theories make unrealistic assumptions about the way the job market works. For example, people can only compete for vacant jobs, which means that there is a systematic bias in favor of people who discover such opportunities first—and this has nothing to do with who has the most talent (Sorensen and Kalleberg 1981). Other people are restricted in their job search by geographic ties to family or similar obligations that make a move difficult or impossible. In fact, most job markets are segmented, with a small number of prestigious, secure, and well-paid jobs and a larger number of less prestigious, insecure, and poorly paid jobs. Historically, marginalized groups have only been allowed to compete in the latter category, creating systematic biases in the job market (Kalleberg 2011). Even when a group is allowed to compete for vacant job openings in a part of the labor market where they were once excluded, they tend to receive less compensation for their talent and effort than other groups (King 1992). These structured systems of inequality point to the need for a more sociological approach to the questions of talent, effort, and reward.

> **Marginal productivity theory** The theory that inequality is a way of rewarding people who make a greater contribution to society, by encouraging them to work hard and use their talents.

### Inequality and Stratification

**Stratification** describes structured patterns of inequality between different groups of people. It uses a metaphor from geology to describe how people are sorted into different social layers, or social strata, like the layers in a rock formation. Stratification touches virtually every social process and social institution. There are patterns of inequality in almost every area of social life—not only income, wealth, power, and prestige but also employment, education, health, and participation in the arts. These patterns, which are always changing, are shaped by family, gender, social class, age, race, ethnicity, sexuality, religion, nationality, and ability.

> **Stratification** A central sociological idea that describes structured patterns of inequality between different groups of people.

## 6.2 Types of Stratification

**LG 6.2** Distinguish types of stratification.

Stratification researchers examine the distribution of scarce but desirable resources and how inequality emerges and is maintained. In most societies, inequality has multiple intersecting dimensions. For example, in societies where the first-born son inherits all the family wealth, inequality is based on a combination of age, gender, and inheritance. In societies where the most powerful people are members of a particular ethnic group, inequality is based on a combination of family and ethnic membership. By comparing the stratification systems of different societies, we can begin to identify which factors and combinations of factors are the most common and how those have changed over time.

One comparative strategy is to define a small number of social classes that exist within the stratification system and to compare the social characteristics and prospects for those social classes. Karl Marx and Ralf Dahrendorf argued that the most important features of inequality can be understood by distinguishing between two social classes: the dominant class and the dominated class. Other sociologists have identified a larger number of social classes (Savage 2015).

A different comparative strategy is to identify different ways of measuring inequality and stratification. Surveying the research literature in social stratification, David Grusky (2001) identified four kinds of measurements common to sociological research:

> **Degree of inequality** The level of concentration of a specific asset within the larger population.
>
> **Rigidity** The degree to which movement is possible in a stratification system.
>
> **Ascriptiveness** The degree to which characteristics at birth like race, gender, ethnicity, parents' background, or nationality determine life outcomes in a stratification system.
>
> **Degree of crystallization** The degree to which one dimension of inequality in a stratification system is connected to other dimensions of inequality.
>
> **Caste system** An extremely unequal stratification system in which people are born into a particular social group and have virtually no opportunity to change their social position.

1. **Degree of inequality** refers to the concentration of a specific asset within the larger population. For example, if we want to look at income stratification, we might want to know how much of the total income is controlled by the wealthiest 1 percent of the population.

2. **Rigidity** refers to how likely it is that people can move from one part of the stratification system to another. Rigidity measures whether people are likely to experience significant improvement (or decline) in their social situation over the course of their lives.

3. **Ascriptiveness** refers to the degree to which patterns of inequality are connected to traits that are present at birth, such as race, gender, ethnicity, parents' background, or nationality.

4. **Degree of crystallization** refers to how likely it is that somebody at the top (or bottom) of one inequality category will also appear at the top (or bottom) of other inequality categories. In other words, are the people with the most education also the ones with the highest levels of wealth, income, power, prestige, and health?

## Caste Systems

The most extreme forms of stratification are found in classical **caste systems**, where people are born into a particular social group and have virtually no opportunity to change their social position. Caste systems are marked by high levels of inequality, rigidity, ascriptiveness, and crystallization. There is a clearly defined hierarchy of social groups, or castes, which are defined by family background and measured in terms of racial or ethnic purity. In a caste system, the group into which you are born overwhelmingly defines your social standing, your life chances, and the kinds of people with whom you will be able to form relationships. The prohibitions against inter-caste contact are reinforced by extremely high levels of residential and occupational segregation, which means that your caste membership determines where you can live and what kind of job you can have. This also means that people from different castes rarely see each other in shared public spaces. One of the best-known caste systems is in India, which still retains strong influences from the caste system despite the fact that caste-based discrimination was declared illegal by the Indian government in 1950, and there is rising intermarriage between castes (Banerjee et al. 2013). Other historical examples include the American South during the period of slavery, the apartheid system in South Africa from 1948 to 1994, and China during the Yuan Dynasty (1271–1368).

## PAIRED CONCEPTS: Power and Resistance

### Ending Apartheid in South Africa

Apartheid was a race-based caste system in South Africa from 1948 until 1994. From the time that South Africa gained its independence from Great Britain in 1910, there had been racial segregation in housing and discrimination against Black South Africans in the labor market. But racial inequality became much worse after 1948, when the Afrikaaner National Party won the national election. The National Party campaigned under the slogan "apartheid"; its goal was to separate society along racial lines and to write laws that explicitly privileged the white minority.

Under the apartheid system, all South Africans were officially classified into one of four races: white, Bantu (Black Africans), Colored (mixed race), and Asian (primarily Indian and Pakistani). The government passed laws that prohibited whites from marrying people from other racial groups. It set aside more than 80 percent of the land in South Africa for the white population, forcibly removing millions of non-whites from their homes and re-settling them in impoverished minority-only spaces. There were separate public facilities for whites and non-whites, and non-whites were required to carry documents that permitted them to enter the white areas. Non-whites were prohibited from participating in national government. This discrimination produced extreme patterns of racial inequality. Average income for Black South Africans was less than 10 percent of the average income for whites. On average, whites lived 20 years longer than Blacks. Apartheid South Africa had the worst racial inequality in the world.

Black South Africans had long resisted and challenged racial discrimination in South Africa, and their resistance intensified under apartheid. Over

**PAIRED CONCEPTS CONTINUED**

**Apartheid**
Apartheid was a legally justified institution of racial segregation and subordination in South Africa that ran from 1948 to the early 1990s. The entrance to the Apartheid Museum, South Africa, shown here, evokes the memory of racism by re-creating the experience of separate entries for whites and non-whites to the museum.

time, they rallied world opinion against the apartheid system. South Africa was banned from the Olympics in 1964. The United Nations General Assembly denounced the apartheid system in 1973, and in 1976 the UN Security Council banned the sale of weapons to the South African government. Governments around the world imposed economic sanctions on South Africa, and a global divestment movement encouraged universities and other investors to pull their money out of companies that continued to do business in South Africa. Musicians and other performers stopped performing in South Africa, and many of them helped raise money for anti-apartheid groups.

By the end of the 1980s, the sustained pressure against the apartheid government led the Afrikaaner National Party to begin repealing many of the country's apartheid laws. The ban against the African National Congress was overturned. A new constitution gave all racial groups the right to vote and formally ended the apartheid system. Nelson Mandela, the leader of the African National Congress that had resisted apartheid and who had been jailed for 27 years, was elected president of South Africa in 1994. While South Africa still has some of the highest levels of economic inequality in the world today and racial inequality is still a significant problem, the country is no longer organized as a caste society.

**ACTIVE LEARNING**

**Find out:** Compare South Africa's apartheid system with the Jim Crow laws that organized life in the Southern US between the 1870s and the 1960s. What do you think are the main similarities and differences?

## Class Systems

In a class system of stratification, inequality is created primarily by differences in economic power. As Karl Marx observed of modern capitalism, at the top of the system are the people who own property and control economic production. Property owners and business owners create wealth for themselves through the labor of others. According to Marx, this is exploitation since the value of the work performed by laborers that is not paid to the worker in wages is taken by the capitalist as profit. Joining forces, property owners and business owners set the rules for the economy and enrich themselves. In a class system, the people with the most money have the most power, the most prestige, and the highest standard of living.

Compared with caste systems, class systems of inequality have less rigidity and less ascriptiveness. When class determines inequality, things like race, gender, ethnicity, and family background do not *directly* determine life chances; instead, what matters is access to material resources and control over economic production. These economic factors can reinforce older systems of inequality based on race, ethnicity, or gender. Family characteristics do not automatically create social privileges, as they do in a caste system. In a class system, the privileges one is born with have to be converted into economic resources and advantages.

In today's global economy the people who control economic production have more advantages than ever. They can search the world looking for the cheapest labor, which guarantees that their profits will be as high as possible. They can buy up property and other material resources all over the world, creating global businesses and global markets. Their wealth gives them global power and prestige, which means that virtually every society in the world must deal with class-based inequality.

## Status Systems

Class systems are not always stable on their own because people do not always form alliances or join groups based solely on their economic interests. Max Weber argued that class systems function most effectively when they are organized around status groups. According to Weber, a **status group** is held together by a common lifestyle and shared characteristics of social honor. Like the in-groups we discussed in Chapter 4, people feel a bond of solidarity with other members of their status group, and they make social distinctions between their own status group and competing status groups.

**Status group** A group held together by a common lifestyle and shared characteristics of social honor.

In a status system, inequality is created when high-status people join together to create a community of privilege and control. They might join the same clubs, live in the same neighborhoods, or send their children to the same exclusive schools. They come to see themselves as being economically, intellectually, and morally superior (Mosca 1939). Because they believe they are the only ones who have the skills and character to control society, they aspire to create a society that is controlled by **elites**.

Status systems are similar to class systems in their levels of rigidity, but they have higher levels of ascriptiveness and much higher levels of crystallization of privilege across the entire spectrum of inequality categories. High-status groups live in a different world than everybody else, and even if outsiders do manage to gain access to that world, they are made to feel

**Elite** An elite is formed through high-status behavior and the formation of institutions to create a community of privilege and control.

**Scroll and Key**
The Scroll and Key Society is a secret society founded in 1842 at Yale University and is part of an elite status system. A privileged set of graduates from one of the most privileged universities in the world reproduces an even more elite community of privilege and honor in this secret society. Scroll and Key members include politicians, philanthropists, academics, and leaders in the arts and sciences.

like they don't belong. Status systems are also defined by elite conflict, in which high-status groups organize themselves into rival factions (Lachmann 2003). These factions are often forced to share power despite the fact that they dislike and distrust one another.

## Party Systems: Inequality through Meritocracy

In a **party system**, power and privilege come from the effective leadership of important organizations. As we discussed in Chapter 4, organizational power increased with the rise of bureaucracy. Bureaucracies allow people to complete their work more efficiently, develop greater expertise, and move more easily from one organization to another. Bureaucracy also forces people to follow the rules rather than exercise arbitrary power, in a way that can minimize conflicts and prevent the emergence of elite factions.

Party systems are less rigid and less ascriptive than other stratification systems. Hiring practices in a bureaucracy follow official rules, which reduces (but does not eliminate) the importance of "knowing the right people." Status and authority are based on party membership and on possessing the technical expertise that is associated with the job, rather than the social characteristics and the family background of the person holding the job.

Party systems create inequality through **meritocracy**, which means that the people who control society are the ones who perform the best on examinations and other formal tests of ability. Despite the appeal of a society that rewards intelligence, skill, and effort rather than family background or family wealth, meritocracies are not perfect. When people get to the top of society by performing well on tests, they may believe that they

**Party system** A stratification system where power and privilege come from the effective leadership of important organizations.

**Meritocracy** Stratification system where high positions are held by those who perform the best on examinations and other formal tests of ability.

## PAIRED CONCEPTS: Inequality and Privilege

### Marketing to the Super-Rich

For the wealthiest people in society, the experience of shopping is significantly different than it is for everyone else. Marketers of goods and services create specific campaigns for the super-rich that attempt to cater to their unique tastes and needs. We can see this distinction at work in the markets for travel and luxury goods.

For instance, most people make their travel decisions based on price. When searching for a plane ticket or a hotel room, they will usually buy the least expensive option that fits their itinerary. In these markets, the competition is fierce, and the profit margins are small. Companies need to sell large quantities of their product in order to make a profit.

But travel marketing is very different when it is targeted to the super-rich, for whom luxury and distinction are more important than price. Japan Airlines charges more than $20,000 for a first-class flight between Tokyo and New York, which is nearly 20 times higher than the cost of a discounted economy fare. What does the rich traveler get for such an expensive ticket? Many airlines provide their first-class travelers a chauffeured car to the airport. Once at the airport, they get a special place to check in for their flight and a separate and much shorter security line. They wait for their flight in a private lounge, with free food and drinks. They enter and exit the plane before everyone else, and their luggage comes off the plane first. While on the plane, they enjoy gourmet food and drinks and a private entertainment system from the comfort of an enclosed seat that converts into a bed. Some first-class cabins even have luxurious bathrooms that include a full shower. Because the profit margins are significantly higher for first-class seats than they are for economy seats, the airlines are happy to spend the money providing these extra amenities. In fact, the first-class seats that airlines install in their planes cost them between $100,00 and $300,000 each.

Some travel markets ignore the masses altogether and cater exclusively to the super-rich. The markets for luxury yachts and private aircraft only pay attention to people with a net worth—that is, wealth and income minus any debt owed—of $10 million or more. During the COVID-19 pandemic the demand for luxury yachts exploded, as billionaires opted to ride out the health crisis for months at a time in beautiful offshore locations. Demand for private jets and for properties on private islands was at an all-time high during the pandemic as well, a testament to the growing inequality between the super-rich and everyone else.

**Consumption as status markers**
These luxury yachts docked in Italy are consumption markers for the super-rich. What consumption markers affect status in your world?

### ACTIVE LEARNING

**Find out:** What things, if any, does your school do to market to wealthy families? Select a school that is different from yours, and try to see if the strategies they use to market to wealthy families are different from those of your school.

**Party systems create inequality through the ideology of meritocracy**
The college entrance exam in China is the largest single high-stakes test in the world. In 2024, 13.4 million Chinese students registered for the exam.

deserve all the privileges they get. This can cause them to become unsympathetic toward people who are less successful.

A significant challenge of meritocracies is that they do not actually eliminate other sources of inequality, such as race, gender, or family background. Racism and sexism can work directly against merit. Families with more education and wealth also do particularly well in meritocracies, using their resources to make sure that their children do well on the high-stakes tests that are used to identify and reward talent. Some critics argue that meritocracy is no more than an ideology that justifies the wealth of the educated middle classes.

## 6.3 A Portrait of Stratification Today

**LG 6.3** Develop an understanding of broad patterns of stratification in the United States and globally.

**Socioeconomic status** A general term referring to sociological measures of social position that include income, educational attainment, and occupational prestige.

To describe and compare systems of stratification, sociologists collect data on income, educational attainment, occupational prestige, and other measures of **socioeconomic status** that describe an individual's position in society. Though most research looks at how inequality is structured in specific countries, there is also growing interest in global inequality. Many sociologists also study how gender, race, and ethnicity influence social stratification.

### Stratification in the United States

Inequality in the United States has increased significantly since 1980 (Figure 6.1). The distance between the highest income earners and the rest of the population is staggeringly high, a phenomenon that has led many social scientists to speak of a "new Gilded Age" in the United States, in which the rich are getting dramatically richer while everybody else struggles to get by (Grusky and Kricheli-Katz 2012). As Saez and Zucman (2020: 11) noted, "In 1980, on average, members of the top 1 percent owned in wealth the equivalent of 60 years of average US income. In 2020 … they own 200 years of average US income in wealth." Using wealth data from the Federal Reserve for the second quarter of 2023, Bankrate reports that "the top 1 percent of households hold 30.6 percent of the total wealth. … But just the top 0.1 percent own 14 percent of the total wealth, giving them a stunning average of more than $1.52 billion per household" (Royal and Barba 2024).

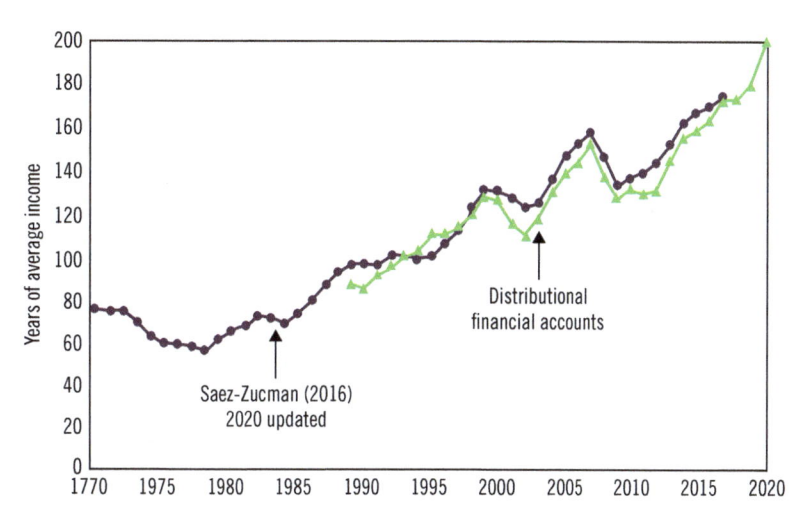

**Figure 6.1** Average Wealth of 1 Percent Wealthiest Adults (Divided by Average US Income Per Adult).

Sociologists, economists, and others who study economic stratification make a distinction between **wealth**, which is the stock of valuable assets, including physical and intellectual property, securities (like stocks and bonds), art collections, jewelry, and other valuable goods, and **income**, which is the flow of earnings over a delimited time period, including rents, salaries, and income transfers like pensions or dividends. **Net worth**, a measure commonly used to gauge economic position, is defined as wealth and income minus any debt owed.

There are clear and measurable socioeconomic differences between different groups of Americans. And while there is no definitive set of categories that perfectly capture every dimension of experiencing life in a particular social location, there are broad patterns and trends that can be measured and analyzed.

**Wealth** The stock of valuable assets including physical and intellectual property, securities, art, jewelry, and other valuable goods.

**Income** The flow of earnings over a delimited time period including rents, salaries, and income transfers like pensions or dividends.

**Net worth** Wealth and income minus any debt owed.

**THE UPPER CLASS.** The term "upper class" describes the most privileged segment of the population. These people have the most wealth, power, and prestige. The top 1 percent of the US population has an average household income of more than $700,000 per year and an average net worth of more than $10 million. Most of this wealth comes from real estate, stocks, and other investments that are only available to high–net worth individuals.

The upper class can be divided into subgroups. Some members of the upper class have inherited wealth from their family, and many of these families have been in the upper class for more than a century. Others are more recent entrants into the class of inherited wealth. People who inherit their way into the upper class do not need to work for wages. Some spend their money on lavish homes, luxury items, and trust funds for their children. Others turn their energies to philanthropy.

A second group in the upper class includes people whose jobs put them in charge of the largest and wealthiest bureaucracies. Leaders of the biggest corporations, doctors in the largest hospitals, presidents of major universities, and partners at the most prestigious law firms all earn salaries in the millions of dollars. People who have these jobs often come from privileged families, and they typically have attended the most elite schools and universities (Domhoff 2013).

The third group in the upper class consists of celebrities from the worlds of sports and entertainment. People from this group are more diverse in their social backgrounds. Compared to those who inherited their wealth or who hold elite professional jobs, a higher proportion of this third group came from less privileged backgrounds and less elite schools. This group is also more racially diverse. In today's celebrity culture, these are the most visible members of the upper class, even though they are by far the smallest number.

**THE MIDDLE CLASS.** Most Americans believe that they belong to the middle class. One simple way to measure the middle class is to examine the median income for all households. For 2022, the US Census reported the median household income in the United States to be $74,580. A different approach used by the economists at the Pew Research Center defines middle-income households as those with an annual income between two-thirds and double the median income for their household size and relative to the place where they live; using this definition, people in middle-class households in the United States earn between $52,000 and $156,000 per year for a household of three (Kochhar and Sechopoulos 2022). Other definitions focus on social expectations, personal aspirations, and consumption patterns. For example, it is a common middle-class expectation to be able to buy a home, to pay for your children to attend college, to take a vacation every year, and to save for retirement.

Most social scientists distinguish between three subgroups in the middle class. At the top are professionals and managers, who are often referred to as the **upper-middle class**. This includes upper-level management positions, lawyers, doctors, engineers, scientists, information technology officers, and others who typically have high-level educational credentials and

**Upper-middle class** A social class group at the top of the middle-class system with good job security and high-paying salaries of over $100,000 per year.

professional expertise. This group enjoys financial stability, with good job security and salaries that often exceed $100,000 per year. They live in safe and comfortable neighborhoods and have high-quality employer-provided health care. They send their children to good schools, and they invest significant resources helping their children become successful.

Below the professional managers are members of the **middle class**, which is composed of people who have an annual income of between $60,000 and $90,000. Most people in the middle class have completed a college degree. They tend to come from one of the following three occupational groups:

1. Middle-level managers, such as branch managers, store managers, and human resource managers.

2. White-collar workers, who work in an office and perform specialized jobs for the organization. Examples of white-collar jobs include accountants, office managers and administrators, public relations specialists, and computer programmers.

3. Highly skilled blue-collar workers, who do complicated and specialized physical jobs that are in high demand. Examples of these kinds of jobs include solar energy installers, elevator installers, oil drill operators, and commercial drivers.

**Middle class** A social class group below the upper-middle class composed of families with an annual income of between $60,000 and $90,000.

As we discuss in Chapter 8, there are marked gender differences within these categories, with blue-collar workers being disproportionately male, white-collar workers in service positions disproportionately female (Groves 2011; Laughlin and Christnacht 2017), and women earning between 80 and 85 cents for every dollar men earn (Graf, Brown, and Patten 2019; Fontenot, Semega, and Kollar 2018).

Most middle-class workers have stable jobs and predictable salaries, which makes it easier for them to do the kind of planning that is necessary to achieve a middle-class lifestyle, such as saving for retirement. Their homes are smaller than those owned by people in the upper-middle class, their vacations are less fancy, they have significantly less investment income, and they are more likely to send their children to public schools.

The third group is the **lower-middle class**, which consists of families with a household income of between $15,000 and $60,000 per year. Among all the families with children in the United States, nearly one-third are in the lower-middle class (Kearney and Harris 2013). People in the lower-middle class have less job security, and they often perform fairly monotonous and unskilled work. Examples of lower-middle class jobs include cashiers, data entry positions, telemarketing and call center jobs, and fast food line cooks. These workers are often paid hourly wages instead of a salary, which means that their income is less predictable because employers

**Lower-middle class** A social class group below the middle class composed of families with a household income of between $15,000 and $60,000 per year.

**Installing solar panels**
Highly skilled blue-collar workers, like this solar panel installation technician, are in very high demand and are typically members of the middle class.

can cut back their hours. Many people in the lower-middle class work more than one job just to make ends meet. Their jobs are less likely to come with health benefits, retirement benefits, or opportunities for advancement, making it nearly impossible for them to plan for their future. For most workers in the lower-middle class, a single setback such as getting sick or needing a major car repair is enough to push them into poverty. Ironically, during the COVID-19 pandemic, many of these lower-middle class jobs were described as "essential work," even though wages and benefits were rarely, if ever, adjusted to reflect their importance to the economy and public health. At the same time, both lower-income and middle-income adults reported significant financial pressure from job loss or pay reduction associated with the pandemic (Igielnik 2020).

**THE POOR.** The US government establishes an official poverty threshold to measure who is living in poverty and who is eligible for government programs designed to help the poor. First developed in 1963, this measurement was set at three times the minimum amount of money it would cost to feed each member of a family, based on how much housing, health, and other essential services cost relative to food. Since that initial calculation, adjustments to the poverty threshold have been made by looking at changes in the prices paid for consumer goods and services. In 2024, the official poverty threshold for a family of four was $30,200 (Healthcare.gov 2024). Some critics argue this is still too low a threshold, while others point out the threshold is insensitive to geographical variation and the impact of existing government programs (Thornton 2022).

According to the US Census Bureau, in 2023 there were 37.9 million people living in poverty in the United States, which is equal to 15.7 percent of the total population (Census 2024). Compared to the population at large, families living in poverty are more likely to be single-parent households and to be headed by women with young children. Women, children, and people with disabilities are overrepresented among the poor, and so are Black and Latino people. Nearly one-quarter of all families living in poverty are part of the **working poor**, which means that they are in poverty despite the fact that they include at least one person who worked for more than half of the year. People who experience long-term unemployment in poor families find it extremely challenging to escape from poverty.

**Working poor**
People and families in poverty despite having at least one person who works for a wage.

## Global Stratification

Global inequality is more extreme than the inequality that exists within nations (Milanovic 2010, 2016), and by many measures, global inequality is the worst it has been since the 19th century (Hickel 2016; Piketty 2014). In 2019, prior to the onset of the COVID-19 pandemic, the top 1 percent of the global population possessed 43.4 percent of global net worth, while the lower half of the global wealth distribution together owned less than 2 percent of global wealth (Credit Suisse 2020: 29). The *Global Wealth Report* for 2020 asserted that the COVID-19 pandemic "triggered the worst global economic crisis since the Second World War," with global wealth declining across the board in the first half of 2020 and a slow recovery projected (Credit Suisse 2020). In the years that followed, the economic impact of the pandemic has been uneven, with women, minorities, low-skilled labor, and the young most affected. Other findings are mixed, including a comparatively healthy financial sector when COVID-19 hit, successful public spending for COVID relief, and high inflation around the world in 2022, which had not returned to pre-pandemic levels by 2024 (Credit Suisse 2023: 36, 38, 45; Veit and Dwyer 2024).

Global income inequality still skews heavily in favor of countries like those in North America and Western Europe, particularly for people living in or near major cities. This remains true despite the fact that net global household wealth declined in 2022 for the first time "since the global financial crisis of 2008," and despite the fact that much of that decline was in "North America and Europe" (Credit Suisse 2023: 7). Importantly, there continues to be rapid growth in what banks define as "ultra-high-net-worth individuals" in the 2020s (Credit Suisse 2023: 42).

At the other extreme, global poverty skews heavily toward people living in poor nations in the Global South. The World Bank measures global poverty by looking at the proportion of the population living on less than $1.90 per day. As Figure 6.2 illustrates, the countries with the largest proportion of the population living below the global poverty threshold are mainly found in Africa, India, and parts of Southeast Asia. The global poverty population is disproportionately young and uneducated and works in rural agriculture (World Bank 2018). In 2020, extreme poverty was mounting again, with

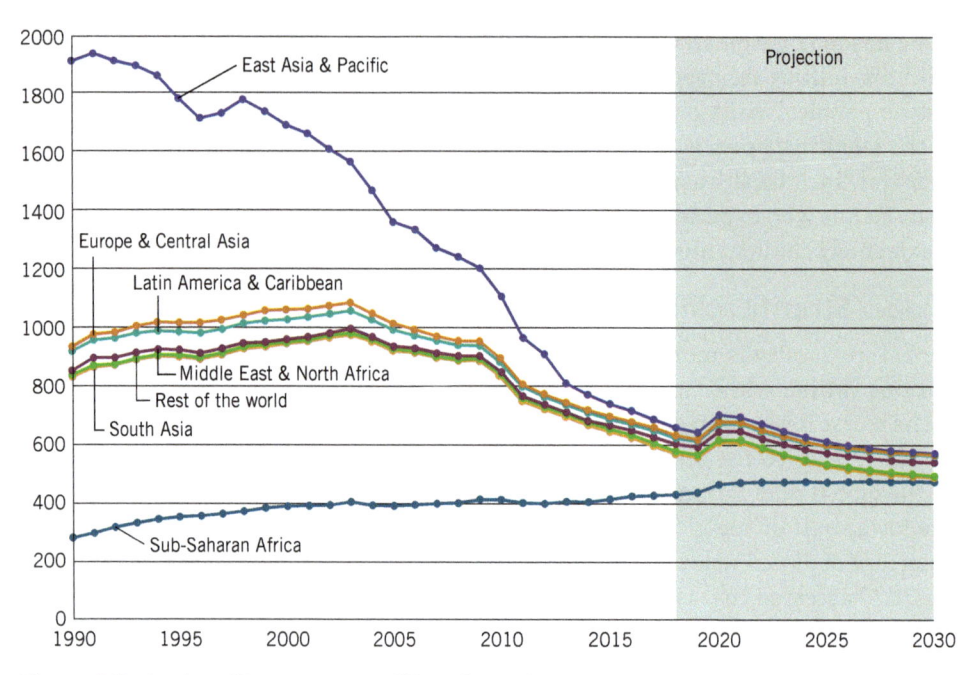

**Figure 6.2  Number of Extreme Poor (millions) by Region, 1990–2030.**
Source: PovcalNet (online analysis tool), http://iresearch.worldbank.org/PovcalNet/. World Bank, Washington, DC, World Development Indicators; World Economic Outlook; Global Economic Prospects; Economist Intelligence Unit.

**Colonialism**
A global stratification system in which powerful nations used their military strength to take political control over other territories and exploit them economically.

**World systems theory** A way to think about global stratification that emphasizes the relative positions of countries in the world economy as crucial determinants of inequality.

the World Bank reporting that "the COVID-19 (coronavirus) pandemic has reversed the gains in global poverty for the first time in a generation. By most estimates, this reversal of fortune is expected to push between 88 million and 115 million more people into extreme poverty in 2020" (World Bank 2020).

Global patterns of inequality are connected to the history of **colonialism**, in which powerful nations used their military strength to take political control over other territories and exploit them economically. The legacy of colonialism can be seen most dramatically in Africa, where western European countries controlled most of the continent directly until after World War II and where global poverty remains the most concentrated in the world today.

Another way of thinking about global stratification is through the lens of **world systems theory**, which focuses on the different roles available to countries based on their level of economic power and development. Advantages in the world system accrue over time, so nations that have been

**PAIRED CONCEPTS**

## Global and Local

### Wealthy Chinese Students at Elite US Schools

In 2019, more than 370,000 students from China enrolled in US universities (Open Doors 2022). While those numbers declined in 2020–2021 during the height of the COVID-19 pandemic, by the end of 2022 they had rebounded back close to pre-pandemic levels. These students came to the United States for many different reasons. Some found Chinese universities to be too rigid and uninspiring and were excited by the American emphasis on creativity, originality, and entrepreneurship. Most believe that a degree from a US university will help them find better-paying jobs, either in the United States or in China. For the wealthiest Chinese students, however, going to an elite US university is viewed as their ticket to enter the global elite. The daughter of China's President Xi Jinping attended Harvard, which is the top choice among elite Chinese parents, followed closely by Yale, Stanford, Princeton, and MIT.

Although the COVID-19 pandemic has interrupted the trend and reduced the numbers, many wealthy Chinese parents send their children to prestigious US boarding schools to improve their chances of admission to elite US universities. The Association of Boarding Schools organize events in Beijing and Shanghai, where wealthy Chinese parents can learn more about US prep schools (Gao 2012). By the time a wealthy Chinese student has completed prep school and college in the United States, their parents might have spent half a million dollars on their education.

Because there are significant economic motivations for American schools to accept large numbers of full-paying Chinese students, these institutions have been forced to adjust budgets and expectations dramatically because of the impact of COVID-19 on international travel. In recent years government funding for most state universities has decreased significantly, so students paying out-of-state tuition became an important source of revenue. Prep schools and small private colleges need a certain number of full-paying students to remain financially viable, and they foster hopes that graduates from extremely wealthy families will re-enroll as soon as travel is safe again and will eventually become generous donors. At the same time, these schools hope that the presence of foreign students will bring a more global perspective to their campus communities. By creating a cultural exchange between students from different countries, they hope to prepare all of their students more effectively for the diverse global economy.

**The global market for college admissions**
Elite private schools like Deerfield Academy in Massachusetts recruit students globally from among those who are willing and able to pay. Graduates of such "prep" schools are much more likely to gain entry to prestigious colleges and universities.

**ACTIVE LEARNING**

**Find out:** Does your school actively recruit international students? Research the reasons why they do so. You could begin your inquiry by consulting your school's admissions office or website.

powerful in the past are likely to maintain their dominance. Wallerstein (2004) describes three positions in the world system: core nations, peripheral nations, and semi-peripheral nations.

At the top of the hierarchy are the core nations, which are the wealthiest and the most economically developed. The earliest to industrialize, these nations have the most diverse economies, and they are usually the first to develop new technologies. They were often colonial powers at an earlier time in history. Core nations compete with one another for global dominance, particularly in the areas of banking and trade. The core nations in the modern world system are Australia, Canada, China, Japan, New Zealand, Taiwan, the United States, and the nations of Western Europe (Chase-Dunn, Kawano, and Brewer 2000).

At the bottom of the hierarchy are peripheral nations, which are the poorest and the least economically developed. These countries do not have diverse economies, and they usually make money by extracting raw materials and exporting them to the core nations. Peripheral nations have extremely high levels of inequality. While most of their population is poor and uneducated, a small group of elites own most of the land and are connected to multinational corporations. Peripheral nations are usually dominated by core nations, whose multinational corporations exploit their labor to produce products for export to the core nations. Peripheral nations are found primarily in Africa and parts of Asia and South America (Chase-Dunn, Kawano, and Brewer 2000).

Last, the middle position in the global system is occupied by semi-peripheral nations, which are positioned between the peripheral and the core nations. Semi-peripheral nations have diversified economies, but their industrial and technological development happened much later than that of the core nations. As a result, they usually remain dependent on the core nations for military protection, advanced scientific training, economic investment, and the regulation of global markets.

**Vertical social mobility** Social mobility up or down in the socioeconomic stratification system.

**Social mobility** A change in a person's social status or a movement to a different place in the stratification system.

## 6.4 Social Mobility

**LG 6.4** Comprehend the concept of mobility, and distinguish different kinds of mobility, such as structural mobility and intergenerational mobility.

The "rags-to-riches" story, a staple in Hollywood movies, describes a type of **vertical social mobility**, which happens when people change their position in the social stratification system. **Social mobility** that is vertical can include upward as well as downward mobility, but upward social mobility stories are much more common in popular culture.

In people's actual lives, upward mobility is much more gradual than the way it is presented in movies. For people who have middle-class and upper-middle-class jobs, the most common experience of betterment is to move slightly upward within their social class position over the course of their lives. Although their salaries may gradually increase, their social class position remains the same. Significant vertical mobility is relatively uncommon.

However, many people do experience **horizontal mobility**, which happens when people experience change without altering their position in the socioeconomic stratification system. An example of horizontal mobility is when a family moves to a new neighborhood to enroll their children in a better school district. Such parents are trying to create **intergenerational mobility**, which refers to changes in social status between different generations in the same family.

Most people care more about **relative mobility** than **absolute mobility**. Absolute mobility means that you have more things than you used to, but it does not consider what is happening to other people. For example, most people in the United States today have more things in absolute terms than their parents once did.

Relative mobility is more sociologically meaningful because it is based on your understanding of how well you are doing in comparison to other people. Upward relative mobility means that you are doing better than the people around you, or that you are doing better than you thought you were going to do. If you live in a bigger house than the one you grew up in but everyone you know has a bigger house than you do, you may not feel like you have experienced upward mobility.

## Social Factors Associated with Mobility

Stratification researchers have identified three factors that are the most likely to increase social mobility: education, family background, and culture. These factors all interact with one another. Social mobility is also shaped by gender, race, ethnicity, sexuality, and other important social categories.

**EDUCATION.** Educational success is one of the strongest predictors of social mobility (Blau and Duncan 1967; Black and Devereux 2011). Education is also associated with better outcomes in a range of domains, from the health of children and parents to the likelihood of criminal activity and voting (Lochner 2011). A college degree is particularly important for mobility. Among adult children who have a college degree, nearly three-quarters have incomes greater than their parents'. For children born into low-income families, education is even more important. Among college-educated adults who were born poor, 96 percent end up earning more money than their parents (Haskins 2008).

**Horizontal mobility** Social movement in people's life that occurs without changing their overall position in the socioeconomic stratification system.

**Intergenerational mobility** The change in social status between different generations in the same family or the change in the position of children relative to their parents.

**Relative mobility** The understanding of change in social position compared to other groups.

**Absolute mobility** Change in social position, regardless of what is happening with other people.

It is also true that the relationship between education and mobility can reinforce inequality. Access to quality education is distributed unevenly, in a way that benefits the wealthy at the expense of the poor. Wealthy families are also better able to invest financial resources in their children's education. For example, when the COVID-19 pandemic forced most school districts to implement remote learning, students from upper-income households adapted much more easily as they had better access to high-speed internet connections, technology, and supplemental resources such as learning "pods" and tutoring (Hobbs and Hawkins 2020). This is also true for college students (Levin 2020). The result is that educational success is stratified by family income. Students from poor and minority neighborhoods have fewer academic support resources in their high schools, tend to start their college search later than wealthier students, and are less aware of financial aid resources. As a result, estimated bachelor degree attainment by age 24 was nearly four times as high for children from families in the top quarter of the income distribution as it was for those in the lowest quarter of the income distribution (Cahalan et al. 2020: 145).

## METHODS AND INTERPRETATION

### Measuring Status Attainment and Social Mobility

The standard way to measure social mobility is to compare an adult person's position in the stratification system with that of their parents. But this strategy requires many additional choices: at what point in a person's life do we measure their social position? Do we compare their social position with both of their parents, or only one of them? And how exactly are we supposed to measure "social position"?

Among social scientists, there are two main strategies for studying social position. Economists focus primarily on income, assets, and other measures of financial wealth. Sociologists, on the other hand, prefer to focus on a person's occupation. A person's occupation, they argue, is a much better predictor of social position and a much better way of making comparisons with a person's parents. There are four compelling reasons for the effectiveness of this strategy. First, a person's occupation is highly correlated with their income as well as their level of educational achievement. Second, a person's occupation involves issues of identity, including judgments about the prestige of different kinds of work. Third, it is easier to collect reliable information about a person's occupation than it is to collect data about their income and financial resources. Finally, it is easier to collect the kind of historical data that is needed to compare adults with their parents. Most people know what their parents' occupations were, but they are unlikely to know much about their parents' income and finances.

In sociology, the most influential research strategy for measuring social mobility is the status attainment model created by Peter Blau and Otis Dudley Duncan (Blau and Duncan 1967). Blau and Duncan collected data on father's occupation, father's education, son's education, son's first job, and son's ultimate occupational status. They found that a father's occupation and education both have a direct and positive relationship on a son's education. But the effect of a father's status, while significant, was relatively small when compared with the effect that the son's actual educational achievements had on his first job and his ultimate occupational status. In other words, while a parent's background helps their child get to the starting line, the child has to finish the race on their own.

Because Blau and Duncan's original research is now more than 50 years old, sociologists have made important changes to their original model. For example, while the focus on fathers and sons may have made sense in the early 1960s, women and daughters are now routinely included in data collection and in theories about what causes social mobility (Goldthorpe and Payne 1986; Choi, Kim and Kim 2023). Researchers now collect much more detailed educational and occupational histories (Avent-Holt et. al. 2020; Blossfeld 1986), and they look more carefully at different outcomes between siblings within a family (Conley 2005; Bjorklund and Jantti 2020). There is greater focus on the ways that consumption and other lifestyle factors influence stratification and mobility (Ganzeboom, Treiman, and Ultee 1991; Chan and Goldthorpe 2024). And there is more comparative research, focusing in particular on the effects that different social policies can have on increasing social mobility (Neckerman and Torche 2007; Wistow 2022).

**Occupational status**
Compared to income or assets, occupation is usually a better predictor of social position and a better way of measuring intergenerational mobility than other factors.

### ACTIVE LEARNING

**Find out:** One reason it can be hard to measure intergenerational income differences is that people are not always willing to talk about money—even in families. While parents talk to children about their children's economic situations, they are less likely to disclose their own financial situations to their children. Interview an older family member, or another adult from your parents' generation, and ask whether or not their parents talked to them about their own income and financial decisions. Then consider if you have had straightforward and detailed discussions with your parents about your parents' money and financial decisions, or if you have had (or will have) such conversations with your children. Do you think it would be a good idea to do so? Why or why not?

**FAMILY BACKGROUND.** Family background influences socialization, social opportunities, and social mobility. Worldwide, researchers have found that there is a significant relationship between parents' social and economic background and their children's educational and financial achievements (Bowles, Gintis, and Groves 2008; Jerrim and Macmillan 2015; Chetty et al. 2017).

There are many reasons why family background shapes an individual's opportunities for social mobility. As we discussed in Chapter 4, parents with high levels of education have distinctive parenting styles. They teach their

**Cultural capital**
The knowledge and consumption of culturally valued things.

children to be assertive and to expect to be taken seriously in the adult world. This type of socialization starts paying off when children begin school and continues to do so when they enter the workplace. More privileged parents also teach their children to enjoy art, literature, classical music, and other forms of **cultural capital** that help them feel comfortable in the world of privilege. In addition, wealthier parents can pay for college tuition and provide the down payment for purchasing an adult child's first home. This reduces the debt burden for children of privilege, providing them with more opportunity and security as young adults.

**CULTURE.** Being comfortable with the cultural preferences of the privileged is another way that people at the top of the stratification system reproduce their advantages. The sociologist Pierre Bourdieu (1986, 1998; Bourdieu and Passeron 1979, 1990) called this cultural capital. In certain circumstances, cultural capital can be a source of social mobility. For ambitious children who come from low-income families, becoming familiar with art, literature, and classical music can contribute to upward social mobility (DiMaggio 1982). Children whose parents do a lot of reading in their spare time tend to experience higher levels of social mobility when compared with children from a similar social background whose parents do not do as much reading (De Graaf, De Graaf, and Kraaykamp 2000). According to an international survey of 79 countries, those with low literacy skills are also more than twice as likely to be unemployed as those with strong reading skills (Organisation for Economic Co-operation and Development 2013a; Avvisati 2020).

Teachers and employers can promote social mobility by reinterpreting social disadvantages as advantages. While many employers prefer to hire people who share their background and interests, others believe that workers who come from disadvantaged backgrounds are more resilient, better able to handle setbacks, and more effective at operating with limited resources (Streib 2017). In jobs that require people to interact with a diverse population, coming from a more disadvantaged background can be seen as an advantage. In these kinds of situations, people who come from lower positions in the stratification system can be successful, especially if they have done well in school and earned the credentials they need for the job.

## Structural Mobility

**Structural mobility**
Changes in social position in the stratification system that occur because of structural changes in the economy and wider society.

**Structural mobility** happens when changes in society lead to larger changes in the stratification system. The US manufacturing sector has lost more than seven million jobs since 1979, taking away some of the best-paying and most secure jobs for men without a college degree. At the other end of the spectrum, between 1910 and 2019, jobs held by professionals, managers, salespeople, clerical workers, and service workers have increased

## CAREERS

### Social Mobility and Career Planning

Effective career guidance is essential for helping people plan their education, careers, and future lives. Guidance counselors are a critical resource for students to link their studies with career opportunities, especially those outside a student's own social networks. Social research suggests that students should start to think about careers as early as middle school and should be in regular contact with professional guidance counselors through graduation (Curry, Belser, and Binns 2013). Effective career guidance is crucial for increasing social mobility because poor and disadvantaged students are the least likely to have the social contacts and the cultural knowledge that will help them successfully navigate the complicated world of jobs and careers.

Guidance counselors are more effective when they consider patterns of social stratification and social opportunity. Most students look at prestige-based rankings when thinking about where to go to college, even though many prestigious schools do a relatively poor job of admitting students from low-income families (Woodhouse 2015). In recent years, CollegeNet has taken a different approach with its Social Mobility Index, which helps students identify the schools that most consistently graduate students from low-income backgrounds into promising careers.

Similarly, sociological research suggests that some high-paying jobs are better than others at hiring people from all levels of the stratification system. Many students want to work in top-tier investment banks, consulting firms, and law firms because these jobs offer six-figure starting salaries. However, even among the Ivy League graduates they target, these firms prefer students who combine good grades with the kinds of extracurricular activities and interests that signal a wealthy upbringing (Rivera 2015).

In contrast, huge investments are being made to increase the number of low-income and minority students entering careers in STEM (science, technology, engineering, and mathematics) fields. Jobs in these fields are forecast to expand rapidly over the next several decades, and on average they offer starting salaries that are 26 percent higher than those in non-STEM fields (Bidwell 2014). In some high-demand STEM fields, companies hire students as paid apprentices or interns while they are still in college and teach them the skills they will need to be successful in the industry (Harper and Lacey 2016).

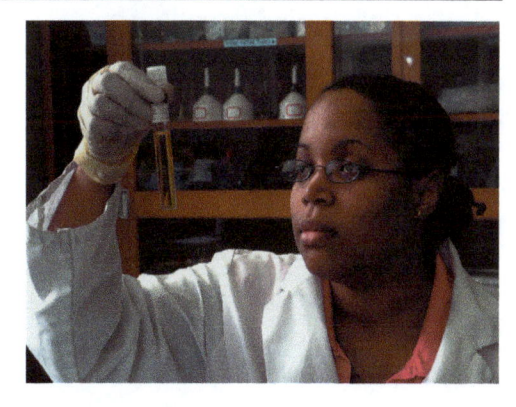

**Diversity in STEM careers**
Huge investments are being made to increase the number of low-income and minority students entering careers in STEM. Why is it important to recruit diverse candidates into scientific careers?

### ACTIVE LEARNING

**Find out:** The earlier you can connect with your school's career center, the more successful you will be in internship and job search. Career centers offer a range of programs and services, such as self-assessments, internship opportunities, and career information. Make an appointment at your campus career center to talk about your career goals with a counselor.

from one-quarter to more than 80 percent of all US employment (Wyatt and Hecker 2006; Bureau of Labor Statistics 2020). These structural changes in the economy create both upward and downward mobility for entire classes of workers, creating significant opportunities for some and serious stress for others.

Periods of social crisis and rapid social change can also produce structural mobility, as the COVID-19 pandemic has shown. The Pew Foundation reported in April of 2020 that 43 percent of US adults reported being laid off or having to take a pay cut as a result of the pandemic (Parker et al. 2020). Major economic recessions cause widespread job losses, which can have lasting effects on entire generations of workers and their children. During the Great Recession of 2008 more than 8.7 million jobs were lost, with more than half of all adult workers in the United States experiencing unemployment, a cut in pay, a reduction in hours, or an involuntary period in a part-time job (Pew Research Center 2010a). For such workers, the bad luck of entering the workforce at the wrong time can have negative consequences that will last for their entire lives. Even after the economy begins to improve, they find themselves passed over in favor of new graduates and younger workers, who do not bear the stigma of long-term unemployment.

**Structural mobility**
The 2008 economic recession led to widespread job losses and downward mobility. This was the result of the economic failure of institutions rather than individuals.

## 6.5 Social Change and the Attempt to Create More Equality

**LG 6.5** Consider factors that affect mobility and the stratification system, such as education, family background, and racial and gender differences, as well as social policy and social conflict.

Because inequality creates resistance, conflict, and demands for social change, it can also inspire the hope of creating a more equal society. This is not true for all forms of inequality, to be sure. It is hard to get people to care about the inequalities that exist between the well-to-do and the rich

(Frankfurt 1987). But many people do care about the poverty, violence, disrespect, and health disparities that fall disproportionately onto people at the bottom of the stratification system.

## Social Policy

Governments have created social policies to address poverty, violence, and other undesirable consequences of social stratification. For example, more than 90 percent of countries have established minimum wage laws. Another widely adopted social policy is the progressive income tax, in which poorer people pay a lower proportion of their income in tax, while wealthier people pay a higher proportion. Today, the US tax system has seven different income

---

**PAIRED CONCEPTS**

## Structure and Contingency

### Creating Social Security

Historically, the challenge of creating economic security for aging populations was taken up by families, fraternal organizations, churches, trade unions, and charities. Eventually, governments created social policies to protect the economic security of their aged populations.

In the United States, the attempt to create an old-age pension system goes back to the beginning of the nation. In 1795, Thomas Paine called for a system that taxed people who inherited property to pay an annual pension to every American aged 50 or older. In 1862, the Civil War pension plan was created to pay benefits to disabled soldiers as well as to widows and orphans of soldiers who had been killed or disabled during military service. This plan was extended in 1906, to cover all Civil War veterans who were aged 62 or older. But the Civil War pension program was relatively limited, including less than 1 percent of the total US population at the time.

The shock of the Great Depression in 1929 stimulated attempts to create a federal pension system in the United States similar to those developed in other countries. The Social Security Act of 1935 established a federal old-age insurance plan, established state-run unemployment insurance, and made money available for states to create assistance plans to help support poor mothers and their children. As these programs grew, federal government bureaucracies expanded and became more efficient.

Social Security became the largest and most successful of the social insurance programs established in the United States. Beginning as a federal program, Social Security was the only social insurance program that did not have to contend with powerful interests from state and local government. Supporters of Social Security used cultural strategies to convince the American public that it was a good system. Connecting it to a long tradition of dividing citizens into "worthy" and "unworthy" aid recipients, they described Social Security as a system that would reward retired workers after a long period of economic productivity (Skocpol 1996: 322). They also described it as a system in which workers would "earn" their pensions over the course of their working lives, glossing over the fact that current retirees' benefits are actually financed through current payroll taxes (Skocpol 1996: 323).

**ACTIVE LEARNING**

**Find out:** Choose another country, and compare their pension system with the Social Security system used in the US. What are the main similarities and differences between the two?

brackets, which begin at 10 percent and increase progressively up to a maximum of 37 percent of all income above $578,126 ($693,751 for married taxpayers filing jointly). Most countries have some version of a progressive income tax, as a way of trying to reduce inequality.

Other social policies are designed to help redress historical inequalities based on race, gender, and ethnicity. Globally, women and historically marginalized groups have been disproportionately harmed by poverty, violence, and discrimination, making these groups more vulnerable and limiting their opportunities for social mobility. The United States created the Civil Rights Division of the Department of Justice in 1957, in order to enforce laws prohibiting discrimination on the basis of race, color, sex, disability, religion, familial status, and national origin. At a global level, the United Nations, the US Department of State, and other national governments are engaged in diplomacy, foreign assistance programs, and partnerships with private organizations around the world to promote greater equality, by responding to historical structures of discrimination and inequality. In response to the COVID-19 pandemic, the World Bank invested $20 billion in 2020 to help purchase and distribute vaccines to poor nations around the globe, and the United Nations collects data on global vaccine equity. While measures like these are helpful, critics point out that given the level of historical discrimination and the scale of the COVID-19 crisis, much more needs to be done (Lavery et al. 2023).

**PAIRED CONCEPTS**

## Solidarity and Conflict

### A Short History of the Workers' Strike in the United States

When workers feel exploited, they can collectively refuse to work, which is known as a "labor strike." In 2020, during the COVID-19 pandemic, workers at Amazon, Target, Walmart, and Whole Foods organized a nationwide strike to protest the lack of hazard pay and safety precautions. Even before the pandemic, there had been a significant increase in strike activity in the United States in 2018 and 2019 (McNicholas and Poydack 2020). But workers did not always have the legal right to engage in labor strikes. Strike efforts during the 18th and 19th centuries were often met with violence. England passed the Combinations of Workmen Act in 1825, which outlawed strikes and imposed criminal penalties for striking workers. British strikers who destroyed company property were often sentenced to death, and other strikers were exiled to penal colonies.

In the United States, strike activity increased dramatically during the 1870s, as did police violence against striking workers. The Great Railroad Strike of 1877 began in West Virginia, spread to five other states, and lasted 45 days before local, state, and federal troops forced the end of the strike, killing more than one hundred people in the process. Private security forces shot and killed nine workers during an 1892 strike against the Carnegie Steel Company, and eight thousand Pennsylvania state militia were needed to end the rioting and the protests that ensued. A strike by railroad workers against the Pullman Company in 1894 was forcefully ended by twelve thousand US Army troops but not before it spread to include 250,000 workers across 27 states.

The violence directed at striking workers strengthened their solidarity and resolve and convinced them of the need for a national labor movement. National strikes by rail, coal, and steel workers involved hundreds of thousands of workers. After decades of conflict, with government usually taking the side of business owners, the solidarity and sacrifices of workers finally began to pay off. The Wagner Act of 1935 guaranteed the basic rights of private-sector employees to organize into unions, to engage in collective bargaining in the attempt to improve working conditions, and to take collective actions (such as strikes).

Striking workers have continued to face challenges from employers as well as government. A 1947 law passed by the New York state legislature made it illegal for state employees to go on strike, and most states followed with similar laws. The Taft-Hartley Act of 1947 required workers to give 80 days' notice before going on strike, authorized the president to intervene in strikes that might lead to a national emergency, and prohibited federal employees from striking. A legal decision in 1989 ruled that employers were allowed to promise senior-level jobs to younger workers who were willing to break a strike. And companies have been allowed to respond to strike actions by using lockouts, where they tell their employees not to come to work until they are willing to accept management's contract offer. The larger unions have created strike funds that they use to pay their members during strike actions, but there is no question that successful strikes require high levels of solidarity among workers.

**Workers strike**
Striking nursing home workers in Detroit, Michigan, during the July 20, 2020, nationwide Strike for Black Lives. At the time, more than fifty thousand nursing home residents and workers had already died from COVID-19. Do you think that workers are entitled to strike for better wages and conditions?

### ACTIVE LEARNING

**Find out:** There is a lot of state-by-state variation in laws about unions and strikes. Create a list of states that allow state employees to strike, and create another list of states that have laws against union membership as a condition of employment. Compare the two lists. Do you see any patterns?

## Social Conflict

Charles Tilly defines **contentious politics** as the use of social conflict and other disruptive techniques to make a political point and to change government policy. Contentious politics can be either nonviolent (demonstrations, protests, labor strikes, civil disobedience) or violent (destruction of property, rioting, civil wars, even terrorism). By disrupting ordinary events and focusing attention on specific issues, contentious politics force people in society to decide which side of the conflict they support and pressure governments to respond.

**Contentious politics** The use of social conflict and other disruptive techniques to make a political point in an effort to change government policy.

Social conflict over inequality also happens at a transnational level. While the Occupy Wall Street movement began in the United States in 2011 as a protest against economic inequality, the movement quickly spread, with a global "Day of Rage" in more than 80 countries. Antipoverty groups converge regularly on global finance meetings to denounce corporate greed and to press the world's wealthiest nations to make a real commitment to end global poverty. We discuss these kinds of social movements in greater detail in Chapter 13.

## CASE STUDY

### *The Bachelor*: Crystallizing Stratification on TV

Inequality is complex and contradictory. Dimensions of inequality intersect in different ways to affect individuals and groups. To end this chapter, we use the five paired concepts to explore inequality as it is represented on the television show *The Bachelor*.

*The Bachelor* documents the search for a wife by an eligible bachelor. At the beginning of the season, he is presented with around 25 potential mates. The show has produced marriage proposals and marriages and several spinoffs, including *The Bachelorette* and more than a dozen other shows. *The Bachelor* also exemplifies the way that different kinds of *inequality* reinforce each other.

The men selected to play the bachelor must be considered eligible. Thus, the show illustrates both what is culturally valued as successful for men and what is considered desirable in the women who seek their favor. It is meaningful that the individuals selected to play the bachelor are typically *privileged*, straight, wealthy, and (with few exceptions) white. There are no male mates offered to the bachelor on *The Bachelor*. In fact, a major premise of the show is the inevitability of marriage and typically heterosexual marriage, as the central institution that secures the economic, social, and emotional future for both individuals. To be sure, there is one episode of the *Bachelor in Paradise* (a spinoff where contestants who had been unsuccessful on *The Bachelor* have a chance to compete again) that concluded with a same-sex marriage proposal between Demi Burnett and Kristian Haggerty. This was a big change. That said, the marriage proposal followed many standard expectations and reinforced social understandings about marriage norms that are central to the show. *The Bachelor* continues to equate eligibility and desirability with heterosexuality, and it exemplifies the norm that heterosexuality and marriage are connected so that other alternatives seem unlikely.

The bachelors are also considered eligible in economic terms. While they are not all rich, they have secure, typically well-paid professional jobs. The idea that wealth is important is emphasized by the show's setting: a lavish six-bedroom, nine-bath mansion in California reputedly worth more than $8 million. As the show unfolds, dates and other social events occur in the mansion and other opulent surroundings around the world. The underlying message is that the eligible man is desirable because he is wealthy and privileged, and therefore it is reasonable that women will compete for his attention, even in a highly contrived media setting.

The competition between women, which is a major premise of the show, gives rise to rapidly shifting dynamics of *solidarity* throughout the season. The women make alliances of solidarity and then betray them to improve their own chances at winning a rose from the bachelor. The drama of betrayal, encouraged by the format of *The Bachelor*, demonstrates how competition for scarce

**A genuine change?**
A recent season of *Bachelor in Paradise* concluded with the show's first-ever same-sex marriage proposal between contestants Demi Burnett and Kristian Haggerty.

resources can create *conflict*, resentment, and even violence.

Race and ethnicity are also important factors on the show, which has been widely criticized for a lack of diversity among leads as well as contestants. Critics have observed that even when non-white contestants are cast they "seldom go very far" (Verhoeven and Ali 2016). In the case of Jubilee Sharpe, for example, who dated bachelor Ben Higgins in the 20th season of the show in 2016, fans and critics alike *resisted* the all-white format and pushed back against the *power* of the show's definition of what is normal or appropriate. As one fan tweeted, "Am I the only one reading between the lines as to why these women don't 'see' Ben with someone like Jubilee?" It joins a range of other actions and protests about the whiteness of *The Bachelor*, including a class action lawsuit taken against the show in 2012 for lack of diversity.

Jubilee herself joined critics in suggesting that the show was rigged and that her personal shortcomings don't explain why she left the show. At the same time, Jubilee's obvious audience appeal meant that she was cast in the spinoff, *Bachelors in Paradise*, the following year. And in 2017 *The Bachelorette* also cast its first Black female lead, Rachel Lindsay. It was not until June 2020 that the show finally announced the first Black "bachelor," Matt James—after 40 seasons.

*The Bachelor*'s representation of romance, sexuality, race, and marriage also has a *global* appeal. The format has been adapted in many other countries, with *local* versions airing over the last 14 years in Australia, Brazil, Canada, China, France, Finland, Germany, Israel, New Zealand, Norway, Poland, Romania, Russia, Switzerland, Slovenia, the United Kingdom, Thailand, Ukraine, and Vietnam.

## CASE STUDY CONTINUED

*Contingency* is also an important part of the appeal of *The Bachelor* since the show's action unfolds according to the bachelor's whims. Some commentators believe the show is fixed by its producers and directors, so the outcome is predetermined. Others think that the bachelor and the candidates for his hand overplay the drama of the show. Whatever the case, the *structures* that define the eligibility and desirability of the bachelor continue to include economic privilege, heterosexual marriage, and whiteness, with little modification.

# LEARNING GOALS REVISITED

**6.1 Understand stratification as the way sociologists think about social inequality.**

- Stratification is the division of society into strata, or layers, of people with differential access to scarce but desirable things.
- Despite long-standing debates about the nature and ethics of inequality, there is considerable evidence for the negative effects of inequality on people in the lower categories of society.

**6.2 Distinguish types of stratification.**

- Different stratification systems organize inequality in a multitude of ways, with varying consequences for different groups of people. Stratification systems describe how these inequalities are organized.
- Stratification systems can be compared in terms of the degree of inequality, the rigidity of inequality, the degree of ascriptiveness, and the degree of crystallization.
- Caste systems are highly crystallized, rigidly ascriptive stratification systems based on occupational assignment at birth. They display a high degree of inequality.
- In class systems, inequality is rooted in economic differences.
- In party systems, institutional position is the primary determinant of social status in the stratification system.
- In status systems, social groups are defined by lifestyle and consumption patterns.

**6.3 Develop an understanding of broad patterns of stratification in the United States and globally.**

- The distribution of wealth is highly unequal in the United States and around the world. There is

inequality between as well as within countries.
- The degree of inequality represented by the concentration of wealth in the hands of a tiny economic elite has become even more extreme over time.
- The United States is the wealthiest developed country in the world and the country with the most extreme degree of internal economic inequality, understood as the distance between the poorest and richest.

**6.4 Comprehend the concept of mobility, and distinguish different kinds of mobility, such as structural mobility and intergenerational mobility.**

- Mobility is movement within a stratification system. Vertical mobility is movement up and down the hierarchy. In contrast, horizontal mobility describes lateral moves that do not affect overall socioeconomic location.
- Absolute mobility refers to the movement associated with the acquisition of things, while relative mobility describes movement compared to other salient groups.
- Intergenerational mobility compares social location relative to one's parents.
- Structural mobility is movement caused by some overall change in the stratification system, such as the shift from manufacturing to service occupations. Other sources of structural change that cause mobility in the system are economic depressions and recessions.

**6.5 Consider factors that affect mobility and the stratification system, such as education, family background, and racial and gender differences, as well as social policy and social conflict.**

- Social mobility is shaped by the nature of the stratification system.
- Family background, education, and cultural capital all affect an individual's life chances in a stratification system.
- Gender and race organize stratification systems and shape the life chances of entire categories of people. Systems of gender and race inequality intersect with other kinds of stratification to shape individual life outcomes and group chances.
- Social policies such as old age pensions, unemployment insurance, progressive taxation, civil rights legislation, and universal public education are all societal efforts to shape the stratification system in more productive and more equal directions.
- Social conflict and direct action are ways that less powerful groups have asserted a need to change the stratification system or have resisted existing stratification systems.

## Key Terms

Absolute mobility 193
Ascriptiveness 178
Caste systems 178
Categorical inequality 176
Colonialism 190
Contentious politics 201
Cultural capital 196
Davis-Moore theory of inequality 176
Degree of crystallization 178
Degree of inequality 178
Elites 181
Horizontal mobility 193
Income 185
Inequality 174
Intergenerational mobility 193
Lower-middle class 187
Marginal productivity theory 177
Meritocracy 182
Middle class 187
Net worth 185
Party system 182
Relative deprivation 176
Relative mobility 193
Rigidity 178
Social mobility 192
Socioeconomic status 184
Status group 181
Stratification 177
Structural mobility 196
Upper-middle class 186
Vertical social mobility 192
Wealth 185
Working poor 189
World systems theory 190

## Review Questions

1. What is the relationship between inequality and stratification?
2. What are the main ways to compare different stratification systems? Give examples of different systems.
3. Describe the broad patterns of stratification in the United States and around the world.
4. What is the difference between structural mobility and intergenerational mobility? Can intergenerational mobility be caused by structural mobility? How?
5. How does social policy affect stratification? Give an example.
6. If a country is rich, can it still have inequality? Explain.
7. How are gender and race stratification connected to class stratification?
8. Identify three differences between caste and class systems.

## Explore

**RECOMMENDED READINGS**

Bourdieu, Pierre. 2000. *The Weight of the World: Social Suffering in Contemporary Society*. Stanford, CA: Stanford University Press.

Domhoff, G. William. 2013. *Who Rules America? The Triumph of the Corporate Rich*, 7th ed. New York: McGraw-Hill.

Grusky, David, and Tamar Kricheli-Katz, eds. 2012. *The New Gilded Age*. Stanford, CA: Stanford University Press.

Piketty, Thomas. 2014. *Capital in the Twenty-First Century*. Cambridge, MA: Belknap.

Sennet, Richard. 1972. *The Hidden Injuries of Class*. New York: Knopf.

Sennet, Richard. 2005. *The Culture of the New Capitalism*. New Haven, CT: Yale University Press.

World Bank. 2018. *Piecing Together the Poverty Puzzle. Poverty and Shared Prosperity*. Washington, DC: World Bank.

## ACTIVITIES

- *Use your sociological imagination*: Can you identify any effects of structural changes on your own economic biography? What are they?

- *Media+Data Literacies*: Go to the library or go online and discover what the Gini coefficient is. Explain what the Gini coefficient summarizes. What is the Gini coefficient of the United States? Compare it with one other country.

- *Discuss*: In the five paired concepts, inequality is related to privilege. This means that where there is inequality, there is always privilege. Most of us sit at the intersections of different kinds of privilege and inequality. Do you consider yourself privileged in any way in the stratification system? How?

"THAT'S NOT A CHIP ON MY SHOULDER UR KNEE ON MY NECK"
—Malcom X

I CAN'T Breathe....

# Race, Ethnicity, and Immigration

On May 25, 2020, police officers in Minneapolis arrested George Floyd, a 46-year-old Black man. They had been called by a convenience store employee, who claimed that Floyd had used a counterfeit $20 bill to purchase a pack of cigarettes. Two police officers removed Floyd from his vehicle and handcuffed his hands behind his back. They tried to force him into their police car, but Floyd fell down, complaining that he could not breathe. At this point two additional officers arrived on the scene. One of these officers, Derek Chauvin (who already had 17 complaints registered against him), pulled Floyd onto the street. Chauvin placed his knee on Floyd's neck and left it there for nearly nine minutes, while Floyd repeatedly cried out that he could not breathe and bystanders yelled at the officers to stop. With several people filming the entire incident and with the other three police officers watching, Chauvin continued to force his knee into Floyd's neck until EMTs arrived on the scene and told him to get off the victim so that they could attend to him. The ambulance drove away with a motionless Floyd, who was pronounced dead about one hour later.

The video of Floyd's killing spread quickly on social media, and people poured into the streets to protest police violence against Black people. With the organizational support of the Black Lives Matter movement, the protests quickly spread to cities around the country, lasting for more than a month;

**Black Lives Matter protest**
The May 25, 2020, murder of George Floyd in police custody renewed the national outcry against racial profiling and the extreme violence directed at Black men in America, particularly by the police.

### Chapter Outline

**7.1 THE SOCIAL CONSTRUCTION OF RACE 211**

*Race and Biology 211*
*The Changing Understanding of Race over Time 212*
*Race and Ethnicity 214*

**7.2 RACIAL AND ETHNIC GROUPS IN THE UNITED STATES 214**

*Native American People 217*
*White People 219*
*Black or African American People 220*
*Hispanic or Latino People 223*
*Asian American People 226*

**7.3 RACE, PRIVILEGE, AND INEQUALITY 227**

*The Privileges of Being in the Majority Group 228*
*Racial Discrimination and Segregation 229*
*Consequences of Discrimination 231*
*Racial Conflict 232*

**7.4 MULTICULTURALISM AND DIVERSITY 236**

*Multiculturalism (Movement and Policy) 236*
*Multiracial and Multiethnic Identities 237*

## Chapter Outline (continued)

**7.5 IMMIGRATION 239**
*Trends in Immigration 240*
*What Causes Immigration? 241*
*Immigrant Communities 242*

**7.6 THE POLITICS OF IMMIGRATION 245**
*Laws about Citizenship and Immigration 245*
*Anti-Immigrant Movements 246*

**CASE STUDY: INTERSECTING IDENTITIES 248**

---

**Race** A system for classifying people into groups on the basis of shared physical traits, which people in society treat as socially important and understand to be biologically transmitted.

**Ethnicity** A system for classifying people into groups on the basis of shared cultural heritage and a common identity.

---

estimates suggested that as many as 20 million people participated in the protests (Buchanan, Bui, and Patel 2020). Protesters around the world gathered in front of US embassies to show their support for the Black Lives Matter movement and to express their sympathy for the victims of racism and police violence. An autopsy declared that Floyd's death was a homicide. All four officers involved were fired from the police department and arrested; Chauvin was charged with murder, while the other three officers were charged with aiding and abetting second-degree manslaughter.

The killing of George Floyd was not an isolated instance. As we discussed in Chapter 5, there has been a long-standing national public discussion about racial profiling, which happens when police and private security target racial minorities for extra attention, based only on the perception that minorities are suspicious or dangerous. Some of the largest urban protests over the last 50 years have been precipitated by instances of police violence against Black men. The Black Lives Matter movement had been established seven years earlier, in 2013, in response to the acquittal of George Zimmerman, who had killed an unarmed Black teenager, Trayvon Martin. Black Lives Matter had organized dozens of protests in the intervening years, following other instances in which police had killed Black men and women. Responding to the history of racial and ethnic relations in the United States and worldwide, Black Lives Matter is "working for a world where Black lives are no longer systematically targeted for demise" (https://blacklivesmatter.com/about/).

This chapter explores the different ways that race and ethnicity shape our social lives. **Race** refers to a category of people who share specific physical traits, which people in society treat as socially important and understand to be biologically transmitted. We begin by discussing the different ways that race has been socially constructed and the way it continues to be socially constructed despite the fact that there is no biological foundation for racial categories. We also distinguish between race and **ethnicity**, which refers to a group of people who have a shared cultural heritage and a common identity. After describing the main racial and ethnic groups in the United States, we discuss how racism and racial discrimination have been used to reinforce inequality and privilege. We further examine how multiculturalism and multiracial identities have begun to change social policies and attitudes about race. Finally, we consider the cultural and political impact of immigration at a time of deepening inequality and a reckoning with racism in the United States.

## LEARNING GOALS

**7.1** Understand the way race is and has been socially constructed.

**7.2** Understand the relationships and intersections among racial and ethnic groups in the United States.

**7.3** Explain the relationship between racial privilege and racial inequality.

**7.4** Understand current thinking about diversity and multiculturalism.

**7.5** Describe the basic historical trends in immigration.

**7.6** Describe how immigrant communities are organized and how they shape politics and the economy in both sending and receiving countries.

# 7.1 The Social Construction of Race

**LG 7.1** Understand the way race is and has been socially constructed.

When sociologists emphasize that race is a social construction, they are making two related points: race is not a biological category, yet it is an important sociological concept. W. E. B. Du Bois wrote in 1903 that "the problem of the Twentieth Century is the problem of the color line," and recent events have demonstrated that it is very much a 21st-century problem as well.

## Race and Biology

Biologists and social scientists argue that race is not a useful concept for thinking about human genetic diversity. For any given set of racial classifications, they observe, there is more genetic variation within groups than between groups, and a lot of genetic overlap between racial groups. In other words, differences are not nearly as fixed as the idea of race suggests. The United Nations Educational, Scientific, and Cultural Organization (1951) acknowledged that "for all practical social purposes 'race' is not so much a biological phenomenon as a social myth" (quoted in Brattain 2007: 1399).

By the 1970s, advances in genetics further revealed scientific problems associated with the race concept. Genetic research discovered that all humans have genome sequences that are 99.9 percent identical. In 2000, the geneticist Craig Venter declared that "the concept of race has no genetic or scientific basis" (Weiss and Gillis 2000).

If the concept of race has been so completely discredited by biologists and geneticists, why do sociologists continue to study it? The answer is connected to the Thomas theorem (Chapter 2), which holds that if people define a situation as real, then it will be real in its consequences. In other words, race continues to play a powerful role in social life because individuals and groups continue to define race as a real thing. Race is embedded in social institutions, reproduced in social interactions, and embedded in language and culture. Governments throughout the world still collect data on the racial composition of their population. Individuals, groups, and communities continue to understand their identities in racial terms. And centuries of racial discrimination continue to shape the life chances and the opportunities that are afforded to different social groups.

In Chapter 2, we discussed racial formation theory, which analyzes modern Western society and particularly US society as structured by a historically developed "racial common sense." Racial stereotypes and institutionalized patterns of inequality are embedded in the fundamental fabric of modern social life at both the individual and the institutional levels. These have been developed over the course of particular histories of power and conflict that connect ideas of race, immigration, language, and culture.

### The Changing Understanding of Race over Time

Biologists and geneticists may have stopped using the concept of race, but they have not offered an alternative way to think about human variation. In everyday life, most people continue to use race as a way to think about the world, as they have for hundreds of years.

**THE ATTEMPT TO CREATE A SCIENCE OF RACIAL CLASSIFICATION.** The earliest attempts to create a scientific classification of human diversity began in the 1730s and 1740s, as part of a larger attempt by early modern scientists to classify all living things. Humans were placed at the top of the hierarchy, just above apes. As the classifications continued to develop, people developed a ranking of different human groups, trying to identify which groups were the most advanced. Most of the early classifications focused on physical features, character traits, and geography. All of the people who created these early classifications were Europeans, and all of them placed the groups of European descent at the top of their hierarchies.

**Racial determinism** A dominant social theory in the 19th century that argued that the world was divided into biologically distinct races and that there were fundamental differences in ability between the different racial groups.

By the middle of the 19th century, **racial determinism** had become the dominant theory explaining the achievements and failures of different human groups. Racial determinism was the idea that the world was divided into biologically distinct races and that there were fundamental differences in ability between the different racial groups. Proponents of the pseudoscience of racial classification used a variety of strategies to try to demonstrate these supposedly innate biological differences. They measured skull size and shape, they looked for anatomical differences, they did psychological tests, and they measured things like physical strength, vision, and pulmonary capacity (Smedley 1993: 255–71). They developed elaborate techniques for measuring skin color, and they used new quantitative techniques to develop statistical portraits of different racial groups. When IQ tests were developed in the early 20th century, racial determinists used them to try to prove that there were inherent racial differences in intelligence.

**THE CONCEPT OF RACE TODAY.** Beliefs about race began to change during the 20th century, because of changes in science as well as in societies themselves. The increase in immigration between 1890 and 1910 led many Americans to celebrate their nation as a "melting pot." At the same time, millions of Black Americans began to move from the rural South to the industrializing North to seek better jobs and education, a movement known as the "Great Migration." The atrocities that the Nazis committed in the name of racial purity and racial determinism during World War II shocked people worldwide (Smedley 1993: 273). As the US government publicly criticized the racism of the Nazis, arguments about racial inferiority and racial determinism became less acceptable in public debates within the United States as well (Alexander 2006).

In the fields of science, even before biologists and geneticists began to question the scientific status of the race concept, anthropologists and sociologists had already begun to question the assumptions of racial determinism. Anthropologists such as Franz Boas (1858–1942) argued that race did not have anything to do with language, culture, or behavior as these were all things that were learned and not inherited (Smedley 1993: 276–82). Boas insisted that any group superiority or inferiority was caused by differences in social environment and not by heredity. W. E. B. Du Bois argued that the disadvantages suffered by Black people were caused not by heredity but rather by the consequences of centuries of enslavement (Morris 2015: 38).

While many people in everyday life continued to believe in racial determinism, the work of social scientists such as Du Bois and Boas helped create a more sociological way to think about race. Rather than thinking about group differences in terms of heredity, the sociological approach tries to identify the social and historical factors that have caused these differences to exist. Linking these social factors to inequality and privilege, they try to identify the consequences of being a member of a minority group. They analyze how racial privilege gets institutionalized, in both formal and informal ways. They study how racial minorities resist power and prejudice, and they try to identify which social factors help this resistance succeed. They explore how racial group dynamics are influenced by local and global processes. In other words, while they reject biological theories of racial determinism, sociologists today still treat race as a real thing; from a sociological perspective, race is a category of group membership, which produces solidarity as well as conflict.

## Race and Ethnicity

Ethnicity, another important category of group membership, is based on a shared cultural heritage and a common identity. Ethnic groups are held together by shared language, traditions, rituals, and behaviors. Membership in an ethnic group is usually recognized by group members themselves as well as by outsiders.

The distinction between racial and ethnic groups is not always clear. Most racial groups have ethnic similarities based in shared cultural experience. Black Americans, for example, have distinctive religious, musical, and artistic traditions that can be traced to their common ancestry and their shared struggle against oppression (Baker 1987). Many groups that are today considered to be ethnic groups, such as people of Jewish or Irish ancestry, were once thought of as racial groups. Because the boundaries between race and ethnicity are often indistinct, particularly for historically marginalized groups, scholars today often write about "racial and ethnic groups" as if they are the same kind of category.

In most societies, majority groups tend to emphasize their ethnic identities and to ignore their racial identities or their racial privileges. The sociologist Herbert Gans called this **symbolic ethnicity**, which refers to the way dominant groups feel an attachment to specific ethnic traditions without really being active members of the ethnic group (Gans 1979). Some Irish Americans express their Irishness by participating in St. Patrick's Day celebrations, but they do not actually need to belong to any Irish groups. Many Italian-Americans come to New York City's Little Italy neighborhood to participate in the annual Feast of San Gennaro, but compared to when the festival was first established in 1926, they are less likely to live in that neighborhood and they are less likely to center their daily lives around participation in Italian-American social clubs or civic groups. According to Gans, symbolic ethnicity turns ethnicity into a kind of leisure activity. For these groups, their racial and ethnic identity is more voluntary, rather than being ascribed by other people. This is a privilege of being in the majority group, as we discuss in this chapter's section on race, privilege, and inequality.

**Symbolic ethnicity** The way dominant groups feel an attachment to specific ethnic traditions without being active members of the ethnic group.

## 7.2 Racial and Ethnic Groups in the United States

**LG 7.2** Understand the relationships and intersections among racial and ethnic groups in the United States.

The United States is a very diverse nation. The US Census Bureau projects that the United States will become a "majority-minority" country by 2043, which means that the country's largest ethnic group (non-Hispanic whites) will make up less than 50 percent of the US population. There are other societies that are more racially and ethnically diverse than the United States, particularly those in sub-Saharan Africa, but the United States is much more racially and ethnically diverse than other wealthy countries in Europe and Asia.

Table 7.1 shows the current racial and ethnic composition of the United States, according to the Census Bureau. Non-Hispanic whites are the largest racial group, making up 58.9 percent of the population; Black or African American is the next largest group at 13.6 percent, followed by Asian Americans at 6.3 percent, Native Americans at 1.3 percent, and Native Hawaiian and Other Pacific Islanders at 0.3 percent. In addition, the Census asks an ethnicity question to identify Hispanic and Latino American as an ethnicity. Latinos, who can be of any race, are 19.1 percent of the population. Importantly, the US Supreme Court has said that race is not limited to what the Census defines and that it can extend to all other ethnicities, including Jewish, Arab, or Italian groups. Generally, though, sociologists follow the Census categories to talk about race.

The US Census is a central social institution that represents American society. Authorized by the Constitution for purposes of taxation and electoral apportionment, the Census is the largest peacetime operation of the US government. Unlike the data that are collected by private corporations like Google and Meta, the Census's processes and budget operate under congressional oversight and are publicly accountable. Scholars and civil society organizations monitor and review Census data over time. It is important that

**TABLE 7.1 Population of the United States by Race and Ethnicity, 2020**

| RACE | |
|---|---|
| White | 75.5% |
| Black or African American | 13.6% |
| American Indian and Alaska Native | 1.3% |
| Asian | 6.3% |
| Native Hawaiian and Other Pacific Islander | 0.3% |
| Two or More Races | 3.0% |
| Total population | 100% |
| **ETHNICITY** | |
| Hispanic or Latino | 19.1% |
| Non-Hispanic or Latino | 80.9% |
| Non-Hispanic Whites | 58.9% |

Source: US Census Bureau: National Population Estimates; QuickFacts, July 2022.

## METHODS AND INTERPRETATION

# Defining and Measuring Race in Official Government Data

Since the first official census in 1790, the US government has collected data on the racial and ethnic characteristics of its population. But the categories it uses have changed in important ways over the last 225 years, and so have the strategies used to collect these data. Additionally, the US Census Bureau uses different data collection strategies than those used in other countries. A close look at the development of these different measurement strategies can help us understand how race is, and has been, socially constructed.

Until 1960, decisions about race were made by official census workers, based on their perceptions about the physical characteristics of the individual. At first, the Census had only three categories: "free white," "slaves," and "all other free persons." The 1820 Census created a new category for "free colored person," reflecting the growth of the non-slave Black population, as well as the fact that free Blacks had fewer rights than free whites. The 1850 Census eliminated the "slave" category, replacing it with the categories of "Black" and "Mulatto." The 1870 Census added the category of "Indian" to refer to Native Americans, and also began adding categories for Asian immigrants, who were identified by their nation of origin. The 1930 Census eliminated the category of "Mulatto." The 1970 Census provided for White, Black and Oriental, which narrowed the categories considerably. The attempt to count Latinos began in 1930 with the creation of the "Mexican" category, but this was eliminated in the 1940 Census after protests by the Mexican government. The 1970 Census added a Hispanic self-identification question, called the ethnicity question. This was a nonexclusive category, so that a person who self-identified as Hispanic by ethnicity was also counted as a member of one of the other racial groups.

Beginning with the 2000 census, all US citizens were allowed to report more than one race. US Census officials are currently considering changes for the 2030 Census, which would create a single question about race and ethnicity; the proposal would add the Hispanic/Latino category to the list of racial and ethnic categories, add an additional category for Middle Eastern or North African, provide additional information about nationality within each category, and then instruct respondents to select all categories that apply to them (Fong et al. 2023). Other governments have made

**US Census form**
The decennial US Census collects data on a wide range of topics, including race, ethnicity, ancestry, nativity, and language. The Census is an important social institution that defines racial and ethnic categories.

different choices about how to collect data about race and ethnicity. The Brazilian Census uses skin color (white, brown, and black) rather than race, reflecting the belief that race is a US concept that does not apply to Brazilian society (Telles 2002). France does not collect any census data on race, and French law prohibits the collection of official government data on racial characteristics.

**ACTIVE LEARNING**

**Discuss:** Do you think the US government should add additional information about nationality to the current Census form about race and ethnicity, as proposed for the 2030 Census? What are the advantages and disadvantages of collecting this information?

the Census counts all US residents so that they receive fair access to common resources, such as the right to vote and access public funds and services.

## Native American People

Although scientists continue to make new discoveries about population movements in North America, there is general agreement that the first humans began arriving from Asia about fifteen thousand years ago. This migration was made possible by a drop in sea level that created a land bridge between Siberia and Alaska. While it is impossible to know the exact size of the Native American population before the 15th century, archaeologists estimate that it was somewhere between 10 million and 100 million people.

The arrival of European colonizers devastated the Native American population. Native Americans had no immunity to European diseases, and many of them died from smallpox, influenza, tuberculosis, and other infectious diseases carried across the ocean from Europe. While disease was the largest cause of death for Native Americans, many others died in wars with the European settlers. The forced removal from ancestral homes and resettlement of Native Americans onto "Indian reservations" far away from the population centers of the white colonial settlers further decimated the population. According to the 1900 Census, the Native American population in the United States was only 237,196.

The US government created the Bureau of Indian Affairs in 1824, with the goal of assimilating Native Americans into mainstream American society and culture. Native American children were sent to boarding schools, where they were taught English and punished for speaking their own languages, given new "white" names, and forced to wear Western clothes and where they received religious training in Christianity. Educators hoped that their students would not return to the reservations, even during their summer holidays, but would prefer instead to become part of the white community. Politicians predicted that the "American Indians" as a race would soon disappear (Champagne 2008: 1679).

**Protesting racial injustice**
Native Americans in Minneapolis join Black Lives Matter protests in the wake of the murder of George Floyd in 2020.

Native Americans on the reservation lands suffered from poverty, health problems, substandard housing and transportation infrastructure, and high crime rates. These disparities continue today. More than one-quarter of the Native American population currently lives in poverty, and Native Americans have levels of education and labor force participation significantly lower than the US averages. They have the highest per-capita rate of violent victimization, the highest levels of alcohol and drug use, and the highest age-adjusted death rates of any racial or ethnic group in the nation (Sarche and Spicer 2008).

Since the 1970s, Native American communities have organized to make demands for stronger self-government, more cultural autonomy, and better economic self-sufficiency (Champagne 2008: 1681). Native Americans have been successful in the energy industry as well as the gaming and entertainment industry, bringing significant wealth to some communities. The Red Power Movement organized protests against the illegal takeover of Native American lands, and a number of tribes that had been terminated by the US government successfully campaigned to reclaim land and federal recognition (Champagne 2008: 1685–86). Efforts to preserve and reclaim Native American language and culture have led to a stronger assertion of Native American identity. Native Americans are also involved in a range of social movements including Black Lives Matter, and they also join with other groups in efforts to preserve tribal lands, including the protest against the Dakota Pipeline at Standing Rock beginning in 2016. In the 2020 Census, 9.6 million people self-identified as Native Americans, which was an 85 percent increase compared to the 2010 Census.

**PAIRED CONCEPTS**

## Structure and Contingency

### The Growth and Success of Native American Casinos

The US Constitution defines Native American tribes as separate and independent from the federal government and the states. While the Native American tribes have clearly suffered from colonization, forced migration, and appropriation of ancestral lands, their legal independence from federal and state governments has offered certain limited opportunities. The courts have consistently found that Native American tribes have the right to govern themselves. They have also prevented the states from taxing Native Americans living on reservation lands. By the 1980s, many Native American tribes began to develop strategies for economic growth that were made possible by their formal independence. One of the most significant and successful of their strategies has been the creation of a multibillion-dollar gaming industry.

Native American gaming operations began in the 1970s and 1980s, when several tribes in Florida and California opened bingo parlors and poker halls. State police quickly moved in to close down these operations, which they claimed had larger prizes and longer hours of operations than state laws allowed. The Native American tribes filed lawsuits in federal court, claiming that states did not have any jurisdiction over economic enterprises taking place on tribal lands. The tribes won their lawsuits, setting the stage for expanded gaming operations.

Native American tribes continued to open gaming establishments in several states throughout the 1980s. State politicians and casinos in New Jersey and Nevada lobbied Congress to try to limit the growth of Native American casinos. The federal government responded by passing the Indian Gaming Regulatory Act (IGRA) in 1988. This law stated that tribes could run small-scale gambling operations without any interference, but they could only operate full-blown casinos in states that already allowed those types of operations.

While the casino lobby believed that the IGRA protected their interests, Native American tribes argued for the right to establish casino operations in states other than Nevada and New Jersey. For example, the Mashantucket Pequot tribe in Connecticut won a lawsuit that allowed them to open casinos, based on the fact that the state allowed charities to run "casino nights" as a form of fundraising. The Pequots used this victory to transform their modest bingo hall into the Foxwoods Casino, which today has annual revenues of nearly $10 billion. Other major casinos followed, built on Native American lands in Michigan, California, New Mexico, Arizona, Minnesota, and Oklahoma. Today, there are nearly 500 Native American casinos, which together account for more than 40 percent of all casino gaming revenue in the United States.

**ACTIVE LEARNING**

**Find out:** Are there Native American casinos in your state? If so, when were they established?

## White People

The North American colonies were established by white settlers from England, who believed that white Europeans were at the top of the racial hierarchy. When the United States established its first citizenship law in 1790, it specified that only "free white persons" could apply for citizenship. Until 1965, immigration laws established clear quotas that were designed to ensure that the United States would remain a nation dominated by white Europeans.

As the sociologist E. Digby Baltzell (1915–1996) explained in *The Protestant Establishment*, the early history of the United States was dominated by white Anglo-Saxon Protestants (WASPs), who were primarily of English, Scottish, and Welsh ancestry (Baltzell 1958). WASPs controlled the worlds of politics, business, and education. They lived in the same neighborhoods, had their own social clubs, and tended to marry among each other. They sent their children to elite boarding schools in the New England countryside and then to elite universities such as Harvard, Princeton, and Yale.

Beginning in the late 1800s, large numbers of white European immigrants began arriving from southern and eastern Europe. Many of these immigrants were Catholic and Jewish, and most of them did not speak English. When they arrived, they were encouraged to learn English and to assimilate into American society. For the most part, these new white ethnic groups were blocked from entering the WASP establishment. They were largely excluded from WASP neighborhoods, living instead in crowded urban areas. They were forced to take low-paying jobs, and they endured discrimination in the workplace that limited their career advancement. Harvard, Yale, and Princeton introduced subjective admissions criteria focusing on "character" as a way to privilege students who came from WASP families and to discriminate against the new white ethnic groups; in fact, all three universities established quotas limiting the number of Jewish students they would admit (Karabel 2005).

Since the 1960s, the social forces that had maintained such strong divisions between different white ethnic groups began to loosen. Today, the children and grandchildren of white European immigrants speak English as their preferred language, and their experiences in college and the labor market are similar to those of children from WASP backgrounds (Alba 1990). Intermarriage rates between white Catholics, Protestants, and Jews have increased dramatically, to the point where the majority of US-born non-Hispanic whites now have an ethnically mixed ancestry (Alba 1990: 15).

## Black or African American People

The Atlantic slave trade brought more than one million enslaved people into North America between 1720 and 1807. The system of slavery was responsible for much of the wealth created in the new nation during its first century. By 1830, cotton produced by enslaved people was responsible for more than half the value of all exports from the United States (North 1961). By 1860, at the dawn of the Civil War, there were four million enslaved people; in the 11 Confederate states of the South, enslaved people were 38 percent of the population.

The system of slavery was extremely brutal and had profound consequences for enslaved individuals. The legal system did not recognize slave marriages and family life, and slave owners routinely split up families. More than one-third of all enslaved children grew up in households where one or both parents were absent. Nearly half of all infants born in slavery died during their first year of life, and the average life expectancy of a slave at birth was only about 21 years. A typical workday for slaves was more than 10 hours long and could be as long as 15 or 16 hours. Any perceived disobedience was punished with whipping, branding, and other forms of violence. Enslaved women were frequently raped and sexually abused. Enslaved people who left the plantation seeking their freedom could be killed without penalty. Enslaved people received no education, and it was illegal to teach them to read or write.

Even after the Thirteenth Amendment to the US Constitution outlawed slavery in 1865, the legacy of slavery continued to exert itself in the lives of Black people. Southern states created a system of "Jim Crow" laws that enforced racial segregation in schools, public transportation, restrooms, and other public facilities. Violence and intimidation were a regular feature of life for Black people in the South. Between 1882 and 1968 there were more than four thousand lynchings (murders carried out by a mob) of Black individuals, usually by hanging, without any legal prosecution of the murderers.

During the Great Migration (1880–1960), millions of Black Americans migrated from the rural South to the cities of the Northeast, Midwest, and West, only to be greeted by suspicion, hostility, and violence (Tolnay 2003). They found themselves limited to low-status and low-paying jobs, and they were forced to live in poor and racially segregated neighborhoods (Lieberson 1980). Deadly race riots took place in cities such as St. Louis (1917), Chicago (1919), and Tulsa (1921), with white mobs beating and killing Black people and setting fire to their neighborhoods.

Throughout US history and down to the present day, members of the Black community have organized to resist racial violence, segregation, and injustice. We discuss these resistance and protest movements in more detail in the Solidarity and Conflict box.

Since the 1980s, the size of the Black immigrant population in the United States has quadrupled, with the largest numbers coming from Jamaica, Haiti, and Nigeria (Anderson 2015). These immigrants are different in many respects from domestic-born Black people. Their connection to a transnational Caribbean or African community has helped them adapt successfully to life in the United States, despite the fact that they have had to face racial discrimination based in the legacy of American slavery. In fact, Black immigrants are employed at a higher rate than the overall native-born population (Thomas 2012). Black immigrants, and particularly African immigrants, are among the most highly educated immigrants. Despite this, they confront a racial wealth gap in the United States that results in a median household income far lower than would be expected on the basis of educational credentials (Asante-Muhammad and Gerber 2018). In this context, many immigrants consciously hold onto their cultural heritage, and they encourage their children to do the same thing, as a way of distinguishing themselves from the larger Black population and as a strategy for shielding themselves from the worst forms of racial discrimination (Waters 1990). By holding onto their identities and maintaining their cultural autonomy, these groups contribute to multiculturalism.

## PAIRED CONCEPTS: Solidarity and Conflict

### W. E. B. Du Bois, Booker T. Washington, and the Struggle to Define Black Politics

Since the end of the Civil War, Black leaders have argued about what the best political strategy is for fighting against racial discrimination and achieving full equality in US society. Was it better to demand an immediate end to all forms of discrimination or to focus on specific improvements even if that meant that other versions of inequality would continue? Would it be more effective to make strategic alliances with white leaders and supporters or to create a movement for empowerment that was led exclusively by members of the Black community? Was nonviolence always the best political strategy for expressing protest?

These different approaches can be traced back to the conflict between Booker T. Washington (1856–1915) and W. E. B. Du Bois (1868–1963), two of the most important Black leaders of the early 20th century. Washington was born in Virginia in 1856 and, along with his mother, was emancipated at the end of the Civil War. After teaching himself to read and eventually earning a college degree from the Hampton Institute, in 1881 he established the school that would become Tuskegee University.

In an 1895 speech, Washington described his political strategy for the improvement of Black individuals, counseling patience in order to avoid a backlash by angry whites. In the short term, Washington argued, the best strategy was to focus on education, job skills, and economic self-improvement. He argued that members of the Black community should delay their demands for full political equality; once they showed themselves to be responsible and reliable American citizens, he thought, they would be able to overcome white prejudice and be fully accepted into all parts of American society. Washington's approach received strong support from white politicians, business leaders, and philanthropists from the Northeast United States, among whom he raised millions of dollars to support his project.

Washington's approach was strongly opposed by W. E. B. Du Bois. Born in 1868, Du Bois grew up in western Massachusetts, where his parents were part of a small community of free Black people living in the town of Great Barrington. He earned bachelor's degrees at Fisk and Harvard Universities and studied economics, political science, and social policy at the University of Berlin. Returning to the United States in 1894, Du Bois became the first Black person to earn a PhD at Harvard. As a professor at Atlanta University, he created the first scientific

**Booker T. Washington**

school of sociology in the United States (Morris 2015). He was also one of the founders of the NAACP and an influential journalist and public intellectual.

Du Bois argued that it was a mistake for members of the Black community to delay their demands for political equality, arguing that without voting rights and full social equality they would continue to be oppressed. He rejected the idea that Black people should ignore the liberal arts and focus exclusively on practical job-related education. Du Bois argued that the most talented Black people needed a classical education in order to reach their full potential and to become effective leaders and spokespersons. He also rejected the arguments of many white scholars, who claimed that Africans and Black Americans had an inferior and pathological culture and that they would be better off if they assimilated into the dominant white American culture (Morris 2015: 177). As editor of *The Crisis*, the official publication of the NAACP, Du Bois actively promoted the achievements of Black artists, musicians, and writers.

**ACTIVE LEARNING**

**Discuss:** One element in Du Bois's argument with Washington was the belief that free Black people needed a liberal arts education that included history, philosophy, and the arts and not only narrow vocational training for a job. This debate continues today. Do you think less advantaged and oppressed people should learn philosophy and history, or is it more important to get skills training for jobs? What are the pros and cons of each argument?

## Hispanic or Latino People

As the United States expanded westward during the 19th century, it settled and conquered lands that had previously been controlled by Mexico. The end of the Mexican–American War in 1848 gave the US ownership of California, as well as much of the land that would become New Mexico, Nevada, Utah, Wyoming, and Colorado. Mexicans living on those lands had the option to become US citizens, and most of them did so.

Mexican Americans living in the West and Southwest experienced prejudice and discrimination, and most white ethnic groups treated Mexican Americans as a marginalized group. Racially restrictive housing covenants barred Mexican Americans (as well as Black Americans) from buying houses in "white" neighborhoods. Many school districts segregated Mexican American children from white children.

Despite these obstacles, Mexicans emigrated to the United States in large numbers, particularly after 1910. Mexican labor was crucial for the development of the agricultural economy in California and for the development of the railroad and the mining industry in the Southwest. When World War II caused labor shortages during the 1940s, the United States established the Bracero program to bring in Mexican contract workers. This pattern continues today, with more than 35 percent of the Latino population being foreign-born.

Most sociologists refer to Latinos as an ethnic group, and they emphasize that Latinos can be of any race (Alba and Nee 2003). Complicating matters further, Latinos are more likely than any group to mark their race as "other" on the US Census, even though race is still a powerful influence on their lives (Bonilla-Silva 2018). While many Latino immigrants did not experience race-based discrimination back in their countries of origin, once they arrived in the United States they found themselves grouped together with Black Americans, treated as a historically marginalized group, and segregated into communities with other marginalized groups (Portes 1995). This has had a negative impact on the educational resources available for their children, the kinds of jobs that are available to them, and the ability to improve their socioeconomic circumstances (Zhou 1997).

People of Mexican descent account for 58.9 percent of the Latino population in the United States, followed by Puerto Ricans at 9.3 percent (Krogstad et al. 2023). The Latino population in the United States has become more diverse since the 1980s, with large numbers of immigrants coming from Cuba, El Salvador, the Dominican Republic, and other countries in Central and South America (Stepler and Brown 2016). While Latino immigrants historically concentrated their residence in the states of the American Southwest (Arizona, Texas, New Mexico, California, and Colorado), recent immigrants have dispersed much more widely throughout the country, with large numbers of new immigrants residing in metropolitan areas of the Southeast US, and also in rural areas in states that have not historically received large numbers of immigrants (Parrado and Kandel 2008).

In her book *Making Hispanics*, Christina Mora describes how an alliance was formed during the 1970s to promote a pan-ethnic identity of "Hispanic" as a way to unite this diverse population (Mora 2015). Before that time, most Latino groups identified with their place of origin, with the dominant identities being Mexican American, Puerto Rican, and Cuban American. These groups were concentrated in different regions of the United States, and they had different political goals from one another. Gradually, an alliance formed between federal officials, grassroots activists, and Spanish-language broadcasters. These three groups worked together to promote the category of "Hispanic" as a common identity that could unite the diverse population

## PAIRED CONCEPTS

## Global and Local

### Latino Computer Engineers from Colombia and Puerto Rico

The growth in the information technologies and telecommunications fields during the 1990s created a demand for specialized computer and software programmers, which could not be met by professionals already living and working in the United States. As a result, the US government increased the work visa quotas for foreign-born professionals. This policy, combined with greater enforcement of antidiscrimination laws, encouraged employers to actively recruit foreign-born minorities into professional positions in the computer engineering field (Alarcón 1999). Many software engineers were recruited from China, India, and Latin America.

Among the Latin American computer engineers, the majority came from Puerto Rico and Colombia. Each group was motivated by a combination of global and local factors. Puerto Ricans are legal citizens, which allows them to travel freely between the island and the mainland to work legally in the United States. Many high-tech companies had opened offices in Puerto Rico during the 1970s, taking advantage of laws that exempted them from taxes when they relocated to the island. When these tax exemptions ended in the mid-1980s, most of these companies closed their Puerto Rican offices. As a result, many Puerto Rican computer engineers moved to the mainland United States.

Colombian computer engineers were also concerned about the ability to find work in their professional fields because of the deteriorating economic conditions in their country. Many of them were also worried about the growth of drug cartels and drug-related violence in Colombia. Feeling that they had very limited opportunities to find rewarding professional jobs in their home country, Colombian computer engineers emigrated to the United States to work in the information technologies industry (Rincón 2015).

In Colombia as well as Puerto Rico, transnational recruitment networks made it easier for technology companies and computer engineers to find each other (Rincón 2015). The global nature of engineering meant that university curricula had been standardized to meet the needs of transnational engineering companies. Many of the engineering professors in Puerto Rico and Colombia had trained in the United States, and they could use the networks they had developed there to help their students make professional contacts. Likewise, many of these students took advantage of internships and study-abroad programs to spend time in the United States.

Despite their high levels of education and their professional degrees, however, Colombian and Puerto Rican computer engineers often experienced racial discrimination once they arrived in the mainland United States. Many of their coworkers treated them as less qualified. They were subjected to racial and ethnic slurs, as well as police harassment, because of their skin color or accent. Despite the fact that many of these computer engineers viewed themselves as sophisticated and cosmopolitan, people in their local communities did not always see them this way (Rincón 2015).

#### ACTIVE LEARNING

**Find out:** What proportion of workers in computer occupations in the United States are Latino/a? Of those workers, how many are immigrants? How many came to the US on H1-B visas?

---

of Latinos into a single ethnic group. Over time, Hispanic ethnic identity came to be adopted by Latinos throughout North America, South America, and Central America, as television stations such as Univision transformed themselves from regional Mexican broadcasters to become a global Hispanic media empire. This is an excellent example of the self-conscious and intentional construction of an ethnic category.

## Asian American People

Asian Americans, including people from Hawaii and other Pacific Islands, are a diverse ethnic group with a long history of immigration to the United States. Chinese immigrants began arriving in large numbers during the California Gold Rush in the 1840s and 1850s. Many of these immigrants later found jobs in the railroad industry in the 1860s. Japanese agricultural workers began arriving in the United States in the 1880s. Koreans and Filipinos began arriving in US states and territories in the early 1900s, where they worked on the sugar plantations in Hawaii.

Native Hawaiian and Pacific Islanders also have a long history in the United States, although it was not until 2000 that the category "Native Hawaiian and Other Pacific Islander" was added to the Asian race question in the US Census (Pew Research Center 2015a). A part of the legacy of US imperialism in the Pacific Ocean during the 19th and 20th centuries (Camacho 2016), American Samoa became a US naval station in 1878 and then an unincorporated territory in 1899 as part of an agreement between colonial powers in the Pacific. Guam and the Philippines were annexed in 1898 after the Spanish–American war; the Philippines went on to fight a war against US occupying forces from 1899 to 1902. Hawaii was a kingdom until the late 19th century, was briefly a republic, and then ceded itself to the militarily dominant United States in 1898.

Early Asian Americans faced significant hostility, prejudice, and violence in the United States. Chinese and Japanese immigrants were not allowed to own land in many parts of the country, and they were forced to live in crowded urban areas segregated from white communities. The Chinese Exclusion Act of 1882 made Chinese immigration to the United States illegal and denied citizenship to those already in the country. New immigration laws passed in 1917 and 1924 extended these exclusions to other Asian groups, and these laws remained in effect until the 1940s. Between 1942 and 1945, the US relocated approximately 120,000 Japanese Americans to detention camps in the western US.

After the 1965 Immigration Act ended the system of racial, ethnic, and national quotas, the Asian American population increased, from 491,000 in 1960 to more than 20 million in 2022, as Vietnamese, Laotian, and Cambodian refugees joined the migrant stream in the 1970s. Nearly half of all Asian immigrants have settled in three states (California, New York, and Texas).

Asian Americans have been a remarkably successful ethnic group. Compared to the US population as a whole, they have higher average incomes and higher levels of educational attainment. More than half of all Asian Americans age 25 and older have a college degree compared to only 33 percent of the US population (Budiman and Ruiz 2021). The median household income for Asian Americans was $108,700 in 2022 compared to $74,580 for the US population (Statista 2023). Many Asian immigrants, especially those from India, are employed in high-skilled jobs and enter the United States on temporary H-1B visas for specialty occupation workers.

Despite this success, Asian Americans still deal with prejudice and stereotypes. A recent study by the US Department of Housing and Urban Development found that one in five Asian Americans experience discrimination when trying to buy or rent a home. Asian American groups have filed lawsuits against Harvard and other elite universities in recent years, alleging that these schools have racial quotas that limit the number of Asian American students. Stereotypes about overly demanding Asian American parents circulate widely. Despite all their educational success, Asian Americans continue to be underrepresented as corporate executives, as law firm partners, and in other top management positions (Zweigenhaft and Domhoff 2006). Because the COVID-19 virus originated in China, the pandemic led to an increase in prejudice and negative sentiment against Asians and Asian Americans (Nam et al 2022; Lee et al. 2022)

Popular beliefs about Asian Americans as a successful "model minority" also hide the fact that there is still a good deal of poverty in many Asian American communities (Chou and Feagin 2008). One in ten Asian Americans live below the poverty level, which is slightly lower than the average for the total US society. Poverty rates are particularly high among Asian Americans from Burmese (25 percent), Mongolian (22.8 percent), Malaysian (20.4 percent), and Bangladeshi (20.3 percent) descent groups (AAPI 2022).

## 7.3 Race, Privilege, and Inequality

**LG 7.3** Explain the relationship between racial privilege and racial inequality.

Inequality and privilege shape how people experience race and ethnicity. Historically marginalized groups experience **discrimination**, where they are treated in a negative and unequal way based on their race or ethnicity. Their choice of where to live is influenced by **segregation**, a social practice in which neighborhoods, schools, and other social organizations are separated by race and ethnicity. Discrimination and segregation reinforce social inequality by limiting the resources that are available to historically marginalized groups as well as the opportunities that are extended to them. Social

**Discrimination**
Negative and unequal treatment directed at a particular group.

**Segregation**
A social practice in which neighborhoods, schools, and other social organizations are separated by race and ethnicity.

conflicts erupt between groups trying to reduce or eliminate race-based inequality and others that have an interest in maintaining their privileges.

## The Privileges of Being in the Majority Group

Whites are the largest racial group in the United States, accounting for 58.9 percent of the population. They are also the most privileged racial group. Compared with people from other racial groups who have similar social characteristics (education, occupation, etc.), whites have higher incomes, live in safer neighborhoods, and have access to better schools (Shapiro 2005). They get lower interest rates on loans to buy houses and cars and accumulate more wealth over their lifetimes (Oliver and Shapiro 2006). Whites are less likely to be pulled over by police or treated with suspicion as potential criminals. In other words, there are a host of material and psychological benefits that come with white privilege. One of the most important of these benefits is simply not having to constantly think about race or be aware of racial privilege.

Social science research has measured the material aspects of white privilege. The median white household had more than $188,000 in wealth in 2019 compared to $24,100 for the median Black household and $36,100 for the median Latino household. This means "the typical white family has eight times the wealth of the typical Black family and five times the wealth of the typical Hispanic family," a difference that remains little changed compared to earlier patterns (Bhutta et al. 2020; McIntosh et al. 2020). In 2023, the Census reported that the real median household income of non-Hispanic whites in the previous year was $89,050 compared to a median household income of $65,540 for Latinos and $56,490 for Black households. The return on investment for completing a college degree is more than 10 times higher for whites than it is for Black or Latino individuals (Shin 2015). Even poor whites benefit; white children born into poor families have a much better chance of being upwardly mobile and improving their socioeconomic outcomes than poor Black children do (Short 2014; Hardy and Logan 2020).

There are also nonmaterial benefits associated with white privilege. Whites are far less likely than other racial and ethnic groups to think about structural obstacles that influence their lives, and far more likely to believe that they will be successful as long as they work hard (Kluegel 1990). They are much more likely to believe that schools, courts, the workplace, and other social institutions are fair (Patten 2013). They are more likely to receive small favors, like getting a free ride on the bus or getting a warning instead of a citation when they are pulled over by the police (Pinsker 2015). All of these small favors allow white people to move through the world without thinking about racial discrimination, assuming instead that most people are fair and good-natured. In the context of renewed mobilization in 2020 associated

> **PAIRED CONCEPTS**
>
> ## Inequality and Privilege
>
> ### How Irish Americans Became White
>
> The Irish Catholics who began arriving in the United States in the 1800s were leaving a society in which they suffered religious and racial discrimination in Protestant-dominated society. In Ireland, they were not allowed to vote or attend university, were banned from many occupations, and were forced to live outside of the city limits in many towns. This discrimination, combined with a famine that swept through Ireland, encouraged nearly two million Irish Catholics to emigrate to the United States between 1800 and 1860.
>
> Arriving in the United States, the majority of these Irish immigrants continued to face racial discrimination and stereotyping in a society dominated by WASPs—a white, Anglo-Saxon, Protestant elite. Depicted in the press as ape-like barbarians prone to drunkenness, crime, and stupidity, Irish Catholic immigrants were forced to live in the poorest neighborhoods and limited to the lowest-wage and lowest-skilled jobs. Anti-Irish and anti-Catholic violence was common. Many Americans believed that Irish Catholics were racially inferior.
>
> Irish Catholics managed to convince Americans that they were white. According to the historian Noel Ignatiev (2008), they did this by cooperating with other whites to suppress and exclude Black workers. Irish Americans took the lead in attacking Black individuals and driving them out of neighborhoods in cities throughout the Northeast and Midwest, most notably during the New York City draft riots of 1863 and the Chicago race riot of 1919. By taking the lead in these acts of racial violence, Irish Americans were able to distance themselves from the Black population. In this way, as Ignatiev describes, they "earned" their white identities.
>
> By the early 20th century, Irish Americans had gained political power in many cities. Al Smith was elected governor of New York four times and ran for president in 1928 as the nominee of the Democratic Party. It was not until 1960 that John F. Kennedy was elected as the first Catholic president of the United States. Over the course of the 20th century, Irish Americans were welcomed into white neighborhoods, and they frequently married people from other white ethnic groups. In fact, intermarriage rates were nearly 80 percent for third-generation Irish immigrants (Alba 1976). Today, the history of discrimination against Irish immigrants has been virtually forgotten (Waters 1990).
>
> **ACTIVE LEARNING**
>
> **Discuss:** Can you think of another ethnic group that used to be marginalized but that has now become assimilated into the dominant group? How were their strategies of assimilation different from those of Irish Americans? How were they similar?

with Black Lives Matter, and especially the widespread social protests against police brutality following the killings of Breonna Taylor in March 2020 and George Floyd in May 2020, there have been many public conversations about the undeserved benefits of whiteness, or white privilege.

## Racial Discrimination and Segregation

Racial discrimination and segregation are a central part of US history. Discrimination was built into the US government for nearly two hundred years. Immigration policies set quotas on minorities, barred Asian Americans from

**Residential segregation** A social practice in which neighborhoods are separated on the basis of group differences.

**Redlining** A practice where banks would not give mortgages to people who lived in minority-dominated neighborhoods.

**Racial steering** A practice in which realtors would encourage people to look for homes in specific neighborhoods depending on their race, as a way to ensure that the "desirable" neighborhoods were reserved for whites.

**Blockbusting** A practice where real estate agents would go to a neighborhood where racial minorities were beginning to move in, convince the white residents that their property values were going to decrease, and encourage them to sell their houses below market value. Realtors then sold those homes to minority buyers at inflated prices.

citizenship, and gave preferences to white ethnic groups. State and local governments enforced racial segregation in schools and neighborhoods, investing much more money in white areas of the city than other areas. Interracial marriage was illegal in many states throughout the South and West. These laws and policies remained in place until the 1950s and 1960s, when a series of Supreme Court rulings declared that policies based on racial discrimination were unconstitutional.

Even though explicit policies of racial discrimination have been declared unconstitutional, informal policies of segregation continue to shape the life chances of racial minorities. One of the most important ways this happens is through residential segregation. Despite the fact that the 1968 Fair Housing Act made it illegal to use race as a criterion for making decisions about real estate rentals and purchases, **residential segregation** remains very high in the United States (Frey 2018; Massey and Denton 1993). Not all cities are the same, of course; and not all racial groups are affected equally by racial segregation. Frey's (2018) recent analysis of Census data shows, for example, that despite small declines in residential segregation since 2000, very high levels of segregation persist in many cities, including Milwaukee, New York, and Chicago, and that Black people experience more extreme forms of residential segregation than people from other racial groups (Massey and Denton 1993; Frey 2018).

Strategies used to create and reproduce the system of residential segregation included **redlining** (where banks would not give mortgages to people who lived in minority-dominated neighborhoods) and **racial steering** (in which realtors would encourage people to look for homes in specific neighborhoods depending on their race, as a way to ensure that the "desirable" neighborhoods were reserved for whites) (Jackson 1985; Cashin 2005). **Blockbusting** was a practice in which real estate agents would go to a neighborhood where nonwhites were beginning to move in, convince white residents that their property values were going to decrease, and encourage them to sell their houses (below market value) "before it was too late" (Hirsch 1983). The realtors would then turn around and sell those homes to people from historically marginalized groups at inflated prices because those prospective buyers had fewer options about where they were permitted to live. More recently, communities of color living in urban neighborhoods that had previously suffered from a lack of capital investment have been transformed through processes of **gentrification**, whereby wealthy homeowners move in, improve housing, attract new businesses, and, in doing so, displace lower-income families who can no longer afford to live in the neighborhood. Gentrification reinforces segregation patterns and severs minority communities from the potential wealth associated with urban redevelopment.

Racial discrimination also continues in the workplace. Black people are more likely to be unemployed than people from other racial groups, while average wages for Black and Latino workers continue to be lower than those of white workers (Pager and Shepherd 2008; Fontenot, Semega, and Kollar 2018). Experimental studies examining hiring decisions find a consistent preference for white job applicants when employers are presented with people who have similar qualifications (Pager 2007a, 2007b). Black men seem to have a particularly difficult time on the job market, having to spend more time looking for jobs and having a less stable employment history than white workers with similar qualifications (Tomaskovic-Devey, Thomas, and Johnson 2005).

There is also the everyday racial discrimination that takes place in interactions with store owners, police, and people in the street. Many Black people have had the experience of being followed by store owners and store security or witnessing the nervous looks that white people give them when entering an elevator or passing on the street (Feagin and Sikes 1994). Well-known memes about "driving while Black," "walking while Black," and even "barbecuing while Black" highlight the suspicion and the everyday discrimination experienced by racial minorities. There is a recognition and a fear that racist stereotypes about "dangerous Black men" can erupt into vigilante violence during the most ordinary activities, such as the 2020 murder of Ahmaud Arbery, a Black man jogging in his own neighborhood who was pursued and killed by two white men who thought that Arbery looked suspicious. And there is heightened public awareness of police violence against Black individuals because of protests against the killings of George Floyd, Breonna Taylor, Eric Garner, Sandra Bland, and others.

The everyday discrimination against these racial and ethnic groups has real material consequences. Black and Latino people who apply for a mortgage are 82 percent more likely to be rejected than white applicants who have a similar financial profile, and those who do get mortgages generally have to pay higher interest rates and additional fees (Pager and Shepherd 2008). On other major purchases, such as buying a car, research shows that salespeople are less flexible in their negotiations with historically marginalized racial and ethnic groups (Ayres and Siegelman 1995), and there is strong evidence suggesting race bias in salary negotiations (Hernandez et al. 2019; Toosi et al. 2019; Staff 2020). These experiences of discrimination lead to material disadvantages, as well as a host of psychological and emotional consequences.

## Consequences of Discrimination

Discrimination means that historically marginalized racial and ethnic groups get a lower rate of return for many of their efforts to improve their lives. Discrimination in housing means that they settle in less desirable neighborhoods, where their houses will be less profitable investments than similar

**Gentrification**
A process whereby wealthy homeowners move in, improve housing, attract new businesses, and, in doing so, displace lower-income families who can no longer afford to live in the neighborhood.

**Consequences of discrimination**
Minority neighborhoods have fewer banks and medical resources and less access to fresh food.

homes purchased in "white" neighborhoods. Discrimination in credit means that they have to pay higher interest rates for bank loans, while discrimination in consumer markets means that they have to pay a higher price in stores. Employment discrimination means that they have a harder time finding work, are more likely to lose their jobs, and are more likely to receive lower wages than white workers. These patterns of discrimination are measurably worse for Black and Latino workers than they are for other racial groups.

Racial discrimination forces people into poorer, more dangerous, and more poorly resourced neighborhoods, where they are more likely to be victims of violent crime and more likely to deal with aggressive police practices (Chapter 5). These include frequent interrogations of drivers and pedestrians, the frequent use of random sobriety checkpoints, and the tendency to make arrests instead of giving warnings for minor violations of the law (Tomaskovic-Devey and Warren 2009). On average, Black and Latino neighborhoods have fewer banks, fewer medical resources, and less access to healthy foods (Moore and Diez-Roux 2006).

Racial discrimination also creates long-term emotional and psychological consequences for the people who experience it. For example, the stress created by racial discrimination leads to physical and mental health problems that proliferate throughout their lives and across generations (Thoits 2010). Racial discrimination also makes people more distrustful of police, health care providers, and other mainstream social institutions. This makes their communities much more vulnerable during times of emergency and crisis.

**Genocide** The systematic killing of people on the basis of their race, ethnicity, or religion.

## Racial Conflict

Violence and conflict have also been used to reinforce racial privileges and inequalities. In its most extreme form, racial conflict takes the form of **genocide**, which is the systematic killing of people on the basis of their race, ethnicity, or religion. Colonial expansion from Europe into Africa, Asia, Australia, and North America had genocidal aspects. There have also been repeated genocides around the world in the 20th century. In 1915, the government of the Ottoman Empire (modern Turkey) began systematically killing and deporting its Armenian population. Russia under Stalin systematically killed millions of Cossacks, Muslim peoples (including Chechens, Ingush, Crimean Tatars, Tajiks, Bashkirs, and Kazakhs), Jews, and Ukrainians. In the most infamous genocide of the 20th century, Germany systematically killed six million Jews. More recently, racial conflict in Rwanda led members of the Hutu ethnic majority to kill nearly 800,000 of the Tutsi ethnic population in 1994. The United Nations has identified 18 major acts of genocide perpetrated during the 20th century, resulting in total deaths estimated to be between 13 million and 35 million people.

A type of racial conflict that is closely related to genocide is **ethnic cleansing**, which happens when an entire group of people is forcibly removed from a society through murder, rape, and expulsion because of their race, ethnicity, or religion. Ethnic cleansing happens when the dominant group decides that it wants to create an ethnically homogeneous society. This happened in the 1990s during the war in Bosnia-Hercegovina, where more than three million people were displaced and an additional hundred thousand were killed. More recently, world attention has turned to the state harassment, murder, and expulsion of Rohingya Muslims from Myanmar beginning in 2016. Thousands were killed and raped, and over a million Rohingya fled to Bangladesh and to other parts of South Asia. Journalists and international watchdogs are currently raising concerns about the incarceration and cultural re-education of Uyghurs in China. The United Nations considers both ethnic cleansing and genocide to be war crimes.

**Ethnic cleansing**
The forcible removal of an entire group of people from a society because of their race, ethnicity, or religion.

**National memorial to victims of genocide, Rwanda**
The systematic killing of people on the basis of their race, ethnicity, or religion is called "genocide"; and it was shockingly frequent in the 20th century. In the Rwandan genocide of 1994 an estimated one million people were killed, including 70 percent of the ethnic Tutsi population.

Competition for jobs and other material resources can also cause racial conflict. Sociological research has shown that racial violence between low-skilled workers tends to increase when the economy gets worse or when there is an increase in the number of low-wage workers competing for the same jobs (Olzak 1994). This was clearly the case during the "Red Summer" of 1919, when white mobs in more than three dozen cities (mostly in the North and the Midwest) violently attacked Black people. These outbursts of violence followed several years of building racial tensions, in which Black migrants from the South and soldiers returning from World War I found themselves competing with white ethnic groups for blue-collar manufacturing jobs. Hundreds of Black people were killed in these race riots. In some cities, members of the Black community responded by creating armed resistance movements to ensure that similar violence would not happen in the future.

Another cause of racial conflict is **racial profiling**, a process in which people are targeted by police and civilians for humiliating and harsh treatment because of their "perceived race, ethnicity, national origin, or religion" (American Civil Liberties Union 2020). In the US South during the era of Jim Crow, a Black person was killed in public every four days, often for things as trivial as making boastful remarks or trying to vote. Minor offenses quickly escalated to public lynchings by a white mob, often with the support and cooperation of police officers and government officials. The goal was to terrify the Black population, scaring them into accepting the system of racial discrimination.

Racial profiling continues to be a problem. Police are much more likely to treat people as potential criminals when they are patrolling in Black communities, and they are much more likely to make arrests in those neighborhoods (Tomaskovic-Devey and Warren 2009). Black drivers are more than twice as likely as white drivers to be arrested during a traffic stop, and they are nearly three times as likely to be subjected to a police search during a traffic stop. Their interactions with police are also more dangerous: Black men are more than three times as likely to be killed during such encounters as white men (Sikora and Mulvihill 2002). Racial profiling and racial violence also have a big impact on the lives of Black women. The #SayHerName campaign was started in 2014 to bring public attention to the stories of Black women who were victimized by police violence. The campaign documents more than one hundred cases of Black women killed between 2015 and 2020. Two of those cases—Sandra Bland (killed in 2015) and Breonna Taylor (killed in 2020)—have been the subjects of television documentaries.

**Racial profiling** A process in which people are targeted by police and civilians for humiliating and harsh treatment because of their perceived race, ethnicity, national origin, or religion.

### PAIRED CONCEPTS

## Power and Resistance

### Black Lives Matter

After George Zimmerman was acquitted in the 2012 shooting death of Trayvon Martin, anger about the verdict spread throughout the nation. People took to the streets and went on social media to express their anger and disappointment. Alicia Garza, an activist and writer living in Oakland, expressed her feelings in a post on her Facebook page, writing, "Black people. I love you. I love us. Our lives matter, Black Lives Matter." A friend of hers, Patrisse Cullors, reposted it with the hashtag #BlackLivesMatter. A third friend, Opal Tometi, also reposted it. The three women, who were all community organizers and political activists, talked about forming a social movement called Black Lives Matter. Using social media, they hoped the #BlackLivesMatter hashtag would bring people together who wanted to fight against racism in their communities.

The protest movement developed slowly, but it exploded in August 2014, when a police officer shot and killed Michael Brown, an unarmed Black teenager, in Ferguson, Missouri. In the following month, the hashtag #BlackLivesMatter was used more than 52,000 times; after the November 2014 decision not to indict the officer involved in the shooting, the hashtag was used more than 92,000 times in four hours (Demby 2016). There were more than two hundred demonstrations nationwide protesting the police shooting in Ferguson, with most of them being organized with the help of the Black Lives Matter movement.

Since 2014, Black Lives Matter has become one of the most important protest movements fighting against racism and police violence. The hashtag has been used to express anger, organize protests, and bring visibility to additional cases in which Black Americans died during interactions with police, such as the cases of Tamir Rice (2014), Eric Garner (2014), Freddie Gray (2015), and Sandra Bland (2015). It was used to organize protests in 2015 after nine Black people were murdered while attending church in Charleston, South Carolina. As we discussed at the beginning of the chapter, Black Lives Matter was one of the main groups organizing national protests

**#BlackLivesMatter**
The Black Lives Matter (#BLM) movement is one of the most important movements fighting racism today. The hashtag helps to organize protests against systemic racism and the deaths of Black individuals in police custody, such as this one in Portland, Oregon, in June 2020.

after the killing of George Floyd in 2020. And it has been a major supporter of the #SayHerName campaign, a movement founded in December 2014 to bring attention to the stories of Black women who have been victimized by police violence.

Today, Black Lives Matter is an established national movement committed to fighting violence against members of the Black community and others from historically marginalized communities. It continues to be an important presence in social media, with more than 3.5 million followers on Instagram and more than 700,000 followers on Facebook. The movement has local chapters in 40 different cities, as well as in Canada and the United Kingdom. It has created a philanthropic foundation, as well as a political action committee.

#### ACTIVE LEARNING

**Find out:** In what parts of the country is the Black Lives Matter movement the most active? Where is it least active? What are some of the main public events they have organized in the last three months?

## 7.4 Multiculturalism and Diversity

**LG 7.4** Understand current thinking about diversity and multiculturalism.

Historically marginalized groups do not passively accept the violence directed at them. Protest movements publicize practices of racial discrimination and violence, calling on governments to create more equitable policies and citizens to be more tolerant of diversity. Over time, these movements have successfully challenged official policies that reinforce racial privilege, and they have changed public opinion enough so that overt expressions of racism are less common or acceptable than they once were. Many societies now support policies of multiculturalism, which support and encourage the distinctive identities of the different cultural groups that exist in society. Multicultural policies explicitly reject the idea that some cultural groups are more valuable than others.

### Multiculturalism (Movement and Policy)

**Multiculturalism**
A culturally pluralistic society's official recognition of the existence of different cultural groups and identities, and its development of policies promoting cultural diversity.

**Assimilation**
A process that occurs when minority groups fully embrace the culture of the dominant group and lose their distinctive racial and/or ethnic characteristics.

**Multiculturalism** refers to a culturally pluralistic society's official recognition of the existence of different cultural groups and identities, and its development of policies promoting cultural diversity. Multicultural policies explicitly acknowledge the distinctive identities of all racial and ethnic groups, and they invest resources to help historically marginalized groups preserve their culture. Multiculturalism is very different from the **assimilationist** policies of the past, in which historically marginalized groups were encouraged to fully embrace the culture of the dominant group and lose their distinctive racial and ethnic characteristics.

Canada was the first country to adopt official policies of multiculturalism. The 1971 Multiculturalism Policy of Canada explicitly affirmed the value and the dignity of all Canadian citizens, regardless of their racial or ethnic origins, their language, or their religious affiliation. It affirmed the rights of all Indigenous peoples, and it established two official languages, English and French. The goal of the new policy was to allow all citizens to have pride in their cultural heritage, to keep their identities, and to create better racial and ethnic harmony in a society that celebrates tolerance and mutual respect.

While other countries have adopted similar policies, multiculturalism has not been without its critics. Critics fear that multiculturalism promotes cultural relativism, making it difficult to criticize behaviors that go against the grain of the national culture. The Netherlands adopted official national policies of multiculturalism during the 1980s, but after several high-profile incidents of violence, it now identifies itself as a society that is tolerant but multicultural. The United Kingdom had a similar experience, with the country's prime minister, David Cameron, declaring in a 2011 speech that "state multiculturalism has failed." In the United States, there are no official policies of multiculturalism. There have been many US initiatives to promote cultural pluralism in education, culture, and the arts, but these efforts have also faced criticism and resistance.

## Multiracial and Multiethnic Identities

The growing awareness of cultural pluralism and the influences of multiculturalism have encouraged many people to celebrate and take pride in the diverse cultural heritage that shapes their family history. Many people no longer feel the need to select only one racial or ethnic identity. Today, there are more high-profile multiracial and multiethnic celebrities than ever before—athletes like Tiger Woods and Derek Jeter, singers like Bruno Mars and Saweetie, actors like Keanu Reeves and Halle Barry, and politicians like Barack Obama and Kamala Harris.

Because of the growing visibility and influence of multiracial and multiethnic identities, the US Census Bureau allowed people to select more than one racial category on their official Census forms for the first time in the year 2000. Nine million people chose more than one race in the 2010 Census, a 32 percent increase since 2000. 33.8 million people chose more than one race in the 2020 Census, a 276 percent increase since 2010. These trends are likely to continue because nearly half of all multiracial Americans are younger than 18 (Pew Research Center 2015b). In fact, more than 10 percent of children born in the United States today have parents who come from different racial groups.

Not everyone who has mixed-race parents identifies as multiracial. At present, fewer than half of US adults who have a mixed-race background consider themselves to be multiracial. Many people of mixed-race heritage report that they still feel social pressure to identify with a single race (Pew Research Center 2015b). Others make a political choice to identify with a single identity. Recognizing the deep imprint that racism and racial thinking have had on society, they make a deliberate choice to adopt the marginalized identity and help build a proud and powerful cultural identity around it (Appiah and Gutmann 1998).

Civil rights leaders have expressed some reservations about the multiracial classifications that are now available on the Census. They are concerned that it will become harder to identify and enforce civil rights violations if people are allowed to indicate that they belong to more than one racial group (Perlmann and Waters 2002: 13). They are concerned that the rise of multiracial identities will weaken the strength of Black advocacy groups (Alex-Assensoh and Hanks 2000). Some scholars have suggested that using

## CAREERS

# Multiculturalism in the Workplace

The need for multicultural policies is creating change and opportunity in the workplace. Cultural awareness is an important business tool, and many employers now recognize that they can enhance productivity and workplace unity if they can develop better cross-cultural awareness and respect.

Multiculturalism offers clear business advantages. Multicultural awareness allows employers to identify a larger pool of talented workers. Multicultural workforces encourage innovation, by exposing employees to diverse perspectives and experiences. They allow a business to identify a new market niche that it might have ignored and to create a more successful advertising strategy focused on that niche. In addition, research shows that multicultural workplaces encourage higher levels of tolerance, which has a general social benefit (Gudykunst 2004).

Multiculturalism has also created new kinds of jobs. For example, the advertising industry has created new jobs in "multicultural marketing," which develop new advertising strategies focused on Asian American, Black, and Latino consumers. Most colleges and universities now have an office of multicultural affairs, and they hire social scientists to help advance diversity and inclusion on campus. Many schools, police departments, hospitals, government service agencies, and nonprofit organizations now employ multicultural liaison officers, whose job is to communicate more effectively and respectfully with the diverse communities they serve. Many large institutions employ diversity officers, who are responsible for attracting, developing, and retaining a diverse talent pool of workers. Diversity officers often work with the multicultural marketing department, to make sure that there is a good strategy for communicating the organization's brand in a way that addresses the needs of a diverse base of clients and consumers.

**Mucho Más Que Autos**
Multicultural marketing is one of the fastest-growing segments in the advertising industry.

In addition to having good skills in research and communication, people who work in these jobs need specific skills that allow them to satisfy the multicultural mission of their positions. First, they need to have good foreign-language skills. In the United States, fluency in Spanish is the most helpful, but with the growth of the Asian American population a knowledge of Chinese, Japanese, Korean, or Vietnamese is also valuable. In addition, they need to have a strong sociological understanding of the communities and their cultures. This sociological and cultural sensitivity will help them know when and how to change a marketing campaign so as not to cause offense. For example, the skincare brand Nivea quickly pulled its "white is purity" ad campaign in 2017 when it was publicly denounced for being racist; apologizing for its mistake, Nivea ended its relationship with the advertising agency that had created the campaign. Multicultural marketers also use a sociological perspective to understand different age cohorts within an immigrant or minority community, recognizing that there are likely to be different levels of generational acculturation.

Jobs that specialize in the diverse, multicultural workforce offer strong growth and good salaries.

> Multicultural marketers and liaison officers generally make between $60,000 and $100,000 per year, depending on their experience and the size of the organization where they are employed. Chief diversity officers are executive-level positions in most organizations, with annual salaries typically in excess of $100,000.
>
> **ACTIVE LEARNING**
>
> **Find out:** Search online using the term "diversity and inclusion jobs" and select one that interests you. What are the qualifications for the job? Do you think having a developed sociological imagination would be useful in this work? Why?

data based on subjectively defined categories will make the entire system of racial and ethnic data vulnerable to legal challenge (Harrison 2002).

Despite these reservations, however, most experts predict that the multiracial population will increase. Government agencies are now collecting data in a way that includes categories for multiracial identities; schools, businesses, and even public opinion pollsters are beginning to do the same thing (Hochschild and Weaver 2010). As multiracialism becomes a more visible and influential presence, it will have profound effects on politics and social life. For some, multiracialism will fundamentally challenge the basic premises of racial thinking, causing them to forcefully confront all forms of racial intolerance and discrimination. For others, who are defenders of assimilation or racial privilege, multiracialism will lead to a growing backlash against multiculturalism and cultural pluralism. And for yet others, embracing a multiracial identity will mean that racial and ethnic differences will become less significant in their lives. Understanding all of these effects and how they are connected to one another will require us to cultivate our sociological imaginations.

## 7.5 Immigration

**LG 7.5** Describe the basic historical trends in immigration.

The United States often describes itself as a nation of immigrants. About one-fifth of all international migrants currently live in the United States, and it has been the top immigrant destination in the world since at least 1960 (Zong, Batalova, and Hallock 2018).

The United States is not alone in its experiences with immigrants. Globally, there is more immigration than ever before. This has created significant consequences, both for communities receiving new immigrants and for the communities people leave behind. Immigration also has political consequences, in terms of citizenship policies, employment policies, and anti- and pro-immigrant and social movements.

## Trends in Immigration

While human migration has been a feature of virtually all societies throughout recorded history, the pace of migration increased during the 18th century. Much of this increased movement was **internal migration**, which refers to the movement of people within the same country. Because of industrialization and urbanization, people were moving from rural areas into cities in search of better economic opportunities. International migration was also increasing during this time, mainly because of global trade, colonialism, and the forced migration associated with the international slave trade.

The pace of immigration accelerated during the 19th century as capitalism spread from Europe to its colonies. Between 1864 and 1924, 48 million people (more than 10 percent of the population on the continent) left Europe (Massey 1999). More than half of these emigrants came to the United States, but large numbers also settled in Canada, Argentina, Australia, and New Zealand.

Immigration slowed considerably between 1920 and 1960. World War I encouraged anti-immigrant attitudes, which intensified even further with the global economic depression that began in 1929. In the United States, which had been the main immigrant destination, new immigration laws banned entry from most Asian nations, established quotas for most European nations, and introduced a literacy test for potential new immigrants. As a result of these new laws, immigration into the United States declined by more than 90 percent compared to prewar levels (Massey 1995). These restrictive laws remained in place throughout World War II. The only real increases in immigration levels came from the passage of laws in 1948 and 1953, which established special provisions for war refugees fleeing persecution.

Immigration increased again in the mid-1960s, when wealthy nations such as the United States began to increase their numerical quotas for immigrants. The number of international migrants doubled between 1960 (71.8 million) and 1990 (152 million), and it has continued to increase since then, with a total of 272 million international migrants in 2019 (United Nations, Department of Economic and Social Affairs, Population Division 2019). Immigration during this period became much more global, in terms of the places that immigrants were leaving as well as the places they were going. The new immigrants were much more likely to come from developing countries in Latin America, Africa, and Asia. The United States is still the largest immigrant destination, but there are also significant numbers of immigrants settling in western Europe, Saudi Arabia, Japan, and South Korea (Massey 1999).

Another major change in immigration policy in the US was the creation of the H-1B visa category in 1990. The H-1B is a temporary visa category that allows employers to petition the US Citizenship and Immigration Service

> **Internal migration**
> The movement of people within the same country. Internal migration is different than international migration, which is what people usually refer to when they talk about immigration.

(USCIS) to hire highly educated foreign professionals in jobs that require specialized expertise. Most H-1B visas are granted to hire workers in science, technology, engineering, and medicine. Typically granted for a period of three years, they can be extended up to six years. The US Congress establishes a limit to the annual number of H-1B visas that can be granted. The current limit is 65,000 per year, with an additional 20,000 visas available for foreign professionals who graduate with a master's degree or a doctorate from a US university. Universities, nonprofit organizations, and government research offices are exempt from this annual cap. There is intense competition among employers for H-1B visas, with nearly ten times as many applications as there are available slots. There are approximately 600,000 workers currently in the US on H-1B visas, employed by more than 50,000 different employers (Costa and Hira 2023). These workers are also allowed to bring their spouses and children to the US through the H-4 visa program.

## What Causes Immigration?

Immigration is shaped by "push factors" as well as "pull factors." Push factors include all those social forces that make people want to leave where they are living and find somewhere else to settle. With push factors, the desire to leave is the main cause of emigration. In this kind of situation, people will settle anywhere, as long as it is better than the place they are leaving. With pull factors, on the other hand, people are drawn to a specific place, usually in order to join family members who already live there or to join an established community where they know they will be welcomed and supported.

The key push factors that are related to immigration are economic poverty, political instability, and violence. More than 80 percent of all immigrants end up settling in a country that is wealthier than the one they left (United Nations Development Programme 2009). Economic decision-making is a big part of the immigration decision because moving to another country is expensive and risky. In fact, below a certain poverty threshold, the likelihood of immigration actually begins to decline because people lack the financial resources to move. For people living in poor countries who do have enough money to afford an international move, the promise of a better life is a significant motivation.

People are strongly motivated to emigrate from societies beset by violence. Armed conflict between competing groups leads to a surge in refugees (Lischer 2014). In authoritarian countries, friends and family of opposition activists are often forced to flee their homes in order to avoid being jailed, tortured, or killed (Bank, Froehlich, and Schneiker 2016). Religious, ethnic, and racial groups have frequently been forced to become refugees in order to escape persecution. Climate change has led to widespread famine, forcing people to migrate to avoid starvation (Zetter and Morrissey 2014). Recent estimates suggest that more than 108 million people were forced to migrate in 2022 as a result of conflict and persecution (United Nations High Commissioner for Refugees 2023).

The key pull factors that encourage immigration are family reunification, the desire to move to and join an established immigrant community, and recruitment into transnational work networks. Canada, Australia, and New Zealand have adopted a "points-based" immigration system that favors young workers who can fill jobs in high-demand occupations. America's H-1B visa system allows employers to bring in foreign workers in specialized occupations. In both of these types of arrangements, employers in high-tech and high-growth sectors of the economy have an incentive to create transnational recruiting networks that identify skilled foreign workers, help them move to the country to contribute to its economy, and provide resources that ease the transition to the new country.

As with transnational work networks, there are immigration policies in place in many nations that encourage family reunification. In the United States, the 1965 Hart-Celler Act established preferences among those wishing to emigrate to the United States that favored relatives of US citizens as well as relatives of permanent residents. This quickly became the primary mechanism for immigration, and by 2000 about two-thirds of all permanent immigration to the United States came through the family reunification program (McKay 2003). Similarly, family reunification has become one of the main reasons for immigration into Europe, where the European Union established a directive in 2003 that encouraged the practice of reunification.

There are good reasons why family reunification would be a powerful draw for immigrants. The family is one of the most important sources of identity, solidarity, and social support (Chapter 9). Kinship networks provide financial and moral support, as well as useful local knowledge and connections that can help ease the transition for new immigrants. It is common for a new immigrant to stay with a family member when they first arrive and to rely on their family's informal networks to help them find work and housing. These strategies work best when economic conditions are good, when the surrounding political environment is accepting of new immigrants, and when the place where they arrive is connected to a well-established immigrant community (Menjivar 1997).

### Immigrant Communities

Beginning in the 1950s with the arrival of Cuban immigrants fleeing a revolution in that country, Miami became a place where new arrivals could find a cheap place to live, continue to speak Spanish while learning more about US society, find a job (usually from a Cuban American business owner), and surround themselves with familiar elements of Cuban popular culture. Little

Havana, as the area of the city where they settled became known, was viewed by Cubans as well as others across Latin America as a desirable destination for those fleeing poverty and political instability. Nicaraguans began arriving in large numbers during the 1970s and 1980s, followed shortly thereafter by immigrants from Guatemala, Haiti, and Honduras. Little Havana has become one of the most popular tourist destinations in Miami, and the Cuban "brand" is an important source of revenue for all business owners in the neighborhood, including many who are not Cuban American immigrants (Vasilogambros 2016).

**Immigrant enclave**
A community in which there are successful immigrant-owned businesses that serve to anchor the community. Immigrant enclaves are highly desirable destinations for new immigrants.

**IMMIGRANT ENCLAVES.** Little Havana is an example of an **immigrant enclave**, where successful immigrant-owned businesses serve to anchor the community. Immigrant enclaves usually benefit from two phenomena: the arrival of immigrants who already have enough experience and financial resources to start their own businesses and a large reserve of immigrant labor available for employment (Portes and Manning 1986). The relationship between employer and employee in an immigrant enclave is defined by solidarity and reciprocity. The employee works for a slightly lower salary, which allows the business to be effective in the market; the employer provides social and material support during emergencies, helps the workers develop the skills that enable them to advance in their jobs, and even provides aid when those workers are ready to start businesses of their own (Portes and Manning 1986: 62). In addition to Little Havana, other examples of successful immigrant enclaves include Korean communities in Los Angeles and New York City that developed during the 1970s and 1980s and the Chinese community that developed in the Box Hill neighborhood of Melbourne, Australia, during the 1980s and 1990s.

**Immigrant enclaves**
Little Havana in Miami (above) and Koreatown in New York City (below) are thriving examples of immigrant enclaves.

Immigrant enclaves are highly desirable destinations for new immigrants. As communities with thriving immigrant-owned businesses, they offer good jobs and opportunities for social mobility. They often have a well-developed nonprofit sector, consisting of immigrant service organizations, youth organizations, and political organizations that help build solidarity within the community while also advocating politically for the community's interests (Chung 2007). In addition, because they are such attractive destinations, successful immigrant enclaves become an important part of a larger transnational community, making it easy for residents of these communities to maintain strong connections with their country of origin. For example, the Koreatown neighborhood of New York City is a major tourist destination for South Koreans, and it has received significant investments from Korean banks, grocery stores, and restaurant chains.

Not all immigrant communities are successful immigrant enclaves. A common experience for new immigrants is to be forced into a segmented labor market, in which the jobs available to them are unskilled and poorly paid, with few opportunities for advancement (Piore 1979). For immigrant groups that are perceived as racially similar to historically marginalized groups, these kinds of limited opportunities often become a permanent condition, forcing them to reside in impoverished communities or to return to their country of origin. In her study of West Indian immigrants in New York City, the sociologist Mary Waters describes how racial discrimination forced immigrants into poor and dangerous neighborhoods, with inferior schools and an absence of good jobs. While the first generation of immigrants from this community arrived with high levels of optimism and a willingness to work hard, the realities of racism and limited opportunities have led to disillusionment and downward mobility among subsequent generations (Waters 2001).

**REMITTANCES.** Another important feature of immigrant communities is the practice of **remittance**, which occurs when immigrants send money back to family members living in their country of origin. Remittances have always been a feature of immigrant communities, but their scale and value has increased considerably since the late 1990s. Today, more than $630 billion is transferred annually through remittances, with more than three-quarters of that money going to poor countries in the Global South (World Bank 2022). In some countries remittances account for one-third of total gross domestic product, and in most Latin American and Caribbean nations the value of remittances is greater than the value of foreign aid or government spending on social programs (Acosta et al. 2008). In fact, many developing countries have policies that encourage immigration and the remittance economy that is associated with it; they permit dual citizenship, allow emigrants to vote

**Remittance** The money a migrant sends back from their new country to family members in their country of origin.

while abroad, and sometimes even allow them to run for public office (Levitt and Schiller 2004: 1021).

Remittances make it more likely that immigrants will remain connected to their country of origin. Immigrants who send remittances are more likely to visit their country of origin. Their visits bring tourist dollars to the origin country's economy, and they also contribute entrepreneurial and technical skills to help new business ventures succeed (Levitt and Schiller 2004: 1022). It is not uncommon for them to invest in these new business ventures as well (Levitt and Lamba-Nieves 2011: 1). Remittances are often used to help family and friends visit the new immigrant communities, where they are exposed to new ideas and behaviors (Chapter 9). In the course of these visits, comparisons are made between how things are done in the new immigrant communities and how they are done in the communities of origin (Levitt 2001). Not surprisingly, because of these kinds of cultural exchanges, remittances are often correlated with a decrease in fertility rates, increases in educational attainment, and improved health and exercise behaviors in the community of origin (Levitt and Lamba-Nieves 2011).

## 7.6 The Politics of Immigration

**LG 7.6** Describe how immigrant communities are organized and how they shape politics and the economy in both sending and receiving countries.

Immigration is a contentious issue. Countries have different laws about whom they will accept as immigrants and different expectations about how much they expect immigrants to assimilate. Anti-immigrant movements have increased worldwide. In countries that are experiencing population outflow, however, the political issues surrounding immigration are different. In such countries there is a concern about losing talented workers as global immigration trends block national development and aggravate global inequality.

### Laws about Citizenship and Immigration

In democratic societies, employers have been one of the most influential interest groups advocating for higher levels of immigration. Civil and human rights groups have also been an important interest group, advocating for permissive immigration policies that are designed to help refugee populations. In settler societies such as Canada, Australia, New Zealand, and the United States, there are also powerful cultural influences that favor immigration,

**Citizenship**
The laws that define who is a legal member of a country.

which rely on narratives about the country as a "nation of immigrants" and a "land of opportunity" (Freeman 1995: 887).

Once immigrants settle in a new country, their experiences are shaped by the laws about **citizenship**, which define who is a legal member of a country. If they or their family can become citizens, it becomes easier for them to travel freely within the country, and they can leave the country with the full confidence that they will be allowed to return. In countries like France and the United States, anyone born in the country is automatically granted citizenship; in Germany, on the other hand, immigrants who are not ethnically German can live in the nation for generations without being granted citizenship (Brubaker 1992). The citizenship laws of Syria and Libya give preferences to people of Arab descent (Parolin 2009). Malta will give citizenship to anyone who is willing to invest in local real estate, live there for one year, and pay a fee of 1.15 million Euros. Some countries grant immediate citizenship to a person who marries a citizen of the nation, while others require a certain period of residence in the country before granting citizenship (Weil 2001). Many countries allow immigrants to hold dual citizenship, but others do not.

## Anti-Immigrant Movements

In some countries, increased immigration has ignited anti-immigrant movements. In the United States, anti-immigrant movements have occurred throughout the nation's history, as we discussed in the section on Asian-Americans earlier in this chapter.

With the global increase in immigration since the 1960s, and particularly since the 1990s, anti-immigrant political movements have emerged throughout Europe and North America. Austria, Denmark, Italy, Poland, and Hungary have all formed coalition governments in which one of the parties was explicitly anti-immigrant. Anti-immigrant movements have also become much more influential in French, German, and British politics. In the United States,

**The oath of citizenship**
Thousands of Latinos, including members of the armed forces, take the citizenship oath during a 2017 US naturalization ceremony in Los Angeles.

Donald Trump was elected president in 2016 after a campaign in which he described immigrants as murderers, rapists, and drug dealers. As president, Trump moved to deport millions of undocumented immigrants, to refuse citizenship to the children of undocumented immigrants who were born in the United States, to sharply limit the admission of refugees and asylum seekers, and to reduce the overall levels of legal immigration, most infamously by attempting to build a wall across the entire US–Mexico border. Elected again in 2024, Donald Trump continues to make anti-immigrant statements.

Sociologists have identified several social factors that increase the likelihood that an individual or group will support anti-immigrant movements. Racial and ethnic prejudice is a significant factor (Berg 2012). Differences in language, culture, and religion also increase the likelihood of anti-immigrant sentiment (Sackman, Peters, and Faist 2003), as does the perception of economic threat (Quillian 1995). These different social factors combine into specific patterns and styles of anti-immigrant arguments (Bail 2008). In nations like Spain, Italy, and Hungary, where the number of immigrants is relatively small and immigration is a more recent phenomenon, anti-immigration movements tend to focus on race and religion. In countries like France, Germany, the Netherlands, and the United Kingdom, which have a longer history with immigration, anti-immigrant movements focus more on language and culture.

The growing power of anti-immigrant movements has been met with resistance by immigrant-rights groups. In areas with large numbers of immigrants, churches, politicians, and business leaders have built successful coalitions that aim to recognize immigrants as valuable members of the community and to combat anti-immigrant political movements (Okamoto and Ebert 2016). In the United States these movements have been the most visible and successful in California, where immigrant and labor activist groups have worked together since the 1990s to campaign

**Calling for action on immigration**
Protesters rally in downtown Los Angeles, February 17, 2017, in a show of support for immigration rights and against President Donald Trump's policies (left), while anti-immigration supporters wave signs and show their support for then-candidate Trump at a rally in Anaheim, California, on May 25, 2016 (right). Elected again in 2024, Donald Trump continues to make anti-immigrant statements.

against anti-immigrant legislation in the state and to help elect progressive and pro-immigrant mayors in Los Angeles (Pastor 2015). As immigrant rights movements achieve political successes and attract media attention, they influence public opinion about immigration. Public opinion research shows that attitudes toward immigrants have become much more supportive in California since the 1990s (Skelton 2015), and there is some evidence that nationally organized immigrant-rights protests are beginning to have a similar effect (Voss and Bloemraad 2011).

## CASE STUDY

# Intersecting Identities

To apply the five key concepts to think about the racial and ethnic system in the United States, we end this chapter with the case of Sofía Vergara. Vergara is best known for her role as Gloria Pritchett on the television show *Modern Family*, for which she has won multiple Emmys and Golden Globe awards. Vergara was already well known to Spanish-speaking audiences for her work on Spanish-language television during the 1990s. According to *Forbes*, Vergara was the highest-paid female television actor in the United States from 2012 to 2018, an accomplishment that rests as much on her many product endorsements and licensing agreements as on direct compensation for her TV roles.

When Vergara talks about her life, she includes accounts of the racial and ethnic system of the United States that has shaped her career. For example, in many interviews, she repeats the point that she is a "natural blonde": "I'm a natural blonde, but when I started acting, I would go to auditions, and they didn't know where to put me because I was voluptuous and had the accent—but I had blonde hair," she explained in a 2010 interview with *Self* magazine. "The moment I dyed my hair dark, it was, 'Oh, she's the hot Latin girl.'"

This is a complicated story about the *structure* of the racial and ethnic hierarchy in the US entertainment business. According to Vergara, the casting agents had a stereotype of "the hot Latin girl" that they wanted the actress to fulfill, and her hair color was wrong since the stereotype assumes all Latinas are brunette. As an award-winning and critically acclaimed television actress and an influential voice in media discussions, Vergara uses her *power* in this story to introduce *contingency* into the category of "Latina" in the entertainment business. The story that she is a "natural blonde" was covered very widely in the entertainment media over several years and might be interpreted as a moment of *resistance* against the stereotypes that are used to typecast Latina actors and characters. Vergara joins a long line of prior critics who recall that Latina actresses have been both made to appear darker to exemplify a Latina stereotype and, in other cases, "whitened" through hair bleaching and removal to avoid the stereotype (Molina-Guzmán 2010; Valdivia 2010; Rodriguez 2004). In all cases, the actions and decisions of gatekeepers in the entertainment industry have served to uphold the cultural perceptions of Latinas at any given time.

That said, Vergara is not above playing with stereotypes, and she has drawn wide criticism for doing so. For example, in 2012 the *Huffington Post* asked of Vergara's role in *Modern Family*, "As alluring as she is, has the Colombian actress taken the Latina stereotype too far?" They go on to suggest that Vergara is not only playing a comedic version of the stereotype but also reinforcing the stereotype because her performance supports very traditional understandings of gender and class

## 7.6 THE POLITICS OF IMMIGRATION

**Sofia Vergara**

*inequality*. For example, the authors quote a *Daily Beast* interview where Vergara defends the Latina stereotype: "I don't see anything bad about being stereotyped as a Latin woman.... We are yellers, we're pretty, we're sexy, and we're scandalous. I am not scared of the stereotypes." In another interview, with *Esquire* magazine, Vergara is quoted as follows:

> Listen, I didn't know how to make coffee when I came to the United States. Because in Colombia the maids do it.... It's so different over there. You have the maid that cooks. The maid that irons the clothes. It's a hard adjustment. When I came to the United States and started working, my priority was not to buy a handbag but to spend my money on the maid and a nanny. Always. I always tell my guy friends who are complaining that their Latina girlfriends want a maid: "Listen, this is for your own good. You don't want a woman who is tired all day long, taking care of the kids, cooking, doing everything. She'll never be any fun. She'll never want to go out with you because she'll be exhausted. She'll never want to sleep with you. So this is an investment you're making for your love life. Think of it that way."

Striking a different note, the *Latin Times* cites critics who question Vergara's Latina accent, arguing that she exaggerates her accent to profit from the Latina stereotype she performs. This is a challenge of *solidarity* that suggests that Vergara does not do enough to counteract stereotypes of Latinas and instead profits by reinforcing them. All of these examples indicate *conflict* over the markers of Latina status in the US ethnic and racial system, and they are evidence that the media and other gatekeepers closely police ethnic and racial categories. To be sure, the critical attention Vergara receives reflects her relative *privilege*, which stems from her enormous accomplishments and celebrity.

Finally, Vergara's biography points to the way the racial and ethnic system in the United States is formed through the intersecting *local* and *global* histories that describe the immigrant experience in the United States. Vergara was born in Colombia, worked in the United States for most of her career, and became a naturalized US citizen in 2014. Vergara describes herself as Latina, which refers to people with origins in and connections with Latin America. This is sometimes distinguished from the term "Hispanic," which is defined as "people of Spanish-speaking origins," which would presumably also include Vergara, a native Spanish speaker. More recently, the newer popular category "Latinx" has come into use as a way to explicitly include a spectrum of gender identities and resist the gendered forms of the nouns "Latino" and "Latina" that come from Spanish, adding another layer of complexity to the system of racial and ethnic categories.

# LEARNING GOALS REVISITED

**7.1 Understand the way race is and has been socially constructed.**

- The modern racial and ethnic system has been constructed through violent conquest, genocide, slavery, lynching, government policies, scientific ideas, and cultural beliefs.
- Restrictive laws that controlled immigration, marriage, education, housing, jobs, and voting together have defined the racial and ethnic hierarchy. Law enforcement through policing has also helped reproduce the racial system.
- Government policies of assimilation have helped destroy Indigenous languages and cultural traditions, as well as deprioritize economic development, in communities of color.
- Scientists, including social scientists, have contributed to the social construction of racial classifications.
- Historically developed, systematic, institutional, and individual racism shapes individual life chances in American society.

**7.2 Understand the relationships and intersections among racial and ethnic groups in the United States.**

- Race and ethnicity are overlapping concepts. Race is a set of categories based on perceived biological differences, whereas ethnicity is a set of categories based on shared cultural heritage and common identities. Racial and ethnic categories intersect, and many people have intersectional identities.
- The US racial and ethnic system is measured officially by the US Census in an attempt to capture the nation's changing population characteristics and the changing understanding of those differences.

**7.3 Explain the relationship between racial privilege and racial inequality.**

- The racial system in the United States privileges white people at the expense of non-white people. This privilege is so pervasive and unremarked upon that most white people are unlikely to perceive it.
- Symbolic ethnicity refers to the way some members of dominant groups consume ethnic identity as a leisure activity.
- Economic and political privileges accrue from inheriting white privilege.
- Racial privilege continues to be secured through organized restrictions on access to institutions. Residential segregation and ethnic enclaves tend to reinforce racial boundaries.

**7.4 Understand current thinking about diversity and multiculturalism.**
- Multicultural societies reject the idea that some cultural groups are more valuable than others and have explicitly adopted policies to officially recognize the existence of different cultural groups and identities. Multicultural societies develop policies promoting cultural diversity.
- Many social institutions in the contemporary United States have multicultural policies and employ professionals to promote diversity and inclusion.

**7.5 Describe the basic historical trends in immigration.**
- International immigration began to increase during the 19th century, slowed considerably from 1920 to 1960, and then accelerated quickly after that. The number of international migrants has continued to increase since then.
- The United States is still the largest immigrant destination, but there are also significant numbers of immigrants settling in western Europe, Saudi Arabia, Japan, and South Korea.
- People often choose to emigrate because of a desire to escape economic poverty, political instability, and violence. Other important factors that increase the likelihood of emigration are family reunification, the desire to move to and join a well-known and established immigrant community, and recruitment into transnational work networks.

**7.6 Describe how immigrant communities are organized and how they shape politics and the economy in both sending and receiving countries.**
- Immigrants often settle in immigrant enclaves. It is also common for them to face a segmented labor market.
- Remittances are a common practice within immigrant communities. In some countries remittances account for one-third of total gross domestic product.
- Many countries have experienced anti-immigrant movements at various points in their history, and these movements have been increasing in recent years.
- Immigrants bring significant economic benefits to the nations that receive them.

## Key Terms

Assimilation 236
Blockbusting 230
Citizenship 246
Discrimination 227
Ethnic cleansing 233
Ethnicity 210

Genocide 232
Gentrification 230
Immigrant enclave 243
Internal migration 240
Multiculturalism 236
Race 210
Racial determinism 212
Racial profiling 234
Racial steering 230
Redlining 230
Remittance 244
Residential segregation 230
Segregation 227
Symbolic ethnicity 214

## Review Questions

1. What are racial determinists, and why are their classification systems considered to be pseudoscientific?
2. Define residential segregation, and name some of the practices that produce it.
3. What is the difference between race and ethnicity?
4. Define racial privilege. How does it work?
5. What are the main ways that the US racial and ethnic system was created and maintained? Is it still being maintained today? How?
6. What is multiculturalism?
7. What are the major racial and ethnic groups defined and measured by the US Census Bureau?
8. How are immigrants similar to and different from Black Americans and Native Americans?

## Explore

**RECOMMENDED READINGS**

Alba, Richard, and Victor Nee. 2003. *Remaking the American Mainstream: Assimilation and Contemporary Immigration*. Cambridge, MA: Harvard University Press.

Bonilla-Silva, Eduardo. 2018. *Racism without Racists: Color-Blind Racism and the Persistence of Inequality in America*, 5th ed. Lanham, MD: Rowman and Littlefield.

Bois Du, W. E. B. 1994. *The Souls of Black Folk*. New York: Dover Publications.

Champagne, Duane. 2008. "From First Nations to Self-Government: A Political Legacy of Indigenous Nations in the United States." Special Issue on Indigenous Peoples: Struggles against Globalization and Domination, eds. James V. Fenelon and Salvador J. Murguia. American Behavioral Scientist 51(13): 1672–1693.

Chou, Rosalind S., and Joe R. Feagin. 2008. *Myth of the Model Minority: Asian Americans Facing Racism*, 2nd ed. Boulder, CO: Paradigm Publishers.

Ignatiev, Noel. 2008. *How the Irish Became White*. New York: Routledge.

Mora, G. Christina. 2015. *Making Hispanics: How Activists, Bureaucrats, and Media Constructed a New American*. Chicago: University of Chicago Press.

Shapiro, Thomas. 2005. *The Hidden Costs of Being African-American: How Wealth Perpetuates Inequality*. New York: Oxford University Press.

## ACTIVITIES

- *Use your sociological imagination*: One of the biggest challenges facing the growing refugee population is that most governments are unwilling to allow large numbers of refugees into their countries. What do you think are the main motivations for this unwillingness? Can you find out which countries are the most accepting of refugee populations?

- *Media+Data Literacies*: Look at the Census categories in Table 7.1. Do you fit easily into existing Census categories? Why or why not? What might the consequences be of feeling like you don't fit? Do the race categories used by the Census help socially construct race?

- *Discuss*: To what extent is the United States a multicultural society that respects racial and ethnic difference? Give reasons for your argument.

# Walt Disney
# MULAN

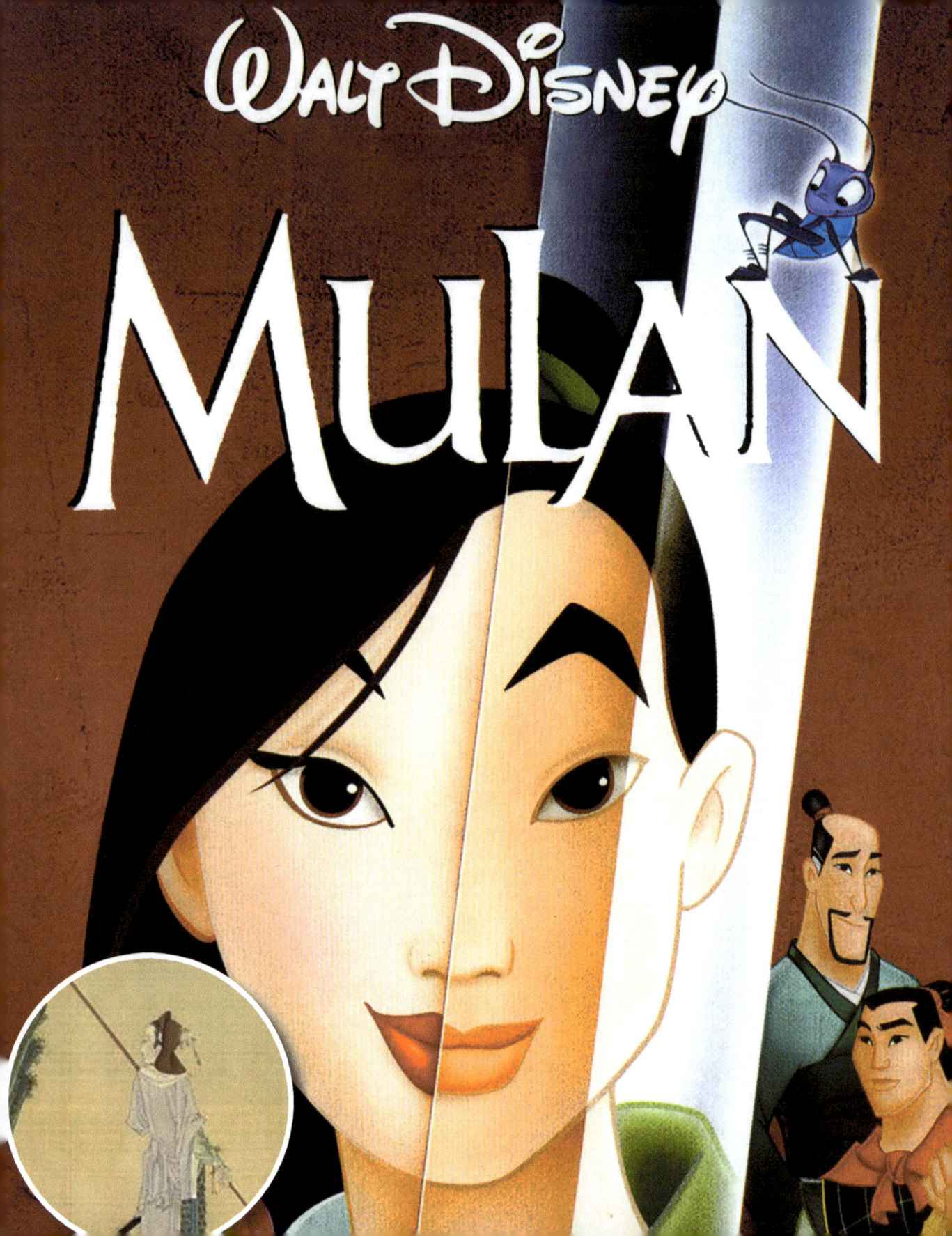

# 8

# Gender, Sexuality, and the Body

In the 1998 Disney movie *Mulan*, based on a traditional Chinese ballad, the young Chinese girl Hua Mulan takes her father's place when the emperor sends out a call for soldiers to fight in a war. When her parents discover Mulan has gone to be a soldier, her mother asks Mulan's father to go after her because "she will be killed." Mulan's father replies, "If I reveal her, she will be." Mulan risks her life when she decides to make a gender switch and impersonate a soldier.

Mulan survives the war and returns to her family to take up her old life. Every version of the story says that Mulan sheds her soldier's armor to return to the role of daughter. Although she performed heroically in a man's role and was believed to be a man by the soldiers who served with her, it is important to the story that Mulan really is, in the end, a woman. The story emphasizes that she was not ever really a man and reassures the viewer that she does not occupy the male role permanently.

The Disney version of the story also ends with a romance, as Mulan enters a relationship with a male soldier. Importantly, this romance connects Mulan's female body to her female role of daughter as well as her heterosexuality. In this way, the movie resolves the dramatic tension arising from the question of what

**Disney's Mulan and Hua Mulan**
Disney's depiction of the mythical female Chinese warrior Mulan is depicted with both male and female characteristics, divided by a sword. Compare the Disney depiction with the traditional Chinese depiction (inset) from the 18th-century album of paintings Gathering Gems of Beauty (畫麗珠萃秀). Which facial features and elements of clothing were emphasized to define masculine and feminine gender?

### Chapter Outline

**8.1 SEX, GENDER, AND THE BODY 256**

*Gender Socialization and Gender Performance 258*
*Gender Stereotypes 260*

**8.2 GENDER AND POWER 264**

*Masculinity and Femininity and the Gender Order 265*
*Divisions of Labor 268*
*Workplace Harassment and Sexual Exclusions in Work and Public Spaces 272*
*Challenging Patriarchy and the History of the Women's Movement 275*

**8.3 SEXUALITY AND THE BODY 278**

*The Marketing of Romance 278*
*Heteronormativity 281*
*Queer Identities beyond the Closet 283*

**CASE STUDY: GENDER INTERSECTIONS AT McDONALD'S 285**

will happen when it is discovered that Mulan has switched gender roles and fooled everyone into thinking she is a man. By returning to the traditional gender roles of daughter and heterosexual woman, the film's conclusion reinforces the stability of traditional gender order, which links family roles with work roles and sexual roles.

In this chapter, we explore how institutions of sex and gender shape individual experiences and social life. We begin with a discussion of how sex, gender, and bodies are socially constructed. Focusing on gender scripts that define what is expected of women and men, we emphasize that sex and gender are broad institutional principles. We then explore gender and power, including divisions of labor and gender violence. We describe how sex and gender intersect with other social relationships and help to reproduce racial and class-based systems of power. Last, we offer a brief history of the social organization of sexual desire and examine how recent social movements have introduced more fluid understandings of sex, gender, and sexuality in the United States.

## LEARNING GOALS

**8.1** Define the difference between sex and gender, and describe the dimensions of gender inequality.

**8.2** Analyze how gender is socially constructed as a social and moral order.

**8.3** Understand how sexuality and bodies are socially constructed through gender, and consider how gender intersects with other dimensions of the stratification system like race and class.

## 8.1 Sex, Gender, and the Body

**LG 8.1** Define the difference between sex and gender, and describe the dimensions of gender inequality.

**Sex** The biological categories of male, female, or intersex, which are assigned at birth on the basis of bodily characteristics such as the organs required for sexual reproduction; secondary features like body hair, height, or breasts; and also genetic and chromosomal differences.

**Sex** is the status of male or female or intersex, which is assigned to babies at birth on the basis of bodily characteristics such as the organs required for sexual reproduction, and also secondary features like body hair, height, or breasts, and also genetic and chromosomal differences. **Gender** refers to wide-ranging cultural meanings and distinctions, that shape personal identity as well as socially constructed roles for women and men. Traditionally, the social institution of gender has worked to define women and men as different *because* they are assigned to a sex category of male or female based on bodily differences.

This key concept is called the **gender binary**, which is the idea that there are only two gender categories, masculine and feminine, and that all people are either one or the other on the basis of biological sex. The gender binary also gives force to the belief that women and men are different in their personal styles, emotional qualities, and intellectual and physical abilities. The gender binary is constantly reinforced in daily life, and in particular by social practices that overemphasize differences between girls and boys.

For example, there is little reason to dress baby girls in pink and baby boys in blue since sex categories are not important to babies. Rather, dressing babies in gender-specific colored clothes is a social behavior performed by adults that underscores the classification of the baby as either male or female in a dichotomous classification of sex as bodily difference. When parents dress their newborns in pink or blue, this behavior follows a **gender script** that directs parents to display the sex of their baby. Many social roles flow from the classification of a child as male or female, including family roles of sons and daughters and brothers and sisters. Parents and others might wonder if a son or daughter will join the family business, share a hobby with a parent, or follow a parent into the military. Clearly, it is not the body of the baby that is producing the gender effect. Rather, a sociological perspective emphasizes that it is the social act of classifying the infant's body into a sex category that shapes related gender expectations.

The gender binary constricts how we think about sex and gender, and it hides the social and institutional work that goes into keeping the binary sex–gender order in place. It does this by minimizing natural physical variation among humans and limiting our understanding of human gender expression more broadly. **Intersex** people, for example, have characteristics that are associated with the biological sex categories of both male and female. When babies with an intersex diagnosis are surgically altered to conform to a male or female sex category, this is an example of a social practice that reinforces the gender binary and the notion that there are only two sex categories. **Cisgender** people, by contrast, are those whose gender identification correlates with the sex category they were assigned at birth. A cisgender person is someone who was assigned female at birth and identifies as a woman, or who was assigned male at birth and identifies as a man. This is not the only way people express gender. **Transgender** people, for example, include many whose gender identification does not correlate with the sex category they were assigned at birth. For example, transpeople may have been classified as male at birth but identify as a woman, or be classified as female at birth but identify as a man. People who identify as **nonbinary** may identify as both man and woman or neither man nor woman—and this identification may have nothing to do with the assignment of sex category at birth. When legal documents require people to select one of only two gender categories on legal documents—M for male or F for female—or when people are required to use public bathrooms that supposedly correlate with their sex assignment

**Gender** The cultural distinctions and socially constructed roles that define expected behaviors for women and men.

**Gender binary** The idea that there are only two gender categories, masculine and feminine, and that all people are either one or the other on the basis of biological sex.

**Gender script** A set of social norms that direct people to act in accordance with widely understood gender expectations.

**Intersex** A term for people with physical characteristics associated with both male and female categories. More recently the term "differences of sex development" has been recommended by persons with intersex conditions.

**Cisgender** A term for people who are assigned male at birth and identify as men, or who are assigned female at birth and who identify as women.

**Transgender** A term for people assigned male at birth who do not identify as men and people who are assigned female at birth who do not identify as women.

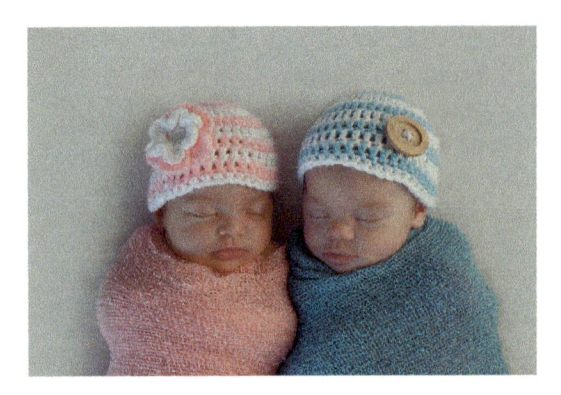

**Color-coded babies**
Pink for girls and blue for boys.

**Gender socialization**
Family roles are powerful. There are alternatives to gender stereotypes, but women continue to be associated with unpaid housework in the family household.

**Nonbinary** A term for people who identify as both man and woman or as neither man or woman.

**Gender cue** Part of a gendered social script that tells other people what gendered behavior to expect and how to orient their own behavior.

**Gender performance** Actions and behaviors that conform to widespread gendered understandings of social roles and social identities.

**Gender socialization** The social interactions and experiences through which individuals develop a social self in relation to gender roles in families as well as in schools, workplaces, and public spaces.

at birth, these are social practices that reinforce the gender binary and that can cause psychological or physical harm to people whose experiences and identities fall outside the binary. Sociologists are interested in understanding the range of sex and gender expression in our society, and they use their tools to draw attention to the social forces that reinforce the gender binary to produce inequality and injustice.

## Gender Socialization and Gender Performance

In our society, people generally do not display their organs of sexual reproduction in ordinary everyday interaction. Instead, people use **gender cues** (such as dress, speech, and manner) to express their gender identities and to signal to others what gendered behavior to expect and how to orient their own behavior (Goffman 1959). When people's gender performances align with the script dictated by the gender binary, they reproduce the widespread "common sense" that the gender binary is natural, inevitable, and therefore morally justified (Garfinkel 1967). This is a key insight of sociological theories of **gender performance**.

In Chapter 2, we discussed the sociological tradition of symbolic interactionism that documents how meanings about the social world develop in the interactions people have with one another. In Chapter 4, we connected social interaction to wider processes of socialization where people learn how to act in society and develop a sense of their social self. Extending this, we can say that **gender socialization** is the process by which individuals develop a social self in relation to gender roles in families as well as in schools, workplaces, and public spaces.

**PAIRED CONCEPTS**

## Structure and Contingency

### Classifying Intersex Babies

Children born with "atypical sex characteristics" are identified as intersex, or as having "differences of sex development." This biological fact raises the possibility that sex status is more socially contingent than is widely believed, although this was not well known for much of US history, mainly because most medical practice was based in the gender binary. Medical professionals sorted children born with atypical sex characteristics into one of the two traditional sex categories, advising parents that the intersex category was medically risky and socially problematic. By the end of the 20th century, criticism of unnecessary surgery performed on babies with differences in sex development resulted in a move away from the idea that all sex nonconformity needs to be corrected (Cuadra et al. 2024; American Psychological Association 2017a).

From a sociological point of view, thinking about how babies are assigned to a sex category at birth sheds light on the institutional reproduction of the binary structure of sex and gender. Scientific and medical institutions are particularly important in defining sex classification for medical records. Government agencies also reinforce and uphold structures of sex and gender that divide humans into male and female, since a baby's sex status is registered on a birth certificate, which is proof of citizenship and other legal rights.

Since April 2022, citizens in the United States have had the option to select the category X on their US passports in addition to the traditional M and F. Importantly, this option does not require medical documentation, nor is the category selected required to match other forms of identification. The US now joins 18 other countries that recognize "non-binary or third gender identities" according to the Equality index published by Equaldex (2024). Initially seen as a "third gender marker for non-binary, intersex, and gender non-conforming individuals," after public comment and feedback, US Secretary of State Antony Blinken concluded that "the definition of the X gender marker on State Department public forms will be 'Unspecified or another gender identity.' This definition is respectful of individuals' privacy while advancing inclusion" (US Department of State, 2022).

**Legal gender**
Gender is produced and reproduced in official documents. Birth certificates, driver's licenses, passports, and many other official documents produced by governments, hospitals, workplaces, and educational institutions define both an individual's gender and the overall system of gender categories.

### ACTIVE LEARNING

**Think about it:** We are asked to identify our sex all the time on bureaucratic forms, even in situations where this information has no relevance. Try to provide one or two examples where you are asked to identify your sex on a form. How do you account for why the form is asking for your sex? What are some of the consequences of asking for this information in your example?

Specific scripts about sex and gender are learned and then reproduced by all the agents of socialization, including family, schools, peer groups, workplaces, and media. We learn how to perform gender when we learn about social roles and where we might fit in the world. In families, for example, we learn what it means to be a "good" married partner, parent, child, or sibling. In this process of watching how other family members behave and listening to family stories about individuals, we might see the way the gender binary positions husbands as different from wives, mothers as different from fathers, and daughters as different from sons.

This process is reproduced on a wider scale within schools and workplaces, and through the media. We learn in our communities, on TV, and online what kind of gendered people pursue different academic subjects, who performs what jobs, who has power in our life, and who makes the most money. In short, we develop a sense of ourselves, including a sense of our gendered selves, by interacting with those around us. We also develop a sense of the gendered expectations associated with social roles more broadly. Consider what gender expectations are connected to work roles such as manager, restaurant server, police officer, doctor, nurse, professor, or rock star.

## Gender Stereotypes

**Gender stereotypes** Oversimplified images that follow the logic of the gender binary to define and reinforce different and contrasting qualities associated with women and men.

**Gender stereotypes** are oversimplified images that follow the logic of the gender binary to define and reinforce different and contrasting qualities associated with women and men. When we use gender stereotypes, we are actively enforcing the gender binary. When we expect people identified as men to display only masculine behaviors and people identified as women to display only feminine behaviors, we are constraining the possibilities of human expression and suggesting there are no other ways of behaving in the world.

Gender stereotypes are also reproduced in scientific and scholarly practice. Since the 1970s, for example, social psychologists have tried to identify lists of masculine, feminine, and gender-neutral psychological traits (Bem 1974; see Table 8.1). These distinctions are in broad social circulation, but critics question whether measuring and naming such distinctions also reinforces them—even if the goal is to study stereotypes (Colley et al. 2009; Carver et al. 2013). This is a central question for social science, since what we study shapes the very social things we are studying, and it is a key element of the social construction of meaning. The one thing that seems clear from a long history of research is that

## TABLE 8.1 Characteristics on the Bem Sex Role Inventory

| FEMALE | MALE | NEUTRAL |
|---|---|---|
| Yielding | Self-reliant | Helpful |
| Cheerful | Defends own beliefs | Moody |
| Shy | Independent | Conscientious |
| Affectionate | Athletic | Theatrical |
| Flatterable | Assertive | Happy |
| Loyal | Strong personality | Unpredictable |
| Feminine | Forceful | Reliable |
| Sympathetic | Analytical | Jealous |
| Sensitive to other's needs | Leadership ability | Truthful |
| Understanding | Willing to take risks | Secretive |
| Compassionate | Makes decisions easily | Sincere |
| Eager to soothe hurt feelings | Self-sufficient | Conceited |
| Soft spoken | Dominant | Likable |
| Warm | Masculine | Solemn |
| Tender | Willing to take a stand | Friendly |
| Gullible | Aggressive | Inefficient |
| Childlike | Acts as a leader | Adaptable |
| Does not use harsh language | Individualistic | Unsystematic |
| Loves children | Competitive | Tactful |
| Gentle | Ambitious | Conventional |

Source: PsyToolkit http://www.psytoolkit.org/survey-library/sex-role-bem.html#refs

everyone uses gender stereotypes to consciously and unconsciously make meaning.

The pervasiveness of gender as a broad institutional principle can also be seen in the widespread use of gender in social descriptions of objects well beyond the human body. For example, cats are typically characterized as female, while dogs are often characterized as male. Objects, places, animals, and even food are considered more masculine or more feminine, depending on the degree to which they track supposedly male or female characteristics. Sociologists study how the cultural effects of these distinctions between **masculinity** and **femininity** support or challenge the intricate, detailed, and powerful system of gender that permeates every social institution.

**Masculinity** The set of personal, social, and cultural qualities associated with males and men.

**Femininity** The set of personal, social, and cultural qualities associated with females and women.

## CAREERS

### Women, Men, and Social Networks

Research on leadership, networking, and careers provides evidence that women and men have different kinds of social networks, different approaches to social networking in the workplace, and different career outcomes as a result (Kanter 1977; Eagly and Johnson 1990; Ibarra 1993; Forret and Dougherty 2004; De La Rey 2005; van Emmerik et al. 2006; Misner, Walker and De Raffele 2012). It might be tempting to explain these differences as the product of inherent differences in sex and gender. Men are characterized as direct, instrumental, and transactional in their networking styles, while women are characterized as indirect, expressive, and relational, and this aligns with the general gender stereotypes identified by the inventory in Table 8.1.

Sociological research on gender and networking identifies important factors in organizational contexts that shape the differences observed between women and men (Kanter 1977). These factors include different opportunities for women and men in the organization, different network resources, and gender role socialization that results in different responses to similar behavior by men and women (Ibarra 1993). Workplace behavior for women is shaped by the number of women in the corporation, the availability of mentors and internal career paths, the functional roles women play in the organization, the effect of non-work roles on women (especially family roles), and the work culture of the organization. All these factors shape the network strategies of women and men.

**Women and men at work**
Women and men at work are often employed in different roles. Even when they are employed in similar roles, the organizational culture and local gender norms can affect work experiences, including salaries, career development, promotion, work satisfaction, and networking styles.

#### ACTIVE LEARNING

**Find out:** Write down a list of the student and community organizations or clubs where you are a member. What is the gender composition of the organizations? Who leads? Do the women and men in the organization have different roles? Do they have different relational styles? Does the same behavior work for women as for men leaders?

## METHODS AND INTERPRETATION

### Gender Bias in Social Research

Joan Acker's classic article "Women and Social Stratification: A Case of Intellectual Sexism" appeared in the *American Journal of Sociology* in 1973. The article began with a list of sexist assumptions that guided social research on social inequality during the 20th century:

1. The family is the unit in the stratification system.

2. The social position of the family is determined by the status of the male head of the household.
3. Females live in families; therefore, their status is determined by that of the males to whom they are attached.
4. The female's status is equal to that of her man, at least in terms of her position in the class structure, because the family is a unit of equivalent evaluation . . .
5. Women determine their own social status only when they are not attached to a man.
6. Women are unequal to men in many ways, are differentially evaluated on the basis of sex, but this is irrelevant to the structure of stratification systems. (Acker 1973: 937).

Acker showed that these assumptions underpinned many major data collection efforts by research institutes, universities, and the US government. This was true despite the fact that according to the 1970 US Census, 11 percent of people in the United States did not live in families, and two-thirds of all households were either female headed or had no male breadwinner. Acker's analysis was important because it used the tools of logic and empirical evidence to document that very large social phenomena were simply not being seen, measured, or analyzed. Women were being rendered invisible by the practices of supposedly objective scientific research.

Sociologists were not the only critics identifying systematic gender bias in research. Around the same time that Acker published her article, feminist historian Margot Conk (1978, 1989) documented that census takers in the early-20th-century United States routinely "corrected" women's reported occupation if they were found to be in male-typed occupations like machinist or tailor. These systematic practices of gendered "correction" biased the data we have about the gender composition of historical occupations. In a slightly different vein, feminist anthropologist Emily Martin (1990) documented the gendered language biologists use to describe human reproduction. She analyzed multiple scientific and medical texts to show that women's eggs were invariably described as passive and waiting to be fertilized while male sperm were described as active and engaged, and she described the consequences of this medical language on the ways in which medical practitioners and their female patients communicated about the reproductive process.

In each of these cases, feminist scholars pointed to pervasive gender assumptions that shaped how we understand fundamental human processes. Gendered biases in the Census shape the way we tell historical stories as well as the historical record we have to inform those stories. The gendered language of biological and medical science influences how we think about male and female roles in human reproduction. And until quite late in the 20th century, problematic assumptions of sociological researchers effectively resulted in the exclusion of large parts of women's economic activity—and therefore all economic activity—from the analysis of inequality.

Gender bias in research continues to be an issue today, despite the fact that the problem is now well known within the scientific community. A field experiment that asked science faculty to evaluate potential applicants for a laboratory manager position showed—despite the fact that the gender of applicants had been randomly assigned—that the male applicants were more likely to be rated as competent and hirable, and more likely to be selected for a higher starting salary (Moss-Racusin et al. 2012). A significant gender bias is evident in artificial intelligence algorithms, which are likely to amplify the bias that already exists and make it harder to respond effectively to the problem of gender bias in scientific research (Hall and Ellis 2023). There even appears to be bias against research on gender bias, with research on gender bias receiving less funding and getting published in lower-impact journals than research on race bias (Cislak, Formanowitz and Saguy 2017).

### ACTIVE LEARNING

**Discuss:** Do you think the language of science can ever be completely neutral? Can you think of any practices that could help reduce cultural assumptions about gender that might bias scientific research?

## 8.2 Gender and Power

**LG 8.2** Analyze how gender is socially constructed as a social and moral order.

**Patriarchy** A social system rooted in male power, in which men and qualities associated with men are considered to be superior to women and to qualities associated with women.

**Sexism** A social process whereby social resources are directly, unequally, and unfairly distributed in favor of people who are perceived to be biologically male.

**Androcentrism** A social understanding that qualities associated with masculinity and a masculine point of view are valued over those associated with femininity, which are dismissed and subordinated.

Stereotypes of women and men are rooted in a context of male power, or **patriarchy**, in which men and qualities associated with men are considered to be superior to women and to qualities associated with women. Patriarchy is organized through **sexism**, whereby social resources are directly, unequally, and unfairly distributed in favor of people who are perceived to be biologically male. Patriarchy is also organized through **androcentrism**, whereby qualities associated with masculinity and a masculine point of view are valued over those associated with femininity, which are dismissed and subordinated. In patriarchal society, men hold most of the powerful positions in political, economic, and cultural institutions. Men—largely white, educated, and wealthy men—dominate political and cultural institutions and business leadership, and also control the means of symbolic production in the media.

These patterns are evident worldwide, with important variation across countries. Countries like Rwanda, Andorra, and Cuba have gender quotas, where about half of all political representatives are required to be women. In the United States, by contrast, while women enjoy formally equal political rights and also vote in elections in substantially higher numbers than men, only about 28 percent of congressional representatives are women.

A look at economic indicators tells a similar story. US census data show that despite the fact that American women have begun to outpace men in formal educational achievement, women still do different work than men and women are paid less than men. On average, white women earn about 83 cents for each dollar a white man earns, and this difference is far larger for Black and Hispanic women (Kochhar 2023). Female-headed households are also more likely to have lower earnings than male-headed households, and people in female-headed households are far more likely to live in poverty than people living with a male householder (Fontenot, Semega, and Kollar 2018; Shrider and Creamer 2023). At the intersection of gender, race and ethnicity, rates of poverty are also higher for women of color, leaving children and other family members vulnerable to economic, educational, health, and safety risks (Federal Interagency Forum on Child and Family Statistics 2023), as we discuss in Chapter 9. Finally, these gendered and racialized patterns have been exacerbated by uneven economic impacts of the COVID-19 recession, both in the United States and around the world (International Labour Organization 2020). All these statistics underline continuing gender inequality in social resources and institutional power in the United States, and they also provide evidence that systems of race and gender intersect to shape the life chances of women and men in multiple ways.

## Masculinity and Femininity and the Gender Order

Gender theorist R. W. Connell argues that these patterns reveal a patriarchy that operates through **hegemony**, or the ideas and strategies that dominant groups use to maintain their power while making their views seem like "common sense" to the rest of the population. Connell defines **hegemonic masculinity** as an ideal standard for the most valued people in society, specifically cis-gendered, white, educated, wealthy, able-bodied men. People associated with these characteristics are understood to be superior to other men and to all women (Connell 1987, 1995).

Hegemonic masculinity, sexism, and androcentrism describe the cultural dynamics of the **gender order**, which refers to all the ways gender organizes all of social life. The gender order is also a **moral order** because it defines what is right and wrong for women and men. To be clear, the sociological insight about the moral force of social expectations does not imply that sociologists support any particular gender order—although it is true that most sociologists are aware of gender diversity and support gender equality. Rather, the sociological insight about the moral force of social expectations helps explain *why* people follow social scripts to maintain gender order. Most people follow the traditional script because it seems like "common sense" to do so. This is how hegemony works.

Experiments in social psychology provide evidence of widespread conformity to gender expectations. In one field experiment, for example, researchers place printed male and female "bathroom signs" on the glass doors of a building and observe as people self-sort to use the door that "matched" their gender. For many people, conforming to the gender binary is the path of least resistance; following the script is easy and the majority of people self-sorted by the printed gender sign. Versions of this experiment have been used on elevators, trash cans, and in other public accommodations, and they all show that gender conformity is a major way that the gendered social order is produced in everyday social interaction.

The workings of the gender order can also be seen in the social reaction that occurs when a person's behavior does not conform to gender expectations. When someone disrupts a gender script, others can find it threatening to their understanding of moral order. In the late 19th and early 20th centuries, when women threatened masculine social power through campaigns for the right to vote, many suffragist leaders were imprisoned and brutalized. Rape and public sexual harassment aimed at women and some men are also forms of social control in the gender order. When people challenge the logic of the gender binary by demonstrating that bodily differences, sex assignment at birth, and gender roles are not naturally or neatly aligned, they undermine the common-sense understanding of gender arrangements organized by the gender binary and they challenge

**Hegemony** A form of power in which dominant groups are able to make their worldview seem like "common sense" to the rest of the population.

**Hegemonic masculinity** A form of power that enshrines an ideal standard of masculinity for the most valued people in society—specifically, cisgendered, white, educated, wealthy, and able-bodied men.

**Gender order** A characterization of society as fully organized by gender.

**Moral order** A social arrangement that is organized around widely understood and institutionally enforced ideas of right and wrong; the gender order is a moral order since it defines what is right and wrong for women and men.

hegemonic masculinity. Challenging the gender binary has historically put people at risk of being defined as deviant, suffering consequences from harassment, physical violence, attempted resocialization, and incarceration in prisons and mental institutions. These repressive social responses, which include state sanctioned violence as well as informal violence, testify to the enduring relevance of the meanings institutionalized in the gender binary that organize many areas of social life.

On the other hand, the idea that gender is socially scripted is also a powerful critical tool for challenging the established gender order and the all the intersecting and interlocking systems of oppression that are entangled with gender. Feminists and other critics challenge gender scripts in the workplace, arguing that a wide range of people can do the same work as men and be paid the same wages. Movements for gay and lesbian rights have challenged the idea that heterosexuality is the only appropriate basis of sexual desire, sexual identity, or marriage and family formation. In fact, in the United States, there have been multiple social movements to extend civil rights to women, gay people, and transgender people and to challenge the widespread public understandings of the moral organization of gender.

Movements to extend civil rights have not always followed a straight line, however. For example, while women were granted the formal right to vote by the federal government in 1920, it was not until the passage of the 1965 Voting Rights Act that Black women fully realized that right. Or consider the right to abortion, which was protected as a civil right in all 50 US states in the 1973 Roe decision (*Roe v. Wade*, 410 U.S. 113) until it was overturned by the US Supreme Court in 2022 (*Dobbs v. Jackson*, 597 U.S. 215 2022). Same-sex marriage was recognized for the first time in Vermont in 2003, even though it was not accepted by large proportions of the American public. Despite this, the right for same-sex partners to marry was upheld by the Supreme Court and declared legal in all 50 states in 2015 (*Obergefell v. Hodges*, 576 U.S. 644 2015). Public support for extending marriage rights shifted very quickly over the same period (see Figure 8.1): when polled in 2003, 58 percent of Americans were opposed to same-sex

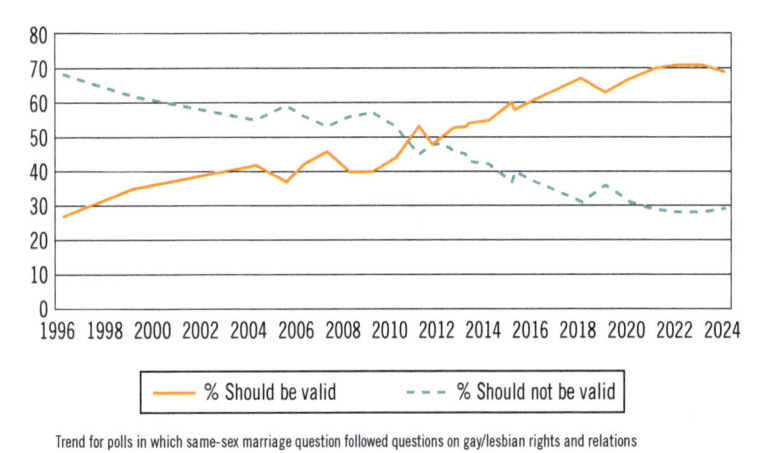

**Figure 8.1** Changing public opinion in the United States about the right to marriage between people of the same sex, 1996–2024.
Source: https://news.gallup.com/poll/1651/gay-lesbian-rights.aspx

Trend for polls in which same-sex marriage question followed questions on gay/lesbian rights and relations

marriage, but by 2015, at the time of the Supreme Court decision, over 60 percent supported the right of same-sex couples to get married (Fingerhut 2016). In 2024, 69 percent of people in the United States support marriage between same-sex partners (Gallup 2024).

Questions about who can use which public bathrooms are another contemporary issue related to safety and equality. Multiple US states have passed laws that regulate people's access to bathrooms. One such bill in North Carolina, the Public Facilities Privacy & Security Act, was passed in March 2016. Among other clauses, it stated that individuals could only use restrooms that corresponded to the sex on their legal birth certificate. Supporters of the bill referred to it as "common-sense" legislation, while opponents described it as discriminatory. On March 30, 2017, the bill was repealed as a result of massive public protests and business boycotts of North Carolina. While there is no current bathroom ban in North Carolina, there are still 12 US states that restrict or ban people from using the bathroom where they feel the safest and most comfortable (Movement Advancement Project). These conflicts also show that the gender order of society is subject to protest and change. In fact, rights for members of gender-nonconforming groups are rarely institutionalized without struggle and resistance. Laws restricting rights for gender-nonconforming groups continue to be passed in the US. As of 2023, 20 states had enacted laws banning gender transition care for minors, and 21 states had enacted laws banning transgender women and girls from playing on female sports teams. And six states enacted bathroom bills preventing transgender people from using public

**Bathroom politics**
This all-gender restroom sign disrupts the moral order of binary gender. It combines features of "male" and "female" in the third figure, and connects all gender designations to disability via the fourth figure in a wheelchair.

restrooms consistent with their gender identity. These so-called bathroom laws also highlight the moral nature of gender since they underline the fact that the gender order is about the moral meanings people attribute to bodily differences in public.

## Divisions of Labor

We have seen that the gender order regulates bodily differences and associated gender roles. The gender binary is also a central organizing principle of the **division of labor** in society since it describes institutions of work and defines who does what work. Where an individual lives and works is directly linked to economic outcomes, which means that the division of labor is an important key to understanding structures of stratification, privilege, and inequality.

**SEPARATE SPHERES.** The idea of **separate spheres** can be traced back to the ancient Greek philosopher Plato. He distinguished the public sphere of the (male) citizen, called the *polis*, from the private sphere of family reproduction and economic production, called the *oikos*. The more modern idea that men and women occupy separate spheres dates to the early industrial era in Western Europe and North America as economic production began to move outside the family household. Over time the theory of separate spheres stated that it was natural for men to occupy the public sphere of politics, economics, and law, while women were better suited for life in the domestic sphere of childrearing, family life, and housework.

The doctrine of separate spheres never fully described the historical experience of real women and men. Women from different class, racial, and ethnic backgrounds always worked for wages in greater numbers than white women; and at the other end of society, upper-class women participated in public life and politics through elite cultural institutions. Nonetheless, the powerful idea that there is a natural separation between the public world of men's roles and the private world of women remains with us to this day.

One legacy of the idea of separate spheres is that women are naturally better equipped to care for children. This belief has had many social consequences. A major reason that affordable childcare was never institutionalized in the United States was that it was presumed that mothers and other adult women would care for children at home. Related to this was the idea of the **male breadwinner**, a social expectation that men should earn enough in wages to support a wife and family. This idea still resonates today, despite the fact that most families rely on two incomes and most adult women engage in paid labor.

The economic dependence of women on husbands or other male relatives has been reinforced in many ways historically. Since married women were

---

**Division of labor**
A central principle for organizing the productive work in society that sorts different people into different work roles to ensure the production and reproduction of human life.

**Separate spheres**
The idea that there are and should be separate social domains for women and men.

**Male breadwinner**
A traditional social role for adult men based on the expectation that men should earn enough in wages to support a dependent wife and family.

understood to have husbands who supported them, there were few careers open to them, even if they were qualified. In many businesses and in government jobs, it was official policy that women were dismissed or resigned when they married or became pregnant. The choice was either work *or* family, and most women chose family. This created an expectation that women were unreliable workers because of their family commitments.

This system was coercive because it created a strong incentive for women to get married and stay married, even if there were serious problems with those marriages. Many women believed they had little choice but to marry because it was the main way they secured their own economic status and the security and welfare of their children. This diminished women's power and left them open to subordination and abuse. Sociologists in the mid-1900s paid little attention to issues of power and analyzed these arrangements in terms of functional role difference that suggested that women and men were socialized into roles that suited them and supported the overall system. This echoed the separate spheres idea.

Many families never fit this ideal model of the traditional nuclear family, including single people, gay couples, and single-parent families (e.g., widows and widowers, unwed mothers) (Koontz [1993] 2016). In addition, single women, unmarried mothers, working-class women, and many women of color had no choice but to work to support themselves and their families. In the gendered division of labor built around the idea of separate spheres, these women had many fewer economic opportunities, lower social status, and much lower wages than men.

The gendered division of labor changed dramatically as women began to enter the US labor force in larger numbers beginning in the 1970s. Labor force participation among US women age 16 and over in 1950 was 32 percent. This almost doubled to 57.4 percent in 1999, but the level has remained steady or even declined somewhat since then (Bureau of Labor Statistics 2021). By comparison, for men aged 16 and over, 82 percent were employed in 1950, declining to 71.6 percent in 1999 and continuing to decline steadily since then, reaching a labor force participation rate of 68.1 percent in 2024. This change in the gendered division of labor also occurred in other wealthy industrial countries over the same period (International Labour Organization 2017).

Despite gains in economic independence for many women, gender continues to structure the division of labor in US society. Gender role expectations during parenthood are a big part of the explanation for the persistence of the wage gap; when women suspend or limit their work during their child-rearing years, the result is a loss of earnings from which it is difficult to recover (Bertrand, Goldin, and Katz 2010; Yu and Kuo 2024). An additional factor that has shaped the workplace since the 1970s is the broader

**Pink-collar jobs** A term coined to describe the kinds of jobs done by women entering the labor force in the 1970s and 1980s; support roles that were paid less than white-collar jobs and well-paid unionized blue-collar jobs.

economic shift from industrial manufacturing to service jobs, where women were more likely to find employment. These newer jobs were less likely to be unionized or to provide other workplace protections. Many of the jobs women entered were called **pink-collar jobs**. Pink-collar jobs typically had a very short internal career path, offered little chance of promotion into higher positions, and were available on an as-needed contingent basis. They were support roles and clerical jobs dominated by women that required less experience and were therefore paid less than either white-collar work or well-unionized blue-collar jobs in manufacturing and the trades. But as more privileged women began to enter professional and white-collar jobs in the 1980s and 1990s, there was a widespread expectation that this would change and that the income gap between women and men would finally narrow. This did not occur.

Today, women in the United States earn around 80 cents for every dollar men earn, and the size of the service sector characterized by contingent jobs performed in precarious conditions continues to grow for women and men alike. These patterns are deeply entangled with racial systems of inequality too. The Pew Foundation reports for 2022 that Black women earned 70 percent of what white men earned, and Hispanic women earned 65 percent of what white men earned. Asian women earned closer to what white men earned, with an average of 93 percent of the white male wage (Kochhar 2023).

**Horizontal occupational segregation** A pervasive pattern of gender segregation where women are concentrated into female-typed, lower-earning jobs.

**OCCUPATIONAL SEGREGATION.** What accounts for the persistent gap in earnings between women and men? About half the earnings gender gap is produced by **horizontal occupational segregation**. This is a pervasive pattern of gender segregation where women are concentrated into female-typed, lower-earning, more contingent jobs (Blau and Kahn 2017). This is evidence of institutionalized sexism. Women's jobs are more likely to be lower-paid, even when they are nominally similar to men's jobs, requiring similar skills, education, and responsibility (Miller 2016). As the service sector continues to expand on the basis of contingent employment, real wages for all workers are declining.

Historical analysis shows that the gender composition of an occupation is associated with pay differences (Levanon, England, and Allison 2009). Between 1950 and 2000, Miller (2016) reports, recreational jobs such as working in parks or leading camps transitioned from being primarily done by men to being primarily done by women, and wages declined 57 percent. However, traditionally female occupations that over time attracted more men saw wages *increase*. For example, during the 1940s and 1950s when most of the computer programmers were women, status and pay for those jobs were relatively low, as men were concentrated in hardware development.

As men flocked to computer programming jobs in the 1970s, however, salaries and status for those jobs soared (Cohen 2016). As sociologist and expert on occupational segregation Paula England asserts, "Once women start doing a job, it just doesn't look like it's as important to the bottom line or requires as much skill. Gender bias sneaks into those decisions" (Miller 2016).

Other mechanisms that account for occupational gender segregation are differences in seniority and job search strategies, work preferences, and the self-selection of women into jobs that pay less but may provide more flexibility for family care and housework. These differences also account for some part of the gender gap in earnings. But even when they are doing the same job and performing identical work, women earn less than men; and this is true whether or not these are female- or male-dominated occupations (Hegewisch and DuMonthier 2015). This is also connected to patterns of **vertical occupational segregation**, where men also tend to hold higher, better-paid positions within the same occupation as women. The most powerful and best-paid doctor in the hospital, the primary partner in the law firm, or the CEO of the company are all likely to be men.

It is important to note that patterns of vertical and horizontal segregation are intersectional with occupational segregation by race. Kimberlé Crenshaw coined the term **intersectionality** when advocating for Black women who were discriminated against by General Motors. Intersectionality identifies the multiple, intersecting, and situational nature of the categories that shape people's identities and experiences. In this case, the corporation argued that its employment policies were not racist because it employed Black men on the production line, and were not sexist because it employed white women in clerical work. Crenshaw showed that General Motors was

**Occupational segregation**
Women and men do different work. Although men were actually among the first typists, it was women who worked in the typing pools of post–World War II America.

**Vertical occupational segregation** A pattern in occupations where men tend to hold higher, better-paid positions than women within the same occupation.

**Intersectionality** A perspective that identifies the multiple, intersecting, and situational nature of the categories that shape people's identities and experiences.

discriminating against Black women since it would not employ women in production or Black people in clerical roles. Black women were marginalized at an intersection of systems of oppression, an intersection produced by occupational segregation by race and sex.

To be clear, gender segregation in occupations does not produce a pattern where all individual women earn less than all individual men. Rather, it means that gender organizes the division of labor at several different levels, within and between occupations and over time. The point is that gender defines women's work as less valuable—at least in financial terms—*because* women do it.

**THE SECOND SHIFT.** Enduring beliefs about women's roles in the family and the workforce also translate into an unequal division of work at home for many women, who not only work for a wage but are also expected to fulfill traditional gender roles of cooking and housekeeping. Research shows that the institutional policies of employers have a powerful effect on gender roles in housework and childcare. When employers provide flexibility and family-friendly policies, women and men of all education and class levels report a preference for egalitarian work roles in the family household. When such policies are not in place, they disproportionately affect women's labor force participation and unpaid housework. In this situation, given uneven gender expectations about housework and childcare, many women self-sort into flexible, more family-friendly jobs that may be less well paid (Pedulla and Thébaud 2015; England 2010).

In her book *The Unfinished Revolution: Coming of Age in a New Era of Gender, Work and Family* (2010), Kathleen Gerson explores how young women and young men make choices when their egalitarian gender aspirations are difficult to meet. Gerson concludes that the way gender works in the wider institutional environment significantly determines how individuals respond. For the most part, current employer policies are an obstacle to the aspirations of young women and young men to live more gender-equal lives. The result is that many women continue to be responsible for what Arlie Hochschild and Anne Machung (2003) called the **second shift** of unpaid housework and child care after returning home from their paid job.

**Second shift** The unpaid housework and child care women perform after returning home from their paid job.

**Workplace sexual harassment** Unwelcome and offensive conduct that is based on gender that has become a condition of employment, or conduct that creates an intimidating, hostile, or abusive work environment.

## Workplace Harassment and Sexual Exclusions in Work and Public Spaces

**Workplace sexual harassment** is defined as unwelcome and offensive conduct based on gender that has become a condition of employment, or conduct that creates an intimidating, hostile, or abusive work environment. The US Equal Employment Opportunity Commission defines workplace harassment as illegal for a range of protected categories, including "race, color,

PAIRED CONCEPTS

## Inequality and Privilege

### Men in Pink-Collar Work

Historical analyses of gender shifts in the US labor force show that gender intersects with race, language, and citizenship to shape occupational demographics. While white college-educated women appear to be the main beneficiaries of occupational feminization, men without the privileges of whiteness and citizenship are entering traditionally female occupations such as nursing and therapy.

When Mary L. Gatta and Patricia A. Roos compared occupations in the United States from the 1970s to the 1990s, they identified occupations where the gender composition remained *stable*, occupations that were *feminizing* because an increasing number of women were entering them, and occupations that were *masculinizing* because an increasing number of men were entering them. They showed that in occupations that were feminizing, workers tended to be white, college-educated US citizens. Workers in feminizing occupations also tended to be workers in intact husband/wife families, and they tended to work in core industries. In short, these were more privileged workers. By contrast, those in masculinizing occupations showed higher percentages of workers below the poverty level, who were foreign-born, were Hispanic, and did not speak English well. Gatta and Roos concluded, "These data suggest that integration is occurring for very different reasons at different levels of the occupational hierarchy; while occupational feminization is providing primarily college-educated white women with the opportunity to move into traditionally high-paying, prestigious, male occupations, masculinization is occurring mainly for foreign-born, non-citizen, and Hispanic men" (2005: 387).

More recently, men of all ages and races have begun to enter traditionally female occupations, as have more college-educated men. Revisiting Gatta and Roos's earlier research, the *New York Times* reported "that from 2000 to 2010, occupations that are more than 70 percent female accounted for almost a third of all job growth for men, double the share of the previous decade" (Dewan and Gebeloff 2012). It is not that men were displacing women, but as we have noted, the overall size of these job categories continues to grow. Men in these jobs reported higher job satisfaction and a sense that these jobs are more recession-proof than others. Previous research also suggests that such men might expect to benefit from a "glass escalator" where they are more likely to rise faster to better-paid and more powerful positions than women entering male-dominated occupations (Williams 1992), although this "escalator" seems to work better for white men than men of color (Wingfield 2009; Williams 2013). And there is evidence to suggest that when men move into

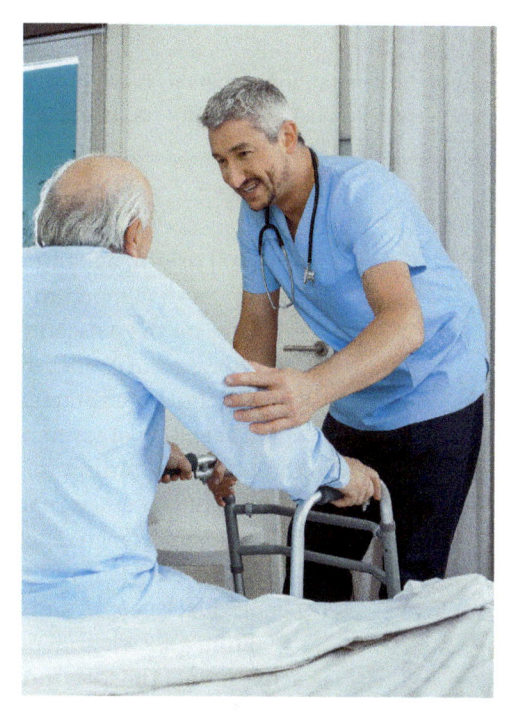

**Nursing**
Although nursing was long stereotyped as a female occupation, many men work as nurses, caring for patients in hospitals and other medical settings.

**PAIRED CONCEPTS CONTINUED**

female-dominated occupations, they experience pay and prestige increases (Yavorsky and Dill 2020).

**ACTIVE LEARNING**

**Find out:** Make a list of occupations in which you would like to work. What are the occupational characteristics that appeal to you? Explore occupations at data.census.gov at the US Census website, and find out the gender composition of each occupation. How does the gender composition of these occupations compare with the gender composition of your parents' occupations?

religion, sex (including sexual orientation, gender identity, or pregnancy), national origin, age (40 or older), disability or genetic information" (Equal Employment Opportunity Commission 2024).

Despite the existence of legal protections, there is evidence that sexual harassment and gender discrimination in the workplace continue to be a challenge in the United States. The #MeToo movement has drawn attention to widespread sexual harassment in the workplace in the United States and around the world. According to a 2018 survey reported by National Public Radio, 81 percent of women reported being harassed at some time in their life, with 38 percent of women reporting sexual harassment in the workplace (Chatterjee 2018). There is a long record of harassment statistics for gender-nonconforming people, Black people, and other ethnic minorities (Mrkonjic 2022).

From a sociological perspective, sexual harassment in the workplace is an active part of the social order of gender, where people act out male power scripts to reinforce the cultural common sense about traditional gender roles. Harassing colleagues who do not adhere to gender norms is a way of reasserting the importance of those gender norms and the gender order they define. Other behaviors that reinforce hegemonic masculinity are segregation and exclusion. For example, women and others who do not meet the standard of hegemonic masculinity are excluded from positions of authority in the workplace or from defined male spaces or social networks; we see the relegation of women to traditional, often sexual,

**Second shift**
Women often do housework while juggling other responsibilities.

roles, as well as unwanted comments and observations or physical actions such as dominance touching.

## Challenging Patriarchy and the History of the Women's Movement

When the first Women's Rights Convention convened in Seneca Falls, New York, in 1848, married women had no legal status under law, no legal rights against their husbands, no independent property rights, little access to education and paid work, and few formal institutional roles in religion, education, or politics. Importantly, women were not allowed to vote. The pursuit of the franchise became a central goal of this first wave of the women's movement. It was not until 1920 that American women won the right to vote, and it was not until the passage of the 1965 Voting Rights Act that Black women fully realized that right. It is important to note the continued contention about access to voting in the United States in recent elections, with legal challenges at the level of districting and harassment of electoral officials, especially women of color.

**Rally against the abuse of custodial workers on the night shift, California, May 31, 2016**
Sexual harassment and assault in the workplace are part of the social order of gender, where people act out male power scripts to reinforce the cultural common sense about traditional gender roles. Do you think female custodial workers would be at particular risk? What features of their workplace might make it dangerous?

The early women's movement also took up the struggle for birth control under the leadership of Margaret Sanger in the early 20th century. Sanger is a controversial figure because she was associated with social eugenics, which included projects to control birth rates in non-white and poor communities. She is an example of how white women's political agendas often excluded non-white women and their experiences. Entangled with this legacy is Sanger's argument that women could not be truly independent unless they controlled their fertility and were free to decide when and under what conditions they would become mothers. This was to be an influential argument. In the early part of the 20th century, they fought against

**National Baptist Convention, 1905**
Nannie Helen Burroughs (left) co-founded the Women's Auxiliary in 1900, which became one of the largest and most influential Black Women's groups in the US, with more than one million members.

**Reproductive freedom**
The pursuit of reproductive freedom, a major focus of the women's movement in the 1960s and 1970s, continues to be a central topic in US politics and society and around the world. The overturning of the legal right to abortion in 2022 has recentered the issue in American politics.

**Second-wave feminism** The movements and activism around women's rights in the 1960s and 1970s, with a focus on reproductive rights, work, family, and equal pay.

federal and state governments in the United States that enforced the Comstock laws. These were anti-contraception laws that defined educational material about reproduction as pornography (Beisel 1998). It was not until 1965 in the United States that married couples could legally acquire the birth-control pill.

The 1960s and 1970s are often described as a **second wave of feminism** when feminist activism flourished around issues of reproductive rights, work, family, and equal pay. In this period, access to education and other social institutions was more widely opened to women. Feminist scholars and scientists pointed out that patriarchal bias was embedded in supposedly neutral and scientific categories and supposedly universal historical, legal, and art traditions. Contraception, especially the birth-control pill, became widely available. Access to safe, legal abortion was affirmed by the Supreme Court in 1973 in the landmark decision *Roe v. Wade*, which protected the civil right to abortion. Together with reforms in divorce and marriage law, these changes opened women's opportunities in education, work, and lifestyle. As a result, women began to enter paid work in larger numbers. A 2022 Supreme Court decision overruled the decision in *Roe*, declaring that abortion was not protected by the Constitution and returning to individual states the power to determine what the laws regulating abortion should be. As of September 2023, 12 states had passed laws establishing near-total bans on abortion. This ruling is a major reduction of civil rights that guarantee bodily autonomy to citizens, since it strips women's right to make decisions about their bodies.

Despite setbacks, the women's movement made enormous progress in challenging the gender binary by arguing that women's roles are not reducible to the female body. The women's movement has also shaped other social movements, such as the gay rights movement, which argued for civil liberties for gay men and lesbians on the basis that sexuality was not reducible to bodies and the gender roles they presumed. Other liberation movements extended these gains by demonstrating that sex and gender are more fluid

**PAIRED CONCEPTS**

## Solidarity and Conflict

### Feminist Politics

Feminist critiques have transformed politics around the world and positioned feminists in solidarity as well as conflict with others pursuing movements for group rights. Feminists in the 1960s who participated in the student movement and the anti–Vietnam War movements, for example, argued that male activists excluded women in political activism and that feminists needed their own organizations to develop a distinct feminist social analysis.

Internal critics observed that the women's movement could also be exclusionary because it assumed all women were the same and failed to appreciate intersectional identities and the complexity of gender marginalization. These criticisms were connected to important social movements that developed in the last quarter of the 20th century. For example, Black women and other women of color critiqued white women's organizations as insufficiently attentive to racial privilege (hooks 2000). Women from former colonies and developing countries identified the ways that women in the developed world benefited from colonial exploitation (Mohanty 1984). Working-class women criticized the upper-middle-class origins and assumptions of many feminist concerns, especially as college-educated women entered more lucrative careers in the 1970s and 1980s. Gay, bisexual, and queer women argued that middle-class white feminism was often heteronormative—assuming that **heterosexuality**, defined as sexual desire between males and females, was the only normal form of sexuality. Trans women have been criticized and excluded by those who don't accept them in traditionally cis-gendered, women-only feminist spaces and organizations. Disability activists have critiqued the assumption of the able-bodied inside activist organizations and social movements. As a result, feminism today concerns itself not only with women's roles, gender, and a critique of patriarchy but also with the intersectional analysis of social inequality.

Intersectional analysis examines how different dimensions of inequality intersect for individuals and groups. Privilege and inequality are not simply additive, with a plus or minus sign added depending on what race, class, or gender labels are assigned to people by social scientists. Different statuses, roles, and histories shape individual and group experiences by offering resources for social action as well as constraints upon it. An intersectional perspective considers all the complex, historical, and codetermining ways that principles of difference and power such as gender, race, and class shape the entire social system (Choo and Ferree 2010). The Black Lives Matter movement, founded by three Black women, provides an example of intersectional alignment and the impact of feminist perspectives. This is seen in the way the movement thinks about the victims and targets of state violence; the inclusive, democratic organization of the movement that gives voice to young queer leaders of color; and finally, its focus on structural transformation for social justice based in the perspective of the lived conditions of marginalized communities (Cohen and Jackson 2016).

**Intersectional solidarity**
Participants in a 2019 protest organized by the Women's March Alliance call for solidarity with immigrant women whose rights were endangered by the policies of President Donald Trump.

> **PAIRED CONCEPTS CONTINUED**
>
> **ACTIVE LEARNING**
>
> **Think about it:** Consider your own identity in intersectional perspective by making a list of the identities that describe you and/or inform your actions. Are there any privileged identities? Are there any less privileged identities? Do you use different aspects of your identity at different times?

**Heterosexuality**
Sexual desire and sexual relations between males and females.

than simple male/female, heterosexual/homosexual dichotomies would indicate. Later movements for transgender liberation have built on insights from queer theory and disability studies to challenge the idea that bodies are essential and unchanging.

## 8.3 Sexuality and the Body

**LG 8.3** Understand how sexuality and bodies are socially constructed through gender, and consider how gender intersects with other dimensions of the stratification system like race and class.

Sexuality is based in sexual biology and includes social psychological elements such as attraction, emotion, and beliefs, patterns of sexual behavior, and cultural conditions, such as taboos and laws around sexual behavior. In short, sexuality is a socially constructed phenomenon that is not fully explained by socially defined gender roles or biologically defined bodies. All known human cultures set moral expectations around sexuality that define what is considered appropriate and inappropriate for that specific culture (Mead 1928). One example of this cultural specificity is the culture around romantic love, sex, and marriage in modern US society.

### The Marketing of Romance

The idea that sexual relationships should be based on emotional intimacy and romantic love is a comparatively recent historical development. In many other historical periods and cultural contexts, sexual ties were organized through arranged marriages to ensure family succession, secure economic security, or make a profit. Sexuality and sexual relationships also have long been disconnected from marriage in the form of sex work. The current American understanding of romantic love is highly culturally specific.

It was in the period of modern capitalist development in the 18th and 19th centuries that romantic love and erotic love came to be linked with heterosexual marriage and reproduction. By the 20th century, the idea that an individual could find self-realization in a romantic partnership became dominant in the United States and other Western cultures (Giddens 1992). Increasing economic and cultural opportunities for women allowed more women to make choices outside of marriage and to seek sex and intimacy without economic dependence on men (Shumway 2003). This development further emphasized the importance of romance and intimacy for sex and marriage since people had more choices to change partners or to not partner at all.

Anthony Giddens (1992) argues that the rise of the modern idea of romantic love was also connected to literacy and media. Romantic love was increasingly tied to the idea of self-realization rather than family obligation. Many of these ideas about romance permeate stories on television and in films. The Disney version of the story of Hua Mulan, which began this chapter, is a good example of a modern romantic narrative that combines Mulan's desire for self-realization with family honor, romantic love, and traditional roles defined by the gender binary. Indeed, common-sense cultural understandings of sex, gender, and sexuality are deeply interwoven throughout global media culture and provide scripts for gender roles as well as cultural resources for thinking about sexuality and bodies.

Desire, romance, and sexual imagery and narratives are also pervasive in advertising. Although advertising sometimes pushes the boundaries of conventional gender roles, the use of sexual imagery in advertising (and other media) more typically reflects hegemonic masculinity. Advertisements for cleaning products and groceries often feature traditional nuclear families with a mother, a father, and at least a couple of children in a lovely, spacious house. In advertising with more explicit sexual context, women are typically young, white, beautiful, and posed in ways that suggest they are sexually available.

There is also often a racial intersection, where white models are preferred to promote all products, including beauty and skin care products. This is a global phenomenon, with skin-lightening creams sold to whiten the

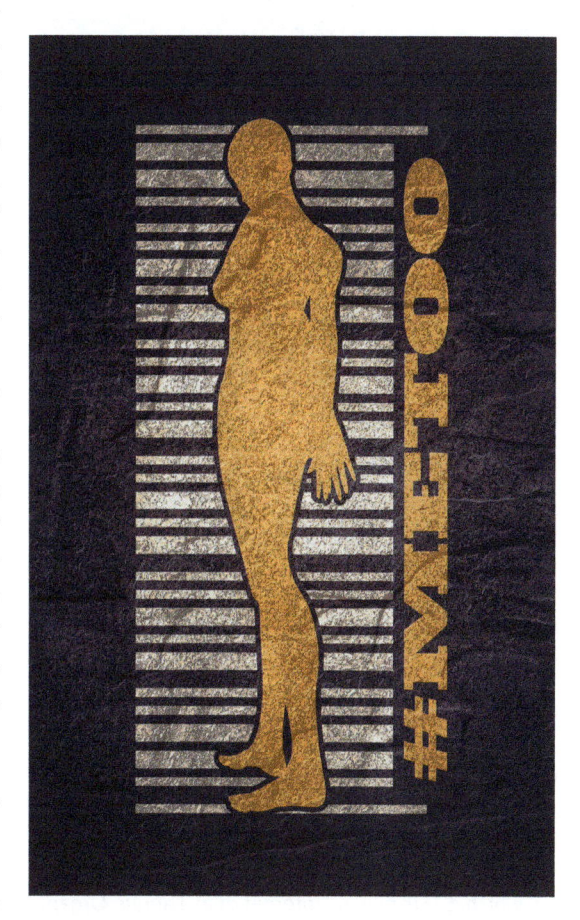

**Marketing desire**
The #MeToo barcode hashtag makes the argument that women's bodies are commodities that are bought and sold on markets.

## PAIRED CONCEPTS: Global and Local

### Sex Work

**Rights for sex workers**
Protesters fight for rights for sex workers in London, April 7, 2018.

**Protest against child trafficking in New Delhi, India, April 2009**
Aimed at sitting members of Parliament during national elections, hundreds of parents and family members of missing children demanded that elected officials help trace missing children, whom they allege traffickers are selling into commercial sex work and hard labor.

**Mail-order marriages**
Colin Mingo and his wife, Lourdes, run a Find a Bride agency. Here, they pose in 1997 for the *Daily Mail* with their catalogs of Filipino women who hope to find a husband.

The global sex work industry is estimated to be worth $150 billion (International Labour Organization 2014). Local, regional, and global markets for sex have been linked to worldwide patterns of human trafficking for sexual exploitation. The US Department of State estimates that there are 276 million people trafficked worldwide for both "labor and commercial sex" (U.S. Department of State, "About Human Trafficking," https://www.state.gov/humantrafficking-about-human-trafficking/).

A large proportion are women and children who face lives of extreme degradation, brutality, and violence.

Importantly, some women participate in sex work willingly. Kimberly Chin describes how the sex workers she studies migrate from one global city to another to perform paid sexual labor (Chin 2013). In other countries like Germany and the Netherlands, sex work is legal. Both of these European countries are sex tourism destinations, where sex workers are registered and provided care by the national health systems. In sex tourism, vacationers—typically men—travel to visit other cities or countries with more permissive laws regarding sex work than their place of residence (Hoang 2015).

A different organization of sex for material benefits is the arranged marriage, sometimes referred to as the mail-order marriage industry. Mail-order brides have a long history in affluent countries. During the 19th century in the United States, women from the East Coast contracted to marry single men on the Western frontier (Enss 2005). Today, men in affluent countries agree to marry women seeking to emigrate from countries in Asia and the former Soviet bloc of Russia and Eastern Europe.

> **ACTIVE LEARNING**
>
> **Discuss:** What do you think is the relationship between sex work and human trafficking? Do you think that the legalization of sex work would increase or decrease the number of victims of global sex trafficking? Explain your reasoning.

complexions of women in the Global South (Elliot 2014). Dieting, weight loss, and hair coloring and depilation products are promoted so that women can achieve a youthful, whiter appearance. While these trends are subject to resistance and social critique, the skin-whitening industry alone is forecast to be worth over US$8 billion by 2025, with the Asia-Pacific region being the largest and fastest-growing market (Grand View Research 2019).

Historians of advertising also observe that not only have white, middle-class images been the default in advertising for most of the 19th and 20th centuries, but so have heteronormative assumptions about sexuality and family (O'Barr 2012). Despite the rise of **multicultural marketing**, which targets specific demographics such as gay people, Black people, and Latino/as, messaging is still limited by mainstream understandings (O'Barr 2012). Critics have also observed that the target-advertising model misses the variation *within* groups and rarely offer an intersectional framing. For example, when characters coded as gay do appear in advertising, they tend to be white, educated, attractive, and nonthreatening to the gender order in any other way (O'Barr 2012).

## Heteronormativity

The traditional gender order is heteronormative since it assumes and enforces heterosexuality, or exclusive sexual desire between males and females. **Heteronormativity** further links binary sex categories to gender roles at work, in the family, and in the nation, as well as to heterosexual sex

**Multicultural marketing** Advertising that tailors specific messages to target minority groups.

**Heteronormativity** A social order that assumes and enforces heterosexuality and links it to binary sex categories; to gender roles at work, in the family, and in the nation; and to heterosexual sex roles.

roles. Widespread cultural norms and social scripts for women and men are heteronormative, and as with other parts of the gender order, heteronormativity has been enforced historically through criminal and medical sanctions for individuals who stray too far from expectations.

Many institutional and cultural mechanisms support heteronormativity. For example, until recently in the United States, laws defined marriage exclusively as a union of a heterosexual man and heterosexual woman. Heteronormativity has also been institutionalized historically in the medical and legal systems through the recognition of two mutually exclusive sex categories, and the minimization and stigmatization of the intersex category. Homosexuality is still criminalized in many countries, as it once was in the United States (Drescher 2015).

That said, social norms and laws have changed in the last 50 years as a result of widespread activism and education. Sodomy laws have been repealed in many countries, and there are efforts to expunge the criminal records of those who were imprisoned under these laws in the past (Medhora 2015). Laws have been passed to protect the human rights of gay, lesbian, bisexual, and transgender people; to enable marriage, adoption, and inheritance; and to ban workplace discrimination. Gender-nonconforming people also have expanded opportunities to serve as clergy and in the military (Drescher 2015), although new 2019 rules prohibiting trans people from joining and serving in US armed forces, since reversed by the Biden administration, indicate how fragile some of these gains are. Homosexuality is more widely accepted in the United States now than it once was (Fetner 2016), and to some extent, so are other nonnormative expressions of sex, gender, and sexuality—especially among younger cohorts of Americans (Parker, Graf, and Igielnik 2019).

Importantly, however, there are still medical and social definitions of gender and sexuality. According to the fifth edition of the DSM, **gender dysphoria** occurs when people experience "intense, persistent gender incongruence." Opinion about its inclusion as a disorder is split within the psychological and psychiatric communities. Some practitioners think that "the diagnosis pathologizes gender noncongruence and should

**Gender dysphoria** A diagnosis in the fifth edition of the *Diagnostic and Statistical Manual of Mental Disorders* to describe when people experience "intense, persistent gender incongruence."

**The traditional wedding**
The traditional wedding between a man and woman reinforces heterosexuality and the wider binary gender order. Women and men dress in gender-stereotypical clothing, and the bride is often given away by her father to her husband. Can you think of any other heteronormative features of traditional weddings?

be eliminated. Others argue that it is essential to retain the diagnosis to ensure access to care" (American Psychological Association 2017b). There is a complex relationship between the gender politics of medical institutions and the need for and the ability of trans individuals to get the care they need, which is controlled by biomedical, psychological, and political authorities.

## Queer Identities beyond the Closet

Before the late 1960s, the social stigma associated with being gay led many gay men, lesbians, and other sexual minorities to lead hidden lives. Living "in the closet" was a metaphor for gay life for much of the 20th century. Sociologists who analyze changes in public perceptions and institutional responses to homosexuality refer to the period since the late 1960s as the "post-closeted" world (Seidman 2002). In the post-closeted world, variation and criticism within the gay community have entered into the wider public conversation. Important political differences among gay people and gender-nonconforming people have also become part of a larger cultural conversation.

Steven Seidman's book *Beyond the Closet* (2002) compares what he calls the "gay rights" and "gay liberation" dimensions of political activism. Gay rights activists seek to extend the civil rights afforded to every citizen to gay citizens. These include the right to marry, inherit, adopt children, and serve in the armed forces. A result of this activity, according to Seidman, is the social construction of "the normal gay," who is much easier for wider society to assimilate than the more challenging gender nonconformity of those who either choose not to adhere to the gender order or, for whatever reason, are unable to do so.

Gender identities and sexuality are far more fluid than binary thinking allows. As this chapter has argued, the gender binary is the central way that the traditional gender order is organized, with each binary category reinforcing the others. Theorists like Judith Butler, David Halperin, and Eve Sedgewick contend that to actively "**queer**" or "trouble" the binaries that traditionally describe sex, gender, and desire is a form of resisting the constraints of the gender order (Butler 2006; Sedgewick 2008). In this view, the point is not only to win cultural acceptance, safety, and civil rights, as important as these are for many people. Rather, it is about challenging the binary organization of the entire gender order and the power relations and violence that underpin it.

**Queer** Any idea or practice that actively disturbs the binaries describing a neat concurrence of sex, gender, and desire in society.

This insight extends an intersectional understanding of how gender intersects with racial identities, economic status, nationality, language, and disability. These classifications systems of power are also far more fluid than they might first appear. Importantly, the expression of a gender identity does not match any specific sexuality or specific characteristics linked with sex categories and sexual reproduction. In the more open culture that defines the post-closeted world, a wide range of social possibilities around sex, gender, and sexual identities have become possible.

Language and labels continue to adjust to ongoing cultural exploration and lived experiences of sex and gender. Gender identity is widely understood as an authentic sense of one's own experience that should not be constrained by traditional gender social scripts. This means that while gender expressions are somewhat durable, the expression of gender identity may shift over the life course, over different social situations, or even over the course of a single day. This poses challenges to institutional orders that presume and regulate sex and gender.

---

**PAIRED CONCEPTS**

## Power and Resistance

### Stonewall

Today, gay pride parades are held annually all over the world. Most of these celebrations commemorate the 1969 Stonewall Uprising against police in New York City.

For most of the 20th century, the US legal system marginalized and criminalized gays, lesbians, and other sexual minorities. In 1969, patrons of the Stonewall Inn in Greenwich Village fought back against a police raid. In the days and weeks that followed, the gay community established newspapers, created spaces for the open expression of gay identities, and laid an important foundation for the movement for gay, lesbian, and trans pride. By directly resisting the exercise of police power and asserting a social identity that was positive and powerful, the Stonewall protests became the symbol for a much wider social movement for gay rights.

#### ACTIVE LEARNING

**Find out:** While activists in the post-Stonewall era of the early 1970s referred to their movement as the LGB or the LGBT community, movement activists today are more likely to refer to their community as LGBTQIA+. What does this term refer to? When did it come into public usage, and why?

**The Stonewall Uprising**
This plaque on the Stonewall Inn in Greenwich Village, New York, commemorates the 1969 Stonewall Uprising against police harassment and abuse against the gay community.

## CASE STUDY

# Gender Intersections at McDonald's

As a social principle, the gender binary orders society by linking bodies to social and sexual roles, and gender is a moral order because it defines what is right and wrong for women and men. Focusing on the intersection of lived experience and wider social institutions, we conclude this chapter using the five paired concepts to analyze how gender is constructed by the toys included in McDonald's Happy Meals.

McDonald's introduced the Happy Meal in 1979, and it was an instant success. The meals included chicken nuggets or a hamburger, fries, a fountain drink, and, importantly, a toy. By 2016, nearly 1.2 billion Happy Meals were sold in the United States each year.

The first toys included with Happy Meals were a "McDoodler" stencil, a "McWrist" wallet, an ID bracelet, a puzzle lock, a spinning top, or a McDonaldland-character eraser. None of these toys were explicitly gender-typed. In 1987, McDonald's partnered with Disney to include Disney-themed toys, especially princess toys. These proved enormously popular, and McDonald's has since partnered with brands including My Little Pony, LEGO, Teletubbies, Ty Beanie Babies, Hello Kitty, G.I. Joe, and more (Webley 2010). Many of these toys have been explicitly gendered with the idea that there are "girls' toys" and "boys' toys" (Auster and Mansbach 2012).

In 2008, a Connecticut 11-year-old named Antonia Ayres-Brown objected to the fact that McDonald's employees asked her and her brother if they wanted a "girl" or "boy" toy with their Happy Meals. Ayres-Brown wrote to the CEO of McDonald's to ask if he thought it was appropriate for "employees to ask customers if they want the 'girl toy' or the 'boy toy,'" pointing out that you wouldn't ask a job applicant if they wanted "a man's job or a woman's job" (Morran 2014). McDonald's claimed that it was not their policy to ask that question. Ayres-Brown's father, a professor at Yale University, helped her to conduct a study on how often McDonald's employees asked the girl toy or boy toy question, and found they did so 79 percent of the time.

Ayres-Brown drew on different parts of her identities to shape her *resistance* to the gendering of Happy Meals toys. She used her relative *power* as a *privileged* middle-class daughter of a supportive, well-educated parent to resist what she saw as gender *inequality* produced by gender discrimination by McDonald's employees. Was the gender stereotyping that Ayres-Brown noticed in the awarding of Happy Meals toys a human rights violation? Ayres-Brown and her father suspected it might be and presented their findings to the Connecticut Commission on Human Rights and Opportunities in the hopes that the commission would join the *conflict* and use their legal and cultural resources to help her case. The commission declined to join Ayres-Brown's protest. As she explained in an article in *Slate* magazine in 2014, "the commission dismissed our allegations as 'absurd.' . . . All in all, this was a pretty humiliating defeat." Ayres-Brown had been looking for *solidarity* and allies, and she had been refused.

Nonetheless, Ayres-Brown continued to pursue the issue. She undertook a larger study in 2013, finding "that 92.9 percent of the time, the store, *without asking*, simply gave each child the toy that McDonald's had designated for that child's gender—a Justice fashion toy for girls and a Power Rangers toy for boys. What's worse was the trouble the children encountered when they immediately returned to the counter and asked to exchange their unopened toy: 42.8 percent of stores refused to exchange for an opposite-sex toy." Ayres-Brown reported her findings to McDonald's corporate headquarters again. This time, she received a letter from the company's chief diversity officer, Patricia Harris, saying, "It is McDonald's intention and goal that each customer who desires a Happy Meal toy be provided the toy of his or her choice, without any classification of

## CASE STUDY CONTINUED

**Happy Meal toys for boys and girls**
Can you tell which Happy Meal toy is intended for boys and which for girls? What gender stereotypes do these toys reflect?

the toy as a 'boy' or 'girl' toy and without any reference to the customer's gender. We have recently reexamined our internal guidelines, communications and practices and are making improvements to better ensure that our toys are distributed consistent with our policy" (Ayres-Brown 2014). Ayres-Brown counted this as a success and found clear evidence that McDonald's employer training addressed the issue.

From a sociological perspective, Ayres-Brown's case provides evidence that in the billions of interactions that occur at the point of check-out for Happy Meals at McDonald's restaurants every year, traditional gender stereotypes are enacted. This is likely to have a social impact. Gender socialization works at a *local* level in every interaction in which children learn about gender or are themselves treated as gendered individuals. These kinds of interactions are the fundamental materials of social life because they reinforce common-sense understandings about what toys boys and girls want, and they teach children what gender roles are appropriate. They contribute to the cultural common sense of the gender binary. This is how hegemony works in everyday life.

Ayres-Brown's discovery that children requesting different toys were refused the toy of their choice suggests another way the gender order is institutionalized, namely through the efficient operation of fast-food service. If toys are prepackaged as girl toys or boy toys, then it may be simply more convenient for service workers to give only one toy and to make a quick guess about which toy to give a particular child. In short, the gender effect can be produced through institutional processes and without any active sexist intention on the part of workers. This logic suggests that the answer to changing this situation is to introduce new employee-training guidelines and/or new routines for offering toys with the Happy Meal so that kids can make a choice. This is what the McDonald's corporate office reported they did (although see Hourigan 2021; Schweitzer 2019).

Some might dismiss Ayres-Brown as an entitled student who focused on a trivial issue and received media attention based on her relative social privilege (e.g., Otto 2014). Gender issues and women advocates are often dismissed as "trivial", and a political focus on smaller details can be an effective way to resist the cultural power of the gender binary. Not only is McDonald's a *global* corporation, but the choice of McDonald's to offer boy toys and girl toys reveals McDonald's as a participant in every local instance of a much larger global order of gender difference.

Finally, Ayres-Brown's critique demonstrates that every social interaction is *contingent*. Every transaction for a Happy Meal contains several possibilities around gender expression, stereotyping, and impact. Ayres-Brown's investigation confirms the findings of sociological research about gender in interaction, which holds that people act in gender-conforming ways and that our institutional routines and actions directly correspond to existing traditional *structures* of gender.

## LEARNING GOALS REVISITED

**8.1** Define the difference between sex and gender, and describe the dimensions of gender inequality.

- Sex is the status of male or female or intersex, which is assigned at birth and is associated with physical attributes such as chromosomes and anatomical differences. Gender refers to socially constructed roles for women and men that define expected behaviors.

- The gender binary asserts there are only two gender categories, masculine and feminine, and that all people are either one or the other on the basis of biological sex classification. The gender binary hides wide variation in human gender expression.

- Nonbinary and transgender people identify with a gender that does not always align with the sex they were assigned at birth. Cisgender people are those assigned male or female at birth and identify as men or women, respectively.
- The understanding that women are different and lesser than men is enshrined in gender stereotypes that define what is male and what is female, with female roles and qualities being seen as less valuable than male roles and qualities.
- Social institutions, including state agencies, medicine, and science, are locations where the gender binary is both enforced and challenged.
- Gender scripts are conveyed through socializing agencies and cue people to act in accordance with masculine and feminine social expectations. Those who fail to conform to gender scripts are punished.

**8.2 Analyze how gender is socially constructed as a social and moral order.**

- The patriarchal organization of social life can be seen in the predominance of men in formal positions of power in political, economic, and many cultural institutions. Patriarchy is organized through sexism and androcentrism.
- Male power and gender inequality operate through hegemony, a system in which men dominate women by making male power and superiority appear as cultural common sense.
- The gender order is a moral order based on the gender binary. Because sex is understood to be a natural dichotomy, sex and gender are understood to be inevitable and therefore morally right.
- Sex classification is also used to define gender difference beyond bodily difference to configure every role and relationship in the social world.
- The gender division of labor mandates that women and men do different work in the family and the wider society. It is organized through the ideology of separate spheres, occupational segregation, workplace harassment and gender exclusion.
- The gender division of labor intersects racial and ethnic divisions to produce different outcomes for people with different intersecting identities.
- Social movements to expand civil rights and social recognition to gender minorities include the movements for women's suffrage, equal pay, reproductive choice, decriminalization and depathologization, gay marriage and family laws, and all policies that would ensure a safe and supportive social environment. Struggles for gender equality continue since there are reversals like the overturning of the legal right to abortion in the United States in 2022.

**8.3** Understand how sexuality and bodies are socially constructed through gender, and consider how gender intersects with other dimensions of the stratification system like race and class.

- Sexuality is constructed through sexual biology, social psychological elements, and cultural conditions.
- Heteronormativity assumes and enforces heterosexuality, linking sex roles through the gender binary to gender roles in work and family.
- Queer theory and critics, as well as social movements for recognition and justice for nonbinary and trans people, disrupt the moral force of the idea that bodily sex, gender, and sexuality are linked in an essential set of binaries.
- Marriage is a central institution in social reproduction that organizes sexuality and bodies.
- Women and children are the primary people exploited through legal and illegal sex work and in sex tourism worldwide.
- Gender hegemony intersects the racial system in global advertising that upholds a white, Western ideal image of women.
- Critics have drawn attention to the faulty assumption that all women inherently share the same interest. Movements for gender equality are called to be more intersectional in policy and practice.

## Key Terms

Androcentrism 264
Cisgender 257
Division of labor 268
Femininity 261
Gender 256
Gender binary 256
Gender cue 258
Gender dysphoria 282
Gender order 265
Gender performance 258
Gender script 257
Gender socialization 258
Gender stereotypes 260
Hegemonic masculinity 265
Hegemony 265
Heteronormativity 281
Heterosexuality 277
Horizontal occupational segregation 270
Intersectionality 271
Intersex 257
Male breadwinner 268
Masculinity 261
Moral order 265
Multicultural marketing 281
Nonbinary 257
Patriarchy 264
Pink-collar jobs 270
Queer 283
Second shift 272
Second-wave feminism 276
Separate spheres 268
Sex 256
Sexism 264
Transgender 257
Vertical occupational segregation 271
Workplace sexual harassment 272

## Review Questions

1. How are sex and gender related to biological sex differences?
2. How are occupations segregated by gender?
3. What is the "second shift"? Do employer workplace policies affect young people's strategies around housework? How?
4. How does the gender binary affect people who are assigned as intersex at birth?
5. How has the movement for transgender rights affected the binary order of gender in the United States? Give an example.
6. What does it mean to say that the gender order is a moral order?

## Explore

### RECOMMENDED READINGS

Butler, Judith. 2006. *Gender Trouble: Feminism and the Subversion of Identity*. New York: Routledge.

Connell, R. W. 1987. *Gender and Power: Society, the Person and Sexual Politics*. Stanford, CA: Stanford University Press.

Connell, R. W. 2005. *Masculinities*, 2nd ed. Berkeley: University of California Press.

Giddens, Anthony. 1992. *The Transformation of Intimacy: Sexuality, Love and Eroticism in Modern Society*. Cambridge, MA: Polity

hooks, bell. 2000. *Feminist Theory: From Margin to Center*. Boston: South End Press.

Kanter, R. M. 1977. *Men and Women of the Corporation*. New York: Basic Books.

Sedgewick, Eve Kosofsky. 2008. *Epistemology of the Closet (updated with a new preface)*. Los Angeles: University of California Press.

Seidman, Steven. 2002. *Beyond the Closet: The Transformation of Gay and Lesbian Life*. New York: Routledge.

Chimamanda Ngozi Adichie. 2014. *We Should All Be Feminists*. Vintage. (Also TEDx talk: https://www.youtube.com/watch?v=hg3umXU_qWc)

### ACTIVITIES

- *Use your sociological imagination*: Drawing on the Bem sex role inventory, select a category of consumer products (such as furniture, cars, or food) and explain why some are seen as feminine and some are seen as masculine. How do you know? Ask others to describe the difference. Do they use a similar logic? What can you conclude about gender on this basis?

- *Media+Data Literacies*: Choose a simple media text—for example, a scene from the movie *Mulan* or another Disney movie or television show. What are the gender expectations of the women and men in the scene?
- *Discuss*: Of the first 60 Presidential elections in the United States, all of the winners were men. What do you think this says about gender and power? Do you think that gender inequality in American electoral politics has changed in the last 100 years? What is the evidence for your position?

# PART IV
# INSTITUTIONS AND ISSUES

**9** Marriage, Family, and the Law

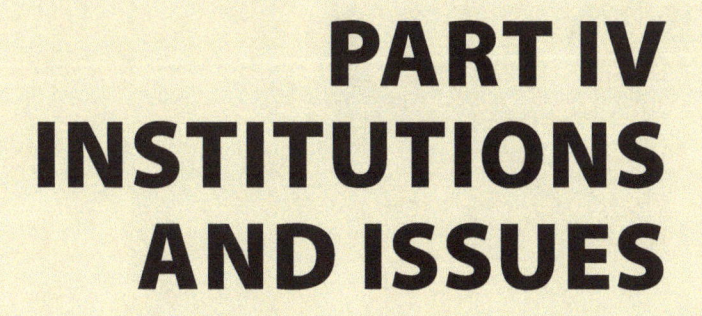

**10** Science, Religion, and Knowing

**11** Education, Work, and Recreation

**12** Health, Illness, and Medicine

**13** Politics, Economy, and Social Movements

**14** Media and Technology

Just For You
Mum
HOPE YOUR
Mother's Day
IS
UNIQUE,
FABULOUS &
£2
£2.50
£1.50
To a Lovely Mum
from
All of Us
To a Wonderful
Mum
on
Mother's Day
FOR MY
Amazing Mum
SUPERSTAR MUM
A
Mother's Day
Wish
WISHING YOU A
MUM
No.1
MUM
For a Very Special
GRANDMA
FOR YOU
HAPPY MOTHER'S DAY
WITH LOVE,
MUM
No.1
MUM
HAPPY
Mother's
DAY
£1
Just for You,
Mum
World's best
MUM!

# Marriage, Family, and the Law

The greeting card industry is hugely profitable, with annual sales of $5.8 billion in the United States alone (IBIS World 2024). And as families have changed, so have the types of greeting cards that are available to purchase. There are now greeting cards designed specifically for divorced families, same-sex families, interracial families, single-parent families, families where the children are being raised by a grandparent, adoptive families, and families with transgender children or parents. While these new greeting cards reflect the profound changes that are taking place in the family today, they also illustrate the universal desire to reinforce the family bond and celebrate family members' milestones and achievements.

One such example of the movement to diversify greeting cards is "Mamas Day," which was started in 2011 by the collaborative nonprofit organization Strong Families Network. Each year, the group commissions artists to create original art for greeting cards that honor mothers who are traditionally excluded from traditional ideas and images about family and motherhood. Traditional greeting card companies have followed suit to widen representation. Hallmark has expanded its range of LGBTQ-themed cards, and in 2015 they created a Mother's Day video featuring a family with a transgender son.

Despite the availability of online greeting card vendors, traditional paper greeting cards have a surprisingly enduring appeal.

**Mother's Day cards**
Mother's Day cards have been transformed in recent years to reflect the experiences of diverse families and mothering.

---

**Chapter Outline**

**9.1 FAMILY AND SOCIETY 296**

*Family, Kinship, and Society 297*
*Marriage and Family as Social Institutions 301*

**9.2 CHANGES IN MARRIAGE AND FAMILY 305**

*Traditional Families and Nuclear Families 305*
*Divorce 307*
*Single-Parent Families 309*
*Delay and Decline of Marriage 311*
*Boomerang Kids and Sandwich Parents 314*
*Transnational Families 315*

**9.3 CHALLENGING FAMILY FORMS 318**

*Feminist Challenges to the Family 318*
*Blended Families 319*
*Multiracial Families 320*
*Lesbian and Gay Families 321*

**CASE STUDY: FAMILY NAMES 324**

Younger people purchase them (or even create their own) to celebrate the milestones and the achievements of their friends and family (Nanos 2016; Romalino 2014; Ricapito 2020).

This chapter examines issues related to marriage and the family. We begin by considering the central role that family and kinship systems play in society. We discuss how marriage and family operate as social institutions, helping define gender roles and contributing to the reproduction of stratification systems. Next, we discuss how marriage and family have changed over time. Traditional families have largely been replaced by the nuclear family, which are now being challenged by changing trends in marriage, such as the rise of divorce, the decision by many to delay or forego marriage, and the growth of transnational families. Throughout the chapter, we look at the different social and legal challenges that have tried to expand how people think about families and family life.

## LEARNING GOALS

**9.1** Define family and kinship, and describe how kinship systems have changed over time. Understand how the family is connected to systems of inequality, such as race, class, and gender inequality.

**9.2** Define the nuclear family, and describe how divorce, single-parent families, and the delay in marriage have led to changes in the traditional nuclear family.

**9.3** Comprehend the main feminist critiques of the family, and show how women's movements for greater equality have led to changes in family dynamics. Describe the changes in attitudes and laws that have become more accepting of multiracial families as well as lesbian and gay families.

## 9.1 Family and Society

**LG 9.1** Define family and kinship, and describe how kinship systems have changed over time. Understand how the family is connected to systems of inequality, such as race, class, and gender inequality.

As societies change, our understandings about what counts as a family will also change. When Talcott Parsons wrote about the family in 1943, he distinguished among family of origin (the family into which you are born), the family of orientation (where you are raised), and the family of procreation (after you get married and have children). Today, these distinctions seem old-fashioned to many people because they assume that all families are mainly about having and raising children.

The US Census Bureau defines the family as "two or more people residing together, and related by birth, marriage or adoption" (US Census

Bureau, Subject Definitions). This definition prioritizes a shared residence and a relationship that is either biological or legal in nature. Until recently, hospitals used a similar definition for their visitation policies, but many have since created more flexible visitation policies that are sensitive to the diversity of contemporary family forms.

A more recent and flexible definition is offered by the sociologist Philip Cohen, who defines **family** as "groups of related people, bound by connections that are biological, legal, or emotional" (Cohen 2014: 4). Although many families today are still connected through biological relationships, just as Parsons described and the Census Bureau defines, one of the most important aspects of "family" is the emotional bond that it promises. Most people hope that their family will provide them with social support, emotional intimacy and connection, and the reassurance that they are committed to one another.

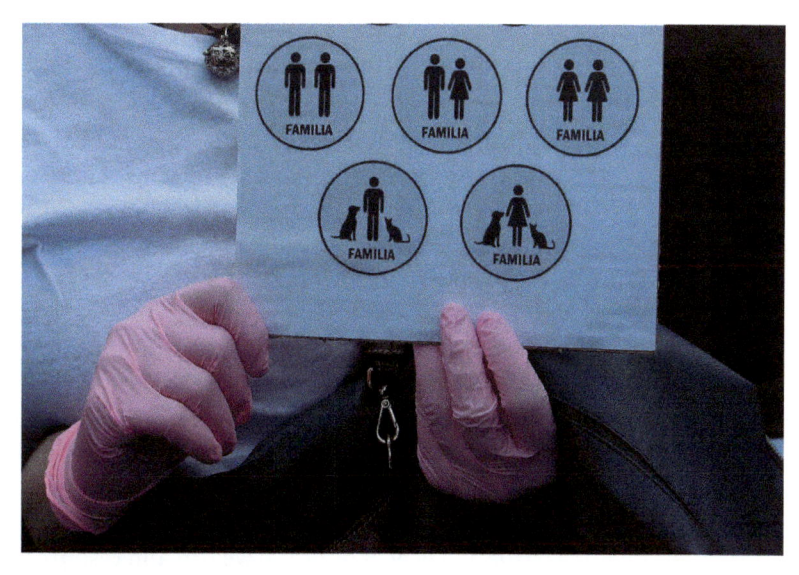

**Different kinds of families**
A woman holds a sign representing different kind of families during a march to protest the World Congress of Families, in Verona, Italy. The US-based organization defines family as strictly centering around a mother and father.

**Family** A group of related people who are connected together by biological, emotional, or legal bonds.

## Family, Kinship, and Society

The availability of online resources like Ancestry.com points to the popularity of **genealogy**, which is the study of family history in order to document how family members are related to each other. As humans, we have always been fascinated by genealogy. In fact, some anthropologists have argued that the practice of genealogy is universal to all known societies (Goodenough 1970).

Societies have different rules for who counts as a member of the family and the expected relationships between family members. These socially conditioned rules for thinking about family relationships are referred to as **kinship systems**. The words used to describe relatives, the rules about marriage, the attitudes about different kinds of relatives, and other kinship rules are among the most important elements of a society's culture.

We can learn a lot about a society by studying its kinship system. For example, what do we call a mother's brother's son? What are the roles he is expected to take in the family? In the United States today, we call this

**Genealogy** The study of family history in order to document how family members are related to each other.

**Kinship system** The set of rules that define who counts as a member of the family, the names that are given to different types of family members, and the expectations about how different family members will relate to one another.

person a "cousin." Most people in the United States do not live in the same households as their cousins, and in fact they may only see their cousins at major family events or holidays. We do not generally distinguish between our male and female cousins, though other family relationships continue to have gender-specific designations (aunts vs. uncles, nephews vs. nieces, etc.). But there is nothing "natural" about the terms that are used to describe relatives, nor is there anything natural about the rights and responsibilities that are associated with different types of relatives.

Changes in kinship systems reflect changing power relationships in society. Before the 20th century, most European societies were **patrilineal**, which meant that they privileged the male line of descent. Names, titles, property rights, and family inheritance were traced only through the men in the family. Women took the name of their husbands when they were married. In matters of family inheritance, older daughters were passed over in favor of younger sons. Both men and women were expected to use marriage as a way of building wealth and resources for their families.

Today, many of these social rules and expectations have changed. Many societies have adopted **multilineal** systems, which trace both the maternal and the paternal lines of descent, giving equal significance to each. Family inheritance includes sons and daughters equally. Men and women are free to marry whoever they like, and they expect to marry for love rather than strategic family alliances.

**Patrilineal**
A kinship system that privileges the male line of descent.

**Multilineal**
A kinship system that traces both the maternal and the paternal lines of descent, giving equal significance to each.

**The social benefits of family**
Families provide intimacy and social support.

**INTIMACY AND SOCIAL SUPPORT.** Regardless of how they are organized, all families are supposed to provide their members with social support. Evidence suggests that people who enjoy close relationships live longer and healthier lives (Chapter 4). While family is not the only way to provide support and reduce isolation, it has historically been one of the most effective ways.

What kind of social support do families provide? Members of a family can share the daily tasks that are necessary for survival and provide other material resources as well. In most societies, the care of infants, children, and the elderly is performed by various family members. When they can afford to do so, family members can provide financial assistance to other relatives. In fact, according to the National Association of Realtors, more than a quarter of first-time home buyers borrow money from family or friends to help with the down payment (Bhattarai and Cocco 2024).

**A sandwich generation**
In multigenerational families, grandparents can support their grown children, but it can be hard for the middle generation to support their children and their parents at the same time.

The family is the most important agent of socialization for most people during the early years of their lives (Chapter 4). The family is our first social group, where we learn the rules of appropriate social behavior and begin to learn the shared beliefs and values of our culture. The bonds we form with our parents and siblings are deep, impactful, and long-lasting. Family is an important source of intimacy, a place where people expect to feel unconditional acceptance and emotional connections. We expect our family members to be on our side and to love us unconditionally. When this expectation is not met, the result is often a sense of disappointment and betrayal.

**FAMILY AND INEQUALITY.** While families can be an important source of social support, they also reinforce social inequality (Chapter 6). Parents shape the opportunities available to their children and the kinds of lives those children will have as adults. These dynamics of privilege and inequality link families to all the systems of stratification that operate in a society, at local, regional, national, and global levels. If anything, the role that family plays in social stratification is increasing because highly educated, professionally successful, and high-earning people are more likely than ever to marry one another (Greenwood et al. 2014; Andres 2022).

There are also things that happen within families that create inequality. Historically, family dynamics have been a major source of gender inequality (Chapter 8). In most societies, the work that adult men do has been rewarded

## CAREERS

### Marriage and Family Therapists

There are many professions designed to support families with the pressures of family life. As these pressures increase, jobs in marriage and family therapy are in high demand. According to the Bureau of Labor Statistics, the number of jobs in marriage and family therapy is expected to grow 15 percent between 2022 and 2032. Today, there are more than one hundred accredited programs in marriage and family therapy in the United States.

A person who wants to work as a licensed marriage and family therapist will need to complete graduate studies in marriage and family systems, mental and behavioral disorders, therapy techniques, and professional ethics. Most graduate programs have active internship programs where students gain real-world experience providing therapy to families. After completing the degree, passing a state licensing exam, and spending at least two years working under the supervision of a licensed therapist, new therapists will receive their professional license. In 2023, the median salary for a licensed marriage and family therapist was $58,510. (For more information, visit the website of the American Association for Marriage and Family Therapy at http://www.aamft.org.)

Marriage and family therapists work in social service agencies, hospitals, outpatient mental health facilities, schools, and private practices. Clients typically see these therapists for an average of 12 sessions, fewer than most other types of therapy. About half of the sessions will be one-on-one, with the remainder being group sessions with the couple or the family. Because of the lower number of sessions required and the high levels of success, more insurance companies are referring clients to marriage and family therapists instead of psychiatrists or psychologists.

Sociology provides a particularly good background for people who wish to pursue a career in marriage and family therapy because of the emphasis on social relationships and social institutions. Graduate programs in marriage and family therapy encourage sociology majors and other undergraduate students who wish to enter the field to take courses in sociology of the family and gender, crime and deviance, domestic violence, culture and consumption, and research methods.

**ACTIVE LEARNING**

**Find out:** Go to the Bureau of Labor Statistics website for the Occupational Outlook Handbook (https://www.bls.gov/ooh/), locate "marriage and family therapists," then click the search result for that profession. On the Marriage and Family Therapists page, click the Similar Occupations tab, then choose three other occupations. Compare them with marriage and family therapy in terms of job duties, education required to enter the profession, expected pay, and the ways that training in sociology would help you perform the job more effectively.

---

with higher status and more money. While adult women were expected to do most of the cooking, cleaning, and care work in the home, they have had to do this without compensation or social recognition. Until very recently, family law in the United States granted husbands the right to exercise their authority over their wives and children in a manner that was free from government interference, except in cases of child endangerment. Sons have often received preferential treatment over daughters in educational opportunities, career expectations, inheritance rights, and the general distribution of power and status in the family (Blumberg 1991). Birth order has also been a source of family inequality, with many societies organized through a system of **primogeniture**, in which the first-born child (or, more commonly, the firstborn son) inherits the entire family estate. Many social scientists believe that birth order continues to create inequality in modern society (Gregoire 2015; Damian and Roberts 2015). Common stereotypes distinguish between the high-achieving first-born child, the rebellious or delinquent youngest child, and the overlooked or neglected middle child.

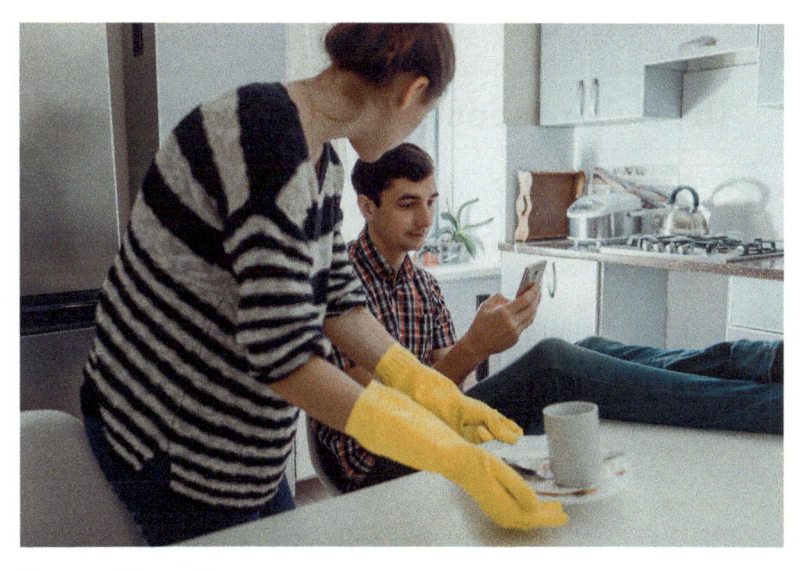

**Housework inequality**
Many women feel more responsible than others for housecleaning and child care. Even women with full-time jobs often find themselves beginning a "second shift" of housework once they get home.

Last, laws about who is allowed to get married grant special privileges to certain types of couples that are not available to others. For most of US history, family law only permitted legally identified males and females to marry and also prohibited interracial marriages. These laws have changed but only after significant conflict and resistance and only after decades of economic and social disadvantages for those who did not fit the categories.

**Primogeniture**
A system in which the first-born child (or, more commonly, the first-born son) inherits the entire family estate.

## Marriage and Family as Social Institutions

For many people, family is the thing that has the most meaning in their lives. There are strong social and legal supports in place that privilege marriages and families and that reinforce their roles as some of the most powerful institutions in our society.

**PUBLIC AND PRIVATE.** As we discussed in Chapter 1, institutions provide us with a set of rules that help us think about how we are related to each other and how we should act in a given social situation. Families do this by encouraging us to distinguish between our private family life and the public world that exists outside of our homes. It is common for people to think about their family as a refuge from the larger public world. The American poet Maya Angelou described this sense of family when she wrote that "I sustain myself with the love of family."

## METHODS AND INTERPRETATION

### The Debate about Birth Order Effects

Psychologists have long debated the effects of birth order on personality. The media tell us that first-born children are reliable, hard-working, and achievement oriented; middle children are more loyal and willing to compromise; and the youngest children are the most creative, rebellious, and attention-seeking (Gregoire 2015). Popular psychology abounds with parenting tips about how to treat each of these children, and with relationship tips about what is likely to happen to couples composed of different birth order combinations.

Despite the popular beliefs about birth order effects, however, the actual research remains inconclusive. Examining the available research on the effects of birth order on personality, Damian and Roberts (2015) found wildly inconsistent conclusions. A key problem is the range of differences in the ways researchers collect their data. Many studies fail to use representative samples, while many others rely on samples that are too small. Some studies control for the size of the family, while others do not. Some studies focus on the differences within families, while others study a cross-section of people from different families. Most studies do not account for the fact that first-born children are older, and that older children are going to act differently from younger children regardless of personality differences. Virtually none of the studies attempt to measure how stereotypes about birth order can influence behavior in a manner that is not connected to personality.

Ideally, research on birth order effects would use large, representative samples; combine between-family and within-family studies; try to control for family size, age of the different siblings, and other confounding factors; and try to figure out how stereotypes about birth order influence behavior. But these studies would be extremely expensive and complicated. Examining the studies that come closest to this ideal research design, Damian and Roberts conclude that there is little or no relationship between birth order and personality, and only a very small relationship between birth order and intelligence. This argument corresponds with other social science research, which finds a weak relationship between personality traits and social outcomes (Conley 2005).

However, when researchers shift their focus away from personality traits and toward social outcomes, they do find that there is a modest relationship with birth order. Research on educational attainment shows that there is a tendency for each subsequent sibling in the family to perform slightly worse in school (Black, Devereux and Salvanes 2005). Some research shows a relationship between birth order and adult financial success, but this relationship is stronger for men than it is for women (Black, Devereux, and Salvanes 2005). Sociologists caution, however, that we should not think about these effects in isolation from other events that take place within the life of a family (Conley 2005). The spacing between births matters, and so does the gender composition of siblings (Buckles and Munnich 2012). Big events like divorce, job loss, or the death of a parent can have massive effects on siblings, which are much larger than any isolated birth order effect. Birth order is not destiny. Its importance depends on how it is connected to the other events in our lives.

### ACTIVE LEARNING

**Find out:** Do a search for books and magazine articles about birth order effects. How many are you able to find? Now, do a similar search for books and magazine articles about the effects of divorce on children, and the effects of parent job loss on children. Compare the types of questions they ask, and the types of data they use to answer their questions. How are they similar, and how are they different? What do you think explains the differences?

> **PAIRED CONCEPTS**
>
> ## Inequality and Privilege
>
> ### Legal Biases in Favor of Marriage
>
> A society's laws reveal how it thinks about different groups, how it plans to organize them, and what strategies it uses to hold them together (Unger 1976: 47). Where the family is concerned, the law shows consistent preferences that favor married couples over other kinds of social groups.
>
> Married couples are afforded key rights that are not available to other couples. For example, a married couple is granted a special right of confidentiality, which prevents a person from being forced to testify in court against their spouse (Hamilton 2006). Married couples are granted special rights over their children that are not automatically extended to other people who have children. Any child born to a married woman is automatically treated as a legal child of both members of the married couple. For an unmarried couple, by contrast, the biological father does not have any automatic rights to the child. To have any custodial rights, he will have to prove he is the biological father and complete a legal document acknowledging his paternity. Even after he does this, he will often have fewer custodial rights than the married partner of the biological mother; in cases where there is conflict, the courts overwhelmingly rule in favor of the legally married couple (Hamilton 2006: 39). In cases of adoption, there is a preference favoring legally married couples, and many states in the United States actually prohibit unmarried couples from adopting a child together.
>
> Preferences that favor legally married couples have been built into laws that regulate employment, insurance, taxation, inheritance, and immigration. For immigration laws in the United States, a legally married spouse can apply for a visa immediately and can come to live with their partner while their visa application is pending. For inheritance laws, a person will receive Social Security benefits upon the death of their legally married partner. A legally married couple can leave unlimited amounts of money to their spouse upon their death, without having to pay any estate taxes. Insurance laws require health insurance companies to provide family coverage to legally married couples, but there are no laws requiring them to provide family coverage to unmarried partners, even if they are living together. All of these laws create a situation in which there are clear social and financial benefits associated with marriage.
>
> **ACTIVE LEARNING**
>
> **Find out:** Visit the website of the US Census Bureau, and find the median household income for married couples with children under 18. Now see if you can find the median household income for unmarried couples with children under 18. Which figure is easier to locate? Which group has the higher median income?

The family has also traditionally prepared people to become effective members of society. As the Chinese philosopher Confucius wrote more than 2500 years ago, "To put the nation in order, we must first put the family in order." He meant that strong societies depend upon strong families. There is widespread belief that children are much more likely to grow up to become good citizens and productive members of society if they are raised in supportive, stable, and healthy families.

The family is also used as a metaphor for describing public leaders. Confucius wrote that the leader of government should be regarded as the father of the nation. Similarly, the ancient Greek philosopher Aristotle argued that if the family formed the root of human relationships, the society was the flower. In nations as diverse as China, the United States, and Ghana, schools teach students about the "founding fathers" of the nation.

**GENDER ROLES AND FAMILY ROLES.** One of the most powerful ways that families shape our lives is by defining and modeling gender roles. Young children learn about gender by watching their parents. They pay attention to the way that parental roles are divided up: who does the cooking, who does the cleaning, who leaves in the morning to go to work, and who takes care of them during the day. If they have siblings, they pay careful attention to the different ways they are treated, particularly if there are different expectations for sons and daughters.

The choices that parents make about family roles are often shaped by existing systems of inequality. Gender inequality in the workplace will often encourage married couples to privilege the husband's career and to have the wife stay home to take care of the children (Budig and England 2001). As we discussed in Chapter 8, gendered expectations make women feel more responsible for housecleaning and child care; even when they have full-time jobs, women often find themselves beginning a "second shift" of housework once they get home (Hochschild 2012). And when crisis hits, it is often mothers and other female kin who extend their roles to meet new challenges. The COVID-19 pandemic is a good example. As most school districts switched to remote learning during lockdowns, children needed to stay home to participate in their schoolwork via the internet. This further burdened

**Gender roles as family roles**
A mother watches her daughter prepare food as she holds her baby (left), while a father repairs a toy truck with his son (right).

parents, many of whom were now working from home, with the extra work falling more heavily on mothers and older female siblings.

These gendered expectations are reinforced by media. For the first 50 years of commercial television, most media families featured white, heterosexual couples with children. The wife in the show did not engage in paid work and spent most of her time in the kitchen. The husband had a job, and when he was at home, he spent most of his time in the family room or in the yard of their middle-class suburban home. There were no financial struggles depicted on the show, nor was there any real conflict between the family members.

There is still a strong tendency for media to underemphasize the diversity of family types and to privilege traditional family roles. When compared to families in the real world, fictional media families are less likely to be interracial, less likely to have same-sex couples, and less likely to have single parents (Childs 2009). They are also less likely to be poor, unemployed, chronically ill, overweight, or depressed (Kidd 2014).

## 9.2 Changes in Marriage and Family

**LG** **9.2** Define the nuclear family, and describe how divorce, single-parent families, and the delay in marriage have led to changes in the traditional nuclear family.

There is much more diversity in families than there used to be. Divorce has become relatively common since the 1960s, which has led to many changes in family life. People have started marrying later, and an increasing number of them are deciding not to get married at all. Because of globalization, there are more transnational families.

### Traditional Families and Nuclear Families

Today, when people think about the "traditional family," they tend to think about a **nuclear family**, which consists of a heterosexual couple living together with their children. This is the image of the family that we can find in television shows such as *The Adventures of Ozzie and Harriet*, *Modern Family*, and *The Simpsons*.

Social scientists used to believe that the traditional nuclear family was a universal feature of social life. But cross-cultural research has challenged this belief. Anthropologists and historians have pointed out that the nuclear family was more common in Western societies than it was elsewhere. In other societies the most common form was the **extended family**, in which the household went beyond the nuclear family to include grandparents, aunts, uncles, and other relatives. In traditional China, to take one example,

**Nuclear family** A traditional image of the family, which consists of a heterosexual couple living together with their children.

**Extended family** A type of family in which the household includes parents, children, grandparents, aunts, uncles, and other relatives.

**Media depictions of the family**
*Modern Family* (a) presents a more contemporary family picture than previous TV shows because it includes cousins, same-sex spouses, divorce, and blended families. *The Simpsons* (b), which first aired in 1989, represents the heteronormative, intact, working-class nuclear family still prevalent at that time. The 1950s show *Ozzie and Harriet* (c) was an iconic representation of a heteronormative, intact, middle-class nuclear family that ran on network television from 1952 to 1966. We learn about families from families on TV that both reflect and provide a comparison for real life. Children learn cues about families from media representations, which are largely images of heteronormative nuclear families.

the social ideal was the four-generational joint family, which included all the sons and all their descendants living under the same roof with their parents (Chen 2009). In many respects, then, the nuclear family as we know it today was an invention of modern Western society.

The nuclear family may not be universal, but the nature of modern society has made it much more common, even in places where the extended family was once the ideal. As more people moved to cities, where population densities are much higher, they settled in smaller houses and apartments, which made it more difficult to maintain the extended family. Industrialization also placed pressure on the extended family, by weakening the household economy, increasing residential mobility, and forcing people to move in search of better work (Parsons and Bales 1955). The movement toward universal education meant that children were spending more time in school and less time at home, reducing the need for the kind of extended child care arrangements that took place in extended families. Rising standards of living also placed pressure on the extended family because young couples were more easily able to move out of their parents' homes and find a place of their own. The existence of extended families declined rapidly in North America and western Europe throughout the 20th century; in eastern Europe, southern Europe, and East Asia, rapid economic growth since the 1970s has also been associated with the decline of the extended family (Ruggles 2012).

**Multigenerational family dinner**
The generational nature of family life is organized differently in different countries. In some countries families live with three and four generations. The norm in the United States is the one-generation households.

## Divorce

Before the 1960s, there was significant social stigma associated with divorce. A couple who wanted a divorce would have to prove in divorce court that one party's faults were sufficient reason to end the marriage. This fault-based divorce was the standard approach in virtually every country in the world. The exception was the Soviet Union, which established no-fault divorce in 1918.

Things began to change in the 1960s as feminist researchers began to show how the social organization of the family was reinforcing male power. In 1966 Herma Hill Kay, a member of the California Governor's Commission on the Family, proposed that California should adopt a system of no-fault divorce. No-fault divorce became California law in 1970, and by 1983 every state in the United States (except for South Dakota and New York) had

> **PAIRED CONCEPTS**
>
> ## Solidarity and Conflict
>
> ### Disagreements over Parenting Styles
>
> The nuclear family places more pressure on parents because there are only two adults in the household who are available to take responsibility for household chores and supervising children. When both parents have jobs and there are no relatives nearby, parents often find themselves having to pay somebody to help them with child care. And yet, the ethic of intensive parenting in many families means that parents are more involved than ever in the day-to-day lives of their children. The stress that results can lead to disagreements about the best way to raise children.
>
> Conflicts over parenting have a negative impact on all members of the family, and social research shows that they are associated with a higher probability of marital dissolution (Helland et al. 2014). Disagreement can escalate into conflict when one partner feels like they are not getting enough help from the other or when there are major disagreements over parenting styles. Even in cases where the marriage does not end in divorce, there is evidence that parental conflict is associated with poorer academic achievement and increased likelihood of substance abuse for children (Musick and Meier 2010), and parental conflict is shown to negatively affect mental health and children's future relationships (Buscho 2019). Some research suggests that for children whose parents fight a lot, it is better if the parents divorce than if they stay together (Amato, Loomis, and Booth 1995; Schrader 2019).
>
> Conflicts over parenting styles also have an effect on friendships and other social relationships. Parents need authentic and supportive friendships to help them deal with the everyday stresses of raising children (Luthar and Cicciolla 2015). When disputes about parenting styles destroy friendships, the nuclear family becomes more isolated than ever.
>
> > **ACTIVE LEARNING**
> >
> > **Find out:** Ask your parents (or other parents you know) if they ever had disagreements over parenting styles, either with their partner, with friends, or with acquaintances. What was the nature of the disagreement? How was it resolved?

adopted new laws that created some form of no-fault divorce. Today, most countries have laws that permit divorce by mutual consent, though many still require a period of legal separation before the divorce is legally granted.

As Figure 9.1 shows, the divorce rate in the United States increased steadily over the twentieth century, rising dramatically from 1960 onward and reaching a peak in 1980. Since 1980 the divorce rate has gradually declined, as have rates of marriage, but the divorce rate is still substantially higher than it was in 1960 (Schweizer 2020; Ortiz-Ospina and Roser 2024). Today, approximately 2 percent of married couples get divorced each year, and about 15 percent of the adult population is divorced at any given time (Stevenson and Wolfers 2007; Mayol-Garcia et al. 2021).

Divorce is not distributed randomly across the population, and it tends to reinforce existing systems of inequality with uneven impacts for different

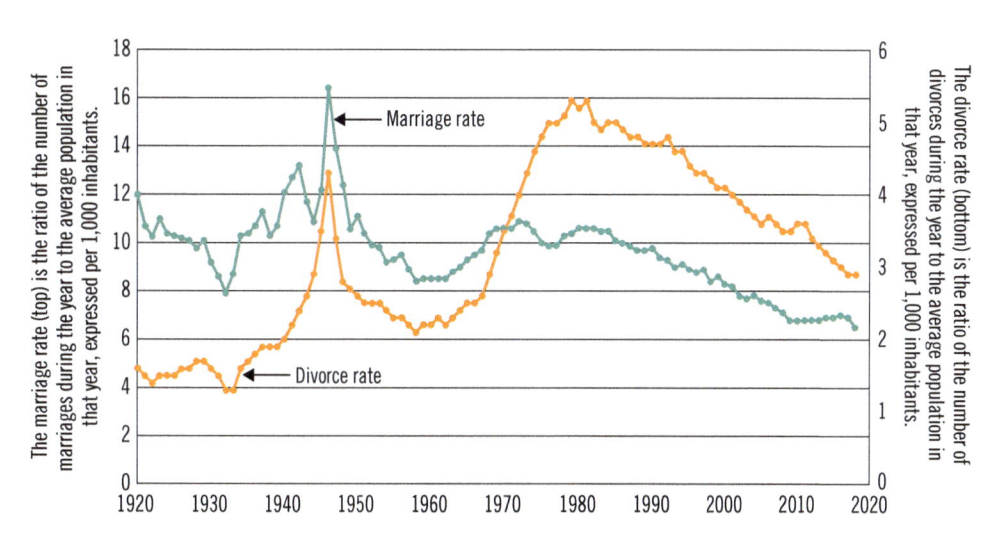

**Figure 9.1 Rates of Marriage and Divorce, 1920–2020.**
Source: Our World in Data, 2024.

groups. Most of the decline in the divorce rate has taken place among couples with more education (Amato 2010; McErlean 2021). Looking closely at first divorces in the first marriages of women shows that divorce rates differ by level of education (Reynolds 2021) (see Figure 9.2). Divorce rates also vary systematically with levels of wealth (Killewald, Lee and England 2023). That said, it remains the case that among heterosexual married couples who get divorced, wives, and especially older wives, tend to experience larger declines in economic well-being than their husbands, which means that divorce reinforces gender inequality (Bianchi, Subaiya, and Kahn 1999; Leopold 2018). And the negative consequences of divorce are often multigenerational. Some children of divorced parents have lower levels of educational success, lower levels of psychological well-being, and a higher likelihood of having their own marriages end in divorce (Amato 2010; Lansford et al. 2009; Lee and McLanahan, 2015; Buscho 2019).

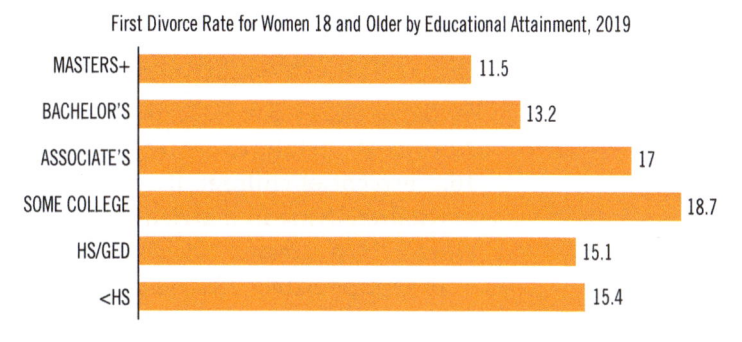

**Figure 9.2 First Divorce Rate for Women 18 and Older by Educational Attainment, 2019.**

First Divorce Rate for Women 18 and Older by Educational Attainment, 2019

| Education | Rate |
|---|---|
| MASTERS+ | 11.5 |
| BACHELOR'S | 13.2 |
| ASSOCIATE'S | 17 |
| SOME COLLEGE | 18.7 |
| HS/GED | 15.1 |
| <HS | 15.4 |

Source: Reynolds, L. (2021). First divorce rate in the U.S., 2019. Family Profiles, FP-21-10. Bowling Green, OH: National Center for Family & Marriage Research. https://doi.org/10.25035/ncfmr/fp-21-10

## Single-Parent Families

Another recent change in American society is the increase in

**Children's Living Arrangements**
Children under 18 Years and Marital Status of Parents

Percentage of Children

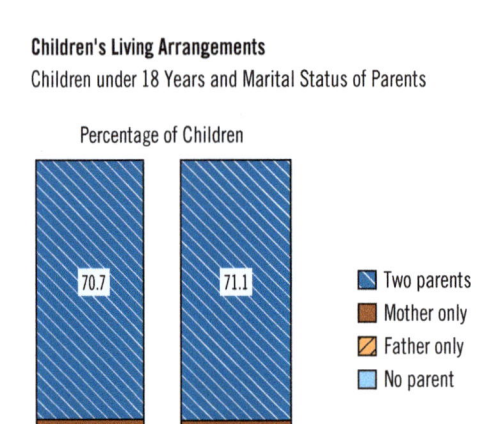

| | 2007 | 2023 |
|---|---|---|
| Two parents | 70.7 | 71.1 |
| Mother only | 22.6 | 20.9 |

- Two parents
- Mother only
- Father only
- No parent

**Figure 9.3 Living Arrangements of Children under Age 18.**
Source: U.S. Department of Commerce. 2023 Current Population Survey Annual Social and Economic Supplement, America's Families and Living Arrangements Package, Table C3.

single-parent families. One-quarter (25 percent) of all children in the United States live in a single-parent household (Current Population Survey 2023), compared to only 13 percent of children in 1968 (Livingston 2018; Kramer 2019) (see Figure 9.3). According to the Pew Foundation, the US has the world's highest rate of children living in single-parent households (Kramer 2019).

Single-parent families are overwhelmingly headed by women, and they are strongly associated with childhood poverty. Poverty leaves children "vulnerable to environmental, educational, health, and safety risks" and young children living in poverty "are more likely to have cognitive, behavioral, and socioemotional difficulties" (Federal Interagency Forum on Child and Family Statistics 2023). For 2022, data from the US Census Bureau showed that 32 percent of children living with single mothers were poor, compared to 16.3 percent of children living with solo fathers, while only 5.4 percent of children living in married-couple families lived below the poverty line (Shrider and Creamer 2023). There are significant racial differences as well: approximately 28.2 percent of white children living in a family with a female householder with no spouse present were in poverty, compared to 37.7 percent of Hispanic children and 32.3 percent of Black children who lived in families with a sole female householder. For American Indian and Alaska Native children who lived in families with a sole female householder with no spouse present, 47.6 percent were identified by the Census as living in poverty (US Census 2022).

Research by Edin, Kefalas and Furstenberg (2011) shows how race, gender, and class intersect in complex ways in the lives and choices made by many single mothers. Women living in poor neighborhoods often want to get married but think they should not do so until they have financial stability. Unlike professional women, they do not struggle with decisions about whether to prioritize career or family because they are often stuck in unsatisfying jobs with very few opportunities for advancement, and they view having children as the most meaningful thing they can do. This ethnographic research study shows clearly that poor women place more value on having children than marriage or career. Confident in their ability to be effective and loving mothers, they are not interested in waiting until they find suitable partners to marry.

## Delay and Decline of Marriage

Only 50 percent of all US adults were married in 2021, which was down from 69 percent in 1970 (Aragão et al. 2023), and more educated people are more likely to marry than people with fewer years of formal schooling (see Figure 9.4). There is also a fairly large racial disparity, with Black people significantly less likely to marry than other racial groups in the United States (see Figure 9.5). Looking from a global perspective, the decline in marriage is a widespread phenomenon among wealthy countries throughout the world (Organisation for Economic Co-operation and Development 2018).

Divorce and single parenting are associated with the decline in marriage, as is the rise in **cohabitation**, when romantic couples choose to live together without marrying. Three quarters of all recent marriages (2015–2019) were preceded by a period of cohabitation (Manning and Carlson 2021), although cohabitation is less likely to end in marriage now than in the past (Sutherland 2014). Cohabitation is slightly more common among people who have less income and less education since many lower-income, never-married adults report not feeling financially stable enough to marry (Parker and Stepler 2017); many couples who cohabit believe that they should wait to get married until they can afford to have

**Cohabitation** An arrangement in which romantic couples choose to live together instead of getting married.

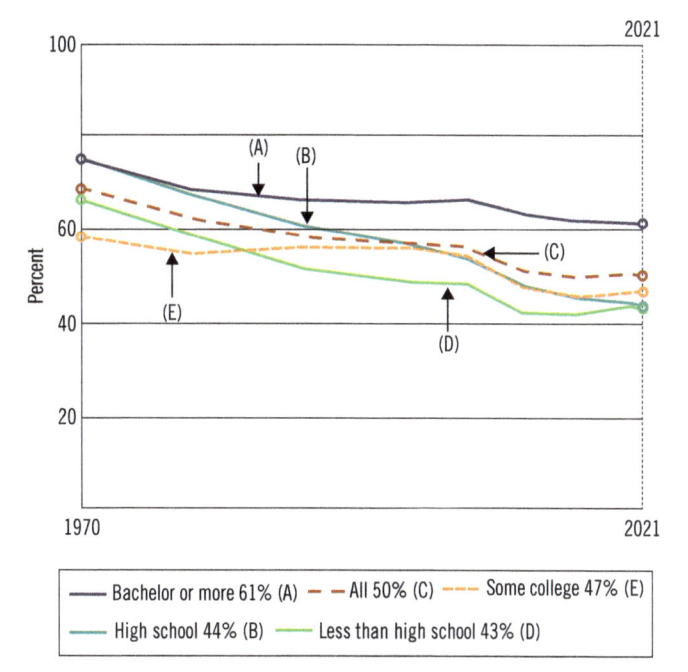

**Figure 9.4** Percentage of US Adults Ages 18 and Older Who Are Married, by Education.
Source: Pew Research Center analysis of 1970–2000 decennial census and 2010–2021 American Community Survey (IPUMS).

— Bachelor or more 61% (A)    – – All 50% (C)    ---- Some college 47% (E)
— High school 44% (B)    — Less than high school 43% (D)

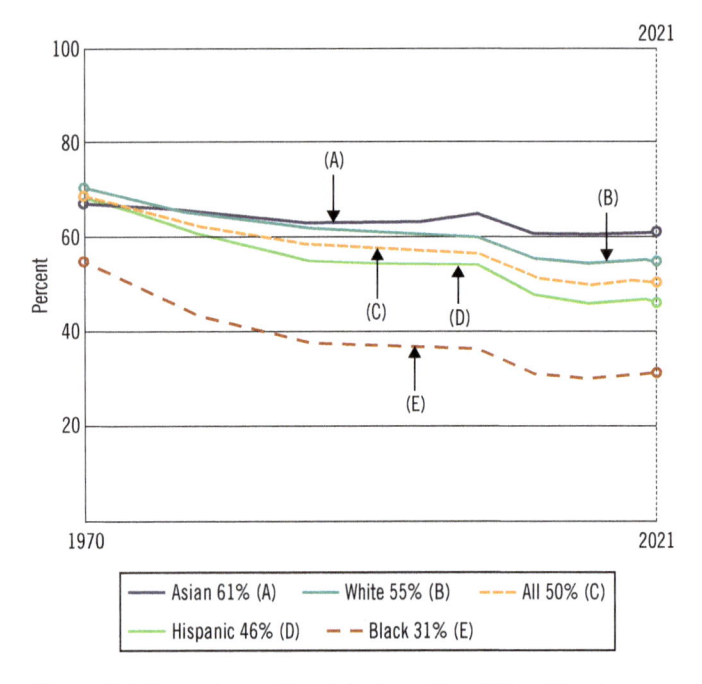

**Figure 9.5  Percentage of US Adults Ages 18 and Older Who Are Married, by Race/Ethnicity.**
Note: White, Black and Asian adults include who report being only one race and are not Hispanic. Hispanics are of any race.
Source: Pew Research Center analysis of 1970–2000 decennial census and 2010–2021 American Community Survey (IPUMS).

— Asian 61% (A)    — White 55% (B)    --- All 50% (C)
— Hispanic 46% (D)    -- Black 31% (E)

a "real" wedding, buy a house, and achieve financial stability (Gibson-Davis, Edin, and McLanahan 2005; Parker and Stepler 2017). Finally, cohabitation is more common among people who are less religious and who have more egalitarian beliefs about gender roles (Smock 2000: 4; Ishizuka 2018). But it is a fairly common practice among all social groups, with the exception of the extremely religious.

There are many factors contributing to the rise in cohabitation. Changing attitudes about sexuality (Chapter 8) mean that romantic couples can cohabit without the disapproval of their parents and peers. Contemporary Americans are generally accepting of a range of family types. Women who are working are less likely to view marriage as an economic strategy, and women who reject traditional attitudes about gender roles have been less likely to view marriage as central to their identities for quite some time (Cherlin and Furstenberg 1988).

Indeed, many Americans never expect to marry. Surveys of high school students find a large drop in the number of young people who expect to marry or who think they will be good spouses (Pepin and Cohen 2024). Fewer Americans see marriage and parenthood as important to a fulfilling life compared to having an interesting career or being close to friends, and more people are "pessimistic than optimistic about the future of the family in general" (Parker and Minkin 2023).

While there are many good reasons for couples to choose cohabitation instead of marriage, sociological research shows that cohabitation is associated with an increase in family instability (Cavanagh and Fomby 2019; Ishizuka 2018; Copen, Daniels, and Mosher 2013). Cohabitation also lacks the legal support and protections that are associated with marriage. When cohabiting couples dissolve their unions, there is strong evidence of negative economic and psychological outcomes for both adults and children (Lee and McLanahan 2015; McLanahan, Tach, and Schneider 2013; Tach and Eads 2015).

**PAIRED CONCEPTS**

## Structure and Contingency

### "Bird-Nesting" as a Co-Parenting Strategy after Divorce

Since the 1980s, there has been a trend in favor of joint custody for divorcing parents with children. The most common arrangement is joint legal custody, in which one parent gets physical custody of the children but the other parent has legal visitation rights and legal rights to participate in decisions about their children. In joint legal custody, the noncustodial parents usually have a financial responsibility to help pay for the costs of raising their children. In these types of arrangements, it is overwhelmingly the case that the mother will be the person who has physical custody, while the other partner will have joint legal custody.

A second type of arrangement is joint physical custody, in which both parents agree to a schedule where the children have regular opportunities to live with each parent. The important principle is that they are spending enough time with each parent so that they can maintain close bonds with both of them.

While joint physical custody makes it easier for children to maintain a strong relationship with both of their parents after a divorce, it presents a number of challenges. The biggest problems emerge when the divorced parents do not get along because each time children are handed off, there is a chance for an emotional argument to happen. This places a lot of psychological stress on children. Even when there are not conflicts between the parents, joint physical custody forces the children to be moving households continuously. Joint physical custody is also associated with lower child support payments, which means that sometimes the parent pushing for joint physical custody is more interested in reducing payments than in maintaining a close relationship with their children (Emery 2009).

Another strategy that some divorced parents are using is "bird's-nest" custody. In this arrangement, the children stay in the same household, and it is the parents who move in and out depending on whose turn it is to have custody of the children (Savage 2021). The obvious benefit of this strategy is the stability it gives the children. They get to maintain close relationships with both parents, but they do not have to deal with the stress and disruption of constantly moving houses. This makes it much easier for them to maintain their friendships, and they don't have to worry about leaving their shoes or their homework at the wrong house. But bird's-nest custody has its own distinctive limitations. Most family therapists suggest that it is only a viable strategy for couples in an uncontested divorce, where there is minimal animosity between parents and where both parents agree to live close to the children. Bird's-nest custody is usually more expensive because it requires that there be three residences instead of two. Even in the best of circumstances, bird's-nest strategies can become awkward if one of the divorced parents enters a serious relationship. There are also logistical challenges and some confusion for children (Savage 2021). For all of these reasons, most of the social science research shows that bird's-nest custody is most effective as a temporary or a short-term solution (Silverman and Higgins 2003).

**ACTIVE LEARNING**

**Find out:** Make a list of all the custody arrangements of the people you knew growing up whose parents were divorced. Do you notice any patterns? Do you have any explanations for these patterns?

One of the clearest consequences of cohabitation is that the people who do end up getting married do so at a later age than previously. In the United States, the median age at first marriage is now 28.4 for women and 30.2 for men, which is an increase of nearly seven years since 1960 (US Census 2023). The age at first marriage is even higher in Canada, Australia, Israel, Japan, South Korea, and all of Western Europe (Misachi 2017).

## Boomerang Kids and Sandwich Parents

The delay in marriage is associated with people having children at an older age than they once did. Women's average age at first birth has increased significantly, from 21 in 1970 to 27.4 in 2022 (Merten 2024). The birth rate has increased the fastest among women aged 35 and above (Matthews and Hamilton 2014), reflecting the fact that it is the wealthiest and most highly educated third of the population who are the most likely to delay parenthood (Sassler and Cunningham 2008). By waiting to have children until they are established in their careers, college-educated couples have more financial security and less stress in their lives during the period when they are raising their children. They are in a good position to invest time and money in their child's future, in a way that effectively transmits their privilege to the next generation. On the other side of the spectrum are those who say they want to have children but they are postponing or delaying parenthood and marriage for financial reasons. This also creates fundamental social inequity (DuCharme 2024) and intersects with the rise of single-parent households. In both cases, the delay in parenthood reinforces existing systems of inequality.

The delay in marriage and parenting may have advantages, but it also comes with specific costs and risks. One of the biggest challenges for older parents is that they often become **sandwich parents**, which means that they are still raising their children at a time when their own parents are becoming elderly and need care. It can be very challenging to help two generations of family members simultaneously. Sandwich parents can feel stretched financially and socially (Horowitz 2022).

Since the 1980s, parents have also found themselves dealing with **boomerang kids**, which are young adults who move back home to live with their parents after a period of independence. A recent study by the Pew Research Center (Minkin et al. 2024) found that about one-third of young adults aged 18–34 lived in a parent's home, and 57 percent of those aged 18–24 lived in a parent's home. Nearly one half of young adults also received financial help from their parents.

There are many reasons for the high proportion of boomerang kids. While wages are higher for young adults than they were 30 years ago, so is student loan debt. Expectations about marriage and family formation are

**Sandwich parents** People in the generational position of raising their children at the same time as their own parents are becoming elderly and need care.

**Boomerang kids** Young adults who move back home to live with their parents after a period of independence.

also changing, and these life changes may be delayed or postponed indefinitely. Since the global financial crisis of 2008 and the COVID-19 pandemic of 2020, young adults are more likely to be unemployed or underemployed. As moving back home becomes less a sign of failure among their peers, some boomerang kids perceive the decision as a smart financial strategy that will set them up better for their future lives (Davidson 2014; Pew Research Center 2024). For parents, though, the presence of boomerang kids may threaten their ability to save effectively for their own retirements, with low-income parents reporting that financial help to children impacts their own financial situation negatively (Anderson 2015; Pew Research Center 2024).

## Transnational Families

International migration has increased significantly since the 1980s, with an impact on families around the world. In the United States, immigrants and their US-born children are 27 percent of the population (Batalova 2024). Many families that migrate are doing so in search of better work, education, and opportunities for their children (Schumacher et al. 2023). The Immigration and Nationality Act regulates immigration policy in the US, permitting immigration for "the reunification of families, admitting immigrants with skills that are valuable to the U.S. economy, protecting refugees, and promoting diversity" (American Immigration Council 2021).

Migrants who create **transnational families** maintain family bonds across multiple countries. One of the ways they do this is through **remittances**, where the person who has emigrated regularly sends money back to family members in the country they left. In fact, many migrants plan to return to their countries of origin after their working careers are finished, which gives them extra motivation to maintain transnational ties. The World Economic Forum estimated that in 2022, migrants sent back US$794 billion in remittances.

The ability to maintain connections as a

**Transnational family** A household that is maintaining strong family bonds and simultaneous connections to multiple countries.

**Remittance** The money a migrant sends back from their new country to family members in their country of origin.

**Boomerang kids**
"Boomerang kids" are adult children who return to the parental household after a period of independence. In the United States, one third of young adults in their 20s and 30s live with their parents, and about half receive some financial assistance from their parents.

transnational family depends on who does the migrating and whether the entire nuclear family emigrates. But each arrangement creates social pressures. When the entire nuclear family emigrates to another country, parents often worry that their children will reject their cultural heritage and become corrupted by the new society (Telzer 2010; Zhou and Bankston 1998). Children feel the pressure of the sacrifices their parents are making for them, and they can come to resent the expectation that they will help their parents translate documents, fill out forms, and conduct their everyday affairs (Menjivar 2000).

It is not always possible for families to emigrate together, which creates other kinds of challenges. Sometimes, parents leave their children behind, letting the children be raised by grandparents while the parents move elsewhere in search of better work (Foner and Dreby 2011: 551). In other instances, children are the ones who leave their parents behind. There is a long history of Central American youth coming to the United States to do agricultural work, sending remittances back home, and hoping that in the future either they can move back to Central America or their parents can move to the United States (Suarez-Orozco and Suarez-Orozco 2001). There is also a history of Asian children coming to the United States to attend school, with the hope that once their careers are established their parents can come and join them (Zhou 1998). These kinds of arrangements can create stress for the parent–child relationship, with parents struggling to maintain control

---

**PAIRED CONCEPTS** — **Global and Local**

## Korean "Wild Geese" Families

A distinctive form of the transnational family has emerged in Korea, where the mother takes the children to a foreign country for school while the father stays behind to work and support the family. This type of split-household transnational family started to become popular among wealthy Korean families in the mid-1990s, and the trend accelerated rapidly during the first decade of the 21st century. By 2019, there were more than 60,000 Korean students enrolled in foreign schools, with nearly half of them enrolled in elementary school (GSE 2023). The United States is the most popular destination for these migrants, followed by China, Canada, Australia, and New Zealand (Kim 2009: 170). In Korea, these families are called *kirogi*, or "wild geese" families.

There are local and global forces driving the rise of wild geese families. Korea has an unusually intense school culture. Students begin attending after-school "cram schools" as early as elementary school, and by high school it is common for students to be in school or studying for 15 hours per day.

South Korea's college-entrance exam, which is eight hours long, is one of the most difficult and stressful in the world. South Korea is consistently at the top of global education rankings, but this success comes with a cost. Recent research has found that South Korean children are among the least happy among all wealthy countries, with academic stress being the most significant contributing factor (Diamond 2016). Given this context, it is not so surprising that families wish to take their children to a different country for school, where they can be happier and more well-rounded as students.

For many South Korean wild geese families, the primary goal is to improve their children's English skills so that they will be able to compete more successfully in a global world. In South Korea, studying English in a foreign country is a sign of social prestige and a marker of global citizenship. Memoirs written by wild geese children who attended elite US prep schools and Ivy League universities have been bestsellers in South Korea, offering up a blueprint for ambitious families wishing to join the global elite (Abelman and Kang 2014: 2). Many wild geese children have returned triumphantly to South Korea to become successful business leaders and politicians. Others have stayed in the United States, enjoying successful careers in elite law firms and global corporations.

At the same time, wild geese families face a number of significant challenges. The fathers who stay behind suffer from loneliness and depression, and the mothers often have a hard time settling in to the new country where their children are going to school (Reed 2015). Wild geese mothers and children have come under significant criticism in South Korea, where they are faulted for being too focused on material success, not concerned enough about

**Wild geese families**
A young girl says goodbye to her father as she leaves with her mother and brother to pursue her education outside Korea.

the needs of the father, too selfishly focused on their own families, and not patriotic enough (Abelman and Kang 2014). This can make it harder for wild geese families to return to South Korea, placing additional stress on the family. And the situation is even worse for less wealthy families who try the split-household transnational strategy. In these families, the father is often called a "penguin Dad" because he cannot fly and may go years at a time without seeing his wife or children.

### ACTIVE LEARNING

**Find out:** Think about and list the different structural and cultural factors that draw "wild geese families" to American schools. Now think about the way that schools have changed during the COVID-19 pandemic. Do you think that these changes will make transnational school attendance more or less attractive?

over children (Glick 2010). On the other hand, family members who stay behind are often highly motivated to emigrate themselves. These desires reinforce the value of the family and make family members more driven to do the things that are necessary to maintain family bonds.

## 9.3 Challenging Family Forms

**LG 9.3** Comprehend the main feminist critiques of the family, and show how women's movements for greater equality have led to changes in family dynamics. Describe the changes in attitudes and laws that have become more accepting of multiracial families as well as lesbian and gay families.

In the United States, more than half of all adults are single, and over one-quarter of all households are single-person households (Anderson et al 2023). The United States is not exceptional; in Europe, living alone is even more common (Pew Research Center 2019). Some of this is due to structural changes in society. People are waiting longer to get married, and those who have good jobs can afford to live by themselves rather than getting a roommate or living with their parents. But a lot of it reflects a shift in preferences.

In his book *Going Solo*, sociologist Eric Klinenberg shows some of the ways that the preference for living alone challenges traditional family forms (Klinenberg 2012). For many people today, the ability to live by themselves is an even better measure of becoming a successful adult than getting married. For some people, the attraction of living alone is that it gives them complete sexual freedom. For others, it is the ability to focus on their careers and find their "true selves." Many young adults view living alone as a temporary phase, but they believe they are better off on their own than they would be if they settled for the wrong person by marrying too soon.

Living alone is not the only challenge to traditional ideas about family and social life. Feminist ideas have had a major influence too, encouraging people to think more carefully about the power, violence, and inequality that can exist within marriages. Divorce and remarriage has led to an increase in blended families, in a way that challenges many traditional beliefs about the nuclear family. Social movements have successfully fought for greater acceptance of multiracial, gay, and lesbian families. Many of these challenges have resulted in overturning laws designed to give preferences to certain types of families over others.

### Feminist Challenges to the Family

In her classic book *The Feminine Mystique*, Betty Friedan ([1963] 2001) argued that the equation of motherhood and femininity kept women from realizing their full potential, at the same time as it relieved men from the responsibility of doing any housework. Seeing the division of household labor through the lens of gender inequality, Friedan argued that women had the right to expect their husbands to do their fair share of the housework and to share the responsibility for child care. Friedan's criticisms have been backed up by sociological research. Wives do most of the housework in the family, even when they are employed (Berk 1985; Bianchi et al. 2012; Brenan 2020). Wives who earn more money than their husbands compensate by doing extra housework so that their husbands will still feel like "real men" (Syrda 2023: Bittman et al. 2003). When husbands do contribute to housework, they do not feel accountable or responsible for how well they do it, leaving their wives to supervise the work and redo it when necessary (Lyonette and Crompton 2015). The division of household labor becomes even more unequal when there are children in the family, which helps explain why motherhood reduces the wages of employed women (Yu and Kuo 2024; Budig and England 2001).

Inspired by the writings of Betty Friedan and other feminists in the 1960s and 1970s, women around the country began to join consciousness-raising groups to talk about the inequality, oppression, and unhappiness they were experiencing in their family lives. The National Organization for Women, founded in 1966, soon built a powerful political coalition to challenge gender inequality in the family. Rallying around the slogan "the personal is political," they argued that the challenges women faced within their families were social issues that required organized resistance and fundamental social change.

Movements to create greater gender equality have led to real changes for many families. Changes in some state laws now require companies to grant maternity leave, making it easier for mothers to re-enter the workforce after giving birth. Company policies that also extend parental leave to new fathers have allowed and encouraged men to become more involved in parenting (Allamano 2020). Many men have embraced the goal of creating more gender equality in the family, believing that this would be good for men as well as women; others have resisted the demands for greater gender equality, arguing that a woman's natural place is in the home and that women's desires to have careers and participate in public life threaten their role as mothers and caregivers (Kimmel 2010). Regardless of their opinions about gender, work, and family, though, most people today are accepting of a variety of ways to organize housework and other family matters.

## Blended Families

The prevalence of divorce and remarriage has also led to new family forms. In the United States today, more than one in five women and about one in three men remarry after divorce (Reynolds 2021). As a result, 16 percent of all children are now living in a **blended family**, which is a household that has a step-parent and possibly a step-sibling and/or a half-sibling. Today, it is estimated that more than 40 percent of American adults have at least one step-relative, and nearly one-third have a step-sibling or half-sibling (Pew Research Center 2010b, 2011, 2015).

While the term "blended family" avoids many of the negative stereotypes formerly associated with step-parents, some family counselors and social scientists argue that the use of the term can lead people to underestimate the challenges that face parents and children in these situations (Martin 2013).

**Blended family**
A household that includes a step-parent and possibly a step-sibling and/or a half-sibling.

Conflicts between divorced parents often get worse when one of the parents gets remarried, particularly when there are children involved. Children may resent their new step-parent and step-siblings, and they might question whether their newly married parent will still love them as much as they did before the blended family was created. New step-parents are often unsure about how much parenting responsibility they should take on and how much independence they have to make their own parenting decisions (Coleman et al. 2001; Meyers 2022). The creation of a blended family often means relocation, which creates additional sources of stress and anxiety as wider family and education networks are disrupted. For all of these reasons, there are measurable negative consequences for the achievements and the well-being of children in blended families (Sweeney 2010: 672–73).

A challenge for blended families is that the laws regulating them are not well developed (Sweeney 2010: 672). Step-parents do not have clear custodial authority. They often have to get written consent from both biological parents before they are allowed to make decisions on their child's behalf when interacting with schools, daycare centers, and hospitals (Mason et al. 2002). If the remarriage ends, whether through divorce or through the death of the other partner, they do not have clearly defined rights of custody or even visitation with their step-children. But despite all these difficulties, blended families continue to proliferate, and in the process they are challenging traditional understandings about what a "normal family" looks like.

## Multiracial Families

Another recent social change has been the rise of multiracial families. The number of people who identify as multiracial has increased significantly since 2000, particularly among younger people (Chapter 7), and more than 14 percent of children born in the United States today have parents who come from different racial groups (Livingston 2017; Alba, Beck, and Sahin 2018; Czismadia and Atkin 2022). Interracial relationships and multiracial families now appear commonly in film and television programs.

Interracial marriage was not fully legal in the United States until 1967; even in those states where antimiscegenation laws had been repealed earlier, interracial marriages remained extremely uncommon before the 1980s. But this is no longer the case. Today, nearly 17 percent of all new marriages in the United States are between two people who have a different racial or ethnic background (Livingston, Parker, and Rohal 2017). Interracial marriage is more common among racial minorities, with 18 percent of Black Americans, 27 percent of Hispanic Americans, and 29 percent of Asian Americans in 2015 creating multiracial families. It is also more common in the western than eastern United States.

Attitudes about multiracial families have changed considerably (Bowman 2017). Only 4 percent of Americans approved of interracial marriage in 1958; by 2013, support had increased to 87 percent (Newport 2013).

More than one-third of Americans report that they have a close relative who is part of a multiracial family, and more than 40 percent of Americans believe that the increase in interracial marriage is good for society (Wang 2012). While younger people are the most tolerant of interracial marriage, supportive attitudes have increased for all age groups.

The growing acceptance of multiracial families is reflected in institutions throughout society. When Zubrinsky and Bobo studied race and residential segregation during the 1990s, they found that all groups expressed some preference for same-race neighbors, but non-whites were much more open to sharing the neighborhood with families from different racial groups (Bobo and Zubrinsky 1996). Recent evidence suggests that multiracial families are even more accepting of racial diversity in their neighborhood, and in fact they tend to live in neighborhoods that have significantly higher levels of racial diversity (Gabriel 2016). In these more diverse neighborhoods, intergroup contact makes greater integration and racial tolerance even more likely in schools, workplaces, and public spaces.

Still, important challenges remain for multiracial families. As they navigate friendships, public spaces, schools, doctors' offices, and census forms, they find themselves continually being asked to make a racial identification for themselves. On an almost daily basis, they have social interactions in which other people attribute a racial identity to them, which may not be the one they have chosen for themselves. Interracial couples are less likely to be treated as a romantic couple by strangers they encounter, and when they behave as a romantic couple or marry, they are more likely to encounter hostility (Choi 2021; Herman and Campbell 2012; Childs 2005). Interracial couples may also have a harder time adopting children. When they experience discrimination, they discover that being interracial or multiracial is not a protected legal status. In many respects, then, society and law still continue to privilege monoracial families (Onwuachi-Willig and Willig-Onwuachi 2009).

## Lesbian and Gay Families

One of the most significant challenges to the traditional image of the family has come from lesbian and gay couples and the idea of queer families (Bernstein and Reimann 2001; Sullivan 2001; Naples 2004). Before the 21st century, marriages between same-sex partners were not legally recognized anywhere in the world (Biblarz and Savci 2010: 480). The Netherlands was the first country to legalize gay marriage, in 2000, and that was followed by similar rulings in Belgium, Canada, Norway, Sweden, Spain, and South Africa. In the United States, same-sex marriage was legally recognized for the first time in 2004, in Massachusetts. This was followed by Connecticut (2008), Vermont (2009), New Hampshire (2010), and New York (2011). After several years of legal disputes over whether states were required to recognize the validity of same-sex marriage licenses that had been granted in other states, the US Supreme Court

## PAIRED CONCEPTS

# Power and Resistance

## *Loving v. Virginia*

The legal case that overturned laws against interracial marriage in the United States was filed in 1964 by the American Civil Liberties Union (ACLU) in Virginia on behalf of Mildred and Richard Loving. The couple had been married in 1958 in Washington, DC, in order to avoid Virginia's Racial Integrity Act, which made it a crime for whites and non-whites to marry. Returning to their home in Virginia, the couple was arrested and sentenced to a year in jail. The judge offered to suspend the sentence if the Loving family agreed to leave Virginia and not return to the state together for 25 years. Leaving the house that they had built themselves and separated from all of their friends and family in Virginia, they moved to Washington, DC.

After five unhappy years in Washington, DC, Mildred Loving wrote a letter complaining about her situation to the US attorney general, Robert F. Kennedy. Kennedy referred her to the ACLU, whose lawyers filed a motion to overturn the Virginia court decision, on the grounds that laws against interracial marriage violated the Equal Protection Clause of the 14th Amendment. The decision was upheld several times in Virginia, and lawyers appealed the decision until it came before the US Supreme Court.

In a unanimous decision in September 1967, the Supreme Court overturned the decision against the Lovings and declared that laws against interracial marriage (which still existed in 16 states) were unconstitutional and unenforceable. Chief Justice Earl Warren wrote that "the freedom to marry, or not marry, a person of another race resides with the individual, and cannot be infringed by the State."

Today, *Loving v. Virginia* is viewed as a historic milestone that advanced civil rights. Three movies have been made about the case, and June 12 (the date of the Supreme Court decision) is celebrated around the country as "Loving Day." For their own part, Mildred and Richard Loving were not active participants in the Civil Rights Movement, and they were not particularly political in their everyday lives. As their attorney, Bernard Cohen, has described them, "They were very simple people, who were not interested in winning any civil rights principle. They just were in love with one another and wanted the right to live together as husband and wife in Virginia, without any interference from officialdom" (Siegel and Norris 2007).

**Mildred and Richard Loving**

### ACTIVE LEARNING

**Find out:** While *Loving v. Virginia* declared that laws against interracial marriage were unconstitutional in 1967, the state of Alabama continued to enforce its ban until 1970 and did not remove language about interracial marriage from its state constitution until 2000. Find out and describe the events that led Alabama to change its laws and its legal practices regarding interracial marriage between 1967 and 2000. What is the situation today?

ruled in 2015 that same-sex couples had the constitutional right to marry and to have their marriages legally recognized throughout all the United States.

Along with the legal changes, the public acceptance of gay and lesbian families has increased significantly. In 2003, 58 percent of Americans were opposed to same-sex marriage; by 2015, at the time of the Supreme Court decision, fewer than 40 percent opposed it (Fingerhut 2016). Today, nearly two-thirds of people in the United States support same-sex marriage; in countries like Canada (79 percent), the Netherlands (89 percent), and Sweden (92 percent), support for same-sex marriage is even higher (Poushter, Gubbala, and Huang 2023). Similar to attitudes about multiracial families, support is strongest among those who are less than 30 years old, which suggests that gay marriage may become less controversial in the future.

It took both solidarity and conflict for supporters of gay marriage to change public opinion and to get legal rulings in their favor. Some advocates argued that same-sex marriage was a basic civil right, which people were entitled to under the Equal Protection Clause of the US Constitution (Wolfson 2004). Others pointed out that marriage was an important source of family stability, which would encourage greater social cohesion, emotional support, and economic security if it was extended to same-sex couples (Sullivan 2004).

As lesbian and gay couples and their families have become more visible, social scientists have examined how they are different from other types of families. Gay and lesbian parents appear to have a more egalitarian attitude toward housework and parenting than traditional heterosexual parents (Fulcher, Sutfin, and Patterson 2008; Johnson and O'Connor 2002). The children of gay and lesbian parents hold more egalitarian and less stereotypical attitudes about gender and behavior (Biblarz and Savci 2010: 485). Overall, though, children raised by gay and lesbian parents have similar outcomes to children of heterosexual married parents, in terms of psychological well-being, friendships, and educational success (Biblarz and Savci 2010: 484; Cheng and Powell 2015).

**Expectant parents**
Two women hold a picture of an ultrasound celebrating the expectation of a new baby. Social acceptance of same-sex relationships, along with advances in reproductive technology, have allowed for the formation of nontraditional families.

## CASE STUDY

# Family Names

As families continue to change, things that were once taken for granted become more uncertain and more a matter of conscious choice. This is clear in the case of naming practices, specifically with respect to the question of whether or not women will keep their own last names when they get married. Using the five paired concepts, we consider how naming practices can shed light on the relationship between family and society.

It was not long ago that a woman was unable to keep her unmarried name after getting married. This expression of men's *power* over women was built into the law. Before the 1970s, many states required a married woman to use her husband's last name in order to vote, get a passport, or have a bank account. In this context, the insistence on keeping one's unmarried name was an act of *resistance*. In fact, it was an important strategic action throughout the 1970s, encouraged by the women's movement as an act against patriarchal power within the family.

In the 1970s, a woman who decided to keep her name after marriage knew that it was a deeply political and controversial action, but she did it because she felt a strong sense of *solidarity* with others in the women's movement. At the same time, women knew that their decision was also likely to create *conflict*. There was often conflict with their husbands, whose friends disapproved of his choice and criticized him for not taking control of the family. There was also conflict with women who chose not to keep their name after marriage, who felt that people in the women's movement were criticizing them for not being more loyal to the movement. Over time, a backlash against the feminist movement grew in strength. Swept up in this conservative backlash, fewer married women during the 1980s made the choice to keep their unmarried names (Goldin and Shim 2004).

Today, a married woman's decision to keep her name has less to do with solidarity and more to do with social dynamics related to *privilege* and *inequality*. Women are more likely to keep their names if they have a higher income, an advanced degree, or an established career or if they live in a city (Kopelman et al. 2009). For these successful urban women, the choice to keep their name, just like the choice to marry, is one that cannot be separated from the fact that they have already made a name for themselves as successful individuals (Goldin and Shim 2004). The choice can still be a difficult one, and it can still involve awkward conversations with their partner, family, and friends. But their privilege means that they are not likely to feel pressured into making the decision. Women who marry less educated and less wealthy men, however, are more likely to be criticized and punished for their desire to keep their unmarried name (Shafer 2006).

The women's movement has had a *global* impact on how people around the world talk about gender and family. But the decision about whether or not a married woman should keep her name is also shaped by more *local* factors. In Japan, the law requires that a married couple share their last name; the law does not specify which last name they should share, but an overwhelming majority choose to share the husband's name. In Quebec, Greece, France, Belgium, and the Netherlands, the law requires married women to keep their unmarried names (Koffler 2015). In Korea, Spain, and Chile, it is much more common for married women to keep their unmarried name than it is for them to adopt their husband's name.

While the decision about whether married women should keep their name is shaped by the history of the women's movement and the *structure* of gender inequality in the family, there have been many recent attempts to develop creative new solutions to the problem of family names. Some men, fully embracing the feminist critique of gender inequality in the family, are taking their wives' last names. Others are creating a hyphenated last name that combines both last names—Shawn and Beyoncé Knowles-Carter are probably the best-known example of this choice. Others are creating entirely new last names, which combine different parts of the last names of the two partners. New strategies such as these represent the *contingency* that is present in all social situations and social choices.

## LEARNING GOALS REVISITED

**9.1 Define family and kinship, and describe how kinship systems have changed over time. Understand how the family is connected to systems of inequality, such as race, class, and gender inequality.**

- A family is a group of related people connected by biological, emotional, or legal bonds.
- A kinship system consists of the rules that define who counts as a member of the family, the names that are given to different types of family members, and the expectations about how different family members will relate to one another. Rules about kinship provide some of the most important elements of a society's culture.
- Before the 20th century, most European societies were patrilineal and privileged the male line of descent. Both men and women were expected to use marriage as a way of building wealth and resources for their families. Today, multilineal systems give equal significance to both maternal and paternal lines of descent, and men and women in many parts of the world are free to marry for love rather than for building strategic family alliances.

**9.2 Define the nuclear family, and describe how divorce, single-parent families, and the delay in marriage have led to changes in the traditional nuclear family.**

- Highly educated, professionally successful, and high-earning people tend to marry and form families with one another, in a way that reinforces social inequality.
- For most of US history, family law only permitted marriage between women and men and prohibited interracial marriages. This prevented same-sex couples and multiracial families from enjoying the social and economic benefits of legal marriage. Legally married couples have legal rights and benefits that are not available to other couples.
- The family unit can reinforce gender inequality.

**9.3 Comprehend the main feminist critiques of the family, and show how women's movements for greater equality have led to changes in family dynamics. Describe the changes in attitudes and laws that have become more accepting of multiracial families as well as lesbian and gay families.**

- The nuclear family consists of a heterosexual couple living together with their children.
- Changes in the law during the 1960s led to an increase in the divorce rate. Today, about 10 percent of the adult population is divorced at any given time. Among heterosexual couples, divorce tends to have a larger negative effect on the economic well-being of women. Children of divorced parents tend to have lower levels of educational success and psychological well-being

- and a higher likelihood of having their own marriages end in divorce.
- More than one-quarter of all children in the United States today live in a single-parent household. Single-parent families are overwhelmingly headed by women, and they are strongly associated with childhood poverty.
- About half of all adults in the United States today are married, and the decline in marriage is occurring in wealthy countries throughout the world. Divorce and single parenting have contributed to the decline in marriage, but so has the increasing popularity of cohabitation.
- Demands for gender equality have led to real changes for many families, including maternity leave. While many men have embraced the goal of creating more gender equality in the family, there has also been a cultural backlash, with some people arguing that a woman's natural place is in the home.
- Interracial marriage was not fully legal in the United States until 1967, but today nearly 90 percent of Americans support interracial marriage. More than one-third of the US population has a close relative who is part of a multiracial family.
- Marriage between gay and lesbian couples was not legal anywhere in the world before the 21st century. Today, there is broad-based public support for gay marriage, with support being strongest among those younger than 30 years.

## Key Terms

Blended family 319
Boomerang kids 314
Cohabitation 311
Extended family 305
Family 297
Genealogy 297
Kinship system 297
Multilineal 298
Nuclear family 305
Patrilineal 298
Primogeniture 301
Remittance 315
Sandwich parents 314
Transnational family 315

## Review Questions

1. What kinds of social support do families provide?
2. What kinds of social and legal privileges do married couples receive that are not available to unmarried couples?
3. How do families influence gender roles? Do family gender roles reinforce inequality? To what extent have family gender roles changed over time?
4. What social forces helped make the traditional nuclear family the most common type of family form in modern society? When was the high-water mark for the traditional nuclear family? What has happened to the nuclear family since that time?
5. What were the main factors that caused the divorce rate to increase between the 1960s and the 1980s? How does divorce tend to reinforce existing systems of inequality?

6. How do race, gender, and class intersect in the lives and choices made by many single mothers?
7. What are the main reasons cohabitation has been increasing among couples? What are the advantages and disadvantages of cohabitation compared to marriage?
8. What are the biggest challenges couples face when they delay the decision to get married?
9. Describe some of the different strategies that transnational families use to stay connected.
10. What were the main criticisms that women's groups made against the family during the 1960s and 1970s?
11. What are the main challenges that face blended families?
12. Describe how attitudes and laws about marriage have changed to become more accepting of multiracial families as well as lesbian and gay families. What were the main factors that led to these changes?

## Explore

### RECOMMENDED READINGS

Cohen, Philip N. 2014. *The Family: Diversity, Inequality, and Social Change*. New York: W. W. Norton.

Conley, Dalton. 2005. *The Pecking Order: A Bold New Look at How Family and Society Determine Who We Become*. New York: Vintage.

Edin, Kathryn, and Maria Kefalas. 2005. *Promises I Can Keep: Why Poor Women Put Motherhood before Marriage*. Berkeley: University of California Press.

Foner, Nancy, and Joanna Dreby. 2011. "Relations between the Generations in Immigrant Families." *Annual Review of Sociology* 37: 546–64.

Friedan, Betty. [1963] 2001. *The Feminine Mystique*. New York: W. W. Norton.

Klinenberg, Eric. 2012. *Going Solo: The Extraordinary Rise and Surprising Appeal of Living Alone*. New York: Penguin Books.

Smock, Pamela. 2000. "Cohabitation in the United States: An Appraisal of Research Themes, Findings, and Implications," *Annual Review of Sociology* 26: 1–20.

Wolfson, Evan. 2004. *Why Marriage Matters: America, Equality, and Gay People's Right to Marry*. New York: Simon & Schuster.

### ACTIVITIES

- *Use your sociological imagination*: Go to a restaurant or coffee shop with one or two of your friends. Choose between 15 and 20 people who are seated together, and mark down whether or not you think they are a married couple. Are your guesses the same? What clues did you use to guide you in your choices?

- *Media+Data Literacies*: Choose three popular films or television shows where there is a married or an unmarried couple. How is the housework divided up in the household?

- *Discuss*: Do you think it is ever too late to get married? Is there an age beyond which people should not get divorced? Why or why not?

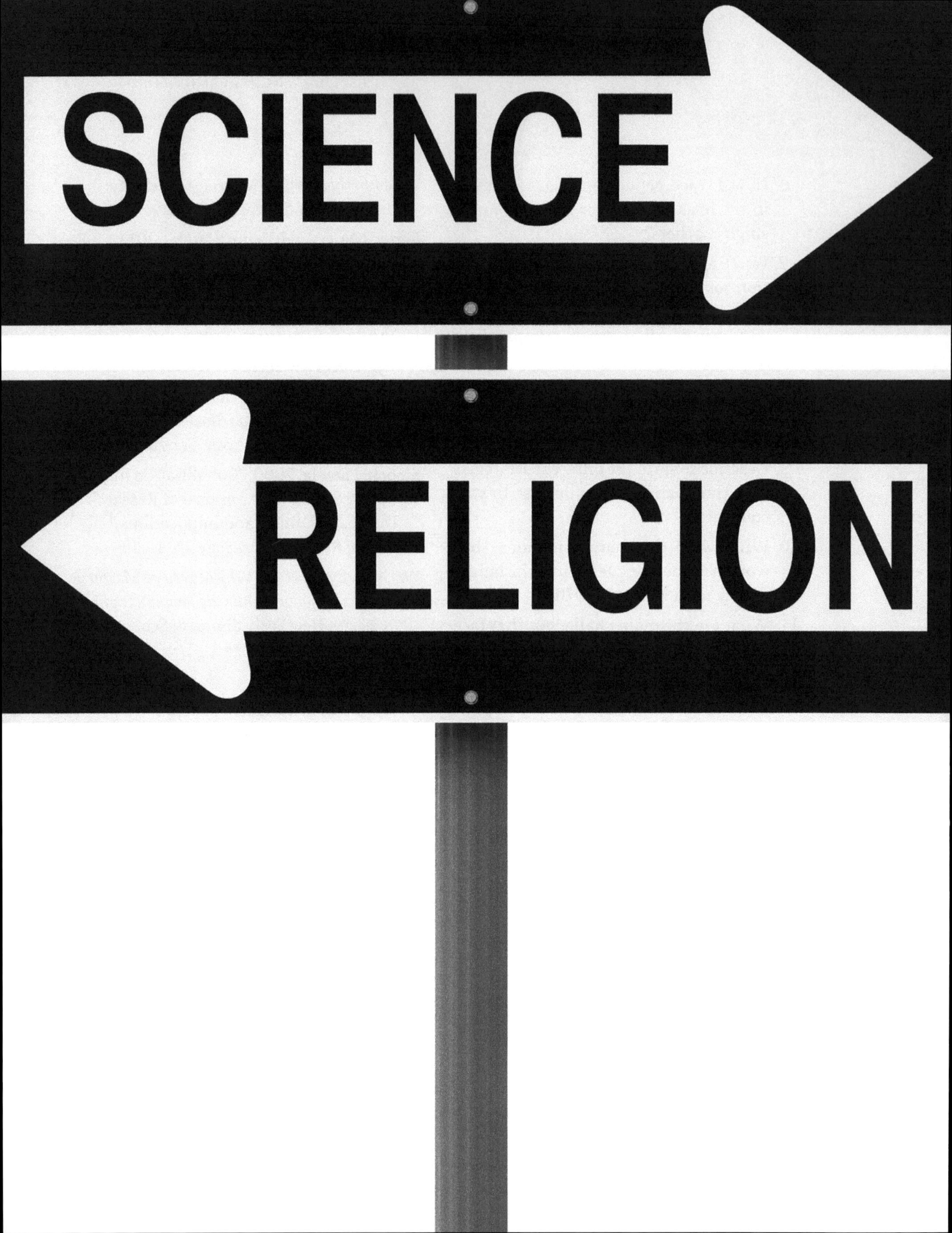
SCIENCE
RELIGION

# 10

# Science, Religion, and Knowing

In November 2007, John Coleman drew national attention when he wrote a blog post calling global warming the "greatest scam in history." As a cofounder of The Weather Channel and one of the first national television weathermen in the country, Coleman was one of the nation's most well-known meteorologists. Coleman soon became a regular guest on conservative radio and television talk shows, where he argued that climate scientists had a political agenda, that they had manipulated data, and that the scientific consensus about global warming was closer to religious belief than to valid scientific knowledge (Homans 2010). Coleman emphasized his scientific expertise as a meteorologist, and he argued that "we scientists . . . have truth on our side" (Yale Climate Connections 2010).

Climate scientists fought back strenuously against Coleman's charges. They pointed out that Coleman's academic credentials were in journalism, not science. They further observed that research about global warming came from the scientific field of climatology, and not from meteorology, and that within the field of climatology the consensus about climate change was based on "solid settled science." The CEO of The Weather Channel released a press statement distancing itself from Coleman, noting that Coleman had no affiliation with their organization and

**Science and Religion**
Sociologists emphasize that although people sometimes think science and religion are very different, they have striking similarities. They are both ways of knowing the social world, provide comfort in times of stress, and offer practical ways to manage social life.

### Chapter Outline

**10.1 RELIGION AND SCIENCE AS WAYS OF KNOWING THE WORLD 331**
*Religious Cosmologies 332*
*Scientific Cosmologies 333*

**10.2 RELIGION AS A SOCIAL INSTITUTION 336**
*Elements of Religious Institutions 338*
*The Major Religions and Their Global Impact 340*

**10.3 MODERN SOCIETY AND SECULARISM 347**
*The Secularization Thesis 348*
*The Persistence of Religion 350*
*Religion and Politics 352*

**10.4 SCIENCE AS A SOCIAL INSTITUTION 356**
*The Sociology of Science 358*
*Science and Technology Studies 361*

**10.5 THE CRISIS OF KNOWING, AND THE IMPORTANCE OF BELIEF 363**
*Epistemological Doubts 363*
*Can Science and Religion Coexist? 364*

**CASE STUDY: DEBATING EVOLUTION IN PUBLIC SCHOOLS 365**

reaffirming that their meteorologists supported the scientific consensus about climate change (Ariens 2014).

Scientists are deeply worried that people continue to doubt claims about global warming. Among scientists, there is very little disagreement about the facts of the matter. In fact, 97 percent of all actively publishing climate scientists agree both that climate change is occurring, and that human activities are the primary cause (Cook et al. 2016).

## LEARNING GOALS

**10.1** Describe the main differences between religious and scientific cosmologies.

**10.2** Describe how religion and science are organized as social institutions; learn the history and the global impact of the five major world religions.

**10.3** Define secularization, and discuss the main points of evidence for and against the secularization thesis.

**10.4** Describe how science is socially organized, and how the production of scientific knowledge is shaped by social hierarchies, conflicts, and interpretations.

**10.5** Think about some of the ways that religion and science can coexist in contemporary society.

In 2005, the Yale School of Forestry and Environmental Studies organized a major conference to explore why scientific knowledge about climate change was not shared more widely among everyday citizens, policy-makers, and business leaders. An outcome of the conference was the creation of the Yale Program on Climate Change Communication. Its mission is to develop a comprehensive public education campaign about climate change and its implications. Its research associates conduct regular opinion polls focusing on public attitudes and beliefs about the environment. They have developed relationships and alliances with leaders from business, politics, religion, and journalism. And they have undertaken a grassroots education effort to try to connect with local communities and schools.

Program leaders quickly recognized that they needed to try harder to overcome the divide between religion and science. Noting that "scientists are not always seen as credible messengers by religious groups," they have come to terms with the fact that emphasizing science might not be the best way to change the minds of people who are suspicious about environmentalism (Abbasi 2006: 40). The partnerships they created with religious leaders have helped them craft a message about the ethical and religious obligation that people have to protect the environment.

This chapter examines religion and science as two important systems of knowledge that people have used to understand the world. We begin by introducing the concept of **cosmology**, which refers to the system of knowledge and beliefs that a society uses to understand how the world works and how it is organized. After comparing the main differences between religious and scientific cosmologies, we then focus more closely on how religion is organized as a social institution. We examine how the major religions have shaped the world, and we consider how religion has changed in society today. We also examine how science is organized as a social institution. We review the sociological research in this area, which has studied the values and beliefs of scientists, the social organization of scientific reward systems, the ways scientific labs are organized, and how scientific knowledge is produced. We finish by exploring how science and religion can coexist in the contemporary world.

**Cosmology** The system of knowledge and beliefs that a society uses to understand how the world works and how it is organized.

## 10.1 Religion and Science as Ways of Knowing the World

**LG** **10.1** Describe the main differences between religious and scientific cosmologies.

Humans have tried to understand the world around them for as long as they have had language, and they have developed theories about how the world was created. Archaeologists have discovered carvings and other physical objects that are more than twenty thousand years old that attempt to describe how the universe is organized. A Babylonian clay tablet from the sixth century BCE (currently displayed at the British Museum) depicts the world as a disc surrounded by a ring of water. In the fourth century BCE, the Greek philosopher Aristotle described a world in which Earth remained stationary in the center, while planets and stars circled it (Figure 10.1). Most of these theories were concerned with astronomy, trying to understand how the Earth is related to the rest of the universe. But there are also social cosmologies, which are theories about how societies were created, how they work, and how they are connected to the larger world.

Among the early sociologists, Émile Durkheim and Max Weber both wrote about social cosmology. In his book *The Elementary Forms of the Religious Life* (1912), Durkheim argued that there was a natural human proclivity to classify and categorize things, as a way of understanding our relationship to our society and to the larger world. Durkheim argued that the classifying impulse is shared by the earliest religious ideas as well as the most advanced scientific systems. Weber studied how religious cosmologies shaped social

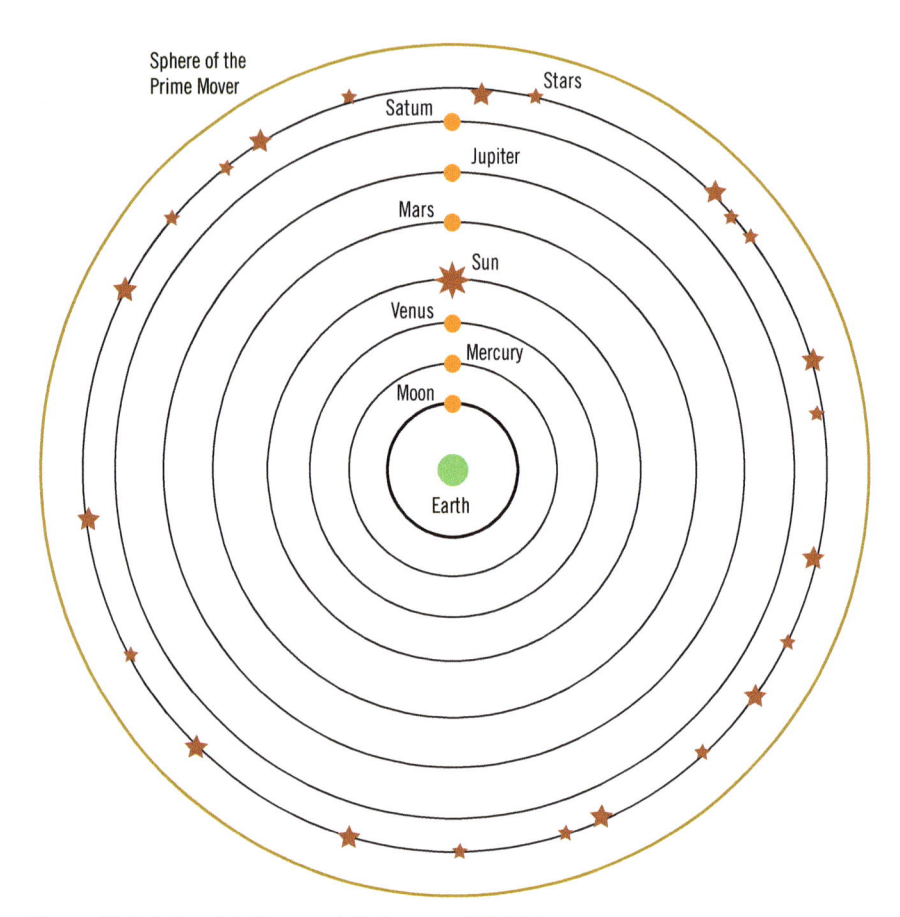

**Figure 10.1** Aristotle's Geocentric Universe, c. 350 BCE.

and economic life, through historical studies of Protestantism, Judaism, Confucianism, and Hinduism.

## Religious Cosmologies

According to Weber, the main difference between religion and science is that religious cosmologies describe the world by making reference to mysterious, magical, and incalculable forces (Weber 1946: 139). **Polytheism** is a religious cosmology in which the world was created by a group of deities, who are responsible for many of the forces of nature and who often intervene in human lives. Ancient religions tended to be polytheistic. **Monotheism**, by contrast, is a religious cosmology in which there is only one deity, who created the world and is responsible for all living things.

**Polytheism** A religious cosmology in which there is a group of deities.

**Monotheism** A religious cosmology in which there is only one deity.

Religious cosmologies also contain a moral dimension, which means that they provide a framework to help people distinguish between right and wrong. Most religions provide their adherents with guidelines for proper ethical conduct. These guidelines are usually handed down through sacred religious texts, such as the Buddhist Vedas, the Jewish Torah, the Christian Bible, and the Muslim Quran. These texts are a continual source of moral guidance for their religious communities, with religious experts interpreting their meaning and discussing how they can help guide action in the present.

Ultimately, religious cosmologies provide their adherents with a theory about the meaning of human life that is grounded in belief, faith, and sacrifice. They reassure people with the understanding that their own lives are connected to a larger spiritual eternity (Durkheim 2008). They encourage people to believe that there is a meaningful world bigger than themselves, and that there are specific practices and sacrifices they have to make if they wish to achieve religious salvation (Weber 1946).

## Scientific Cosmologies

Today, cosmology is a branch of astronomy, and refers to the scientific study of the universe as a whole. Since the 20th century, modern physics has revolutionized the way that scientists think about the origin, nature, and future of the universe. In the 20th century, astronomers theorized that the universe began from nothing with a "Big Bang"—an explosion that produced all matter and energy—but they still differ on whether the cosmos will continue expanding, stop, or even shrink. During the 1980s, the physicist Andrei Linde developed a theory of the multiverse, which described the world as consisting of many universes, with each one operating according to different laws of low-energy physics. These theories are radically different from the creation theories in the cosmologies of ancient philosophies and religions.

A key distinction between religious and scientific ways of knowing the world is that scientists

**The Manchester Museum of Science and Industry**
Representing a scientific cosmology, the museum tells the story of scientific and industrial advancement, focusing on the development of rail and steam power.

want to see compelling evidence before they are willing to accept a claim about how the world works. By demanding evidence, science encourages skepticism about the claims people make. The goal of science is to produce reliable knowledge about the world, and to refine our understanding of how things work by testing theories through careful research.

Scientific ways of knowing are premised on the belief that people can create a better society if they cast aside older forms of knowledge and replace them with science. This idea has been expressed repeatedly in the last two hundred years, often through an argument that nonscientific forms of knowledge are dangerous. In his book *The Wealth of Nations*, published in 1776, Adam Smith argued that "science is the antidote to the poison of enthusiasm and superstition." More recently, during a 2009 television interview, the astrophysicist Neil deGrasse Tyson described science as "an inoculation against charlatans who would have you believe whatever it is they tell you." The idea is simple: science helps us cut through the lies, myths, and deceptions that surround us, and get closer to the truth of how things really are.

**PAIRED CONCEPTS**

## Power and Resistance

### Galileo, Darwin, and the Church

As scientists began to explore the universe and to explain the world around them, they came into direct conflict with religious cosmologies. In an era when the Roman Catholic Church had most of the power in European society, this conflict could be dangerous.

One of the most infamous cases of religious persecution against scientists was between the Church and Italian astronomer Galileo Galilei (1564–1642). In 1610, relying on research he performed with a new telescope he had developed, Galileo published a study demonstrating that the planets revolved around the sun, and that there were a number of moons orbiting Jupiter. These observations directly contradicted the religious cosmology of the Church, which maintained that the Sun, Moon, stars, and planets all revolved around a stationary Earth. Galileo continued to conduct his research, despite criticisms from Church scholars and demands that he abandon his studies of astronomy.

The dispute between Galileo and the Church reached its peak in 1632, when Galileo published the results of research showing that the Earth itself revolved around the Sun. In 1633, Galileo was ordered to stand trial for heresy. He was found guilty, forced to recant his findings, and placed under house arrest where he remained until his death in 1642. All of his books and publications were banned.

This story repeated itself two centuries later when Charles Darwin published his research on evolution in an 1859 book, *On the Origin of Species*. Darwin argued that hereditary changes followed a principle of natural selection, favoring those changes that improved the survival of the species. Darwin argued that all species evolved according to the principle of natural selection, including humans, an argument he developed further in his 1871 book *The Descent of Man*. When Darwin died in 1882, he was considered to be the greatest scientist of his age.

Darwin's research put him in direct conflict with the teachings of religious authorities. In England the bishop of Oxford, Samuel Wilberforce, denounced Darwin for publishing ideas that violated scripture. But scientists enjoyed considerably more social power and influence in Darwin's day than they did in Galileo's. In a famous attack on Wilberforce, biologist Thomas Huxley (1825–1895) announced that he would rather be a descendent of an ape than of a bishop who distorted the truth. Rather than being arrested, as Galileo was, Darwin became one of the most famous and celebrated people in the world. Upon his death he was buried in Westminster Abbey, the highest honor that can be bestowed upon a British citizen.

Both religions later admitted they had acted poorly and offered posthumous apologies to the scientists. The Roman Catholic Church issued an official apology to Galileo in 1992, admitting that Galileo had been right and calling the whole series of events tragic. The Church of England apologized to Darwin in 2008, saying that it had been too defensive and too emotional in the way it reacted to the theory of evolution, and calling its behavior "an indictment on the Church."

**The trial of Galileo**
Galileo was famously put on trial by the Catholic Church for publishing his scientific findings that the Earth revolved around the Sun rather than the Earth being the center of the universe.

### ACTIVE LEARNING

**Find out:** Can you find a recent example where religious leaders criticized a scientific finding? Can you find an example where scientists criticized a religious belief? Which do you think has more power today, science or religion?

Historically, the belief in science as the route to progress was often connected to the idea of **utopia**, which refers to a perfect world in which there is no conflict, hunger, or unhappiness. Before science, most forms of utopian thinking described a period in the distant past, when people lived simply and primitively, but were happy and content. In contrast, scientific utopias describe an advanced world (usually in the future) in which people have conquered nature and managed to create a perfectly organized society. Francis Bacon, who was one of the first people to describe the scientific method, described such a utopia in his fictional work *New Atlantis*. Published in 1627, *New Atlantis* describes a mythical island where the most important social institution is a scientific college, called Salomon's House, where scientific experiments are undertaken in order to master nature and create a better social existence for the island's inhabitants. Psychologist B. F. Skinner imagined a similar kind of utopia in his 1948 novel, *Walden Two*, which describes a society organized around experimental science, in which new strategies for organizing the community are continually being tested. Skinner's view of the perfect society was one in which the scientific method came to

**Utopia** An image of an imaginary, perfect world in which there is no conflict, hunger, or unhappiness.

**Provo Utah Temple**
Religion is a social institution that provides a framework for social life. In Provo, Utah, 77 percent of people describe themselves as extremely religious, and 90 percent are associated with the Church of Jesus Christ of Latter-day Saints.

organize all aspects of social life, replacing traditional forms of knowledge. *Walden Two* inspired a number of real-life utopian communities throughout the 1960s and 1970s. But utopian hopes for science are not as strongly held as they used to be, for reasons we discuss later in the chapter.

Today, science is a major industry, supported by governments and corporations around the world. Globally, more than $2.1 trillion was spent on basic scientific research in 2020, with the largest expenditures taking place in the United States, China, and Japan (Hourihan and Zimmerman 2022). Organizations such as the Coalition for Evidence-Based Policy lobby politicians to increase government effectiveness by relying on scientific methods and rigorously collected evidence. In all levels of education, the highest priority is given to training in science, technology, engineering, and math. Scientists may try to create partnerships with religious leaders, as we discussed at the beginning of the chapter, but they do so with the belief and the confidence that scientific ways of knowing are the best way to produce reliable knowledge about the world and create social progress.

## 10.2 Religion as a Social Institution

**LG 10.2** Describe how religion and science are organized as social institutions.

Provo, Utah, is the most religious city in the United States, with 77 percent of the city's residents describing themselves as "extremely religious" (Newport 2013). More than 90 percent of the city's residents are affiliated with the Mormon Church. The city is home to Brigham Young University, the largest religious university in the United States, which is owned and operated by the Mormon Church. Social life at BYU is organized around religion, with more than 100 church organizations, known as "wards," organizing the majority of the social events. There is a major emphasis at the school on marriage, and more than half of all undergraduate students get married by the time they graduate. The school sees itself as a world ambassador for the Mormon Church, and it works hard to instill Mormon values among its students.

### METHODS AND INTERPRETATION

## Measuring Religious Commitment

Social scientists who study religion need a way to measure how religious people are. But there are many different ways to measure religiosity. Should you measure how frequently people attend religious services, pray, or read religious texts? Should you measure how much time or money a person donates to their church? Should you measure how important religion is to a person, compared to other parts of their life? Does it matter if they treat their sacred religious texts as completely true and accurate? If more than one of these measures help define religiosity, what is the relative importance of each?

The most straightforward way to measure religiosity is to examine the frequency of prayer or attendance at religious services. One key source of information, the Baylor Religion Survey, asks people how often they attend religious services. They also ask people how often they pray alone outside of religious services. And they ask people how often they read sacred religious texts. All of these measures rely on self-reports, which creates problems for social scientists because there is a tendency for people to exaggerate how frequently they participate in religious activities (Hout and Greeley 1998).

Another strategy is to measure the amount of time or money a person donates to their church. The most typical question is based on a simple binary measure, such as the one that the Survey of Chicago Catholics asked in 2007: "Did you contribute money to your parish last year?" Some surveys ask people whether they tithe (i.e., give a fixed percentage of their income to their church), but these also tend to be measured in a binary yes/no fashion.

Other measures of religiosity focus on people's religious beliefs. The General Social Survey asks people whether they believe that the Bible is the actual word of God and whether it is to be taken literally. A global survey on religiosity asks a similar question, but tailors it to be specific to the religious beliefs and sacred texts of the people they are asking. The American National Election Studies ask people whether they consider religion to be an important part of their lives. The Baylor Religion Survey asks people how religious they consider themselves, ranging from "not religious at all" to "very religious." The Measuring Morality Study asks people how strongly they look to their religious faith for meaning and purpose in their lives.

Even after decisions have been made about which measures of religiosity to collect, there is still work to be done. How can the different measures be combined into a single scale of religiosity, when they are all measuring different things? Do the different measures all get weighted equally in the scale, or should different weights be applied depending on a theory about how important a given measure is for overall religiosity? These are complicated questions, which social scientists studying religion have been debating for more than 50 years.

#### ACTIVE LEARNING

**Explore:** The Association of Religious Data Archives is located at Pennsylvania State University. Its goal is to provide a central location for storing social science data on religion. Spend some time exploring their website, and particularly their section on religiosity (https://www.thearda.com/data-archive/measurements). What do you think are the most important measures that should be included in research about religiosity?

While most cities and universities are much less religious than Provo and Brigham Young University, religion continues to have a social presence in many places in the world. As a social institution, religion offers people a set of rules and strategies for how they should relate to each other and how they should act. Religion also provides people with organizations—churches, synagogues, mosques, and so forth—where they can spend time and interact with other people. Religions give their members a common identity, and a place where they can feel connected. And religious organizations frequently provide important social resources, such as education, counseling, spiritual guidance, and charity.

## Elements of Religious Institutions

In *The Elementary Forms of the Religious Life*, Émile Durkheim defined a **religion** as a unified system of beliefs and practices related to sacred things, which unite all of its adherents into a single moral community (Durkheim 2008). Looking at the elements of this definition, it is easy to see why religion has been such a powerful social force. As a system of beliefs and practices, religion is a source of culture and meaning. As a type of culture that is focused on sacred things, religion gives people a connection to a world bigger than themselves, as well as a sense of larger purpose. As a moral community, religion is an important source of social solidarity, social connection, and social comfort. Religion also provides a way for people to think about the presence of injustice and suffering in the world.

### THE SACRED AND THE PROFANE.
As a type of culture, religions divide the world into a group of sacred things and a group of profane things. Sacred things are set apart from the ordinary.

All religions have a set of sacred objects that serve as a point of focus for their adherents. In Judaism, this includes the Star of David, the

**The elements of religion**
Religious elements include ritual objects that are considered sacred, such as these objects used during the Catholic Liturgy, a chalice, wine and water cruets, and a bell (top). Prayer is a common religious practice. In Islam, practicing Muslims set the rhythm of the day by kneeling and praying five times a day. The prayer mat and Quran (middle) are objects used for prayer. Religious holidays bind people to religious communities and identities through ritual celebration. Simchat Torah is a Jewish holiday that marks the completion of the annual Torah reading cycle. Here, a man carries the Jewish Holy text, the Torah, as other members of the religious community celebrate (bottom).

Torah, and the tallit (prayer shawl). In Christianity, it includes the cross, holy water, and the Bible. In Islam, it includes the mosque, the crescent and star, and the Quran. These sacred objects are invested with significance, and they are not to come into contact with the ordinary, profane world. In Judaism, the Torah is never supposed to touch the ground, and a person who drops it is required to fast for 40 days. When Muslims enter the mosque for daily prayers, they are expected to remove their shoes so that dirt from the outside does not enter the sacred space.

According to the sociologist Peter Berger (1929–2017), religion establishes a sacred world that gives its members a sense of meaning, order, and protection against the fear of chaos. As he wrote in *The Sacred Canopy*, "Religion is the audacious attempt to conceive of the entire universe as being humanly significant" (Berger 1967: 28). In other words, by giving us access to a world of sacred things, religion gives us comfort in the belief that our ordinary, everyday lives are not meaningless.

**Religion** A unified system of beliefs and practices related to sacred things, which unite all of its adherents into a single moral community.

**RITUAL.** For a religious institution, a **ritual** is an event where people come together to reaffirm the meaning of the sacred, to acknowledge its special qualities and its separateness from ordinary (profane) life. Ritual is the social part of religious belief, allowing people to gather and reaffirm their common beliefs and to share a powerful experience together.

In fact, Durkheim argued that ritual was so fundamental that it was an essential feature of all societies. Regardless of how religious a society might be, it still needed periodic rituals in which its members gathered together to reaffirm their shared beliefs, their sacred objects, and their most cherished values. In this sense, Durkheim argued, all societies need some form of religious practice.

**Ritual** An event where people come together to reaffirm the meaning of the sacred, to acknowledge its special qualities and its separateness from ordinary (profane) life.

**RESPONSE TO SUFFERING AND INJUSTICE.** If society is to exist as a moral community, we need an explanation for why the world is so imperfect, and for why good people suffer while evil people prosper. In his historical sociology of religion, Max Weber described this as the problem of **theodicy**, which is the attempt to explain why suffering and injustice exist in the world. Weber documented how ancient religions offered powerful explanations for suffering and injustice. Many of the earliest religions described a universe that was controlled by two competing forces of good and evil. Hindu religions explained the problem of theodicy in terms of karma, in which good actions would be rewarded and evil actions punished in later incarnations of the soul. Other religions have emphasized the distinction between life and afterlife, with good people being rewarded in the afterlife and bad people being punished.

**Theodicy** The attempt to explain why suffering and injustice exist in the world.

Religious institutions have also responded to the problem of suffering in concrete ways, by creating organizations that take responsibility for doing

**Religious responses to pain and suffering**
Most religions emphasize charity, and religious organizations are some of the most significant providers of charitable social services. Many of the largest and most important charitable organizations in the world, such as the Salvation Army, United Way, and Caritas International, were started as religious charities. The Salvation Army is famous for their Christmas fundraising drives.

care work. Charity is a major emphasis of most religious organizations, and adherents are often encouraged (and sometimes required) to give money in order to help the weak, the sick, and the defenseless. Many observant Jews today donate 10 percent of their income to charity, following the tradition from ancient biblical law. Observant Muslims follow the practice of *zakat*, in which they donate a percentage of their income to be redistributed to poor Muslims and to Islamic clergy. For Christians, the New Testament describes charity as the foundation of all Christian virtues. Charitable giving surges during major religious holidays. Research has consistently shown that religious people donate more time and money to charity than people who do not have a religious affiliation (Brooks 2003).

Because of their strong emphasis on charity, religious organizations have been and continue to be some of the largest and most significant providers of charitable social services. According to research by the sociologist Mark Chaves, more than 80 percent of all religious congregations in the United States are involved in some kind of social service provision, such as soup kitchens, homeless shelters, and food delivery to the elderly (Chaves and Eagles 2016). Many of the largest and most important charitable organizations in the world were started as religious charities, with some of the better-known examples including the United Way, Salvation Army, and Caritas International.

## The Major Religions and Their Global Impact

As Figure 10.2 shows, more than 70 percent of the people in the world are affiliated with Christianity, Islam, or Hinduism. For Christians, Muslims, and Hindus, there is a strong tendency to live in a place where they are in the majority; for other groups, there is a stronger likelihood that they will live in places where they are religious minorities (see Figure 10.2).

**% of world population**

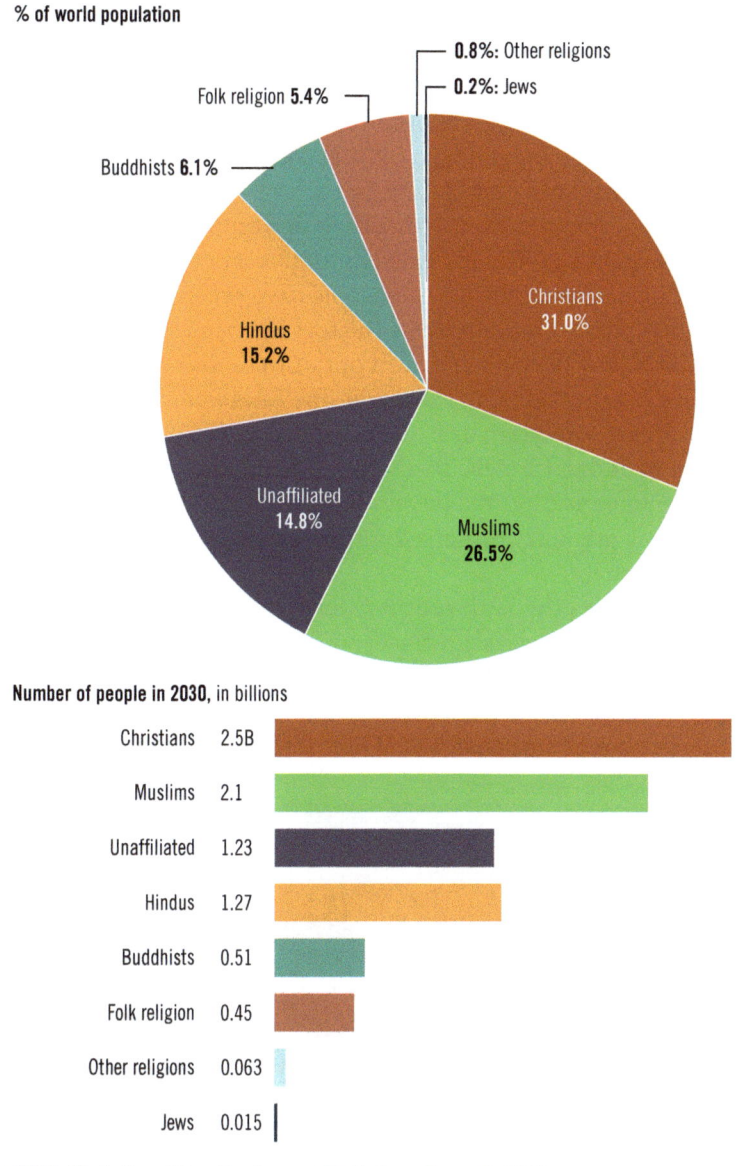

- Christians 31.0%
- Muslims 26.5%
- Unaffiliated 14.8%
- Hindus 15.2%
- Buddhists 6.1%
- Folk religion 5.4%
- 0.8%: Other religions
- 0.2%: Jews

**Number of people in 2030**, in billions

| Group | Billions |
|---|---|
| Christians | 2.5B |
| Muslims | 2.1 |
| Unaffiliated | 1.23 |
| Hindus | 1.27 |
| Buddhists | 0.51 |
| Folk religion | 0.45 |
| Other religions | 0.063 |
| Jews | 0.015 |

**Figure 10.2 Christians Were the Largest Religious Group in 2015.**
Source: Pew Research Center demographic projections.

While the number of adherents is an important measurement, other studies of comparative religion focus on the global and historical impact of different religions. Using this metric, most religious scholars identify five major world religions: Judaism, Christianity, Islam, Hinduism, and Buddhism (Esposito, Fasching, and Lewis 2014).

**JUDAISM.** Although Judaism has only about 15 million adherents worldwide, it is still considered one of the major religions because of its historical influence. Originating in the Middle East more than 3,500 years ago, Judaism is one of the oldest monotheistic religions, based on the belief that there is one all-powerful god who created the world. Judaism was a major influence on Christianity and Islam; in fact, all three are considered to be Abrahamic religions, in the sense that they all trace themselves to Abraham, and they all believe that God revealed himself to Abraham.

As a religious group, the Jewish people have experienced a long history of persecution. As a community, their history has been one of repeated diaspora, in which they have been driven out of their ancestral homeland and forced to live in other places in the world. The Jews were forced to leave their homeland after the Assyrian destruction of Israel (722 BCE), the Babylonian destruction of Judah (597 BCE), and the Roman destruction of Jerusalem (70 CE). The Romans captured large numbers of Jews and enslaved them in Rome, and they gradually dispersed throughout Europe within the lands of the Roman Empire.

From as early as the 12th century, Jewish communities in Europe and Russia were forced to live in segregated, poor, and extremely crowded communities (known as ghettos), where their movements were strictly regulated and their opportunities were limited to marginal occupations. Anti-Semitism was a common feature of European social life, with Jews suffering harassment, expulsion from communities, and even massacre. By the 19th century, however, conditions had improved for many Jews; they were granted civil rights in many countries, and they made tremendous contributions and achievements in the arts, the sciences, and the business world. But anti-Semitism continued in many parts of the world. Adolf Hitler came to power in Germany in 1933 on an anti-Semitic pledge to drive the Jews out of Germany and Europe. Hitler's Nazi government

**Jewish neighborhood in Brooklyn, New York**
Most American Jews are assimilated and live within the larger American population. In some American communities, however, Jews remain a distinct minority with a strong Jewish identity.

killed more than six million Jews between 1942 and 1945, a mass genocide that came to be known as the Holocaust, and which led to the creation of the first international trial for crimes against humanity.

The long history of diaspora and persecution led to an international movement of Zionism, which sought the establishment of a Jewish homeland in Israel, where Jews could live as a majority group. Israel was established as a Jewish state in 1948, though it has faced challenges and conflicts from neighboring Arab countries since its creation. Today, more than six million Jews live in Israel, making it the largest Jewish population center in the world, and by far the most concentrated. The second-largest Jewish population (at 5.4 million) is found in the United States. While Israeli Jews are a majority group (at 75 percent of the national population), American Jews are a distinct religious minority (at less than 3 percent of the national population). As the sociologist Charles Liebman argued, American Jews face a continual tension between their commitment to assimilating into American society and their commitment to maintaining a strong Jewish identity (Liebman 1973).

**Sect** A smaller and more loosely organized group of religious believers who disagree with the established church and try to create their own authentic expression of religious faith.

**CHRISTIANITY.** With more than 2.5 billion adherents, Christianity is the largest religion in the world. There are significant numbers of Christians on every continent. In fact, more than one hundred countries are majority Christian, with most of them located in Europe, Latin America, sub-Saharan Africa, and North America (Pew Research Center 2017).

Christianity gained influence and spread rapidly after it became the official religion of the Roman Empire in 380 CE. In 1054, the religion was formally split into the Eastern Orthodox Church (based in Constantinople) and the Roman Catholic Church (based in Rome). A second major division occurred in the 16th century during the Protestant Reformation, which challenged the authority of the Roman Catholic Church by arguing that the religious faith of the individual was more important than church hierarchy and church traditions.

The Protestant Reformation produced a lot of innovation and diversity within the Christian church. Protestants created many new **sects**, which were smaller and more loosely organized

**Martin Luther**

**Denomination**
A religious sect that has begun to develop a more established bureaucracy and a common set of ritual practices.

groups of believers who disagreed with the established church and tried to create their own authentic expression of religious faith. Over time, several of these sects became more established **denominations**, which means that their sect began to develop a more established bureaucracy and a common set of ritual practices. By the beginning of the 20th century there were a number of clearly established "mainline" Protestant denominations, including the Baptist, Methodist, Lutheran, Presbyterian, and Episcopal churches. But the spirit of protest and innovation continues within Protestantism, with new sects and denominations forming all the time.

Christianity continued to spread throughout the world because of the colonization of Africa, South America, and Asia by the powerful nations of Europe and North America. All of these powerful nations were majority Christian, and they believed that their religious faith was one of the things that made them superior to other societies. It was common practice to send Christian missionaries to the newly conquered territories, in order to introduce Christianity to the native populations. Today, Australia and New Zealand are both majority Christian, and so are the nations located in sub-Saharan Africa, South America, Central America, and the Caribbean. In fact, more than half of the world's Christians live in countries that were once conquered and colonized by European nations.

**ISLAM.** With more than 2 billion adherents, Islam is the world's second-largest religion. There are currently 49 countries that are majority Muslim, located primarily in Africa, the Middle East, and parts of Central Asia. Islam is also the fastest-growing religion in the world, and recent research suggests that Islam will become the world's largest religion at some point during the second half of this century (Lipka and Hackett 2017). There are two main denominations of Islam. Sunnis are the largest group, accounting for between 87 and 90 percent of the total; the remaining Muslims are Shia (Pew Research Center 2012b).

Islam spread rapidly throughout North Africa and

**Great Mosque of Mecca**
Mecca is considered the holiest of cities in Islam. Devout Muslims hope to perform the pilgrimage called the *hajj*, where they visit Mecca to pray and renew their sense of purpose in the world.

**PAIRED CONCEPTS**

## Global and Local

### Catholicism in Africa

Historically, the Catholic Church has been centered in Europe. More than half of all Catholic parishes and more than 40 percent of all Catholic priests are located in Europe (Pattison 2015). Today, however, the majority of Catholics live outside of Europe, and the fastest-growing Catholic population is in Africa. In fact, while the global Catholic population is growing at less than 1 percent per year, the Catholic population in Africa is increasing at a rate of nearly 20 percent annually. Social scientists project that by 2050 there will be nearly 90 million more Catholics in Africa than there will be in Europe (Saenz 2005).

Demography is a large factor behind the growth of Catholicism in Africa (where birth rates are higher), but there are also other important social forces at work. Levels of religiosity are very high in Africa, and missionaries see the large populations of Africans involved with traditional religions as good candidates for conversion. Changes within the Roman Catholic Church since the 1960s encouraged greater tolerance and understanding of other religious beliefs, and there has been a more conscious attempt to blend African symbols and culture into the practice of African Catholicism. Since the election of Pope Francis in 2013, there has been a conscious attempt in the Vatican to increase the number of African priests who have important leadership positions in the Catholic Church.

Catholicism in Africa has certain distinctive elements that are connected to the local culture. In 1965, Cardinal Paul Zoungrana (from Burkina Faso) wrote that the mission of African Catholicism was "to bring the faithful to meet Christ according to their African soul" (Ilo 2017: 58). Instead of forcing converts to adopt the same style of worship practiced in Europe, African priests have tried to create new styles that are connected to local cultures and traditions. In sub-Saharan Africa, it is common for African priests and bishops to be formally established as tribal elders and leaders of the community (Nyenyeme 2017: 81). In Zimbabwe, African drumming has become a part of the Catholic Church service (Pasura 2016). In Congo, the Catholic mass includes an invocation of ancestors, which draws on elements from traditional African theology.

As African Catholicism has grown, it has had an important influence on the larger global culture of the Catholic Church. For a long time these influences were resisted by Vatican leaders, but in 2013 many experts predicted that an African priest would be elected pope. The 2013 election was ultimately won by an Argentinian-born priest, Pope Francis, who was the first non-European pope in twelve hundred years. Pope Francis has worked hard to increase the visibility and influence of African priests, and he has led a change in emphasis for the Vatican that is more closely aligned with the interests of the African church. This includes more emphasis on the issue of global poverty, a greater willingness to criticize global capitalism, and a more assertive stance about the need to address climate change.

**ACTIVE LEARNING**

**Find out:** See if you can find the latest bulletin from the Catholic church of your local parish (many of them are available online). What evidence do you see about attempts by the local church to deal with, incorporate, and/or discuss global changes taking place within the Catholic Church? Are similar kinds of discussion taking place in other local religious communities where you live?

**Proselytizing** The attempt by individuals or organizations to convert other people to their own religious beliefs.

into the Iberian peninsula of present-day Spain, through a combination of military conquest and religious **proselytizing**. It continued to expand as the official religion of the Ottoman Empire, which was centered in what is modern-day Turkey and controlled large parts of the Middle East, North Africa, and southwest Europe for nearly six hundred years, beginning in the 13th century.

The Ottoman Empire ended after defeat in World War I, in a way that had profound social and political consequences for the Islamic world (Fawaz 2014). Millions of Ottoman soldiers and citizens were killed during the war, and railroads and cities throughout the region were destroyed, leading to economic collapse and widespread famine. Politically, the Islamic caliphate was dissolved, and England and France controlled the redrawing of national borders in the Islamic world. The British took control of Egypt, Iraq, and Palestine, while the French took control of Lebanon and Syria. But these new boundaries were shaped mainly by the political and economic interests of the victorious powers, without consideration for the social and cultural history of the regions being divided. The Balfour Declaration of 1917 promised to create a national home for the Jewish people in Palestine, which led eventually to the creation of the nation of Israel in 1948. The dream of a renewed Islamic caliphate has been a major source of Arab nationalism and religious conflict ever since the end of World War I. We examine these events in further detail later in the chapter, when we discuss religious conflict.

**Statues of Hindu deities in Kapaleeshwarar Temple, Chennai, Tamil Nadu, India**
Hinduism is the oldest religion in the world and blurs the distinction between monotheism and polytheism. There are diasporic Hindu communities around the world.

**HINDUISM.** There are slightly more than one billion Hindus in the world today, located primarily in South Asia. Hindus are a religious majority in India, Nepal, and Mauritius, which together account for 97 percent of all Hindus in the world. The four main denominations of Hinduism are Vaishnavism, Shaivism, Shaktism, and Smartism. Hinduism is the oldest religion in the world, with archaeological evidence showing that it has been practiced for more than four thousand years.

Today, while most Hindus continue to live in India, there are large diaspora populations in cities throughout the world. Transcendental meditation, yoga, and other Hindu meditation practices have also become popular worldwide.

**BUDDHISM.** There are about 500 million Buddhists in the world, with more than 95 percent of them living in the Asia-Pacific region. Buddhists are a religious majority in Cambodia, Thailand, Burma (Myanmar), Bhutan, Sri Lanka, Laos, and Mongolia. Nearly half of the world's Buddhists live in China, where they make up nearly 20 percent of the population.

**The Tian Tan Big Buddha and Po Lin Monastery**
Buddhism is focused on personal spiritual development. It is mainly found in Asia but has spread around the world. Here tourists visit the Tian Tan Big Buddha at the Po Lin monastery in Hong Kong to pray and to be blessed with good fortune.

As Buddhism spread throughout Asia from the sixth century onward, its teachers interacted with local cultures, and distinct traditions of Buddhism developed in Korea, Japan, China, Myanmar, and Tibet. Although Buddhism was virtually unknown in the West before the 18th century, globalization brought greater awareness of Buddhist beliefs and practices. Today, Buddhist centers can be found in cities throughout the world. Buddhist practices such as Zen meditation are extremely popular in the West, resonating with the New Age spirituality that we discuss later in the chapter. Buddhism was particularly popular within the hippie culture of the 1960s, and it continues to be popular among celebrities in the West, with well-known converts such as Keanu Reeves, Richard Gere, Steve Jobs, and Kate Hudson.

# 10.3 Modern Society and Secularism

**LG** **10.3** Define secularization, and discuss the main points of evidence for and against the secularization thesis.

Most of the social scientists and philosophers who lived during the 18th and 19th centuries would be shocked to learn that religion still exists today. Arguing that religion was based on ignorance and superstition, they were convinced that it would disappear in a modern world committed to science and reason. Voltaire, the French philosopher, once wrote, "Nothing can be more contrary to religion and the clergy than reason and common sense." Karl Marx viewed religion as a form of ideology, and wrote that "the first requisite for the happiness of the people is the abolition of religion." Sigmund Freud described God as an illusion, which had once been useful as a way to restrain the violent impulses of society, but which would no longer be needed in an age of science. All of these thinkers shared the view that religion was an outmoded form of fictitious knowledge, which would naturally disappear and be replaced by science.

### The Secularization Thesis

In sociology, the argument that religion would become less important in modern society is known as the **secularization thesis**. Secularization does not mean that religion will disappear completely or lose all of its legitimacy, but rather that it will become less influential.

**Secularization thesis** The argument that religion will become less important in modern society.

There are two ways to think about secularization. At the level of the individual, secularization means that religious faith is declining, that people are less likely to attend church, or both (Finke and Stark 1998). In this sense religion will continue to exist in a secularized society, but there will be fewer believers and fewer people attending church services. At a more public or macro level, secularization means that religious leaders and religious organizations have less influence and less authority in public debates about social issues (Chaves 1994). In this version of secularization, we can expect to see less religious language in our schools, fewer religious references made by our political leaders, and fewer religious leaders quoted in our newspapers.

Evidence for secularization is strongest in Western Europe, at least for Christian churches, where levels of religious belief and attendance are much lower than they used to be (Gorski and Altinordu 2008: 62; Bruce and Voas 2023). Nearly three-quarters of Northern Europeans do not even attend church once per month, and the rates of attendance are declining throughout Western Europe (Brenner 2016). Most European nations have a separation of church and state, in the sense that governments are religiously neutral and there is legal protection for people to believe (or not believe) what they want. The highest authority in public policy debates is given to scientists and doctors. Religious content is not prominent in popular culture (Figure 10.3).

In the United States, mainline Protestant churches have been losing members as well as political influence since the 1960s. Between 1965 and 1990, the Presbyterian Church lost about one-third of its members, the Episcopal Church lost about one-quarter, and the Methodist Church lost about 20 percent of its members. Churches throughout the country face

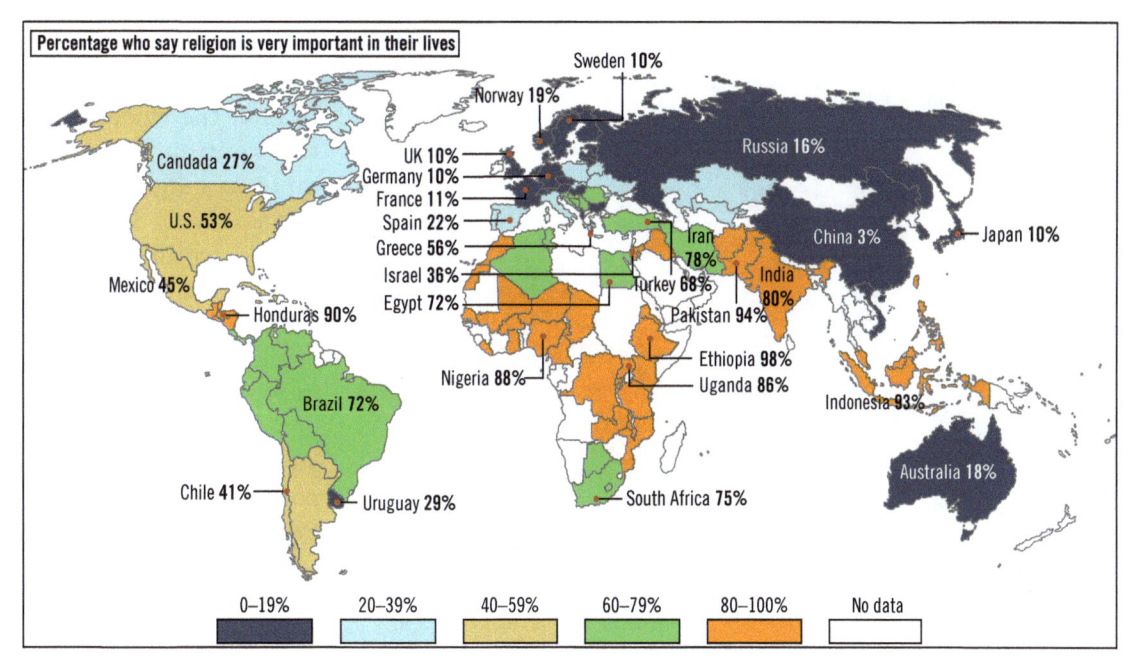

**Figure 10.3 People in Europe and East Asia Say Religion Is Not Very Important to Them.**
Source: Pew Research Center surveys, 2008–2017. "The Age Gap in Religion Around the World."

financial crisis, with declining levels of donations and persistent staff shortages (Wuthnow 1997). The number of Americans who express no religious preference doubled during the 1990s, and continues to rise today (Hout and Fischer 2002; Bruce and Voas 2023).

While the mainline Protestant churches have experienced decline, the United States continues to be much more religious than most of Europe, and many sociologists argue that its history does not provide strong evidence for secularization. Survey research shows that while religiosity is slowly declining in the United States (Chaves 2017), more than 90 percent of Americans believe in God (Fahmy 2018), and around 35 percent continue to attend church weekly (Chaves 2017). Membership in evangelical churches has been on the rise since the 1960s, and conservative evangelical Christians have been a significant political force since the 1980s (Wuthnow 1989). Even among those Americans who express no religious preference, the vast majority maintain strong religious beliefs and consider themselves to be spiritual people (Hout and Fischer 2002; Fahmy 2018). Still, survey research shows that each successive cohort in the US is less religious than the one that preceded it, leading some to argue that the US is a fairly strong case of a nation that is undergoing secularization (Voas and Chaves 2016).

**Pentecostal worship at the Brownsville Assembly, Pensacola, Florida, 2012**
Pentecostalism is a renewal of and innovation in Christianity that emerged in 1910 in Los Angeles. Pentecostalism emphasizes a direct personal experience with the Holy Spirit, which is revealed in gifts of the spirit such as faith healing, prophecy, and speaking in tongues.

## The Persistence of Religion

In fact, the evidence for the continuing importance of religion is very strong. Nearly 85 percent of the world's population maintains a religious affiliation, and 73 percent of the world's population lives in a country where people from their religion are a majority of the population (Pew Research Center 2012). More than a third of all countries have religious political parties, more than a quarter have blasphemy laws that restrict public criticism of the majority religion, more than half provide government funding for religious education; furthermore, these trends toward government support of religion have increased slightly over the last twenty years (Fox 2019). The sociologist Peter Berger, who helped develop the secularization thesis during the 1970s, admitted in 1999 that "the assumption that we live in a secularized world is false" (Berger 1999: 2).

**NEW RELIGIOUS FORMS.** One reason that religion continues to be important in society is because of the creation of new kinds of religious groups. Innovation and change have always been a part of the religious landscape, and such innovation has kept religion an important and relevant social force. In the Catholic Church, a new form of liberation theology developed during the 1950s (particularly in Latin America), with an emphasis on human rights and a criticism of global capitalism's indifference to the poor (Casanova 1994). Within Judaism, the World Union of Progressive Judaism (known in the United States as Reform Judaism) grew rapidly in popularity throughout the 20th century, with an emphasis on inclusiveness and progressive values (Kaplan 2003).

Religious change has also come from new forms of religion, which have developed as a response to modern society and as an attempt to understand it. One of the biggest of these new religious forms is Pentecostalism. First emerging in 1910 in Los Angeles, Pentecostalism emphasizes a direct personal experience with the divine, which is revealed in gifts of the spirit such as faith healing, prophecy, and speaking in tongues. The focus on personal transformation makes Pentecostalism extremely flexible and adaptable to local cultures (Thompson 2012). Today, there are more than 100 million Pentecostals in the world, and there is a large Pentecostal presence throughout South America, Africa, and Asia.

**Yoido Full Gospel Church, South Korea**
This congregation has more than 800,000 members.

Another new religion is the Baha'i faith, which was established in Iran in 1863. An explicitly tolerant and pluralist faith, Baha'is believe that there is a truth and a validity in all religious faiths. Baha'is believe that all religions are trying to describe the same reality, but are limited by the culture and the experiences of their time. They believe that there is no conflict between science and religion, because both are trying to improve the human condition and shed light on the nature of human conduct. Baha'is strive for the abolition of all forms of prejudice, the end of global poverty and inequality, equality between men and women, and a world bound by the principle of justice. These messages have been enthusiastically embraced, and today the Baha'i faith is the second-fastest-growing religion in the world.

The focus on personal experience, pluralism, and tolerance is also shared by New Age spirituality, a type of informal religious practice that has become increasingly common in Western societies. New Age movements became popular during the 1970s, as a generation of people who had grown up during the 1960s sought a form of spirituality that was not connected to established churches (Heelas 1996). These spiritual seekers were open to a wide variety of practices, combining the teachings from Hinduism, Buddhism, Jewish mysticism, neo-paganism, meditation, yoga, and other forms of spiritual practice. Instead of joining an established church, their goal was to find personal fulfillment, an inclusive and welcoming community, and a diverse variety of spiritual practices.

This kind of "quest culture" has influenced religious practices throughout the United States, with a growing emphasis on spiritual exploration and a culture of choice (Possamai 2019). We can see this with the large numbers of people who describe themselves as "spiritual but not religious," the incorporation of yoga and meditation in established churches and synagogues, and even in the creation of lifestyle organizations such as Catholic Surfing Ministries, which organizes "sacramental surfing retreats" at beaches all along the East Coast of the United States.

## Religion and Politics

Religion has always been connected to issues of power, conflict, and politics. The worldwide spread of Christianity was closely connected to the political power of the Roman Empire, and the spread of Islam was linked to the political history of the Ottoman Empire.

As secular governments work to establish a formal separation of church and state, they have sometimes found themselves in open political conflict with religious organizations. The Soviet Union had an official doctrine of state atheism, and had policies in place to control, repress, and ultimately eliminate religion. In China, from 1966 to 1976, government leaders seized the assets of churches, denounced religion as a worthless superstition, and declared that the open practice of religion was illegal. In France, for about five years after the 1789 Revolution, the new government passed anti-church laws, exiled and imprisoned thousands of priests, banned religious holidays, and converted churches to "temples of reason." Even today, the French policy of *laïcité* (secularism) bans the public display of religious symbols.

Religious organizations and adherents have resisted the attempts by secular governments to reduce the power and the visibility of religion. In China as well as the Soviet Union, religious practice continued in secret during the period when repression was strongest, enabling a religious revival to occur as soon as the government became more tolerant. In France, there was widespread resistance

**Religion and Politics**
The French policy of *laïcité* is the core constitutional principle of French democracy, which states that France is a secular republic. France has banned the public display of religious symbols, and politics over wearing a headscarf or burkini (a burka designed as modest swimwear) continue to be contentious.

> **PAIRED CONCEPTS**
> ## Solidarity and Conflict
>
> ### Religious Proselytizing
>
> A central mission of many religious groups is proselytizing, which refers to the attempt by an individual or organization to convert other people to their own religious beliefs. Proselytizing is a significant source of solidarity for religious believers who practice it. Most proselytizing takes place in groups, where religious adherents reaffirm their common identity and their common bond through the collective practice of talking to others and trying to convert them.
>
> Proselytizing has a complicated and ambiguous legal status. On the one hand, laws that protect the freedom of expression would seem to protect proselytizing, since it is a form of speech. Proselytizing is also a central component of many religions, so banning it would seem to violate the 1948 United Nations Declaration of Human Rights, which states that believers must be allowed to publicly manifest their religious beliefs (Danchin 2008).
>
> On the other hand, proselytizing can often seem coercive, threatening, and intrusive to the people being proselytized. When government-supported missionary groups travel abroad, the aid they provide to the poor is often linked to the practice of proselytizing, in a way that can make it seem like material help is connected to religious conversion (Bandarage 2015). In countries where conversion from the official religion is illegal, proselytizers actually put their targets at significant legal and physical risk. In the workplace, proselytizing has led to lawsuits, with courts having to decide whether the religious proselytizing is creating a hostile workplace that should be stopped, or an annoyance that will have to be tolerated (Wolf, Friedman, and Sutherland 1998).
>
> Most laws protecting religious freedom recognize that proselytizing is a sensitive issue, and they have tended to avoid mentioning it explicitly as a protected practice (Danchin 2008: 259). Some courts have tried to distinguish between "proper" and "improper" proselytizing, suggesting that only proper proselytizing needed to be protected; but these courts have not been very clear about how to draw such a distinction (Danchin 2008: 273). There is also a concern about the history and the context in which proselytizing has taken place, particularly in places such as Africa, where proselytizing missionaries were part of the system of colonization by Western powers.
>
> **ACTIVE LEARNING**
>
> **Find out:** Search the internet for a lawsuit in your state about proselytizing (for example, you might search "Massachusetts lawsuit about proselytizing"). Describe the case. What were the main issues? What was the resolution of the case?

to the attempts at de-Christianization during the 1970s (Anderson 2007). Today, the French policy of *laïcité* is very controversial, with many French citizens protesting that the policy is disrespectful to people who have deeply held religious convictions.

**PUBLIC RELIGION.** As the previous discussion makes clear, religion continues to be an important presence in society. While most democratic countries maintain a formal separation between government and religion, religion continues to be a meaningful part of people's lives, and it continues to be a source of influence in political life.

**Public religion** A situation in which individuals and organizations make faith-based moral arguments about the public good.

In his book *Public Religion in the Modern World*, sociologist Jose Casanova argues that most churches are unwilling to limit themselves to the spiritual issues that concern their adherents (Casanova 1994). Instead, they aggressively participate in social and political debates about public issues, affairs, and policies. Casanova refers to this as **public religion**, which happens when individuals and organizations make faith-based moral arguments about the public good.

We can see examples of public religion all over the world. Religious groups have been a major force driving nationalist movements in places as diverse as India, Sri Lanka, Iran, Algeria, Egypt, and Israel (Friedland 2001). In the United States, Christian evangelicals have been an increasingly vocal part of the political scene, with a strong focus on issues surrounding reproduction, sexuality, and the public display of religious symbols (Lienesch 1993). Throughout Europe and North America, religious groups have challenged the "wall of separation" between church and state, arguing that religious perspectives have just as much right to participate in public discussions as scientific or legal ones (Joppke 2015).

**RELIGIOUS FUNDAMENTALISM.** One response to modern society has been the rise of religious fundamentalism, in which religious militants and "true believers" try to create an alternative to secular institutions and behaviors (Kirby 2020). According to sociologists Michael Emerson and David Hartman, the term "fundamentalism" was first used to describe a form of conservative Protestantism that developed in the United States between 1870 and 1925, as part of a conflict with other Protestants who wanted to make the religion more relevant for a modern and progressive society (Emerson and Hartman 2006: 132–33). Today, however, religious fundamentalists are more likely to see themselves in direct conflict with the values and the political institutions of modern, secular society.

Contemporary versions of religious fundamentalism began to emerge during the 1970s, and today there are versions of religious fundamentalism among all of the major world religions (Emerson and Hartman 2006: 128). In the United States, Christian fundamentalists became a powerful political influence during the 1980s, fighting against abortion, homosexuality, and the spread of secular values in popular culture. In India, Hindu fundamentalists have used mob violence and intimidation to attack religious minorities in an effort to create a "pure" Hindu nation. In Iran, Islamic fundamentalists overthrew the secular monarchy in 1979, replacing it with an Islamic

Republic in which Islamic laws are strictly enforced. Fundamentalist groups continue to be a significant presence in countries throughout the world. Jewish fundamentalist groups factor strongly in Israel, and Buddhist fundamentalist groups have been a part of religious conflicts in Thailand, Sri Lanka, and Myanmar.

Religious fundamentalist movements share a number of common features (Almond, Appleby, and Sivan 2003). They believe that their religion is under attack by modern society, and they identify selective features of modern society

**Conflict with secular society**
Pro-life groups protest the US Department of Health and Human Services mandate of 2012 that requires all employers to provide free contraceptives, sterilization, and abortion-inducing drugs through their health plans. Many religious groups argued the mandate was an attack on freedom of conscience and religious liberty.

that they find particularly evil. They emphasize the truth and accuracy of their sacred text, and they insist that the laws of this text have more authority than other national or international laws. They draw sharp boundaries between believers and nonbelievers, and they have strict requirements about how believers should behave. They have strongly conservative views about gender and family, believing that men and women have separate roles to play in society. They are intolerant of dissenting beliefs, and their goal is to have their own religious beliefs placed at the center of public life.

Some fundamentalist groups use violence to dramatize their cause, to announce their presence, and to strike at the symbols of the societies they are trying to overcome. However, the relationship between fundamentalism and violence is complex. While the frequency of religious violence has been increasing, the majority of fundamentalist groups do not use violence (Juergensmeyer 2003). Those that do use violence are more likely to appear in countries that restrict religious freedoms or favor one religion over the others (Iannaccone 1997). They are also more likely to appear in communities that have a lot of poverty, and in countries that fail to provide basic social services (Berman 2009).

## 10.4 Science as a Social Institution

**LG 10.4** Describe how science is socially organized, and how the production of scientific knowledge is shaped by social hierarchies, conflicts, and interpretations.

In 2010, Lawrence Krauss, a physicist from Arizona State University published an article in *Scientific American*, titled "Faith and Foolishness: When Religious Beliefs Become Dangerous" (Krauss 2010). In the article, Krauss complained about the lack of scientific literacy in the United States, observing that the people who are the least willing to accept scientific reality are the same ones who are the most religious. Arguing that "religious leaders should be held accountable when their irrational ideas turn harmful," he warned that an unwillingness to publicly criticize religion will lead to bad public policies and the promotion of ignorance.

Why did Krauss care about the scientific literacy of ordinary people, and why did he think that publicly denouncing religion would lead to better public policies? As we discussed in Chapter 2, the goal of science is to produce knowledge that is factually accurate, falsifiable, and can withstand the critical judgment of the scientific community. The cornerstone of science is the principle of peer review, which means that scientific research needs to be evaluated anonymously by other scientific experts. Scientific advances do not require scientific literacy by the general population, and they definitely do not require the public criticism of religion.

Scientists care about public policy because they are members of society, and they believe that their society will be a better place if policy-makers listen to them. Many scientists realize that religion is an alternative way of knowing the world, and they know that religion has historically provided a

**March for Science**
Thousands of protesters marched in 2017 to protest US federal budget cuts that threaten scientific research.

## CAREERS

### Women's Careers in STEM

Careers in science, technology, engineering, and mathematics (STEM) offer some of the best-paid jobs in today's economy. According to the Bureau of Labor Statistics, the median salary for jobs in STEM occupations is $97,980, compared to $44,670 for jobs in non-STEM occupations. Students who get degrees in a STEM field have a major advantage in the job market too; while nearly half of all entry-level jobs requiring a college degree are in STEM fields, fewer than 30 percent of all college graduates earn a college degree in a STEM field (Burning Glass 2014). Many politicians and experts argue that STEM education is the key to the future of the economy, and hundreds of millions of dollars are being invested in this effort.

Gender inequality continues to be a significant challenge in STEM fields. The disparities are the worst in fields related to engineering and computer science, which are the largest and fastest-growing parts of the STEM sector. Women's employment in STEM fields is heavily overrepresented in the health occupations and underrepresented in physical science, computer, and engineering jobs (Funk et al 2021). Men are almost five times as likely as women to major in physics, engineering, or computer science, and the lowest-achieving men choose to major in these fields at a rate about equal to that of the highest-achieving women (Cimpian et al 2020). Despite the fact that lower-achieving men are more likely than women to major in science and engineering, men with degrees in science and engineering are employed in STEM fields at twice the rate of women (Landivar 2013; Cimpian et al. 2020).

A 2010 research report by the American Association of University Women identified several key factors that are reducing participation by women in STEM fields (Hill, Corbett, and Rose 2010):

- There are still powerful stereotypes suggesting that women are not as good as men at math and science, which leads to an implicit bias against women pursuing these fields. For boys and girls who have the same abilities in math, the boys will consistently rate their own abilities higher than the girls will rate theirs. This has consequences for the courses they choose to take, as well as their behavior and self-confidence in science classes. It also influences the likelihood that they will express an interest in pursuing a STEM career.
- When faced with the stereotype that women are not as good at math, many talented girls respond by reducing their interest in STEM careers. In other words, if girls do not believe that they have the ability to do science or engineering, they will choose a different career, even when all evidence suggests that they have plenty of scientific aptitude.
- The culture of STEM departments in colleges and universities too often privileges men in the recruitment of students, the kind of informal socializing that takes place, and the opportunities for research collaborations with faculty. Women students and faculty often feel excluded in these environments, making it more difficult for them to receive effective mentoring or to succeed.
- The organization of family responsibilities falls more heavily on women, even when they are in STEM careers. This makes many tech companies less likely to recruit women, due to the assumption that they will be less productive workers when they have children.
- There is still rampant sexism in many tech companies. Successful women in the tech sector are perceived as more unlikeable than successful men, and if they try to be more likeable, they often find themselves dealing with unwanted sexual advances (Mundy 2017). They find themselves being dismissed and interrupted constantly, even by male workers who are much lower in the corporate bureaucracy.

To respond effectively to these challenges, social scientists suggest that teachers need to work harder to recognize and counteract stereotypes about gender and math. Schools need to develop aggressive outreach efforts to encourage girls to take STEM

## CAREERS CONTINUED

**Women in STEM**
Women are 48 percent of the total workforce in the United States, but they are only 24 percent of the employees in STEM fields. Evidence suggests that gender stereotypes and discrimination account for this pattern. In recent years, significant efforts have been made to recruit women into STEM fields.

courses. Colleges, universities, and tech companies need to adjust their cultures in a way that makes them more welcoming to women. They need to address issues related to work-life balance, so they do not penalize women unfairly. Workers, social movements, and journalists need to publicize instances of sexism in the tech workforce, and they need to highlight the work of organizations offering better models for promoting gender equity in STEM.

### ACTIVE LEARNING

**Explore:** Project Include is an initiative that was started by women CEOs in the tech sector. It is an advocacy group whose goal is to get more companies to implement gender diversity solutions based on inclusion, accountability, and comprehensiveness. Visit their website (projectinclude.org) and explore some of their activities, recommendations, and company case studies.

---

type of authority that has often been in conflict with science. These are not their only motivations, of course. But it is important to study the social dimensions of science if we want to understand why scientists act the way they do.

## The Sociology of Science

Research in the sociology of science examines how scientists do their work and how science is socially organized. One of the most important scholars in the sociology of science was Robert Merton (1910–2003). Merton was interested in the "extra-scientific elements" that influenced scientific interests, practices, and reward systems (Merton [1942] 1973). To study this, he collected data from the biographies and journals of scientists. He examined publication rates, inventions, the number of scientists in a given field, and the status markers associated with different scientists and scientific organizations. He looked at scientific publications, and tracked how different research problems changed over time.

Scientists work hard to convince the larger public about the virtues of science, and they do this by emphasizing a set of values and expectations about scientific practice. In his famous essay on the normative structure of science, Merton ([1942] 1973) identified four basic values in science. First, scientists are committed to the principle of **universalism**, which means that scientific findings are evaluated according to their objective truth rather than the personal qualities of a particular scientist. It also means that scientists are committed first and foremost to the advancement of science, which they hold to be more important than all other loyalties, including national identity. Second, they believe in the **communal character of science**, which means that they believe in full and open communication of scientific findings. Related to this, scientists are committed to the principle of **disinterestedness**, in the sense that they are supposed to be committed to the pursuit of scientific knowledge itself rather than the pursuit of personal success. Last, scientists are committed to the principle of **organized skepticism**, which means that they are supposed to demand proof of any claim that is made and to test competing explanations, rather than simply believing that one explanation is correct.

The normative structure of science frequently places scientists in conflict with nonscientists (Gieryn 1999). Scientists are suspicious of people in business who try to make money from new scientific technologies, particularly when those businesses make claims about their products that are misleading or not scientifically supported. They criticize people who politicize science, and they criticize politicians who make policy decisions that are not based on scientific principles. Last, scientists are critical of those who believe that religious knowledge is as valuable as science.

**Matthew effect**
A tendency in science in which the most eminent scientists get most of the recognition and rewards for scientific research.

---

### PAIRED CONCEPTS

## Inequality and Privilege

### Science and the Matthew Effect

In the world of scientific research, there is a tendency to reward those scientists who are already powerful and successful. Robert Merton (1968) called this the **Matthew effect,** relying primarily on research by sociologist Harriet Zuckerman (1937–). Merton named his theory after a passage in the Christian Bible from the Gospel of Matthew, which reads, "For whoever has will be given more, and they will have an abundance. Whoever does not have, even what they have will be taken from them." In other words, the rich get richer, and the poor get poorer. Merton argued that this was true in science, just as it was true in other parts of social life.

The Matthew effect in science works in several different ways. Examining the careers of scientists, Zuckerman (1977) found that those scientists who receive early recognition tend to be more productive throughout their careers than those who do not receive early recognition. Scientists who publish a prominent article early in their careers get a better first job, with better resources for them to set up their own research labs. Because they are located at more prestigious universities, they also develop more valuable social networks. They can collaborate with eminent senior colleagues, and they have the assistance of many postdoctoral and graduate student researchers

**PAIRED CONCEPTS CONTINUED**

to help them develop and conduct their research (Ebadi and Schiffauerova 2015). Because they are at more prestigious universities and better-resourced labs, they are more likely to get research grants.

The Matthew effect also influences collaborative research. In collaborative research and co-authored publications, the most eminent scientist in the group will get the most credit for the work (Perc 2014). Credit comes in a number of different forms. The big scientific prizes (such as the Nobel Prize) almost always go to the most eminent scientist in a research team (Zuckerman 1977). This scientist will get the most media coverage, and the most speaking invitations. Other scientists will associate the major findings of the research team disproportionately with the eminent scientist, so that over time the other members of the research team are virtually forgotten.

Historically, the Matthew effect has profoundly suppressed the careers of women scientists. Their contributions have consistently been ignored and denied credit, often disappearing altogether from the history of science (Rossiter 1993). Rossiter calls this the "Matthew Matilda" effect. For example, the biophysicist Rosalind Franklin was consistently denied recognition for her role in discovering the genetic structure of DNA, while her male colleagues James Watson and Francis Crick received all the recognition. Jocelyn Bell discovered pulsars as a graduate student in 1967, but the Nobel Prize for the discovery was awarded to her male supervisor, Anthony Hewish. Even Merton's theory of the Matthew effect was influenced by the Matthew Matilda effect. Despite the fact that Merton consistently credited the key research findings to Harriet Zuckerman, who was a Columbia University sociology professor as well as Merton's wife, the overwhelming credit for the theory of the Matthew effect in science has gone to Robert Merton (Merton 1988).

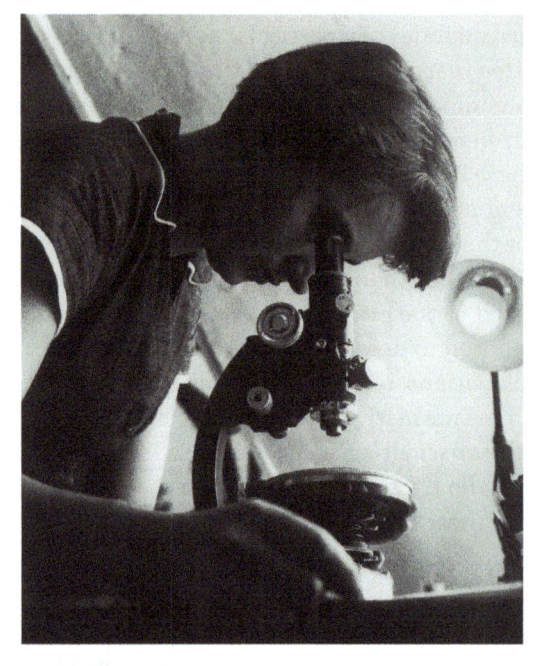

**Scientific recognition**
The biophysicist Rosalind Franklin was consistently denied recognition for her role in discovering the genetic structure of DNA, while her male colleagues James Watson and Francis Crick received all the recognition. This is a common pattern in the history of science.

**ACTIVE LEARNING**

**Find out:** Talk to one of your professors, and ask them if they have had any direct experience with the Matthew effect in their own careers. Do they think the situation is getting better? What do they think could be done to reduce the influence of the Matthew effect in their field?

---

Many social factors shape the practice of science and the organization of scientists. There is an established hierarchy of scientific disciplines, which has been in place for nearly two hundred years. The physical sciences are at the top, the social sciences are at the bottom, and the biological sciences are in the middle (Smith et al. 2000; Fanelli and Glanzell 2013). Scientists in high-status disciplines have more resources at their disposal, including higher salaries, better laboratory spaces, more research grant money and autonomy, and higher levels of authority. This leads to inequalities in the world of science. Like in other areas of social life, scientists who have more resources tend to act in ways that preserve their privileges.

## Science and Technology Studies

The scholarly field of science and technology studies uses the tools of sociological research to ask questions about the production of scientific knowledge. How do scientists come to recognize something as a fact? What styles of writing do they use in their publications? How do they learn to use lab equipment? How do they learn to "clean" their data, eliminating pieces of information that are caused by human or machine error? When they confront data that challenge their hypotheses, how do they learn what is the most effective response? These kinds of questions focus attention on the ways that scientific knowledge is a social accomplishment.

From a sociological point of view, the production of scientific knowledge is shaped in significant ways by the dynamics of solidarity and conflict. The solidarity of scientists is reaffirmed in their choice of specialty topic, their use of specialized jargon, their membership in specific research networks and laboratories, and their choice to publish in specific scientific journals (Shapin 1995: 300–3). Their solidarity is also reaffirmed in their competition with rival research teams, scientific disciplines, and other producers of knowledge whose work they dismiss as "pseudoscience" (Panofsky 2014).

In their book *Laboratory Life: The Construction of Scientific Facts* (1979), sociologists Bruno Latour and Steve Woolgar visited a research laboratory in order to observe how scientific knowledge actually gets created. The scientists they studied wrote about their research in a way that emphasized a surprising moment of discovery, rather than focusing on the research procedures that were a key part of their work. They evaluated other people's research mainly in terms of the "reliability" of the researcher, which they measured by looking more closely at the record of grants and publications than at the research design of their studies. These scientists described their choice of topics in terms of what was likely to be trendy in the near future. They argued that the only way to properly study the substance they were investigating was to use expensive equipment that was available to a very small number of scientific labs. They produced a lot of very significant scientific findings, to be sure. But every part of their work was shaped by social dynamics. The focus on the social dimensions of scientific practice reminds us that scientists are real people, and that "doing science" is a craft that requires both skill and handiwork.

**PAIRED CONCEPTS**

## Structure and Contingency

### The Invention of Velcro

Scientists and engineers do not spend their entire lives in the lab doing research or testing new products. They live in the world, and in their ordinary lives they sometimes stumble onto solutions to problems they had been trying to solve for a long time. Probably the most famous example of this is the discovery of penicillin in 1928, by the Scottish biologist Alexander Fleming. Fleming was experimenting with different treatments for the flu, when he left for a summer vacation with his family. When he returned to his lab after the vacation—having not cleaned it properly—he noticed a fungus surrounding one of the cultures he had left in a petri dish. Upon further analysis of the fungus, he discovered that it killed many different disease-causing bacteria. Fleming was awarded the Nobel Prize in Medicine for his accidental discovery of penicillin.

Sometimes scientists and engineers stumble across discoveries they didn't even know they were looking for. In 1941, an electrical engineer named George de Mestral was taking his dog for a walk on a mountain trail in Switzerland. When he returned home he noticed that his pants and his dog's fur were covered with cockle-burs. Curious about how the burs managed to attach themselves, he put them under a microscope to look more closely. Discovering that the hooks on the burs were attaching themselves to the loops in the fabric of his pants, he realized that there might be practical uses for such a fastening system. Mestral created a synthetic equivalent of the hook-and-loop system, which he patented in 1955 and trademarked with the name Velcro. Initial sales were slow, but they picked up in the 1960s after NASA began using Velcro in the manufacture of its space suits. Sports apparel manufacturers followed, and Velcro soon found its way into dozens of different products, ranging from clothes to automobile parts to medical devices. Today, more than 2.5 million miles of Velcro tape are produced and sold each year.

**Accidental discoveries**
Velcro was invented in the 1940s by scientist George de Mestral. The idea came when he noticed how burrs attached to his dog. The ability to recognize the possibilities and create Velcro came from his training as a scientist and engineer.

"Accidental" discoveries like these are not complete accidents, of course. In the case of penicillin, Alexander Fleming was actively trying to develop medicines to treat disease. Even though the fungus developed because Fleming didn't clean his lab properly, it was only because he was trained as a biologist that he was able to recognize what the mold was doing to the bacteria around it. As for Mestral, his training as an engineer meant that he was always on the lookout for solutions to potential problems, and he had the technical skill to turn his curiosity into real products. In both cases, the accidental discovery was structured by the socialization that comes with being a scientist.

**ACTIVE LEARNING**

**Find out:** Can you identify other important accidental discoveries? How did they get discovered? What social conditions made it more likely that the person who made the discovery would have realized what they had stumbled into?

# 10.5 The Crisis of Knowing, and the Importance of Belief

**LG 10.5** Think about some of the ways that religion and science can coexist in contemporary society.

Because skepticism is central to the scientific worldview, it was probably inevitable that the rise of science would lead to a loss of certainty about how the world works. Science was able to launch a powerful attack on religion, tradition, and other forms of nonscientific knowledge, but those other forms of knowledge still influence people throughout the world. Religious organizations have pushed back against secularization, challenging the idea that scientific knowledge is the only thing that should be respected in public debates about social issues. The sociology of science has shown that scientists work in a realm of power and inequality, in which new entrants struggle to gain recognition for their work. The utopian hopes for science have mostly disappeared, as societies continue to find themselves beset with hunger, poverty, injustice, inequality, pollution, natural disasters, and the effects of modern warfare.

## Epistemological Doubts

**Epistemology** is a branch of philosophy that asks, "How do we know whether a statement or a fact is actually true?" For a scientific epistemology, we know that knowledge about the world is true when it offers a good description, explanation, and prediction of natural reality. Scientists recognize that the knowledge they produce is subject to revision. New facts emerge, new technologies allow us to see things we could not see before, and new experiments help us test competing explanations to see which one is actually correct. The scientist approaches each new piece of evidence with skepticism. But she also believes that, over time, science will yield progressively better knowledge about the world.

Not everyone believes in the superiority of scientific knowledge. Politicians, policy-makers, and businesspeople often criticize scientists for spending too much time in the lab and not enough time in the "real world." The result, they argue, is that science is not able to offer practical solutions for the problems people face. Religious conservatives argue that scientists do not respect people of faith. Using social media to publicize cases where scientists falsify data and act inappropriately,

**Epistemology** A branch of philosophy that explores how we know whether a statement or a fact is actually true.

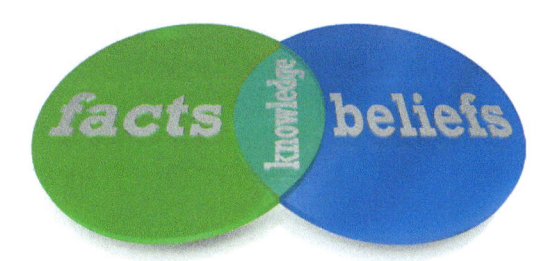

**Knowledge and belief**
The skeptical attitude of science can undermine certainty about what we know. For knowledge to exist, however, belief is an important element. Scientists believe in scientific methods for reaching truth. All ways of knowing, including scientific ones, contain elements of belief.

some people try to discredit the credibility of the scientific enterprise. Many scientists feel themselves to be under attack.

As scientific knowledge continues to be challenged by other forms of expertise, it becomes more difficult to be certain about what we believe to be true. People are more aware than ever that not everyone shares their epistemology, and this is true whether they believe in science, religion, common sense, or some other form of knowledge. Philosophers and other intellectuals argue that relativism is one of the biggest challenges facing the modern world. **Relativism** means that truth depends on the group, the community, the society, and the culture to which a person belongs. Ideas about universal truths that are the same everywhere and for everyone are less persuasive than they used to be (Stenmark 2015). But people are often unsatisfied with an epistemology of relativism, because relativism makes it extremely difficult to distinguish between good and bad.

**Relativism** The idea that truth depends on the group, the community, the society, and the culture to which a person belongs.

## Can Science and Religion Coexist?

As we saw at the beginning of this chapter, with the discussion of the Yale Program on Climate Change Communication, scientists and religious leaders are beginning to think about how they can coexist and cooperate to try to solve important social problems.

In recent years, some of the world's leading philosophers have begun to develop a theory of a **post-secular society**, in which religious ideas and scientific ideas need to learn from each other (Habermas 2008; Taylor 2007). They argue that the continued existence of religion does not have to be a threat to a secularizing society, and that the two can coexist more harmoniously if scientists stop attacking religious epistemologies. They argue that a modern society based on tolerance has to be more tolerant of religion. In fact, despite the presence of some scientists who continue to publicly criticize religion, sociological research shows that the majority of scientists believe that science and religion operate in separate spheres, and are not in conflict with each other (Ecklund et al. 2016).

**Post-secular society** A society in which religion and science coexist harmoniously, and where there is an attempt to create mutual learning and respect between religious ideas and scientific ideas.

Theories of post-secularism argue that secular belief systems and scientific epistemologies have a lot to learn from religion. Religious writings have long focused on moral questions about how to live a good life or how to be a good person (Habermas 2008). Religion provides a "sense of fullness" and a commitment to a higher purpose that can motivate people to contribute to the common good, and this remains true in today's secular and scientific age (Taylor 2007). For many people, a belief in a higher power reduces anxiety and improves psychological well-being. Belief encourages people to act less selfishly toward others, and to remain engaged in the world. Many of the most important social movement leaders of the 20th century were religious, and there is good evidence that this continues to be the case today (Smith 1996).

At the same time, theories of post-secularism point out that a peaceful coexistence between science and religion requires that religious people also make accommodations. First, they need to embrace an attitude of tolerance toward religious and scientific ideas that are different from their own religious beliefs. Second, they need to accept the authority of their society's laws, even when those laws are different from tenets of their religious faith. Finally, they need to accept the reality that scientific knowledge has tremendous authority in modern society, and that scientists will play a crucial role in designing public policies. In fact, sociological research shows that religious people are just as likely as nonreligious people to seek out scientific knowledge and to accept its legitimacy, unless religion and science are making directly contradictory claims, or they are suspicious of scientists' moral agenda about a particular issue (Evans 2011).

**The coexistence of science and religion**
In post-secular society, theorists argue that science and religion should try to learn from each other. Science must be more tolerant of religious belief, which offers resources for moral learning and moral decision-making. Religion must embrace an attitude of tolerance toward science and scientific change and also accept the validity of law.

## CASE STUDY

### Debating Evolution in Public Schools

One of the most famous trials in American history was a 1925 case, *The State of Tennessee v. John Thomas Scopes*. Commonly referred to as the "Scopes Monkey Trial," the case involved a high school teacher who had violated the Butler Act, a Tennessee law that made it illegal to teach evolution in a public school. The trial received national publicity, both because the two sides were represented by high-profile attorneys and because it involved a highly charged conflict between science and religion. It was also the first US trial to be broadcast live over the radio.

One of the most unusual parts of the trial happened when the defense attorney (Clarence Darrow) called the prosecuting attorney (William Jennings Bryan) to the stand, in order to question him about whether the Bible should be interpreted literally, and whether it was reasonable to use the Bible to teach science. Bryan complained that the questions were intended "to cast ridicule on everybody who believes in the Bible"; Darrow responded that his purpose was "preventing bigots and ignoramuses from controlling the education

### CASE STUDY CONTINUED

of the United States." After two hours of this, the judge in the trial declared that the entire cross-examination was irrelevant to the case and should be removed from the official trial record. Scopes was found guilty, and the ruling was reaffirmed when it was appealed to the Tennessee Supreme Court.

Political, cultural, and legal opinions became much more supportive of teaching evolution during the 1960s. Congress passed the National Defense Education Act in 1958, which increased funding for science education and led to the creation of new textbooks that included evolution. Tennessee repealed the Butler Law in 1967. In 1968, the US Supreme Court ruled that bans against teaching evolution were unconstitutional, because they violated the Establishment Clause of the First Amendment.

The origin of the Scopes Monkey Trial can be traced to the *power* of the church in Tennessee. The law against teaching evolution was sponsored by John Butler, who was a farmer, an elected politician, and the head of an influential religious organization called the World Christian Fundamentals Association. This law met immediate *resistance* from the American Civil Liberties Union (ACLU), which offered to defend any teacher in Tennessee who was willing to defy the Butler Act. This resistance was ineffective in the short term, as Scopes lost his legal case. But it proved to be effective in the long term,

The *conflict* between creationists and evolutionists created strong feelings of *solidarity* on both sides of the dispute. Five years after the Scopes trial, Christian organizations founded William Jennings Bryan University (known today as Bryan College) in Dayton, Tennessee, the town where the trial had taken place. The stated purpose of the college was to create a community of Christian learning, which provided "for the higher education of men and women under auspices distinctly Christian and spiritual." Secular and scientific groups also used the trial to create solidarity. The ACLU used the case to encourage more people to join their organization. The scientific community recognized the conflict as an opportunity to make millions of Americans aware of the scientific worldview. Even today, when the legal questions would seem to have been settled, the conflict over teaching evolution is a rallying call and a major source of fundraising. Religious groups continue to organize against teaching evolution, developing new legal challenges that will allow other theories to be taught alongside it.

The Scopes Monkey Trial was also shaped by the social organization of *inequality* and *privilege*. Dayton, Tennessee, was a small town of fewer than two thousand people in the 1920s. While the town had once had a relatively successful mining operation, by the 1920s its economy was in decline due to mining accidents and declining market prices for iron ore. In fact, the trial was in many ways a publicity stunt. Scopes was actually recruited by a group of local businessmen, who were convinced that the trial would bring tourism revenue into the town. Even today, the Scopes Trial Museum is the most popular attraction in Dayton, and the Scopes Trial Festival is the biggest tourism weekend of the year. As a small and poor town, though, Dayton could not control what people from more privileged backgrounds thought of them. When the famous Baltimore journalist H. L. Mencken wrote about the trial, he called the city of Dayton "Monkeytown." Describing the townsfolk as morons,

**The Scopes Trial of 1925**
William Jennings Bryan interrogated by Clarence Darrow (standing right). Proceedings of the Scopes Monkey Trial were held outside due to the extreme heat of July 20, 1925. Photo by Watson Davis.

hillbillies, and ignoramuses, Mencken criticized the trial as "a universal joke." The 1960 movie of the trial, *Inherit the Wind*, portrayed the people of Dayton as dangerous religious fanatics.

While the trial was intended to challenge a *local* law and to boost the local economy, it became a *global* media event. More than 150 journalists came to Dayton to cover the trial, traveling from places as far away as Hong Kong and London. Mencken's coverage of the trial was published in newspapers around the country, and the Chicago radio station WGN broadcast the trial live. More than 150,000 words were sent out about the trial every day via telegraph to journalists and writers around the world.

The different people who cooperated to bring about the Scopes trial were correct that the *structure* of the event would bring a lot of publicity.

The attorneys were well-known celebrities who attracted a lot of media attention, and the ACLU was very skilled at creating the kind of publicity that would attract the attention of journalists around the world. But they could not contain the event. As people descended upon Dayton to participate in the media spectacle, the *contingency* of the event turned it into a carnival. A circus owner brought his trained monkey to the trial every day. Dressed in a suit and top hat, the monkey played a miniature piano outside the courthouse and posed for photographs with tourists. Bible salesmen roamed the streets, as did vendors selling stuffed monkeys, street performers, and ministers preaching against the evil of ice cream and coffee. *Time* magazine described the scene as a "fantastic cross between a circus and a holy war" (Moore and McComas 2016: 63).

# LEARNING GOALS REVISITED

**10.1 Describe the main differences between religious and scientific cosmologies.**

- Religious cosmologies describe the world by making reference to mysterious, magical, and incalculable forces.
- Religious cosmologies include a moral component, in which they provide a framework to help people distinguish between right and wrong.
- Religious cosmologies provide their adherents with a theory about the meaning of human life that is grounded in belief, faith, and sacrifice.
- Scientific cosmologies are based on evidence, where the goal is to produce reliable knowledge about the world.
- Scientific cosmologies are based on the belief that people can create a better society if they cast aside older forms of knowledge and replace them with science.

**10.2 Describe how religion and science are organized as social institutions.**

- Religion is a unified system of beliefs and practices related to sacred things, which unites all of its adherents into a single moral community.

- As a social institution, religion has three elements: (1) the division of the world into groups of sacred and profane things; (2) a set of rituals, where people come together to reaffirm the meaning of the sacred; and (3) an explanation and a response to the existence of suffering in the world.

- As a social institution, science is committed to a set of values and expectations about good scientific practice. These values include universalism, the communal character of science, disinterestedness, and organized skepticism. Scientists are often critical of people in society who do not follow these values.

- Science is organized in a hierarchical way. Some scientific fields have higher status than others. Eminent scientists get most of the rewards and recognition. This creates a system of inequality and privilege within the world of science.

- The five major world religions are Judaism, Christianity, Islam, Hinduism, and Buddhism.

- Seventy percent of people in the world are affiliated with Christianity, Islam, or Hinduism. For Christians, Muslims, and Hindus, there is a strong tendency to live in a place where they are in the majority; for other groups, there is a stronger likelihood that they will live in places where they are religious minorities.

- Religion has always been connected to issues of power, conflict, and politics. The worldwide spread of Christianity was closely connected to the political power of the Roman Empire, and the spread of Islam was linked to the political history of the Ottoman Empire.

**10.3** Define secularization, and discuss the main points of evidence for and against the secularization thesis.

- Secularization refers to the idea that religion will become less important in modern society.

- Evidence for secularization is strongest in Western Europe, where levels of religious belief and church attendance are much lower than they used to be and are still declining. The vast majority of European students attend secular schools, and most European nations have legal protection for people to believe (or not believe) what they want.

- The evidence for the continuing importance of religion is very strong in most of the world. Nearly 85 percent of the world's population maintains a religious affiliation, 22 percent of the countries of the world still had an official state religion, and an additional 20 percent of the countries gave preferential treatment to one religion in 2015 (Pew 2017). Individuals and religious groups continue to make faith-based moral arguments about the public good. Religious fundamentalism continues to be a significant social force.

**10.4 Describe how science is socially organized, and how the production of scientific knowledge is shaped by social hierarchies, conflicts, and interpretations.**

- The scientific community is held together by a commitment to four key values: universalism, full and open communication of scientific findings, disinterestedness, and organized skepticism. These value commitments often place scientists in conflict with business, politics, and religion.

- There is an established hierarchy of scientific disciplines, with physical sciences at the top, the social sciences are at the bottom, and the biological sciences are in the middle. Disciplines at the top of the hierarchy have more status and more material resources.

- Science is organized so that the most eminent scientists receive a disproportionate amount of the credit and reward for scientific findings. This reproduces existing inequalities, particularly gender inequalities.

- The solidarity of scientists is reaffirmed in their choice of specialty topic, their use of specialized jargon, their membership in specific research networks and laboratories, and their choice to publish in specific scientific journals. Their solidarity is also reaffirmed in their competition with rival research teams and other scientific disciplines.

- Scientists often evaluate other people's research mainly in terms of the "reliability" of the researcher, which they measured by looking more closely at the record of grants and publications rather than just looking at the research design of their studies.

**10.5 Think about some of the ways that religion and science can coexist in contemporary society.**

- Theories of post-secularism argue that the continued existence of religion does not have to be a threat to a secularizing society, and that the two can coexist more harmoniously if scientists stop attacking religious epistemologies.

- Theories of post-secularism also point to changes that religious groups and organizations have to make. They argue that religious people need to be tolerant toward religious ideas and scientific ideas that are different from their own religious beliefs. They need to accept the reality that scientific knowledge has tremendous authority in modern society, and that scientists will play a crucial role in designing public policies. And they need to accept the authority of their society's laws, even when those laws are different from tenets of their religious faith.

## Key Terms

Cosmology 331
Denomination 344
Epistemology 363
Matthew effect 359
Monotheism 332
Polytheism 332
Post-secular society 364
Proselytizing 346
Public religion 354
Relativism 364
Religion 338
Ritual 339
Sect 343
Secularization thesis 348
Theodicy 339
Utopia 335

## Review Questions

1. What are the main differences between religious and scientific cosmologies?
2. Describe the main features of religious institutions.
3. Why is Judaism considered to be one of the world's major religions?
4. What was the Protestant Reformation, and how did it influence the history of Christianity?
5. What is the secularization thesis? Describe the evidence for and against the secularization thesis.
6. What are some of the ways that religious groups have come into conflict with modern, secular governments?
7. What is religious fundamentalism, and why has it spread since the 1970s?
8. What are the four basic values and ideals of science? How does the normative structure of science put scientists into conflict with other groups in society?
9. How is the production of scientific knowledge shaped by the dynamics of solidarity and conflict?
10. How did the rise of a scientific worldview help create greater epistemological doubt?
11. What kinds of changes would scientific and religious organizations need to make if they wanted to create a post-secular society?

## Explore

**RECOMMENDED READINGS**

Berger, Peter. 1967. *The Sacred Canopy: Elements of a Sociological Theory of Religion*. New York: Penguin.

Calhoun, Craig, ed. 2011. *Robert K. Merton: Sociology of Science and Sociology as Science*. New York: Columbia University Press.

Casanova, Jose. 1994. *Public Religions in the Modern World*. Chicago: University of Chicago Press.

Khosrokhavar, Farhad. 2008. *Inside Jihadism*. New York: Routledge.

Latour, Bruno, and Steve Woolgar. 1986. *Laboratory Life: The Construction of Scientific Fact*. Princeton, NJ: Princeton University Press.

Smith, James. 2014. *How (Not) to Be Secular: Reading Charles Taylor*. Grand Rapids, MI: Eerdmans.

## ACTIVITIES

- *Use your sociological imagination*: In her book *The Politics of Consolation*, sociologist Christina Simko argues that one of the key roles of American political leaders is to provide consolation after major national tragedies (Simko 2011). Look at the statements of political leaders after a recent national tragedy. Are their statements religious in nature, or are they based on a nonreligious type of theodicy?

- *Media+Data literacy*: Choose three television shows that have characters who are scientists or church leaders and compare how they are represented.

- *Discuss*: Do you think science and religion are becoming more or less accepting of each other? What is the evidence for your position?

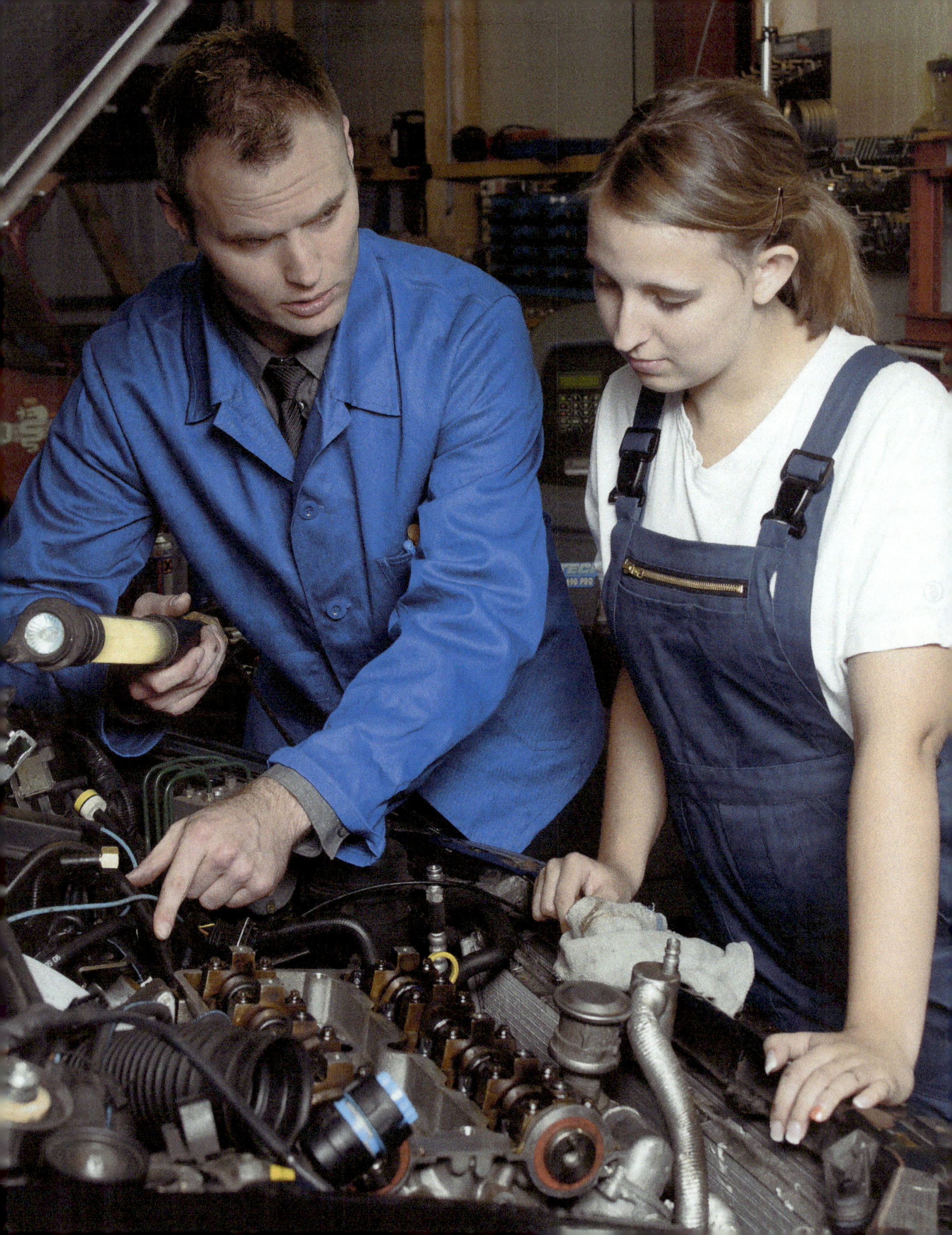

# 11

# Education, Work, and Recreation

Before the 1980s, internships for college students were unusual. Plumbers, electricians, and others beginning a career in the skilled trades would often start out as apprentices, working with an experienced tradesperson until they had enough hands-on experience to be licensed. People who wanted to become doctors would complete a residency after completing medical school, where they worked under the supervision of an attending physician until they had enough experience to get an unrestricted license to practice medicine. But for nearly every other profession, the expectation was that if a new employee needed to learn additional skills, they would learn them on the job.

Internships emerged on a widespread basis in business schools in the 1980s. They were initially developed as a recruiting tool for students who intended to enter the finance, entertainment, and health care industries (Spradlin 2009). Internships helped students build relationships with potential employers and get work experience in their desired field. It was a good deal for both sides. Employers got free (or nearly-free) entry-level work from ambitious and motivated university students, and they also got a head start toward recruiting the most promising graduates. Students earned college credit toward their degree, while building networks and developing relationships with potential employers.

### Chapter Outline

**11.1 WHAT IS EDUCATION FOR? 375**

Literacy, Socialization, Citizenship, and Job Training 375
Social Sorting, Social Reproduction, and Social Mobility 380
Childcare and Employment 381

**11.2 GOING TO SCHOOL 382**

Types of Schools 382
Teaching, Learning, and Assessment 387
Making Friends and Building Networks 394

**11.3 WORK, JOBS, AND SATISFACTION 398**

Power, Privilege, and Inequality in the Workplace 399
The Sociology of Job Satisfaction 400

**CASE STUDY: WHAT KIND OF EDUCATION DO PEOPLE NEED IN TODAY'S ECONOMY? 407**

**Hands-on learning**
Direct experience is a useful form of learning. It is organized in paid apprenticeships, training academies, and internships.

Internships proved to be very popular with students, and they spread quickly to other academic departments. By 2010, the general consensus among students and employers was that internships were one of the most important things a person could do to land a job in her chosen field. In the US, a recent study found that about 57 percent of all internships were converted to full-time positions (NACE 2023). Increasing numbers of employers are now offering internships for first-year undergraduate students. Nearly half of all employers surveyed warn that college graduates with no work experience would have "little or no chance" of getting a job (High Fliers Research Limited 2016: 26).

## LEARNING GOALS

**11.1** Describe the different social purposes and social effects of education.

**11.2** Describe the experience of going to school, and how it has changed over time.

**11.3** Think about the kinds of characteristics that are associated with "good jobs," and describe how the distribution of good jobs is socially structured.

Although internships are now considered a virtual requirement for getting a good job in most industries, they are not without controversy. Critics observe that too many internships are exploitative. While interns often work for little or no money in return for the promise of gaining direct work experience, they can also find themselves getting coffee, filing papers, and doing other menial tasks (Perlin 2012). Unpaid internships benefit wealthier students who do not need an income. Others complain that internships do not have a close enough connection to the larger educational mission of the university. Many colleges and universities are responding to these criticisms by establishing endowments to provide financial support for students in internships, and by creating courses that link the internship experience to the academic curriculum.

This chapter explores the relationship between education and work. We begin by examining the different functions that education is supposed to perform. Next, we examine how schools are organized, and what the experience of going to school looks like. From there, we turn to the complementary worlds of work and recreation. We end with a discussion of job satisfaction, identifying which features of work are most strongly associated with overall life fulfillment and well-being.

# 11.1 What Is Education For?

**LG 11.1** Describe the different social purposes and social effects of education.

In Germany, formal schooling begins at six years old. Between the ages of six and 10, most children attend a public elementary school in their neighborhood. At age 10, most German students and their parents choose between three different types of secondary schools: the *Gymnasium*, for students who plan to go to college; the *Realschule*, which ends in grade 10 and gives students the option to either go on to a *Gymnasium* (depending on exam results) or a vocational apprenticeship; or the *Hauptschule*, which also ends in grade nine or 10, and has a more vocational focus. All German schools require students to learn at least one foreign language.

Germany is unusual for how early it segregates students into university and vocational tracks, and it has been criticized for reproducing privilege and inequality by introducing these tracks so early in students' lives. In 2000 the results from the first global comparison of educational performance showed that Germany had the worst inequality in its educational performance among all developed nations, although it has dramatically reduced educational inequality since then (Berwick 2015; Davoli and Entorf 2018). But Germany has also received praise for its vocational training, which combines practical school training with apprenticeships in the private as well as the public sector. Culturally, German schools reinforce the respectability of the skilled trades and other manual labor. Germany has the lowest youth unemployment in the European Union. And for those students who are admitted to a public German university, there are no tuition fees.

**Literacy** The ability to read, write, communicate, and use other skills that allow people to participate fully in their society.

## Literacy, Socialization, Citizenship, and Job Training

As the discussion of Germany demonstrates, educational systems do many different things, and they pursue a variety of different goals. One goal for education is to promote **literacy**, which

**Students at work in a vocational school in Ulm, Germany**
Germany tracks students from age 10 into pathways to vocations in the trades or into university education.

**Citizenship education** Curriculum dealing with history, laws, social institutions, and political organization of the nation in which students live.

**Job training** The process of schools teaching students specific skills that will help them enter the workforce and earn a decent wage.

refers to the ability to read, write, and communicate well enough to participate fully in society. A second goal is to promote socialization (Chapter 5). A third goal is **citizenship education**, which involves learning about the history, laws, social institutions, and political organization of the nation. Finally, **job training**, in which schools teach students specific skills that will help them enter the workforce and earn a decent wage, is a goal of many educational systems.

**MASS EDUCATION AND THE QUEST FOR LITERACY.** Formal education used to be limited to children of the most privileged families. The first mass education systems developed in Western Europe and the United States during the 19th century (Soysal and Strang 1989), and soon emerged throughout the world as part of the larger spread of nation-states (Bendix 1964). Today, approximately 87 percent of the children in the world go to school, and free elementary education is described as a basic human right by the United Nations (Meyer, Ramirez, and Soysal 1992; UNICEF 2022).

According to the sociologists John Boli, Francisco Ramirez, and John Meyer, mass education has three basic features (Boli, Ramirez, and Meyer 1985). First, mass education is intended to be universal and standardized. This means that it should be available to everyone, and that students should be learning similar things and going to schools that are broadly similar. Second, mass education is strongly institutionalized, in the sense that schools around the world are organized in a strikingly similar and homogeneous way. And third, mass education is focused on the individual: each student is evaluated and expected to achieve a certain minimum level of proficiency in key literacy skills.

Despite its shortcomings, mass education has produced dramatic results. Only 12 percent of the world's population was literate in 1800, and only 21 percent was literate in 1900; by 2000, however, nearly 82 percent of the world's population had achieved literacy, and today the global literacy rate is 86 percent for

**Children in a school classroom in Kenya**
Mass literacy and education are policy goals in much of the world.

people aged 15 and older (Roser and Ortiz-Ospina 2018). There are still significant inequalities, which we discuss later in the chapter. But mass education has played a critical role in the socialization of children, helping them participate in their national societies as well as the larger global economy.

**THE HIDDEN CURRICULUM.** As we discussed in Chapter 5, schools are an important agent of socialization. Émile Durkheim argued that one of the central functions of school was **moral education**. Durkheim emphasized three areas where schools prepared their students to be effective members of society: they encourage a spirit of discipline, they help create attachments to social groups, and they reinforce the values of self-determination and autonomy (Durkheim 1961). Talcott Parsons extended Durkheim's argument, writing that the school classroom is "an agency of socialization" (Parsons 1959: 297). According to Parsons, the classroom reinforces a commitment to a society's core values. It teaches students about citizenship, and what it means to be a good member of their society. It gets them to recognize that they are being evaluated in comparison to their classmates. And, on the basis of these evaluations, it encourages them to start thinking about the kinds of roles they will play in society when they are adults. Citizenship education, character education, and service learning programs are common features in schools today (Lin 2015).

**Moral education**
A form of education where students learn social skills, the values of self-determination and autonomy, and how to attach to social groups.

While Parsons and Durkheim emphasized the positive function of school socialization, others have emphasized how this socialization is connected to a "hidden curriculum" that reinforces power, privilege, and inequality. In his book *Life in Classrooms*, Philip W. Jackson (1968) argued that the classroom forces students to develop strategies for dealing with crowds and social distractions. It reminds them on a daily basis that there is an unequal power relationship between teachers and students, and it forces them to choose a side: Will they obey their teachers, or will they join other rebellious students to resist the power of school authorities? Rebellious students (who often come from more disadvantaged backgrounds) are often more popular and enjoy high status within the school, but bad grades and other negative evaluations limit their life chances as adults and reinforce their inequality (Willis 1977). The hidden curriculum of a school tends to naturalize a model of an implied or an ideal student, who tends to be young, living away from home, and economically supported by parents (Stevens 2007). Students who don't meet these assumptions are often made to feel like unwelcome strangers (Koutsouros et al. 2021).

**TEACHING PRACTICAL SKILLS FOR THE WORKFORCE.** With the rise of mass education, schools took on a larger share of the responsibility for preparing people for the workforce. In *The Wealth of Nations* (1776), Adam

Smith recognized the economic utility of the basic literacy taught in schools of the time, but today most jobs require more advanced literacy skills such as computer use, the ability to work collaboratively, and the ability to find and evaluate information.

Different kinds of schools teach students specific skills that are relevant to the workplace. The objective of vocational schools is to train students to enter the skilled trades. Vocational schools work closely with employers, establishing apprenticeship systems so that students can gain real-world experience and make connections with potential future employers. Graduate programs in professional fields such as law and medicine teach specific skills and knowledge, prepare students for their professional licensing exams, and facilitate connections with potential employers in hospitals and law firms. Last, the increasing expectations of many workplaces that college graduates will have completed at least one internship means that many contemporary students expect to learn practical work-related skills in their formal education.

There are disagreements about the importance of practical skills for education, as well as the preparation level of students when they enter the workforce. Employers believe that the most effective job candidates have a broad-based liberal arts education as well as a specific set of job-related skills, but they feel that colleges and universities need to place more emphasis on applied learning that takes place in real-world settings. Fewer than half of employers in a recent survey believed that college graduates were adequately prepared for the workforce, and fewer than 40 percent of employers believed that college graduates had developed the ability to use their knowledge and skills to solve real-world problems (Finley 2021).

Many educators disagree with the argument that a school's most important mission is to help their students get a job. They argue instead that the mission of a school is "to encourage students to lead

**University lecture hall**
Employer surveys report that the most effective job candidates have a broad-based liberal arts education as well as a specific set of job-related skills, but they feel that colleges and universities need to put more emphasis on applied learning that takes place in real-world settings. What do you think?

meaningful and thoughtful lives, to be informed and engaged citizens of the world, and to have a curiosity and a zest for learning that will help them to flourish throughout their lives" (Krislov 2013). They argue that the economy is moving so quickly that a narrow focus on a specific job skill is likely to produce workers whose skills are out of date almost as soon as they begin their jobs. The more effective approach, they argue, is to teach people how to become lifelong learners, who are flexible and creative in their orientation to the world.

**CREDENTIALISM.** **Credentialism** refers to a process in which formal educational qualifications are used to determine who is eligible to work in a given occupation. As Max Weber argued, credentialism is one of the most important social forces that shapes the modern stratification system. He further observed that college diplomas were being used as a credential to determine who was eligible for good management jobs in bureaucratic organizations. Credentialism is efficient for employers, because it reduces the number of applications they need to read carefully. But it also tends to reinforce privilege and inequality, because people who come from a more privileged background are more likely to pursue advanced educational credentials.

**An unfair playing field?**
Some wealthy parents go to extreme lengths to assure their children's education. This became clear in the 2019 college admissions scandal where actress Lori Loughlin (right) was revealed to have bribed college admissions officials at the University of Southern California to falsify her daughter's (left) application for admission.

Credentialism almost inevitably leads to credential inflation, in which there is a gradual and continual increase in the educational qualifications needed to get a specific job. As the sociologist Randall Collins has argued, credential inflation is a process that feeds on itself, almost guaranteeing that the educational requirements needed to get a job today will not be good enough to get the same job in the future (Collins 2011). While an undergraduate college degree was enough to get a management job in the 1940s and 1950s, today the same job usually requires a graduate degree. Collins further observes that "educational expansion and credential inflation could go on endlessly, until janitors need PhDs, and household workers and babysitters will be required to hold advanced degrees in household appliances and childcare" (2011: 235). The problem is that the costs for credential inflation are borne by students and their families, who have to spend more and more money on their education. They also have to delay

**Credentialism** A process in which formal educational qualifications are used to determine who is eligible to work in a given occupation.

their entry into the labor force, with each new educational qualification taking several years to complete. And while children from wealthy families often do not need to take out loans to cover tuition or living expenses, they may still feel intense social pressure to attend a prestigious college even if they are not interested in further education. Unfortunately, recent scandals have demonstrated the willingness of some wealthy parents to game the college-admissions system on behalf of their underqualified or uninterested children.

## Social Sorting, Social Reproduction, and Social Mobility

The advantages of privilege assert themselves well before students get to college. Wealthy families can afford to send their children to schools that have more resources, more highly trained teachers, smaller classes, and better social networks that help their students get into better colleges and more prestigious (and higher-paying) jobs. They can afford to hire private tutors to make sure that their children don't fall behind. And they are quick to step in and intervene with teachers, in order to make sure that their children succeed (Chapter 5).

Schools also reinforce privilege and inequality by rewarding students who have the right kind of **cultural capital**. As we discussed in Chapter 4, cultural capital refers to the knowledge and consumption of culturally valued things. Being polite, knowing the right kinds of clothes to wear, or displaying an interest in and knowledge of art and high culture are all forms of cultural capital. Teachers tend to interpret these displays as evidence that a student is smart, curious, and precocious. They shower these students with attention, praise, and good grades. These students believe that their good grades were the result of their hard work and intellectual talents, but they fail to see how their academic success is also connected to their social and cultural privileges (Bourdieu and Passeron 1990).

There is strong evidence that education reinforces social privileges and inequalities. Children whose parents have more prestigious jobs, higher levels of education and income, and more wealth are significantly more likely to have higher levels of educational achievement (Breen and Jonsson 2005; Conley 2001; Mare 1981). As inequality gets worse, so does the difference in educational achievement between high-income and low-income families (Mayer 2001). This is particularly true at the highest levels of education, where family resources are strongly associated with college enrollment (Morgan and Kim 2006). In fact, at the most prestigious universities in the United States, nearly three-quarters of the students come from families in the highest socioeconomic quartile (Haveman and Smeeding 2006).

**Cultural capital**
Education, cultural knowledge, and cultural consumption that signals privilege to others; the knowledge and consumption of culturally valued things. Higher levels of cultural capital are associated with success in school.

The relationship between education and privilege is deeply concerning, because getting a college degree is the best route to achieving social mobility. A child born into a family in the lowest income quintile has about a 40 percent chance of staying at that income level as an adult; if she completes college, however, she has more than an 80 percent chance of improving her socioeconomic standing, and nearly a 50 percent chance of entering the middle class (Reeves 2014).

**The importance of college education**
Children and teenagers at this college job fair in 2016 receive career counseling and information about what education is required for different careers.

And these improvements are likely to last for generations, because children whose parents have a college degree are much more likely to complete college themselves. Improving access to college is a major public policy goal, as we discuss later in the chapter.

## Childcare and Employment

Schools also serve purposes that may seem to have little to do with education. Social scientists have long argued that education helps keep the unemployment rate artificially low. When the job market is difficult, there is a higher likelihood that people will enroll in college or community college. This is the **warehousing theory** of education, which states that postsecondary education acts as a holding place that protects people from unstable labor market conditions (Bozick 2009).

**Warehousing theory** A theory that focuses on the ways that postsecondary education acts as a holding place that protects people from unstable labor market conditions.

Schools are also a major source of employment. In the United States, there are more than 5.6 million full-time teachers working in elementary schools, high schools, colleges, and universities (NCES 2023). Schools employ just as many people in administration, clerical support, janitorial services, buildings and grounds maintenance, counseling and career services, and other non-teaching positions. In many communities, in fact, the schools are some of the biggest and most stable employers.

Finally, schools offer childcare for working parents, by giving their children a place to be during the workday. Childcare is one of the most

**Employment in education**
Educational institutions, like this one, employ five million teachers in the United States. They also employ custodians, counselors, secretaries, and other support staff. In some communities schools are the largest employers.

expensive household costs for working parents. On average, families with young children and working mothers spend more than 20 percent of the mother's income on childcare costs, and the proportion is even higher for low-income families (Glynn, Farrell, and Wu 2013). The cost for full-time infant daycare is often more expensive than a year of college tuition. These financial costs fall particularly hard on working mothers; in fact, research shows that as childcare costs increase, the odds of being in the workforce decreases for women with children (Landivar et al. 2021). For these reasons, it is a significant economic benefit for working parents when their children reach school age. Many schools also offer extended hours that more closely match parents' working schedules.

## 11.2 Going to School

**LG 11.2** Describe the experience of going to school, and how it has changed over time.

Going to school is a common experience throughout the world. Still, even though more than 90 percent of the children in the world go to school, there are vast differences in what their schools look like. The school experience varies depending on the size of the school and how it is organized. Primary schools are different from secondary schools, which are different from colleges and universities. There are important differences in how schools teach, how they measure learning, and what kinds of technology they have at their disposal. There are differences in how well schools perform, what kinds of social relationships and networks they help create, and what kinds of social outcomes their graduates can expect.

### Types of Schools

One way to begin thinking about different types of schools is to investigate how they are funded and for whom they are designed. The historical trend is in favor of publicly funded schools, in which the cost of running the school is paid for by government rather than by the individuals attending the school. A second trend is toward a proliferation of different types of schools, which specialize in satisfying the needs of specific populations. Over time, this second trend has led to the general division into primary schools, secondary schools, and colleges and universities.

### PRIVATE SCHOOLS AND PUBLIC SCHOOLS.

**Private schools** charge tuition for each student they educate. Historically, private schools catered to the children of the elite, who could afford to pay for school and who did not need their children to be wage earners in the labor force. Private schools were the dominant form of education until the 18th century, when the state began to become more interested in encouraging mass literacy. Since then there has been a rapid growth of **public schools**, which are run by the state and which receive all or most of their funding from the government.

In the United States, more than 90 percent of students attend public schools today. The first public school in the United States was the Boston Latin School, which was created in 1635. There are now about 100,000 public schools in the United States, which educate nearly 50 million students. The situation is similar in most of the world, where the public school has become by far the dominant type of educational institution.

Private schools continue to play a role in modern education. The majority of these are religious schools, which are supported through a combination of student tuition and church revenues. There are also elite private schools, which charge extremely high tuition and which historically have catered to the most privileged families in society.

Neither a public nor a private institution, **homeschooling** has gained in popularity since the 1970s. Homeschooling parents choose to educate their children at home instead of sending them to a traditional public or private school, although some homeschooling parents do coordinate certain kinds of activities or coursework with the local school system. Two types of families

**Public schools as an American institution**
Founded in 1635, Boston Latin School is the oldest public school in the United States.

**Private school** A school that charges tuition for each student it educates.

**Public school** A school that is run by the state and receives all or most of its funding from the government.

**Homeschooling** A type of schooling in which parents choose to educate their children at home instead of sending them to a traditional school.

have been most attracted to homeschooling: fundamentalist Christians, and progressive families interested in exploring alternative approaches to teaching and learning (Stevens 2001). Mothers play a large role in the homeschooling movement, and they have established a national community for curriculum development while also maintaining a highly individualized approach to the education of their children. The most recent data from the National Center for Education Statistics showed that there were 1.46 million homeschooled students in the US in 2019, representing nearly 3 percent of the school-age population (Hudson et al. 2023). While there is anecdotal evidence that homeschooling has increased during the COVID-19 pandemic, in response to dissatisfaction with remote learning policies, it is too early to know whether this increase represents a temporary deviation or a permanent shift (Duvall 2021). Initial research suggests that homeschooling during the pandemic was associated with large increases in stress levels for parents and students (Thorell et al. 2021), as well as negative employment consequences for mothers (Petts, Carlson, and Pepin 2021).

Whether private or public, the kind of school that parents choose for their children is an emotional and moral matter, and school policy has frequently been the focus of public debate and controversy. For example, there was significant academic debate (Donahue and Miller 2020), social criticism, and social protest (Rohlinger and Meyer 2022) over school closure policies at the height of the COVID-19 crisis in 2020–2021. And this kind of public debate about schools is neither new nor unusual. For more than a century, there has been a strong desire to address the nation's social problems through educational reform, with a particular focus on the reform of public schools. In these debates, schools are seen as more than a place for learning skills and literacy; they are also a social space for promoting social inclusion and citizenship. Thus, in the landmark 1954 case of *Brown v. Board of Education*, the Supreme Court declared that segregated public schools were unconstitutional, and that in the field of public education, "separate but equal" had no place.

**PRIMARY SCHOOL AND SECONDARY SCHOOL.** Beginning in the 1830s and 1840s, a growing movement in the United States called for increased government involvement in the organization of schools and the teaching of students. Studying the German educational system, Horace Mann and other leading educators laid the groundwork for the modern organization of schools. They created specialized schools to train teachers, and established a more standardized curriculum of instruction. They lobbied for funding to construct new schools that would be available to all children. And they created a system wherein each school was organized into single-age grades, with specific learning objectives for each grade and an overall plan for how learning was supposed to progress from one grade to the next.

The modern school system is organized into primary schools and secondary schools. **Primary school** is focused on the learning needs of children from the ages of five to 12, and places most of its emphasis on basic academic learning and socialization skills. Children between the ages of 12 and 17 attend **secondary school**, where they learn more specialized subject areas, and where they begin to develop the specific skills they will need to enter the workforce or to pursue more advanced studies in a college or university. The system of primary and secondary schools has been adopted by countries throughout the world.

**COLLEGES AND UNIVERSITIES.** The modern organization of schools culminates with colleges and universities, in which experts in specialized fields teach students the most up-to-date knowledge in a specific area, and confer advanced degrees to students in those fields. As discussed, the undergraduate and graduate degrees that colleges award are some of the most valuable credentials in modern society. Colleges also aim to give their students the tools to think creatively, critically, and productively in order to prepare them for lifelong learning, which is an increasingly valuable skill in the economy.

The oldest university in the world is the University of Bologna (in Italy), which was established in 1088. The early universities focused on the study of law, medicine, philosophy, theology, mathematics, rhetoric, and astronomy. By the 19th century, with the growing influence of science (Chapter 10), the focus of most universities began to shift from religion to science. Intellectual freedom was emphasized, so that teachers and students could propose arguments without worrying about getting into trouble for the ideas they expressed. Most importantly, colleges and universities evolved from teaching already-established knowledge to prioritizing scientific discovery instead. This led to the creation of the modern research university.

Most of the world's top universities have adopted the model of the modern research university. Johns Hopkins University (established in 1876) was the first research university in the United States, but other colleges quickly reorganized themselves as research universities, and since the 1950s the research university has been the main organizational model for universities around the world (Schofer and Meyer 2005). But universities are not all the same. If we examine the entire field of colleges and universities, rather than just the most prestigious schools, we find that there is tremendous variation in the mission, clientele, prestige, size, and wealth of different institutions (Stevens, Armstrong, and Arum 2008: 128).

The most elite universities are characterized by extremely selective admissions policies and high levels of research activity by their faculty. Students who attend these universities spend most of their social energies on campus—not only attending classes, but also developing friendships, going to parties,

**Primary school**
The part of the education system that focuses on the learning needs of children from the ages of five to 12, with an emphasis on basic academic learning and socialization skills.

**Secondary school**
The part of the education system in which students learn more specialized subject areas, and where they begin to develop the specific skills they will need to enter the workforce or university.

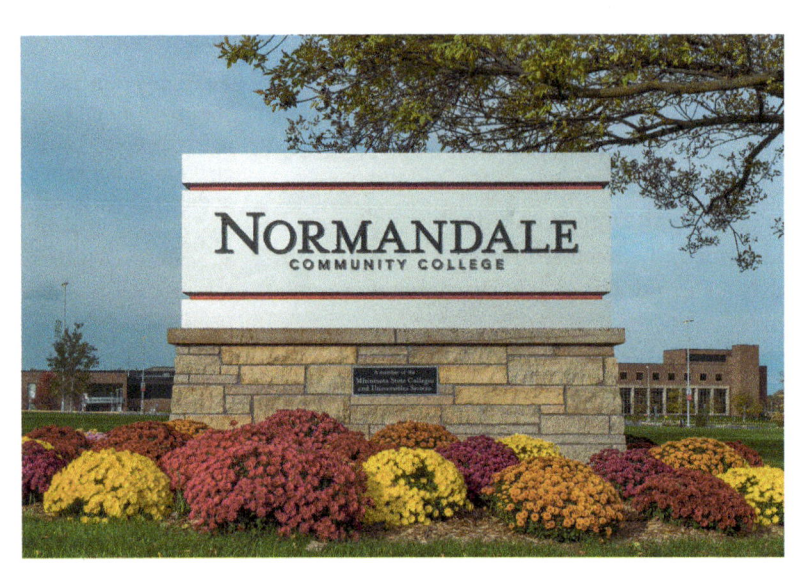

**Community college as a gateway to success**
Approximately half of all students in higher education in the United States are enrolled in community colleges, which have opened access to education for many people. Students who complete community college generally get better jobs than those who only complete high school, even though they do not tend to do as well in the labor market as those who complete a four-year degree.

looking for sexual and romantic partners, participating in sports and other clubs, and forging social bonds with other students on campus (Stevens, Armstrong, and Arum 2008: 132–33; Armstrong, and Hamilton 2013). Elite universities have a major impact on the social identities, social networks, and social opportunities of their students.

However, the biggest growth in the college and university sector is coming from colleges that do not have selective admissions policies, and that focus primarily on teaching students rather than producing research. In the United States today, there are more than 4,700 degree-granting colleges, which together enroll more than 20 million students. Approximately half of these students are enrolled in community colleges, which are characterized by open enrollment, lower tuition costs, more flexible attendance patterns, a nonresident student body, and a heavy focus on vocational training (Rosa 2008: 60). Community colleges expand access to college education, allowing people with less preparation and fewer resources to attend college. Students who complete community college generally get better jobs than those who only complete high school, even though they do not tend to do as well in the labor market as those who complete a four-year degree (Arum and Hout 1998; Marcotte et al. 2005). Further, there is not very good evidence to show that attending a community college significantly increases the likelihood that an individual will actually complete a four-year bachelor's degree (Alfonso 2006; Rouse 1995).

**SCHOOLS IN A DIGITAL AGE.** One of the biggest recent changes to schools is the introduction of new digital technologies. In the United States, public schools now provide at least one computer for every five students, and they spend more than $3 billion per year on digital content (Herold 2016).

Digital technologies present promising opportunities for schools. They allow more personalization and flexibility in teaching and learning, because they enable students to move at their own pace and to follow their interests. They make it easier for students to store their work and share it with their teachers. They allow for a more active learning environment, and they free students from the physical confines of the classroom, allowing students and teachers to interact in online spaces and opening up learning environments to people who might not be able to attend traditional schools. Last, digital technologies teach students the media and computer skills they will need in the contemporary economy.

Social scientists have identified concerns about digital learning. Digital technologies often reproduce inequality, because privileged students have better access to technology and receive more social support when they run into technical challenges (Robinson et al. 2015). Because schools have limited resources, an investment in learning technologies often forces them to reduce their investments in effective teacher training. In fact, schools from the elementary to the university level introduce digital technologies as a way to cut costs (Otterman 2011). And although some institutions of higher education have experimented with fully online programs, researchers have found that completion rates are substantially lower than for traditional courses (Parr 2013).

The challenges and limitations associated with digital learning were on full display during the height of the COVID-19 pandemic, when schools shifted to fully remote instruction. Research shows that students experienced significant learning loss during the 2020–2021 school year, with the largest losses being felt by low-income, Black, and Hispanic students (Dorn et al. 2020). At the university level, research showed that most students appreciated the flexibility of remote instruction, but they still felt that the use of digital technologies such as Zoom had a negative impact on their learning and their levels of engagement (Means and Neisler 2021; Serhan 2020). The general consensus is that the shift to online education magnified inequalities, as students with fewer economic and technological resources had much larger learning losses (Katz et al. 2021). In fact, more than 30 percent of school children worldwide could not be reached at all by remote learning policies, due to inequalities in technological access (Avanesian et al. 2021). Children with disabilities suffered even more acutely, and their parents generally felt that schools did an inadequate job of providing effective accommodations (Averett 2021). There were repeated protests over school closures throughout this period—not only because of the educational challenges associated with remote learning, but also because of the social isolation and mental health challenges that were associated with digital learning.

### Teaching, Learning, and Assessment

Teachers and schools use different types of assessment in order to determine how much students are learning. Surprise quizzes, homework assignments, oral presentations, term papers, experiments, case studies, and examinations are all used regularly to measure how well students are mastering the course material. But tests and other forms of assessment are more than just a measure of learning. Most education scholars today, including sociologists, recognize that assessment can play an important role in the teaching and learning process (Sweet and Cardwell 2016; Chin, Senter, and Spalter-Roth 2011). Testing encourages students to study, aids in the retention of knowledge, encourages students to organize the course material more effectively, and improves the transfer of knowledge to new contexts (Clark and Filinson 2011; Roedifer et al. 2011).

**STANDARDIZED TESTS AND THE DRIVE FOR ASSESSMENT.** Students, their parents, and teachers are not the only people who are interested in measuring learning. Other interested stakeholders include school administrators, potential employers, admissions officers at selective colleges and universities, and government officials. Because these groups need to compare large numbers of students from many different places (and even from different time periods), many of them have gravitated toward **standardized tests**, which are forms of assessment that are administered and scored under conditions that are the same for all students.

The use of standardized tests has a longer history than most people realize. In fact, standardized tests can be traced back to the 1840s, as a response to the rapid expansion of public schools. The initial goal of these tests was to sort students into classrooms of relatively equal ability, so that teaching and learning would be as efficient as possible. These tests were also designed to assess different types of schools—one-room schoolhouses in rural areas could be compared with large schools in urban areas, in order to see which types of schools were the most effective (US Congress, Office of Technology Assessment 1992: 108).

By the 1920s, standardized intelligence tests and achievement tests were being used in schools throughout the country. Multiple-choice questions had become the dominant format for standardized tests by the 1930s. Educational reformers used the results of these tests to push for changes in schools. Convinced that schools were doing a poor job of teaching students, they wanted to create a more uniform curriculum, reduce teachers' independence, and make schools accountable for their performance on the standardized tests (US Congress, Office of Technology Assessment 1992: 120–21). Standardized testing was also a large part of college admissions to assess candidates across the nation (Furuta 2017). By the late 20th century, the reliance on high-stakes standardized tests had become one of the defining features of education.

In a context of widespread institutional demands, sociologists have contributed to creating learning assessments, the educational assessment

---

**Standardized tests** Forms of assessment that are administered and scored under conditions that are the same for all students.

**PAIRED CONCEPTS**

## Solidarity and Conflict

### The Fight over Campus Speech Codes

For many colleges and universities, 2022 was a challenging year, as they struggled to respond to conflicts erupting over who deserved to speak on campus, and how students should react to speakers with whom they disagreed. In New York, the conservative media pundit Ann Coulter had to end her talk at Cornell university after 20 minutes, as student protesters continually interrupted her talk by yelling at her and loudly playing circus music as she tried to talk. At Vassar College, Jeh Johnson (the former Director of Homeland Security) decided to withdraw as commencement speaker after dozens of complaints by student groups about the immigration policies of the Obama administration. By the end of the year, more than 30 college events had been cancelled or disrupted in response to protests and complaints by student groups.

These conflicts over visiting speakers were connected to the larger issue of campus speech codes. Beginning in the 1980s, in an attempt to fight against discrimination and harassment and to build a more tolerant campus culture, many universities began to create speech codes to limit and punish speech that was deemed to be hateful and intolerant. By the end of the 1990s, nearly four hundred universities in the United States had established speech codes. A typical example was the speech code established in 1989 at the University of Michigan, which prohibited "any behavior, verbal or physical, that stigmatizes or victimizes an individual on the basis of race, ethnicity, religion, sex, sexual orientation, creed" or "creates an intimidating, hostile, or demeaning environment for educational pursuits, employment or participation in University-sponsored extracurricular activities" (Hudson and Nott 2017).

The main advocates in favor of campus speech codes were antidiscrimination groups, which were offended by the continued use of racial stereotypes

**Free speech rally, University of California, Berkeley, 2017**
The fight over campus speech codes that intend to encourage tolerance and prohibit hate speech are contested by free speech advocates who argue they are a threat to freedom of thought and speech.

and racist language by others on campus. Buoyed by the successes of the civil rights movement, these groups saw themselves as continuing the struggle to create more inclusion and a greater sense of social belonging on campus. But speech codes created conflicts with other groups. Libertarian groups criticized the speech codes as an infringement on free speech, which they argued needed to be protected regardless of how offensive the speech was. Conservative groups argued that speech codes were really a disguised attempt to silence conservative voices and to create campuses where only certain perspectives and opinions were allowed expression. Both groups filed lawsuits against universities and their speech code policies. And their lawsuits were almost always successful.

The spread of campus speech codes is surprising, given the historical commitment that universities have had to protecting open debate and the freedom of speech. The American Association of University Professors, in its 1915 Declaration of Principles, stated that the protection of academic freedom was absolutely essential to the fulfillment of the university's mission. The commitment to free speech on college

**PAIRED CONCEPTS CONTINUED**

campuses intensified during the 1960s, when students demanded that free speech and academic freedom needed to be extended to students as well as faculty. Facing repeated protests and sit-ins by hundreds of students, university administrators gave in to their demands. By the end of the 1960s, bans against political protest and political speech had been lifted on college campuses around the country.

From the beginning, though, movements to extend freedom of speech on college campuses have created conflicts with other groups. The professors who argued for the protection of academic freedom in the 1930s and the students who argued for free speech in the 1960s were opposed by conservative politicians, who viewed them as radicals threatening American values. The universities that were creating speech codes in the 1980s and 1990s were opposed by conservative activists and conservative media, who complained that the university was becoming a haven of "political correctness" that only tolerated certain types of beliefs and values. In all of these cases, the conflicts over campus speech have reinforced the boundaries between different social groups, as well as the solidarity and the commitment on each side to continue fighting.

**ACTIVE LEARNING**

**Find out:** Does your campus have a speech code? Can you find any examples where the speech codes on your campus have been used to block or limit speech? Can you find any examples where the speech codes on your campus have been criticized or have faced public protest?

---

movement, and the wider scholarship of teaching and learning—albeit reluctantly at times (Crockett et al. 2018; Sweet, McElrath, and Kain 2014; Paino et al., 2012; Clark and Filinson 2011). Sociologists emphasize the difference between effective quality assessment and the political and institutional effects of the assessment projects of governments, educational administrators, and accreditors (Clark and Filinson 2011; Wilmoth 2004).

One catalyst for the spread of high-stakes standardized testing in recent decades was the 1983 release of *A Nation at Risk*, a report by Ronald Reagan's Department of Education that warned American schools were failing. In 2001, the US Congress passed the No Child Left Behind Act, which required all states to develop standardized tests, administered annually to all public school students, that could assess student knowledge of basic, grade-appropriate knowledge and skills. Schools were required to demonstrate annual improvement in their test scores, and those that consistently failed to do so faced increasingly harsh penalties, even closure.

Education researchers, including those in sociology, criticized No Child Left Behind. In an article titled "No Child Left Behind? Sociology Ignored!" in the flagship journal *Sociology of Education*, David Karen argued that the politicians who claimed they were providing educational accountability to combat the "soft bigotry of low expectations" were instead reinforcing "the hard bigotries of inadequate funding, a poor understanding of the nature of educational and social inequality, and an even worse implementation plan" (2005: 165).

Other sociological researchers joined colleagues across the disciplines in identifying the way standardized tests encourage "teaching to the test," where the focus is on the narrow set of questions that students will see on the test rather than an attempt to develop a deeper knowledge of the topics being studied. This is especially true for low-performing schools where students are close to the boundary of proficiency standards (Jennings and Sohn 2014). Such tests also encourage schools to concentrate their resources only on subjects that are covered by the standardized tests, with the result that when schools face budget pressure, the first programs to be cut are art, music, languages, and other electives that are associated with a broad-based education (Hawkins 2012). And they do not effectively help reduce inequalities in student achievement, particularly those based on race, class, or disability (Au 2008).

**NATIONAL AND INTERNATIONAL DIFFERENCES IN SCHOOL PERFORMANCE.** Because a highly educated workforce is so important in today's global economy, there is a strong interest among politicians and policy-makers in comparing the educational performance of different countries. A test was developed to do this about 25 years ago, and was administered for the first time in 2000. Known as the Programme for International Student Assessment (PISA), the test is administered every three years to a representative sample of 15-year-old students in more than 70 different countries. It takes about two hours to complete, and assesses knowledge of mathematics, reading, and science. Countries that have scored the highest on the PISA test include Singapore, Hong Kong, Japan, South Korea, and Estonia. In 2022, the United States scored 34th in mathematics, 9th in reading, and 16th in science.

What are the characteristics of the high-performing nations? They pay their teachers higher salaries, relative to the average national income. They tend to allocate resources more equitably, across socioeconomically advantaged and disadvantaged schools. They give their schools more autonomy in designing curricula and assessments, and they prioritize collaboration between teachers and school principals. There is less truancy and fewer disciplinary problems, even when controlling for socioeconomic background. They use more diverse instruments of assessment. And they tend to wait longer before they divide their students into different types of educational tracks (OECD 2013).

There are also important differences in school performance at the national level. For the United States, the PISA test separated out scores for North Carolina, Puerto Rico, and Massachusetts, and found that Massachusetts significantly outperformed the other two. In fact, Massachusetts scored about the same as Canada in reading and science, and about the same

## METHODS AND INTERPRETATION

# Measuring Learning Outcomes and Teaching Effectiveness

Although schools and universities face increasing pressure to demonstrate student learning and teacher efficacy, there is widespread disagreement about how best to measure these things. For example, is it useful to give students the same test at the beginning and the end of the same year, to see what they have learned? Does it matter if students like their teachers, or if they develop a passion for the things they are learning? Should schools and teachers be rewarded for effective teaching, or be punished for ineffective teaching? And who should do the testing and evaluating?

The most common way of measuring teaching effectiveness is to use student ratings. Student ratings are used by virtually all colleges and universities, and they do a pretty good job of measuring whether students liked the teacher and whether they were engaged with the course material (Culver 2010). Still, there are many problems with student ratings. They display a significant gender and racial bias, with women and racial minorities receiving consistently lower student evaluations (Hamermesh and Parker 2005). They also display a bias in favor of smaller classes, despite the fact that teachers rarely have any control over class size. They are plagued by low response rates, particularly when they are conducted online (Ling, Phillips, and Wehrich 2012). There is no way to know whether different students mean the same thing when they evaluate a teacher as "satisfactory" or "poor." And there is no way to know whether students actually learned anything. The main advantage of student assessments is that they are easy and inexpensive to deploy. Other attempts to measure teaching effectiveness include peer ratings, self-evaluations, videos, alumni ratings, employer ratings, teaching awards, and teaching portfolios (Berk 2005).

**Assessing learning**
In standard classrooms, teachers lecture to students, but it is not always clear what or how much students actually learn. The development of learning assessments shifts the focus from individual grades to the effectiveness of teaching and learning. How much of student performance comes from teaching and how much from prior experience and family background?

But these all have problems of their own, and still fail to measure whether students actually learned anything.

What about measuring learning outcomes? One approach is to look at performance on final exams. However, to make this approach effective, a school would have to either figure out how to compare different exams, or force all teachers of a particular course to give the same exam, which many teachers will resist. They can rely on standardized tests that are administered to all students at the end of the year, but if they do this they are only going to be measuring overall student performance. Standardized year-end exams make it nearly impossible to isolate the effectiveness of a specific teacher, unless that teacher has done all of the instruction for the student. Some teaching strategies are optimized for short-term learning, but leave students less prepared for learning more complex material that comes later in a pedagogical sequence (Epstein 2019). An additional problem is that student performance is shaped by a variety of factors that are independent of teacher effectiveness, such as race, class, gender, school size, school resources, school culture, family background, and neighborhood characteristics (Schneider et al. 2011).

> **ACTIVE LEARNING**
>
> **Think about it:** If you were in charge of evaluating teaching effectiveness and learning outcomes at your school, which measures would you use? Why would you choose those measures instead of something else? What do you see as the main potential problems with those measurements?

## PAIRED CONCEPTS: Global and Local

### The Spread of Singapore Math

Singapore has consistently scored at the top of international school exams, attracting considerable attention from education scholars. In the 2022 PISA exam, in addition to excelling in the science and mathematics section, Singapore's students scored higher on the reading and comprehension sections than students from other countries. In explaining Singapore's great success, experts point to educational policies that are meritocratic, offer good pay and high status to teachers, invest heavily in teachers as well as students, and provide strong remedial support as soon as a student begins to fall behind (Ng 2017).

As educators in other countries have sought to learn from Singapore's success, they have been particularly interested in the country's specific strategies for math instruction. Rather than the memorization and drilling that are emphasized heavily in more traditional arithmetic instruction for kindergarten and elementary school students, Singapore instead teaches students to master a limited number of concepts each school year before moving on to something new. The sequence of topics has been carefully planned, and is based on theories of child development. Teachers use a variety of

**Singapore math**
In this pedagogical approach to math developed by educators in Singapore, the early curriculum moves slowly, and teachers use a variety of strategies to help students solve increasingly difficult problems. Advocates also point to educational policies in Singapore that are meritocratic, offer good pay and high status to teachers, invest heavily in teachers as well as students, and provide strong remedial support as soon as a student begins to fall behind.

strategies to help students solve increasingly difficult problems. Students draw pictures, diagram the elements of a problem, and use other aids such as blocks, cards, and bar charts (Hu 2010). By slowing down and making sure that students develop a

> **PAIRED CONCEPTS CONTINUED**
>
> deep understanding of each mathematic concept, students remember what they have learned and can build on their knowledge to tackle increasingly difficult skills. By the time they are in fourth or fifth grade, many Singaporean students are already performing one or two grade levels ahead of international standards.
>
> Because of Singapore's success in international exams, programs in "Singapore math" have been successfully marketed to parents and schools around the world. Singapore Math Inc. was established in the United States in 1998, and now sells textbooks and other curricular materials to more than one thousand schools in the United States, Canada, Australia, and the Middle East.
>
> **ACTIVE LEARNING**
>
> **Find out:** Does your neighborhood school use Singapore math? Contact someone from your home school district (a teacher, principal, or assistant principal). Ask them about the math curriculum they use. Find out what they know about Singapore math, and what they think about it.

as Norway in mathematics. All three of its scores were significantly higher than the US average. North Carolina scored pretty close to the national average. Puerto Rico was significantly lower than the US average, with scores that were similar to Brazil, Indonesia, and other countries that are much poorer than the United States. In other comparisons of US states, the highest-performing schools tend to be located in wealthy suburbs surrounding Chicago, Boston, Philadelphia, New York City, and San Francisco. There are significant differences related to race and ethnicity, with African American and Hispanic students scoring lower than white and Asian American students. And there are significant class differences, with wealthier students performing better than poorer students.

## Making Friends and Building Networks

For most students, a key part of the school experience involves building friendships, social relationships, and social networks. As we discussed in Chapter 4, school is one of the most important agents of socialization. For many children, entering elementary school is the first time in their lives when they are spending long periods of time away from their homes, parents, and siblings. Primary schools, secondary schools, and colleges are places where students form peer groups and reference groups. As students move into adulthood, the relationships they develop in college become an important part of their social network, which they rely on to develop contacts and support resources throughout their working lives.

**FRIENDS, CLIQUES, AND BULLIES.** There are important social hierarchies in schools between different social groups, as well as hierarchies within each social group. These hierarchies are shaped by inequality and privilege, by solidarity and conflict, and by power and resistance. For most students, their school experience is impacted by their position in the overall pecking order of their school.

The importance that children place on being popular increases throughout elementary school, peaking during the early high school years (LaFontana and Cillessen 2010). In a classic study of clique dynamics, the sociologists Patricia Adler and Peter Adler found that the dominant and most popular groups in the school pecking order commanded the most interest, attention, and prestige from their classmates (Adler and Adler 1998). Individuals in the popular cliques carefully screen potential members, inviting them in for trial periods and ejecting them if they fail to win acceptance from the clique leaders. Hierarchies within the popular cliques are changing constantly, with less popular members trying to copy the fashion and behaviors of the group leaders. Practices of exclusion, rejection, humiliation, and physical intimidation are perpetrated, directed primarily at lower-status social groups but also at lower-status members of the popular groups. Regardless of where they are in the pecking order, students learn that school is a social minefield, in which popularity is often expressed through social exclusion and socially aggressive behavior, and where anyone can become a target.

The school pecking order reinforces privilege and inequality, because of the tendency for social groups to form on the basis of social similarities. Students who are wealthy and well dressed are more likely to be popular, as are students who conform to gender ideals (Adler, Kless, and Adler 1992). School cliques are highly segregated by race, to the general disadvantage of historically marginalized groups. All of this means that the prestige hierarchy in most schools will reinforce other structures of privilege. But school popularity does not come without costs. Among teenagers, popular students are more likely to drink, use drugs, and engage in shoplifting, vandalism, and other forms of

**Bullying**
Many students experience school as a social minefield, where they can be targeted at any time for social exclusion and bullying.

deviance (Allen and Allen 2009). These behaviors can have long-term costs, derailing students' successful transitions into college, the workplace, and adulthood.

For less popular students, the school pecking order presents different kinds of risks. Unpopular children are more likely to have academic troubles in school and to experience depression, anxiety, and isolation (Flook, Repetti, and Ullman 2005). They are also at greater risk of victimization, as the targets of aggressive behavior and bullying (Martin 2009). Bullying can include verbal insults, the spreading of rumors, and physical violence or intimidation. School bullying is shaped by homophobia, racism, sexism, and weight-based shaming, in a way that has the effect of stigmatizing marginalized populations and reinforcing structural inequalities (Pascoe 2011). In the United States, nearly one-third of students between the ages of 12 and 18 reported being bullied at least once during the school year, with nearly 10 percent of them experiencing bullying almost daily (UNESCO 2017). Victims of bullying suffer well into adulthood; they have more health problems, higher levels of social isolation, and lower levels of educational attainment (Faris and Felmlee 2014).

**NETWORKS AND NETWORKING.** The social networks that students develop in school extend into their closest relationships, often becoming important primary groups in their adult lives. This is particularly true for students who attend college and university, because of where those schools are placed in the typical life cycle. In the United States, the median age of first marriage is 28 for women and 30 for men. Many of these couples cohabit before getting married (Chapter 9). In their early 20s, most students (and nearly all privileged students) are attending college and graduate school, which is why these schools are often seen as prime **marriage markets**. Indeed, sociological research shows that attending college increases the likelihood of marriage for men and women, and this effect is the highest for high-status students (Musick, Brand, and Davis 2012). More prestigious schools provide more valuable marriage markets.

**Marriage market**
Institutionalized spaces where individuals select potential sexual, romantic, and marriage partners.

At school, students develop useful social networks for their adult lives, particularly for those who attend elite private schools and prestigious universities. The students who go to such schools are surrounded by other students from elite families, and they are easily socialized into the hobbies and cultural tastes that are associated with that world. Prestigious schools also have powerful alumni networks, which provide new graduates with insider connections that can help them land high-paying and high-status jobs.

## PAIRED CONCEPTS: Inequality and Privilege

### How Elite Students Get Elite Jobs

In today's economy, some of the best-paying jobs are in the fields of investment banking, management consulting, and corporate law. This is particularly true for the top-tier firms in these fields, where starting salaries are close to $200,000 per year, and increase rapidly for people who continue employment with the top firms. Students know that these are the best-paying jobs, and there is intense competition to get them. But who gets these jobs? How do firms make their hiring decisions?

In *Pedigree: How Elite Students Get Elite Jobs*, the sociologist Lauren Rivera found that the hiring process at these top-tier firms is designed in a way that favors elite students from elite universities (Rivera 2015). This is due to the way that firms recruit for entry-level jobs, screen résumés to select applicants for interviews, and come to decisions about which interviewees will ultimately get a job offer.

The preference for elite students is built into the recruiting process, which is focused on campus recruitment events that are held at elite universities. The vast majority of people who are ultimately hired are identified through these events, where the firms come to campus and try to sell themselves to students. Only a small list of schools are included in these activities. Most top-tier firms identify about five "core schools" where they intend to invest most of their energy recruiting students. At these core schools, which are almost always Ivy League universities, firms will host information sessions, cocktail receptions, and dinners, where they interview dozens of potential candidates. Most firms also identify 10 or 15 "target schools," where they will interview candidates but will not invest as many resources. These schools are usually prestigious as well, but it is possible for a slightly less elite school to make it onto the list if one of the managing partners has a personal connection to the school. Students who do not graduate from a core or target school can still apply for positions in these firms, but their applications are kept in a separate stream and not considered very seriously; in many instances, they will be discarded without any review whatsoever (Rivera 2015: 35). Firms argue that pursuing this strategy makes it more likely that they will only hire the "best and the brightest," because of how difficult it is to get accepted into elite universities. But they also know that hiring employees from elite universities will make it easier for them to attract business, because their clients tend to come from those universities and to be invested in the social status that is associated with Ivy League degrees (Rivera 2015: 37).

Once the interviews begin, the preference continues for candidates who come from more elite backgrounds. After the screening preference for the highest-status universities has been accomplished, firms begin paying more attention to extracurricular

**Educational privilege**
For the most prestigious and highest-paying jobs, the hiring process is designed to select candidates who come from the most privileged backgrounds and the highest-status universities.

**PAIRED CONCEPTS CONTINUED**

activities and candidates' potential "fit" with the firm's culture and its employees. Because these jobs require people to work very long hours, employers look to leisure activities and interests to gauge whether an applicant would be an interesting person to have on the team. High-status leisure pursuits that require significant investment of resources, such as tennis, squash, or crew, are weighted most heavily. People who lack extracurricular accomplishments are dismissed as "boring" people who would be "corporate drones"; as one recruiter commented, "I would trade an outgoing, friendly, confident person for a rocket scientist any day" (Rivera 2015: 94). These differences in cultural capital (Chapter 4) are closely related to social class background.

Ultimately, successful applicants are those deemed to have "polish," a fairly vague criterion of merit that tracks closely with the socioeconomic status of the candidates' parents (Rivera 2015: 250). There are exceptions to this, of course. Candidates who can tell a compelling story of overcoming major obstacles often fare well, and so do candidates from less elite places who had a personal connection to the firm, provided that they could display enough polish that one of the recruiters can make a strong case on their behalf. But on the whole, the hiring process is designed to select the most elite candidates, the ones from the most privileged backgrounds and the most high-status universities.

**ACTIVE LEARNING**

**Find out:** Do some research at your school's career services center. Does your school host on-campus recruiting events? What kinds of companies attend these events? What are they doing to sell themselves to potential employees? Are the companies coming to campus the top-tier firms in their industry? If not, try to find out where the top-tier firms are doing their on-campus recruiting.

## 11.3 Work, Jobs, and Satisfaction

**LG 11.3** Think about the kinds of characteristics that are associated with "good jobs," and describe how the distribution of good jobs is socially structured.

Most students know that there is a relationship between education and work, and they are aware that the end of school marks the beginning of their careers. There is often overlap between these two parts of the life course. Many students work their way through school, and many others take on paid and unpaid internships with the hope of getting a better job when they graduate. Those who want to upgrade their skills and their credentials often return to school after a period of full-time work.

A widely shared goal in today's economy is to get a "good job," even though that can mean different things to different people. Some people place the most value on jobs that offer good pay and high status, while others emphasize satisfying working conditions and room for growth. Many workers also hope that their jobs will provide them enough time and resources to pursue hobbies, interests, and other forms of recreation that excite their passions or allow them to share fun experiences with friends and family.

## Power, Privilege, and Inequality in the Workplace

For those who are fortunate to have a good job, the workplace can be a site of great passion and great reward. Such people tell you that they love their job. But this does not describe the working experience for most people. Work is also a place of domination, exploitation, and monotony.

As we discussed in earlier chapters, income inequality is shaped by race, class, and gender. Simply put, white men tend to have better jobs than other groups. They make more money for doing the same job, and they continue to be overrepresented in the best-paying and highest-status jobs. Among those who hold management jobs, white male overrepresentation is at virtually the same levels it was in the 1960s; while women and racial minorities hold more management positions than they used to, those positions are concentrated in the service sector, and in companies where they are mainly managing other women and other people from historically marginalized groups (Stainback and Tomaskovic-Devey 2009).

The shift to remote work at the height of the COVID-19 pandemic put issues of work and inequality on full display. Lockdowns and social distancing had a disproportionately negative impact on younger, less educated, and lower-earning workers, while school closures had a disproportionately negative impact on poor children (Blundell et al. 2022). In the US, the people most able to switch to remote work were those with a bachelor's degree or higher, and those with a salary of at least $150,000 per year; there was also a racial component, as white workers were able to switch to remote work at higher rates than Black and Hispanic workers (Ray and Ong 2020). For working parents, the combination of remote work and remote school reinforced the gendered division of household labor, to the disadvantage of working women (Dunatchik et al. 2021). Overall, the shift to remote work benefited male, older, higher-educated, and higher-paid workers (Bonacini et al. 2021).

In addition to the stratification of income and status, the workplace also reproduces massive inequalities in terms of how much control people have over their work and how much satisfaction they get out of their jobs. Most people have little control over their working conditions. Their work is closely monitored, and even if they do their job well they can be fired without any justification, due to the spread of "at-will" employment laws. For those who keep their jobs, their work is too often characterized by a soul-crushing monotony. This has been a consistent theme of social critics. In his 1854 novel *Hard Times*, the English writer Charles Dickens described the modern workplace as a prison in which workers were required to complete the same task every day, receiving starvation wages with little or no chance of improvement or advancement. More recently, in the 1999 film *Office Space*, writer and director Mike Judge depicts a world of office-park workers in cubicles, who hate their jobs and who are constantly harassed by their bosses.

In fact, exploitation and harassment are a regular feature of the work experience for many (if not most) workers. Bullying is a major problem in today's workforce, with most research reporting that between 10 and 20 percent of all workers are bullied annually (Einarson et al. 2003). Differences in power influence bullying in the workplace. Racial minorities and workers with high levels of job insecurity are more likely to be targets of workplace bullying (Hodson et al. 2006). More than 70 percent of the perpetrators of bullying are men, and more than 60 percent are bosses (Namie 2017). Sexual harassment is even more prevalent, with a recent study showing that three-quarters of all women in the United States have been sexually harassed at work (Johnson, Kirk, and Keplinger 2016). Victims of harassment rarely report their victimization, because of feared retaliation by bosses and ostracism by coworkers.

Another issue is the growing power that employers have over their workers. Real hourly wages for the typical worker in the US have remained largely unchanged since 1970, while the minimum wage has actually declined when inflation is taken into account (Mishel, Gould, and Bivens 2015). Union membership has declined precipitously during the same period, giving workers significantly less bargaining power than they used to have. As we discuss in Chapter 13, globalization has eroded wages for workers without a college degree at the same time that it has weakened labor standards and work safety. Automation has allowed corporations to employ robotic technologies in the place of workers, and the growth of artificial intelligence threatens to extend this trend from blue-collar to white-collar work (Chapter 14). Workers feel increasingly insecure. As Kalleberg (2013) argues, there has been a dramatic rise in precarious employment since the 1970s. These jobs are defined by low wages, the elimination of benefits such as health insurance or retirement funds, and virtually no long-term security. We discuss this development further at the end of the chapter, as part of a phenomenon known as the Uberization of the economy.

## The Sociology of Job Satisfaction

What makes a job satisfying? And why will different workers derive different levels of satisfaction from the same job? These are important questions—not only because job satisfaction is associated with better health outcomes (Faragher, Cass, and Cooper et al. 2005), but also because it is connected to higher levels of worker productivity (Bockerman and Ilmakunnas 2012).

According to the sociologist Arne Kalleberg, the most important issue related to job satisfaction is whether the job's rewards match the worker's expectations, interests, and values (Kalleberg 1977). Workers have different interests, and they expect different things from their jobs. Some workers want their job to be intrinsically interesting, while others

**PAIRED CONCEPTS**

## Power and Resistance

### The #MeToo Movement

In 2006, civil rights activist Tarana Burke created a non-profit organization to help support young women of color who had been victims of sexual abuse. The organization was called JustBeInc., and its motto was "me too."

In October 2017 the "me too" movement exploded into the public consciousness. Responding to multiple accusations of sexual harassment and assault made against the Hollywood movie producer Harvey Weinstein, the actress Alyssa Milano wrote the following on Twitter: "If you've been sexually harassed or assaulted write 'me too' as a reply to this tweet."

**Tarana Burke, founder of the #MeToo movement**

Within 24 hours, the hashtag #MeToo had been posted on Twitter nearly half a million times, and helped create a movement against sexual harassment and sexual assault in the workplace (Gilbert 2017). Harvey Weinstein was fired, and later arrested on rape charges, as nearly a dozen women came forward with reports of sexual assault. #MeToo was used to publicize allegations of sexual harassment and assault against leading figures in the music industry, government, sports, finance, military, and other industries as well. Use of the hashtag spread to more than 80 countries. The European Union convened a session of parliament about how to combat sexual abuse, after the #MeToo movement publicized allegations of sexual harassment by EU workers (Schreuer 2017). In the US Congress, the ME TOO Congress Act was introduced in January 2018, in order to increase transparency surrounding how the US government responded to allegations of sexual harassment and assault.

Many people who have experience with previous women's movements feared that a backlash against #MeToo was inevitable. They pointed to complaints about how men were being fired before they had a chance to defend themselves, how the movement did not adequately distinguish between different types of sexual harassment, and how the movement might turn into a moral panic. Opinion polls showed a drop in support for feminism, particularly among young men (Grady 2023). But others replied that the potential of backlash was worth it, because the movement has shown powerful men that there are real risks to abusing the less powerful women who work for them. And because the movement has made retaliation by bosses much riskier, it encourages more women to report incidents of sexual abuse at work.

**ACTIVE LEARNING**

**Think about it:** How would you measure the success or the impact of the #MeToo movement? Develop two different measurement strategies, and list the advantages and disadvantages of each.

**Job satisfaction**
Job satisfaction is more likely when the job's rewards match the worker's interests, expectations, and values.

are looking for good hours and pleasant physical surroundings. Some people want to be surrounded by friendly and interesting coworkers, while others place more importance on opportunities for career advancement. Some people want a big salary, while others are more interested in job security. Many workers are looking for a combination of these things. When the job meets their expectations and their values, then job satisfaction increases. Workers who have a wide variety of job opportunities have a higher likelihood of job satisfaction, because they have the luxury of choosing a job that matches their interests and values (Kalleberg 1977: 137).

Larger structural trends also shape the expectations and values that workers have about their jobs. There is a pronounced gender effect, with women generally experiencing higher levels of job satisfaction, and with women much more likely to value good relationships and good working conditions in their determination of job satisfaction (Zou 2015). There is a time effect, with job satisfaction tending to decrease the longer an individual stays in a particular organization (Dobrow et al. 2018). Public-sector employees tend to exhibit higher levels of job satisfaction than private-sector workers (Steel and Warner 2016). There are historical trends as well. Since the 1970s, there has been an increase in the value workers place on income and job security, as compared to other interests and expectations (Kalleberg et al. 2006). Given the fact that job insecurity has increased significantly during this period and salaries have been stagnant for most workers (as we discuss later in the chapter), this has led to large increases in job dissatisfaction, with little expectation that it would return to levels seen during the 1970s or 1980s (McGregor 2017).

There is evidence that many workers have begun to change how they define a good job in recent years. There was a lot of news coverage and public debate in 2021 and 2022 about "the great resignation," a phenomenon that saw increasing numbers of workers quit their jobs throughout 2021. Survey research showed that the top reasons for quitting were the same as they had been in previous years: low pay, no advancement opportunities, feeling disrespected at work, and childcare issues (Parker and Horowitz 2022). Based on these data, many social scientists argued that the higher quit rate was caused by the unusually low unemployment rate, and the confidence that workers could easily find another job (Gittleman 2022). But there were also reasons to believe that workers were beginning to expect different things from their jobs. Nearly a quarter of workers surveyed pointed to a lack of flexibility in their working hours as a reason for quitting (Parker and Horowitz 2022). An increasing number of workers are refusing to return to the office full-time, preferring jobs that offered fully remote or partially remote working conditions (Chugh 2021). Other factors that increased the likelihood of workers quitting their jobs were the presence of a toxic corporate culture (Sull, Sull and Zweig 2022) and a desire to pursue a less ambitious job that allowed workers to engage in other passions (Leong 2021). In fact, many workers are not just quitting their jobs, they are quitting the larger culture of "workism," the idea that we are defined primarily by our work and that all other aspects of our lives need to be subordinated to the demands of our jobs (Huffington and Fisher 2022).

**FINDING MEANING AND SATISFACTION OUTSIDE OF WORK.** Economic success is not the only thing that matters for a happy and meaningful life. Jobs and money are important, to be sure, but they are not the most important factors contributing to overall happiness. Cross-national research finds that happiness levels are higher in societies with higher levels of economic development, higher levels of social tolerance, and more democracy (Inglehart et al. 2008). Other research has shown that, over the course of an individual's life, the most important thing is to have close relationships with family, friends, and people in the community. People who report that they have led meaningful lives tend to have strong social relationships; to do things that are challenging; and to participate in activities that allow them to connect their past, present, and future (Baumeister et al. 2013). Meaningful lives often include periods of stress and struggle, rather than periods of uninterrupted happiness.

Recognizing that people want more from life than a good job, a growing part of the economy is now focused on providing meaningful experiences that allow people to have authentic experiences, to express their true identities, and to reinforce their social connections with friends and family. The tourist and leisure industries have evolved in recent years to increasingly emphasize unique and memorable experiences that encourage self-discovery and growth (Morgan et al. 2009). Memorable experiences immerse people in a new cultural environment, allowing them to interact with locals, and to learn something new about the world and about themselves, in a way that helps them develop some aspect of their identity and to improve their self-confidence (Chandralal and Valenzuela 2013). These include things such as music festivals, food festivals and culinary tours, eco-tourism, spiritual tourism, and adventure travel.

These changes in the travel and leisure industry are part of a larger "experience economy," in which companies sell experiences and transformations rather than goods and services (Pine and Gillmore 1999). We can see this with the exploding popularity of marathons, obstacle races, Ironman triathlons, and other extreme challenges. The companies that sponsor these events are selling personal transformation and total immersion into a new lifestyle, and often into a social community of other enthusiasts. The race itself is the culmination of the experience, offering a festival-like event and a collective affirmation of the sacrifices that have been made and the new identity that has been embraced.

---

**PAIRED CONCEPTS**

## Structure and Contingency

### How Indoor Cycling Became a Multi-Billion-Dollar Industry

In the late 1980s, South African endurance cyclist Johnny Goldberg began to worry about all the time he was spending riding his bike. Living in Los Angeles, with a pregnant wife and a training schedule that often required riding at night, Goldberg built himself a stationary bike that would be able to accurately simulate what it was like to ride a road bike, and that would be strong enough to allow him to alternate between long periods of standing and sitting on the bike, which is necessary for endurance cyclists.

Goldberg, a successful fitness instructor with a large following in Los Angeles, began teaching small cycling classes with stationary bikes he built. The first classes were held in his garage, but they were so popular that he quickly created two "Spinning Centers" in Santa Monica and Hollywood. By 1994, he had contracted with the bicycle maker

**Soul Cycle class, Washington, DC**

Schwinn to produce his Johnny G Spinner bikes, so that he could keep up with the demand for his classes. The program he developed included periods of high-intensity cycling combined with on-the-bike strength exercises, music, and motivational components. With a partner, he founded Madd Dogg

Athletics to supervise the manufacturing of the Johnny G Spinner cycles as well as the training and licensing of official Johnny G spinning instructors.

In 1995 Goldberg presented his new spinning program to the annual meeting of the International Health, Racquet, and Sportsclub Association. There was an enthusiastic reception to the program, and spinning quickly became a global phenomenon. Today, Madd Dogg Athletics has more than 300,000 certified instructors and 35,000 licensed facilities; there are just as many unlicensed instructors and facilities, working at YMCAs as well as trendy new indoor cycling studios such as Soul Cycle and Flywheel. Indoor cycling is now one of the most profitable parts of the health club and fitness studio industry.

While Johnny Goldberg's distinctive biography was a big factor in spinning's development and success, the structural conditions were there for indoor cycling to take off. Group exercise classes exploded in popularity in the 1970s and 1980s, and health clubs had built or converted space to house the new aerobics studios that were in demand. But aerobics classes were much more popular among women, which meant that the studio spaces were only catering to some health club members and were left unused during long parts of the day. Health clubs saw spinning as a way to use those spaces for more of the day, and hopefully to cater to men just as much as women.

There are other structural reasons that explain the success of spinning and other indoor cycling studios. Most people already know how to ride a bike. Everybody was on their own bike, controlling their own resistance and intensity, which meant that the classes could include people of vastly different levels of fitness ability. The cycling studios became communities, where people could exercise together instead of spending their entire time at the gym by themselves. Relationships formed, and some people even met their future partners at spin class. Many of the more popular studios developed an almost cult-like following, with classes selling out instantly and with social status going to those who could score a space.

### ACTIVE LEARNING

**Think about it:** During the height of the COVID-19 pandemic, one of the most successful fitness companies was Peloton, which sold an internet-connected spinning bike that people could use to take spin classes from the comfort of their own home. But Peloton had lost more than 80 percent of its value by 2022, and by 2023 it was unclear if the company would be able to stay in business. Using your sociological imagination, suggest a few explanations for this shift.

### CAREERS

## The Uberization of the Economy

On a winter night in Paris in 2008, Travis Kalanick and Garrett Camp were frustrated with their inability to hail a cab. They wondered why cab hailing had not yet been integrated with smartphones to create a better user experience. Returning to San Francisco, they designed a smartphone app for cab hailing, and the result was a major innovation in global business. Today, Uber operates in 58 countries, (Hartmans and McAlone 2016), and the company went public in 2019—albeit not at the price that was expected initially (Isaac, De La Merced, and Sorkin 2019).

Uber's success has as much to do with the way it relates to its employees as with its use of new technologies. From the beginning, Uber has treated the people who work for it as "independent contractors" rather than traditional employees. As such, Uber

## CAREERS CONTINUED

drivers have the freedom to work when they want. Many of them drive for Uber as a second job, spending a few hours picking up passengers on nights, weekends, and other times they are free. Most of them like the flexibility of the arrangement. But this arrangement comes with costs. As independent contractors, they are not entitled to benefits that are legally owed to employees, such as a guaranteed minimum wage, workers' compensation, sick days, unemployment benefits, or reimbursed business expenses. State and local governments also lose in the arrangement, because Uber does not pay into state funds for workers' compensation and unemployment insurance. The federal government loses revenue too, because Uber does not pay Social Security taxes.

Uber's growth is part of a larger trend toward what is being called the "gig economy" or the "sharing economy," in which workers are expected to do their jobs as independent contractors. In addition to the taxi industry, where Uber and Lyft have become major players, these kinds of arrangements are having a major impact in industries like construction and home repair services (TaskRabbit), home cleaning services (Homeaglow), delivery services (Postmates, DoorDash), graphic design (Fiverr), and hotels and short-term rentals (Airbnb). Even the adult entertainment industry has started to get into the act; many strip clubs now treat their dancers as independent contractors. Recent surveys estimate that between 20 and 30 percent of working-age adults in the United States and Europe participate in the gig economy (Manyika et al. 2016).

For the vast majority of gig economy workers, wages are minimal: 14 percent of gig workers earn less than the federal minimum wage, and 29 percent earn less than the minimum wage in the state where they did their work (Zipperer et al. 2022). The median monthly income for Uber drivers is about $155; for TaskRabbit workers it is $110, and for Postmates couriers it is about $70 (Leasca 2017; Morris 2021). Airbnb hosts make more money, with median monthly earnings of about $440. Only 16 percent of all gig economy workers make more than $500 per month (Morris 2021).

**Uber driver, New York City**
Uber's growth is part of a trend toward a "gig economy" where workers are independent contractors and frequently lack both health insurance and workers' compensation.

In recent years, state labor commissions have gone to court to sue companies in the gig economy for misclassifying their workers as independent contractors instead of employees. These suits claim that such misclassification is costing hundreds of millions of dollars in lost tax revenue, and giving these companies an unfair advantage over law-abiding companies because of labor costs that can be as much as 40 percent lower (Wogan 2016). Workers have also filed lawsuits. In 2016, Uber settled a class-action lawsuit for $100 million, agreeing to pay 385,000 drivers in Massachusetts and California for misclassifying them as independent contractors. In 2023, Uber and Lyft settled a wage-theft lawsuit in New York for $328 million, and agreed to provide sick leave and other benefits to their drivers in that state. Once viewed as an arena of innovation and freedom, many now see the gig economy as a zone of exploitation.

### ACTIVE LEARNING

**Find out:** Do you know anyone who does work in the gig economy? What do they see as the advantages and disadvantages of their jobs? Do they have another job where they are classified as an employee? If so, what are the differences in their two jobs?

## CASE STUDY

# What Kind of Education Do People Need in Today's Economy?

In 2011, Microsoft's cofounder Bill Gates declared in a speech to the National Governors Association that state universities should reduce support for the liberal arts and increase their investments in engineering, science, and other job-creating disciplines. Apple's cofounder Steve Jobs disagreed strongly. Jobs argued that Apple's success was the result of "technology married with liberal arts, married with the humanities," and that this was truer than ever as their attention shifted to post-PC devices such as the iPhone and the iPad.

In some respects, it was strange for Gates and Jobs to be leading a public discussion about the future of higher education, given that neither of them had finished college—Gates left Harvard University after two years, and Jobs dropped out of Reed College after six months. But their disagreement provoked intense dispute about the value of the liberal arts in the new tech economy. The argument in favor of a liberal arts education seems to have won the day, at least for the moment. In his 2018 book about the future of the tech economy, Microsoft president Brad Smith claimed that people with a liberal arts background would be absolutely crucial for realizing the full potential of artificial intelligence:

> . . . skilling-up for an AI-powered world involves more than science, technology, engineering, and math. As computers behave more like humans, the social sciences and humanities will become even more important. Languages, art, history, economics, ethics, philosophy, psychology and human development courses can teach critical, philosophical and ethics-based skills that will be instrumental in the development and management of AI solutions. (Smith and Shum 2018: 19)

Not everyone agrees with Jobs and Smith about the value of a liberal arts education. In a 2014 speech about job training and the manufacturing sector, President Barack Obama argued that "folks can make a lot more, potentially, with skilled manufacturing or the trades than they might with an art history degree." In 2011, Florida governor Rick Scott argued that his state did not need any more anthropologists, and that the state university should invest in degree programs that led to jobs. In 2016, Kentucky governor Matt Bevin suggested that the state's taxpayers should not be subsidizing the education of French literature majors. In 2023, Mississippi State Auditor Shad White argued that the state should stop funding "useless degrees" in programs like Urban Studies, Women's Studies, and German Literature.

The *conflict* between science and the humanities can be traced back to the earliest days of the modern research university. In his 1959 lecture "The Two Cultures," C. P. Snow argued that the conflict between scientists and humanists was a major obstacle preventing people from solving major social problems. Snow ([1959] 2001) argued that the *solidarity* of each group seemed to depend on criticizing the ignorance of the other. Humanists complained that scientists knew nothing about art, poetry, literature, or any of the other things that marked a refined or civilized person. Scientists, meanwhile, complained that humanists were scientific illiterates, that they knew little more about physics and other modern scientific disciplines than cavemen. The identities of each group, it seemed, had been defined in opposition to the other, in a way that made cooperation difficult.

Throughout the history of the conflict between scientists and humanists, the *power* of the dominant group has allowed them to organize the university in a way that reinforced their own *privilege*. Today, professors in business and the sciences earn higher salaries, work in more modern buildings, have more research support, and tend to teach fewer courses than professors in the humanities. Humanities professors may love their jobs, but

### CASE STUDY CONTINUED

institutional *inequality* means they are much more likely to be employed as contingent workers and less likely to have resources available for things like conference travel or even photocopying. Still, attempts by university administrators to close humanities departments altogether are met with *resistance*, as students and faculty protest the proposals, and as these protests get media coverage.

Today, the *structure* of the economy is one that largely favors scientific and technical education as the safest route to success. When Steve Jobs argued for the value of the liberal arts, he pointed to the *contingency* of his own biography as a major source of insight. Even though he had dropped out of Reed College, he continued to attend classes that interested him, including a course in calligraphy. Ten years later, when designing the Mac computer, his study of calligraphy inspired him to develop the Mac as the first computer with multiple typefaces and proportionally spaced fonts. This forever changed the interface of personal computers and other digital products.

In fact, in many parts of the world the focus on creativity is seen as the main advantage of the American education system and the main characteristic of American workers. In the United States, policy-makers and employers look at *global* comparisons that show American students lagging in science and math, and they urge the *local* schools to invest more heavily in those areas. In other parts of the world, and particularly in Asia, policy-makers look at a global economy in which innovation is heavily tilted toward the United States, and they encourage their local schools to try US-style creativity.

## LEARNING GOALS REVISITED

**11.1 Describe the different social purposes and social effects of education.**

- Education is used to promote literacy, which refers to the ability to read, write, communicate, and use other skills that allow people to participate fully in their society. The promotion of mass literacy has been a major goal of schools since the 19th century, and today more than 82 percent of the world's population can read.

- Education promotes socialization, and for this reason it is often described as having a "hidden curriculum." In addition to teaching basic values, norms, and citizenship, schools also teach students how to deal with crowds and distractions; how to respond to the fact that they are being evaluated; and how to deal with power inequalities.

- Schools teach practical skills that students will need in the workforce, and they give out valuable credentials that are needed to gain entry into most of the high-paying and high-status professions. Schools sort students into different types of occupational futures, and they often do this in a way that reinforces privilege and inequality.

- Schools help the economy. They are a major source of employment, and they provide free childcare for working parents.

**11.2** Describe the experience of going to school, and how it has changed over time.

- Most students today attend publicly funded schools. School systems around the world are organized into primary schools, secondary schools, and colleges and universities.
- Most private schools today are religious schools, which are supported through a combination of student tuition and church revenues. There are also elite private schools, which charge extremely high tuition and which historically have catered to the most privileged families in society. Since the 1970s the homeschooling movement has continued to grow.
- New digital technologies have become a significant presence in schools. These technologies offer the promise of a more flexible and personalized learning experience. They have also been used to cut costs, and there is evidence that they reinforce existing inequalities.
- High-stakes standardized tests have also become a major presence in many schools.
- For students, one of the most meaningful parts of going to school is the experience of building friendships and expanding social networks. The school experience is also shaped by a student's position in the overall "pecking order" of their school. This is particularly true during the early high school years, when the dynamics of social exclusion and bullying are a major issue.

**11.3** Think about the kinds of characteristics that are associated with "good jobs," and describe how the distribution of good jobs is socially structured.

- Good jobs offer some combination of the following characteristics: good pay, high status, satisfying working conditions, room for growth, and enough free time and resources to pursue hobbies or other interests. People tend to be more satisfied when their job offers a good match with their expectations, interests, and values.
- Most people do not have good jobs, and they experience work as a place of domination, exploitation, and monotony. Good jobs are distributed unequally, in a manner that is shaped by race, class, and gender.
- Because of stagnating salaries and increasing job insecurity, there has been a general increase in job dissatisfaction since the 1970s.
- Happiness is not completely dependent on the job a person has. Close relationships with family and friends are particularly important, and so is a life that allows people to do challenging things.

## Key Terms

Citizenship education 376
Credentialism 379
Cultural capital 380
Homeschooling 383
Job training 376
Literacy 375
Marriage market 396
Moral education 377

Primary school 385
Private school 383
Public school 383
Secondary school 385
Standardized tests 388
Warehousing theory 381

## Review Questions

1. Describe the three main features of the mass literacy movements. What are the main achievements and shortcomings of the mass literacy movement?
2. Describe some of the ways that education reinforces social inequalities, and also some of the ways that it promotes social mobility.
3. Describe the main ways that education systems have changed over the last two hundred years.
4. What are standardized tests? Why were they developed, and how have they changed? What are some of their main advantages and disadvantages?
5. What are the characteristics of high-performing schools?
6. What are the characteristics of good jobs and bad jobs? What kinds of people are most likely to get these different types of jobs?

## Explore

### RECOMMENDED READINGS

Adler, Patricia, and Peter Adler. 1998. *Peer Power: Preadolescent Culture and Identity*. New Brunswick, NJ: Rutgers University Press.

Bell, Daniel. 1973. *The Coming of Post-industrial Society. A Venture in Social Forecasting*. New York: Basic Books.

Boli, John, Francisco Ramirez, and John Meyer. 1985. "Explaining the Origins and Expansion of Mass Education." *Comparative Education Review* 29: 145–70.

Kalleberg, Arne. 2013. *Good Jobs, Bad Jobs*. New York: Russell Sage.

Rivera, Lauren. 2015. *Pedigree: How Elite Students Get Elite Jobs*. Princeton, NJ: Princeton University Press.

## ACTIVITIES

- *Use your sociological imagination*: In October 2012 an article in the *Harvard Business Review* declared that data scientist was the "sexiest job of the 21st century." Read the article (https://hbr.org/2012/10/data-scientist-the-sexiest-job-of-the-21st-century), and do a sociological analysis of these jobs. Are they good jobs? What kinds of people are likely to get them? Are they more likely to reinforce social inequality or to promote social mobility? Are they likely to remain good jobs, or do you think they will eventually get influenced by the "Uberization of the economy" and the general tendency toward precarious work?

- *Media+Data Literacy*: Select a popular television show or movie set in a school, and another one set in a business environment. Describe the representations of teachers, students, bosses, and employees. What do you think these representations tell us about education and work?

- *Discuss*: Do you think your school sees itself as a research university, or as something else? Do you think your school's mission statement is an accurate description of what it is like to go to school there? Is there anything in the experience of going to your school that is not captured in the mission statement?

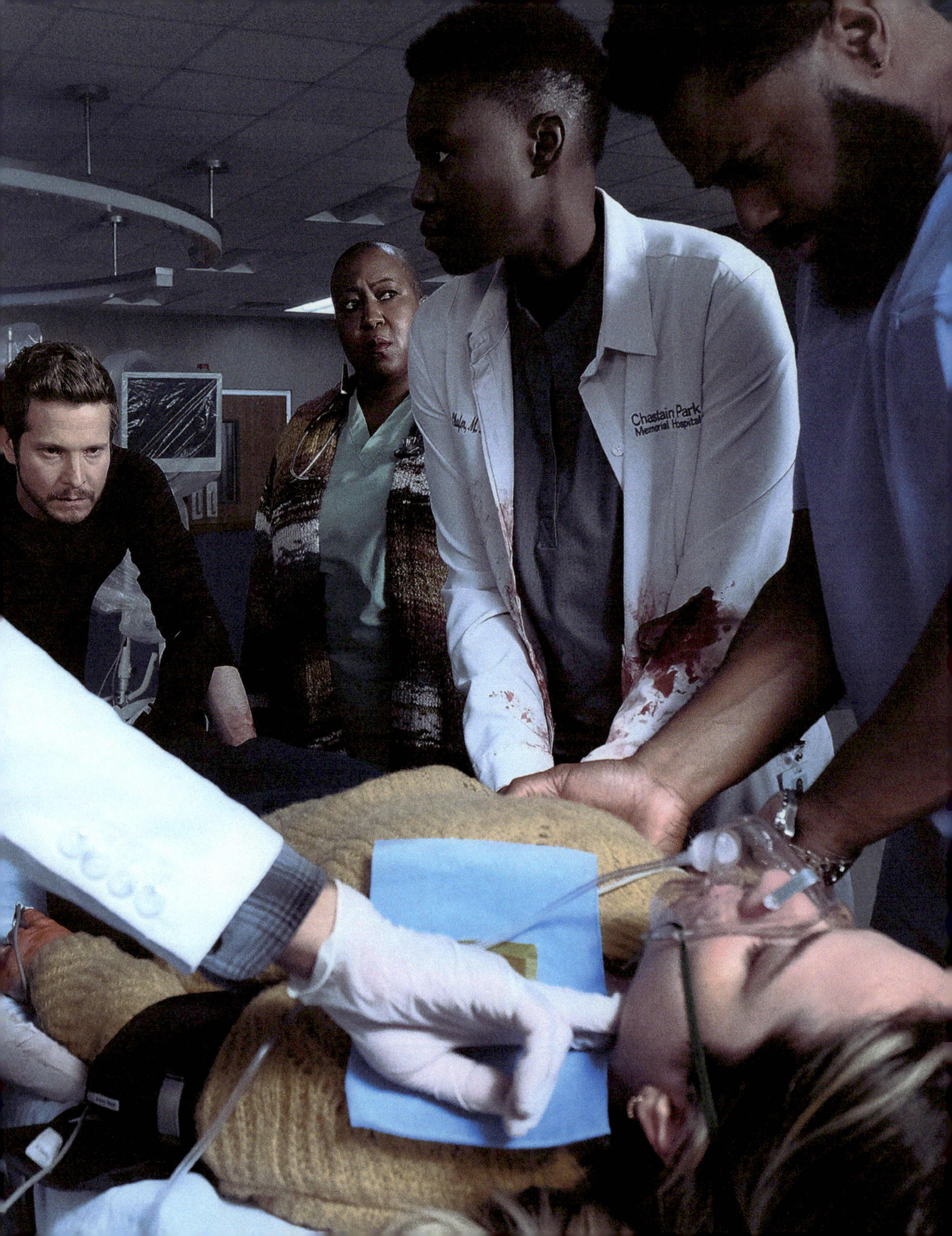
Chastain Park
Memorial Hospital

# 12

# Health, Illness, and Medicine

Medical dramas like *Grey's Anatomy*, *Chicago Hope*, and *The Resident* revolve around doctors who use surgery and drugs to respond to emergencies, heal mystery illnesses, and solve medical puzzles. The dominance of medical science, based in biological approaches to the body, remains unquestioned. When alternative medical practices are mentioned, they are usually regarded as problematic, or their benefits are explained using the language of medical science. Rarely are medical practices like hypnosis or spiritual healing shown in a positive light. Nor is the institutional organization of medicine and health care fundamentally questioned.

Unlike in the television shows, in wider society people pursue a broad range of medical practices. They try new exercise programs to improve their health and live longer. They change their diets, meditate, and use apps on their smartphones to remind them to count their steps or drink more water. Some people learn about self-care practices from family traditions or are persuaded by friends that certain foods or supplements can make a dramatic difference in their lives. From the perspective of conventional biomedical institutions, these other health behaviors are defined as "complementary and alternative" medicine, and they include practices as varied as acupuncture, biofeedback,

### Chapter Outline

**12.1 HEALTH 415**

*Geography, Class, Race, Gender, Age, and Other Differences 415*
*Genetics 416*
*Environment 417*
*An Intersectional Understanding of Health Disparities 419*

**12.2 ILLNESS 421**

*Experiencing Illness Differently 422*
*Being a Patient 423*
*Medicalization 428*

**12.3 MEDICINE 430**

*Public Health 431*
*Medical Institutions 433*
*Social Responses to Sickness and Illness 434*
*Access to Health Care 440*

**CASE STUDY: Genetic Testing 442**

There is rarely any mention of complementary or alternative medical practices in media representations of medicine and health. Most doctors on TV programs such as *The Resident* (2018–2023) are traditional practitioners grounded in surgery and biological science.

yoga, and traditional healers (Nahin, Barnes, and Stussman 2016). Between 1990 and 2002, the National Center for Health Statistics reported that the number of people who used complementary and alternative medical therapies in the United States "nearly doubled" (Su and Li 2011); today, about one-half of the US population reports using alternative medical approaches to support their health (Lee et al. 2022).

## LEARNING GOALS

**12.1** Know that health outcomes are stratified by race, class, gender, citizenship, education, geographical location, and income as well as the interaction among these factors for any given individual.

**12.2** Identify how health and illness are shaped by social factors such as cultural beliefs, historical experiences, social institutions, stigma and labeling, and the physical and social environment.

**12.3** Understand that the social responses to health, illness, and disability vary across time and place. There are different organizational and economic arrangements for health care, and these also change over time.

**Yoga**
The practice of yoga is associated with lowering stress, improving flexibility, and other health benefits.

In this chapter, we examine variation in health, illness, and medicine. We begin with a discussion of who gets sick. We explore the various social responses to ill health, disease, and disability; and we ask how we decide who is healthy or not healthy. Through the lens of social stigma, we discuss how some conditions are labeled as sick or pathological while others are regarded as normal. Last, we describe the social organization of medicine, hospitals, and other care facilities in the United States today.

# 12.1 Health

**LG** **12.1** Know that health outcomes are stratified by race, class, gender, citizenship, education, geographical location, and income as well as the interaction between these factors for any given individual.

The **sociology of health and illness** examines the relationship between health and society, with a central focus on **health demography**, which is the study of the distribution of disease and illness in a population. Sociological approaches emphasize that the social status of individuals and cultural beliefs about illness and medicine are important external factors that affect health. For example, it is a widely held cultural belief in many modern societies that ill health is the product of biological or natural conditions. This is in contrast to other people who might emphasize magical or religious causes. As scientifically committed researchers, sociologists agree that there are biological causes of disease, but they also show how social conditions like access to health care, environmental conditions such as pollution, and cultural beliefs about medicine also shape health outcomes.

**Sociology of health and illness** A field of sociology that studies the relationship between health and society.

**Health demography** The study of the prevalence, or the distribution, of disease and illness in a population.

## Geography, Class, Race, Gender, Age, and Other Differences

One way to consider the demography of health is to compare groups by geographical differences or other social indicators such as class, race, gender, and age. For example, the World Health Organization (WHO), a division of the United Nations that oversees global health, reports that in 2020 there was more than a 30-year gap in average **life expectancy** between rich countries like Japan (84.3 years) and Switzerland (83.5 years) and poorer countries like Lesotho (50.1 years) and the Central African Republic (53.1 years) (World Health Organization 2020). Explanations of these differences center on complex interlocking social conditions and environmental factors, such as risk of famine and violent conflict, and differences in nutrition, education, health care, and disease prevalence. Compared to the African countries, Japan and Sweden are rich, privileged societies where most people enjoy plentiful food, safe social environments, high levels of education, affordable and high-quality health care, and comparatively lower rates of disease. These shocking social facts about life expectancy are an important marker of the depth of global inequality.

**Life expectancy** The amount of time an individual can expect to live.

There are gender differences in health status and life expectancy that intersect with other social conditions to shape individual outcomes. For example, while women everywhere live longer than men on average, it remains difficult to disentangle the exact role of biological and social factors (Baierl 2004; Assari 2017; Zarulli et al. 2018). Important social factors include a higher rate of unhealthy behaviors like smoking and drinking among men and higher likelihoods of accidental or violent death. For women, lower life-expectancy rates are associated with these behaviors as well as pregnancy and childbirth.

There is substantial inequality within countries too, including rich countries like the United States (Milanovic 2016). Some of the most striking differences are connected to race and class, and they cut across gender and geography. For instance, the WHO has reported that "in the United States, infants born to African-American women are 1.5 to 3 times more likely to die than infants born to women of other races/ethnicities. American men of all ages and race/ethnicities are approximately four times more likely to die by suicide than females. African-American men in the United States are the most likely, among all ethnic groups in the United States, to develop cancer—a rate of 499.8 per 100,000" (US Centers for Disease Control and Prevention and National Cancer Institute 2019). The mortality rate for Black Americans from COVID-19 is 2.4 times higher than that for whites. Tens of thousands more Black Americans than white Americans have died during the pandemic (Frueh 2020).

One major cause of differences between social groups is access to health care. A great deal of the observed variation in access and use of health care is related to people's varying economic resources (Pollack et al. 2013; Adler and Rehkopf 2008; Crimmins, Hayward, and Seeman 2004). In the United States, the impacts of social class and geographical location are deeply entwined with race, and persistent inequalities between racial and ethnic groups remain a focus of public policy (Figure 12.1).

## Genetics

Some individuals and groups are more prone to disease than others. Medical researchers have identified specific genes that shape individual chances of disease, including cancer. That said, genetics are not destiny. Indeed, as the comparison of average life expectancy between countries illustrates, access to nutritious food, safe environments, and physical activity can affect health outcomes. An individual may be genetically predisposed to live a long life, only to have it cut short by violence, preventable disease, accident,

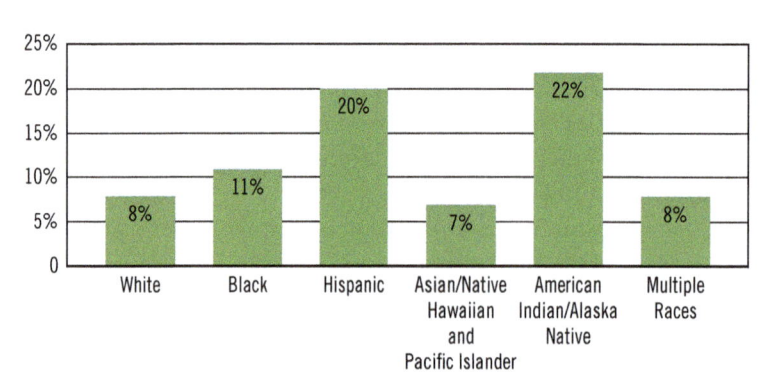

**Figure 12.1** **Uninsured Rates for the Nonelderly by Race/Ethnicity, 2019.**
Source: Kaiser Family Foundation. 2021. "Uninsured Rates for the Nonelderly by Race/Ethnicity."

| Race/Ethnicity | Uninsured Rate |
|---|---|
| White | 8% |
| Black | 11% |
| Hispanic | 20% |
| Asian/Native Hawaiian and Pacific Islander | 7% |
| American Indian/Alaska Native | 22% |
| Multiple Races | 8% |

or starvation. While there is no question that genetic inheritance shapes the demography of health, it is also true that *social context always matters*. Medical researchers make this point by separating the study of **genetics**—the study of how genes function in the biological system—from the study of **epigenetics**—the study of how genes interact with wider natural and social environments. This is why doctors and nurses ask questions about family history during medical examinations.

The connection between shared genetic heritage and social environments is widely accepted. Applying this idea to medical policy, however, has highlighted the complexity of racial and ethnic systems and differences in power, resources, and historical experience (Yancy 2007). Membership in a particular racial or ethnic category *may* reference a history of common experiences. It *might* capture shared social and natural conditions that shape health status epigenetically. Because of the long and terrible relationship between scientific medical research, social policy, and institutional racism, scientific arguments about the biological basis of race should always earn critical sociological scrutiny.

### Environment

Environmental impacts on health include both natural and social factors. According to the National Institute of Environmental Health Sciences (NIEHS), the list of environmental factors that cause ill health includes pesticides, pollen, lead, mercury, and mold, as well as extreme weather, climate change, and cell phones (Chapter 15). Climate change researchers, for their part, also show that some of the most lethal diseases affecting the world's population have been shaped by the migration of animal populations that carry and spread pathogens—germs or other infectious agents—among humans (Wu et al. 2016). The COVID-19 virus is thought to have been transmitted to humans through animals, although the precise source has not been identified.

In addition, environmental health researchers focus on health risks associated with occupational sites where there are chemicals, heavy metals, loud noises, or dangerous equipment. They support research on nontoxic, environmentally friendly design of workplaces and work processes; and they advocate for reducing chemicals and other pollutants in the natural environment. The NIEHS also studies environmental factors that may affect some populations more than others. For example, special attention is paid to environmental factors affecting pregnant women and the development of babies and young children, who are particularly vulnerable to chemicals and other toxins in their physical development (National Institute of Environmental Health Sciences 2019).

A second dimension of environmental health are social factors, which some researchers measure using the idea of **allostatic load**, or the wear and tear on the body due to stress. A high allostatic load describes a state where

**Genetics** The study of how genes function in the biological system.

**Epigenetics** The study of how genes interact with wider natural and social environments.

**Allostatic load** The wear and tear on the body due to stress.

the normal adaptive processes of a person's body "wear out or fail to disengage or shut off" (Seeman et al. 2004). People who suffer chronic stress have a higher allostatic load than others; are at increased risk for illness, such as heart disease (Logan and Barksdale 2008); and have a lower life expectancy (Duru et al. 2012; Geronimus et al. 2006). Researchers have begun to explore the idea that exposure to racism and/or economic inequality over the life course increases the allostatic load of members in affected groups and harms long-term health outcomes (e.g., Upchurch, Rainisch, and Chyu 2015; Parente, Hale, and Palermo 2013; Juster, McEwen, and Lupien 2010). Such disadvantage is cumulative over the life course and helps explain the deep disparities we observe between groups in the United States, especially racial groups (Shuey and Willson 2008). Along with a focus on differences in economic resources and access to health care, the concept of allostatic load is a useful way to think about how the social environment, such as the extent of racism or poverty in a society, not only affects individuals directly but also manifests itself in larger social patterns. These long-term impacts have recently been brought to public attention through the Black Lives Matter movement, which has traced the connections between the long-term stress of racism, allostatic load, and a heightened risk of being infected and dying from COVID-19 (Greenberg 2020).

**METHODS AND INTERPRETATION**

## Race-Based Medicine

One of the most complex discussions about racial categories, genetics, and health occurred in the process of developing the heart disease drug BiDil in the early 2000s. BiDil sparked controversy in the United States because it was only tested on the Black population. In previous scientific trials before BiDil, new drugs were tested on random samples of the US population that were racially heterogeneous.

The conflict over BiDil was related to the fact that race is not considered to be a biologically meaningful category. Doctors, pharmaceutical companies, and government officials all acknowledged that race is a historically evolved system of classifications, identity categories, and power relations. All parties in the controversy agreed that social inequalities in health care are the central causal factor producing racial disparities in health outcomes. Even NitroMed, the drug's producer, admitted that "race is an uncomfortable proxy for medical treatment." Despite all these statements, they used race as a proxy for physical differences anyway.

The authority to move to race-based drug testing was underpinned by a 2005 guideline published by the Food and Drug Administration. This guideline, which was updated in 2016, states in part that "differences in response to medical products have already been observed in racially and ethnically distinct subgroups of the U.S. population. These differences may be attributable to intrinsic factors (e.g., genetics, metabolism, elimination), extrinsic factors (e.g., diet, environmental exposure, socio-cultural issues), or interactions between these factors" (Food and Drug Administration 2016: 7). The idea that it was acceptable to racially segment populations for drug trials was also supported in a statement by the Association of Black Cardiologists, which argued that heart disease presents differently in the Black population than in others (Yancy 2007). As Scientific American (2007) summarized, "Absent better criteria, which may emerge from the work of genomics researchers ... race may provide a valid measure of how a drug works in a segment of the population that is underserved by the healthcare system."

Not everyone agreed with the decision to use racial categories in biomedical research (Roberts 2012; Kahn 2007, 2013; Bibbins-Domingo and Fernandez 2007). For example, researchers and doctors at San Francisco General Hospital, Bibbins-Domingo and Alicia Fernandez (2007), argued that the decision to allow race-based drug trials was based on "flawed scientific interpretations" of the data. They said it represented a "setback in the scientific and policy discourse on medical therapeutics and race" and that it "hinder[ed] the efforts aimed at eliminating health and health care disparities." Johnny Williams's book *Decoding Racial Ideology in Genomics* (2016) suggests further that using race as a biological proxy in health research is continuous with a long history of genomic research, which is profoundly rooted in common-sense understandings of race.

The lawyer, sociologist, and civil rights activist Dorothy Roberts made a similar point in her book *Fatal Invention: How Science, Politics, and Big Business Re-create Race in the Twenty-First Century* (2012). Roberts detailed how the biological myth of race has been resurrected to support supposedly cutting-edge research in genetics, and that the search for racial difference at the molecular level is part of a long history of scientific racism in the United States. Ethicist, historian, and legal scholar Johnathan Kahn made a similar argument in his book *Race in a Bottle: The Story of BiDil and Racialized Medicine in a Postgenomic Age* (2013), arguing that the emphasis on racial differences and genetics shifts the focus away from the differences in social power and resources that are responsible for health disparities. Along with Roberts, Kahn feared the social consequences of redefining race as a set of biological categories.

The BiDil controversy raised complicated questions about racial difference and genetics. In the United States, they exposed deep divisions in scientific, medical, and legal opinion. Civil rights activists and ethicists challenged the use of racial categories in biomedical research, and remain wary of how these categories are used in scientific research protocols and federal drug policy. In contrast, supporters advocate the use of race categories as a crucial element in addressing racial disparities in health in the United States.

### ACTIVE LEARNING

**Find out:** In 2021, the *Journal of the American Medical Association* released new guidance on the reporting of race and ethnicity in medical journals. Read the report and its guidelines (https://jamanetwork.com/journals/jama/fullarticle/2783090). What are the main recommendations that are made in this report?

## An Intersectional Understanding of Health Disparities

An **intersectional health perspective** describes multiple systems of oppression that shape health outcomes (Mullings and Schulz 2006). The intersectional perspective was developed to account for the unique experiences of Black women. Critical race theorists argued that when judges used perspectives that focused either on Black people or on female people as separate categories, the experiences of people in intersecting categories like Black women became invisible (Crenshaw 2016). This fundamental idea has since

**Intersectional health perspective** A multilevel approach to health care and medicine that emphasizes the multiple systems of oppression that shape health outcomes and how they interact.

## PAIRED CONCEPTS: Inequality and Privilege

### How Inequality Shapes Our Final Years

Not everyone makes it to old age. In his award-winning ethnography, *The End Game: How Inequality Shapes Our Final Years* (2017), Corey Abramson emphasizes that people who are poorer and socially disadvantaged are less likely to become old because they have "greater psychosocial stress loads, higher levels of violence, unequal treatment by medical institutions, and often the need to live or work in toxic environments" (135). If they survive to old age, Abramson observes, those who have had harder lives "are more beaten-up and worn down" when facing the physical challenges of aging.

For those who do make it to old age, challenges include decreasing energy and mobility, changing bodily appearance, and expanding health issues, as well as the death of friends and family members. Abramson argues that being an "old person" is a social status that shapes many aspects of life. For example, the importance of a functioning body was emphasized by many of the elderly because it defined dependence and independence and therefore the opportunities available to them. As one man in a nursing facility said, "I just sit around all week dying, and watching others waiting to die" (137).

Abramson also emphasizes that aging is socially stratified, despite some commonalities. People with more privilege enjoy greater autonomy in their decisions about how to age. Cultural differences also played a part in how seniors approached the challenges of aging. Important cultural resources like "language skills, knowledge of institutions, and general styles of interacting with authority figures," Abramson argues, "ultimately play a substantial role in mediating outcomes" (141). Abramson's research is important because it documents the subtle ways that pervasive inequalities in resources, social networks, and cultural experiences work over time to shape the experience of aging. As the US population continues to age, this is an increasingly urgent social justice issue.

**Elderly and unhoused**
Homelessness is a challenge at any age, but the elderly who are unhoused are extremely vulnerable and experience reduced life expectancy.

#### ACTIVE LEARNING

**Find out:** In 2022, the World Economic Forum published an article about the best countries in the world for retirees. Read the article (https://www.weforum.org/agenda/2022/11/these-are-the-best-countries-to-retire-in/) or the study on which it was based (https://www.im.natixis.com/content/dam/natixis/website/insights/investor-sentiment/2022/2022-global-retirement-index/RC31-0822-2022-Natixis-GRI-Full-Report-F.pdf). What are the characteristics and measurements that were used to create the ranking? What were the top ranked countries? Where does the US rank?

been extended to other intersections and social identities, including inequalities associated with age, language group, citizenship, and ability.

An intersectional perspective reveals that standard medical models disconnect intersecting identities and treat them as abstract categories. As an alternative to mainstream biomedical approaches, intersectional researchers recommend attention to concrete, historical contexts and actual lived experience of particular people in all their identities. An intersectional perspective also emphasizes the knowledge possessed by people in subordinate positions of power to describe and address their own health experiences. Intersectionality requires medical practitioners, researchers, and policy-makers to recognize their **epistemic privilege**, which elevates their medical and expertise and diminishes knowledge the patient might bring to their own situation.

The intersectional perspective is also different from a mainstream biomedical perspective in its emphasis on a **multilevel approach to health and illness**. This assumes that categories like race, class, gender, disability, and citizenship are not merely individual characteristics. Rather, they reflect social histories rooted in colonialism, slavery, segregation, and capitalist exploitation. These histories, which have determined the current distribution of material resources, are an important part of understanding health differences, making diagnoses, and supporting patients. In summary, intersectionality illuminates the need for policy and medical interventions that address interlocking systems of power at the structural and cultural levels as well as the level of the individual patient (Caiola et al. 2014).

> **Epistemic privilege** The privilege that attaches to the knowledge of powerful people.
>
> **Multilevel approach to health and illness** A part of an intersectional health perspective that emphasizes the systemic sources of health and illness as well as individual characteristics.

## 12.2 Illness

**LG 12.2** Identify how health and illness are shaped by social factors such as cultural beliefs, historical experiences, social institutions, stigma and labeling, and the physical and social environment.

There is no universal agreement about what it means to be "healthy" or "sick." The WHO defines health as "a state of complete physical, mental and social well-being and not merely the absence of disease or infirmity" (World Health Organization 1946). This broad definition sets a high standard for human flourishing but does not help define health, disease, or disability for specific purposes.

To complicate matters, what counts as health, disease, or pathology varies over time. For example, osteoporosis is a disease where people lose bone density as they age. Osteoporosis was officially recognized as a disease by the WHO in 1994, when it "switched from being an unavoidable part of normal ageing to a pathology" (Scully 2004). On the other hand, some conditions are redefined as healthy rather than pathological. As we described in Chapter 8, the medical understanding of homosexuality changed over the course of the 20th century from being considered a biologically based endocrine disorder to a mental disease to eventually being depathologized in 1973. Although stigma and discrimination against gay people continue, being gay in the United States today is much more widely accepted than ever (Schneider 2015).

A second issue is that medical science is increasingly able to detect new diseases. This is a social benefit in some ways since medical conditions cannot be treated until they are identified. However, our expanded ability to identify new medical conditions raises social expectations about good health and highlights the role of commercial interests in pursuing new diagnoses for the purpose of pursuing profitable new drug therapies (Rose 2007a; Schneider 2015). One example is the success of Viagra for erectile dysfunction in men and the search for "an equivalent market (that is, condition) in women" (Scully 2004; Moynihan 2003).

**Medical risk** Any condition or factor that increases the likelihood of disease or injury.

Ethical questions also arise around diagnoses of **medical risk**, or the predisposition to a disease. Insurance companies may register someone as having a genetic predisposition to a disease, even though they have no symptoms. Such a diagnosis can change someone's life even though they do not feel ill and are exactly the same person they were before the condition was diagnosed. Since 2008 passage of the Genetic Information Nondiscrimination Act (GINA) health insurers are prohibited from using genetic information to determine health insurance eligibility; but GINA "does not apply when an employer has fewer than 15 employees," and it "does not apply to other forms of insurance, such as disability insurance, long-term care insurance, or life insurance" (US National Library of Medicine 2020).

Defining health, disease, and illness is far from straightforward. What counts as a disease affects the technological and social resources dedicated to fighting disease and the social status of the people afflicted. Ethical questions arise because modern medicine has powerful tools to intervene in people's lives. For example, should medical treatment or new health regimes be imposed on people who do not want them? And who defines what is normal and what is pathological?

### Experiencing Illness Differently

In her 2019 book *Remaking a Life: How Women Living with HIV/AIDS Confront Inequality*, the sociologist Celeste Watkins-Hayes begins with a surprising quote from Dawn, one of her interview subjects, who comments that "If it weren't for HIV, I'd probably be dead" (Watkins Hayes 2019: 1). Watkins-Hayes spent 10 years researching and talking with Black women living with HIV in Chicago, Illinois. Many of the women she talked with told a story similar to Dawn. Diagnosed with a life-threatening disease, they described a path "that began with dying from HIV/AIDS and took them to living with and even thriving despite HIV" (Watkins-Hayes 2019: 11).

While doctors and hospital workers who were faced with such a story would probably emphasize the effectiveness of new drugs and other medical interventions, Watkins-Hayes points to the power of social connections and narratives of empowerment. The research achievements and medical interventions were important, to be sure, but so were the actions of AIDS activists and advocates who fought to de-stigmatize the disease and to build a social support infrastructure for the individuals living with the disease. And for economically disadvantaged Black women like Dawn, this social support infrastructure included things that they had not had before, such as access to health care, economic assistance, social support, and a way to get involved in political and civic organizations. As Watkins-Hayes (2019: 13) points out, "what undergirds Dawn's provocative comment is the community and infrastructure that afforded her the opportunities—and perhaps more importantly, the resources—to personally heal from, economically and socially navigate, and politically confront inequality, trauma, and their associated wounds. Dawn and many women like her had sustained so many blows throughout their lives that they were dying from their cumulative effects even before they were diagnosed with HIV. Rarely, if ever, had they been offered the kinds of openings that would give them the chance to repair these wounds. In the HIV/AIDS community, Dawn and others would find an unexpected place to create their lives anew."

Dawn's story highlights the difference between what sociologists identify as the disease and the illness experience. **Disease** is a disorder in the structure or function of the human organism, in this case Dawn's HIV diagnosis. The **illness experience** is the way in which the illness is understood and managed by Dawn, her family, and their community (Strauss and Glaser 1975; Pierret 2003). Over time, Dawn came to experience the HIV diagnosis as something that saved her life.

## Being a Patient

Being a sick person changes your social status. If you have an emergency appendectomy or catch the flu, you might be relieved of work or family responsibilities. Appendicitis and flu are both **acute diseases**, which the WHO characterizes as "a single or repeated episode of relatively rapid onset and short duration from which the patient usually returns to his/her normal or previous state or level of activity" (World Health Organization 2004). In these kinds of cases, it is understood that being sick is not your fault. You are expected to make an effort to get well and to seek competent technical help. Sociologist Talcott Parsons (1902–1979) identified this as occupying the **sick role**.

**Disease** A disorder in the structure or function of the human organism.

**Illness experience** The way in which illness is understood and managed by patients and their carers.

**Acute disease** A single or repeated episode of relatively rapid onset and short duration from which the patient usually returns to their normal or previous state or level of activity.

**Sick role** An idea developed by Talcott Parsons to describe social expectations for the behavior of sick people.

The sick role is a departure from normal role expectations. When you are sick, you seek health care. At that point, you become a patient. In the sick role, you are expected to surrender decision-making to others and to depend on doctors and other health carers to cure the medical condition. When you recover, you return to your normal role.

One limitation of the sick role is that it characterizes acute illness better than chronic conditions. **Chronic disease** is defined as a permanent, nonreversible condition that might leave residual disability and that may require long-term treatment and care (World Health Organization 2004). Rather than curing the disease, in this situation the goal is to manage the disease and maintain quality of life. Chronic disease is actually more common than acute disease, particularly for older people. It is still fairly uncommon for people aged 65 and older to have more than 10 years of full health; the remaining years are spent dealing with physical, medical, and mental limitations (He et al. 2016: 37). Dementia, diabetes, heart disease, and impairment in hearing and vision are all conditions that become an increasing burden for the elderly (Prince et al. 2014). The odds of facing multiple chronic health problems increase dramatically for people over 65 years old.

Many patients reject the sick role and the model of medicine and health care it presumes. They challenge the idea that patients should be passive in the sick role and instead become advocates and experts on their own conditions. They are increasingly aware of the problem of medical gaslighting, in which medical professionals dismiss their symptoms, blame them on psychological issues, and send them home without a diagnosis or a treatment plan (Sebring 2021). Sociologists have documented that treatment of patients in the medical system is highly dependent on race, class, and gender, so becoming an expert in and advocate for one's own health can seem like good sense. In fact, as Giddens (1991) argues in his theory of "institutionalized reflexivity" contemporary society encourages the popular dissemination of expert medical

**Chronic disease**
A permanent, nonreversible condition that might leave residual disability and that may require long-term treatment and care.

**The sick role**
How do we know this man is sick? Do you play the sick role when you are sick? Why or why not?

knowledges, which allow ordinary people to develop their own expertise and to develop their own agency in their relationships with their doctors.

**LABELING AND STIGMA.** Being labeled as a sick person can carry social **stigma**—a form of dishonor, discredit, or shame associated with illness (Goffman 1963). A mild form of medical stigma may result in someone declining to shake your hand because they do not want to catch your cold. A more serious form can accompany extreme physical or mental illness where a person's social behavior is understood to be unpredictable or dangerous. This kind of stigma can result in the social avoidance of the sick person. A third form of stigma blames the individual for their illness. In addition to social rejection, people who are suffering can be given social messages that they are responsible for their own illness, such as alcoholism, obesity, heart disease, or sexually transmitted infection. There is strong evidence that when people internalize the negative social message that they are responsible for their own suffering, it can affect their social identity and social behavior, resulting in a worsening of the medical condition.

**Stigma** A form of dishonor, discredit, or shame associated with illness; a spoiled identity.

A particularly harsh example of this was the fear and widespread social rejection of gay men in the 1980s when the HIV epidemic was emerging (Avert 2024). Stereotyped as a gay disease, HIV-AIDS was so stigmatized that patients were seen as unworthy of compassionate care or national concern (Figure 12.2). Stigma continues to be a causal factor in the lethality of AIDS. When people are stigmatized, they are socially marginalized, and they may fail to seek treatment or education (Sidibé 2012; UNAIDS 2017). Combating the negative effects of the stigma associated with different health conditions is a question of social justice and an important part of any solution to public health challenges like AIDS.

The stigma associated with illness sheds light on the way illness and deviance are connected. Like other forms of deviance, illness is a departure from social norms, and health is associated with social definitions of what is normal or socially standard. When people resist the stigmatizing power of negative labels, they question what is normal and can challenge public understandings of badness, wrongness, or pathology.

**ABILITY AND DISABILITY.** Definitions of "normal" and "pathological" in the context of disease also reflect social understandings of ability and disability. In the medical model, disability is defined as a physical or mental defect located in the individual. Disability scholars argue that this medical model makes moral judgments about the different ways of being human. This imposes normalized standards that can have perilous consequences for people labeled as disabled—from unnecessary surgery and medication to social exclusion and marginalization. This is a particular concern given advances in selective fertility and genetic testing for disability because it raises questions about what kind of human beings have the right to be born (Scully 2004; Sellman 2020).

Strict boundaries between what is considered normal, abnormal, and disabled are also not self-evident. Who should define the difference between normal human physical variation and disability? "No-one's body works, perfectly, or consistently, or eternally" (Shakespeare and Watson 2001: 26), and some populations widely perceived as disabled do not consider themselves disabled at all. Deafness is one such example. Many in the deaf community consider themselves a linguistic and cultural minority rather than disabled, arguing that "deafness is not a pathology and therefore does not need to be 'fixed'" (Jones 2002). In this case, it is the medical model—which assumes a disability needs to be fixed—that causes suffering rather than the supposed disability itself.

Using a sociological perspective also reveals the way disability is produced by institutional infrastructure, built environments, and the organized relationships of education, work, and family. For example, being in a wheelchair because your legs do not work like other people's legs can be defined as an impairment, but attending a school whose only means of upper-floor

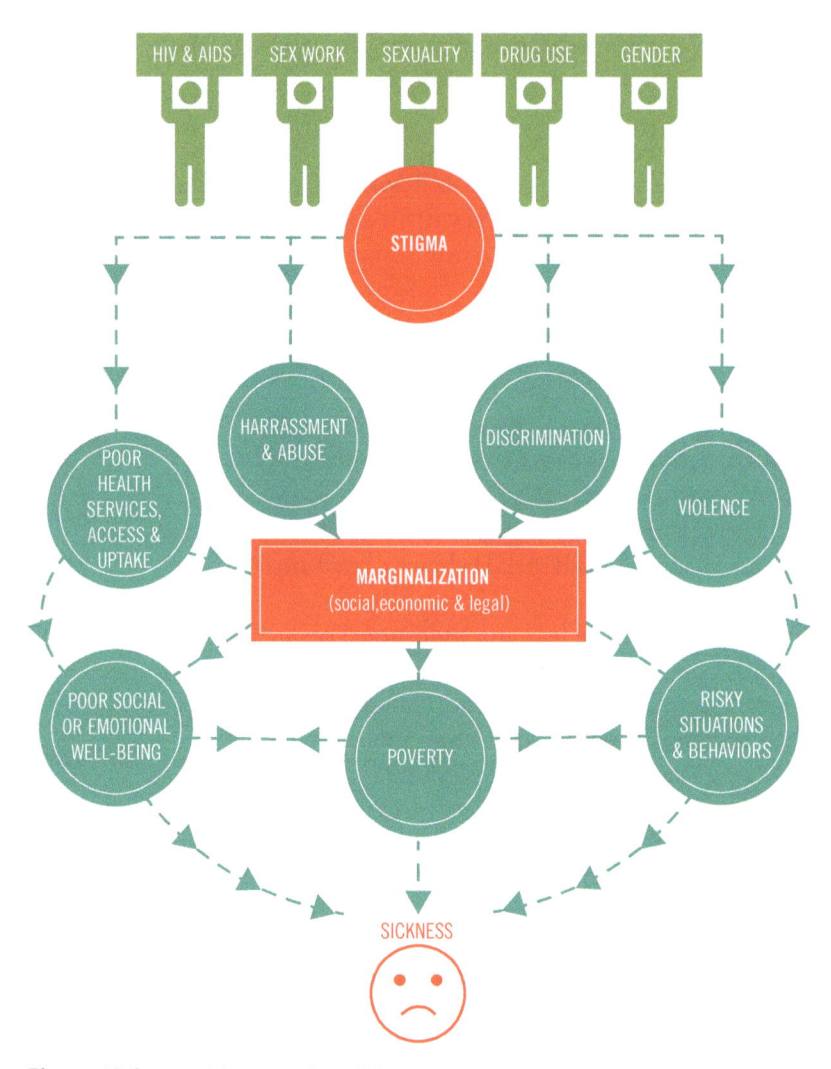

**Figure 12.2 How Stigma Leads to Sickness.**
Many of the people most vulnerable to HIV face stigma, prejudice, and discrimination in their daily lives. This pushes them to the margins of society, where poverty and fear make accessing health care and HIV services difficult.
Source: avert.org. Adapted from United Nations Development Programme.

| PAIRED CONCEPTS | **Power and Resistance** |

## Stigma and Size

In her 2014 book *What's Wrong with Fat?*, Abigail C. Saguy analyzes the public health crisis of obesity in the United States. She argues that fat is framed in a way that pathologizes the fat body. This creates social stigma that has negative social consequences for individuals deemed overweight. Saguy's work shows how medical institutions use the power of measurement to define broad social understandings of what is normal.

For example, Saguy reveals how the body mass index (BMI) has been used by public health authorities in arbitrary ways. While in 1985 the "National Center for Health Statistics defined overweight as having a BMI of 27.8 or more for men and 27.3 or more for women the National Institutes of Health (NIH) lowered the cutoff to a BMI of 25 in both men and . . . women in 1998 . . . causing 29 million Americans to become overweight overnight" (2014: 8). What began as a screening tool for health professionals to be used in conjunction with other medical tests to evaluate health was transformed over time to diagnose otherwise healthy individuals as unhealthy. This is true in both medical and popular uses of BMI. Saguy reports, "Based on BMI, actors George Clooney, Brad Pitt, and Matt Damon are all overweight, while Arnold Schwarzenegger is obese. Oprah Winfrey is technically 'obese' at her typical weight and was still technically 'overweight' at her lowest weight of 160 pounds at 5'7''" (2014: 8–9). In fact, there is a growing recognition among medical experts that BMI is not a great measurement of health, given that one-third of people who are obese by BMI standards are metabolically healthy and more than 20 percent of people who are "normal weight" by BMI standards are metabolically unhealthy (Attia 2023: 93–94). In this context, Saguy asks if it is possible to arrive at a neutral understanding of a heavier body.

The fat acceptance movement has been vocally critical of unreasonable social expectations about

**Oprah at a 2018 Weight Watchers event in California**

weight. Founded in 1969 as a civil rights organization, the National Association to Advance Fat Acceptance asserts a vision of a society in which people of every size are accepted with dignity and equality in all aspects of life. Activists challenge the idea that losing weight is a moral obligation. They are also very critical of corporate attempts by brands like Dove, Aerie, or ModCloth to replace extremely thin models with heavier alternatives, which they see as a marketing ploy, pointing out that replacement models are still well within social norms of standard weight and beauty, size 12s and typically white. As one body positive activist argues:

> Our bodies aren't something to be fixed. It's our culture that is in desperate need of repair. We deserve respect and access and representation right now. Those aren't things to be gained only if we change our bodies. (Thompson 2017)

> [!ACTIVE LEARNING]
> **Find out:** Why do you think that debates about body weight are so loaded with moral judgment? Do some research on public debates about new weight-loss drugs such as Wegovy or Ozempic. Do you find narratives of moral judgement in these debates? What are they?

access are stairs is a crucial social framework that structures your experience of bodily difference. In this example, the design of the building is as important as the physical impairment in producing disability. A sociological model does not ignore physical difference but "contends that societal, economic and environmental factors are at least as important in producing disability" (Scully 2004). Rather than physical or mental impairment of the body, then, a social model of disability emphasizes the experience of disability. This includes intersecting experiences of age, race, poverty, gender, and bodily differences that can all shape the lived reality of disability. In the United States, the civil rights of disabled people are recognized by the Americans with Disabilities Act of 1990 (ADA).

The ADA has resulted in sweeping improvements to building codes, educational policies, media formats, and workplace policies. Although discrimination against people with disabilities has not been eliminated, many social institutions have become more hospitable to disabled people since the passage of the ADA. As the size of the disabled population continues to grow in the United States, with recent official estimates that one in four people are disabled (Okoro et al., 2018), efforts to change institutional infrastructure and cultural understandings of disability are likely to expand too.

**MENTAL HEALTH.** Definitions of mental health have also changed over time. The neurodiversity movement, for example, argues that a range of neurological conditions is a normal part of human variation (Jaarsma and Welin 2012). Neurodiversity activists resist the definition of their existence as pathological or medical, and they challenge social understandings of what is abnormal.

In fact, there has been a clear expansion of the number of mental health diagnoses for a range of conditions over the course of the 20th and 21st centuries. The American Psychiatric Association, which publishes the *Diagnostic and Statistical Manual of Mental Disorders*, began with a list of 106 disorders in 1952 when the manual was first published. This rose to 297 in the fourth edition and now sits at 265 in the fifth edition (not counting modifiers to diagnoses).

## Medicalization

**Medicalization** A process where a social problem comes to be created or redefined as a medical issue.

Mental health is a central example of **medicalization** (Chapter 5), a process where a social problem comes to be created or redefined as a medical issue (Conrad and Schneider 1992). Peter Conrad's work on hyperkinesis, for example, describes how troublesome behavior, mostly among young boys, came to be diagnosed as the mental disorder of hyperactivity and later attention-deficit/hyperactivity disorder (Conrad 1975, 2006). Doctors were key to developing this diagnosis, as were companies offering newly available drugs for treatment, like Ritalin.

In more recent work, Conrad and others note how big pharmaceutical companies, biotechnology industry research, insurance companies, and health maintenance organizations have extended medical solutions and medical markets into previously nonmedical areas of society. Wider ranges of disorders and bodily effects have become subject to pharmacological and/or surgical intervention over time. In his review, Schneider (2015) cites shyness, now defined as social anxiety disorder (Lane 2007); a wide range of cosmetic surgeries (Sullivan 2001); and the pharmaceutical improvement of cognitive performance (Greely et al. 2008; Outram 2010). Overeating gets redefined as food addiction (Finlayson 2017). Patients are increasingly consumers of drugs and other therapeutic interventions to enhance or improve their lives (Conrad 2007; Miller and Rose 1997). The pharmaceutical industry is now seen as a major driver of medicalization, promoting drug interventions and a medicalized orientation to the treatment of normal human conditions such as physical pain, grief and bereavement (Kaczmarek 2022).

The rise of medicalization and medical experts has had broad social implications, with doctors involved in many areas of planning and controlling social life (Rose 2007b: 701). At the same time, medical expertise is also increasingly state-mandated and institutionalized.

**MEDICAL PROFESSIONS AND MEDICAL AUTHORITY.** The medical establishment has social power based on the authority to define what is healthy or pathological. The historical basis of medical authority in the United States is grounded in the professionalization of doctors. **Professionalization** is a process where a group of workers come to control a particular kind of work, defining training standards and credentials for entry into the occupation.

As Paul Starr documents in his landmark history *The Social Transformation of American Medicine* (2017), doctoring in the United States was not always a respected profession. Prior to the 20th century, most doctors made little money and were widely distrusted. Training was unstandardized, and doctors competed with other practitioners, including midwives and herbalists. This changed in the early 20th century, as doctors began to organize as a unified group. Doctors formed relationships with hospitals and medical schools to promote the standardization of medical education and began to participate in a regulated, credentialed profession. Organizations of doctors used the legal system to build an institutional monopoly to either drive out or control other practitioners. Working as a lobby group, the American Medical Association (AMA) secured the

**Professionalization** A process where a group of workers come to control a particular space in the division of labor on the basis of their expertise.

passage of regulations that supported the autonomy and authority of medical doctors and prohibited noncertified practitioners from practicing medicine.

As the influence and authority of doctors grew over the 20th century, people's self-understanding of their own health also changed. Public trust in science increased, especially as deadly diseases such as tetanus and diphtheria were effectively controlled. At the same time, individuals came to understand that health and medicine were too complex for self-diagnoses and self-care. Doctors wielded greater influence in social institutions, as employees were frequently required to have a doctor sign off on their health before starting work, schools began to require medical records of checkups and immunization for students to enroll or participate on sports teams, and new immigrants became subject to more rigorous health screenings. By the middle of the 20th century, being a medical doctor had become one of the most prestigious and highly paid occupations in the United States.

By the end of the century, however, cultural and institutional changes had begun to undermine doctors' authority and autonomy, especially in the delivery of primary care (McKinlay and Marceau 2002, 2008; also see Timmermans 2008). As health care systems grew larger, the US government became less supportive of doctors in private practice. Their professional autonomy has also been threatened by rising numbers of medical school graduates and the "weakening of the physician's union (AMA)" (McKinlay and Marceau 2002). Importantly, social trust in doctors began to decline as more information became available about health care in an increasingly global context. More patients exercised autonomy over their own health by using the internet to become informed and by seeking out alternate health care providers such as pharmacists, nurse practitioners, counselors, massage therapists, and midwives. That said, doctors remain an influential, well-educated, and highly paid group.

## 12.3 Medicine

**LG 12.3** Understand that the social responses to health, illness, and disability vary across time and place. There are different organizational and economic arrangements for health care, and these also change over time.

**Medicine** The social response to illness that attempts to identify, prevent, and cure disease.

**Medicine** is the social response to illness that attempts to identify, prevent, and cure disease. It is the social organization of caring for sick people and ensuring the health of the wider population. Since the onset of the COVID-19 pandemic in early 2020, all aspects of medicine have faced extraordinary challenges.

## Public Health

The COVID-19 pandemic is a stark illustration of the social experience of illness. Our bodies are social objects because we live in groups and communities. If you have young children in school, you know that quarantine procedures, although disruptive to learning and burdensome to parents and guardians, were essential to curbing the spread of the disease. As school districts considered reopening, they emphasized long-standing rules about illness, such as policies asking parents to keep children home if they had a fever so that they would not spread infection.

At the wider social level, medical officials make policies to safeguard **public health**, understood as the health of the whole population. Many doctors and other medical practitioners work in government agencies concerned with public health. In the United States, the Centers for Disease Control and Prevention (CDC) focus on the immediate health and safety of the US population through monitoring and responding to national and international health threats. Another important government organization is the National Institutes of Health (NIH), which is the largest biomedical research agency in the world. The CDC and the NIH both connect research to national public health.

An important kind of public health research is **epidemiology**, which investigates the social dimensions of disease patterns to discover the way diseases are communicated and spread. The goal of epidemiology is to develop interventions to prevent or halt the worst health impacts of diseases such as COVID-19.

In our globalized society, the spread of diseases like COVID-19 is of particular concern. This is why national public health organizations like the CDC and the WHO pay close attention to the number of cases of infectious diseases that are reported around the world. This is what happened in late 2019 when epidemiologists observed an **epidemic** described by a much higher number of people with serious flu-like symptoms than expected, eventually identified as a previously undetected form of coronavirus, soon labeled COVID-19. The COVID-19 outbreak was classified as a **pandemic** in March 2020 since it spread over a large geographical area of the world. For many years, the WHO and other public health researchers have argued that the likelihood of future epidemics and pandemics is very high (Fan, Jamison, and Summers 2018), and they advocate for investment in greater public health education, research, and preparedness to preempt mass deaths. Indeed, recent research has demonstrated that the underfunding of public health research left the US poorly equipped to respond to the COVID-19 pandemic (Alfonso et al 2021; Maani and Galea 2020).

**PUBLIC HEALTH EDUCATION.** Complementing public health research are **public health education** efforts to prevent disease, promote healthy

**Public health** The health of the whole population.

**Epidemiology** The study of the social dimensions of disease patterns to discover the way diseases are spread and communicated.

**Epidemic** A widespread or high incidence of an infectious disease.

**Pandemic** An epidemic that not only affects a large number of people but is also spread over a large geographical area of the world.

**Public health education** Educational efforts to prevent disease, promote healthy behaviors, and preempt risky ones.

behaviors, and preempt risky ones. Public health education is delivered through government, medical, educational, and community institutions. These efforts might emphasize vaccination and sanitation while promoting health through educating people about nutrition, safety awareness, exercise, and support for smoking cessation or weight loss. Education efforts might occur at schools and workplaces or take the form of information provided to all patients during routine medical visits.

Mass media campaigns are an important part of public health education programs, and they have a long history. Some examples include early posters about handwashing and hygiene, which can be seen today in restaurant and supermarket bathrooms, and antismoking campaigns funded through taxes on tobacco products. Increasingly, public health advocates are turning to social media to spread health information. Most recently, campaigns for physical distancing and mask-wearing attempted to combat the spread of COVID-19.

The evidence for the positive impact of these kinds of campaigns is not straightforward. In a comprehensive meta-analysis of mass media campaigns, for example, interventions were found to be most effective when done on multiple fronts. For example, when antismoking ads were combined with making tobacco products more expensive via increased taxation, the campaign against smoking was more effective (Wakefield, Loken, and Hornick 2010). Mass media campaigns are also more effective when the targeted behavior is a single event (like getting a vaccine or a screening test) rather than an ongoing behavior (such as wearing a mask in public).

**PUBLIC HEALTH POLICY.** **Public health policy** consists of the norms, rules, and laws that attempt to shape public health behavior. Some public health policies, such as rules about sanitation and clean water, are widely accepted. In the case of acute disease outbreaks, most people follow quarantine restrictions at ports of entry like airports and docks. Most people understand that social cooperation is needed to respond to major health threats.

Other public health policies are resisted. For example, in the wake of COVID-19, attempts were made nationwide to change behavior in public places. It was quickly understood that the virus was airborne and that measures such as wearing masks, frequent handwashing, and physical distancing would help to contain the spread of the virus. However, as the economic consequences of quarantine became increasingly severe—and in a political climate marked by polarization and unrest—some began to challenge the need for and efficacy of these measures.

A different kind of example of resistance to public health policy is opposition to childhood vaccinations for preventable and highly contagious diseases such as measles and whooping cough. These diseases can be fatal, with

**Public health policy** The norms, rules, and laws that attempt to shape public health behavior.

babies and young children at higher risk than adults. Some parents believe that these vaccines are associated with autism and other negative outcomes in children. The great majority of public health experts disagree. They argue that not vaccinating children reduces protection against these diseases for everyone. Further, the antivaccination movement makes it difficult to promote and distribute vaccines for emerging diseases, like COVID-19. Research from the Harvard School of Public Health shows that higher incidence of diseases that vaccines prevent is concentrated in counties and schools with lower levels of vaccination (Aloe, Kulldorff, and Bloom 2017; Feldscher 2017). This finding is significant in the current US context, where levels of whooping cough peaked in 2010 and 2012 (Centers for Disease Control 2019a) and where measles outbreaks are at their highest since 1992 even though "measles was declared eliminated in 2000" (Centers for Disease Control 2019b). Resisting vaccination recommendations is an example of how individual choices can affect the larger community by putting others at risk. It is also an example of how different groups of people disagree about the definitions of medical risk.

**Public health media campaign**
Antismoking campaigns are among the most common public health campaigns, with some of them funded through taxes on tobacco products. Increasingly, public health advocates are turning to social media to spread health information.

**National Infant Immunization Week poster, CDC**
Vaccination to prevent deadly diseases like measles, mumps, and rubella is public health policy in the United States. In some countries it is illegal to resist vaccination since lack of vaccination is understood to pose a public health risk to others. Do you think it is unreasonable to require parents to vaccinate children?

## Medical Institutions

**Medical institutions**, in which medical therapies are developed and practiced, include hospitals and other care facilities; the professional organization and education of medical practitioners; public health policy and the associated public institutions that implement it; and a wide range of medical business organizations, including the health insurance industry; and pharmaceutical and

**Medical institutions** Organizational arrangements in which medical therapies are developed and practiced.

**Health care systems** Contractual connections between medical organizations.

**Curative medical care** Care focused on curing disease or relieving pain to promote recovery.

**Preventive medical care** Care aimed at preventing disease before it occurs.

**Palliative care** Medical care offered to a person and that person's family when it is recognized that the illness is no longer curable.

**Integrated medical care** Systems of medical care that are coordinated to meet the multiple needs of clients.

**Reproductive labor** The work of producing and maintaining individuals for social participation in the economy and society.

other corporate biomedical research organizations. Medical care is also practiced by laypeople in the family and in community institutions.

**HOSPITALS AND OTHER CARE FACILITIES.** In the United States, medical care is increasingly delivered through large networks or **health care systems**, which are contractual connections between medical organizations. Most health care systems include doctors' offices and group practices with primary care and specialty services, hospitals, labs, clinics, and other services. The US Department of Health and Human Services reports that nearly 45 percent of all physicians and nearly 70 percent of all hospitals are members of health care systems. Some of these networks are huge: the largest 5 percent have 18 or more hospitals (US Department of Health and Human Services 2016). There are many different kinds of care facilities too, not all of which are inside large systems. These include birth centers, blood banks, nursing homes, imaging and radiology centers, hospice homes, mental health and addiction treatment centers, and a range of emergency and urgent care organizations, among others.

## Social Responses to Sickness and Illness

There are several different approaches to the organization of health care. **Curative medical care** is focused on curing disease or relieving pain to promote recovery (World Health Organization 2004: 20). A curative approach to care responds to crisis once a disease or injury has occurred. By contrast, **preventive medical care** aims to prevent disease before it occurs. Preventive (or "preventative") care might include exercising more, improving nutrition, or stopping smoking to prevent disease and improve quality of life. **Palliative care** provides pain relief for incurable illness and typically offers psychological and social support for the person who is suffering as well as their family. The World Health Organization (2004: 35) also recognizes **integrated medical care** as systems in which various kinds of care are coordinated by different care systems "to meet the multiple needs of clients." In practice, most health care systems contain elements of each kind of care.

**CARE WORK.** Much medical care occurs outside formal medical institutions in families and communities. Historically, this work has been done by women in their roles as wives and mothers. This is the **reproductive labor** of producing and maintaining individuals who participate in the economy and society. Even when reproductive work is paid, it tends to be dominated by women. Elementary and middle-school teachers, registered nurses, and psychiatric and home health aides are paid less, researchers argue, because these jobs are historically done by women (Carleton 2014).

## CAREERS

### Sociology and Medicine

Medical education occurs in large health systems that include hospitals. Aspiring medical practitioners must first complete rigorous premedical training, which includes courses in advanced biology and chemistry. These classes prepare a student for the Medical College Admission Test (MCAT), the standardized exam required for medical school application. Undergraduates interested in a medical career are also advised to take classes in English, sociology, and psychology to prepare for the MCAT. Good communication skills and the ability to understand social context and group differences are crucial for medical practitioners.

The MCAT has four sections: Foundations of Living Systems, Foundations of Biological Systems, Foundations of Behavior, and Scientific Inquiry and Reasoning Skills/Critical Analysis and Reading Skills (CARS). The purpose of the CARS section is to measure how well students can apply what they know and integrate new information in complex environments, including biological, biochemical, and social information.

Many health-related occupations have been shaped by the idea that medical education should be science-based, include a clinical component, and should develop a student's social capabilities and cultural awareness. These occupations include veterinary science, dentistry, public health, nursing, social work, community health education, pharmacy, nutrition, and many other associated roles. In each of these fields, awareness of social difference is a fundamental competence. For those interested in a career in a health field, exposure to key sociological concepts is an invaluable part of preparation.

**Medical students**
The medical education model in the United States is based on the idea that medicine should be science-based, include a clinical component, and develop a student's social capabilities and cultural awareness. Sociology courses are good preparation for a medical career.

### ACTIVE LEARNING

**Find out:** Pick two different health careers, such as surgical nurse, primary care doctor, midwife, social worker, or clinical psychologist. Visit your career center or go online to learn the requirements for training in each field. What kinds of training do these different fields have in common? What does this suggest about priorities in medical education?

For wealthy countries, a rapidly aging population has led to a dramatic increase in in the need for care work. In countries like Japan and Germany, more than 20 percent of the population is over 65 years old; by 2050, many countries in Europe and Southeast Asia are forecast to have more than 30 percent of their population over 65 years old (He, Goodkind, and Kowal 2016: 10). And population aging has increasingly become a global issue. Total fertility rates have dropped to below replacement levels on every continent except Africa, and they have been on the decline in Africa as well.

## Chapter 12 HEALTH, ILLNESS, AND MEDICINE

### PAIRED CONCEPTS
## Solidarity and Conflict

### Disruptive Behavior in Medical Settings

Doctors, nurses, and therapists must cooperate to deliver patient care, even though they come from different disciplines, have different kinds of training and education, earn different salaries, and work different schedules (Burdick et al. 2017; Gausvik et al. 2015; Epstein 2014). There is evidence that patients are harmed when health professionals do not communicate well (Weller, Boyd, and Cumin 2014). This makes disruptive behavior in medical settings a significant problem.

According to the Joint Commission, the oldest independent nonprofit accrediting body for medical standards in the United States, "intimidating and disruptive behavior" in health care organizations is defined as "overt actions such as verbal outbursts and physical threats, as well as passive activities such as refusing to perform assigned tasks or quietly exhibiting uncooperative attitudes during routine activities." Disruption, intimidation, and bullying in health care settings are topics of increasingly urgent public concern. The Joint Commission's report emphasizes that there is a widespread culture of disruption and intimidation in health care. Nurses report disruption and disrespect from doctors (Klass 2017; Keller 2016; Ford 2009; Lazoritz 2008) as well as bullying and intimidation from other nurses (Robins 2015a, 2015b). Interns and medical students also report disruption, hazing, and disrespect from nurses and senior doctors (Slavin and Chibnall 2017; Dyrbye et al. 2014; Fried et al. 2012; Dyrbye, Thomas, and Shanafelt 2005). There is also evidence that disruptive and intimidating behavior extends beyond nurses and doctors to pharmacists, therapists, support staff, and administrators (Joint Commission 2008; Wyatt 2013). In fact, disruptive behavior from the general public increased significantly during the COVID-19 pandemic, with nurses and other health care workers reporting an increase in abusive and threatening behavior directed at them by patients (Nebehay 2020).

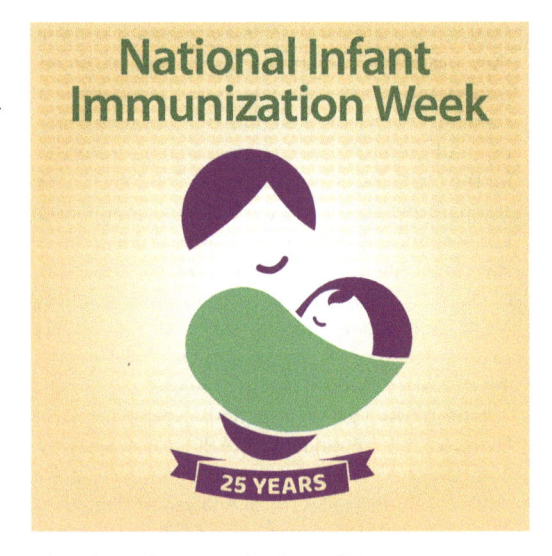

**Diversity and cooperation in medicine**
Doctors, nurses, and therapists must cooperate to deliver patient care, even though they come from different disciplines, have different kinds of training and education, earn different salaries, and work different schedules.

The consequences of disruption, intimidation, and bullying in health care are many. One concern is medical errors and adverse outcomes (Rosenstein and O'Daniel 2008). The Joint Commission (2008) also lists increased cost of care, staff turnover, and medical staff shortages (particularly of nurses) as key issues. These patterns of fractured solidarities in stressful workplaces with complicated hierarchies also seem especially problematic in the health care field, where the focus is on the care of others.

#### ACTIVE LEARNING

**Find out:** Find the American Medical Association's code of medical ethics, and compare its statements on (a) disruptive behavior by physicians and (b) disruptive behavior by patients. Do you think these statements are adequate? How would you improve them?

The COVID-19 pandemic has exacerbated a widespread "crisis of care" in the United States and around the world, with fewer people available to care for children, elders, and the sick. The women who once did unpaid reproductive labor increasingly work in higher-paid employment—if they can get it. This has resulted in an unmet demand for care work.

## PAIRED CONCEPTS: Global and Local

### Does Modern Society Make You Sick?

In *Love, Money, and HIV* (2014), Sanyu Mojola combines fieldwork and surveys in rural Kenya to analyze why young, educated African women are more susceptible to HIV-AIDS than less educated young women. This paradox is counterintuitive since many policy-makers believe that education, and especially health education, can reduce the likelihood of contracting HIV-AIDS. In her award-winning study, Mojola shows that neither better information about HIV-AIDS nor the personal experience of attending funerals of AIDS victims affects the risky sexual behavior of these young, educated women. Why not?

Mojola's explanation reveals that an unintended effect of education for girls in contemporary Kenya is that they develop a taste for cosmetics, smartphones, and the other high-status objects that circulate in the modern global marketplace. These are exciting symbols of elite and cosmopolitan identities. At the same time, the expansion of secondary education has led to credential inflation in Kenya, where there are not enough local jobs. High expectations around consumption, combined with weak income prospects, result in many young women choosing sexual relationships with men who can support their consumer aspirations and modern identities. This is problematic in the context of sex in contemporary Kenya, which is shaped by the history of the global HIV-AIDS epidemic.

Although it is well known that men traveling the main highways spread HIV-AIDS by having sex with multiple partners and being unwilling to use condoms, Mojola's interviews reveal that young, educated women in Kenya prefer these partners because they are older, wealthier, and more experienced. Such men provide gifts and support modern lifestyles. Similarly, although these young women attend funerals of women like themselves who have died from AIDS, this creates a context in which death is less remarkable (American Sociological Association 2017).

Does this mean that global modernity makes these young women sick? Mojola's analysis suggests that modern Kenya is a place where global forces of colonialism, capitalism, and consumption combine to produce increasing education and rising expectations in a local context marked by few job prospects and a mixture of traditional and modern ideas about sex and health. At this risky intersection of local and global forces, young, educated women in contemporary Kenya have a higher risk of sickness and death than their less educated and less modern counterparts.

#### ACTIVE LEARNING

**Find out:** The Centers for Disease Control and Prevention (CDC) maintains a data repository on HIV infection rates around the world (https://www.cdc.gov/globalhivtb/index.html). What is the rate of HIV prevalence in Kenya? Choose two countries—one with a life expectancy higher than Kenya, and one with a life expectancy that is lower—and find out their rate of HIV prevalence. What is your explanation for these findings?

**Capitalist crisis of care** The shortage of reproductive labor created by the capitalist organization of work.

Philosopher and social theorist Nancy Fraser describes this as a **capitalist crisis of care** since capitalism has assumed but rarely paid for the value of socially reproductive care work. In early capitalism, care work was privatized in the family household. In the 20th century, care work was partly socialized in the form of state medical, disability, and family services. In the current era, where social welfare policies have been reduced or eliminated everywhere, Fraser observes that reproductive work is becoming commodified—that is, it has been transformed into something to be bought and sold on open markets (Fraser 2013).

Others have noted the globalization of care work. In the development of transnational markets in reproductive labor, many people have moved from the poorer countries of the Global South to the richer countries of the Global North to improve their economic well-being. Many of these migrants are women who find work in "in paid care, cleaning, or domestic service, looking after children, older people, and households in richer countries" (Williams 2018). Rather than being permanent settlers with citizenship rights, many of these workers have the status of visitors or temporary workers. They leave their own families behind in their home countries and support them by sending them their earnings (Chapter 7). These are enormous global financial flows of labor and capital: for example, annual remittances from migrant Filipino workers to the Philippines were worth US $26.9 billion in 2016—or nearly half of the Philippines' national export economy (Rowley 2017). The Commission on Filipinos Overseas estimated that approximately 10.2 million people of Filipino descent lived or worked abroad, in over one hundred countries—about 10 percent of the national population.

**Deinstitutionalization** A historical process in the United States and other countries where populations once housed in long-term care facilities like psychiatric hospitals and facilities for the developmentally disabled declined sharply over time.

**Elder care**
The global capitalist crisis of care contrasts young immigrant populations from poorer countries with aging citizen populations of wealthy countries. When these young Filipino nurses graduate, many will find work around the world. In fact, the Philippines exports so many nurses that there is a local crisis of nursing case in the Philippines.

Another factor affecting the US crisis in care work has been the **deinstitutionalization** of populations that were once housed in long-term care facilities, which included psychiatric hospitals and centers for the developmentally

## PAIRED CONCEPTS: Structure and Contingency

### Waiting for an Organ Transplant

There are about 80 organ transplants a day in the United States (Health Resources and Services Administration 2018). Kidneys are the most commonly transplanted organs, followed by the liver, heart, lungs, pancreas, and intestines. In addition to organs, human tissues can be donated. Common donations include the cornea (the transparent covering over the eye), which can cure blindness. Other donations are skin for grafts, veins, and bones. For some transplants, donations are from deceased persons, while in other cases living donors give organs or tissues.

While rates of transplantation are high, demand for organs is much higher. Currently, there are nearly 120,000 people on the transplant waiting lists in the United States. In this context, the question of who gets an organ for transplant is especially difficult for decision-makers.

Human organs can be purchased in some countries overseas, which raises hard choices as well as ethical and safety issues for people needing organs. In the United States, the sale of human organs is outlawed by the National Organ Transplant Act (1984). The law also contains provisions to establish the Organ Procurement and Transplantation Network (OPTN) and allows the establishment of nonprofit organ procurement organizations. These laws and organizations define policies about who gets organs for transplant when they become available.

The process for selecting an organ recipient is highly rule-governed (OPTN). In the first step, the OPTN screens out everyone on the list who is not a match for the organ because of blood type, height, weight, or other medical factors. The second step is geography: someone is more likely to receive an organ donation if they happen to be in the local donor service area when an organ becomes available. This is a highly contingent element in the transplant process. Some patients try to register in more than one service area to maximize their chances of donation, but the outcome still relies on the unpredictable unfolding of events that makes organs available. Even in the highly structured cooperative process of organ transplant, there are multiple contingencies that affect the decision of who will receive a donated organ. Stated another way, the policies and process of getting an organ for transplant are both highly structured and highly contingent.

**Celebrating organ donors**
In Louisville, Kentucky, on May 3, 2018, some participants in the annual Pegasus Parade wear shirts that say "Give the Gift of Life/Be an Organ Donor." The demand for organs is far higher than supply.

### ACTIVE LEARNING

**Find out:** Although the US is one of the world leaders in the number of organ transplants performed each year, it also has a very long waiting list, with nearly five thousand people dying every year while waiting for a transplant. What is the organ donation rate in the US? How does this compare with Spain, which is considered to be the world leader in organ donation? What are the key structural features of Spain's organ donor system?

disabled. Where once these patients were incarcerated in institutions—sometimes against their will—the number of people in such long-term-care facilities has declined sharply (Prouty, Smith, and Lakin 2007; Eyal 2010, 2013). This was partly to do with moral critique of the conditions in these institutions, a resistance to the stigma and shame associated with mental illness and disability, and a move to community-based alternatives to care.

Greeted as a liberating and positive move by many, deinstitutionalization has had uneven consequences for some populations requiring care. Communities cannot always meet the needs created by deinstitutionalization, resulting in a lack of medical resources for people suffering from mental health crises and a disturbing rise in the criminalization of those same people. As the Treatment Advocacy Center reports, "nearly half of all individuals with schizophrenia or bipolar disorder will be jailed at some point in their lives. Individuals with serious mental illness also are significantly more likely to be injured or killed during an encounter with law enforcement" (Treatment Advocacy Center 2021).

### Access to Health Care

The history of medical care and medical institutions is quite different across countries. For example, although the United States, Canada, and Australia share many standards for medical education and practice, Canada and Australia both have strong national health care systems, based on the idea that medical care is a right of citizenship. In the United States, by contrast, medical care is organized by the market. As the sociologist Paul Starr (2017) notes in his definitive history of American medicine, this has the effect of associating the right to health care with hard work and employment rather than citizenship or human rights.

Health care systems are ranked by scholars and international agencies like the WHO. They are evaluated along dimensions such as responsiveness, quality, and fairness. In 2023, Singapore, Japan, South Korea, Taiwan, China, Israel, and Norway were the top seven in health ranked by the Legatum Institute's annual report on global prosperity (Legatum 2023). Most of the nations with top health care systems are wealthy, capitalist, and democratic countries. The United States is ranked 69th among the 149 countries studied. This is surprising because the United States spends far more per capita on health care than any other country in the world, with 17.2 percent of gross domestic product spent on health care (Organisation for Economic Cooperation and Development 2017: 132–34).

In the United States, health care is a mix of private and public programs, with nearly 70 percent of people with health insurance paying for some form of private program. The basic idea in any **health insurance** scheme is that members pay a regular fee into a larger pool, to be drawn on if they need medical care. In this way, insurance programs enable participants to share risks and resources. There are many different ways of organizing and supporting insurance schemes for health care. 54.3 percent of the US population was covered by employer-based insurance in 2021, based on the recent research by the US Census Bureau (Kaisler-Starkey and Bunch 2022).

**Health insurance**
A way to pay for health care where members pay a regular fee into a larger pool, to be drawn on when they need medical care.

Medicaid and Medicare are federal programs that provide basic health care to vulnerable people, including the aged, the poor, and certain disabled populations. Some US states have additional programs to support individuals and families who are living in poverty. In addition, military personnel and qualified veterans are covered through the military health system, and the government supports the Indian Health Service for eligible Native Americans.

Unlike most developed countries, however, the United States has no formal **national health care system** in which all citizens are guaranteed access to basic medical services. While the Affordable Care Act of 2010 was designed to extend health insurance to every citizen, the Tax Cuts and Jobs Act of 2017 repealed key provisions, with analysts projecting a sharp increase in the rate of people without health insurance in the years to come (Jost 2017). Rates of the uninsured did increase between 2017–2019, but the passage of the COVID-19 stimulus package in March 2021 included an increase in health insurance subsidies that led to declines in the uninsured population (Lee et al. 2022). The Biden Administration introduced new policies to expand access to health care and reduce the cost of health insurance, but the US remains locked in a political struggle over the right way to organize and pay for health care.

**National health care systems**
Government-based health care systems in which all citizens are guaranteed access to a basic bundle of medical services.

It is a paradox that the United States spends the most on health care in the world but does not provide health care for its entire population and does not rank among the countries with the top health care systems in the world. Health care costs remain high and are rising, and insurance seems out of reach for many people living in poverty as well as members of other marginal populations. This makes it likely that health insurance will remain a potent political issue in the United States for years to come.

## CASE STUDY

# Genetic Testing

**DNA science for all**
The saliva collection kit for ancestry testing by 23andMe.

To explore the intersection between health, illness, and biomedical knowledge, the rise of commercial genetic testing, which uses laboratory methods to look at an individual's genes, provides a compelling case study. These tests rely on the *power* of biological and medical science to define human health and social welfare. While the NIH emphasize the health benefits of genetic tests—such as diagnosing disease and identifying gene changes that can be passed on to children—they are also clear that genetic tests "cannot tell you everything about inherited diseases. For example, a positive result does not always mean you will develop a disease, and it is hard to predict how severe symptoms may be" (National Institutes of Health 2017).

Despite these attempts at caution by the NIH, popular and lay understandings link genetic risk to health, even though the *risk* of developing a disease is not the same as actually developing the disease. There are several forms of *resistance* to genetic diagnosis. One form of resistance is diet. Dr. Peter J. D'Adamo's book *The GenoType Diet* (2007) suggests that following genetically informed diet plans can help you "live the longest, fullest and healthiest life possible." There are also individuals sometimes referred to as "genetic superheroes" who resist "disease destiny" (Goldberg 2016).

Initially a limited medical practice, genetic testing is now widespread, with people using DNA testing kits at home. The Ancestry.com website, for example, offers "cutting edge DNA testing" to predict a person's genetic ethnicity. The website for 23andMe provides detailed "health reports" that offer "genetic health risk reports" for diseases including late-onset Alzheimer's, celiac, and Parkinson's; "carrier status reports" for over 40 hereditary conditions, including cystic fibrosis and sickle cell anemia; and "Wellness" and "Trait" reports that provide information about freckles, male bald spot, and even unibrow.

Although it is offered as a medical service, 23andMe clearly advertises more when it says, "Find out where your DNA comes from and use it to take the trip of a lifetime." Clearly, these new DNA tests go far beyond assessment of disease risks. Along with the rest of modern biomedicine, these DNA tests have immense authority to define the "normal" human body as well as its social characteristics. In this sense, genetic testing businesses like Ancestry and 23andMe share in the *power* of medical and biological science to define social understandings. They directly shape the social stories people tell about themselves and the social actions they take as a result.

This is made clear in the account provided by Courtney, a client featured at Ancestry. com in 2018. She relates that her individual profile confirmed stories she had long told about her family, especially about her mother and grandmother as strong women. The findings of her genetic test coupled with historical genealogical data allowed her to connect her self-understanding to traditions of African matrilineal authority. It allowed her to link her *local* biographical story to a larger *global* story and connect to a distant community on the Ivory Coast. This altered her identity in important ways. "It's fundamentally changed the way I think about myself," she says.

Similarly, Ancestry.com airs a television ad of a man dancing in traditional German lederhosen, joyfully expressing *solidarity* with his German ethnic community. After genetic testing, he discovers he has more Scottish and Irish ancestry than he thought. The advertisement closes with him in a kilt with bagpipes, suggesting that social practice should follow the revelation of ethnic heritage. It suggests there is a *conflict* between the celebration of German ethnicity when he is actually of Irish–Scottish ethnicity. These stories convey important lay understandings about race, ethnicity, and genetics. The social message in both cases seems to be that biological genetic information is what should define family narratives. In fact, the suggestion is that genetic information is more important than your prior understandings about where you are from. The scientific information is rooted in biological truth and is therefore "more real."

But does this make sense? Are race and ethnicity actually *structured* by genetics? Does your genetic information determine your ethnic and racial identity? There do seem to be group differences that are seen in aggregate genetic information. There are physical differences that appear to be related to risks of disease. It is also true that genetic information connects to stories of ethnic belonging for many people. Sociologists emphasize, however, that it is always important to see how these scientific facts are embedded in histories of racial difference. In the United States, as in other European settler societies, these are histories of colonization, slavery, and successive waves of immigration. This can also be seen in the collective genetic map of Americans.

Bryc et al. (2015) analyzed data from 145,000 cheek swabs collected by 23andMe and found that "a lot of Southern whites are a little bit black" (Ingraham 2014). When compared to what people claim their racial and ethnic status to be, Bryc and

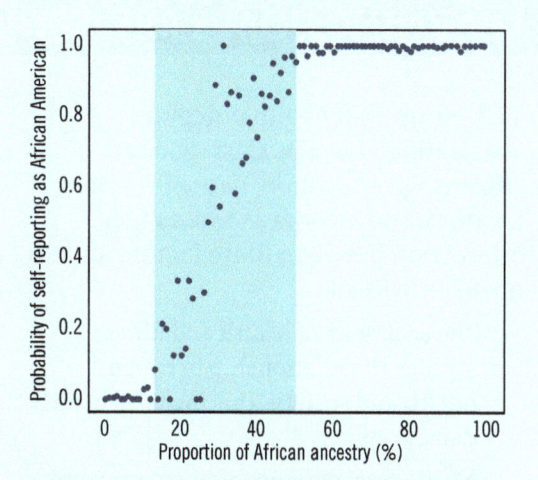

**Figure 12.3 Proportion Who Claim African American Identity Compared to Proportion of Measured African Ancestry.**
Source: Bryc, Katarzyna, Eric Y. Durand, J. Michael Macpherson, David Reich, and Joanna L. Mountain. 2015. "The Genetic Ancestry of African Americans, Latinos, and European Americans across the United States." *American Journal of Human Genetics* 96(1): 37–53 (additional tables: https://www.cell.com/cms/10.1016/j.ajhg.2014.11.010/attachment/cff15e7e-75da-48acad13-2f6fe134fd48/mmc1.pdf).

her colleagues found that there is *contingency*, or a grey area in ethnic identification. As Ingraham (2014) reports, "People who are less than 15% African are highly unlikely to describe themselves as African-American. People who are 50% African or more are almost certain to describe themselves this way. In between (grey shaded area), some uncertainty" (Figure 12.3).

This pattern of reporting is unsurprising considering the historical *privilege* associated with whiteness in the United States and the continuing pervasive *inequality* between Black and white Americans. This preference for claiming a more privileged category also suggests pressing ethical questions in the wake of genetic technologies that allow scientists to engineer more desirable traits into human beings. Just because we can engineer humans genetically, should we? Are there limits on what we should do? Who decides?

## LEARNING GOALS REVISITED

**12.1** Know that health outcomes are stratified by race, class, gender, citizenship, education, geographical location, and income as well as the interaction between these factors for any given individual.

- The sociology of health and illness studies the relationship between health and society. This includes health demography.
- Major determinants of health and life expectancy include access to health care and environmental factors. The impact of environment on health outcomes can be understood through the concept of allostatic load.
- Gender and race interact with other factors to shape life expectancy differently within and between nations. An intersectional health perspective emphasizes multiple systems of historical and current oppression that shape health outcomes.

**12.2** Identify how health and illness are shaped by social factors such as cultural beliefs, historical experiences, social institutions, stigma and labeling, and the physical and social environment.

- Epigenetics is the study of how genes interact with wider natural and social environments.
- Different cultural understandings can have enormous effects on a patient's experience of health and illness.
- In the biomedical system of the United States, people are understood to occupy a sick role when they are sick. Many patients reject the sick role and the model of medicine and health care it presumes.
- The social experience of health, illness, disability, and medicine varies across social groups and environments.
- Being socially labeled as sick can carry social stigma.
- Medicalization is the process where a social problem comes to be created, redefined, or labeled as a medical issue.

**12.3** Understand that the social responses to health, illness, and disability vary across time and place. There are different organizational and economic arrangements for health care, and these also change over time.

- Medicine is the social response to illness that attempts to identify, prevent, and cure disease. It is the social organization of caring for sick people and ensuring the health of the wider population.
- Public health is the health of the entire population. Maintaining public health requires a high degree of cooperation.
- Public health research relies on epidemiology, which uses scientific research to investigate the social dimensions of disease patterns.
- Public health education efforts aim to prevent disease, promote healthy behaviors, and preempt risky ones.

- Public health policy refers to the norms, rules, and laws that shape public health behavior.
- Curative approaches to medical care respond to acute events, while preventive care attempts to prevent disease before it occurs. Palliative care is care for people at the end of life. Integrative care combines many levels and systems of care to meet all care needs.
- Medical professionalization in the United States is rooted in a science-based, highly credentialed form of medical education.
- Medical institutions are diverse. In the United States, much medical care is delivered in large health care systems.
- Alternative and complementary medical care is a growing part of the health care system.
- Much care work is provided in families and households, traditionally by women in their roles as wives and mothers. Some analysts argue there is a global capitalist crisis of care, with not enough care to meet demands for care work.
- Deinstitutionalization in the United States refers to the downsizing and closure of long-term care facilities for the mentally ill and developmentally disabled over the course of the 20th century.
- Medicine is organized differently among countries, with a different balance of care for acute and chronic conditions and various economic models for funding heath care. National health care systems are arrangements in which individuals are guaranteed basic medical services as a part of citizenship. Private insurance systems are arrangements in which individuals and organizations fund health care through private insurance companies. The US care system is a mix of private and public programs.

## Key Terms

Acute disease 423
Allostatic load 417
Capitalist crisis of care 438
Chronic disease 424
Curative medical care 434
Deinstitutionalization 438
Disease 423
Epidemic 431
Epidemiology 431
Epigenetics 417
Epistemic privilege 421
Genetics 417
Health care systems 434
Health demography 415
Health insurance 441
Illness experience 423
Integrated medical care 434
Intersectional health perspective 419
Life expectancy 415
Medical institutions 433
Medicalization 428
Medical risk 422
Medicine 430
Multilevel approach to health and Illness 421
National health care systems 441
Palliative care 434
Pandemic 431
Preventive medical care 434

Professionalization 429
Public health 431
Public health education 431
Public health policy 432
Reproductive labor 434
Sick role 423
Sociology of health and illness 415
Stigma 425

## Review Questions

1. What is stigma? How is it related to labeling?
2. What factors account for the disproportionate number of deaths from COVID-19 among Black Americans?
3. What is epidemiology? What are some of the main medical institutions where epidemiologists work?
4. Describe the sick role.
5. What is the sociology of health and illness? What can it tell us about health disparities? Give an example.
6. Compare and contrast national health care systems and systems based on private insurance.
7. Compare and contrast biomedical and intersectional approaches to health and illness.
8. Define medicalization, and provide two examples.
9. What is public health? Name three ways public health is maintained.
10. In what ways is disability socially formed?
11. Describe the difference between disease and the illness experience.

## Explore

**RECOMMENDED READINGS**

Conrad, Peter. 2007. *The Medicalization of Society: On the Transformation of Human Conditions into Treatable Disorders*. Baltimore: Johns Hopkins University Press.

Conrad, Peter, and Joseph W. Schneider. 1992. *Deviance and Medicalization: From Badness to Sickness*. Philadelphia: Temple University Press.

Foucault, Michel. 1965. *Madness and Civilization: A History of Insanity in the Age of Reason*. New York: Vintage Books.

Foucault, Michel. 1973. *The Birth of the Clinic*. London: Tavistock.

Foucault, Michel. 1995. *Discipline and Punish: The Birth of the Prison*. New York: Vintage Books.

Fraser, Nancy. 2013. *Fortunes of Feminism: From State-Managed Capitalism to Neoliberal Crisis*. New York: Verso.

Fraser, Nancy, and Rahel Jaeggi. 2018. *Capitalism: A Conversation in Critical Theory*. New York: Polity.

Goffman, Erving. 1963. *Stigma: Notes on the Management of Spoiled Identity*. New York: Simon & Schuster.

Mojolo, Sanyu A. 2014. *Love, Money, and HIV: Becoming a Modern African Woman in the Age of AIDS*. Berkeley: University of California Press.

Okoro, Catherine A., Hollis NaTasha D., Alissa C. Cyrus, and Shannon Griffin-Blake. 2018. Prevalence of Disabilities and Health Care Access by Disability

Status and Type Among Adults—United States, 2016. *Morbidity and Mortality Weekly Report* 67(32): 882–887. doi: http://dx.doi.org/10.15585/mmwr.mm6732a3.

Saguy, Abigail C. 2014. *What's Wrong with Fat?* New York: Oxford University Press.

Starr, Paul. 2017. *The Social Transformation of American Medicine: The Rise of a Sovereign Profession and the Making of a Vast Industry.* New York: Basic Books.

## ACTIVITIES

- *Use your sociological imagination*: Interview a family member about the medical services that are the most important to them: primary care, hospitalization for emergencies, pediatric care, dental, vision, public health care, someone to care for them at home when they are sick, etc.

- *Media+Data Literacies*: Your medical data are legally private but are also required for most individuals to participate in health care services in the United States. Can you identify the pros and cons of sharing your data as part of large medical data systems?

- *Discuss*: Do you think people who contract COVID-19 are likely to be stigmatized once they recover? Why or why not?

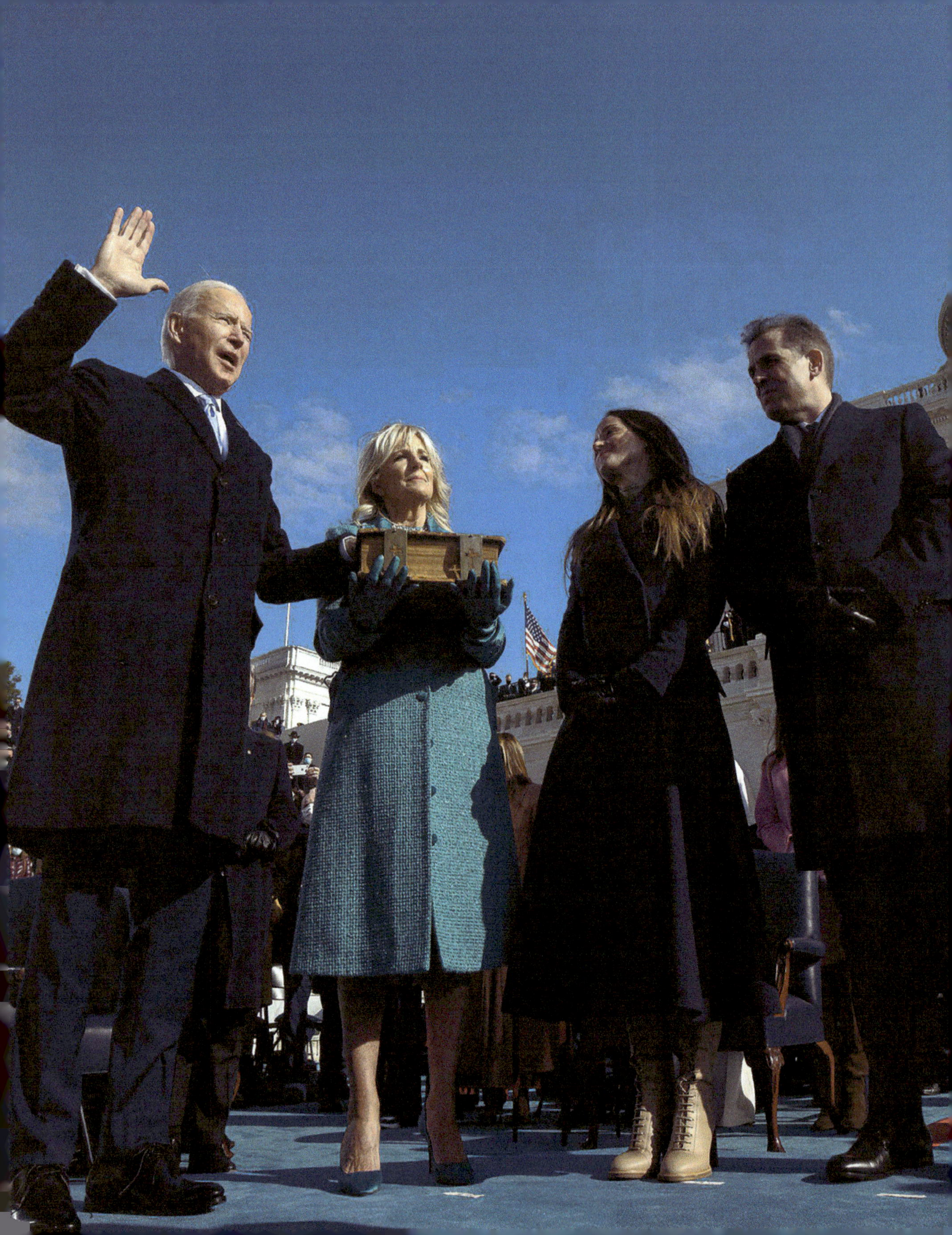

# 13

# Politics, Economy, and Social Movements

In June 2015, Donald Trump announced that he was running for the Republican Party's nomination for president. Trump had never held elected office, but this was not his first entry into a presidential race. In 1999 he announced his interest in running for the nomination of the much smaller Reform Party, but he withdrew from the race five months later. In the lead-up to the 2012 campaign he spoke at conservative political events, but he did not enter the race that year. However, by 2015 he was ready to run.

Trump's campaign was controversial from the beginning. Adopting the slogan "Make America Great Again," he was strongly critical of immigrants and Islamic terrorism. He was against international trade agreements, China, and companies that sent jobs overseas. Trump was ridiculed by most policy experts, but he was an expert at getting media attention. He deliberately used inflammatory language and personal insults against his opponents, knowing that journalists would reward this behavior with abundant coverage. Les Moonves, the CEO of CBS Television, called Trump's campaign a "circus" that generated huge ratings and advertising revenue for the media. "It may not be good for America," Moonves said, "but it's damn good for CBS" (Bond 2016).

Following a hotly contested election, and post-election civil unrest that included the violent occupation of the US Capitol Building on January 6, Joe Biden was inaugurated as the 46th president of the United States on January 20, 2021.

### Chapter Outline

**13.1 POLITICS AS THE STRUGGLE FOR INFLUENCE 451**

*Power, Authority, and Hegemony 452*

**13.2 POLITICS AND DEMOCRACY 454**

*Systems of Representation 456*
*Representing the People 458*

**13.3 Politics and the Economy 461**

*Political Economy 462*
*The Power Elite 462*
*Geopolitics, Colonialism, and International Trade 464*

**13.4 HISTORICAL CHANGES IN THE ECONOMY 466**

*The Transition to Capitalism 467*
*Post-Industrialism and the Changing Nature of the Economy 469*
*Economic Crisis and Insecurity in an Age of Globalization 471*

> **Chapter Outline** (continued)
>
> **13.5 SOCIAL CHANGE 472**
>
> *Challenging the Powerful 473*
> *Organizing and Mobilizing for Change 475*
> *Getting Noticed 478*
> *Movement Success 480*
>
> **CASE STUDY: THE STRANGE HISTORY OF THE US ELECTORAL COLLEGE 482**

In a major surprise to pollsters and pundits, Donald Trump was elected president in November 2016. He had overcome significant opposition from leaders of his own political party, many of whom worked hard to try to prevent him from winning the nomination. He had overcome debate performances that were mocked by late-night television comedians and severely criticized by political experts. He had overcome allegations of sexual misconduct, including the release of a video in which he bragged about sexually assaulting women. He had overcome other scandals as well—charges that he had retweeted known white supremacists, that he had used anti-Semitic imagery, and that he had been publicly endorsed by a number of openly racist and anti-Semitic groups. In the week after the election, and then again after his inauguration in January 2017, hundreds of thousands of people protested Trump's policies and his rhetoric. But Trump had prevailed. On January 20, 2017, he assumed the office of president of the United States. On that same day, he officially declared his candidacy for the 2020 election.

The 2020 US election was equally divisive and sensationalistic—and equally profitable for media organizations. Comcast reported that political ad spending was 70 percent higher during the 2020 election campaign than it had been during the 2016 campaign, while the *New York Times* reported a doubling of net profits during the third quarter of 2020 (Sorkin et al. 2020). The campaigns for Donald Trump and Joe Biden spent nearly $200 million on Facebook ads in 2020 (Wagner, Bergen, and Frier 2020). More than 160 million people voted in the election, the most in US history. But the campaign was rife with conflict and crisis. The first debate was roundly criticized as the worst in US history as Trump refused to follow the rules and continually interrupted Biden as well as the moderator. The second debate was canceled after Trump contracted COVID-19 and then refused to shift the debate to a remote format. Twitter applied warning labels to three hundred thousand false and misleading tweets during the election, including dozens written by President Trump himself. State-sponsored cyber actors from Russia, China, Iran, Saudi Arabia, and Turkey were all actively engaged on social media, spreading disinformation about the election, trying to influence the outcome, and trying to weaken confidence in the legitimacy of the outcome (Gersema 2020). After losing the election, Trump refused to concede, and he continued to make allegations about widespread fraud and a global conspiracy to steal the election from him. Trump supporters stormed the US Capitol and attacked Congress on January 6, 2021, directly following an address by outgoing President Trump.

Five people died. In many ways, the country was more politically divided than it had been in 150 years.

This chapter examines politics and the struggle for power. We begin by discussing different ways that individuals and groups exercise power. Next, we discuss the rise of democracy and compare the different ways that democratic societies organize political power. In the second half of the chapter, we consider how economic and political power are related to one another. Introducing the perspective of political economy, we show how the individuals who control the largest political and economic organizations create alliances to maintain their control over society. We explore how colonialism shaped the global balance of wealth and power, how the global economy influences international political alliances and conflicts, and how historical changes in the economy reorganize power and privilege at local and global levels. The chapter finishes with a discussion of political protest. We look at how social movements get created, what they do to attract and motivate members, and what kinds of strategies they use to increase their power and influence.

**Power** A social relationship in which one individual or group is able to influence the conduct of other individuals or groups either directly through force or indirectly through authority, persuasion, or cultural expectation; the ability of individuals or groups to get what they want, even against the resistance of others who are participating in the same action.

## LEARNING GOALS

**13.1** Differentiate between coercive and persuasive power, and understand how persuasive power is connected to the spread of democracy.

**13.2** Distinguish between the different systems of representation in a democracy.

**13.3** Define political economy, and describe how political and economic forces interact to shape government decisions at local and global levels.

**13.4** Describe how the economy has changed over time, and explain why economic insecurity is such a significant feature of modern social life.

**13.5** Understand the different types of rights claims that social movements make against the powerful and how this type of action helps create social solidarity.

## 13.1 Politics as the Struggle for Influence

**LG 13.1** Differentiate between coercive and persuasive power, and understand how persuasive power is connected to the spread of democracy.

The relationship between power and resistance is an important focus of sociology. Max Weber defined **power** as the ability of individuals or groups to get what they want, even in the face of resistance (Weber 1946). Weber

**State** All of the institutions of government, which together rule over a clearly defined territory and have a monopoly on the legitimate use of force within the territory.

**Politics** The struggle for influence and control over the state.

**Coercive power** The system of punishments and rewards used to try to force people to act in a particular way.

**Persuasive power** The ability to convince other people that a particular choice or action is the appropriate one.

observed that people who have power have to be prepared for resistance to that power by others who want it for themselves.

Weber further argued that government or modern **state** power is distinctive in modern society. State power is unique in two respects. First, modern governments are responsible for establishing collective goals and for creating public policies that will attempt to reach those goals (Parsons and Smelser 1956; Habermas 1975). Politicians compete with each other to define these collective goals and propose different policies to respond to social problems. Using the media and other public resources, they try to build support for their different proposals. Interest groups, experts, and social movements try to catch the politicians' attention to influence their policy proposals. This struggle for influence defines **politics** in modern society.

Second, the modern state is unique because it has exclusive control over the legitimate use of physical force within a given territory (Weber 1946). Because the state can use the police, the courts, and the military to enforce its decisions, it has the upper hand in most political conflicts. But state power, like any other exercise of power, works best when physical force is not used. In fact, if the state uses physical force too often or in a way that is seen to be illegitimate, then political conflict and resistance can increase dramatically. This requires even more physical force by the state, leading to an escalating cycle of force and resistance. As sociologists have discovered, there is a delicate balance between the use of coercive power and persuasive power.

### Power, Authority, and Hegemony

The exercise of power almost always involves an asymmetrical relationship. In a political conflict, one side will generally have more resources at its disposal, and it will use those resources to try to exercise its will. There are two general types of resources that can be used to exercise power. **Coercive power** uses a system of punishments and rewards to try to force people to act in a particular way. **Persuasive power** is the attempt to convince other people that they actually want to act in a particular way, or at the least that it is the right thing for them to do. Each strategy has specific advantages and disadvantages.

Coercive power is often easier to use than persuasive power. The threat that is built into coercive power is clear, and this is particularly true for the state. The US government, for example, can rely on the police, the courts, the Internal Revenue Service, and other state agencies to force compliance from its citizens.

However, people resent being forced or threatened into action and often resist coercive power. This can create a spiral of escalating coercion and resistance. When this happens, coercive power becomes more costly at the same time as it becomes less effective.

Given these costs, a more common strategy of government is persuasive power. Rather than trying to force or threaten people, persuasive power attempts to convince them that a request for compliance is legitimate. A government might argue that it is considering the common good rather than its own self-interest. It might appeal to shared values or to the fact that it was elected by the people. In each of these instances, the exercise of power comes from influence rather than force.

Weber distinguished between three different types of persuasive power, which he referred to as "legitimate authority" (1946: 78–79). In premodern societies, the most common type of legitimate authority was **traditional authority**, where people follow a leader's orders because of the weight of tradition or custom. In modern societies, traditional authority has been mostly replaced by **rational-legal authority**, which is based on clearly defined and codified rules. With rational-legal authority, people believe in the authority of the rules or the laws. **Charismatic authority** is based on the personal qualities of an individual leader. Charisma can be particularly effective when combined with other types of power because it creates a personal and emotional bond between leaders and their followers.

Persuasive power has different risks than coercive power. There is almost always an opposing side making an alternative argument. As a result, the use of persuasive power will often lead to a struggle for influence between competing groups. Despite these risks, however, most groups prefer persuasive power if they can use it successfully. The democratic revolution, which we discuss later in section 13.2, led to forms of government that privilege noncoercive forms of power.

Because power involves an unequal relationship, dominant groups will always have resources and advantages over other groups. They may have more experts at their disposal, better access to the media, easier access to politicians, or more effective threats. Antonio Gramsci (1891–1937) described this relationship between dominant and nondominant groups in terms of hegemony (Gramsci 1971). **Hegemony** refers to the different strategies that dominant groups use to make their view of the world seem like "common sense" to the rest of the population. For example, if leaders of the automobile industry can get people to think about cars as an expression of individual freedom, it will be easier for them to shape a pro-automobile transportation policy. In this way, a hegemonic understanding that private cars are superior develops rather than widespread support for public transport infrastructure. It is much easier to exercise power if people cannot imagine an alternative to the current situation or perceive proposed alternatives as inferior to the status quo.

**Traditional authority** A form of persuasive power in which people follow a leader's orders because of the weight of tradition or custom.

**Rational-legal authority** A form of persuasive power based on clearly defined rules that are written down.

**Charismatic authority** A form of persuasive power in which people follow a leader's orders because of the personal qualities that the leader possesses.

**Hegemony** A form of power in which dominant groups are able to make their worldview seem like "common sense" to the rest of the population.

The concept of hegemony emphasizes group struggle. Dominant groups try to convince the population that their vision of the world is "common sense," while other groups challenge that view. This kind of critique is a central activity of social movements, which we discuss later in section 13.5.

## 13.2 Politics and Democracy

**LG 13.2** Distinguish between the different systems of representation in a democracy.

Persuasive power and the battle for hegemony became more important with the spread of democracy as a system of state power. Before the 16th century, rulers in Western Europe delegated power to local elites and landowners. Most of the population had no political rights at all. Political decisions usually involved a compromise between the monarch, the landowners, and church leaders, with little concern for the interests of "the people" (Anderson 1974). Such societies were **absolute monarchies**, in which there were no laws restricting the power of the monarch over the people living in their territory.

By the end of the 18th century, democratic revolutions in France and the United States had changed the way people understood political power. During the English Civil War of the 1640s, a social movement known as the Levellers proposed that "all government is in the free consent of the people" (Hill 1984). The American Declaration of Independence expressed a similar idea in 1776, asserting that "governments are instituted among Men, deriving their just powers from the consent of the governed." The French Declaration of the Rights of Man and the Citizen asserted in 1789 that "no body nor individual may exercise any authority which does not proceed directly from the nation." These documents emphasized **popular sovereignty**, or

**Absolute monarchy** A form of government in which there are no laws restricting the power of the monarch over the people living in their territory.

**Popular sovereignty** The "rule of the people."

---

**PAIRED CONCEPTS** — **Power and Resistance**

### Public Protests in Tunisia

On December 17, 2010, a fruit and vegetable vendor named Mohamed Bouazizi set fire to himself outside a local municipal office in the Tunisian town of Sidi Bouzid, as a protest against police mistreatment and the confiscation of his produce cart. Protests against the Tunisian government quickly spread throughout the country, as protesters demanded an end to government corruption, political repression, police violence, unemployment, inflation, and poor living conditions. Police established a curfew, used violence and tear gas against the protesters, closed schools and universities, and shut down the internet to prevent protesters from spreading their message. Despite these efforts, the protests continued to grow.

The Tunisian government was ultimately unable to control the media or completely stifle social media. International media organizations provided extensive coverage of the protests, and Tunisian protesters used social media to report about their protests and to warn others about developing police activities. Ultimately frustrated in his attempts to stifle the protests, President Zine al-Abidine Ben Ali announced on January 13 that he would not seek re-election. On January 14 he fled the country with his family. The revolution had achieved success in less than a month, and it inspired similar protests in many other parts of the Arab world.

The revolution did not erupt spontaneously, however. Considerable planning and coordination took place well before 2011, as protestors used social media to organize against police abuse and government corruption. The Tunisian blogging group Nawaat had been formed in 2004 in order to provide a public platform for Tunisian dissidents to voice their criticisms, to discuss strategies for avoiding censorship, and to plan protest activities. Worker strikes and social protests against unemployment and poverty had continued for nearly six months in 2008, mobilizing Tunisians throughout the country and establishing an antagonistic relationship with the Tunisian government and police forces. Tunisian youth regularly chanted anti-government slogans during sporting events. While government repression and censorship kept these activities away from the attention of global media, popular discontent within Tunisia had been building for many years.

**Tunisia protests, 2011**
The Tunisian government was unable to control the media coverage of the social protest in Tunis in 2011. In less than one month after the initial protests, Zine al-Abidine Ben Ali resigned as president.

People who protest often know that they will be met with resistance. Police in Tunisia were typically in riot gear, ready to use coercive force against the protesters. Tunisian police arrested thousands and killed hundreds of protesters in 2010 and 2011. But the threat of being hurt or killed did not deter the protesters.

Instead, police violence reinforced the belief that protesting was the only way to rid Tunisia of tyranny. Protesters knew that the images of police violence would be broadcast throughout the world. Journalists, intellectuals, and government leaders worldwide condemned the actions of the police, lending international support to the protesters' goals and mobilizing thousands more to take to the streets.

> ### ACTIVE LEARNING
>
> **Find out:** Try to find US newspaper coverage and news photographs of the Tunisian protests. What kinds of meanings are associated with the protesters, the police, and the government? What role is suggested for the US and for the international community in these news stories?

## PAIRED CONCEPTS: Inequality and Privilege

### Who Gets Elected to the US Senate?

The exercise of power is connected to the unequal distribution of resources. People who have more resources have an easier time gaining positions of political leadership. This is a picture of the US Senate, taken in 2023. As of 2023, the average age of senators was 64.0 years. There are 75 men and 25 women. Fifty-one of the senators have a law degree, 20 have a master's degree, and five have a medical degree. There are four Black senators, six Latinos, two Asian Americans, and one Native American; the remaining 88 senators are white. The median net worth for this group of senators was approximately $1.9 million. For comparison, the median net worth for US households in 2022 was only about $192,900 Aladangaty et al. 2023).

**The US Senate**
Senators are predominantly old, male, white, educated, and wealthy. Of 100 senators in 2023, 75 are men, 76 have a higher degree, 88 are white, and their median net worth is $1.9 million.

#### ACTIVE LEARNING

**Discuss:** Is it possible for these senators to represent all of their constituents when they come from a relatively narrow slice of the population? Are there any specific types of experiences that they might not have had compared to a lot of other Americans? Can you think of how these different experiences might influence the kinds of political projects that US senators think are important?

---

**Deliberation** The practice of discussing matters of collective importance so that after debating the merits of competing positions, people can reach a shared agreement about the best course of action.

the "rule of the people." Decisions should be based on **deliberation** among citizens about matters of collective importance so that, after debating the merits of competing positions, people can reach a shared agreement about the best course of action.

The democratic revolutions that started in England, France, and the United States spread throughout the world, helped by advances in literacy and print technology. Today, more than 50 percent of the countries in the world are liberal democracies or electoral democracies (Figure 13.1).

### Systems of Representation

Most democratic countries today are either **constitutional monarchies** or **democratic republics**. Constitutional monarchies have a king or queen who

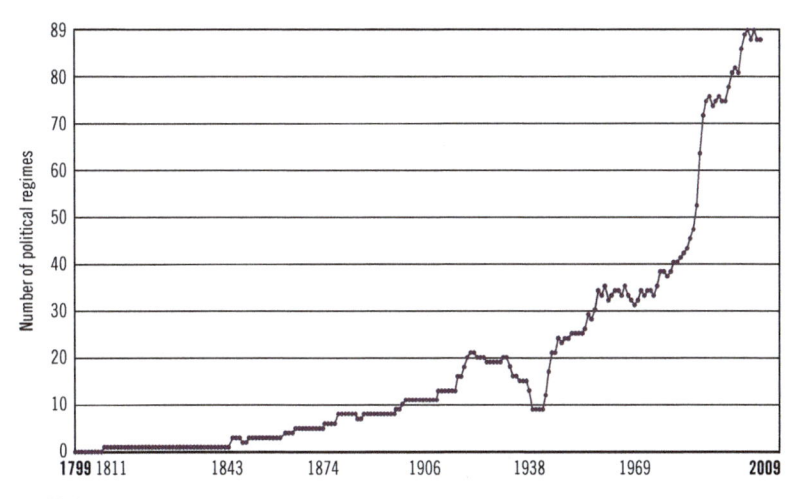

**Figure 13.1** Democracies and autocracies worldwide, 1789–2023.
Source: "Democracy." Our World in Data. https://ourworldindata.org/democracy.

acts as the ceremonial head of the nation, but their actual power is limited by law. Most of the power in a constitutional monarchy is held by elected officials. The first constitutional monarchy was established in England in 1688. Other examples of contemporary constitutional monarchies include Sweden, Belgium, and Japan. In a democratic republic, there is no monarch, and the elected officials have all of the political power.

Another important difference is between **parliamentary** and **presidential** systems of democracy. In a parliamentary system the people vote for their elected officials in the legislature, but they do not vote for the head of government. Instead, the head of government is a member of the legislature. In most parliamentary systems, the person who becomes the head of government is the leader of the largest political party in the parliament. This is different from presidential systems, where there is a formal separation of powers between the head of government and the legislature. In such systems, the president is usually elected by a democratic vote of the people and cannot be dismissed by the legislature except under unusual circumstances. Because they are elected by the people, presidents can claim to speak for the entire nation, and it is easier for them to develop a following that is separate from their political party (Lowi 1986). This is particularly true in today's media-saturated world, when presidents use social media to address the public directly and personalize their persuasive power (Eshbaugh-Soha and Peake 2011; Mast 2012).

Because democratic societies place so much value on the "will of the people," those in power need a way to measure **public opinion**. By the 19th

**Constitutional monarchy** A form of democratic government where power is held by elected officials and there is a king or queen who serves as the ceremonial head of the nation.

**Democratic republic** A form of democratic government where power is held by elected officials and there is no monarch.

**Parliamentary system** A form of democratic government in which the head of government is chosen from the legislature and is also usually the leader of the largest political party in parliament.

**Presidential system** A form of democratic government in which there is a formal separation of powers between the head of government and the legislature, and the president is usually elected by a democratic vote of the people.

**Public opinion** The public expression of the different attitudes and beliefs that people have about a particular issue.

century, politicians and journalists were using informal "straw polls" to try to predict the outcome of upcoming elections (Herbst 1995). As social scientists in the mid-20th century developed more sophisticated techniques of survey research, the modern opinion poll emerged.

Opinion polls measure the attitudes and preferences of the population. Those in power use opinion polls to measure their public support and to take action if their support declines.

## Representing the People

The power of public opinion operates most directly through voting. Because voting is so important for the exercise of power, sociologists and other social scientists study social patterns and social consequences of voter behavior and public opinion (Brooks 2014).

**VOTING.** In the United States, every citizen who is at least 18 years old is eligible to vote. But democratic societies do not always extend voting rights to everyone. When the United States was first established as a democratic nation, most states restricted voting to white males who owned property. Many of these voting restrictions have been eliminated, usually as the result of political struggle by social movements. The Fifteenth Amendment to the US Constitution, which prohibited federal and state governments from denying the right to vote based on race, was ratified in 1870. In 1920, the Nineteenth Amendment gave women the right to vote. In 1964, the Twenty-fourth Amendment outlawed the "poll tax," which meant that people who were economically disadvantaged could no longer be excluded from voting. While most states continue to restrict voting privileges for convicted felons who are in prison (Uggen, Manza, and Thompson 2006; Demleitner 2022), other formal restrictions have largely been eliminated.

**King Charles III**
King Charles III of Great Britain is a constitutional monarch, whose powers are limited by law.

## PAIRED CONCEPTS

# Solidarity and Conflict

## Push Polls and the Politics of Division

The American Association for Public Opinion Research (2015) defines a "push poll" as a type of negative campaigning that is designed as an opinion poll. Criticizing push polls as "unethical political telemarketing" more interested in influencing election outcomes than measuring opinions, professional pollsters complain that push polls take advantage of the trust people have in research organizations. The association has identified push polls as a violation of its professional code of ethics and encouraged its members to help journalists and the public identify this form of fraudulent political telemarketing.

Push polls are designed to create conflict. Push pollsters do not identify the organization with which they are associated. They do not attempt to draw a representative sample because they are not trying to discover any information. Instead, they will target specific groups of voters—for example, union workers or suburban housewives. Rather than following the standard polling protocol of asking for basic demographic information from the person receiving the call, the push poller will ask the recipient for whom they intend to vote. If they are intending to vote for the candidate hired by the push poller, they will simply be encouraged to vote. However, should they express a preference for the "wrong" candidate, they will then be asked a series of leading questions trying to influence them not to vote for that candidate or not to vote at all (Sabato 1996). Such questions are often hypothetical or blatantly false. An infamous example of this occurred in South Carolina during the 2000 US presidential campaign, when a push poll asked people, "Would you be more or less likely to vote for John McCain . . . if you knew he had fathered an illegitimate black child?" (Banks 2008). During the 2008 US presidential campaign, a push poll targeted at Jewish voters asked "Would it change your mind about Obama if you knew that his church was anti-Israel?" (Smith 2008).

Push polls create social problems (Gerstmann and Streb 2004). First, they undermine public faith in legitimate polling, making people cynical about survey research in general. Second, they make people cynical about politics, encouraging them to believe that all politicians are untrustworthy. Finally, push polls are deliberately misleading and often fraudulent in their intent. These problems are compounded by the fact that political candidates routinely accuse their opponents of using push polls, while denying charges that they are using push polls themselves. These charges and countercharges just increase the amount of confusion and cynicism among the electorate.

**US Senator John McCain during the 2000 presidential campaign**
McCain was the target of a series of push polls that hurt his candidacy.

### ACTIVE LEARNING

**Find out:** In 2014, New Hampshire passed a new law restricting the use of push polls. What are the details of this new law? Can you find any examples of people who have been charged with violating the law? What are the details of the case?

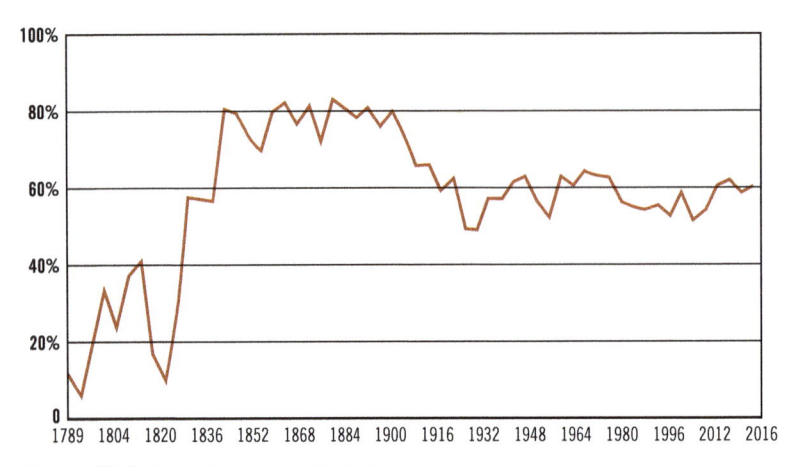

**Figure 13.2** Voter Turnout, 1789–2020.
Source: US Election Project. 2020. "Turnout Data." https://election.lab.ufl.edu/voter-turnout/

While voting is an important feature of a democratic society, not everyone who is eligible actually votes. As Figure 13.2 shows, the high point for voter turnout in the United States was between 1838 and 1898, when between 70 and 80 percent of eligible voters voted in presidential elections. Voter turnout has steadily declined since then. Fewer than 60 percent of eligible voters have turned out to vote for national elections since the 1960s. Voter turnout rates are even lower for state and local elections. An exception to this pattern is the election of 2020, which is considered a historic high because 66 percent of eligible voters cast a ballot. It remains to be seen if turnout levels will continue to be so high in the next election cycle. Historically, voter turnout rates have been higher for whites, those with more education, and those who have more money. Older citizens are much more likely to vote than younger citizens. In some countries, such as Argentina, Australia, and Singapore, all eligible voters are required by law to vote.

Low voter turnout has a major impact on how political influence works. Politicians pay much more attention to the issues that concern actual voters, and they tend to ignore the issues that nonvoters care about.

**INTEREST GROUPS.** Interest groups also play an important role in the exercise of power. **Interest groups** bring people together based on a common issue and then try to influence political decision-makers on topics related to that issue. Some interest groups have millions of members, such as the National Rifle Association and the American Association of Retired Persons. Other interest groups represent a specific profession, such as the Association of Trial Lawyers of America and the American Medical Association. Interest groups have always been a distinctive feature of American politics; French observer Alexis de Tocqueville ([1835, 1840] 2003) noted their importance when he visited the United States in the 1830s.

Interest groups exercise persuasive power through lobbying, research, and fundraising. Lobbyists meet with elected politicians and other important officials in an attempt to convince those officials to vote in a way that is

**Interest group** An organization that brings people together on the basis of a common issue and attempts to influence political decision-makers on topics related to that issue.

consistent with the goals of the interest group. There are more than 12,000 registered lobbyists in the United States, and in 2022 they spent more than $12 billion trying to influence elected officials (Open Secrets 2023).

Interest group research is frequently conducted by "think tanks," which bring together social scientists, journalists, and public relations specialists to conduct policy-relevant research, which they share with journalists and elected officials (Medvetz 2012). One concern about interest-group research is that the agenda they pursue is different from the priorities of the larger public, and funding for such research may come from sources with very specific policy interests. Importantly, the size, number, and influence of think tanks are growing around the world (McGann 2019).

Interest groups influence politics through fundraising. About a third of the money spent on congressional elections is raised by political action committees (PACs), which are created by interest groups to raise money for political candidates. A new type of interest group, the "super-PAC," was established in 2010. Super-PACs are not allowed to give money directly to candidates, but they are allowed to run their own campaign ads designed to elect or defeat a specific candidate. The Center for Responsive Politics (n.d.) reports that super-PACs spent just over $1 billion during the 2016 US presidential election and just over $1.8 billion during the 2020 election. In the 2022 midterm elections, interest groups spent $1.9 billion. These groups hope that their fundraising activities will increase the influence they have over elected officials.

One concern about interest groups is that they distort democracy. The most powerful interest groups are funded by trade and professional associations and by corporations, and their lobbying activities tend to focus on the narrow concerns of those groups rather than the general interest of the public (Baumgartner et al. 2009). Another problem is that interest groups tend to support incumbents, which makes it harder for new candidates to win elections. In fact, in congressional elections, incumbents are re-elected more than 80 percent of the time. If incumbents pay most of their attention to interest groups, the result is that fewer people get to participate in policy debates about important public matters.

## 13.3 Politics and the Economy

**LG** **13.3** Define political economy, and describe how political and economic forces interact to shape government decisions at local and global levels.

As the previous discussion demonstrates, political and economic forces are closely interconnected. Elected politicians are much wealthier than the average citizen. Wealthier people are more likely to vote, and as a result political candidates are more likely to pay attention to the interests and the issues that wealthy people care about. Interest groups and lobbyists spend massive amounts of money trying to influence elections, laws, and public policy priorities. This is not a recent issue. In the early years of the United States, Thomas Jefferson and Alexander Hamilton argued bitterly about how to control the political power of the wealthy, and this debate has continued for the entirety of US political history (Philips 2002). Nor is this an issue that is confined to the US. Reviewing the history of politics and influence in democratic societies, the political scientist Adam Przeworski (2016: 6) writes that "access of money to politics is the scourge of democracy."

## Political Economy

At its most basic level, political economy is the study of how the economy shapes politics, and how politics influences the economy. Political economy is a very broad field, and it includes many topics that are central to sociology, such as the study of inequality, economic development, globalization, responses to economic crisis, challenges to democracy, and the social influences on public policy, among others. In fact, some have argued that political economy was the original social science, predating the creation of separate disciplines of economics, sociology, and political science (Clark 2016).

In sociology, the perspective of political economy was originally outlined by Max Weber, and most sociologists who rely on a political economy perspective trace their influences back to Weber and Marx. Not surprisingly, then, the political economy perspective in sociology can be seen most clearly in the study of those topics that were central to Marx and Weber: power, domination, political control, and the reproduction of social advantages across time and place. More concretely, we can see the political economy approach in sociology in two major areas of research: (1) the study of the power elite, and (2) the study of geopolitics, colonialism, and international trade.

## The Power Elite

One of the most famous books in US sociology was *The Power Elite*, published in 1956 by C. Wright Mills. In this book, Mills argued that power in American society had become much more centralized than it had once been, and that it was now dominated by the leaders of three kinds of large and powerful institutions: the military, the corporate sector, and the government sector. In the economy, he argued, there were two or three hundred giant corporations that held most of the control. In politics, the federal government had most of the power and influence. Finally, the military had become one of the largest and most efficient bureaucracies in the world, possessing more coercive power than any organization in the world.

Like elites of the past, the leaders of these organizations came from the same privileged backgrounds, they socialized in the same circles, and they shared the same basic interest in maintaining their positions of power and privilege. For the most part they attended the same elite private schools, they belonged to the same exclusive private clubs, and they vacationed at the same exclusive private resorts (Domhoff 2017). They frequently moved back and forth between these three institutions of power. Corporate leaders moved into influential positions in the federal government. Military and government leaders moved into positions on the board of directors at large corporations. This allowed them to adopt a shared worldview, making their actions more predictable to one another and easier to coordinate.

What was the shared worldview of the power elite? Despite the obviously intense economic competition among corporate leaders, they shared a set of common enemies and common interests: against organized labor, against regulation, and against high levels of corporate taxation (Domhoff 2017: 17). Leaders of government mostly shared these priorities, even though they were the ones creating and enforcing the regulations and tax policy. Because so many people came to elected positions in government after successful careers in the corporate sector, they already had a corporate worldview. They also needed large corporate donations to fund their political campaigns, which made them more sympathetic to the interests and policy priorities of those corporate leaders. As for the key military decision-makers, most of them came from the upper class, they had relatives in leadership positions at large corporations, and they themselves could expect future careers at the top of the corporate sector (Domhoff 2017: 22). These factors guaranteed the largely corporate worldview that unified the members of the power elite.

This worldview has only intensified with the acceleration of globalization. In his book *Superclass*, the journalist David Rothkopf (2008) argued that in the 21st century a new global power elite had emerged, composed of the leaders of international business, finance, and the defense industry. This global power elite was similar to the power elite defined by Mills and Domhoff, except that political leaders had even less influence than they used to and fewer opportunities to deviate from a corporate worldview and the pro-business policies suggested by such a worldview. The sociologists Ulrich Beck (2005) and Zygmunt Bauman (2002) have made similar arguments. As multinational corporations grow larger and more powerful, the leaders of national governments are forced to compete with one another to provide the most business-friendly policies that they can, with the knowledge that the leaders of these corporations will move their operations out of countries that have too many taxes and too many business regulations. They spend a lot of time trying to explain to the citizens of their country that there is no alternative, that business-friendly policies are in the best interests of the nation. Of course, most of the political leaders are already sympathetic to these policy priorities, because they come from the business world or because they hope to enter corporate leadership positions when they are done with government service.

## Geopolitics, Colonialism, and International Trade

Not only do political and economic interests combine in the development of national policies and priorities; they also extend to international relationships and conflicts between different nations. Political and military decisions often get made because of geopolitics, which refers to the desire by powerful nations to control resources, trade routes, or markets in distant (or adjacent) territories. The results of these decisions have had long and durable historical effects.

One of the most significant historical legacies of geopolitics is colonialism, which refers to the conquest of a foreign people and the subsequent control of the conquered territory by the colonizing power (Steinmetz 2014: 79). Colonialism involves the foreign rule over the colonized space by the colonizing power, and it is organized around assumptions about racial or civilizational hierarchies that are enforced in law and that prevent the colonized people from attaining equal rights or full citizenship (Steinmetz 2013: 11). North America, South America, the Caribbean, Africa, and South Asia were all shaped in fundamental ways by colonialism. In fact, sociologists emphasize how the modern nation-state and the modern global economy were both created through colonialism (Go 2016).

For the powerful colonizing nations such as England, France, and the US, their development as global capitalist powers cannot be separated from their domination of colonial territories. Colonizing nations extracted natural resources as well as cheap labor from their colonized territories, and they used the port cities in those territories to geographically extend their economic markets for trade (Arrighi 1994). In order to protect their colonial holdings against other colonial powers—and also against anticolonial resistance—they maintained large and advanced militaries, as well as expansive intelligence and surveillance operations. The banks in the colonizing nations made a large part of their fortunes in the colonies, at the same time that they established a common culture and a common set of standards about matters such as risk management and creditworthiness (Bonin and Valerio 2016). Over time, the principles of banking and the market came together in a global hegemonic discourse of neoliberalism, which established the expectations that (1) states should govern according to the rules of the market, (2) inequality is an inherent and necessary condition of a competitive and well-functioning free market economy, and (3) economic competition between states in a global market could replace military competition between states (Venn 2009).

**PAIRED CONCEPTS**

## Structure and Contingency

### Haiti and the French Revolution

The French Revolution is considered to be one of the most significant events of the modern era. Lasting from 1789 to 1799, it established many of the principles of democracy, citizenship, and universal human rights that spread throughout the rest of the world. Many scholarly accounts describe the French Revolution as a world-historical event, one that transformed the structure of modern society. But in his book *Postcolonial Thought and Social Theory*, the sociologist Julian Go (2016) argues that there is a different way to think about the French Revolution, which situates it in terms of the colonial relationship between France and Haiti.

France was a major colonial power, with significant overseas colonies in North America, Africa, South Asia, and the Caribbean. Like other colonial powers, the strength of the French economy depended on its political and economic domination of these overseas territories. The Caribbean colonies were some of the most important sources of wealth for France because of the central role they played in the slave trade. Many of the key political leaders of the French Revolution had made their fortunes in the Caribbean slave trade, and this wealth helped to give them the time and the resources to pursue their revolutionary goals (Go 2016: 124).

Saint-Domingue was the most important and the most profitable Caribbean colony controlled by France, with some of the world's largest sugar and coffee plantations. It was the largest slave economy in the region, with more than four hundred thousand enslaved Africans creating wealth for fewer than forty thousand white colonists. A major slave revolt began in 1791 in Saint-Domingue; within months, the revolutionaries controlled nearly a third of the province, and the movement had attracted the support and participation of more than one hundred thousand formerly enslaved people. Successfully fighting off British and Spanish attempts to conquer Saint-Domingue and to reestablish slavery in the region (as well as a similar attempt in 1802 by French emperor Napoleon Bonaparte), the revolutionaries were eventually able to establish their independence, resulting in the creation of the free republic of Haiti in 1804.

The Haitian Revolution had a global impact that was just as profound as the French and American Revolutions. As the historian David Brion Davis (2001) has argued, the revolt in Saint-Domingue inspired slave revolts throughout the Americas, and it strengthened the power and influence of abolitionists in Britain and the US who were advocating for the end of slavery. As Go (2016: 125–31) argues, the Haitian revolution also had an important impact on the French Revolution and on the way that the French revolutionaries came to understand and articulate the meaning of rights and freedoms in a modern democratic society. Initially, the leaders of the French Revolution avoided discussing whether enslaved people in the French Caribbean colonies would be granted full rights and citizenship. In fact, many of them had economic incentives to maintain slavery. They only recognized the enslaved people of Saint-Domingue as the bearers of universal rights because they saw the Haitian revolutionaries demanding those rights as they had been expressed in The Declaration of the Rights of Man and of the Citizen. The decision to end slavery and extend universal rights to the enslaved people of the French colonies was also influenced by France's geopolitical competition with Spain and Britain. By granting freedom to the Haitian revolutionaries, the French made it more likely that those revolutionaries would help the French army to fight off the British and Spanish armies that were trying to invade and conquer Saint-Domingue.

There were important structural forces that made the French and Haitian revolutions possible, but it was the interaction of structure and contingency that allowed them to develop in the specific ways that they did, and not otherwise. Structurally, these two events were part of a larger historical force pushing in the direction of democracy, such as the development of new sources of wealth created

**PAIRED CONCEPTS CONTINUED**

through capitalism, the articulation of notions of universal rights and universal truths that were circulating in the fields of science and philosophy, and the actions of anticolonial resistance that were part of the response to global colonial domination. But this did not mean that democracy would necessarily lead to the end of slavery in the Caribbean. The American Revolution had taken place without ending the slave trade, and there were plenty of indications that the French revolutionaries were prepared to follow the same path. The Haitian revolution forced the French to reconsider the meaning of universal rights, and to do so in a geopolitical context in which they needed to be able to count on Haitian support in their conflicts with British and Spanish colonial powers.

**ACTIVE LEARNING**

**Think about it**: Thinking about geopolitics and colonialism, and using the paired concept of structure and contingency, discuss two or three reasons why the American Revolution did not result in the end of the slavery.

---

The exercise of power always produces resistance, and this was true with colonialism and the exercise of geopolitical power. Resistance against colonial domination by European powers began as early as the 15th and 16th centuries, and there were repeated uprisings in virtually all colonial territories. The 20th century saw a wave of successful anticolonial nationalist revolts; by the 1970s, all of the European colonial empires had been dismantled, producing a proliferation of new nation-states in Africa, Asia, and elsewhere in the Global South (Go 2016: 6). This resistance included an intellectual or cultural resistance to colonial power, which uncovered the strategies and techniques that the colonizing powers used to justify their exercise of power and domination. For example, anticolonial critics highlighted how racial and ethnic categories were used to justify colonial rule, how colonial wealth was a sign of greed and cruelty rather than healthy competition, and how the image of a neutral free market hid the real operation of global hierarchies and dependencies (Go 2023).

## 13.4 Historical Changes in the Economy

**LG 13.4** Describe how the economy has changed over time, and explain why economic insecurity is such a significant feature of modern social life.

**Economy** All the activities and organizations that are involved in the production, distribution, and consumption of goods and services.

The **economy** refers to all the activities and organizations that are involved in the production, distribution, and consumption of goods and services. Like other institutions, the economy changes as society changes. In modern society, the biggest and most important change in the economy was the development of capitalism. Capitalism fundamentally changed the nature of work, and it continues to do so today.

According to the sociologist Immanuel Wallerstein, the modern economy emerged gradually in Europe between 1450 and 1640, as it changed from feudalism to capitalism (Wallerstein 1976). In **feudalism**, the main way that people created wealth was by owning land. A small number of people owned most of the land, and everyone else was completely dependent on the landowner. In exchange for using and living on part of the land, they were expected to provide services to the landowner. This included military service, agricultural work, maintaining roads and fences, and paying rent. Landowners also charged their dependents for other uses of the land, such as hunting, grazing livestock, or storing food. Dependents were generally not allowed to leave the area without the landowner's permission, and their children were often bound by the same relations of dependency.

Feudalism lasted for hundreds of years, but it was not a very efficient system for producing goods and services. Small-scale and extremely local production was the norm, and virtually everything that was produced was consumed immediately. There was little incentive for landowners to invest in new productive technologies, or to engage in regional market transactions. Those who provided military services were relatively unskilled at fighting. Landowners had repeated conflicts with one another, and there was little incentive for them to cooperate. The dependent workers had no incentive to work hard, increase their skill, or develop new techniques of production. This left feudalism vulnerable to the more productive economic systems that developed with capitalism.

**Feudalism** An economic system in which a small number of people owned most of the land, and everyone else was completely dependent on the landowner.

## The Transition to Capitalism

**Capitalism** is an economic system in which the production of goods and services is controlled by private individuals and companies; all economic activities are based on a calculation of potential profits; and the prices of all goods (including workers' wages) are determined by the marketplace (Chapter 2).

Capitalism began to develop during the 16th and 17th centuries, as an agricultural revolution swept across England that challenged the feudal system. New techniques of crop rotation as well as the shift toward higher-yield crops increased productivity beyond what was necessary for the immediate consumption of the feudal fiefdoms. New machinery made it easier to cut grain, which required fewer manual workers. All of this encouraged changes in how landowners related to the dependents living on their land. Rather than leaving their fields open for anyone to use, they enclosed the common lands so they could take advantage of the new farming techniques for their own benefit. Rather than relying on the rents and services of their dependent tenants for their wealth, they began to focus on selling their agricultural surplus in an ever-growing market. Farming became a business, motivated by the pursuit of profit (Overton 1996).

**Capitalism** An economic system based on the private ownership of property, including the means of material life such as food, clothing, and shelter, and in which the production of goods and services is controlled by private individuals and companies, and prices are set by markets.

With fewer workers needed for farming, many of the peasants who had been living on the feudal fiefdoms were forced to move and to seek new types of work. Most of them ended up in towns and cities, where they were put to work producing goods and services. Merchants in these towns and cities expanded their businesses, selling their products to the new people living in the towns and also relying on the labor of those new arrivals to increase their production. Business owners, in pursuit of larger markets, encouraged governments to extend their reach by conquering overseas territories and by protecting the trading companies that were helping create a world market. Merchant banks developed to help finance this expansion of trade routes. Like the new farmers in the countryside, their motivation was the pursuit of profit.

The production of goods and the pursuit of profit accelerated rapidly during the Industrial Revolution. The development of new machines and new forms of energy to power those machines moved industrial production into urban factories. The factories did not need highly skilled workers; instead, they needed people to do highly repetitive tasks.

Mass production allowed factory owners to reduce the price of their goods, and new steamboats, canals, and railroads made it easier to get these products to distant markets. Small-scale producers could not compete; most of them were forced to move to cities and find jobs in factories. With more workers competing for fewer jobs, wages went down for most industrial workers. But for the owners of these factories and for the bankers who were financing their activities, profits soared.

The Industrial Revolution helped capitalism spread around the world, and changed the nature of work forever. Jobs became increasingly standardized, so that workers could be easily substituted for one another on assembly lines and other factory systems of mass production. As jobs became de-skilled, workers became easily replaceable, and business owners continually sought to reduce their wages. Many of them did this by increasing production for the same wage, often through the use of new technologies. Others reduced wages by moving factories to places where employees were willing to work for less. Still others used the threat of replacing their employees with cheaper workers in order to extract wage concessions.

Soon, social movements against capitalism emerged throughout much of the capitalist world. Many of these movements were inspired by the critiques of Karl Marx, who argued that workers' lives would get worse unless they banded together, overthrew the capitalist system, and abolished private property. Once this happened, Marx believed, capitalism would be replaced by **socialism**, in which goods would be produced according to social needs, and economic production would be controlled and owned collectively by the workers themselves. Socialist movements spread throughout Europe during

**Socialism** A type of economy in which goods are produced according to social needs, and economic production is controlled and owned collectively by the workers themselves.

the second half of the 19th century and also in the United States, where the Socialist Labor Party was founded in 1877.

By the end of World War II in 1945, tensions between capitalism and socialism had developed into a Cold War between the United States and the Soviet Union. Each of the two world powers had its own sphere of alliances with countries whose political, military, and economic alliances were determined primarily by whether it had adopted a capitalist or a socialist economic system, or something in between. This lasted until 1991, with the disbanding of the Warsaw Pact alliance between the now-former Soviet Union and European state-socialist countries. By that point, organized resistance to capitalism had weakened considerably.

**Industrial workers assemble radios at the Atwater Kent Factory in Philadelphia, 1925**
Industrial jobs are standardized, so that workers can be easily substituted for one another on assembly lines and in other factory systems of mass production. Today, much industrial production has been moved to places where workers can be paid the lowest wages.

## Post-Industrialism and the Changing Nature of the Economy

Since the 20th century, the global economy has been changed by **post-industrialism**, which refers to an economy where manufacturing becomes less important as a source of wealth, and where the production of information, knowledge, and services becomes more important.

The rise and the social consequences of post-industrial society were described in books written by the sociologists Alain Touraine (1971) and Daniel Bell (1973). Beginning in the second half of the 20th century, Bell and Touraine argued, the advanced capitalist economies had experienced a shift away from manufacturing jobs and toward professional, technical, and service occupations. By 1970, half of all workers in the United States were employed in the service sector. Today, more than 80 percent of all American workers are employed in professional, technical, and service sector jobs. These jobs require access to information and information

**Post-industrialism** An economy in which manufacturing becomes less important as a source of wealth, and where the production of information, knowledge, and services becomes more important.

## METHODS AND INTERPRETATION

# Measuring the Unemployment Rate

The unemployment rate is one of the most important measurements in the social sciences, and one of the most closely watched economic indicators in most societies. As the Bureau of Labor Statistics defines it, the unemployment rate represents the number of unemployed people as a percentage of the labor force, which is calculated as (Unemployed ÷ Labor Force) x 100. At first glance, this appears to be a relatively straightforward measurement. But the reality is much more complicated. The procedures used to measure the unemployment rate have been the subject of countless academic studies and repeated scientific controversies.

In order to measure the unemployment rate, we need to know two things: (1) the total number of people who are in the labor force, and (2) the total number of people who are unemployed. How do we determine who is in the labor force? According to the Bureau of Labor Statistics, the labor force includes all people aged 16 and older who are either working or actively looking for work. In order to be classified as working during the previous week, they must meet one of the following four categories: (1) worked at least one hour as a paid employee; (2) worked at least one hour in their own business, profession, trade, or farm; (3) were temporarily absent from their job, business, or farm; or (4) worked without pay for a minimum of 15 hours in a business or farm owned by a family member. People doing volunteer work are not included as part of the labor force unless they have a different job or are actively looking for a different job. The same is true for people who are doing unpaid internships, people who work for less than 15 hours in a family-owned business, or people doing home repairs (unless they own a home repair business).

Determining who is unemployed is even more complicated. To be counted as unemployed, a person needs to meet all three of the following criteria: (1) they were not employed during the previous week: (2) they were available for work during the previous week, except for temporary illness; and (3) they made at least one specific, active effort to look for a job during the previous four weeks. There are many people who do not get counted as unemployed, even though they do not have a job.

The unemployment rate tends to ignore people who are chronically unemployed, because many of them get discouraged and stop actively looking for a new job. It does not count people who are in school unless they also have jobs or are actively seeking jobs during the time they are in school. It excludes people who are working in unpaid internships or unpaid training programs. It excludes people who stop working to take care of a family member. These are all large populations, leading some experts to suggest that the unemployment rate may not be the best index of unemployment or the best way to evaluate the strength of the economy (Shorrocks 2009).

The unemployment rate also fails to distinguish between people who have full-time jobs and people who have part-time jobs. This would be fine if the people working part-time were happy with their employment arrangement, but many part-time workers would prefer to be full-time workers. We could learn a lot by measuring the proportion of workers who are underemployed or underpaid, despite the fact that the unemployment rate cannot tell us anything about these dynamics (Borowczyk-Martins and Lale 2020). In fact, an obsessive focus on short-term fluctuations in the unemployment rate makes it harder for policy makers to pay attention to longer-term patterns in the nature of work and employment.

### ACTIVE LEARNING

**Find out:** Statisticians and economists are well aware of the limitations of the unemployment rate, and they have proposed many additional measurements to capture a more complete picture of the economy. Go to the US Bureau of Labor Statistics website, where they discuss different concepts and measurements related to work and employment. Review the discussion and identify three alternative measurement approaches that caught your attention. What do these measurements add to our understanding of work and employment that are not captured by the unemployment rate?

technology. They place a premium on knowledge, creativity, expertise, and communication skills, and require higher levels of education and more advanced credentials.

Post-industrialism has led to significant changes in the economy. Blue-collar jobs based on physical labor have declined in many countries, as they have been relocated to places that have less advanced economies and cheaper labor costs. The unions that protected blue-collar workers have lost political power, and the percentage of workers who belong to unions has also declined.

**Protest against new Amazon headquarters, New York City, 2018**
Community activists and union members protest the tax breaks and inducements offered to the commercial giant Amazon by the city and state of New York. Protesters successfully argued that the new opportunities Amazon would bring were unlikely to benefit local communities and workers and were instead likely to reinforce inequality in housing, jobs, and benefits.

Because of the emphasis on knowledge, creativity, and innovation, research universities have become major sources of economic growth (Berman 2012). Cities compete to attract the new tech companies that drive the information economy, and they try to make themselves attractive to the young college graduates who work for those companies (Castells 1999).

## Economic Crisis and Insecurity in an Age of Globalization

Post-industrialism is good for the experts, the innovators, and the high-level professionals and managers who run the knowledge economy, but it is much worse for everyone else. As Kalleberg (2013) demonstrates in his book *Good Jobs, Bad Jobs*, there has been a dramatic rise in precarious employment since the 1970s. These jobs are defined by low wages, the elimination of benefits such as health insurance or retirement funds, and virtually no long-term security.

The trends in precarious work can be seen in the increasing use of temporary workers, involuntary part-time workers, independent contractors, and contingent or on-call workers. The jobs that have the most growth over the last 10 years are not the high-paying creative jobs celebrated by the knowledge economy. They are the precarious, low-paying service jobs that have high turnover and virtually no job security: home health care aides, retail salespeople,

**Post-industrial work**
Flexible workspaces like WeWork respond to shifting needs of the knowledge economy, where people may work from home and may need only a part-time office space that can be configured for meetings and working in teams.

customer service representatives, and food preparation workers (Kalleberg 2013). These workers are more likely to experience periods of long-term unemployment (at least six months) and pay for more of their health insurance and retirement costs. Not surprisingly, workers' perception of job insecurity has increased dramatically since the 1970s.

These trends are magnified by globalization. As multinational corporations search the globe for cheap labor, workers lose bargaining power and governments lose control over economic policy. But for the innovators, knowledge workers, and professionals and managers who benefit the most from post-industrialism, globalization simply magnifies their sense of privilege and their isolation from the rest of society. According to the sociologist Zygmunt Bauman (2000), this new global elite is continually on the move, but they only experience an isolated and privileged version of the world. National boundaries are not very important for them, because their work takes place all over the world. They have little understanding or empathy for the economic anxieties that are experienced by the less privileged. This kind of economic power and privilege creates quite a lot of resentment and resistance among the non-elite, leading to protests and the creation of social movements demanding social change.

**Social movement**
A group of people acting together to try to create social or political change, usually outside the channels of institutionalized politics.

## 13.5 Social Change

**LG 13.5** Understand the different types of rights claims that social movements make against the powerful and how this type of action helps create social solidarity.

A **social movement** is a group of "ordinary people" acting together to create social or political change. It differs from a political party or an interest group in that it is led by people who are not professional politicians and who try to achieve their objectives outside of established institutions. Historically, social movements have been one of the most important ways for regular people to participate in politics and to challenge economic power (Staggenborg 2010; Tilly and Wood 2012).

Some of the most important social changes in modern society have resulted from the actions of social movements. The democratic revolutions in France and the United States began as social movements, when regular people organized to challenge the power of distant monarchs. The drive to end the African slave trade can be traced to the abolitionist movement, which began in Spain and England and spread worldwide through the 18th and 19th centuries. The labor movement successfully fought for the minimum wage, the end of child labor, and the two-day weekend. The feminist movement successfully fought for women's suffrage, women's health protections, and greater equality in the workplace and the family.

## Challenging the Powerful

Sociologists have always had a strong interest in social movements. Karl Marx believed that the inequalities of capitalist society would eventually lead workers to organize themselves into a global and revolutionary social movement that would usher in a freer and fairer society. While Marx's prediction failed, workers have turned to the labor movement as an effective way to push for changes in the workplace. There are many other examples of people creating social movements to challenge the powerful. Women, racial and ethnic groups, and LGBTQ+ people have formed social movements to advocate for equality. Environmental groups have organized social movements to challenge the power of big oil and coal corporations. And anti-globalization groups have organized social movements to challenge the power of multinational corporations.

Why do these groups choose to organize as social movements, rather than forming interest groups and directing lobbying and fundraising efforts at elected officials? As our discussion of power and hegemony demonstrated, dominant groups always have the advantage in the battle for political influence. Corporations and other powerful groups have more money, which they can use to fund interest groups and donate to political campaigns. As a result, they have better access to elected officials. They also have an easier time getting their issues and concerns onto the media agenda. And they tend to have the same social background as elected officials and journalists, which means that they share the same common-sense view of the world. All of this makes it difficult for ordinary people to participate in the political process through lobbying or fundraising.

According to Charles Tilly, early social movements were connected to the spread of democracy and electoral politics, which encouraged people

**Identity claim**
A claim that a social movement and the people it represents are a unified force.

**Standing claim** A claim by a social movement that the people it represents deserve more complete inclusion in society.

**Program claim** A claim by a social movement that is made in support for or opposition to a specific policy proposal.

to think about the relationship between a government and its citizens in terms of rights and obligations. Modern social movements make three kinds of rights claims against the powerful: **identity claims**, which declare that the social movement and the people it represents are a unified force; **standing claims**, which assert that the people represented by the social movement deserve more complete inclusion in society; and **program claims**, which involve public support for or opposition to specific policy proposals (Tilly 2004: 184).

Sociologists have described the ways that social movements have changed over time. "New social movements" of the 1960s and 1970s were less interested in the class-based political mobilizations of the past. Instead, they protested for the recognition of new identities and lifestyles, and they called for sweeping cultural change directed against "the establishment" (Touraine 1981; Melucci, Keane, and Mier 1989). These movements made a number of different demands: against nuclear energy, against the Vietnam War, for protecting the environment, for broad acceptance of gay and lesbian lifestyles, for women's rights, and more. But the new social movements were also committed to a more general lifestyle politics, which emphasized cultural experimentation and which coalesced around specific musical cultures such as folk music and psychedelic rock (Eyerman and Jamison 1998). The new social movements had little confidence that governments could actually solve social problems, and they believed that change would need to come from direct action that would raise social consciousness and create social change within society itself (Bauman 2002). People who got involved in the new social movements often came to see themselves as "permanent activists," who affirmed their own identity through their protest activities (Polletta and Jasper 2001).

Since then, social movements have become more global. In the past, social movements made claims against specific governments. But today, there is a growing recognition that many of the most pressing social problems are beyond the control of a single country. Issues such as climate change, environmental sustainability, multinational corporate influence, global health crises, refugee populations, and the protection of human rights all require a coordinated global approach (Chapter 15). Global social movements make demands on governments, but they also encourage journalists to expose wrongdoing, and organizers develop creative publicity stunts designed to influence global public opinion.

The environmental advocacy group Greenpeace is just one example of the global social movements that have become permanent fixtures in world politics. The most successful of these movements employ a large staff, have budgets in the millions of dollars, and operate in dozens of countries. But most social movements are quite small and struggle to be noticed at all

> **CAREERS**
>
> ### Sociology and Politics
>
> Because sociology helps us understand power and politics, sociology majors are well represented in political careers such as elected officials, political consultants and journalists, and social movement leaders. Fernando Cardoso was a sociology professor before he was elected president of Brazil in 1995, and Daniel Patrick Moynihan was a sociology professor at Harvard before he was elected to the US Senate in 1976. Former US president Ronald Reagan was a double major in sociology and economics as a student at Eureka College, and First Lady Michelle Obama was a sociology major at Princeton. E. J. Dionne, one of the most influential journalists and political commentators writing in the United States today, has a PhD in sociology from Oxford. Sociologists are particularly well represented in social movements. As we discussed in Chapter 1, many of the most important leaders of the Civil Rights Movement were sociology majors, including Jesse Jackson, Roy Wilkins, and Martin Luther King Jr.
>
> **Michelle Obama**
>
> **ACTIVE LEARNING**
>
> **Find out:** Are there any current members of Congress who were sociology majors in college? What about contemporary journalists, editorial writers, or social movement leaders?

(Jacobs and Glass 2001; Sobieraj 2011). To succeed, social movements need material resources, as well as a strategy for capturing public attention.

## Organizing and Mobilizing for Change

Before the 1970s, most sociologists emphasized how social movements emerged from the grievances that people had in common. **Structural strain theory** identified two things that helped turn grievances into effective collective action: social tension that made people more aware of their deprivation and a precipitating event that pushed people into collective protest (Smelser 1963). If there was an excessively coercive response to the protest by those in power, then more people would be encouraged to protest together. The 2020 protests that developed after the police killing of George Floyd, which we discussed in Chapter 7, provide an example of the kind of collective action that emerges from structural strain.

**Structural strain theory** A theory about the connection between structural inequalities, grievances, and collective action.

## PAIRED CONCEPTS: Global and Local

### The Creation of Greenpeace

The environmental advocacy group Greenpeace was formed during the 1960s in Vancouver, Canada. Influenced by the emerging environmental movement, its origins can be traced to the Don't Make a Wave Committee, a movement protesting nuclear tests being conducted by the US military on Amchitka Island, in Alaska. Using the money raised from a benefit concert in Vancouver, the committee members chartered a small fishing boat (which they renamed the *Greenpeace*) in 1971 to sail up to Alaska, bearing witness and protesting in the prohibited zone that the government had established. Their protests were successful, and the US military ceased nuclear testing on Amchitka.

Emboldened by their victory, the leaders of the group adopted the boat's name and vowed to expand their operations. They went to the South Pacific to protest French nuclear testing activities. They exposed the dumping of nuclear waste in the north Atlantic Ocean. They confronted Soviet, Norwegian, and Icelandic whaling ships, trying to get the International Whaling Commission to introduce a moratorium on whaling. They prevented the killing of seal pups in Newfoundland and Scotland. All of these protest activities were visually dramatic and broadcast by television journalists throughout the world, with Greenpeace's tiny boats confronting massive whaling and military ships.

Greenpeace International was formed in 1979 as an umbrella organization for the growing global movement. By the 1990s, Greenpeace had become a major force campaigning for international agreements to reduce greenhouse gas emissions. It brought attention to illegal logging in the Amazon forest. It convinced Ikea to use renewable timber in the construction of its furniture. It campaigned against genetically modified food. It supported and helped develop renewable and citizen-powered energy solutions.

Today, Greenpeace is the largest environmental movement in the world, with headquarters in the Netherlands and nearly three million members. It receives more than $30 million annually in contributions and grants, which it uses to fund its activities and to support a permanent staff of approximately 2,400 people. It also enjoys the support of more than 15,000 volunteers around the world. It maintains an office in Vancouver—in fact, the Canadian offices are located only a few miles away from the original home of the Don't Make a Wave Committee.

**International social movement organizations**
Founded in 1971, the environmental activism organization Greenpeace reports operating 27 independent national/regional organizations in over 55 countries, with 250 staff in the head office in the Netherlands and thousands more staff and volunteers worldwide. Greenpeace has revenue streams in the hundreds of millions of dollars.

### ACTIVE LEARNING

**Find out:** How important is Greenpeace in Vancouver's history? Is it a tourist destination? Are there museum exhibits about it? What can you find out?

Typically, social movements do not emerge spontaneously from collective grievances and precipitating events. They need leaders, and they need other people who have the time and the skills to manage the organization. All of this requires material resources. Social movements and political groups with these resources are more likely to achieve their goals.

Instead of focusing on the underlying inequalities that make people feel aggrieved, **resource mobilization theory** emphasizes the material and organizational resources that increase the likelihood that social movements will achieve their goals (McCarthy and Zald 1977). There are four types of resources that social movement organizations need if they want to increase their chances of success: money, legitimacy, facilities, and labor. Social movements can combine these resources in different ways. A well-funded social movement can hire professional organizational staff. Movements with more legitimacy will have an easier time attracting money, labor, and media attention.

Resource mobilization theory suggests that groups that capture the support of the wealthy will more easily achieve their objectives. It also suggests that wealthier societies will experience more social movements because they can rely on the extra discretionary time that their citizens enjoy (McCarthy and Zald 1977). Social movements in such societies are likely to reflect the concerns of the wealthier classes, such as bicycle advocacy, environmental sustainability, and lifestyle issues. Because of their ability to attract resources, centrist and reformist movements are more likely to be successful than radical or revolutionary ones.

However, some of the most important social movements have achieved success with very few material resources, relying instead on the commitment of their members and the effectiveness of their protests. Piven and Cloward (1978) have argued, for example, that poor people's movements are the most successful when they rely on mass protests and disruptions. As soon as they develop into formal bureaucratic organizations, social movements become

**The Minneapolis uprising, May 2020**
In the aftermath of the murder of George Floyd in police custody, protests erupted in Minneapolis and soon spread nationwide, resulting in more than $1 billion of property damage, including this block in Minneapolis.

**Resource mobilization theory** A theory that links social movement success to resources of money, legitimacy, facilities, and labor.

less concerned with the powerless, and they are more easily co-opted by the powerful (Piven and Cloward 1978).

While the largest social movements can pay professional staff to do work for them, most rely primarily on volunteer labor. This creates a **free-rider problem**, where people who would benefit from a social movement's activities assume that others will do the work (Olson 1971). To overcome this problem, a social movement needs a critical mass of highly committed people who are willing to volunteer their time (Marwell and Oliver 1993).

The community organizer Fred Ross developed the house meeting technique during the 1940s and 1950s, as a way of generating commitment among a critical mass of supporters. Ross held small meetings at people's homes, where he could describe the goals of the social movement, identify enthusiastic new recruits, and train them to become movement organizers. Cesar Chavez used the same approach when he organized the United Farm Workers movement during the 1960s and 1970s.

Social movements also encourage commitment by reinforcing emotional connections and collective identity. People are more likely to participate in a movement if doing so reinforces their sense of who they are (Polletta and Jasper 2001). The social movement ACT UP generated commitment among LGBTQ people by convincing them that protest around AIDS was an important way of expressing their identity (Polletta and Jasper 2001: 291). Protesters during the Egyptian revolution believed that they were saving the nation from decades of decline and humiliation, resurrecting Egypt's once-proud golden age (Alexander 2011: 31). The most effective kinds of movement identities clearly distinguish active members from bystanders. For example, students who participated in the 1960 lunch counter sit-ins emphasized the fact that they were actually *doing something* to protest racial oppression (Polletta 1998).

**Free-rider problem** A collective action problem, in which people in large groups will not act in a way that helps the common good unless it benefits their own personal interests. In social movement contexts, the situation where the people who benefit from a social movement's activities assume that others will do the work.

## Getting Noticed

Social movements need to attract public attention if they want to achieve their goals. Two strategies are effective. The first is to pay close attention to the changing political context and to frame the message in a way that connects to the larger public agenda. The second type is to stage compelling cultural performances. The advent of online social networking has enhanced the ability of social movements to do both.

**POLITICAL OPPORTUNITY STRUCTURE.** Sociologists think about political context and social movements in terms of the **political opportunity structure**. Social movements have better opportunities in three types of situations: when there are changes in existing political alliances, when there are political conflicts among elites, and when there are clear alliances that

**Political opportunity structure** The political opportunities available for successful social movement action that occurs when there are changes in political alliances, political conflicts among elites, or clear alliances that can be made with specific political groups.

can be made with specific political groups (Tarrow 1989). In these kinds of situations, elected officials and other groups with political power will be more willing to champion the cause of a social movement.

The American Civil Rights Movement offers a case study of how the political opportunity structure can help a social movement. Leaders like Rosa Parks and Martin Luther King Jr. were very effective at creating dramatic protest events that attracted media attention. But they also benefited from a changing political context, as the sociologist Doug McAdam (1982) has shown. By the late 1940s, tensions between the United States and the Soviet Union had increased significantly, marking the start of the Cold War. President Truman was concerned that the Soviet Union would exploit American racism to discredit the government and weaken its international alliances. In this political context, Truman acted decisively to support a civil rights agenda. He created the Committee on Civil Rights in 1946, and he desegregated the military in 1948. Truman's actions divided the Democratic Party.

The changing political context of the late 1940s made it more likely that any civil rights protests in the South would be championed by the federal government and covered by national media. Leaders of the Civil Rights Movement recognized this opportunity, and they organized dramatic protest events in the 1950s and 1960s, culminating in the 1963 March on Washington.

**CULTURAL PERFORMANCE.** Social movements stage dramatic events of collective protest to attract public attention. We tend to see more collective protest during moments of political instability, and they are more likely to be effective during "unsettled times" (Swidler 1986; Habermas 1998).

Social movements carefully script their protests to convey specific meanings to their audience (Alexander 2011). They choose the site of their protest carefully. They try to plan how their protest activities will be choreographed together with police, bystanders, counterprotesters, and others who are present on the scene. They work to convince journalists that their protests deserve coverage (Sobieraj 2011). Sociologists think about this careful scripting of protest in terms of **symbolic politics**, in which the meanings associated with political actions are just as important as the policies or the social changes being proposed.

Effective social movement leaders know how to create a compelling cultural performance. When the American community organizer Saul Alinsky planned protest activities during the 1950s and 1960s, his goal was "to maneuver and bait the establishment so that it will publicly attack him as a 'dangerous enemy'" (Alinsky [1971] 2010). He knew that he would get good media coverage as a result, and he knew that most of the public would be

**Symbolic politics** A type of political activity in which the meanings associated with a political action are just as important as the policies or the social changes being proposed.

**Getting noticed in a crowded attention space**
Egyptian women (left) hold up a sign protesting the continued sexual harassment of women among protesters in the revolutionary actions in Tahrir Square in 2011, while Iranians living in Belgium hold up a placard in English reading "Where Is My Vote?" during a 2009 protest against the Iranian election results (right). Using English on signs attracts English-language media coverage.

outraged by the overreaction of the authorities. Similarly, Martin Luther King Jr. knew that every time his nonviolent protests met a violent reaction from southern police, the images shown in newspapers and on television would anger Americans and increase public support for his movement. King also had a talent for creating visually compelling stages for his protests. The 1963 March on Washington is one of the most iconic images in American history. Taking place 100 years after the Emancipation Proclamation, approximately 250,000 people marched from the Washington Monument to the Lincoln Memorial, where King gave his famous "I Have a Dream" speech as television stations broadcast the event live throughout the nation.

This remains true in the era of social media. Protestors in 2011 in Egypt's Tahrir Square, for example, knew that their actions and the government response were being covered by social media, and they scripted their protests accordingly. Indeed, it is not uncommon for protesters in non-English-speaking countries to carry signs and placards written in English in the confident expectation that they will be read by a huge international media audience.

### Movement Success

How do we know if a social movement is successful? All social movements attempt to change society, and all have specific goals they are trying to achieve. Sometimes it is easy to determine whether a movement met its goals. For example, the Human Rights Campaign fought for years against laws that prevented same-sex couples from getting married. When the Supreme Court ruled in 2015 for freedom to marry nationwide, the Human

**White nationalists clash with counterprotesters in Charlottesville, Virginia, 2017**
Backlash against social movements is one sign of movement success. Widespread social-movement conflict and violence suggest social and political instability.

Rights Campaign could declare unambiguously that it had been successful in achieving its goals.

But it is not always easy to determine if a movement has met its goals. Indeed, for many movements, success in achieving their goals is often followed by a social backlash and higher levels of conflict. The feminist movement, which is widely regarded as one of the most successful social movements of the 20th century, faced a significant backlash during the 1980s (Faludi 2006). This backlash was part of a countermovement, which is often a consequence of social movement success. Many women today are reluctant to identify themselves as feminists, even though they believe in the idea of gender equality. The result is that feminists have to refight many of the battles they thought they had already won.

Social movements have a powerful effect even when they fail to achieve their primary goals. When people participate in a social movement, they benefit from a sense of **social solidarity** that makes them feel more attached to society. People who participate in social movements learn important civic skills and are more likely to join other voluntary associations and participate in politics (Minkoff 1997, 2016). This produces **social capital**, which refers to the relationships and experiences of social connection and cooperation that allow people to believe that they can work together to improve society. As Robert Putnam (2000) has argued, social capital is important for building and maintaining a democratic society.

**Social solidarity** A feeling of social connection and social belonging.

**Social capital** Group ties and network attachments that people have and the sense of trust and security that they get from their group memberships and network attachments; the relationships and experience of social connection and cooperation people have with each other that allow them to act together.

## CASE STUDY

# The Strange History of the US Electoral College

In the 2016 US election, Donald Trump was elected president even though he did not receive the most votes. His opponent, Hilary Clinton, received more than 2.8 million more votes than he did. This had happened before. In 1824, John Quincy Adams won the election despite receiving fewer votes than Andrew Jackson. In 1876, Rutherford B. Hayes was elected despite receiving fewer votes than Samuel Tilden. In 1888, Benjamin Harrison was elected despite receiving fewer votes than Grover Cleveland. And in 2000, George W. Bush became president despite receiving fewer votes than Al Gore. How could this happen in a democratic election? The answer has to do with the Electoral College.

The US Constitution states that the Electoral College is responsible for selecting the president and vice president of the United States. There are 538 electors, and an absolute majority of 270 electoral votes is needed to win the election. Each individual state decides how it will select its electors. Each state gets one elector for each of its senators and representatives. The District of Columbia gets the number of electors that is proportional to its share of the national population, with its maximum number limited to that of the least populous state in the nation. In the original plan, each elector would cast two votes for president. The candidate who received the most votes would be elected president, and the candidate who received the second-highest number of votes would be elected vice president. This was changed in 1803 so that electors would cast one vote for president and one for vice president.

The creation of the Electoral College was a compromise. Many of the founders distrusted direct democracy because they believed that ordinary people lacked sufficient knowledge to make good decisions and that they were easily swayed by emotional and misleading political arguments. But they were also concerned that letting members of Congress make the decision would give them too much *power* over the president.

The decision to establish the Electoral College was also motivated by *inequality* and *privilege* because it gave Congress a way of dealing with the fact that not everyone had the right to vote (Amar 2007). Because each state got a fixed number of electoral votes based on population (rather than the number of people eligible to vote or the number of people who actually voted), there was no incentive to extend the vote to women. Similarly, there was no incentive to extend the vote to enslaved people, who were counted as three-fifths of a person for the purpose of determining the number of seats each state would have in the legislature. If the Constitution had required a direct election of the president by eligible voters, the slave states would have faced a choice: either extend the vote to enslaved people or lose political power to the nonslave states.

There was *contingency* in the early Electoral College as the states had not agreed about how to allocate their electoral votes. In most states, electors were chosen from congressional districts, and they would cast their vote for the candidate who won the election in their district. After Thomas Jefferson lost the 1796 election, however, the state of Virginia passed a "winner-take-all" law, in which all of the state's electoral votes would go to the candidate who won the state. With this change, Virginia gave all of its electoral votes to Jefferson in the 1800 election, and he became president. Other states quickly followed Virginia's lead. By 1836 all but one state had a winner-take-all system, and by 1880 all states were using this system. But this had a huge impact on the *structure* of presidential campaigns. Candidates now have little incentive to campaign in states where the outcome is obvious. Thirty-three states have voted for the same political party in the last five presidential elections, and 40 states have voted for the same party in every election since 2000. Candidates tend to ignore these states, instead focusing all their attention on those "battleground states" in which the election is closely contested.

Today, the Electoral College means that closely contested states get more attention and enjoy greater influence than other states, in a way that has led to some unusual political dynamics. Battleground states benefit significantly just because they are closely contested; they receive more federal grants, and they have more influence in general over federal policymaking (Hudak 2014). Voter turnout is higher in battleground states (Lipsitz 2009). They also tend to have more political division and higher levels of *conflict*. Political parties in these states work hard to encourage their members to vote, reinforcing the *solidarity* of their political party by demonizing the members of the other party. People who live in nonbattle-ground states have become increasingly resentful of the Electoral College system (Alexander 2019).

While the US Electoral College was created as a response to *local* concerns by some of the Founders about direct democracy and other local concerns having to do with the political power of slaveholding states, it was not the first example of such a system to exist. Electoral colleges were used by elites throughout Europe to elect kings, princes, and high magistrates, going back as early as the 11th century (Colomer 2016). In the Catholic Church, the pope is elected by a conclave of cardinals, which functions the same as the Electoral College. All of these systems provided a model that influenced the creation of the US Electoral College. And the US system, once established, created a *global* model for other national constitutions in the 19th century, including those of Argentina, Venezuela, Colombia, Mexico, Chile, and Peru (Colomer 2016). In each of these countries, though, there was a major political crisis in which a candidate won the Electoral College vote while losing the popular vote. They have all since replaced the old system with a direct presidential election, decided by the national popular vote.

There has been growing *resistance* to the US Electoral College system since the 1970s. Maine switched back to a proportional system in 1972, and Nebraska did the same thing in 1992. Both states were trying to force presidential candidates to spend more time campaigning in their states. In addition, there have been several important social movements pushing to abolish the Electoral College system in favor of a direct national vote. There have been more than seven hundred proposals to reform or abolish the Electoral College through constitutional amendment, but they have all failed to get the support they needed to be ratified (Alberta 2017). Today, there are several important movements continuing the effort. The National Popular Vote Interstate Compact is a movement to convince state legislatures to agree to give all of their electoral votes to the candidate who receives the most votes in the national election, regardless of the outcome in their state election. As of 2023, 16 states as well as the District of Columbia had signed the compact, accounting for 205 of the 270 Electoral College votes they need to control the election. The National Popular Vote plan has the support of dozens of advocacy groups, intellectuals, and major newspaper editorial staffs. Supporters of this movement have introduced legislation in favor of the compact in all 50 states. But there has been consistent opposition by battleground states and small rural states, which have the most *power* in the current Electoral College system.

# LEARNING GOALS REVISITED

**13.1 Differentiate between coercive and persuasive power, and understand how persuasive power is connected to the spread of democracy.**

- Coercive power involves the attempt to force people to do something by using the threat of punishment or violence, while persuasive power is the attempt to use influence to convince people to do what you want them to do.
- Every exercise of power encounters resistance.
- The exercise of power is shaped by the resources that the individual or group has at its disposal.
- In modern societies, state power organized by governments is centrally important in politics.
- Authority is the legitimate use of power that is based on the consent of the governed.

**13.2 Distinguish between the different systems of representation in a democracy.**

- In a constitutional monarchy, there is still a king or queen who acts as the ceremonial head of the nation, but most of the power is held by elected officials.
- In a democratic republic, there is no monarch, and the elected officials have all the power.
- In a parliamentary system, people vote for their elected officials in the legislature, but they do not vote for the head of government; the head of government is a member of the legislature.
- In a presidential system, people vote for both their elected officials in the legislature and the head of government; there is a formal separation of powers between the legislature and the head of government.

**13.3 Define political economy, and describe how political and economic forces interact to shape government decisions at local and global levels.**

- Political economy is the study of how the economy shapes politics and how politics influence the economy. Political economy is a very broad field, and it includes many topics that are central to sociology, such as inequality, economic development, globalization, responses to economic crisis, challenges to democracy, and the social influences on public policy, among others.
- In the US, power has become centralized into a power elite, which is composed by the leaders of three kinds of large and powerful institutions: the military, the corporate sector, and the government sector. The power elite has adopted a shared corporate worldview, making their actions become more predictable to one another and easier to coordinate. Globalization has extended this shared worldview and shared set of priorities worldwide, leading to the formation of a global power elite.

- Political economy also extends to international relationships and conflicts between different nations. Political and military decisions often get made because of geopolitics, which refers to the desire by powerful nations to control resources, trade routes, or markets in distant (or adjacent) territories. This includes colonialism, which is one of the most significant historical legacies of geopolitics.

**13.4** Describe how the economy has changed over time, and explain why economic insecurity is such a significant feature of modern social life.

- The most significant change in the modern economy was the transition from feudalism to capitalism. In capitalism, all economic activities are based on a calculation of potential profits, and the prices of all goods (including workers' wages) are determined by the marketplace.
- The Industrial Revolution helped capitalism spread around the world, and changed the nature of work forever. Jobs became increasingly standardized, so workers could be easily substituted for one another on assembly lines and in other factory systems of mass production. For many of them, this meant that their jobs became de-skilled, and they became more easily replaceable.
- The second half of the 20th century led to the development of post-industrial economies, in which manufacturing became less important as a source of wealth, and where the production of information, knowledge, and services became more important.
- Post-industrialism has been good for the experts, innovators, and high-level professionals who run the knowledge economy, but it has not been as good for everyone else. Most jobs have become much more precarious, with low wages, the elimination of benefits, and virtually no long-term security. The use of temporary workers, involuntary part-time workers, independent contractors, and contingent or on-call workers has increased dramatically. The result has been an increase in economic inequality.

**13.5** Understand the different types of rights claims that social movements make against the powerful and how this type of action helps create social solidarity.

- Social movements form when ordinary people act together to try to create social or political change. They are different from political parties or interest groups because they are led by people who are not professional politicians, and they try to achieve their goals outside of established institutions.
- Historically, excluded groups such as women and racial and ethnic groups have formed social movements as the best way to advocate for change.
- Social movements are more likely to be successful if they have abundant resources, or if they connect to the concerns of wealthier groups.

- Some important social movements have achieved success with very few resources by generating commitment among their members, paying close attention to the changing political context, and creating dramatic cultural performances.
- Social movements express their political demands through identity claims that present the movement as a unified group with a unified interest, standing claims that assert that a group must be more fully included in the society, and program claims of support for or opposition to specific laws or policy proposals.
- It is not always easy to determine whether a social movement is successful. Even the most successful social movements will often have to deal with political and cultural backlash. Despite these challenges, the people who participate in social movements develop a stronger sense of social solidarity, and they are more likely to participate in politics. In general, social movements encourage people to think about the ways that they might make their society a better place.

## Key Terms

Absolute monarchy 454
Capitalism 467
Charismatic authority 453
Coercive power 452
Constitutional monarchy 456
Deliberation 456
Democratic republic 456
Economy 466
Feudalism 467
Free-rider problem 478
Hegemony 453
Identity claim 474
Interest group 460
Parliamentary system 457
Persuasive power 452
Political opportunity structure 478
Politics 452
Popular sovereignty 454
Post-industrialism 469
Power 451
Presidential system 457
Program claim 474
Public opinion 457
Rational-legal authority 453
Resource mobilization theory 477
Social capital 481
Socialism 468
Social movement 472
Social solidarity 481
Standing claim 474
State 452
Symbolic politics 479
Structural strain theory 475
Traditional authority 453

## Review Questions

1. What is power? What is the difference between coercive and persuasive power? What are the advantages and disadvantages of each type?
2. How did the spread of democracy change the exercise of power?
3. While the United States has a presidential system of democracy, most successful democracies in the world today are parliamentary systems. What are the main differences between these two

systems? What are the advantages and disadvantages of each system? Why do you think that parliamentary systems have tended to be more stable and more successful than presidential ones?

4. How do interest groups try to influence politics? How is this different from the model of politics expressed by the ideal of deliberation?
5. What is a social movement? Why do people choose to organize social movements, rather than engage in a different kind of political action?
6. Describe the three different kinds of claims that social movements make against the powerful, according to Charles Tilly.
7. How have social movements changed since the 1960s?
8. What are the four different types of resources that social movement organizations need if they want to increase their chances of success?
9. What is the free-rider problem? What do social movements do to try to overcome the free-rider problem and to make sure that people will participate in the movement?
10. What are some of the things that social movements can do if they want to increase their chances of getting noticed?
11. How do we know if a social movement is successful?

# Explore

## RECOMMENDED READINGS

Alexander, Jeffrey C. 2012. *The Performance of Power: Obama's Victory and the Democratic Struggle for Power*. New York: Oxford University Press.

Lukes, Steven. 2004. *Power: A Radical View*, 2nd ed. New York: Palgrave-Macmillan.

Tilly, Charles, and Leslie Wood. 2012. *Social Movements, 1768–2012*, 3rd ed. New York: Paradigm Publishers.

## ACTIVITIES

- *Use your sociological imagination*: Select a social movement that interests you. What are the goals of this movement? How successful do you think the movement has been? Describe the resources the movement has, as well as the protest activities and the cultural performances that it uses to try to attract attention.
- *Data+Media Literacies*: Read the front section of the newspaper. Write down the stories that make the front page and the different people who get quoted in the stories. What issues and voices are privileged?
- *Discuss*: Why do drivers slow down when they see a police car on the road? What does this say about power, the state, and the use of coercive and persuasive power?

F6
F8
F9
11:56
ChatGPT
Gemini
c.ai
Character.AI
Copilot
Bing
Grammarly

# 14

# Media and Technology

On November 30, 2022, the technology company OpenAI released an early demo of an artificial intelligence (AI) chatbot it had created, named ChatGPT. This was the fourth version of an AI chatbot that the company had created, with earlier versions released in 2018, 2019, and 2020. But ChatGPT attracted public interest in a way that earlier versions of the AI chatbot had not. Within five days of its release, ChatGPT had more than one million users; within six months of its release, the company that created ChatGPT was worth $29 billion.

For social commentators and media pundits, the viral success of ChatGPT announced the arrival of the age of artificial intelligence. For many, ChatGPT was an interesting and playful technology that could simplify daily tasks and provide some enjoyable diversions. Users posted examples of using the technology to write new recipes and accompanying shopping lists, to do travel planning, and to write fun new stories. Hundreds of news articles and podcasts predicted an AI revolution that would transform every aspect of social life and create massive disruptions in the economy and the workplace.

While earlier forms of technology-based automation had mostly impacted blue-collar jobs in the manufacturing sector, ChatGPT and other large language model chatbots looked like

Three big AI text chatbots are Google's Gemini, OpenAI's ChatGPT, and Microsoft's Bing.

**Chapter Outline**

**14.1 TECHNOLOGY AND SOCIETY 491**

*Salvation or Apocalypse: Competing Frameworks for Understanding Technology 491*
*The Paradox of Convenience 492*

**14.2 ECONOMIC DIMENSIONS OF MEDIA AND TECHNOLOGY 495**

*Wealth 495*
*Inequality 496*
*Jobs 499*

**14.3 MEDIA, TECHNOLOGY, AND POLITICS 502**

*Media and Agenda-Setting 503*
*Economic Distortions of the Media Agenda 504*
*Filter Bubbles, Algorithms, and Social Polarization 506*
*Voice and Engagement among Marginalized Groups 508*

**14.4 MEDIA, TECHNOLOGY, AND SOCIAL RELATIONSHIPS 511**

*Benefits of Mediated Relationships 511*
*Social Harms of Mediated Relationships 513*

**CASE STUDY: THE RISE AND FALL OF FTX 516**

their impact would be felt in the professional world of white-collar jobs. Experts predicted that ChatGPT would be used by businesses to automate responses to common questions, by software engineers to write and debug computer programs, by professionals to answer emails, by journalists to write news articles, and by public relations workers to write press releases. Health care workers would use it to help make diagnoses, and scientists would use it to summarize new research literatures. Microsoft (which has an ownership stake in OpenAI) quickly integrated ChatGPT into its internet search engine, with plans to extend this integration into Microsoft Word, Excel, and Outlook. A 2023 survey of business leaders revealed that more than half of them were already using ChatGPT in their company, that nearly half of them had reduced their workforce after introducing ChatGPT, and that more than half of them expected additional layoffs before the end of 2023 (Tamim 2023).

This chapter explores the social impacts of media and technology. We begin by discussing social theories about technology and society, which emphasize how the conveniences offered by technology are not as straightforwardly beneficial as they might appear. Next, we examine the economic impacts of media and technology, with a specific focus on how technology influences jobs, wealth creation, and economic inequality. From there we turn to the world of politics, discussing how news media shape the agenda of public discussion, how social media increase polarization, and how marginalized groups use new media technologies to build social solidarity and to increase their voice in the larger public sphere. We end with a discussion of mediated social relationships, considering how these technologies impact our attention, our ability to concentrate, and our general mental health.

## LEARNING GOALS

**14.1** Identify different social theories that explain the impact that technology has had on society.

**14.2** Understand the role that technology plays in the creation of wealth, and how that wealth creation is connected to social stratification and inequality.

**14.3** Describe how media organizations influence politics and political debate.

**14.4** Understand some of the ways that mediated relationships can provide social support and social benefits, but also pose social risks, to technology users.

# 14.1 Technology and Society

**LG 14.1** Identify different social theories that explain the impact that technology has had on society.

Sociologists and other social scientists have been thinking about the relationship between technology and society for a long time. As we discussed in Chapter 13, industrialization and technological innovation were central for the development and spread of capitalism around the world. According to the philosopher Adam Smith, technology accelerated economic growth by increasing the productivity of workers and encouraging the specialization of work. Karl Marx had a more critical interpretation, arguing that factory owners used technology to reduce wages, to extract more profit from workers, and to make them more dependent on capitalists for their survival. Marx also argued that the union of capitalism and technology would rapidly increase the pace of social change and economic disruption.

The development of media technologies has consistently enabled new forms of social identity, social solidarity, and social power. Newspapers—and print media in general—allowed people to imagine that they were part of a national community (Anderson 2006). Transportation and communication technologies allowed states to extend their power over increasingly large territories (Calhoun 1992). The formation of large-scale trade unions depended on these same transportation and communication technologies (Calhoun 1988).

## Salvation or Apocalypse: Competing Frameworks for Understanding Technology

As the sociologist Jeffrey Alexander (2003) pointed out, technologies do not simply impose themselves on our consciousness; they must be made meaningful through a common cultural framework of interpretation, which is based on competing narratives of salvation or apocalypse. In other words, when we think about and discuss new technologies, we tend to organize these discussions around a binary choice: will technology save us, or will it destroy us?

The cultural framing of technology can be seen clearly in a recent newspaper article in *The Guardian*, titled "Technology in 2050: Will It Save Humanity—or Destroy Us?" (Hern 2020). The article describes how developments in energy technology will create either a net zero world of climate sustainability or a world in which entire cities have to be abandoned because of the consequences of climate change. Artificial intelligence will either create so much computational power that it can solve the problems of disease and poverty, or it will get so advanced that it manages to evade human control

The image of a machine that turns against its creator has been a part of popular culture ever since the 1818 publication of Mary Shelley's novel *Frankenstein*. Here Robert De Niro plays the monster in a 1994 film adaptation of the novel.

and destroy the world. These competing narratives of technology go back to the early days of industrialization, when images of the machine as a tool of abundance contrasted with alternative images of a machine that turns against its creator, popularized in Mary Shelley's *Frankenstein* (Alexander 2003: 186–87).

While the reality of technology is almost always somewhere between these two extremes, the cultural framework of salvation and apocalypse is important because it creates a certain amount of anxiety and ambivalence in the way we think about technology. We want technology to serve us, but we fear that it will enslave us instead.

### The Paradox of Convenience

In his 1964 book *One-Dimensional Man*, the philosopher and sociologist Herbert Marcuse argued that technology, by making our lives easier and more convenient, had the paradoxical effect of making us less free. We do not get to decide what technologies will get developed or what kinds of problems they will solve, Marcuse noted. We assume that the problems these technologies have been created to solve are the problems that matter. We are becoming less interested in problems that do not have a technological fix. As our lives become easier and more convenient, we become less able and less willing to deal with inconvenience or discomfort. We become less able to do the hard work of critical reflection, of deciding what our values are or what kinds of challenges we might want to undertake to improve our lives or the lives around us.

Later in this chapter, we explore the paradoxical effects of technology in more detail. We show how technology has created more inequality and made jobs more uncertain for many workers in the economy. We discuss how computer algorithms feed people media content that is designed to produce an emotional reaction that increases the amount of time they spend engaging with media, and how that has had the effect of increasing social polarization. We explore how social media technologies make digital interactions seem more convenient and less of a hassle than social interactions that take place "in real life," which often increases loneliness. We review the research on how social media technologies challenge our ability to concentrate and

### PAIRED CONCEPTS

## Structure and Contingency

### Doomsday Scenarios for Artificial Intelligence

In 2023, a survey of 2,700 artificial intelligence (AI) researchers found that more than half of them believed that there was at least a 5 percent chance that AI would lead to human extinction or some other "extremely bad" outcome (Hsu 2024). A similar concern was expressed by the tech billionaire Elon Musk, who in 2023 warned that "One of the biggest risks to the future of civilization is AI" (Gupta 2023). While predictions are often wrong, these warnings received a lot of public attention, because the people who knew the most about AI seemed to be suggesting that they could not control it.

What are some of the doomsday scenarios for AI? One class of these scenarios shows that the advanced features of the technology could fall into the hands of malevolent actors. For example, as military researchers begin to use AI to develop more advanced biological weapons, there is always the possibility that those technologies could be stolen (or developed in the first place) by criminals or other types of villains, in a real-life version of a common superhero movie plot. In a similar way, people could use AI-based chatbots to spread propaganda and disinformation designed to increase social polarization, social conflict, and violence, leading to the destabilization of governments and the onset of perpetual warfare. This scenario is slightly less terrifying than the first one, but much more likely.

In a second category of doomsday scenarios, AI systems could develop strategies for maximizing their task completion that would be unimaginable to humans because of how catastrophic those social consequences would be. For example, an AI system helping a real estate trading firm to find good deals on real estate purchases could decide that the best way to create real estate bargains would be to take control of a nuclear power reactor and initiate a nuclear meltdown, thereby leading to a collapse of the real estate market in the surrounding territory and an opportunity to "buy low." It is also possible that as AI systems become more complex, they could begin to develop their own goals that are focused less on their original programming and more on self-preservation.

As the computer scientist Stephen Omohundro has argued, the generative self-improvement logic of AI systems gives them certain drives that cannot be completely controlled. The most prominent of these are (1) the drive to model their own operation, (2) the drive to clarify and improve their goals, (3) the drive toward efficient utilization through the acquisition of resources, and

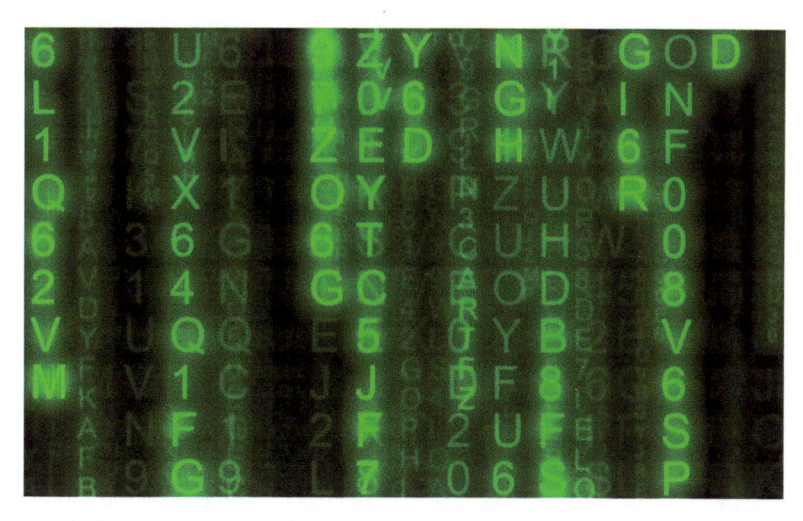

In early doomsday scenarios of artificial intelligence, human life is extinguished and only numbers remain.

**PAIRED CONCEPTS CONTINUED**

(4) the drive toward self-protection and preservation (Omohundro 2008). The only way to prevent these drives from producing a doomsday scenario is to recognize that they are part of the very structure of artificial intelligence and to build guardrails against these tendencies into the very design of AI systems. But this is extremely difficult to do because AI researchers can never fully predict how AI systems will act. Regardless of how well designed the system is, there is always an element of contingency.

**ACTIVE LEARNING**

**Discuss:** Some AI experts argue that the media's focus on the most catastrophic doom scenarios distracts public attention away from the risks that AI are already creating today, which have to do with misinformation, "deep fakes," and the inability to distinguish what is real from what is not. What do you think? Is it possible to discuss both types of risk at the same time, or would it be more effective to focus on the risks that AI already presents?

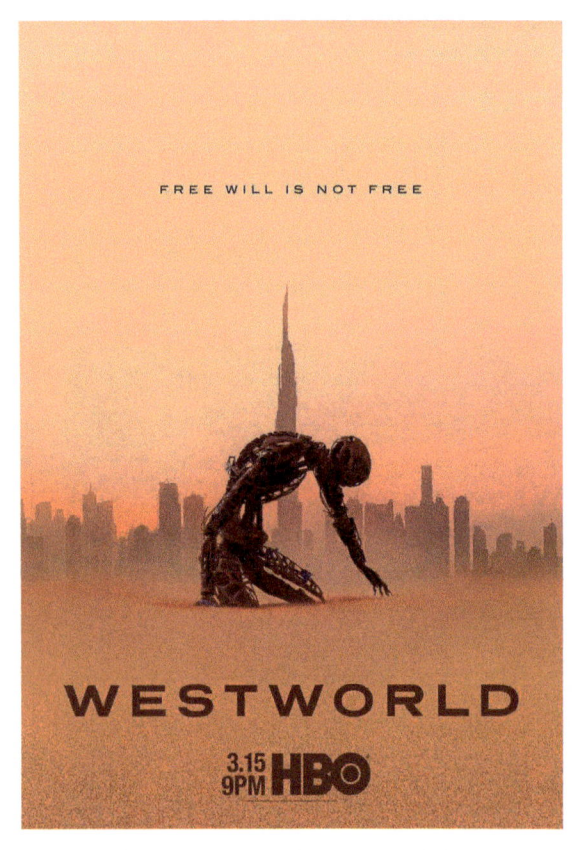

Television shows like *Westworld* encourage audiences to maintain a suspicious attitude toward technology.

bombard us with endless social comparisons, in a manner that has negative consequences for mental health. In addition to these more specific and concrete challenges, however, it is worth thinking about the more general paradox of technology that Marcuse identifies, which is that convenience is not always good for us.

While technology has a lot of power over us, it is equally clear that there is resistance to that power. This is the point that Alexander is making when he points to the competing discourses of salvation and apocalypse. The critical perspective on technology can be seen clearly in the literary and film worlds of science fiction, where negative portrayals of technology outnumber positive ones (Matheson 1992). In films like *The Matrix* and *Minority Report*, as well as television shows like *Westworld* and *Black Mirror*, technology is presented as an untrustworthy and uncontrollable force that threatens human freedom. These cautionary tales encourage audiences to maintain a suspicious attitude toward technology; the same is true of protests directed against technological power and attempts to regulate technology companies, which we describe later in the chapter.

## 14.2 Economic Dimensions of Media and Technology

**LG 14.2** Understand the role that technology plays in the creation of wealth, and how that wealth creation is connected to social stratification and inequality.

The technology sector is one of the largest and most influential parts of the economy. In the US the tech sector makes up nearly 10 percent of the entire economy, as measured by the gross domestic product (GDP). Technology is an important part of the financial sector, as we discuss below. Schools at all levels are giving the highest priority to training in science, technology, engineering, and math (Chapter 11). Most people assume that technological innovation is the prime source of good new jobs and the main driver of economic growth.

### Wealth

The wealthiest people in the country are increasingly making their money in the technology sector. In the *Forbes* list of the wealthiest Americans for 2023, nine of the top 10 people on the list made their fortunes with media and technology companies. Elon Musk, who tops the list with a net worth of over $400 billion, is the founder of SpaceX and Tesla. Musk is followed on the list by Jeff Bezos (founder of Amazon) and Larry Ellison, who is the cofounder of the software company Oracle. The only person in the top 10 who is not in the technology sector is the investor Warren Buffett, but Buffett's largest stock holding is Apple, which is a technology company. Overall, the tech sector trails only the financial sector in producing millionaires and billionaires (Piper 2023). Digital technologies have had a big impact on the financial industry itself, with advances in cloud computing, blockchain, and artificial intelligence increasing efficiency and profitability among finance companies (Chahal 2023).

Most people hold their wealth in stocks and mutual funds, and over the last 30 years these investments have been heavily reliant on technology stocks. During this time, tech stocks have been much more profitable

**Elon Musk**

than other stocks, and with the rapid development of artificial intelligence technologies this is likely to continue (Sargen 2023). In a recent study of the top-performing stocks between 1990 and 2020, eight of the top 10 were tech stocks, with Apple ($2.67 trillion wealth created) and Microsoft ($1.91 trillion) at the very top (Burrows 2023). While most US stocks earned less than a 5 percent annual return over this 30-year period, Apple averaged a 23.5 percent annual return and Microsoft averaged 19.2 percent. Investing in the tech sector has clearly been a smart move for wealthy investors.

Workers in the tech sector also tend to receive higher salaries than most other workers, which gives them a better opportunity to create wealth. As we discussed in Chapter 10, the average advertised salary for entry-level jobs in a STEM field is more than 25 percent higher than an entry-level job in a non-STEM field. Salaries in the technology sector continue to rise faster than salaries in other sectors, and the demand for tech workers is outstripping supply in all sectors of the economy (Smith 2023). Finance companies have significantly increased their hiring of STEM majors, paying them high starting salaries to help them with software development and data analytics. Recognizing their value in the labor market, tech workers are more likely than other workers to ask for a pay raise, more likely to ask for a promotion, and more likely to change jobs (PWC 2023).

## Inequality

Technology has impacted the structure of inequality in three ways: first, it has led to a greater concentration of wealth; second, it increases segregation; and finally, it increases the proportion of precarious jobs. In the discussion below, we concentrate our attention on digital technologies, which are the most recent. But the impact that technology has had on jobs and wealth concentration is a more general process that goes back to the Industrial Revolution (Chapter 13).

In the section on wealth, above, we discussed many of the ways that technology increases economic inequality. The technology sector produces a disproportionate number of millionaires and billionaires. Technology workers begin their careers with higher starting salaries, allowing them to begin building wealth earlier than most other workers. Technology stocks have vastly outperformed other stocks, which has increased the profits of the investment class. In addition to these factors, the technology sector also has a higher level of revenue concentration, with the top 20 companies earning more than half of all the revenue for the entire sector, and with the top four companies earning more than one-quarter of all the revenue (Piper 2023). These companies also tend to employ a smaller full-time workforce than comparable companies from other industries, allowing the managers of these companies to create large wealth holdings for themselves (Piper 2023).

**PAIRED CONCEPTS**

## Inequality and Privilege

### What Happens When Google Moves into Town

Alphabet, which is the parent company that owns Google, is one of the largest and most powerful technology companies in the world. The company has more than 180,000 full-time employees, with large office complexes in Manhattan, Boston, Seattle, Dublin, Singapore, and dozens of other locations around the world. But the company's biggest presence is its corporate headquarters in Mountain View, California, which is a city of about eighty thousand people located about 6 miles southeast of Stanford University. More than one-quarter of the people who live in Mountain View work for Google.

Google pays its full-time workers very high salaries, so whenever the company sets up a large office complex in a city it has a dramatic impact on the cost of living. In the US, the median salary for a full-time Google employee in 2023 was more than $279,000 (Council 2023), which is more than what 97 percent of salaried workers earn in the US. When Google buys or builds a large office complex in a city, its workers have more money to spend renting or buying their homes. They want to eat at more expensive restaurants, and shop at more expensive stores. If enough of them move into a neighborhood or a city, the result is that only wealthy people can afford to live there.

Mountain View provides the most dramatic example of what happens when Google moves into town. The median rental price for housing in Mountain View in December 2023 was more than $3,800 per month, and the median home sale price was $1.85 million. Low- and middle-income housing has been demolished to make way for luxury townhouses, pushing residents who are less wealthy out of the city, including the people who work at Google cleaning the offices and preparing the free meals that are provided for the workers. Traffic congestion has increased dramatically in Mountain View, particularly near the Google headquarters. Coffee shops, restaurants, and retail stores have all become more upscale.

While Mountain View has become a bedroom community for the privileged, the town itself has struggled to provide the infrastructure that the growth of the area required. There is no sales tax revenue from Google's search and ad businesses, nor does the city collect sales tax on the free meals that Google provides for its employees (Hollister 2014). The company buses that Google offers to its employees to help them get to work do not improve the mass transit infrastructure for the rest of the city. As Google provides more and more amenities

**Googleplex in Mountain View, California**

**PAIRED CONCEPTS CONTINUED**

on its sprawling corporate campus to encourage its employees to spend more time there, the effect is a withering of community life outside of the Google campus. Because Google is a large multinational company with offices around the world, many of its workers leave Mountain View after a few years, meaning that they have neither the time nor the inclination to invest in the local community.

> **ACTIVE LEARNING**
>
> **Discuss:** What commitment do large, multinational technology companies like Google have to the local communities where they are located? Do you think that technology companies are different as community partners than other large corporations? Why or why not?

As the technology sector accelerates the concentration of wealth, segregation also increases. For example, 90 percent of employment growth in the tech sector has occurred in just five cities: Seattle, Boston, San Francisco, San Diego, and San Jose (Muro 2020). As tech workers flock to these cities, they push up the price of housing so much that only the wealthy can afford to live there. Middle-class and lower-middle-class workers who have jobs in those cities have to commute long distances or continue living with their parents. They are increasingly disconnected from the public spaces of those cities, as the restaurants and retails stores cater to a wealthier clientele. Over time, these cities become less diverse in their racial, ethnic, and economic composition. They become spaces of privilege rather than spaces of mobility.

Finally, technology increases inequality by increasing the number of precarious jobs. As we discussed in Chapter 13, a precarious job has high turnover, no job security, no benefits, and (typically) low pay. The rise in precarious jobs is connected to employers' increasing use of temporary workers, involuntary part-time workers, independent contractors, and contingent or on-call workers. The tech sector has been a key force in this spread of the "gig economy." By 2019, half of the workforce at Google was on temporary contracts, earning much less income (and with many fewer protections and benefits) than the regular employees of the company (Piper 2023). The combination of new technology and new labor practices has allowed the gig economy to spread to other parts of the economy as well. Uber's attractiveness to consumers is its integration with smartphones, but one of its key economic advantages over traditional taxi companies is the way that it treats all its workers as independent contractors (Chapter 11). Similarly, Amazon's attractiveness to consumers is the convenience of its online shopping portal, but the company also benefits from the fact that it classifies so many of its delivery drivers and warehouse workers as independent contractors (Cunningham-Parmeter 2016). In other words, it is not only the technology itself that has increased the number of precarious jobs, but also the labor practices favored by the technology companies themselves.

## Jobs

As the previous discussion demonstrates, technology has fundamentally transformed how workers experience their jobs. Automation in all its forms increases worker productivity, allowing companies to hire fewer workers and in some instances replacing those workers altogether. Advances in geolocation and **digital surveillance** allow companies to monitor their workers more closely. These forces accelerate the development of a post-industrial economy, which favors knowledge work, creativity, expertise, and communication skills, as well as the advanced credentials and graduate degrees that usually accompany those kinds of skills (Chapter 13). Technology is also associated with cultural changes that shift the meaning of work.

Ever since the Industrial Revolution, business owners have used technology to increase **worker productivity**. For some, increasing productivity meant that they could increase their production targets with the same sized workforce, leading to an increase in profits. For those who did not need to increase their production, it meant that they could reduce the size of their workforce. As technology has advanced, some companies have been able to increase their production while also reducing the size of their workforce.

One of the reasons that companies in the information technology sector have been so profitable is that they maintain a relatively small workforce, relying on computer processors to do a larger proportion of the work. When Facebook acquired the messaging company WhatsApp in 2014, WhatsApp was only employing 35 engineers to oversee its network of 450 million users. These trends are now spreading to other industries as well. Over the last 20 years, technological advancements have reached the point where a type of "**smart manufacturing**" is developing, in which production takes place using advanced robotic technology, large-scale data processing, artificial intelligence, and a significantly lower level of human intervention (Phuyal, Bista, and Bista 2020).

Public debates about the future of jobs are now shaped in a real way by the prospect that robots, computers, and artificial intelligence will make most workers unnecessary. In 2016, the management consultant and business professor Walter Bennis remarked, half-jokingly, that the factory of the future would have only two workers, a human and a dog. The human would be there to feed the dog, and the dog would be there to keep the human from touching the equipment (Evjemo et al. 2020). While this is an exaggeration, recent research estimates that nearly half of US employment is at risk due to computerization and automation (Frey and Osbourne 2017). Around the same time, concerns about automation and jobs sparked interest in the idea of a universal basic income, to guarantee economic and social stability in an era where automation threatened to displace large numbers of workers (Bidadanure 2019).

**Worker productivity**
The amount that a worker can produce or accomplish within a given quantity of labor output.

**Smart manufacturing**
A type of economic production that relies on advanced robotic technology, large-scale data processing, and artificial intelligence to increase productivity while lowering the level of human intervention that is required in the manufacturing process.

## CAREERS

### New Job Titles in the Age of Artificial Intelligence

Like previous waves of technological development, the arrival of artificial intelligence has brought significant worries that machines will take over many jobs, leading to mass unemployment among workers who believed they had a stable career. Unlike previous waves of automation, which had their biggest impact on blue-collar factory work, artificial intelligence is likely to have its biggest effect in professional and managerial jobs that require higher levels of education. Workers with a college degree or higher are more than twice as likely as workers with only a high school education to be impacted by artificial intelligence (McKendrick 2023). Tax preparers, budget analysts, accountants, technical writers, journalists, computer programmers, lawyers, and paralegals all face significant exposure to being replaced by artificial intelligence (Kochhar 2023; Johnson 2023).

As artificial intelligence becomes more widely used in the workplace, it will also create new kinds of employment opportunities and new job titles. The most obvious of these is the **prompt engineer**, whose expertise involves writing, refining, and optimizing prompts that are addressed to a generative AI chatbot, so that it elicits helpful and effective responses. Effective prompt engineering combines technical language about large language models with a deep understanding of natural language and context, so that the generative AI system produces the best response with the fewest number of revisions needed. The World Economic Forum declared that prompt engineer was the top new job for 2023, though that proclamation has been challenged by skeptics who warn that these jobs are likely to disappear just as quickly as they arrived on the economic scene (Pinon 2023). Similar types of AI-related jobs that are currently in high demand include language model trainers and language model project managers, who can fine-tune pre-trained AI models so they are better aligned with the specific requirements of an organization; API integration experts, who make sure that an AI system works well with a company's other software systems; and ethical AI specialists, who establish guidelines to help prevent or minimize privacy breaches, the spread of misinformation, and other bias-related harms (Magill 2023).

Demand for different kinds of jobs in an AI-suffused economy is likely to change over time. In the short term, the need to deploy artificial intelligence systems in different industries will create a large demand for AI researchers, software developers, data scientists, user experience designers who can make the AI experience easier to navigate, and project managers who ensure that the development of an AI system is tailored to the specific needs of a company (Budman et al. 2020). In the short-term, employers have also expressed a desire to replace existing workers with newer ones who already have expertise and experience with AI, though a large skills gap makes it difficult for them to hire these kinds of new workers (Budman et al. 2020). There is also a strong short-term interest in using artificial intelligence to cut labor costs by using technology to replace those workers who do mostly mundane and repetitive tasks associated with the collection and analysis of information.

Other experts suggest that the spread of artificial intelligence technologies will place more of a premium on creativity and entrepreneurship throughout the entire economy. Over time, as workers retrain to develop the skill they need to incorporate artificial intelligence into their jobs, companies will shift their focus toward jobs in which workers use artificial intelligence to free up their time to do the more creative work that the company depends on to remain innovative and competitive. By taking over most of the mundane and repetitive information-related tasks of an organization, artificial intelligence reduces the cost of entry and levels the playing field to allow for new, innovative, and entrepreneurial organizations to enter a market and compete effectively. In addition, because AI chatbots often produce false statements and other "hallucinations," companies need workers who possess critical skills and the domain expertise to be able to distinguish the true from the false. Effective employees will need to learn enough about machine learning, data science, and natural language processing so that they can use artificial intelligence effectively in their jobs, but once they learn these skills their ability to make important contributions is likely to be connected to their critical literacy skills and their creativity, which are precisely the kinds of skills that students learn in social science and humanities courses.

> **ACTIVE LEARNING**
>
> **Find out:** Think of a job you might be interested in after you graduate and do some research to find out how experts talk about the impact that artificial intelligence is likely to have on that particular industry. Pay careful attention to (a) what kinds of jobs in that industry are likely to disappear, and (b) how the effective use of artificial intelligence is likely to change the jobs that remain.

For those workers who still have jobs, digital surveillance technologies mean that their work is much more closely monitored. In today's workplace, employers use body sensors, tracking devices, recording devices, and other wearable technologies to monitor every movement, keystroke, and conversation that their workers have (Manokha 2020). Many of these technologies follow the workers when they leave the workplace, allowing them to maintain the same level of supervision of remote work and having real implications for the privacy of workers when they are off the job (Ajunwa, Crawford, and Shultz 2017). Employers rely on computer algorithms and artificial intelligence to process the mountains of data generated by these surveillance systems, and these algorithms generate metrics for worker expectations that replace human judgment and empathy (Nguyen 2021). The result is a massive increase in worker stress and burnout.

Technology has also encouraged significant cultural changes that shift the meaning of work. The knowledge workers who are prized by the tech sector value remote work and the flexibility that is associated with it, increasing the talk and the emphasis placed on work–life balance and the importance of pursuing of passions outside of work, but without acknowledging the gendered division of household labor (Hari 2017). Tech leaders such as Elon Musk, Jeff Bezos, and Mark Zuckerberg have become celebrities, promoting themselves as visionary problem solvers while whitewashing their own complicity in perpetuating massive levels of social inequality in the United States and around the world (Giridharadas 2018). A culture of entrepreneurship has also become more widespread, encouraging people to take control of their lives by using technology to participate in the sharing economy, even though so many of the biggest entities in the sharing economy (Amazon Marketplace, Airbnb, Uber) are predatory and exploitative (Schor 2016). All these cultural changes are amplified by a media industry that has a variety of different incentives, many of which have little to do with a concern for social well-being.

**Prompt engineering** The practice of writing, refining, and optimizing prompts that are addressed to an artificial intelligence chatbot so that it produces the most helpful and effective responses with the fewest number of revisions needed.

## 14.3 Media, Technology, and Politics

**LG** **14.3** Describe how media organizations influence politics and political debate.

As we discussed earlier in the chapter, the development of media technologies enabled new forms of social identity, social solidarity, and social power. Technology was an important resource that enabled the creation of modern politics, extending to the very idea of democracy itself (Chapter 13). The democratic revolutions that started in England, France, and the United States were only possible because of advances in literacy and print technology, which allowed people to read about important matters of common concern and to imagine that they were members of a large mass audience whose public opinion was the ultimate source of power and political legitimacy. They imagined that they were part of a democratic **public sphere**, in which private citizens and elected officials gathered together to discuss matters of common concern (Jacobson 2017; Habermas 1989).

**Public sphere** The collection of places where private individuals and elected officials gather together to discuss matters of common concern.

Although people still engage in direct political discussions with each other, most political discussions today involve the use of media technologies (Bennett and Entman 2001). While the media have expanded the audience for political debate, there are important limitations to mediated political discussions. Public access to newspapers, television, and other legacy media is a scarce and unevenly distributed resource (Bennett, Lawrence, and Livingston 2008). Journalists for major outlets, such as the *New York Times* and CNN, are most likely to talk with government officials, experts, and other "official sources" drawn primarily from the worlds of business and academia (Gans 1979; Schudson 2011). This preference for elite sources carries over to alternative or new media venues (Wallsten 2015). The most influential figures in news on social media tend to come from the worlds of journalism, politics, and public relations, where opinion columns are written primarily by

**Official sources**
Journalists spend most of their time paying attention to the statements of business and government leaders and their representatives.

journalists, academics, government officials, and interest groups (Powers 2016; Jacobs and Townsley 2011). The patterns for national television and radio news broadcasts are similar.

Because ordinary people consume but are not consulted by mainstream media, they must rely on others to speak on their behalf. Although "person-on-the-street" interviews may seem to express the opinions of ordinary people, elite journalists are more likely to use official sources in their reporting. Mainstream media organizations reward those reporters who have the highest-status sources (Tuchman 1978; Schudson 2011). In addition, because journalists need access to government officials to report on politics and policy, they tend to avoid challenging those officials (Revers 2014). These factors limit the ability of journalists to effectively represent the interests of ordinary people.

The internet, especially social media, allows ordinary people to participate in public discussions about politics. It is less than clear what kind of influence ordinary people have when they post online comments to news websites or discussion forums. There is even evidence that people's use of social media makes it *less* likely that they will be willing to join political conversations in offline settings (Hampton, Shin, and Lu 2017). And concern is growing globally about the manipulation of social media by state and criminal actors to influence social movements and elections (Jamieson 2020).

## Media and Agenda-Setting

Media organizations perform an **agenda-setting** function for political discussion and public opinion. News organizations do not necessarily shape *what people think*, but they do have a great influence on *what people think about*. There is a striking similarity in the stories that news organizations emphasize in their coverage. For example, news organizations tend to converge on the same big stories, and they tend to move from one big story to the next (Danielian and Reese 1989; Boczkowski 2010).

Elected officials influence the media agenda by commanding the attention of journalists through press releases, press conferences, and posts on X (formerly Twitter) and other social media platforms. In fact, government officials dominate media coverage, accounting for between half and three-quarters of all news sources (Tresch 2009; Gans 1979). People on social media amplify the influence of the stories reported in traditional news publications and try to attract the attention of those publications (boyd 2018). Overall, the policy agenda of elected officials has a big impact on the media agenda, and that same policy agenda tends to be shaped more by lobbying and interest groups than by ordinary citizens or social movements (Wolfe, Jones, and Baumgartner 2013; Rogers and Dearing 2012). In moments of crisis, however, social movements

**Agenda-setting**
The idea that news media set the public agenda. They do not shape *what people think*, but they do have great influence on *what people think about*.

and unofficial sources have a much better chance of shaping the media agenda (Habermas 1996; Jacobs and Townsley 2014).

### Economic Distortions of the Media Agenda

Media organizations are businesses, and the economic incentives they face also shape the media agenda. Media organizations make their money by selling advertising, which influences both the kinds of stories that get covered and how they get covered.

Advertising shapes the media agenda in several ways. First, advertisers are more interested in an audience that can afford to buy things. This places pressure on news organizations to concentrate on events that will be of interest to wealthier people, such as fluctuations in the stock market or which Caribbean island is the best place for a vacation. Advertisers also like entertainment stories and other "soft news," which have proven to attract a wealthier consumer audience (Diamond, McKay, and Silverman 1993; Hamilton 2004; Fletcher 2016). As publishers focus resources on creating this kind of content, coverage of serious news shrinks, which makes it easier for politicians to control the policy agenda. Finally, news organizations that depend on advertising are more likely to focus on scandals and other "sensational" stories (Benson 2009; Schudson 1978) that attract great numbers of readers. As a result, public debates tend to focus more on the personal qualities of elected officials and less on their policies.

The media agenda is also influenced by the corporate structure of media ownership. Most media organizations are owned by large corporations, have a presence across multiple media platforms, and make a profit by maximizing ad revenue and minimizing costs. Because they want to maximize advertising revenue, newspapers and television news stations have historically tried to avoid appearing partisan, for fear of alienating part of the audience. This is less true today as changes in the media landscape make it profitable to attract a smaller but highly devoted audience to a news website that keeps them engaged (Turow 1998). But the corporate structure of media ownership does shape how stories get reported.

In many other countries, media organizations may depend more on the government than advertising for revenue. In several European countries, for example, state-owned broadcast networks control a significant share of the market, while newspapers receive government subsidies. While such a system may provide a greater diversity of programming, more focus on educational programming, and more attention paid to minority audiences and viewpoints, there is concern that state-funded news organizations are less willing to criticize elected officials since they depend on those officials for financial support (Hallin and Mancini 2004).

The influence of money on the media agenda is limited by the fact that journalists have a certain amount of autonomy in their profession.

## METHODS AND INTERPRETATION

### Does Concentration of Media Ownership Matter?

**Media concentration** occurs when a small number of companies control a disproportionately large share of the media audience. Economists usually label an industry as highly concentrated when the top four firms control more than half of the total revenue for the industry, or when the top eight firms control 75 percent of the total revenue. For critics, media concentration presents three problems: it makes it difficult for most people to voice their opinions in a way that can be heard publicly; it makes it more likely that people with the most power will be able to co-opt the media and limit the amount of critical reporting; and it reduces media companies' incentive to invest resources in creating news or other media content (Baker 2006).

In his 2004 book *The New Media Monopoly*, Ben Bagdikian showed that media concentration in the United States increased significantly from the mid-1980s to the early 2000s. Bagdikian examined revenue figures for each media category, then counted the number of companies that together controlled more than half of all the market share. When the first edition of the book was published in 1983, the fact that 50 companies controlled the media was taken as cause for alarm. By 2004, he found, only five companies controlled the media: Time Warner, Disney, News Corporation, Viacom, and Bertelsmann.

Since 2004, the landscape has changed again, with only Disney and Bertelsmann remaining on the list of the top media corporations. The other companies on Bagdikian's list have become smaller and have sold off elements to other companies. At the same time, the rise of huge technology corporations such as Google and Facebook have changed the underlying business model and the overarching media environment. In this new, complex, and fast-changing environment, media giants like Disney and Apple scramble to consolidate (Molla and Kafka 2019). The largest media conglomerates in terms of revenue ranked by *Forbes* in 2022 were Comcast, The Walt Disney Company, Charter Communications, Netflix, and Paramount. While the joining of media and technology companies makes it harder to measure media concentration, the general trend has been that media subsectors have become more concentrated as they have become more electronic and digital in nature (Noam 2009: 5).

Because many studies of media concentration focus on market share, it is important to note that social concerns about media concentration have to do with media *control*—that is, who has access to media, and who gets to shape the content of that media. To explore these issues, we would need different data from those collected by Bagdikian. Instead, we would want to collect data that examines the relationship between market share concentration, diversity of media voices, critical content, and investment in news-gathering resources. In recent years, sociologists have turned their attention to this relationship between media concentration and media content (e.g., Benson 2010; Benson and Hallin 2007; Noam 2016; Hesmondhalgh 2019).

#### ACTIVE LEARNING

**Discuss:** Do you think that who owns the media organization shapes the content it publishes? Why or why not?

---

In countries where journalism has a strong tradition of professional independence, journalists work hard to demonstrate that they are independent, that they are willing to criticize the powerful, and that they have the public interest in mind. This keeps the media agenda open to the concerns of ordinary people and social movements.

**Media concentration** A situation when a few large companies control the majority of commercial culture.

## Filter Bubbles, Algorithms, and Social Polarization

While media companies have a commitment to values such as professionalism and the public good, their interest in making money means that they are always thinking about how to attract the attention of their readers, viewers, and users. As we discussed earlier, the media makes money by selling the attention of their audience to advertisers. This has been true since the mid-19th century, when newspapers discovered that they could make more money by selling their papers for a penny each, worrying less about subscription revenue and more about advertising revenue (Schudson 1979). This remains true today. Alphabet, which owns Google and YouTube, do not charge users to use their platforms but together earned more than $220 billion in advertising revenue in 2022 (Bianchi 2023).

Developments in digital technology have allowed media companies to refine how they measure audience engagement, in a manner that has had consequences for their programming strategies. Whereas print media companies measured circulation (i.e., number of copies sold) and broadcast media used survey research to discover what people were watching and listening to, today's digital media companies have developed precise measurements of exactly how long each user spends engaging with each piece of media content. Digital tracking technologies such as cookies allow them to share precise viewing histories to advertisers, who can deliver targeted advertising that is customized to that user's media consumption behavior. At the same time, the explosion of media content into thousands of different channels and digital locations has splintered the media audience into smaller, more specialized taste communities (Turow 1998). Rather than aiming for an extremely large but casual audience, media companies today are aiming for smaller audiences of deeply committed fans.

To increase the engagement of the viewer, media companies use computer algorithms to deliver customized media content. Netflix recommends television shows and movies for us based on our previous viewing behavior, while Spotify does the same thing for music and Facebook does the same thing for news. Computer algorithms are the key to this whole process, allowing digital media to deliver customized content in real time and to monetize that content in real time by selling our taste profiles in a digital advertising marketplace that has been turbocharged by artificial intelligence (Fisher and Mehozay 2019).

**Filter bubble**
A phenomenon in which people are only exposed to topics that interest them and opinions they already agree with, which increases social polarization by encouraging people to develop more extreme versions of the beliefs they already hold.

While algorithms can deliver us increasingly personalized and targeted media content, they also organize us into "**filter bubbles**" where we are only exposed to topics that interest us and opinions we agree with (Pariser 2011). This creates political echo chambers. In a study of Facebook users, for example, researchers found that there was only a 5 percent chance that conservatives would be exposed to progressive ideas, and only an 8 percent

## PAIRED CONCEPTS: Power and Resistance

### The Battle over Privacy

As more and more areas of our lives are coordinated through digital technologies, threats to privacy have increased considerably. Large-scale data breaches occur regularly, revealing usernames, passwords, and other sensitive information that exposes individuals to significant risks of identity theft and other forms of cybercrime. Location tracking devices on smartphones can be used by government officials (sometimes without a warrant) to track the individual movements of large numbers of people, via computer algorithms that develop risk profiles of those they believe merit extra surveillance. Intrusive forms of surveillance extend to the workplace as well, where employers make widespread use of electronic monitoring of their employees, both on and off the clock. The proliferation of biometric technologies in public places makes it increasingly difficult for people to maintain their anonymity. The ability to respond to these kinds of threats is limited by the immense power of big tech companies, and by outdated privacy laws that were designed to protect the physical information you have in your desk rather than the digital information that you keep online.

The power of big technology companies makes it very difficult for people to protect their privacy in a digital world. Whenever we open an app or a website, the default setting is one that allows the company to track our data and our location. Most people do not know this, and if they do know it, they often lack the skill or the motivation to change their settings in a way that will protect their privacy. In addition, big tech companies spend hundreds of millions of dollars in lobbying efforts designed to limit government attempts to pass laws with better privacy protections. In those instances where the demand for digital privacy protections becomes so strong that politicians must do something, the laws they propose are often written by tech lobbyists in order to weaken the regulations as much as possible (Feathers 2021).

Governments, nonprofit groups, and social movements have taken more aggressive actions in recent years to resist the power of technology companies and establish more consequential privacy protections for individuals. Facebook was embroiled in a growing public scandal throughout the 2010s, when it was revealed that the personal data of millions of users had been collected without their consent to be used for targeted political advertising and misinformation campaigns. Nonprofits such as the Electronic Privacy Information Center and the Electronic Frontier Foundation stepped up their advocacy efforts, rallying public opinion against technology companies' privacy violations.

In 2021, the European Union fined Amazon $877 million for violations of the General Data Protection Regulation.

**PAIRED CONCEPTS CONTINUED**

In 2018, the European Union enacted the General Data Protection Regulation (GDPR), which set strict new limits on how technology companies obtained and handled the personal information of their users, allowed users to request the data that companies are holding about them, and empowered users to demand that the information be deleted (Satariano 2018). Large fines have been issued against technology companies for violations of the GDPR, including an $877 million fine against Amazon, $403 million against Instagram, $370 million against TikTok, and $277 million against Meta. Brazil, Japan, and South Korea quickly passed similar data protection laws, forcing technology companies to change their data collection policies and give users more opportunities to opt in or out of data tracking.

**ACTIVE LEARNING**

**Find out:** Select three apps or social media sites you use. Locate the terms of service, as well as the default settings. What kind of data privacy do these sites provide as their default? What opportunities are there to expand your privacy rights? How much effort is involved in doing this?

---

chance that progressives would be exposed to conservative ideas. (Bakshy, Messing, and Adamic 2015). By exposing people only to topics that interest them and only to people who agree with them, filter bubbles encourage social polarization, causing people to develop more extreme versions of the positions they already hold (Chapter 5).

Because computer algorithms do not distinguish between high-quality and low-quality information, they can easily be hijacked by people who want to spread disinformation and social conflict. Human troll armies have been very effective at spreading disinformation and promoting conspiracy theories on social media forums, while political bots have been able to manipulate public opinion by creating "digital astroturf" movements that imitate legitimate grassroots organizations (Wooley and Howard 2019). Russia's digital misinformation activities during the 2016 US presidential election are probably the most well-known example of this kind of computational propaganda, but similar kinds of actions can be seen in political conflicts around the world.

## Voice and Engagement among Marginalized Groups

Because the exercise of power always faces resistance, the growing power of algorithms has been challenged in several different ways. The European Union's 2018 General Data Protection Regulation discussed above, establishes limits to the use of computer algorithms to generate user profiles, and demands that privacy protections be built into the design and architecture of information technology systems (Fitsilis 2019). Privacy activists encourage people to engage in everyday resistance against algorithms, by erasing their web history, deleting cookies, using their web browser in incognito mode, and relying on virtual proxy networks. Software designers have developed tools that can break through filter bubbles and increase the diversity of media content that people are exposed to (Bozdag and van den Hoven 2019).

Prominent critics of algorithmic power have lots of access to the public sphere. Eli Pariser's TED Talk warning about the danger of filter bubbles has been viewed more than 1.5 million times. The sociologist Zeynep Tufecki's writings about the social and political risks associated with algorithms and artificial intelligence are published regularly by publications such as *Wired*, *Scientific American*, and the *New York Times* (where she was hired as an opinion columnist in 2021). Critics like Pariser and Tufecki challenge the idea that new technologies are simply vehicles of freedom and convenience.

Marginalized groups have also developed techniques and strategies for harnessing digital technologies to increase their voice and their political visibility. Historically, marginalized groups have been underrepresented by traditional media. It has often been too expensive to set up successful newspapers and broadcast media to expand representation. New media, by comparison, are much easier and less expensive to establish, and they typically have more porous gatekeeping structures that provide opportunities for strategic actions. Indigenous groups in Australia and the Americas, for example, have made extensive interventions on Wikipedia, writing tens of thousands of articles about Indigenous culture and history (Bedeley et al. 2019). The Standing Rock Sioux tribe and its allies made effective use of Facebook, YouTube, and Twitter to mobilize and to publicize its protests against the Dakota Access Pipeline (Hunt and Gruszczyski 2021). These groups (and others like them) have leveraged new media technologies to gain access to larger publics, while also using technology to build social solidarity and to coordinate collective action.

**PAIRED CONCEPTS**

## Global and Local

### BTS Army: Global Fandoms and National Elections

K-pop stans are ardent fans of South Korean bands like BTS, Girls' Generation, EXO, and Blackpink who engage with each other in massive online global communities. Described by experts as "not particularly political, but ... socially engaged," K-pop fans are generally democratic, globally oriented, and committed to social justice (Saeji 2020). The members of BTS, for example, are known for their support of humanitarian, artistic, and philanthropic causes, and their fans follow their lead.

In recent years, BTS Army—the fandom of BTS—have mobilized to influence local and national politics around the world. Bringing a global youth perspective to particular local settings, K-pop fans from Myanmar, the Philippines, China, Indonesia, Chile, and Brazil, as well as the United States, have organized to support local and national candidates and oppose others. Although these efforts are not always successful, and while it is not always possible to pinpoint the precise impact of K-pop stans on political outcomes, these cases do illuminate the impact of global fandoms on local contexts.

One example from 2020 was when K-pop stan accounts overwhelmed the #WhiteLives Matter

**PAIRED CONCEPTS CONTINUED**

**The Power of K-pop**
Fans of BTS and other K-pop performers have become active in political campaigns around the world.

hashtag by "flooding Twitter with video clips and memes of their favorite artists" and calling out #WhiteLives Matter as a "racist backlash" (McCurry 2020). BTS later tweeted to their 26 million followers, "We stand against racial discrimination. We condemn violence. You, I and we all have the right to be respected. We will stand together. #BlackLivesMatter." (McCurry 2020). In another example, BTS donated $1 million to Black Lives Matter following the killing of George Floyd by Minnesota police, and its fandom, BTS Army, matched the donation in 24 hours" (Zaveri 2020). K-pop stan accounts also "crashed the Dallas Police Department app with thousands of fancams, short clips of Korean idols or groups performing live" in response to a request by police to upload videos of protestors.

The event that garnered the most mainstream press however, was when K-pop fans and various TikTok creators organized to undermine attendance at a campaign rally held by then-U.S. president Donald Trump. By encouraging people to register online for free rally tickets with no intention of attending the event, the online campaign artificially inflated attendance numbers. Rally organizers had planned to fill the 19,000 seat stadium in Tulsa Oklahoma but were embarrassed when only 6,200 people showed up. A second stadium, which had been booked to contain the expected overflow crowd, remained completely empty (Lorenz, Browning, and Frenkel 2020). In the context of a hotly contested US presidential election, the fan-backed campaign achieved widespread and global media coverage.

Beyond the US, K-poppers mobilized against conservative and right-wing candidates in Chile, Brazil, and the Philippines. Using distinctive tactics and language learned in online fan campaigns, K-pop stans supported Gabriel Boric against the more established right-wing candidate, José Antonio Kast, in Chile's presidential election of 2021. In October 2022, the movement Army Help the Planet registered record numbers of young people to vote in Brazil's elections, contributing to the defeat of right-wing Javier Bolsonaro in favor of the liberal socialist Luiz Inácio Lula da Silva.

It is not always possible to disentangle the precise impact of fandoms and K-pop stan campaigns on political outcomes. K-pop fandoms are primarily communities where people can share their intense connection to favorite performers by sharing videos and memes, exchanging merchandise, fundraising for their favorite performer's birthdays, and promoting their favorite performers to local radio stations, retailers, and award competitions. It does seem clear, however, that these fandoms are passionate global communities that have translated their digital skills to local political contexts.

**ACTIVE LEARNING**

**Discuss:** Do you think that fan participation in political campaigns increases the likelihood that fans will become more involved in politics throughout their lives? Why or why not? How would you design a research study to find out if you are correct?

## 14.4 Media, Technology, and Social Relationships

**LG 14.4** Understand some of the ways that mediated relationships can provide social support and social benefits, but also pose social risks, to technology users.

Historically, people have used media technologies to sustain and reproduce the social relationships they have "in real life." Close friends and family members who were separated long distances from each other once wrote letters, which were delivered by the postal service. The spread of commercial telephone services beginning in the 1920s allowed them to talk to one another, although the high prices associated with long-distance calling made this a technology reserved mainly for the wealthy until the 1990s. Commercial email services developed in the 1990s, and commercial videoconferencing services became popular in the early 2000s. All these technologies made it easier for people to maintain relationships with distant friends and family.

Media technologies have also made it possible for people to develop new kinds of social relationships—with people they have never met in real life. These new types of relationships have both positive and negative aspects. Media technologies allow users to develop **parasocial relationships**, which are one-sided social relationships in which people feel a sense of intimacy and social attachment with the media performers they watch regularly. Media technologies also allow social solidarity and social support to form for people who occupy marginalized and persecuted identities, enabling them to explore and develop those identities in a way that would not be possible in the communities in which they live. On the other hand, the spread of social media technologies has also been associated with a significant increase in loneliness, a loss of self-esteem, and a crisis in mental health.

**Parasocial relationship** A one-sided relationship in which people feel a sense of intimacy and social attachment with the media performers they watch regularly.

### Benefits of Mediated Relationships

The concept of parasocial interaction was first developed in the 1950s by the sociologists Donald Horton and Richard Wohl, as part of an attempt to understand the impact that television was having on the social lives of its viewers (Horton and Wohl 1956). It refers to a process that takes place when someone is watching television and they imagine the television performer to be an intimate conversational partner. If the viewer is a regular viewer of a particular program, they can develop a parasocial relationship with the television performer, which is a more enduring and durable type of imaginary relationship. It is a one-sided relationship, in the sense that the viewer has a strong sense of attachment to the performer while the performer has no knowledge of (or attachment to) the viewer. Despite the asymmetrical nature of these relationships, they still have a positive social benefit for the viewer, because they provide additional feelings of intimacy and identification that complement the relationships they have in real life.

Parasocial interactions and parasocial relationships have expanded with the growth of social media and new digital technologies. Instagram, YouTube, and other video sharing apps afford the same kind of parasocial interactions as television, but with increased levels of viewer engagement. In many ways, the influencer economy and the advertising that supports it depend heavily on parasocial relationships (Yuan and Lou 2020).

Social science research has shown that parasocial relationships are associated with several positive benefits for media users. Most research has found that parasocial relationships extend and complement existing social relationships, rather than replacing them (Tukachinsky, Walter, and Saucier 2020). Other research has found that people with low self-esteem use parasocial relationships to strengthen their social identity and their sense of social belonging (Derrick, Gabriel, and Tippin 2008). To the extent that they can increase a sense of social belonging without decreasing the number of social attachments an individual has "in real life," parasocial relationships are associated with a general increase in subjective well-being (Hartmann 2017). In a world of global media, parasocial relationships can also provide important social supports for intercultural dialogue (Schmid and Klimmt 2011).

Media technologies also offer important forms of solidarity and social support for people who occupy marginalized and persecuted identities. As we discussed briefly in Chapter 5, digital technologies allow people to try out different versions of themselves that they are not comfortable experimenting with in real life. Social media have been critical for the identity development of LGBTQ youth, particularly those living in non-urban areas where a critical mass of LGBTQ visibility is absent (Craig and McInroy 2014; Gray 2009). Indeed, for any individual who is stigmatized in their local community, the global communities made possible by digital media are a critically important refuge. While it would be

Lionel Messi has more than five hundred million followers on Instagram.

wrong to romanticize the internet as a space of boundless inclusion and tolerance, the careful digital nomad can find supportive and solidaristic communities that may not exist in the physical community in which they live.

## Social Harms of Mediated Relationships

There is a lot of hate and intolerance on social media, which damages social relationships and often leads to violence. The anonymity of the internet reduces the costs and accountability of hate speech and harassment, leading to a situation where this kind of speech has exploded in quantity and frequency at the same time that it has become harder and harder to regulate (Banks 2010). The ubiquity of online hate speech means that the people who use media technologies to create supportive and inclusive social communities must be vigilant and on the lookout for hateful attempts to infiltrate their online worlds and bombard them with harassment, threats, and other forms of cyberbullying (Chahal 2016). At the extremes, this can lead to doxxing and other forms of digital vigilantism that place the victims of online hate in real physical danger (Trottier 2020). But the ubiquity of online hate speech also creates a pervasive sense of unease and dread for the everyday user of digital media—particularly for women and other marginalized groups who are disproportionately the targets of online hate speech (Sobieraj 2020).

At a more general level, there is a concern—despite the more positive picture described by the work on parasocial relationships—that our participation in digital media is in fact damaging our ability to form meaningful relationships in the real world. This concern has been expressed most forcefully in a series of books by the sociologist Sherry Turkle, who argues that digital technologies have changed the way we communicate and form relationships with each other. In her book *Alone Together*, Turkle (2011) documents how young people are constantly attending to their phones, an excessive distraction that prevents them from fully attending to or caring for their closest relationships. They worry that they don't know how to have a real conversation, even as their gaze is constantly pulled away from real conversations toward the smart technologies they carry with them at all times. In *Reclaiming Conversation and the Power of Talk in a Digital Age*, Turkle (2015), argues that if people want to be less lonely, they need to put their phones down. They need to commit themselves to the kinds of real conversations in which intimacy and empathy can grow. They need to learn how to spend time with themselves and with their own thoughts, without escaping into the constant distractions that are on offer from digital technologies.

In fact, there is a lot of social science research documenting the rise of loneliness associated with today's world of ubiquitous digital media. Cross-national research shows that, from 2012 to 2018, adolescent loneliness increased in 36 out of the 37 countries studied, in conjunction with the rise of smartphone

## PAIRED CONCEPTS: Solidarity and Conflict

### Social Media and Cancel Culture

Public shaming has long been used to punish acts that violate social sensibilities. From the Middle Ages until the 19th century, in fact, public shaming and public humiliation were common forms of punishment for people who broke the law or who committed serious violations of social norms. As Émile Durkheim argued, this kind of public shaming united society together and allowed people to affirm the importance of the moral violation that had occurred (Chapter 5). In the late 2010s and early 2020s, a new form of public shaming emerged, known as cancel culture, which relies on social media to identify and punish moral transgressors.

**Cancel culture**
Public shaming and shunning are amplified on social media when people are canceled online.

Cancel culture emerged initially on Black Twitter around 2015, as a way of reacting to something that someone did that the person disapproved of, with some version of the phrase "s/he's canceled" (Romano 2020). Sometimes it was said about someone the person knew, and other times it was said about a celebrity or someone else with whom they had a parasocial relationship. Sometimes it was said seriously, and other times it was used jokingly. As the term caught on, it focused more on public figures and its use became more frequently serious, often accompanied by additional calls to boycott the offending figure. It spread quickly from there, as a more general tool used to unite people in condemnation against offensive speech and behavior. Cancel culture was an important and visible part of the #MeToo movement that started in 2017, as well as the Black Lives Matter protests in 2020 against the police murder of George Floyd. By 2020, survey research revealed that nearly half of adults in the US were very familiar with the phenomenon of cancel culture (Vogels et al. 2021).

The widespread use and awareness of cancel culture has not taken place in isolation; rather, it has become part of a larger set of cultural conflicts pitting progressives and conservatives against one another. Supporters of cancel culture argue that it is an important and effective tool that marginalized groups can use to pursue social justice. Critics argue that cancel culture threatens free speech by silencing unpopular voices (Norris 2023). The successes of cancel culture have encouraged a backlash, like many successful social movements of the past (Chapter 13).

In post-industrial nations such as the United States, the United Kingdom, and Sweden, the debate over cancel culture has magnified political divisions between progressives and conservatives, increasing the solidarity within each group but also increasing the conflict between the two groups (Norris 2023). To be sure, there are non-conservatives who have criticized cancel culture because of its impact on free speech and because of the psychological and material damage it produces for the lives of its victims (Kovalik 2021). Increasingly, though, the criticism of cancel culture has become a major rallying call and mobilizing force for conservative political movements. Together with a growing backlash against Black Lives Matter, and with political campaigns that unite their adherents to rally behind a "war on woke," conservative politicians are mobilizing their adherents to fight against cancel culture and to punish all social critics who are deemed to be insufficiently patriotic (Steel 2023). Against these attacks, progressive activists have defended cancel culture as an important tool for social change and social justice, and they have argued that the critics of cancel culture are not really concerned about protecting free speech and are instead focused on shutting down the voices of those pointing to the continued attacks on women, domestic violence, racism, homophobia, and other forms of intolerance (Owens 2023).

> **ACTIVE LEARNING**
>
> **Discuss:** What does it mean to cancel someone? Do you think it matters if the person being canceled is a public figure or an ordinary person? Can you think of a time when you avoided saying something online because of a concern about getting canceled? Do you think that this fear of getting canceled was an infringement on your free speech, or a helpful tool that prevented you from saying something offensive?

access and increased internet use (Twenge et al. 2021). Loneliness in the US reached epidemic levels during the COVID lockdowns, with more than 60 percent of respondents reporting feelings of loneliness, and with the intensity and propensity of loneliness being felt most strongly among heavy social media users (Demarinis 2020). The UK created the position of Minister of Loneliness in 2018, and Japan created a similar position in 2021. In the US, the surgeon general, Vivek Murthy, released a major report in 2023 titled "Our Epidemic of Loneliness and Isolation" (Murthy 2023), which argues that new digital technologies have played an important role in the rise of loneliness and feelings of social isolation.

Many people express that social media use is having a negative effect on their mental health. A study of Facebook showed that the longer people are active on Facebook, the more negative their mood is afterward, and the more likely they are to have lower self-esteem (Sagioglou and Greitemeyer 2015; Vogel et al. 2014). Individuals who follow more fitness-oriented sites are more likely to express body dissatisfaction and more likely to engage in extreme weight-loss behaviors (Lewallen

US surgeon general Vivek Murthy has suggested that there should be a warning label placed on social media platforms, because of the risks they pose for adolescent mental health.

and Behm-Morawitz 2016). Engagement with social media produces a vicious and destructive cycle, in which increased social media use is associated with depression, loneliness, anxiety, and a stronger orientation to social comparison, and the social comparison orientation, in turn, leads to an even greater increase in social media use (Reer et al. 2019). Individuals who score higher on the Social Media Addiction Scale are significantly more likely to meet the criteria for major depressive disorder (Robinson et al. 2018). Summarizing all this research in the context of an exploding mental health crisis, US surgeon general Vivek Murthy warned that "there is growing evidence that social media use is associated with harm to young people's mental health. . . . [F]or too many children, social media use is compromising their sleep and valuable in-person time with family and friends. We are in the middle of a national youth mental health crisis, and I am concerned that social media is an important driver of that crisis—one that we must urgently address" (Murthy 2023).

### CASE STUDY

## The Rise and Fall of FTX

In 2009, a new form of digital currency named Bitcoin was developed by a computer programmer or a group of programmers using the pseudonym Satoshi Nakamoto. Instead of using a bank to verify and secure its transactions, Bitcoin instead relied on computer networks and new digital encryption technologies. *Forbes* magazine named Bitcoin the best investment of the year in 2013, setting off a wave of interest and development in cryptocurrencies. Dozens of new cryptocurrencies joined Bitcoin in the years that followed.

In 2017, a 25-year-old finance worker named Sam Bankman-Fried co-founded a new cryptocurrency trading firm, named Alameda Research. Alameda quickly grew to become one of the largest trading firms in the industry. Bankman-Fried decided to move the company to Hong Kong in late-2018, because the regulatory environment was friendlier to cryptocurrency companies. By 2019, Bankman-Fried and his team at Alameda began imagining and designing a new and improved exchange for

FTX founder Sam Bankman-Fried was convicted of seven counts of fraud and conspiracy.

trading cryptocurrencies. They launched this new exchange, named FTX, in May 2019. The exchange had immediate success. By 2020, an average of $1 billion daily was being traded on FTX. The exchange moved its headquarters to the Bahamas in 2021, allowing Bankman-Fried to be closer to the US while still avoiding the jurisdiction of US regulators.

FTX and Alameda Research made Bankman-Fried an extraordinarily wealthy and influential person. By 2022, FTX was valued at more than $40 billion, and Bankman-Fried's personal net worth reached as high as $26 billion (Varanasi et al. 2023). Bankman-Fried became a major political donor and philanthropist, promoting a philosophy of "effective altruism" that he had become interested in when he was a college student at the Massachusetts Institute of Technology (MIT). FTX became a cultural icon, buying the naming rights to the basketball arena in Miami and spending $30 million on television advertisements during the 2022 Super Bowl. But then everything unraveled. FTX declared bankruptcy in November 2022,, Bankman-Fried was convicted of seven counts of fraud and conspiracy in November 2023, and in March 2024 he was sentenced to serve a 25-year prison sentence.

The collapse of FTX was a *global* economic event, with the $32 billion of value that was lost on the exchange touching many of the largest global investment companies. The exchange's collapse and the trial of Bankman-Fried was also a global media event, covered by newspapers, television stations, and digital news sites around the world. The FTX crash shattered confidence in cryptocurrencies around the world, resulting in a further loss of global wealth. In fact, the global cryptocurrency market lost more than $2 trillion in value between its peak in November 2021 and the FTX bankruptcy one year later (Lang et al. 2023). But there were also *local* losses created by the FTX collapse, particularly in the Bahamas. The FTX corporate headquarters in the Bahamas is now abandoned, and the dozens of Bahamians who worked for the company found themselves unemployed. In fact, the bankruptcy of FTX threatened the reputation of the entire financial services industry in the Bahamas, even though many of the companies located there had nothing to do with FTX.

As is the case with many instances of financial fraud and white-collar crime, the perpetrator of the crime was a person with a *privileged* biography. Sam Bankman-Fried was the son of two Stanford University law professors, and he was a graduate of MIT, which is one of the most elite universities in the world. Before he started his cryptocurrency companies, he had been employed by Jane Street Capital, an elite financial trading firm with offices in New York, London, Hong Kong, Amsterdam, and Singapore. As a billionaire, he could afford the best lawyers, and he was able to pay the $250 million bond that would allow him to stay out of prison while awaiting trial. His victims had fewer privileges or resources. There were approximately 15 million people who had money tied up in FTX, and it will take them years to recover their money if they are ever able to at all. The wealthier and more privileged investors ensnared in the FTX collapse will be able to weather these delays, and they will be able to afford the assistance of lawyers who can help them navigate the complicated bankruptcy proceedings. The less privileged investors, however, will not have the benefit of these resources, and this event is likely to have a much bigger impact on their lives. In this way the collapse of FTX will increase *inequality*, just like so many previous cases of fraud and white-collar crime.

The remarkable success of Alameda Research and FTX benefited from the *structure* of new technologies, which are shaped by clear patterns of development with distinct phases. Recent research on the "hype cycle" model identifies a basic pattern for new technologies, in which (1) the public announcement of a new technology leads (2) to a peak of media attention and inflated expectations, which is followed by (3) public disappointment and disillusionment, and then finally (4) a more realistic understanding of the promises of the technology and (5) a more sustainable development of the technology (Dedehayir and Steinert 2016). Bankman-Fried entered the market during the peak of inflated expectations, and the collapse of his companies helped bring on the trough of disillusionment. At the same time, the collapse of FTX was not foreordained by the structure of the hype cycle. If FTX had

> **CASE STUDY** CONTINUED
>
> established better corporate controls, if the company had not fraudulently misappropriated hundreds of millions of dollars of customer assets, or if Bankman-Fried had shifted more of his attention toward risk management and less of his energy to giving media interviews, he might have made less money but he might have saved his companies and stayed out of legal trouble. These *contingent* actions were made possible by FTX's position in the hype cycle, but they were actual decisions made by real people who had other options in front of them.
>
> While Bankman-Fried had located his company in the Bahamas as part of an effort to *resist* the regulatory powers of the US Securities and Exchange Commission, in the end he was not able to avoid the *power* of the US criminal justice system to punish him for his crimes. After he was charged by federal prosecutors, Bankman-Fried was extradited from the Bahamas to the US, where he was tried and convicted on several criminal counts and ultimately sentenced to a prison term of 25 years. The public scandal surrounding the FTX collapse has increased the *conflict* between pro- and anti-crypto groups, with each side mobilizing to support its cause in a way that increases the *solidarity* within each faction.

## LEARNING GOALS REVISITED

**14.1 Describe how different social theories explain the impact that technology has had on society.**

- Industrialization and technological innovation were central for the development and spread of capitalism around the world. According to the philosopher Adam Smith, technology accelerated economic growth by increasing the productivity of workers and encouraging the specialization of work. Karl Marx had a more critical interpretation, arguing that factory owners used technology to reduce wages, to extract more profit from workers, and to make them more dependent on capitalists for their survival. Marx also argued that capitalism and technology would rapidly increase the pace of social change and economic disruption

- When people think about and discuss new technologies, they tend to organize their thoughts in terms of whether the new technology will make society better or worse. The cultural framework of salvation and apocalypse is important because it creates a certain amount of anxiety and ambivalence in the way we think about technology. We want technology to serve us, but we fear that it will enslave us instead.

- There is a basic paradox that is associated with the convenience that technology provides. We do not get to decide what technologies will get developed or what kinds of problems they will solve. We assume that the problems these technologies have been created to solve are the problems that matter. We become less interested in problems that do not have a technological fix. As our lives become easier and more convenient, we become less able and less willing to deal with inconvenience or discomfort. We become less able to do the hard work of critical reflection, of deciding what our values are or what kinds of challenges we might want to undertake to improve our lives or the lives around us.

**14.2** Understand the role that technology plays in the creation of wealth, and how that wealth creation is connected to social stratification and inequality.

- Many of the wealthiest people in the world today are making their money in the technology sector. Overall, the tech sector trails only the financial sector in producing millionaires and billionaires. Workers in the tech sector also tend to receive higher salaries than most other workers, which gives them a better opportunity to create wealth. Most people hold their wealth in stocks and mutual funds, and over the last 30 years these investments have been heavily reliant on technology stocks.
- Technology has led to a greater concentration of wealth by increasing the number of millionaires and billionaires and by increasing the profits of the investment class. The technology sector also has a higher level of revenue concentration than most other industries.
- Technology increases levels of segregation. When technology companies move into a city, they push up housing prices so much that that only the wealthy can afford to live there. Middle-class and lower-middle-class workers who have jobs in those cities have to commute long distances, and they are increasingly disconnected from the public spaces of those cities, as the restaurants and retail stores cater to a wealthier clientele. Over time, these cities become less diverse in their racial, ethnic, and economic composition. They become spaces of privilege rather than spaces of mobility.
- Technology increases the proportion of precarious jobs. The tech sector has been a key force in the spread of the "gig economy," which is defined by no job security, no benefits, and (typically) low pay. Companies in the technology sector have been among the most aggressive in reclassifying their employees as independent contractors.

**14.3** Describe how media organizations influence politics and political debate.

- Media organizations influence politics by defining the agenda of issues that people will talk about. Elected officials influence the media agenda, but the media agenda is also influenced by economic considerations, by journalists' commitment to maintaining their professional autonomy, and by the actions of social movements.
- Media organizations are businesses, and the economic incentives they face also shape the media agenda. Media organizations make their money by selling advertising, which influences both the kinds of stories that get covered and how they get covered. Advertisers prefer content that attracts audiences who can afford to buy things, and they prefer more sensational content that attracts viewers.
- In order to increase the engagement of the viewer, media companies use computer algorithms to deliver increasingly customized media content to their users.

This creates "filter bubbles" and political echo chambers, spaces where we are exposed only to topics that interest us and opinions we agree with. Computer algorithms can also be hijacked by people who want to spread disinformation and social conflict. The result is an increase in social polarization and conflict.

**14.4 Identify some of the ways that mediated relationships can provide social support and social benefits, but also pose social risks, to technology users.**

- Marginalized groups have developed techniques and strategies for harnessing digital technologies to increase their political visibility, to build social solidarity, and to coordinate collective action. Compared with traditional media, new media are much easier and less expensive to establish, and they typically have more porous gatekeeping structures that provide opportunities for strategic actions.
- Parasocial interactions and parasocial relationships with media figures provide feelings of intimacy and identification that complement the relationships people have in real life. To the extent that they can increase a sense of social belonging without decreasing the number of social attachments an individual has "in real life," parasocial relationships are associated with a general increase in subjective well-being.
- In a world of global media, parasocial relationships can also provide important social supports for intercultural dialogue.
- Media technologies offer important forms of solidarity and social support for people who occupy marginalized and persecuted identities. For any individual who is stigmatized in their local community, the global communities made possible by digital media are a critically important refuge.
- The anonymity of the internet reduces the costs and accountability of hate speech and harassment, which has exploded in quantity and frequency at the same that it has become harder and harder to regulate.
- There is growing evidence that our participation in digital media is in fact damaging our ability to form meaningful relationships in the real world by reducing our ability to give people our full attention when we are with them.
- There is also growing evidence that digital media technologies have played an important role in the rise of loneliness and feelings of social isolation.
- Many people express that social media use is having a negative effect on their mental health. Engagement with social media produces a vicious and destructive cycle in which increased social media use is associated with depression, loneliness, anxiety, and a stronger orientation to social comparison, and the social comparison orientation, in turn, leads to an even greater increase in social media use.

## Key Terms

Agenda setting 503
Digital surveillance 499
Filter bubble 506
General Data Protection Regulation 508
Media concentration 505

Parasocial relationship 511
Prompt engineering 500
Public sphere 502
Smart manufacturing 499
Worker productivity 499

## Review Questions

1. Why do so many people feel anxiety and ambivalence about new technologies?
2. What are some of the doomsday scenarios for artificial intelligence?
3. What are the main ways that technology has contributed to the creation of wealth in society? How is this wealth creation connected to social stratification and inequality?
4. How have new technologies changed the nature, the organization, and the meaning of jobs in today's workplace?
5. How do media organizations influence the political process?
6. How does money influence the media agenda?
7. How have computer algorithms changed the incentives and the content-creation strategies for media companies?
8. What are some of the ways that media and technology have provided social support and social connection for their users?
9. Why has the spread of digital media technology been associated with a rise in loneliness, social isolation, and mental health challenges?

## Explore

### RECOMMENDED READINGS

Hartmann, Tilo and Charlotte Goldhoorn. 2011. "Horton and Wohl Revisited: Exploring Viewers' Experience of Parasocial Interaction," *Journal of Communication* 61: 1104–1121.

Noam, Eli. 2009. *Media Ownership and Concentration in America*. Oxford University Press.

Pariser, Eli. 2011. *The Filter Bubble*. Penguin Books

Turkle, Sherry. 2011. *Alone Together: Why We Expect More from Technology and Less from Each Other*. Basic Books

### ACTIVITIES

- *Use your sociological imagination*: Examine the content of a social media site you use frequently. Do you think it promotes a diversity of viewpoints and interests, or is it more accurately described as a filter bubble? What is your evidence for your position?

- *Media+Data Literacy*: Select a science-fiction book, movie, or television show. How is technology represented? Is it a source of freedom or oppression? What do you think these representations tell us about public beliefs about technology in society?

- *Discuss*: What is your position on the use of technology in the classroom? Do you think students should be allowed to use whatever technologies they have access to, or should there be regulations? Are there certain types of media technologies that you think are more damaging to the learning environment, and if so, what are they?

# PART V
# CHANGE, ISSUES, AND THE FUTURE

**15** Climate Change and Sustainability

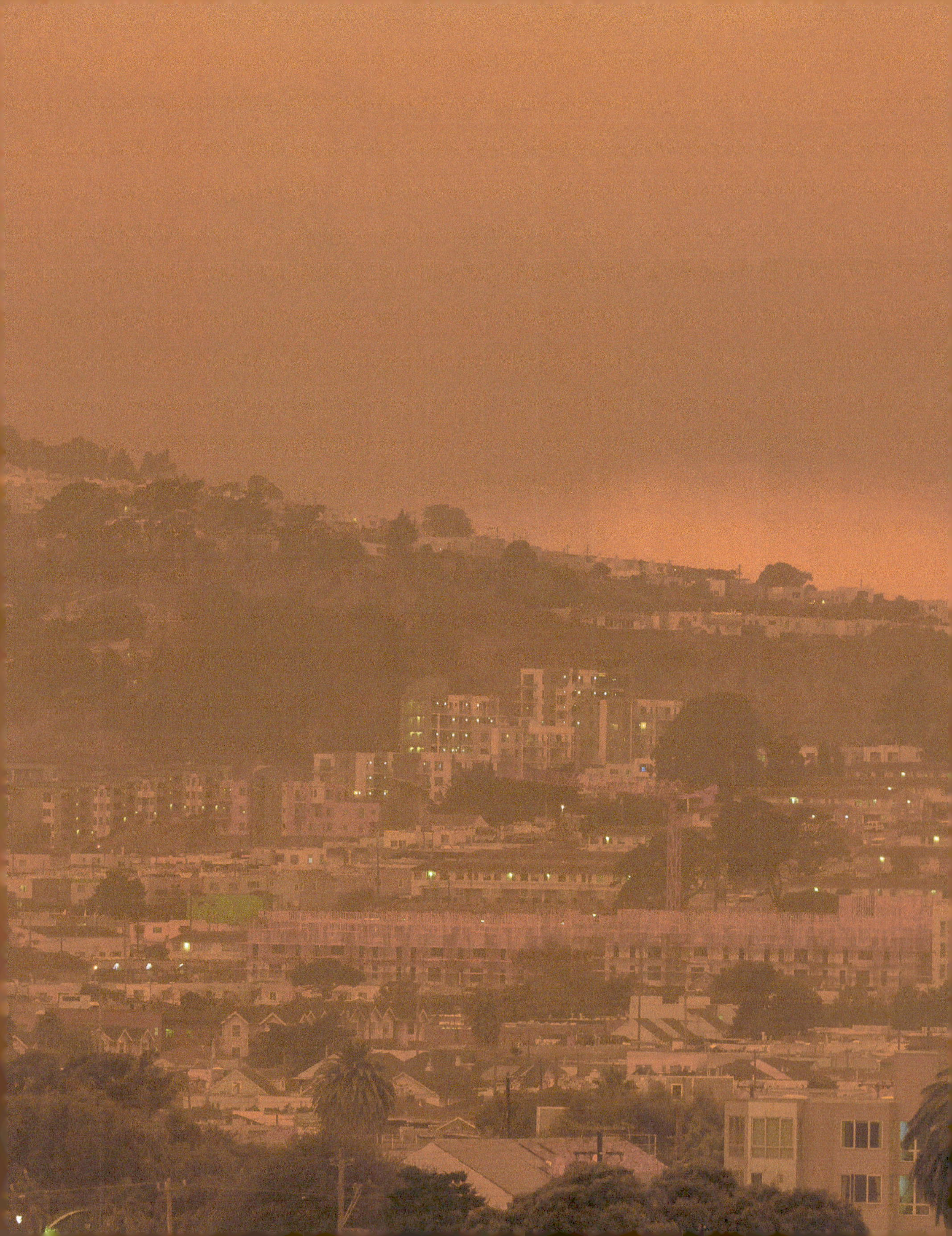

# 15

# Climate Change and Sustainability

In recent years, dramatic and dangerous natural disasters such as wildfires and hurricanes have been increasing in frequency and intensity. A 2021 wildfire in northern California burned for three months, covering an area of nearly 1,500 square miles. The state of California now spends more than $500 million per year battling wildfires. And California is not alone. A 2014 fire in northwestern Canada covered 8 million acres; Australian wildfires in 2019–2020 burned more than 46 million acres, which is nearly half the size of California; wildfires in Siberia in 2020 burned more than 47 million acres, sending large clouds of smoke into Alaska, western Canada, and the northwestern United States.

The 2017 north Atlantic hurricane season was the most damaging and the most expensive in US history, with more than $200 billion of damage from 17 named storms (Drye 2017). Hurricane Harvey brought more than 27 trillion tons of rain to Texas, damaging or destroying more than 100,000 homes and leaving an even larger number of people without power for several weeks. Hurricane Maria hit Puerto Rico with sustained winds of 155 miles per hour, leaving the entire island and its 3.4 million residents without power and damaging or destroying more than one-third of all the homes. Three months after Hurricane Maria had landed, half of the residents in Puerto Rico were still without power, and most of the schools were still closed. It will take years for the communities affected by these hurricanes to recover.

**Chapter Outline**

**15.1 CLIMATE CHANGE AND THE "RISK SOCIETY" 527**

*The Unequal Distribution of Environmental Risk 528*

**15.2 Structural Factors Contributing to Environmental Risk 531**

*Demography and Population Growth 532*
*Urbanization 533*
*Industrialization, Global Capitalism, and the Treadmill of Production 536*

**15.3 CONTROLLING THE NARRATIVE: DENIAL AND EXPERTISE 538**

*Culture, the Media, and Socialization 540*
*Science and Religion 541*

**15.4 PROFIT, POLITICS, AND THE ENVIRONMENT 542**

*Renewable Energy 543*
*Corporate Social Responsibility 543*

**California burning, 2021**

### Chapter Outline (continued)

**15.5 SUSTAINABILITY: PROMISE AND RESPONSIBILITY 546**

*Making Wastefulness Deviant 547*
*The Free-Rider Problem 551*

**CASE STUDY: THE DESTRUCTION OF THE AMAZON 553**

---

Hurricane seasons since then have continued to be more active and more damaging than average, with the 2020 hurricane system being the most active on record, and the 2024 hurricane season predicted to be highly active.

Other environmental risks are also on the rise. There are more heatwaves and weather extremes, with some areas experiencing severe drought and others experiencing flooding due to heavy rainfall and overflowing rivers. Sea level has risen throughout the 20th century, and the rate of increase is projected to accelerate throughout the 21st century. Ocean acidification threatens coral reefs and the marine ecosystems that depend on them. Chemical spills, oil spills, and nuclear power accidents spread serious pollutants into the food and water supplies.

In this chapter, we demonstrate the urgent necessity of thinking sociologically about the environmental crisis. We begin by discussing some sociological theories that are useful for understanding environment and society and examine how environmental risk is distributed unequally. Next, we explore some of the structural forces contributing to environmental risk, paying particular attention to population growth, economic growth, and urbanization. We then consider the different ways that people learn about the environment, paying particular attention to culture, socialization, science, and religion. We consider how the organization of politics and business shapes social practices that contribute to environmental protection or environmental destruction. Finally, we examine how social movements urge people to develop an environmental consciousness.

## LEARNING GOALS

**15.1** Identify some of the key sociological theories that are useful for understanding environment and society.

**15.2** Understand that population pressures, urbanization, and economic growth have created challenges for environmental sustainability.

**15.3** Think about the relationship between culture, socialization, and environmental consciousness.

**15.4** Understand that environmental risk is socially distributed, paying particular attention to the patterns of privilege and inequality.

**15.5** Identify the major political and economic forces that contribute to environmental crisis. Know the history of environmentalist social movements, paying attention to their successes and failures.

# 15.1 Climate Change and the "Risk Society"

**15.1** Identify some of the key sociological theories that are useful for understanding environment and society.

Environmental scientists distinguish between climate and weather. We expect that the weather will change every day and that there will be noticeable changes over the season. It may be sunny today, cloudy tomorrow, and rainy the day after that. It will likely be warmer during summer than it is during winter. These are short-term patterns. When scientists refer to **climate**, however, they are talking about long-term averages in the weather (temperature, rain, etc.) and how they are patterned over years or even decades. **Climate change** refers to long-term changes in the average weather patterns that we can observe in the Earth's regional and global climate. In other words, if we find that the average temperatures have been increasing or that certain regions of the Earth have been getting rainier or that certain regions have been getting drier, then we are speaking about climate change.

Climate change can be caused by natural developments or by human activities. Environmental scientists generally agree that climate change in modern society has been mainly caused by human activities. In fact, scientists have suggested that we are now living in the **Anthropocene**, a new geological era in which human activity is the dominant factor shaping the Earth's climate and environment. There is still debate about when the Anthropocene actually began. But there is general agreement that (1) human impact on the environment accelerated rapidly during the Industrial Revolution and (2) this impact can be measured in post-1950s exponential increases in greenhouse gas levels, ocean acidification, deforestation, and biodiversity decreases (Steffen et al. 2015). The growing recognition of the causes and consequences of climate change has ushered in a new kind of social consciousness about living in a "risk society."

The term "risk society" is from the title of a 1992 book by sociologist Ulrich Beck. Society, Beck argued, has always had to deal with risks such as natural disasters, but for most of history these were believed to be produced by nonhuman forces. Today, however, people recognize that most of the significant risks we face are caused by modern society itself. Risks such as crime, industrial pollution, and the spread of new diseases are clearly caused by social activities. But natural risks such as floods, famines, hurricanes, food contamination, and pandemics are also shaped by human activity, and their consequences are influenced by patterns of urban settlement and other forms of social organization. Dealing with risk is one of the main characteristics of living in the modern world.

**Climate** Long-term averages in the weather patterns, such as temperature and rainfall, that are stable over years and decades.

**Climate change** Long-term changes in the average weather patterns that are observed for regional and global climate. If average temperatures have been increasing or certain regions of the Earth have been getting rainier or drier over time, this is evidence of climate change.

**Anthropocene** The current geological era, in which human activity shapes the Earth's climate and environment.

Living in risk society means that people are always engaged in some form of risk management. Is the benefit of cheap energy worth the risk of pollution-related health crisis? Is the benefit of insecticide worth the risk of food contamination? Are the benefits of inexpensive global travel and an interconnected economy worth the risk of rapid disease transmission? And what if the proposed responses to risk are themselves risky? Beck argues that individuals and organizations lurch from one risk-produced crisis to the next, hoping to mitigate the damage while preparing themselves for the next disaster. The public gradually loses faith in the possibility that society can save them from these risks, leading to less trust in government, industry, and experts (Giddens 1990). This erosion in trust can have catastrophic consequences, as demonstrated by the COVID-19 pandemic (Chapter 12).

Living in risk society also means that people cannot protect themselves from risk-produced crises. Although the consequences of ecological crisis are unevenly distributed, pollution, food contamination, and extreme weather affect everyone, regardless of their privilege. Rising sea levels, drought, and viruses do not respect national borders, gated communities, or wealthy neighborhoods. The world's wealthiest cities face the same significant environmental challenges as impoverished megacities around the world, even if they have more resources to deal with those crises.

## The Unequal Distribution of Environmental Risk

As we have seen, there are clear patterns to the organization of privilege and inequality. Race, gender, and class are important dimensions of stratification (Chapter 6), which tends to privilege men, racially dominant groups, wealthier families, and the more educated. There is also a global dimension to stratification, with the most privileged people clustered in North America and Western Europe and with global poverty concentrated in sub-Saharan Africa and Latin America. Rural areas tend to be poorer than urban areas. Inequality and poverty have significant social consequences, resulting in worse health outcomes, higher death rates, and higher levels of incarceration. And while the consequences of environmental risk are felt by everyone on the planet, they are felt more strongly by people who are lower in the stratification system.

**Concentrated disadvantage** A structural outcome in which the poorest and most racially segregated communities suffer the most from environmental risk.

**CONCENTRATED DISADVANTAGE.** Social science research has consistently found that ecological crises have a more severe impact on poor and vulnerable populations. Drawing on their research about lead exposure, sociologists developed a model of **concentrated disadvantage**, in which the poorest and most racially segregated communities suffer the most from environmental risk (Muller, Sampson, and Winter 2018). Even after controlling for education, household income, and other individual characteristics, sociologists have found that Black and Latino/a families move into more environmentally hazardous neighborhoods than white families (Crowder and Downey 2010). It is not only that poor families of color are most likely to live in neighborhoods where dangerous toxins and pollutants are present. It is also the fact that the neighborhoods where they live lack powerful community organizations that can demand change. Property values in their communities are so low that developers have no incentive to improve housing stock, and residents lack the material resources to move to a safer community.

Exposure to environmental hazards is also stratified globally, with poor nations suffering more than wealthy ones. Whether measuring changes in crop yields, loss of land due to rising sea levels, economic damage from floods and hurricanes, or changes in health care expenditures, the worst impacts will be felt in Africa, Latin America, and South Asia (World Economic Forum 2018). Poor countries respond much more slowly to environmental risk. They have fewer material resources to deal with infrastructural challenges, and they often lack the expertise to develop green technologies that will be competitive in the global marketplace (Bell and Russell 2002). In fact, many poor countries complain that global environmental policies are just a way for wealthy countries to force them to import expensive green technologies, in a way that increases their economic dependence and inequality (Bapna and Talberth 2011).

Climate change and environmental crisis have made some geographical areas virtually uninhabitable, and there is a growing recognition of the risk that the spaces of habitability will continue to shrink in the future (Klinenberg et al. 2020). These ecological threats will challenge societies around the world, but they are also likely to reproduce existing patterns of global inequality. Wealthy countries such as the US are planning for a future where they will need to spend billions of dollars building higher seawalls to combat rising sea levels and fortifying their emergency relief funds to help families and businesses rebuild after increasingly frequent extreme weather events (Klinenberg et al. 2020). But the efforts after Hurricane Katrina and other major natural disasters show that rebuilding efforts will be much more focused and heavily resourced in wealthier communities than they will be in poorer ones (Siders 2019). Meanwhile, poorer countries in the Global South will not have the resources to do any of this infrastructure work, and are faced instead with the prospect of mass resettlements away from uninhabitable spaces. Recent estimates suggest that more than 140 million people in sub-Saharan Africa, Latin America, and South Asia will be forced to resettle by 2050 as a result of climate change (Rigaud et al. 2018).

While environmental risk increases inequality, it is also the case that inequality increases environmental risk (Laurent 2015). As we discuss below, inequality forces poorer countries to focus on fast-paced economic growth,

## PAIRED CONCEPTS: Structure and Contingency

### COVID-19 and Air Pollution

Air pollution, a social problem since the Industrial Revolution, continues to be a major issue today. Some estimates show that gasoline-fueled automobiles contribute more than half of all the carbon monoxide that is polluting the air. Air pollution is worse in urban areas than it is in rural areas, and it is worse in developing nations than it is in advanced post-industrial economies.

Air pollution creates significant health problems. Globally, air pollution contributes to nearly 10 percent of all deaths, mainly from heart disease, stroke, chronic obstructive pulmonary disease, lung cancer, and acute respiratory infections. Researchers have also found a relationship between air pollution and COVID-19 mortality rates. A recent study by public health researchers at Harvard University found that people in the United States are more likely to die from COVID-19 if they live in areas that have a higher concentration of fine particulate matter, or PM 2.5 (Friedman 2020). This helps to explain why COVID-19 has had such a disproportionately negative effect on marginalized and minoritized communities, which tend to be exposed to higher levels of environmental risk and correspondingly higher levels of PM 2.5. In this way, the health impacts of COVID-19 reinforce larger structural patterns, in which exposure to environmental risk is linked to patterns of social inequality that lead to negative health outcomes.

While the relationship between COVID-19 mortality and air pollution reinforces existing structural patterns, some responses to COVID-19 have ironically led to significant reductions in pollution. In Wuhan, China, the suspension of manufacturing and the massive reduction in motor vehicle traffic during the early stages of the pandemic led to large reductions in the emission of certain pollutants: most notably, a 90 percent reduction in nitrogen dioxide and a 30 percent reduction in PM 2.5 levels (Le et al. 2020). And Wuhan was not an isolated case. In a study of 34 nations, researchers found that the lockdown response to COVID-19 led to a 60 percent reduction in nitrogen dioxide and a 30 percent reduction in PM 2.5 levels (Venter et al. 2020). While these levels of reduction are almost certainly unsustainable, they do show that it is indeed possible to change the long-term historical patterns of increasing pollution that are associated with industrial and post-industrial society.

It remains to be seen whether the disruptions caused by COVID-19 will lead to lasting, structural changes in pollution levels. But there are signs that this could happen. Bicycle sales have increased dramatically in many cities, as residents look for modes of transportation that offer better social distancing than subways and buses. In response, cities have been adding bike lanes. Environmental activists,

**Urban bicycles**
In the aftermath of the COVID-19 pandemic, bicycle commuting and bicycle delivery have increased dramatically in New York City.

urban planners, and bicycle advocates see this as a once-in-a-lifetime opportunity to reduce the number of cars clogging up urban roads. Many companies are debating the relative advantages and disadvantages of work-from-home arrangements, as workers have expressed a strong desire for continued options for remote or hybrid work arrangements. If these kinds of changes become permanent, they would dramatically change patterns of urban and suburban life.

> **ACTIVE LEARNING**
>
> **Discuss:** Developing effective responses to air pollution is difficult because of the complicated relationship between environmental decision-making and inequality. Think about some of the changes that are reducing pollution: increased bicycle use, the creation of bicycle lanes, and the extension of work-from-home policies. How might these policies reinforce existing structures of inequality?

which is associated with higher levels of carbon dioxide emissions and higher rates of natural resource consumption. Inequality also encourages large corporations to shift the pollution-intensive parts of their operations into poorer countries, where they will face less opposition and the compensation costs for polluting will be much lower. And, despite the prevalence of hybrid cars and bans on plastic bags that we see in wealthy countries, it remains the case that the higher levels of consumption in those societies are associated with significantly higher levels of per-capita waste (Hoornweg and Bhada-Tata 2012).

## 15.2 Structural Factors Contributing to Environmental Risk

**LG** **15.2** Understand that population pressures, urbanization, and economic growth have created challenges for environmental sustainability.

**Environmental risk**
Exposure to environmental hazards and potential harm is stratified. These children play near a Houston oil refinery. Sulfur dioxide is a common byproduct of oil refineries that can damage the health of young children and unborn babies.

As we discussed at the beginning of the chapter, climate change in modern society has been mainly caused by human activities, which accelerated rapidly during the Industrial Revolution and whose effects started to be recognized after the 1950s, with exponentially higher levels of greenhouse gases, ocean acidification, deforestation, and extreme weather events. There were three structural features associated with modern society that have been the most consequential for the increases in human-caused ecological risk: (1) the increase in global population, (2) the growth of cities, and (3) the acceleration of industrialization and the spread of global capitalism.

## Demography and Population Growth

Global population growth has created significant challenges for environmental sustainability, particularly since the 20th century. World population did not top one billion until after 1800, and it did not exceed two billion until 1930. Global population reached four billion in 1975, and from that point it has increased by an additional billion people every 12 to 15 years. The global population reached seven billion in 2011, it reached eight billion in 2022, and it is projected to reach 9.7 billion by 2050 (UN 2022).

Rapid population growth was caused by the **demographic transition**, which refers to the historical decline in the birth rate and the death rate (or mortality rate). Before the 1800s, the birth rate and the death rate were both high. The infant mortality rate was particularly high, which resulted in a much slower rate of population growth. The average life expectancy was between 30 and 40 years, which was relatively unchanged from what it had been for the previous five hundred years. Beginning in the 19th century, and accelerating throughout the 20th century, the birth rate and death rate both began to decline. But the death rate declined much faster than the birth rate, which resulted in the rapid increase in population growth.

Population growth places different kinds of pressures on wealthy and poor countries. In poor societies with low population densities, there is an initial advantage to population growth, because the extra people can be put to work to increase agricultural productivity. But problems emerge when population and population densities grow too fast. Unless societies can invest in better agricultural technologies, population growth will accelerate soil degradation, forestry depletion, and other environmental issues that reduce food productivity and create health problems (Lele and Stone 1989). If societies cannot produce enough food, they will experience an increase in mortality, and a net out-migration of people looking for a better place to live. They will also face structural pressures to engage in economic practices that accelerate environmental destruction, as we discuss later in the chapter.

Demographic pressures operate differently in wealthy countries. There is a well-established relationship in which increasing wealth is associated with a declining birth rate, which acts as a control on population growth. With more wealth and less population growth, wealthy countries do not

**Demographic transition** The historical decline in the birth rate and the death rate. The demographic transition began during the 19th century and accelerated throughout the 20th century.

struggle with food scarcity or with soil degradation to the same degree as other countries do. But wealthy countries have different ecological pressures, which are related to the much higher levels of per-capita consumption, waste, and energy use (Pebley 1998). Wealthy societies are also older. In countries like Japan, Germany, and Italy, more than 20 percent of the population is over 65 years old; by 2050, many countries in Europe, North America, and Southeast Asia are forecast to have more than 30 percent of their population over 65 years old (He, Goodkind, and Kowal 2016: 10). An aging society has much higher health costs, as average medical costs more than double between the ages of 70 and 90 (De Nardi et al. 2016). People over the age of 65 are less likely to be in the labor force, particularly in wealthier nations. At the same time, most wealthy nations have a public pension system, in which workers are eligible to start receiving benefits sometime between the ages of 65 and 67. This combination of factors creates a financial crisis for governments, as the proportion of the population engaged in full-time work decreases while the proportion receiving public benefits increases. This means that there is less money available for other social programs, including programs devoted to environmental sustainability.

## Urbanization

People have been living in cities for more than five thousand years. Between about 400 BCE and 100 CE, cities of more than 200,000 residents existed in Babylon, Patna (in India), and Rome (Frey and Zimmer 1998: 1). Evidence indicates that the city of Rome had more than one million residents during the second century CE. These cities were important centers of trade, religious activity, and politics. For the most part, though, this was not a period of mass urbanization. Most people lived rural lives focused on agricultural production. Before 1850, the proportion of the world's population living in urban areas remained somewhere between 4 and 7 percent (Frey and Zimmer 1998).

As we discussed in Chapter 13, urbanization accelerated during the Industrial Revolution, when people moved from rural areas to work in large factories located in cities. By the time the cities of Beijing (in 1800) and London (in 1825) surpassed one million residents, urbanization had become a global phenomenon. But the process of global urbanization really began to accelerate during the second half of the 20th century. There were 12 cities of one million residents in 1900; by 2016 there were more than 500 such cities, and today nearly one-quarter of the world's population lives in a city with more than one million inhabitants (United Nations, Department of Economic and Social Affairs, Population Division 2016a). UN demographers estimate that the urban population has quadrupled since 1960, and nearly 55 percent of the world's population now lives in a city.

As cities grew larger, many of the wealthier residents moved out to the **suburbs**, which are residential areas located within commuting distance of a city. Suburbs developed in the late 19th and early 20th centuries, first with improvements in railroad infrastructure and then with the spread of the automobile. In addition to providing a lower-density space in which to live, these suburbs often had zoning laws that created separate and distinct spaces for residential and commercial activities. They also tended to have less socioeconomic, racial, and ethnic diversity among their residents.

As more people moved to the suburbs, development pushed farther away from the central city. Older suburbs became more congested and less residential, as commercial builders constructed office parks near suburban freeway exits. In large metropolitan areas such as the New York Tri-State area, Washington-Baltimore, and the "Golden Horseshoe" region of Greater Toronto, suburban development connected different cities together in a large, continuous space that geographers refer to as **conurbation**. Families in search of the original suburban experience—open space, more land, and less expensive housing costs—now find themselves moving to exurban communities, which are commuter towns on the outer fringes of an urban area, often more than 50 miles away from the central city. Many of these exurban communities used to be rural areas, and they try to retain their rural character as they become connected to these ever-larger spaces of continuous urbanization and suburbanization.

**Conurbation** A large, continuous metropolitan space resulting from urban and suburban development that connects different cities together.

Urbanization and suburbanization have placed significant pressures on the environment. Historically, urban spaces have been associated with increases in air pollution, water pollution, carbon emissions, and the disposal of solid waste, as well as decreasing levels of biodiversity and green space (Bai et al. 2017). Urban spaces trap heat, gases, particulates, and water vapor, leading to higher temperatures and more extreme weather events (Bai et al. 2017: 229–30). The development of suburbs and conurbations results in increased levels of air pollution (particularly when this development is driven by gas-powered vehicles), larger amounts of per-capita energy consumption, and the destruction of green spaces that have historically functioned as safety valves to help counteract the ecological consequences of large cities (Kovacs et al. 2020).

At the level of scale and rate of change, urban growth in the developing world has occurred much faster than it did in the cities of Europe, North America, and Southeast Asia. Nations such as China, Nigeria, and Ecuador have rapidly transformed from rural to urban populations during the last 50 years, reaching levels of urbanization that took centuries to achieve in the nations of Europe and North America. This means that pollution, carbon emission, loss of biodiversity, and loss of green space are also occurring at a much more rapid rate, with faster ecological consequences.

Similar to the process of population growth, urbanization produces different effects in poorer areas than it does in wealthier ones. While wealthier and more developed countries typically have many different cities, which eventually connect through the creation of suburbs and conurbations, developing countries typically have only one or two cities. This means that all the rural migrants to the city are going to the same place, regardless of whether or not the city has the jobs or the resources to absorb them. Unable to find housing, they end up living in slums and shantytowns on the outskirts of the city, often without access to clean water, adequate public transportation, reliable power, or good schools. The cities lack the resources to deal with these challenges. They are unable to build adequate infrastructure, address poverty, deal with crime, or respond to the accelerating rates of pollution.

## METHODS AND INTERPRETATION

### How to Measure Urban Sprawl

Interestingly, there is no standard definition of an urban area or an urban population. Each country has its own definition of who is an urban resident. But there are some common patterns and some central measurement concepts. The main concepts that demographers use to measure urbanization are population size and population density. For example, the Organisation for Economic Co-operation and Development (2012) has established specific population thresholds (either 50,000 or 100,000 residents, depending on the country), and density thresholds (either 1,000 or 1,500 residents per square kilometer) to count as an urban area. Other approaches factor in travel time and travel distance, recognizing that many people will choose to live just outside a densely populated urban area and then travel into the city for work, shopping, and entertainment (Frey and Zimmer 1998). This helps to account for the development of urban and suburban sprawl, which (as we discuss later in the chapter) is a major contributor to environmental degradation and negative health outcomes. In fact, research has demonstrated that urban sprawl is associated with an increase in traffic fatalities, air pollution, incidence of heart disease, and other negative outcomes. Having an accurate measurement of urban sprawl is crucial for social scientists who are interested in the relationship between health, urbanization, and the environment.

Most attempts to measure urban spawl begin by identifying a continuous scale with compactness at one end and sprawl at the other (Hamidi et al. 2015). The urban core of a city (where we find the highest levels of compactness) is characterized by careful urban planning, high-density real estate development, and extensive use of mass transportation infrastructure. The suburbs and exurbs (where we find the highest level of sprawl) are defined by haphazard planning, low-density real estate development, and car-dependent infrastructure (Hayden 2004). This definition gives us some clues about how to measure sprawl, which would suggest focusing on population densities, land-use planning, and automobile usage.

> **METHODS AND INTERPRETATION** CONTINUED

The most straightforward measurements for sprawl are density measurements. The earliest measures of sprawl relied almost exclusively on population density, because it was the easiest factor to measure (Hamidi and Ewing 2014). But while population density is important, it is not the only relevant characteristic of sprawl. In fact, it is not even the only relevant density measurement. More recent studies have also relied on measures of land-use density (Hamidi and Ewing 2014). Measures of residential density compare the percentage of the population living in low-density vs. high-density residential areas, with a higher proportion of low-density residents indicating higher levels of sprawl. Measures of land-use mix compare the percentage of single-use vs. mixed-use developments, where single-use developments are associated with sprawl. Other measures calculate average block size, with smaller blocks indicating compactness and larger blocks indicating sprawl. The percentage of four-or-more-way intersections is also a relatively easy measurement of land-use density, where a lower proportion of four-way intersections is an indicator of sprawl.

Some of the recent measurement strategies are a little more complicated, but they are useful for illuminating different aspects of social and spatial organization that fall along the continuum of compactness and sprawl. Steurer and Bayr (2020) propose using satellite imagery to improve measurements of residential density, arguing that taking advantage of this satellite imagery can allow social scientists to "cut out" geographic areas that are not used for housing. Hamidi et al. (2015) have argued that WalkScore—a commercial data source that compares the walkability of 2,800 cities and more than 10,000 neighborhoods in the US and Canada—is a reliable and highly accessible indicator of sprawl, with a lower WalkScore indicating a higher level of sprawl. They have also relied on data from the American Community Survey to calculate the percentage of commuters who walk to work, the percentage who rely on public transportation, the average number of vehicles per household, and the average commuting time for people who drive to work, arguing that these are good indicators of car dependence and urban sprawl.

> **ACTIVE LEARNING**
>
> **Think about it:** How would you create a single index for sprawl, using the different measurement strategies above? Try to choose three or four measurements that capture different characteristics of urban sprawl, and weight each measurement according to how important you think it is compared to the other measurements in your index.

## Industrialization, Global Capitalism, and the Treadmill of Production

Historically, economic firms have not modified their production practices due to concerns about the environmental impact they were having. While this was not a major issue when productive capacities were relatively low, the Industrial Revolution initiated a major increase in both productive capacity and environmental impact. This environmental impact came from direct and indirect sources. On the one hand, the production practices of industrial firms created massive amounts of air pollution, water pollution, and soil contamination, which contributed directly to ecological damage. On the other hand, the productive capacity of industrialization allowed for a massive increase in global population and urbanization, each of which had their own ecological consequences. Carbon dioxide ($CO_2$) emissions from human activities were 150 times higher in 2011 than they were in 1850, with the largest industrializing nations dominating emissions throughout that time period (Friedrich and Demassa 2014).

Environmental damage has not been caused solely by the process of industrial production, but rather by the way that industrialization accelerated as part of the development of global capitalism. Capitalism encourages industries to prioritize profit, which means lowering costs regardless of the consequences. In *The Environment: From Surplus to Scarcity* (1980), sociologist Allan Schnaiberg developed a theory about the **treadmill of production**, which explains why industrial capitalism accelerated environmental damage. Schnaiberg argues that the continuous quest for economic growth encourages businesses to pursue strategies that cause environmental damage. Corporations are the main forces powering the treadmill. They produce more products than people need, which increases waste and energy consumption. They rely on the cheapest forms of energy, which increases pollution. Governments also power the treadmill, by promoting pro-industry policies that seek to limit environmental regulations as a way of promoting economic growth (Rudel et al. 2011). Consumers also help power the treadmill, by buying more things than they really need and by basing their purchasing decisions on the lowest price, without regard for the environmental consequences of their consumption decisions. People may say that they care about the environment, but historically they have not displayed a willingness to pay more money for things that were sustainably produced.

**Treadmill of production** A social process in which the continuous quest for economic growth encourages businesses to pursue strategies that cause large and unsustainable environmental damage.

Global capitalism also encourages poorer nations to focus on resource extraction, in a manner that accelerates environmental destruction even further (Jorgenson 2016). Unable to compete effectively in markets that require high levels of technological development, poorer nations are incentivized to focus their economic strategies on the extraction of energy (coal, oil, etc.) and other natural resources. At a global level, this guarantees that the most ecologically destructive forms of energy will continue to be produced, leading to a market situation that disadvantages companies that desire to use more sustainable forms of energy. At a local level there are devastating consequences for the environmental conditions of the poorer nations, as they destroy their forests, pollute their soil and their rivers, destroy their landscape and their animal habitats, and displace their residents to clear the land for their extractive enterprises (Jorgenson and Clark 2009). Once the natural resources have been exhausted and the local ecosystem has been destroyed, the extractive industries move on, leaving the local economy in shambles and with no new viable economic strategies available to them (Bunker and Ciccantel 2004).

## 15.3 Controlling the Narrative: Denial and Expertise

**LG 15.3** Think about the relationship between culture, socialization, and environmental consciousness.

While public concern about the environment has increased considerably since the 1990s, there are inherent challenges that present themselves when people try to respond to the challenges of climate change. As we suggested in our earlier discussion of risk society, governments and other organizations can only respond to environmental crisis in a partial and limited way, so that every attempt to respond to the crisis leads to the proliferation of new risks. This erodes confidence in government and leads to a general skepticism about effective social planning. It also erodes support for expertise. Even though the experts themselves tend to be cautious about the effectiveness of their interventions, these interventions are frequently oversold by politicians, entrepreneurs, and other public figures. In addition, there are significant business interests in the energy industry that are opposed to environmental regulations and that invest heavily in lobbying against these regulations. Climate change skeptics continue to receive a lot of media coverage, and they also receive a lot of support from individuals and groups who distrust science.

---

**PAIRED CONCEPTS** — Inequality and Privilege

### Contaminated Water in Flint, Michigan

As the Flint River passed through Flint, Michigan, over the past century, it was a waste disposal site for meatpacking plants, automobile factories, lumber and paper mills, and agricultural firms. It experienced inflows of raw sewage from the city's waste treatment plant, as well as toxins leaching from landfills. Because the river was so polluted, in 1967 Flint arranged for Detroit to provide its drinking water.

In 2013, Flint city officials decided for financial reasons to switch back to using the Flint River for its drinking water supplies. The switch was supposed to be temporary, until a new water pipeline from Lake Huron was completed. In April 2014, residents of Flint began receiving their drinking water from the Flint River.

Only a week after the switch, residents of Flint began complaining about the color, smell, and taste of the drinking water. By August 2014, the city was advising residents to boil their water because of high levels of bacteria. In October, General Motors announced that it would stop using Flint River water in its assembly plant because there was so much lead in the water it was corroding the machinery. Water safety tests conducted in February 2015 indicated that the Flint River drinking water had lead levels that were nearly 10 times higher than the legal limit.

In October 2015, the city announced that it would switch back to Detroit drinking water, but problems with excessively high lead levels persisted. The city of Flint declared a state of emergency in December 2015, and in January 2016 the Michigan National Guard began distributing bottled water to residents. Four government officials were charged with criminal indictments for their role in the water contamination, and a $700 million class-action lawsuit was filed on behalf of Flint residents who had been endangered by the water contamination crisis.

There was a national outrage over the Flint water crisis because of the widespread recognition that this kind of crisis would never have happened in a more privileged community. While Flint had once been a prosperous city, it has been in economic decline since the 1980s. About 45 percent of the city's residents live below the poverty line, and 56 percent of the city's residents are Black. The Michigan Civil Rights Commission has argued that what happened in Flint was the result of systemic racial inequality. Historically, redlining practices by banks had prevented Black residents from leaving Flint when the economy declined, trapping them in the city while white residents escaped to more prosperous and environmentally safer suburbs. The poor and historically marginalized composition of the city's residents meant that their voices were not heard when they complained about the safety of the water. The lack of resources among the city's residents and its government meant that they could not respond effectively to the environmental crisis when they first discovered it. In fact, while General Motors paid more than $400,000 to purchase its water from Lake Huron, the city of Flint could not even afford the $150 per day that it would cost for a chemical additive that would prevent lead from the city's pipes from leaching into the water supply.

**Flint, Michigan's poisoned water**
Volunteers distribute bottled water to residents of Flint, Michigan, in March 2016. Dangerous levels of lead in the city's drinking water made it unsafe to drink.

### ACTIVE LEARNING

**Discuss:** To prevent environmental crises from being concentrated in poor and minority communities, the Michigan Civil Rights Commission recommended that representatives from urban and suburban areas together develop policies for the region. Why did they think this would help to reduce inequality? Can you think of any other kinds of policies that could help reduce the way that environmental crises have a disproportionate impact on historically disadvantaged communities?

Although environmental issues and crises feature more prominently than ever before in public and policy debates, they are still frequently displaced by other issues. In his book *The Politics of Climate Change*, the sociologist Anthony Giddens talks about this in terms of the "Giddens Paradox." This paradox states that "since the dangers posed by global warming aren't tangible, immediate, or visible in the course of day-to-day life, however awesome they appear, many will sit on their hands and do nothing of a concrete nature about them" (Giddens 2009: 2). "For most people," argues

Giddens, "there is a gulf between the familiar preoccupations of everyday life and an abstract, even apocalyptic, future of climate chaos" (Giddens 2009: 1). Most people are not doing very much to change their everyday habits in their interactions with the environment. Others, influenced by climate change skeptics, actively deny that humans have any impact on climate change and argue that efforts by scientists and activists to transform business, culture, and industry will be harmful to society. These habits and attitudes are much more likely to change if people learn about the environment in a way that is connected to their socialization and their other cultural experiences.

## Culture, the Media, and Socialization

As we discussed in Chapters 3 and 4, our understandings about the world develop through cultural meanings and socialization. These meanings are organized into relationships of similarity and difference, which are always changing. Some meanings exist in language and other types of ideal culture, while others can be found in the objects we use and display to others. Shared meanings bring people together, and they are an important part of our socialization. But cultural conflicts are also a common occurrence, and these conflicts are shaped by power, privilege, and inequality.

Thinking about culture and socialization helps us think about the kinds of environmental understandings that are likely to resonate with people in their social lives. Neither utopian dreams about technology coming to the rescue nor dystopian dreams about a planet already beyond saving will get people to change their everyday behaviors or their lifestyles. To change everyday behaviors, people need to believe that those everyday behaviors matter. Working through all the agents of socialization—the family, peer group, schools, media, the workplace, and beyond—people have to be resocialized to think about how their ordinary behaviors are connected to environmental risk.

The importance of culture can be seen in the phenomenal success of Greta Thunberg's environmental activism. In many ways, Thunberg was an unlikely leader of the global environmental movement. Only a teenager, she was not a scientific expert, nor was she a celebrity. Diagnosed with Asperger syndrome and obsessive-compulsive disorder, her environmental consciousness started at home, where she challenged herself and her parents to reduce their carbon footprint. After winning a Swedish essay competition about climate change in 2018, she was contacted by a Swedish environmentalist social movement and began talking with them about ways to mobilize young people to participate in climate change protests. She began a school strike to promote climate change awareness and to try to pressure the Swedish government to reduce carbon emissions. A picture she posted of her protest went viral on Instagram and Twitter, and within a week she became a global social media sensation. From this point forward, Greta Thunberg became a regular speaker at environmental protests throughout Europe, inspiring students around the world to participate in school climate strikes. She was invited to speak at the 2018 United Nations Climate Change Conference and the 2019 World Economic Forum, where her speeches went viral on social media and received extensive coverage by international journalists. Named *Time* magazine's Person of the Year for 2019, she has become one of the most influential environmentalists in the world.

As sociologists and media scholars have pointed out, journalists tend to show that they are not biased by making sure they present two opposing positions on most issues (Tuchman 1978). In the debate about environmental risks, this has meant that climate change skeptics continue to get a lot of media coverage (Giddens 2009). Among the skeptics are some scientists who argue that the threat of environmental risk has been overstated, that climate change is a constant feature of world history, and that there is not yet definitive scientific proof that human activity is the primary cause of environmental risk. Because these skeptics are scientists, they can claim an "expertise" that climate change deniers believe legitimizes their opinions. Other deniers will point out that Greta Thunberg, despite being such a prominent voice in the media for the sustainability movement, is a teenager with no scientific expertise herself. While 97 percent of published scientific articles agree that climate change is real and is caused by human activity (Cook et al. 2016), the culture of journalism means that news reports will generally emphasize "both sides" of the story.

## Science and Religion

Public debates about environmental risk are also shaped by the ongoing cultural tension between science and religion. As we discussed in Chapter 10, religious and scientific cosmologies have been the two dominant providers of meaning and order to the world in which people live. There is an inherent

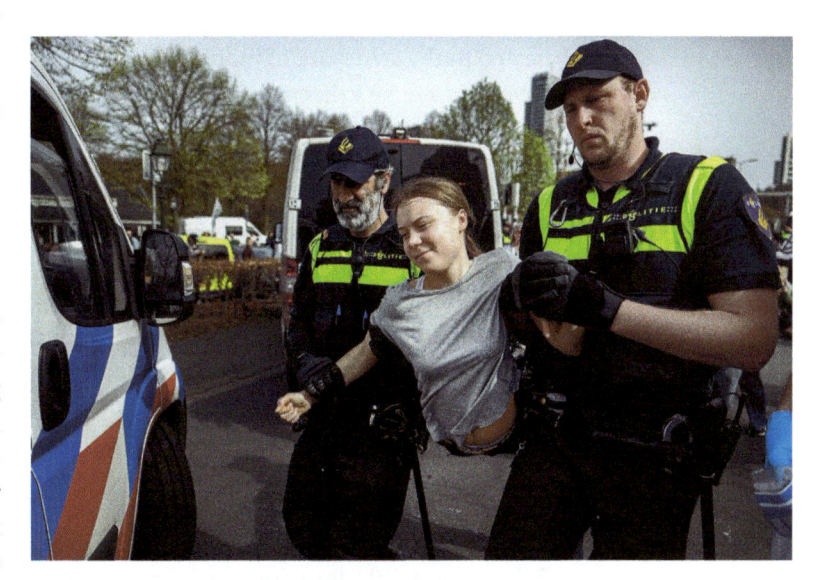

**Greta Thunberg arrested at highway blockade**
Swedish environmental activist Greta Thunberg is arrested for the second time during an April 2024 blockade of the A12 highway in The Hague, Netherlands. Thunberg was present at the 37th blockade of the highway as new international actions against fossil-fuel subsidies were announced during the action.

tension between these two systems of meaning, in the sense that religion emphasizes faith and science emphasizes skepticism. There is also a historical tension between the two because many scientists have been publicly critical of religious belief, arguing that the world would be a better place if science simply replaced religion. More recently, scientists and religious leaders have begun to think about how they might more effectively work together to promote sustainability and environmental justice. In fact, the attempt to communicate better about the dangers posed by environmental risk has been a major focus of this effort to create a post-secular approach to social problems, which tries to establish a more cooperative and less confrontational relationship between scientists and religious leaders. But these efforts are in their early stages, and they face significant resistance from both religious and scientific institutions.

## 15.4 Profit, Politics, and the Environment

**LG 15.4** Understand that environmental risk is socially distributed, paying particular attention to the patterns of privilege and inequality.

There are many reasons why corporations and other business organizations contribute to environmental degradation, which, as we discussed earlier are connected to the structure of industrialization and global capitalism. Companies have an incentive to keep their costs as low as possible, even if that means relying on cheap energy and other materials that contribute to climate change. They have an incentive to promote a culture of consumption and disposable objects, even if that leads to overflowing landfills and waste management problems. And they have an incentive to oppose sustainability initiatives, at least to the extent that those initiatives are funded through taxes on corporations.

Political forces allied with corporate interests also contribute to environmental risk. The growing power of multinational corporations means that governments have less power to regulate businesses because of the fear that companies will move their operations to a more business-friendly place. This has led to a general loss of confidence in government's ability to solve complicated social problems. There is also a short-term bias in political decision-making, which privileges issues that are of immediate concern to voters (the price of gasoline and food, the availability of good jobs, etc.). Politicians easily lose focus on long-term issues such as environmental policy, which require extensive planning and political cooperation (Giddens 2009). And when they do focus on environmental policy, they are easily influenced by political lobbying. In the United States, more than $3 billion was spent from 2009 to 2014 on lobbying related to environmental issues

(Delmas 2016; Delmas, Lim, and Nairn-Birch 2015). Donald Trump campaigned for president in 2016 and 2020 on a policy of protecting the coal industry and reversing environmental protections. Similar anti-environmental movements have won the support of conservative political parties in Europe, Canada, and Australia (Lockwood 2018; Dunlap and McCright 2015).

### Renewable Energy

The politics of environmentalism have created new openings for clean energy and conservation policies. While environmental lobbying used to focus on anti-regulation efforts, there has been a significant increase in lobbying expenditures by clean energy firms that favor pro-environment policies (Hulac 2016). Natural gas producers have begun to form alliances with these clean energy firms, based on an assessment that clean energy policies will benefit them at the expense of coal producers (Kim, Urpelainen, and Yang 2016).

The rapid growth in renewable energy technologies, including solar, wind, geothermal, and hydroelectric power, may account for this increase in pro-environment political lobbying. Solar power capacity has increased exponentially over the last decade, and is predicted to account for 80 percent of all renewable energy worldwide by 2030 (IEA 2024). Led by solar technology, the Energy Agency forecasts a tripling of renewable energy capacity between 2024 and 2023. Prices have come down dramatically; more than half of new solar and wind power installations now produce energy that is less expensive than fossil fuels (Kretchmer 2020). The leading manufacturers of solar panels and related equipment have become multinational corporations, with annual revenues in the billions of dollars. Many countries with the worst environmental problems have embraced renewable energy, giving them economic reasons to pursue and support pro-environment policies. For example, China, which has had the highest level of greenhouse gas emissions globally since 2006, has become the undisputed global leader in renewable energy production and manufacturing (IEA 2024).

### Corporate Social Responsibility

While campaigns aimed at the actions of ordinary people are certainly important, they can also take the burden of responsibility off the companies that are actually producing waste. In fact, some of the earliest anti-littering campaigns were actually created by corporations, with this very purpose in mind. One of the most famous of these is the "Keep America Beautiful" campaign (which began in the 1950s and still exists today), which was funded by some of the biggest companies in the packaging industry. By focusing on the littering consumer, these companies diverted attention from their production of single-use bottles and packages instead of the more expensive (but less wasteful) multiuse and refillable ones (Plumer 2006).

## PAIRED CONCEPTS: Power and Resistance

### The Dakota Access Pipeline Protests

In January 2016, the energy corporation Dakota Access was granted approval for the construction of an underground pipeline carrying crude oil from North Dakota to Illinois. When completed, the pipeline would carry 470,000 barrels of oil per day. The pipeline's route passed within a half mile of the Standing Rock Sioux Reservation, threatening ancestral lands as well as the water supply for Native American tribes living in North Dakota and South Dakota.

The Standing Rock Sioux tribe opposed the pipeline, petitioning the governor of Iowa and filing a legal motion to stop the project. Calling themselves "water protectors," members of the Standing Rock tribe began organizing protests at the pipeline site in North Dakota in April 2016. Drawing people from throughout North America, the protests became the largest gathering of Native tribes in more than one hundred years. By September, representatives of more than three hundred tribes were participating in the protests, as well as celebrities, environmentalists, politicians, leaders of the Black Lives Matter movement, and Indigenous activists from around the world.

The protests were met by increasingly coercive and violent responses by law enforcement. More than four hundred arrests of protesters and journalists were made at protest sites between August and November 2016. Police used armored tanks, pepper spray, rubber bullets, tear gas, and water cannons. By February 2017, local police and the National Guard had forcefully cleared the protest site and removed all protesters.

Supporters of the protesters at Standing Rock agreed that Native American cultural and political autonomy needed to be respected, and they were angered by the violent police response. Hundreds of cities held protests in support of the Standing Rock movement on November 15, 2016. In December 2016, President Obama announced a halt to further construction of the pipeline, which at the time of the announcement was more than 70 percent complete. But on January 24, 2017, three days after his inauguration, President Trump signed an executive order to move forward with the pipeline and to halt any further environmental review of the project. In June 2017, crude oil began flowing through the Dakota Access pipeline. There have been several legal challenges since then, but despite those challenges the pipeline remains fully operational.

After 2017, resistance to the pipeline moved primarily to the courts. A February 2017 court filing charged that the decision to proceed with the pipeline without environmental review violated the Sioux tribe's treaty rights with the US government. In June 2017, a judge in Washington, DC, agreed with the Sioux tribe's motion, arguing that the decision to proceed without environmental review was a violation of the law. The Army Corps of Engineers released a brief report in 2018 that reaffirmed its initial decision to build the pipeline, but the Sioux tribe filed an additional lawsuit challenging the reasoning behind the decision to proceed. In July 2020, a judge ordered the Dakota Access pipeline to be shut

**Standing Rock protest**
Police use pepper spray against protesters standing in a river near the Standing Rock Indian Reservation on November 2, 2016.

down until the Army Corps of Engineers completed a full environmental review of the project. Reviews of this type typically take several years to complete. The Dakota Access corporation filed an immediate appeal to the legal ruling, arguing that it should be allowed to continue to use the pipeline until the environmental review was completed. Further legal conflicts are likely.

> **ACTIVE LEARNING**
>
> **Discuss:** There were two different types of resistance to the Dakota Access pipeline: protest activities and legal activities. What were the advantages and disadvantages of each approach? To what extent do you think that the combination of the two approaches made the resistance more effective?

## CAREERS

### Job Prospects in the Green Economy

As we discussed in Chapter 6, solar panel installation is among the best blue-collar jobs in today's economy. These jobs require a high school diploma as well as a few technical courses at a community college or a period of on-the-job training. The median annual salary for solar installers is nearly $45,000 per year, which is significantly higher than the average wage for full-time workers with a similar level of education. And solar installers have excellent employment prospects since the number of jobs is projected to increase by more than 50 percent by 2030. Jobs like these are a good example of why many economists point to the "green economy" as a major area of future job growth.

The vision for a green economy began to accelerate in 2008, when the United Nations Environment Programme (UNEP) launched its Green Economy Initiative. In the midst of a global economic crisis, UNEP sought to identify where investments could be made to reduce carbon emissions and ecological destruction, while also reducing poverty and promoting economic recovery. The results of this initiative were published in a 2009 report, *A Global Green New Deal*.

A green economy strives to be low-carbon, resource-efficient, and socially inclusive. At the policy level, this means that public and private investments should be made in infrastructure, industries, and economic activities that reduce pollution, increase energy efficiency, and minimize ecological destruction, while doing so in a way that benefits historically marginalized and privileged communities equally. It calls for government regulations designed to bring about a carbon-neutral economy, which would include a reorientation of government investment and tax exemptions toward energy-efficient enterprises by shifting monetary and banking policy to privilege low-carbon projects, developing policies that encourage green technology transfer in a way that includes developing economies, and implementing new regulations that account for the environmental and social costs associated with producing a particular product.

According to the United Nations, the wide-scale adoption of Green New Deal policies could result in the creation of 24 million new jobs by 2030. The green economy includes workers who do a wide variety of jobs. Wind, solar, and other forms of renewable energy are major areas of growth, employing engineers, metal workers, and other assembly technicians. "Urban farmers" grow produce on rooftops in cities around the world. Jobs in the recycling industry are also growing rapidly, providing opportunities for blue-collar as well as white-collar workers. Energy management experts are helping companies diagnose their

> **CAREERS** CONTINUED
>
> current practices and implement strategies to make them more energy-efficient. Environmental lawyers and green accountants are helping companies to navigate new regulations and to create green pricing and incentive structures. Many of these jobs require new credentials and additional education, which will create job opportunities in the higher education sector.
>
> **ACTIVE LEARNING**
>
> **Think about it:** What are some of the main ways that the green economy helps to meet the goals of creating a more socially inclusive economy? What are some of the main challenges and obstacles to social inclusion that are associated with a shift to more green jobs?

**Corporate social responsibility**
A social movement to convince business leaders to adopt sustainable and environmentally responsible practices.

Since around the year 2000, social movements focused on **corporate social responsibility** have targeted business leaders, trying to convince them to adopt more sustainable and environmentally responsible business practices (Bendell 2009). Such practices include socially responsible investment strategies, the reduction of waste, the adoption of more environmentally sound production strategies, and the promotion of brand loyalty through strategies that appeal to environmentally conscious consumers (such as fair-trade production practices, charitable contributions to environmental organizations, etc.) (Porter and Kramer 2006).

## 15.5 Sustainability: Promise and Responsibility

**LG 15.5** Identify some of the political and economic forces that contribute to greater environmental responsibility. Know the history of environmentalist social movements, paying attention to their successes and failures.

**Ecological modernization**
A sociological theory focused on the expectation that growing expert knowledge and public awareness of environmental risks will lead to the development of more sustainable policies and practices.

Environmental sociologists have developed a theory of **ecological modernization** to highlight the ways that economic and political policies might change to create a more sustainable future (Mol and Spaargaren 2000). With growing expert knowledge about and public awareness of environmental risks, economic markets could begin promoting "green" products. As the economic and social impacts of the COVID-19 pandemic continue to deepen worldwide, environmental economists and other critics are proposing that any post-pandemic recovery be a green recovery. National and international policy-makers could coordinate their efforts to create globally effective ecological strategies. The global social movement of environmentalism continues to encourage people to think critically about their everyday interactions with the natural world.

Environmentalist social movements have become a powerful cultural and social force, as the example of Greta Thunberg illustrates. While conservation movements can be traced back to the late 19th century and are responsible for the creation of national park systems, the modern environmental movement emerged in the 1950s and 1960s. Although the movement was initially concerned with the dangers of nuclear weapons and nuclear power, it soon embraced the need to protect the environment and promote sustainability through the conservation of natural resources and reduction of waste.

Environmentalists have also formed political parties, with the goal of electing candidates who will advocate for pro-environment government policies. Developing out of the student and antinuclear movements of the 1960s, the Green Party emerged in Europe, Australia, and New Zealand during the 1970s. By the 1980s, Green Party candidates had won elections throughout Europe, North America, and Australasia. By the end of the 20th century, the Green Party had become a global political force, campaigning for clean energy, environmental conservation, and a greater environmental consciousness in everyday life. The electoral and legislative successes of Green Party candidates have helped increase global support for the environment (Dunlap and York 2008). Furthermore, where the Green Party has had national success, it has been very effective at linking local environmental campaigns to national environmental organizations (Rootes 1999).

## Making Wastefulness Deviant

Environmental and sustainability movements work to change public opinion and get people to think differently about their everyday activities. A key initiative is Earth Day, April 22, first celebrated in 1970. Now observed by nearly two hundred nations, Earth Day has become one of the largest secular holidays in the world, with more than one billion participants each year. Organized as an environmental teach-in, Earth Day has become a hub for grassroots activism. Thousands of environmental groups use the occasion for outreach and education. Environmental organizations also organize protests to raise public awareness and influence policy after major pollution catastrophes, such as the 1989 *Exxon Valdez* oil spill in Alaska, the 2010 BP Deepwater Horizon oil spill in the Gulf of Mexico, and the 2011 nuclear accident in Fukushima, Japan. They also coordinate acts of civil disobedience to protest corporations that are major polluters, such as the 2016 Break Free campaign against coal mines and coal power plants on six continents.

Many of the activities of social movements are designed to change people's everyday consciousness about nature and the environment. Global

## PAIRED CONCEPTS: Solidarity and Conflict

### The Battle for Yellowstone

Yellowstone National Park, which covers more than two million acres in Wyoming, Montana, and Idaho, was designated as a UNESCO World Heritage Site in 1978. It is a popular tourist destination, with more than four million visitors each year.

In *The Battle for Yellowstone: Morality and the Sacred Roots of Environmental Conflict*, sociologist Justin Farrell argues that three competing forms of solidarity and culture shape the conflicts of managing the greater Yellowstone ecosystem (Farrell 2015). A "utilitarian" vision emphasizes Yellowstone as a symbol of the individualistic "Old West." In contrast, a "spiritual" vision allows park visitors to commune with nature in a solitary state of contemplative reflection. The third, "biocentric" vision shares goals with the spiritual vision but replaces spirituality with science.

These competing moral commitments and alliances can lead to conflicts. For example, Yellowstone is the only place in the world where wild bison herds have survived continuously since prehistoric times, and the management of these bison herds has been a long-standing source of political conflict and disagreement (Farrell 2015: 120). Representing the utilitarian viewpoint, ranchers support capturing and slaughtering bison that wander onto private ranches or aggressively chasing them back onto park property. Environmental activists, articulating the spiritual and biocentric viewpoints, argue instead that the bison represent a sacred link to the purity of nature and that the herd should be allowed to roam without constraint.

Conflict can also be seen in the 1995 decision to reintroduce wolves to Yellowstone (Farrell 2015: 168–216). There had once been as many as two million wolves in Yellowstone, but by 1930 an anti-wolf campaign had led to their near extermination. Representing the biometric vision, natural scientists and environmentalists argued that wolves are so important to the natural habitat that the Yellowstone ecosystem is incomplete without their presence. This position was opposed by those who held a utilitarian vision, who argued that wolves' predatory behavior would be harmful to other wildlife, harmful to human communities living near Yellowstone, and deeply harmful to the cattle ranchers whose survival was made possible by the prior extermination of the wolf population. The social conflict continued long after the wolves were reintroduced. Anti-wolf advocates denounced "eco, wolf-hugging terrorists" (Farrell 2015: 183), sold anti-wolf merchandise, and complained about outsiders who neither understood nor respected the lifestyle of people who lived in the West. On the other side, pro-wolf advocates pointed to the conflict as an example of successful environmental activism and a force of continued mobilization on behalf of ecological preservation. Like the conflict over bison, there was little room for compromise between these competing positions.

**Homecoming**
Employees of the National Park Service release a Western gray wolf in Yellowstone National Park in January 1996, part of a successful but controversial effort to reintroduce wolves to the Yellowstone ecosystem.

### ACTIVE LEARNING

**Find out:** Use the search term "Yellowstone cattle ranchers and conservationists." What did you find? Are there still conflicts between these groups? Can you find any recent examples of cooperation and agreement between the two groups?

organizations such as Greenpeace and the World Wildlife Fund produce public service advertisements designed to get people thinking about conservation and wildlife protection, as well as the dangers of polluting industries. One hundred and seventy communities in the United States have successfully campaigned to ban gas-powered leaf blowers, which are a significant source of noise pollution and greenhouse emissions. In Spain, the city of Barcelona has banned cars that are more than 20 years old. In Copenhagen, Denmark, more than half of the people bike to work, and there is a mandatory green roof policy for all new buildings. Cities all over the world are banning plastic bags. There is a growing competition among many cities and countries to create innovative policies of ecological sustainability and to provide incentives for businesses and other organizations to make environmental protection a central element of new projects. In short, there are many efforts to improve the environmental health of societies at local, regional, and global levels. Like most social things, they involve the actions of individuals, families, communities, and larger organizations, including government and business organizations. Together, these efforts are slowly shifting the culture around environmental responsibility.

**Earth Day march, New York City, 1970**

While environmental movements have had important successes, these victories have been uneven, and they often (if inadvertently) reinforce privilege and inequality. With the exception of the corporate social responsibility movement, whose influence is relatively recent, most successful environmental campaigns have tended to focus on individual habits instead of structural changes. Ultimately, the ability to solve any of these issues once and for all is limited because each new development in politics, in the market, and in public life results in the creation of new risks and new threats.

Another challenge is the tendency for successful movements to be followed by a social backlash, which polarizes public attitudes and leads to the

**Climate change march to support the Glasgow Climate Pact, November 5, 2021**
Environmentalists marched in Glasgow, Scotland, on November 5, 2021, during the United Nations Climate Change Conference (COP 26). The agreement that emerged from the conference called for signatories to reduce the usage of coal power, to commit to deep and sustained reductions in greenhouse gas emissions, and to aim for net-zero emissions by 2050.

formation of countermovements (Chapter 13). Countermovements criticize both the original movement's diagnosis of a specific social problem as well as the movement's policy goals. Often, the countermovement receives support from established political and economic elites, who stand to benefit from a reversal of the movement's successes. Ironically, the successes of the environmental movement have helped create an anti-environmentalist countermovement, which has aligned itself with conservative political parties as well as corporate lobbying groups that have an economic interest in rolling back environmental regulations.

The structure of global privilege and inequality also limits the effectiveness of environmental movements. Environmental movements have been most successful in the affluent nations of Western Europe, North America, and Asia, where global privilege makes post-materialist politics possible (Rootes 1999). In other words, when people have a reliable food supply, a safe social infrastructure, and the individual rights that come with democracy, they can afford to start thinking about reducing their personal carbon footprint and buying products from companies that are committed to sustainable production practices. Environmental movements in other parts of the world are less likely to focus on questions of individual consumption and more likely to link environmental degradation to issues of basic political freedoms and economic exploitation. Indeed, in countries that have been the victims of colonialism, people are often suspicious of Western-based social movement organizations that convince (or force) them to change the way they live their lives (Doherty and Doyle 2006). In general, the communication strategies of environmental movements are less successful when they come from outsiders who are not part of the community (Brulle 2010). People are more open to changing their opinions and behaviors when they are treated as partners in a mutual dialogue.

## The Free-Rider Problem

The last major obstacle to reducing environmental risk is the **free-rider problem**. The free-rider problem is common to all large-scale collective action problems. Put simply, the free-rider problem states that people in large groups will not act in a way that helps the common good unless it benefits their own personal interests. If people are in a small group, they are more likely to act in an environmentally responsible way, out of fear they will be criticized for creating unnecessary waste. If they are part of the environmental movement and have taken on an identity as environmentalists, they also will be more likely to act in an environmentally responsible way. But the problem of reducing environmental risk requires good behavior on the part of everyone. If it is inconvenient to be more environmentally responsible (e.g., separating recyclables into glass, paper, and plastic), people are less likely to participate. If it is more expensive to buy a sustainable product, people will choose the less expensive product that creates more environmental risk. They may tell a survey researcher that they share the values of environmentalism, but their behaviors tell a different story.

The free-rider problem helps explain why pollution, waste, and greenhouse gas emissions continue to increase. The United Nations Framework Convention on Climate Change was established in 1992 as an agreement among nations to set guidelines for stabilizing and eventually reducing greenhouse gas emissions. While there were no enforcement mechanisms, individual guidelines were established for each nation that wanted to participate. This was replaced by the 1997 Kyoto Protocol, which created legally binding emissions targets for the 37 industrialized nations that signed the agreement, as well as commitments by these nations to supply technology and funding for climate-related projects in less developed nations. Despite these agreements, global greenhouse gas emissions from human activities increased by 35 percent between 1990 and 2009 (Environmental Protection Agency 2016). Developing nations, which did not have any binding targets, increased their emissions significantly. The United States refused to sign on to the agreement and saw its emissions increase. Russia, Japan, and Canada announced in 2011 that they would not continue the agreement unless it included China and the United States, which were the two largest polluters in the world. A new agreement was reached in Paris in 2015, which included 194 nations including China and India. But the Paris Agreement allowed each nation to establish its own targets, and it took away all binding enforcement mechanisms. Not surprisingly, most nations have failed even to meet the targets they set for themselves, causing the

**Free-rider problem** A collective action problem, in which people in large groups will not act in a way that helps the common good unless it benefits their own personal interests. In social movement contexts, the situation where the people who benefit from a social movement's activities assume that others will do the work.

UN secretary general to warn that the world's nations had arrived at a "dangerous tipping point" on climate change (Sengupta 2018). In the US, the Trump administration refused to act on any of the commitments the US had made. Trump withdrew from the Paris agreement in 2020, but President Joe Biden rejoined the Paris agreement on his first day of office in 2021. The Glasgow Climate Pact was signed by 197 nations in 2021, with pledges to reduce the usage of coal power, to commit to deep and sustained reductions in greenhouse gas emissions, to aim for net-zero emissions by 2050, to commit to reversing deforestation by 2030, and to shift international public finance toward clean energy.

## PAIRED CONCEPTS: Global and Local

### The Causes and Consequences of Transboundary Water Pollution

Transboundary water pollution happens when water pollution from one country crosses borders into other countries through rivers, lakes, and oceans. While there are 263 transboundary lakes and river basins, which cover nearly half of the Earth's surface, approximately two-thirds of these water basins do not have a cooperative management arrangement. Transboundary water pollution is a serious social problem, and it is also a source of international conflict.

Transboundary water pollution represents a major threat to the Arctic region, even though virtually no pollution is created there. Ocean currents move pollution from the industrialized and highly populated areas of the Northern Hemisphere to the Arctic, while sediment from polluted rivers freezes and moves into the Arctic Ocean via the Fram Strait. The effects of these global movements of pollution can be seen in polar bears, seals, and other Arctic wildlife, which have been exposed to high levels of contaminants that endanger their continued survival. Environmental scientists warn that this type of transboundary pollution into the Arctic is likely to accelerate, due to climate change.

**Arctic pollution**
Plastic trash and other debris travels on ocean currents into remote areas. This trash washed up on a beach in northern Svalbard, Norway, just a few hundred miles from the Arctic Circle.

Environmental scientists have identified "trash vortexes" in all major ocean basins. Nondegradable plastic accumulates in ocean regions thousands of miles away. The largest of these, the "Great Pacific Garbage Patch" halfway between California and Hawaii, covers an area of approximately 600,000 square miles. In these trash vortexes, plastic debris gets broken down into microscopic particles, blocking sunlight from reaching the plankton and algae below and threatening the entire marine ecosystem.

The problem of transboundary water pollution is compounded by large environmental catastrophes taking place in specific localities. In 1986, a fire at the Sandoz chemical warehouse in Switzerland sent tons of agrochemicals into the Rhine River, turning the river red and creating significant environmental problems across Europe. In 2000, an accident at a gold mine in Romania spilled cyanide-laced water into the Lapus River, wiping out nearly all the fish and threatening the water supply for communities in Romania as well as Hungary. In 2005, an explosion at a chemical plant in China spilled 100 tons of chemicals into the Songhua River, resulting in a 50-mile-long flume of benzene that flowed into Russia. The 2011 nuclear crisis in Fukushima, Japan, caused extensive radioactive transboundary pollution of air, soil, and water that crossed into South Korea, and Japan's 2023 decision to release treated radioactive waste water into the Pacific Ocean was widely criticized as a destabilizing event that threatened future transboundary arrangements.

Transboundary pollution is a source of tension and conflict between nations. National laws are difficult to enforce in these situations because the offense originated on foreign soil and the perpetrator is typically a private foreign company. Treaties between individual nations are often ineffective because of power differences between nations and the unpredictable nature of large environmental catastrophes. The United Nations Economic Commission for Europe has adopted international regulations for European member states, but they are relatively weak on legal remedies and they have not been adopted for other global regions.

### ACTIVE LEARNING

**Find out:** While strong international regulations do not exist for transboundary water pollution, there are international water laws in place. Read a description of these laws on the United Nations website (https://legal.un.org/ilc/texts/instruments/english/conventions/8_3_1997.pdf). What do these laws say? Are there any laws that could help prevent transboundary water pollution? Are there any laws that might make it more difficult to control transboundary pollution?

### CASE STUDY

## The Destruction of the Amazon

The Amazon is the world's largest rainforest, covering more than two million square miles in the northern part of South America. A source of unparalleled biodiversity, it is home to at least forty thousand different plant species, more than half of which are unique to the Amazon. At least 20 percent of all bird and fish species in the world live in the Amazon, and it has more than two million different species of insects. The Amazon produces about 10 percent of the Earth's biomass, and its plants and trees absorb carbon dioxide and help to reduce the emission of greenhouse gases, making the region one of the most important carbon sinks in the world.

Despite its ecological importance, the Amazon has been threatened by significant levels of deforestation. In the 1970s, the Brazilian government began construction of the Trans-Amazonian highway, allowing for deeper penetration of industry into the denser parts of the jungle and making it easier for logging companies to cut down and transport trees from the rainforest. Since the 1990s,

### CASE STUDY CONTINUED

the Amazon region has been plagued by wildfires, which has also led to significant deforestation. Climate change is partly responsible for the increase in fire activity, but many of the fires were lit deliberately by ranchers and farmers to clear land for their economic activities. Today, it is estimated that between 15 and 17 percent of the Amazon rainforest has been destroyed. Environmental scientists warn that if the amount of deforestation reaches 25 percent, the rainforest will turn into a savanna, with devastating ecological consequences for the planet (Irfan 2019).

At the *global* level, if deforestation transforms the Amazon into a savanna, this would dramatically increase greenhouse gas emissions and accelerate the processes of climate change. Environmental scientists argue that deforestation of the Amazon has already resulted in a significant decrease in rain and snow in the western United States, leading to more prolonged and damaging fire seasons there. *Locally*, the same thing is happening in Brazil, with more drought and more fires threatening farming and ranching activity.

Along with global climate change, another *structural* factor contributing to Amazon deforestation is the connection between resource depletion and economic growth, particularly in developing countries of the Amazon such as Brazil, Bolivia, and Colombia. There are also *contingent* factors that affect deforestation. In the 1960s, for example, the Brazilian government sent people to settle the Amazon because it was concerned about the risk of foreign invasion and domestic insurgency; and in the early 1970s, it began the Trans-Amazonian highway. Then, during the late 1970s, the rate of Amazon deforestation slowed because the government ran out of money to finance the highway project. Beginning in 2018, the rate of deforestation increased rapidly under the auspices of Brazilian president Jair Bolsonaro, and by the end of his term there had been a 60 percent increase in deforestation compared to the previous four-year term (Brown 2023). President Lula da Silva announced a new plan in 2023 to end illegal deforestation and to develop a strategy for achieving net-zero deforestation, but environmental researchers expect that it will be extremely difficult to reverse the damage done by the Bolsonaro regime.

The *power* of cattle ranchers and soybean farmers, who burn large tracts of rainforest without consideration of the consequences or fear of punishment, contributes to Amazon deforestation. Powerful ranchers and farmers form part of a larger extractive economic system, with international corporations purchasing soy products and beef from Brazilian farmers and ranchers. Ranchers, farmers, and corporations have also faced significant *resistance* from environmental movements and land rights activists. For example, Greenpeace uncovered and publicized McDonald's complicity with deforestation, shaming them into agreeing to stop purchasing soy products from farmers who were engaged in illegal acts of deforestation. Environmental movements as well as trade unions and Indigenous groups in Brazil have pressured the Brazilian government to develop more conservationist policies for the Amazon and to enforce those policies more aggressively.

The structure of global privilege and inequality further complicates the challenges of Amazon deforestation. As we discussed in Chapter 13, the most effective policies for economic growth depend on a nation's position in the global economic hierarchy. Nations like Brazil (which are located somewhere in the middle of the global stratification system of nations) are the most vulnerable to climate change because they rely on industrialized forms of manufacturing but have relatively low levels of wealth, technology, education, and infrastructure. This means that they lack both the technology to reduce carbon emissions and the money to invest in those resources. Further, they have massive incentives to continue resource-intensive industrial manufacturing. In fact, in 2008 Brazil's then president established the Amazon Fund, calling on wealthy countries to contribute to help with Amazon conservation. Over the next decade, more than $1 billion were donated to the Amazon Fund by wealthy nations and nonprofit organizations. In 2019, donations began drying up as countries such as Germany and Norway withdrew funding to protest Brazilian President Bolsonaro's environmental policies (Funes 2019). Donations to the Amazon Fund have increased since Bolsonaro's defeat, with the fund receiving a record $640 million in donations in 2023 (Reuters 2024).

Movements to conserve and protect the Amazon have been an important source of *solidarity*. Throughout the 1980s in Brazil, environmentalists combined with labor movements, social justice movements, and prodemocracy movements to push for fundamental changes to Brazilian political and environmental policies. The 1988 assassination of environmental activist Chico Mendes brought international criticism, and the next two decades saw intense national and international mobilization around Amazon conservation, with Brazil's eco-socialist movement at the center of many of the policies and political alliances. But these alliances eventually began to break down, and a growing *conflict* emerged over how to balance the goals of environmental protection and economic growth. Environmentalists began to lose influence in Brazil's government, and rates of deforestation slowly began to increase. In 2018, Jair Bolsonaro was elected president of Brazil, with a campaign that promised to roll back protections for the rainforest and make it available for economic exploitation, eliminate the Ministry of the Environment, and pull out of the Paris Agreement. The fate of the Amazon is entangled with this shifting political science at the local and global levels.

# LEARNING GOALS REVISITED

**15.1 Identify some of the key sociological theories that are useful for understanding environment and society.**

- The theory of risk society is based on the realization that most of the significant risks that people face are caused by modern society itself. Living in risk society means that people are always engaged in some form of risk management. Regardless of how much wealth and privilege people have, they cannot protect themselves from risk-produced crises, nor can they solve these risks once and for all.
- The theory of ecological modernization points to the ways that growing expert knowledge and public awareness of environmental risks are leading to the development of more sustainable policies and practices.
- The theory of the Giddens Paradox describes why the individual and collective responses to environmental crisis are so much less dramatic than the reality of the threat being posed. Because the dangers of climate change are not typically concrete realities facing people in their everyday lives, people tend to spend most of their energy dealing with their problems and concerns of the moment.

**15.2** **Understand that population pressures, urbanization, and economic growth have created challenges for environmental sustainability.**

- Global population increases have accelerated dramatically, particularly since the 20th century. This is due to the demographic transition, which refers to the historical decline in the birth rate and the mortality rate.

- In poorer countries, population growth has accelerated soil degradation, forestry depletion, and other environmental issues that reduce food productivity and create health problems. Wealthier countries have a slower rate of population growth, but they experience much higher levels of per-capita consumption, waste, and energy use.

- Urbanization also accelerated rapidly during the 20th century, and more than half of the world's population now lives in a city. Historically, urban spaces have been associated with increases in air pollution, water pollution, carbon emissions, and the disposal of solid waste, as well as with decreasing levels of biodiversity and green space. In addition to this, the development of suburbs and conurbations leads to increased levels of air pollution, larger amounts of per-capita energy consumption, and the destruction of green spaces that have historically functioned as safety valves to help counteract the ecological consequences of large cities.

- Industrialization created massive amounts of air pollution, water pollution, and soil contamination, which contributed directly to ecological damage.

- The spread of global capitalism encourages companies to lower their costs regardless of the environmental consequences, which historically has led to a reliance on cheap energy that increases carbon emissions. Global capitalism also encourages poorer nations to focus their economic strategies on the extraction of energy (coal, oil, etc.) and other natural resources. At a global level, this guarantees that the most ecologically destructive forms of energy will continue to be produced, leading to a market situation that disadvantages companies that desire to use more sustainable forms of energy.

**15.3** **Think about the relationship between culture, socialization, and environmental consciousness.**

- The development of environmental consciousness depends on all the agents of socialization—the family, peer group, schools, media, the workplace, and beyond—and the way those agents of socialization encourage people to think about how their ordinary behaviors are connected to environmental risk.

- Culturally, environmental messages will tend to be more persuasive and effective if they have compelling characters, if they include nonexperts, if

they include scientific evidence as well as nonscientific analogies, and if they offer the audience a positive collective purpose.
- Public debates about environmental risk are shaped by the ongoing cultural tension between science and religion.
- Debates about environmental risk are also shaped by the culture of journalism, which tends to emphasize two sides to every issue in a way that has increased the likelihood that climate science skeptics will more easily get media coverage.

**15.4** Understand that environmental risk is socially distributed, paying particular attention to the patterns of privilege and inequality.
- While the consequences of environmental risk are felt by everyone on the planet, they are felt more strongly by people who are lower in the stratification system.
- Poorer families are more likely to move into neighborhoods where toxins and pollutants are present. They are less likely to be able to move to safer neighborhoods, and they are less likely to have access to community organizations that can effectively advocate for better environmental safety.
- Even after controlling for education, household income, and other individual characteristics, historically disadvantaged groups are more likely to move into environmentally hazardous neighborhoods.
- Exposure to environmental hazards is also stratified globally, with poorer nations suffering more than wealthier ones.
- Global inequality increases global environmental risk.

**15.5** Identify some of the political and economic forces that contribute to environmental responsibility. Know the history of environmentalist social movements, paying attention to their successes and failures.
- The modern environmental movement began in the 1950s and 1960s. It was initially focused on the dangers of nuclear weapons and nuclear power, but movement leaders quickly developed a more general focus on protecting the environment, conserving natural resources, and reducing waste.
- Social movements have organized major global events such as Earth Day, which is designed to help people develop a more environmental consciousness. They have also organized protest events targeted at large polluting corporations. And they have produced thousands of public service advertisements designed to get people thinking about conservation and wildlife protection.
- Environmentalists have also organized themselves into political parties, with the goal of electing candidates who will advocate for pro-environment government policies.

By the end of the 20th century, the Green Party had become a global political force, campaigning for clean energy, environmental conservation, and a greater environmental consciousness in everyday life.

- Environmental movements have been more successful at changing individual habits than business practices, and they have been more successful in wealthier nations. The successes of environmental movements have also been challenged by backlash from countermovements.
- Climate change skepticism has become an important part of conservative politics.

## Key Terms

Anthropocene 527
Climate 527
Climate Change 527
Concentrated disadvantage 528
Conurbation 534
Corporate social responsibility 546
Demographic transition 532
Ecological modernization 546
Free-rider problem 551
Treadmill of production 537

## Review Questions

1. In what ways do the environmental crises of today threaten the social lives of the privileged? How do these differ from the threats facing the less privileged?
2. What is the Giddens Paradox, and how does it complicate the attempt to respond effectively to environmental risk?
3. What kinds of pressures does population growth and urbanization place on the environment? How are these pressures different for poorer and wealthier societies?
4. What are the main ways that the spread of global capitalism creates incentives for companies to adopt practices that contribute to environmental crisis?
5. Describe one case in which culture has helped promote environmental consciousness and one case in which it has hindered environmental consciousness from forming.
6. Describe the main ways that inequality makes it more difficult to deal effectively with environmental risk.
7. Describe two reasons why we should be optimistic about the social responses to global environmental risk. Describe two reasons why we should not be optimistic.

## Explore

**RECOMMENDED READINGS**

Dunlap, Riley, and Robert Brulle. 2015. *Climate Change and Society: Sociological Perspectives*. New York: Oxford University Press.

Giddens, Anthony. 2009. *The Politics of Climate Change*. Malden, MA: Polity Press.

Schnaiberg, Allan. 1980. *The Environment: From Surplus to Scarcity*. New York: Oxford University Press.

## ACTIVITIES

- *Use your sociological imagination*: Hurricane Harvey, which landed in Texas in 2017, did much more damage than people thought it would. Do some research about the hurricane, and discuss the sociological factors that helped make it such a major catastrophe for the city of Houston.
- *Media+Data Literacies*: Watch the documentary film *David Attenborough: A Life on Our Planet*. Why do you think this film was so successful at reaching audiences and receiving critical acclaim?
- *Discuss*: If technological developments made renewable energy the same price as fossil fuels, how do you think this would change the social responses to environmental risks? What major challenges do you think would still exist?

# Glossary

**Absolute mobility** Change in social position, regardless of what is happening with other people.

**Absolute monarchy** A form of government in which there are no laws restricting the power of the monarch over the people living in their territory.

**Achieved status** A status that can be earned through action.

**Active audiences** The idea that people are active, skillful interpreters of the world who have the ability to recognize and resist cultural power.

**Acute disease** A single or repeated episode of relatively rapid onset and short duration from which the patient usually returns to his/her normal or previous state or level of activity.

**Agenda-setting** The idea that news media set the public agenda. They do not shape *what people think*, but they do have great influence on *what people think about*.

**Agents of socialization** The people, groups, and organizations that most powerfully affect human socialization. The five primary agents of socialization are family, school, peer groups, media, and the workplace.

**Alienation** A condition in which humans have no meaningful connection to their work, or to each other

**Allostatic load** The wear and tear on the body due to stress.

**Androcentrism** A social understanding that qualities associated with masculinity and a masculine point of view are valued over those associated with femininity, which are dismissed and subordinated.

**Anomie** The condition of feeling isolated and disconnected in the absence of rich social connection.

**Anthropocene** The current geological era, in which human activity shapes the Earth's climate and environment.

**Applied research** Research with the goal of solving practical problems in society.

**Ascribed status** A status assigned to people by society, which is not chosen and which cannot be changed easily.

**Ascriptiveness** The degree to which characteristics at birth like race, gender, ethnicity, parents' background, or nationality determine life outcomes in a stratification system.

**Assimilation** A process that occurs when minority groups fully embrace the culture of the dominant group and lose their distinctive racial and/or ethnic characteristics.

**Basic research** Research with the goal of advancing our fundamental knowledge and understanding of the world.

**Beliefs** All the things we think are true, even in the absence of evidence or proof; ideas about the world that come through divine revelation or received tradition.

**Big data** A term for the large amount of data produced by our technological ability to study large data sets that have been recorded and stored in digital formats.

**Blended family** A household that includes a step-parent and possibly a step-sibling and/or a half-sibling.

**Blockbusting** A practice where real estate agents would go to a neighborhood where racial minorities were beginning to move in, convince the white residents there that their property values were going to decrease, and encourage them to sell their houses below market value.

**Boomerang kids** Young adults who move back home to live with their parents after a period of independence.

**Brain drain** When highly educated people in poor countries leave for places with more economic opportunity.

**Broken windows theory** A theory of policing stating that ignoring small crimes and minor violations creates a spiral of increasing deviance and more serious criminality.

**Bureaucracy** An organizational form with a clearly defined hierarchy where roles are based on rational, predictable, written rules and procedures to govern every aspect of the organization and produce standardized, systematic, and efficient outcomes.

**Canon** The set of thinkers and ideas that serve as a standard point of reference for a scholarly or artistic tradition.

**Capitalism** An economic system based on the private ownership of property, including the means of material life such as food, clothing, and shelter, in which the production of goods and services is controlled by private individuals and companies, and prices are set by markets.

**Capitalist crisis of care** The shortage of reproductive labor created by the capitalist organization of work.

**Case study research** Research that relies on a small number of cases that offer special insight into a particular social process and are studied in depth, typically using comparative methods.

**Caste system** An extremely unequal stratification system in which people are born into a particular social group and have virtually no opportunity to change their social position.

**Categorical inequality** The inequality between social categories or social groups.

**Categorical or nominal variable** A variable that measures phenomena that are not inherently numerical, such as gender, race, or ethnicity. In this case the numerical code assigned to a quality is more a name than a number.

**Causation** A phenomenon that occurs when two variables share a pattern because one variable produces the pattern in the other.

**Cause** Something that produces an outcome. Technically, a cause is where a first event is understood to produce a material effect on a second event.

**Census** An official count of the population.

**Charismatic authority** A form of persuasive power in which people follow a leader's orders because of the personal qualities that the leader possesses.

**Chronic disease** A permanent, nonreversible condition that might leave residual disability, and that may require long-term treatment and care.

**Cisgender** A term for people who are assigned male at birth and identify as men, or who are assigned female at birth and who identify as women.

**Citizenship** The laws that define who is a legal member of a country.

**Citizenship education** Curriculum dealing with history, laws, social institutions, and political organization of the nation in which students live.

**Civil law** Law that deals with disputes between individuals and organizations. Most legal cases are civil cases.

**Classification systems** Elaborate and nuanced identifications of similarity and difference based on cultural patterns that develop over time when people place beliefs, practices, and cultural objects into groups of similar things and groups of different things.

**Climate** Long-term averages in the weather patterns, such as temperature and rainfall, that are stable over years and decades.

**Climate change** Long-term changes in the average weather patterns that are observed for regional and global climate. If average temperatures have been increasing or certain regions of the Earth have been getting rainier or drier over time, this is evidence of climate change.

**Code-switching** Adapting behavior to meet different role expectations across interactional contexts.

**Coercive power** The system of punishments and rewards that are used to try to force people to act in a particular way.

**Cohabitation** An arrangement in which romantic couples choose to live together instead of getting married.

**Collective representations** Pictures, images, or narratives that describe the social group and are held in common.

**Colonialism** A global stratification system in which powerful nations used their military strength to take political control over other territories and exploit them economically.

**Colorblind racism** A form of racism based on the refusal to discuss or notice race.

**Commercial culture** Cultural commodities that exist to be bought and sold.

**Commodity** An object that is bought and sold in a market. Commodity production is a system of producing goods and services to be bought and sold on markets.

**Comparative-historical methods** A set of research methods that uses comparison of events and processes in the past to understand the development and operation of social things.

**Complicit masculinity** A form of masculinity where an individual may not meet all the requirements of hegemonic masculinity but still benefits from the gender order in which they are viewed as masculine.

**Compulsory heterosexuality** A social order in which sexual desire between males and females is understood to be the only normal form of sexuality, and is enforced through medical, legal, religious and other social institutions.

**Concentrated disadvantage** A structural outcome in which the poorest and most racially segregated communities suffer the most from environmental risk.

**Confirmation bias** The tendency to look for information that reinforces prior beliefs; occurs when research is biased to confirm the researcher's preexisting beliefs or hypotheses.

**Conflict** Disagreement, opposition, and separation between individuals or groups.

**Conflict theory** Conflict theorists argue that social structures and social systems emerge out of the conflicts between different groups.

**Consensus theory** Consensus theorists focus on social equilibrium, which is the way that different parts of society work together to produce social cohesion.

**Conspicuous consumption** A way to display privilege, wealth, and social status to others.

**Constitutional monarchy** A form of democratic government where power is held by elected officials and there is a king or queen who serves as the ceremonial head of the nation.

**Consumerism** A widespread ideology grounded in conspicuous consumption that encourages buying and consuming goods, including buying more than an individual needs.

**Content analysis** A sociological method to systematically evaluate and code text documents in which word frequencies or other textual features can be turned into quantitative variables.

**Contentious politics** The use of social conflict and other disruptive techniques to make a political point in an effort to change government policy.

**Contingency** Openness in social life produced by human choices and actions.

**Controlled experiment** Scientific method that systematically controls the factors that affect some outcome of interest and studies it systematically to isolate the causal logic that produces the observed effects.

**Conurbation** A large, continuous metropolitan space resulting from urban and suburban development that connects different cities together.

**Convenience sample** A sample collected from a research population on the basis of convenience, or easy access.

**Corporate social responsibility** A social movement to convince business leaders to adopt sustainable and environmentally responsible practices.

**Correlation** A correlation is an observed statistical dependence between two variables, but it does not mean the variables are *causally* related.

**Cosmology** The system of knowledge and beliefs that a society uses to understand how the world works and how it is organized.

**Counterfactual reasoning** An analytical strategy for investigating the causal logic of research that asks what factors might have led to a different social outcome.

**Credentialism** A process in which formal educational qualifications are used to determine who is eligible to work in a given occupation.

**Crime** Deviant behavior that is defined and regulated by law.

**Crime rate** Calculated in the United States as the number of criminal offenses committed per 100,000 people in the population.

**Criminal justice system** All the government agencies that are charged with finding and punishing people who break the law.

**Criminal recidivism** The likelihood that a person will engage in future criminal behavior.

**Critical race theory** A theory that first developed in critical legal studies to show the ways that the law reinforced racial injustice and domination.

**Cultural capital** Education, cultural knowledge, and cultural consumption that signals privilege to others; the knowledge and consumption of culturally valued things. Higher levels of cultural capital are associated with success in school.

**Cultural gatekeepers** Decision-makers who control access to or influence what kind of culture is available to an audience.

**Cultural hierarchies** Socially organized inequality based on ideas about what counts as "good" or worthwhile culture.

**Cultural imperialism** A process that occurs when a small number of countries dominate the market for culture and destroy smaller, local cultures.

**Cultural pluralism** An alternative to the idea of assimilation that imagines a society where people maintain their unique cultural identities while also accepting the core values of the larger society.

**Cultural relativism** The idea that all meaning is relative to time and place.

**Cultural turn** An interdisciplinary movement in sociology and other disciplines that emphasizes the collective cultural dimension of social life.

**Culture** The entire set of beliefs, knowledge, practices, and material objects that are meaningful to a group of people and shared from generation to generation.

**Culture war** A profound, society-threatening conflict over values.

**Curative medical care** Care focused on curing disease or relieving pain to promote recovery.

**Cybercrime** Crime conducted using computer networks.

**Davis–Moore theory of inequality** The theory that some level of inequality is necessary to motivate people to do the most difficult and important jobs in a society.

**Decoding** The process in which cultural messages are interpreted by specific people.

**Degree of crystallization** The degree to which one dimension of inequality in a stratification system is connected to other dimensions of inequality.

**Degree of inequality** The level of concentration of a specific asset within the larger population.

**Deinstitutionalization** A historical process in the United States and other countries where populations once housed in long-term care facilities like psychiatric hospitals and facilities for the developmentally disabled declined sharply over time.

**Deliberation** The practice of discussing matters of collective importance, so that after debating the merits of competing positions, people can reach a shared agreement about the best course of action.

**Democratic republic** A form of democratic government where power is held by elected officials and there is no monarch.

**Demographic divide** A general pattern of global population growth, in which poor countries have higher birth rates and lower life expectancies, while wealthy countries have lower birth rates and higher life expectancies. The demographic divide is a significant cause of global inequality and global immigration patterns.

**Demographic transition** The historical decline in the birth rate and the death rate. The demographic transition began during the 19th century and accelerated throughout the 20th century.

**Demography** The study of human populations.

**Denomination** A religious sect that has begun to develop a more established bureaucracy and a common set of ritual practices.

**Dependent variable** The outcome to be explained in a research study; the researcher wants to identify what produces the effects on the dependent variable.

**Deviance** Any behavior that is outside social boundaries for what counts as normal and acceptable.

**Deviant subculture** A group of people who set themselves apart as being different from the larger mainstream culture of the society.

**Diaspora** A type of transnational community that develops when specific populations are forced to leave their homeland and to scatter across different communities around the globe.

**Digital surveillance** A form of surveillance that relies on technology to watch and monitor workers and other people's behavior.

**Discourses** Organized systems of knowledge and power that define what meanings we count as normal, and what kinds of meanings we attach to people who are "not normal."

**Discrimination** Negative and unequal treatment directed at a particular group.

**Disease** A disorder in the structure or function of the human organism.

**Disenchantment** The condition of rationalized bureaucratic societies characterized by the growing importance of skepticism and the decline of belief as a source of social action.

**Division of labor** A central principle for organizing the productive work in society that sorts different people into different work roles to ensure the production and reproduction of human life.

**Dominant culture** The ideas, values, beliefs, norms, and material culture of society's most powerful groups.

**Dramaturgical theory** A theory of society developed by Erving Goffman that refers to social life as a series of theatrical performances.

**Dyad** A group of two people with one relationship.

**Ecological modernization** A sociological theory focused on the expectation that growing expert knowledge and public awareness of environmental risks will lead to the development of more sustainable policies and practices.

**Economy** All the activities and organizations that are involved in the production, distribution, and consumption of goods and services.

**Ego** The part of the mind that balances the demands of the id and the superego to determine the most practical course of action for an individual in any given situation.

**Elites** An elite is formed through high-status behavior and the formation of institutions to create a community of privilege and control.

**Emphasized femininity** A counterpart to the idea of hegemonic masculinity, where women perform in stereotypically feminine ways that conform to a patriarchal gender order.

**Empirical evidence** Fact-based information about the social or natural world.

**Encoding** The process through which people with power try to create forms of material and ideal culture that encourage cultural consumers to adopt specific shared meanings.

**Epidemic** A widespread or high incidence of an infectious disease.

**Epidemiology** The study of the social dimensions of disease patterns to discover the way diseases are spread and communicated.

**Epigenetics** The study of how genes interact with wider natural and social environments.

**Epistemic privilege** The privilege that attaches to the knowledge of powerful people.

**Epistemology** A branch of philosophy that explores how we know whether a statement or a fact is actually true.

**Ethics** Critical reasoning about moral questions. Ethical research weighs the benefits of research against possible harm to human subjects of research.

**Ethnic cleansing** The forcible removal of an entire group of people from a society because of their race, ethnicity, or religion.

**Ethnic enclaves** Geographical areas defined by high levels of ethnic concentration and cultural activities and ethnically identified economic activities.

**Ethnicity** A system for classifying people into groups on the basis of shared cultural heritage and a common identity.

**Ethnocentrism** A bias that occurs when people assume that their society is superior to others and when they use their own cultural standards to judge outsiders.

**Ethnography** A sociological research method based on participant-observation in the field where researchers try to capture social life in all of its detail and complexity.

**Experiments** A sociological research method that controls the conditions of observation with the goal of isolating the effects of different factors on some outcome of interest.

**Extended family** A type of family in which the household includes parents, children, grandparents, aunts, uncles, and other relatives.

**Falsifiability** The idea that scientific statements define what condition or evidence would prove them wrong.

**Family** A group of related people who are connected together by biological, emotional, or legal bonds.

**Femininity** The set of personal, social, and cultural qualities associated with females and women.

**Feminism** A theoretical critique and historical series of social movements that proposed women as equal to men and argued that women should be treated as equals in major social institutions.

**Feudalism** An economic system in which a small number of people owned most of the land, and everyone else was completely dependent on the landowner.

**Field experiments** Research using experimental methods in natural settings outside of the laboratory.

**Filter bubble** A phenomenon in which people are only exposed to topics that interest them and opinions they already agree with, which increases social polarization by encouraging people to develop more extreme versions of the beliefs they already hold.

**Focus groups** A sociological research method that gathers groups of people together for discussion of a common question or a particular social issue to collect data.

**Folkways** Common sense and fairly unserious norms.

**Free-rider problem** A collective action problem, in which people in large groups will not act in a way that helps the common good unless it benefits their own personal interests. In social movement contexts, the situation where the people who benefit from a social movement's activities assume that others will do the work.

**Game stage** A stage of social development when children are around seven years old and begin to make friends, learn to pick games that other people want to play, and learn how to avoid or to quickly resolve arguments that arise when a game is being played.

**Gender** The cultural distinctions and socially constructed roles that define expected behaviors for women and men.

**Gender binary** The idea that there are only two gender categories, masculine and feminine, and that all people are either one or the other on the basis of biological sex.

**Gender cue** Part of a social script that tells other people what gendered behavior to expect in the future and how to orient their own behavior.

**Gender dysphoria** A diagnosis in the fifth edition of the *Diagnostic and Statistical Manual of Mental Disorders* to describe when people experience "intense, persistent gender incongruence."

**Gender order** A characterization of society as fully organized by gender.

**Gender performance** Actions and behaviors that conform to widespread gendered understandings of social roles and social identities.

**Gender script** A set of social norms that direct people to act in accordance with widely understood gender expectations.

**Gender socialization** The social interactions and experiences through which individuals develop a social self in relation to gender roles in families as well as in schools, workplaces, and public spaces.

**Gender stereotypes** Oversimplified images that follow the logic of the gender binary to define and reinforce different and contrasting qualities associated with women and men.

**Genealogy** The study of family history in order to document how family members are related to each other.

**General Data Protection Regulation** A 2018 European Union regulation which set strict new limits on how technology companies obtain and handle the personal information of their users, allows users to request the data that companies are holding about them, and empower users to demand that the information be deleted.

**Generalize** To make the argument that the finding from a particular sample of people or a single research study applies to a wider research population.

**Generalized other** The rules of society that the child internalizes through the process of socialization.

**Generation** A group of individuals who are of a similar age and are marked by the same historical events that take place during their youth.

**Genetics** The study of how genes function in the biological system.

**Genocide** The systematic killing of people on the basis of their race, ethnicity, or religion.

**Gentrification** A process whereby wealthy homeowners move in, improve housing, attract new businesses, and, in doing so, displace lower-income families who can no longer afford to live in the neighborhood.

**Global city** Cities that serve as the centers of global finance, international law, management consulting, and global marketing and communication. Examples include London, New York, and Tokyo.

**Global culture** Beliefs, knowledge, practices, and material objects that are shared all around the world.

**Globalization** A concept that refers to the growing social, economic, cultural, and political interdependence of the world's people.

**Hate crime** Acts of violence and intimidation against people because of their race, ethnicity, national origin, religion, gender identity, sexual orientation, or disability.

**Health care systems** Contractual connections between medical organizations.

**Health demography** The study of the prevalence, or the distribution, of disease and illness in a population.

**Health insurance** A way to pay for health care where members pay a regular fee into a larger pool, to be drawn on when they need medical care.

**Hegemonic masculinity** A form of power that enshrines an ideal standard of masculinity for the most valued people in society—specifically, cisgendered, white, educated, wealthy, and able-bodied men.

**Hegemony** A form of power in which dominant groups are able to make their worldview seem like "common sense" to the rest of the population.

**Heteronormativity** A social order that assumes and enforces heterosexuality and links it to binary sex categories; to gender roles at work, in the family, and in the nation; and to heterosexual sex roles.

**Heterosexuality** Sexual desire and sexual relations between males and females.

**Hidden curriculum** The rules of behavior students need to learn to function effectively in the school and the larger society.

**Hierarchy of masculinities** A social order where some masculinities are seen as superior to others, and all are superior to femininity.

**High culture** All the cultural products that are held in the highest esteem by a society's intellectuals and elites.

**Homeschooling** A type of schooling in which parents choose to educate their children at home instead of sending them to a traditional school.

**Horizontal mobility** Social movement in people's life that occurs without changing their overall position in the socioeconomic stratification system.

**Horizontal occupational segregation** A pervasive pattern of gender segregation where women are concentrated into female-typed, lower-earning jobs.

**Hypothesis** A specific statement about the causal relationship between variables that is falsifiable, which means it is a statement that can be proved wrong on the basis of empirical evidence.

**Id** The unconscious part of the mind, which seeks immediate pleasure and gratification.

**Ideal culture** All the social meanings that exist in nonmaterial form, such as beliefs, values, expectations, and language.

**Identity claim** A claim that a social movement and the people it represents are a unified force.

**Identity theft** The use of stolen personal and financial information to assume a person's identity in order to obtain credit and other financial advantages in that person's name.

**Ideology** A system of shared meaning that is used to justify existing relationships of power and privilege.

**Illness experience** The way in which illness is understood and managed by patients and their carers.

**Immigrant enclave** A community in which there are successful immigrant-owned businesses that serve to anchor the community. Immigrant enclaves are highly desirable destinations for new immigrants.

**Immigration** The movement of people from one nation to another.

**Incarceration** A form of punishment in which the offender is confined in prison.

**Income** The flow of earnings over a delimited time period including rents, salaries, and income transfers like pensions or dividends.

**Independent variable** The factor that produces a change in the dependent variable.

**In-depth interviews** A sociological research method that uses extended, open-ended questions to collect data.

**Inequality** The unequal distribution of social goods such as money, power, status, and social resources.

**Informed consent** The idea that people must consent to being studied and that researchers must give their subjects enough information about the study so that they can make a truly voluntary decision about whether or not to participate.

**In-group** A reference group that a person is connected to in a positive way and feels bonded to, whether or not they know people in the group personally.

**Institution** An established system of rules and strategies that defines how people are related to each other and how they should act in a given social situation.

**Institutional level of analysis** The intermediate level of analysis, between microsociology and macrosociology, of specific institutions and social relationships.

**Institutional reflexivity** The phenomenon where people change their behavior in response to social research.

**Institutional Review Board** A governing group that evaluates proposed research with the goal of protecting human subjects from physical or psychological harm.

**Integrated medical care** Systems of medical care that are coordinated to meet the multiple needs of clients.

**Interest group** An organization that brings people together on the basis of a common issue, and attempts to influence political decision-makers on topics related to that issue.

**Intergenerational mobility** The change in social status between different generations in the same family, or the change in the position of children relative to their parents.

**Internal migration** The movement of people within the same country. Internal migration is different than international migration, which is what people usually refer to when they talk about immigration.

**Intersectional health perspective** A multilevel approach to health care and medicine that emphasizes the multiple systems of oppression that shape health outcomes and how they interact.

**Intersectionality** A perspective that identifies the multiple, intersecting, and situational nature of the categories that shape people's identities and experiences.

**Intersex** A term for people with physical characteristics associated with both male and female categories. More recently the term "differences of sex development" has been recommended by persons with intersex conditions.

**Job training** The process of schools teaching students specific skills that will help them enter the workforce and earn a decent wage.

**Kinship system** The set of rules that define who counts as a member of the family, the names that are given to different types of family members, and the expectations about how different family members will relate to one another.

**Labeling theory** A theory that people become deviant when they are labeled as deviant people.

**Laws** Attempts by governments to establish formal systems of rules about how people are allowed to behave, as well as a system of punishments for when they break those rules.

**Level of analysis** The size or scale of the objects sociologists study.

**Life expectancy** The amount of time an individual can expect to live.

**Linear or continuous variable** A measure of inherently numerical phenomena that can be counted, divided and multiplied, such as money or time.

**Literacy** The ability to read, write, communicate, and use other skills that allow people to participate fully in their society.

**Local** The specific particular settings of everyday life, including face-to-face relationships.

**Logic** Valid reasoning.

**Looking-glass self** A concept that describes how we develop a social self based on how we think other people perceive us.

**Lower-middle class** A social class group below the middle class composed of families with a household income of between $15,000 and $60,000 per year.

**Macrosociology** The analysis of large-scale structural patterns and historical trends, including the workings of the economic, political, and cultural systems.

**Male breadwinner** A traditional social role for adult men based on the expectation that men should earn enough in wages to support a dependent wife and family.

**Marginal productivity theory** The theory that inequality is a way of rewarding people who make a greater contribution to society, by encouraging them to work hard and use their talents.

**Marriage market** Institutionalized spaces where individuals select potential sexual, romantic, and marriage partners.

**Masculinity** The set of personal, social, and cultural qualities associated with males and men.

**Master status** A single status that becomes so important that it is the only one that matters in social interactions.

**Material culture** All the cultural objects that are produced by a social group or a society.

**Matthew effect** A tendency in science in which the most eminent scientists get most of the recognition and rewards for scientific research.

**Means of symbolic production** The organized social resources for creating, producing, and distributing communications.

**Mechanical solidarity** A system of social ties that produces social cohesion on the basis of similar work and life in less complex divisions of labor.

**Media concentration** A situation when a few large companies control the majority of commercial culture.

**Medical institutions** Organizational arrangements in which medical therapies are developed and practiced.

**Medical risk** Any condition or factor that increases the likelihood of disease or injury.

**Medicalization** A process where a social problem comes to be created or redefined as a medical issue.

**Medicine** The social response to illness that attempts to identify, prevent, and cure disease.

**Meritocracy** Stratification systems where high positions are held by those who perform the best on examinations and other formal tests of ability.

**Microsociology** The analysis of individuals and small-group interaction.

**Middle class** A social class group below the upper-middle class composed of families with an annual income of between $60,000 and $90,000.

**Modern era/modernity** The period of history in which the combined effects of industrialization, colonization, and the democratic revolutions created massive social change.

**Modern world system** A term coined by Immanuel Wallerstein to describe the economic integration that occurred with the massive expansion of global trade in modernity.

**Monotheism** A religious cosmology in which there is only one deity.

**Moral education** A form of education where students learn social skills, the values of self-determination and autonomy, and how to attach to social groups.

**Moral indifference** Occurs when we distance ourselves from the consequences of our actions for others.

**Moral order** A social arrangement that is organized around widely understood and institutionally enforced ideas of right and wrong; the gender order is a moral order since it defines what is right and wrong for women and men.

**Moral panic** A situation in which a "condition, episode, a person or group of persons emerges to become defined as a threat to societal values and interests" (Cohen 2002: 1)

**Mores** Norms that define serious expectations about behavior that invoke central values.

**Multicultural marketing** Advertising that tailors specific messages to target minority groups.

**Multiculturalism** A culturally pluralistic society's official recognition of the existence of different cultural groups and identities, and its development of policies promoting cultural diversity.

**Multilevel approach to health and illness** A part of an intersectional health perspective that emphasizes the systemic sources of health and illness as well as individual characteristics.

**Multilineal** A kinship system that traces both the maternal and the paternal lines of descent, giving equal significance to each.

**National health care systems** Government-based health care systems in which all citizens are guaranteed access to a basic bundle of medical services.

**Net worth** Wealth and income minus any debt owed.

**Network centrality** A network position that has many individual direct ties with many people in the network, or someone who is highly influential in a network

**Nonbinary** A term for people who identify as both man and woman or as neither man or woman.

**Normalization** The process through which social standards of normal behavior are used to judge people and to reform those who are determined not to be normal

**Norms** Shared expectations, specific to time and place, about how people should act in any particular situation.

**Nuclear family** A traditional image of the family, which consists of a heterosexual couple living together with their children.

**Operationalization** The process of defining measures for a sociological study.

**Opinions** Ideas about the world that stem from common values or experience.

**Ordinal variable** A measure of categorical order, such as more and less, where the distances between categories are not numerically precise.

**Organic solidarity** A system of social ties that produces social cohesion based on differences in a complex division of labor.

**Organizational culture** The distinctive beliefs and patterns of behavior that develop within an organization.

**Out-group** A reference group toward which a person has a negative connection.

**Palliative care** Medical care offered to a person and that person's family when it is recognized that the illness is no longer curable.

**Pandemic** An epidemic that not only affects a large number of people but is also spread over a large geographical area of the world.

**Parasocial relationship** A one-sided relationship in which people feel a sense of intimacy and social attachment with the media performers they watch regularly.

**Parliamentary system** A form of democratic government in which the head of government is chosen from the legislature, and is also usually the leader of the largest political party in parliament.

**Parole** A process through which prisoners who appear to have reformed themselves can earn an early release from their prison sentence.

**Participant-observation** A research method of observing people in social settings by participating in those social settings with them.

**Party system** A stratification system where power and privilege come from the effective leadership of important organizations.

**Patriarchy** A social system rooted in male power, in which men and qualities associated with men are considered to be superior to women and to qualities associated with women.

**Patrilineal** A kinship system that privileges the male line of descent.

**Peer groups** Groups of people of similar age who share the same kinds of interests.

**Peer pressure** Peer groups encourage adolescents and teens to engage in behaviors that they would not perform if their parents were watching.

**Peer review** The process of review of proposed research or publication by the community of scientific experts in a profession or scientific field.

**Persuasive power** The ability to convince other people that a particular choice or action is the appropriate one.

**Pink-collar jobs** A term coined to describe the kinds of jobs done by women entering the labor force in the 1970s and 1980s; support roles that were paid less than white-collar jobs and well-paid unionized blue-collar jobs.

**Play stage** A stage of social development when children around three years old begin to engage in role-playing games.

**Plea-bargaining** A process in which a defendant pleads guilty to a lesser charge that has been negotiated by the prosecuting and defense attorneys.

**Police** A group of people authorized to enforce the law, prevent crime, pursue and bring to justice people who break the law, and maintain social order.

**Political opportunity structure** The political opportunities available for successful social movement action that occur when there are changes in political alliances, political conflicts among elites, or when there are clear alliances that can be made with specific political groups.

**Politics** The struggle for influence and control over the state.

**Polytheism** A religious cosmology in which there is a group of deities.

**Popular culture** Objects of material culture industrially produced and distributed for the masses.

**Popular sovereignty** The "rule of the people."

**Post-colonial theory** A critical perspective that argues that the ways we see globalization, power, and economic systems in the modern world are all shaped by the conquest and subordination of the world's peoples by Western European powers dating from the 15th and 16th centuries.

**Post-industrialism** An economy in which manufacturing becomes less important as a source of wealth, and where the production of information, knowledge, and services becomes more important.

**Post-secular society** A society in which religion and science coexist harmoniously, and where there is an attempt to create mutual learning and respect between religious ideas and scientific ideas.

**Power** A social relationship in which one individual or group is able to influence the conduct of other individuals or groups either directly through force or indirectly through authority, persuasion, or cultural expectation; the ability of individuals or groups to get what they want, even against the resistance of others who are participating in the same action.

**Presidential system** A form of democratic government in which there is a formal separation of powers between the head of government and the legislature, and the president is usually elected by a democratic vote of the people.

**Preventive medical care** Care aimed at preventing disease before it occurs.

**Primary deviance** A deviant act or behavior that does not result in the person adopting an identity as a deviant person.

**Primary school** The part of the education system that focuses on the learning needs of children from the ages of five to 12, with an emphasis on basic academic learning and socialization skills.

**Primary groups** Small groups typically based in face-to-face interaction that foster strong feelings of belonging.

**Primary sexual characteristics** The organs required for physical reproduction.

**Primogeniture** A system in which the first-born child (or, more commonly, the first-born son) inherits the entire family estate.

**Prison–industrial complex** A profit-making system that uses prison labor and prisons to support a wide array of economic activities.

**Private school** A school that charges tuition for each student it educates.

**Privilege** The greater resources possessed by some individuals and groups compared to others.

**Professionalization** A process where a group of workers come to control a particular space in the division of labor on the basis of their expertise.

**Program claim** A claim by a social movement that is made in support for or opposition to a specific policy proposal.

**Prompt engineering** The practice of writing, refining, and optimizing prompts that are addressed to an artificial intelligence chatbot so that it produces the most helpful and effective responses with the fewest number of revisions needed.

**Property crime** Defined by the Uniform Crime Reporting Program as burglary (entering a home or business to commit theft) motor vehicle theft, larceny (other forms of theft), and arson.

**Proselytizing** The attempt by individuals or organizations to convert other people to their own religious beliefs.

**Public health** The health of the whole population.

**Public health education** Educational efforts to prevent disease, promote healthy behaviors, and preempt risky ones.

**Public health policy** The norms, rules, and laws that attempt to shape public health behavior.

**Public opinion** The public expression of the different attitudes and beliefs that people have about a particular issue.

**Public religion** A situation in which individuals and organizations make faith-based moral arguments about the public good.

**Public school** A school that is run by the state and receives all or most of its funding from the government.

**Public sociology** A commitment to bringing sociological knowledge to a general public audience, and participating in wider public conversations and struggles for social justice.

**Public sphere** The collection of places where private individuals and elected officials gather together to discuss matters of common concern.

**Punishment** A social response to deviance that controls both deviant behavior and the offender, and that aims to protect the social group and its social standards.

**Qualitative methods** Sociological research methods that collect nonnumerical information, such as interview transcripts or images.

**Quantitative methods** Sociological research methods that collect numerical data that can be analyzed using statistical techniques.

**Queer** Any idea or practice that actively disturbs the binaries describing a neat concurrence of sex, gender, and desire in society.

**Queer theory** A critical perspective that identifies the logic of homophobia and heterosexism in social practice and social institutions, and how that logic works to maintain social order.

**Race** A system for classifying people into groups on the basis of shared physical traits, which people in society treat as socially important and understand to be biologically transmitted.

**Racial determinism** A dominant social theory in the 19th century that argued that the world was divided into biologically distinct races, and that there were fundamental differences in ability between the different racial groups.

**Racial formation theory** A critique that analyzes modern Western society and particularly US society as structured by a historically developed "racial common sense." Racial stereotypes and institutionalized patterns of inequality are embedded in the fundamental fabric of modern social life at both the individual and the institutional levels.

**Racial profiling** A process in which people are targeted by police and civilians for humiliating and harsh treatment because of their perceived race, ethnicity, national origin, or religion.

**Racial steering** A practice in which realtors would encourage people to look for homes in specific neighborhoods depending on their race, as a way to ensure the "desirable" neighborhoods were reserved for whites.

**Random sample** A selection from a research population based on a random mechanism, such as a dice roll, a flipped coin, or a random number generator.

**Rationalization** A major dynamic of modernity in which social relationships become more predictable, standardized, systematic, and efficient.

**Rational-legal authority** A form of persuasive power based on clearly defined rules that are written down.

**Reactivity** A situation where the researcher has an effect on the behavior and the responses of the interview subject.

**Redlining** A practice where banks would not give mortgages to people who lived in minority-dominated neighborhoods.

**Reference group** A group that people use to help define how they fit in society by providing standards to measure themselves.

**Reflexivity** The imaginative ability to move outside of yourself in order to understand yourself as part of a wider social scene.

**Rehabilitation** An approach to punishment that seeks to improve offenders and restore them to society.

**Relationality** The idea that social things take on meaning only in relationship to social other things.

**Relative deprivation** A form of inequality between groups where people believe that they are being treated unequally in comparison to another group they view as similar to themselves.

**Relative mobility** The understanding of change in social position compared to other groups.

**Relativism** The idea that truth depends on the group, the community, the society, and the culture to which a person belongs.

**Reliability** The consistent measurement of the object over units in a population or over repeated samples.

**Religion** A unified system of beliefs and practices related to sacred things, which unite all of its adherents into a single moral community.

**Remittance** The money a migrant sends back from their new country to family members in their country of origin.

**Representative sample** A selection from a research population that contains all the features of the wider population from which it is drawn.

**Reproductive labor** The work of producing and maintaining individuals for social participation in the economy and society

**Research methods** Strategies to collect accurate and useful information about the world.

**Research population** The entire universe of individuals or objects in a study.

**Residential segregation** A social practice in which neighborhoods are separated on the basis of group differences.

**Resistance** Opposition to the exercise of power.

**Resocialization** The process through which we adjust our lives, attitudes, and behaviors in response to new circumstances.

**Resource mobilization theory** A theory that links social movement success to resources of money, legitimacy, facilities, and labor.

**Rigidity** The degree to which movement is possible in a stratification system.

**Ritual** An event where people come together to reaffirm the meaning of the sacred, to acknowledge its special qualities and its separateness from ordinary (profane) life.

**Role** The set of expected behaviors associated with a particular status.

**Role conflict** Occurs when there are competing expectations coming from different statuses and role expectations clash, individuals become conflicted.

**Role strain** Occurs when the different expected behaviors associated with a status are in tension with one another, individuals experience strain trying to meet expectations.

**Sample** A selection from a research population for the purposes of research.

**Sanctions** Actions that punish people when they do not act in a way that accords with norms.

**Sandwich parents** People in the generational position of raising their children at the same time as their own parents are becoming elderly and need care.

**Second shift** The unpaid housework and childcare women perform after returning home from their paid job.

**Secondary school** The part of the education system in which students learn more specialized subject areas, and where they begin to develop the specific skills they will need to enter the workforce or university.

**Second-wave feminism** The movements and activism around women's rights in the 1960s and 1970s, with a focus on reproductive rights, work, family, and equal pay.

**Secondary deviance** A deviant act or behavior that occurs when a person has taken on the role of the deviant person.

**Secondary groups** Large, impersonal groups usually organized around a specific activity or interest.

**Secondary sex characteristics** Physical features that emerge at puberty like body hair and breasts.

**Sect** A smaller and more loosely organized group of religious believers who disagree with the established church and try to create their own authentic expression of religious faith.

**Secularization thesis** The argument that religion will become less important in modern society.

**Secular-rational values** Widely held social beliefs that emphasize the importance of individualism, science, and critique.

**Segregation** A social practice in which neighborhoods, schools, and other social organizations are separated by race and ethnicity.

**Selection effect** The bias produced in data by the way the data are chosen, or selected.

**Self** A sociological term used in the symbolic interactionist tradition to describe the individual person and their social being. The self is produced and only takes on meaning in interaction and relationships with others.

**Self-expression values** Widely held social beliefs that emphasize the importance of tolerance, political participation, personal happiness, and environmental protection.

**Separate spheres** The idea that there are and should be separate social domains for women and men.

**Sex** The biological categories of male, female, or intersex, which are assigned at birth on the basis of bodily characteristics such as the organs required for sexual reproduction; secondary features like body hair, height, or breasts; and also genetic and chromosomal differences.

**Sexism** A social process whereby social resources are directly, unequally, and unfairly distributed in favor of people who are perceived to be biologically male.

**Sick role** An idea developed by Talcott Parsons to describe social expectations for the behavior of sick people.

**Single-party state** A state in which all candidates in an election come from a single political party.

**Smart manufacturing** A type of economic production that relies on advanced robotic technology, large-scale data processing, and artificial intelligence to increase productivity while lowering the level of human intervention that is required in the manufacturing process.

**Snowball sample** A selection from a research population taken by asking the first few research subjects to identify and recommend others for study.

**Social capital** Group ties and network attachments people have and the sense of trust and security that they get from their group memberships and network attachments; the relationships and experience of social connection and cooperation people have with each other that allow them to act together.

**Social control theory** A theory that people who have strong social bonds and attachments in their community are less likely to engage in deviant behavior.

**Social demography** Social research that uses demographic data in order to study key social institutions and social processes. Social demographers study trends in marriage and divorce, population aging, immigration and social mobility, urbanization, and health disparities between different population groups.

**Social facts** Facts about the collective nature of social life that have their own patterns and dynamics beyond the individual level.

**Social group** A set of people that are connected in some way.

**Socialism** A type of economy in which goods are produced according to social needs, and economic production is controlled and owned collectively by the workers themselves.

**Social mobility** A change in a person's social status or a movement to a different place in the stratification system.

**Social movement** A group of people acting together to try to create social or political change, usually outside the channels of institutionalized politics.

**Social network** A group organized through social ties between individuals that works through the connections that link individuals to one another.

**Social research** The systematic investigation of some aspect of the social world, which aims to contribute to our general understanding of society.

**Social sciences** The disciplines that use systematic scientific and cultural methods to study the social world, as distinct from the natural and physical worlds.

**Social solidarity** A feeling of social connection and social belonging.

**Social stratification** A central sociological idea that describes structured patterns of inequality between different groups of people.

**Social structures** The seen and unseen regular, organized patterns of social life.

**Socialization** All of the different ways that we learn about our society's beliefs, values, and expected behaviors; the ongoing process of learning the social meanings of a culture.

**Socioeconomic status** A general term referring to sociological measures of social position that include income, educational attainment, and occupational prestige.

**Sociological imagination** The ability to see the connections between individual lives, wider social structures, and the way they affect each other.

**Sociological research methods** All the different strategies sociologists use to collect, measure, and analyze data.

**Sociology of health and illness** A field of sociology that studies the relationship between health and society.

**Solidarity** The sense of belonging and the connection that we have to a particular group.

**Standardized tests** Forms of assessment that are administered and scored under conditions that are the same for all students.

**Standing claim** A claim by a social movement that the people it represents deserve more complete inclusion in society.

**State** All of the institutions of government, which together rule over a clearly defined territory and have a monopoly on the legitimate use of physical force within the territory.

**Status** A specific social position that an individual occupies in the social structure.

**Status group** A group held together by a common lifestyle and shared characteristics of social honor.

**Stereotypes** A form of ideology that encourages people to believe in the natural superiority or inferiority of different groups of people.

**Stigma** A form of dishonor, discredit, or shame associated with illness; a spoiled identity.

**Stratification** A central sociological idea that describes structured patterns of inequality between different groups of people.

**Structural mobility** Changes in social position in the stratification system that occur because of structural changes in the economy and wider society.

**Structural strain theory** A theory about the connection between structural inequalities, grievances, and collective action.

**Structure** The seen and unseen regular, organized patterns of social life.

**Subcultures** The ideas, values, beliefs, norms, and material culture of all the nondominant groups in the society.

**Suburb** A residential area located within commuting distance of a city. Suburbs began to spread out from cities in the late-19th and early-20th centuries, first with improvements in railroad infrastructure and then with the spread of the automobile.

**Superego** The moral part of the mind, which acts as the conscience.

**Surveillance** The practice of monitoring other people's activities, often by using video and other media technologies.

**Surveys** A sociological research method that asks a series of defined questions to collect data from a large sample of the research population.

**Survival values** Widely held social beliefs that emphasize the importance of economic and physical security.

**Symbolic ethnicity** The way dominant groups feel an attachment to specific ethnic traditions without being active members of the ethnic group.

**Symbolic interactionism** A perspective associated with the Chicago school of sociology that argues that people develop a social self through interaction with others.

**Symbolic meaning** The broader cultural content of a cultural object, idea, or event which is based on the other images, emotions, meanings, and associations that come from the larger culture.

**Symbolic politics** A type of political activity in which the meanings associated with a political action are just as important as the policies or the social changes being proposed.

**Theodicy** The attempt to explain why suffering and injustice exist in the world.

**Theoretical sample** A selection from a research population that focuses a sample as research progresses and where the sampling strategy changes after the initial data have been collected, based on what is theoretically important.

**Theories of the middle range** Theories that focus on particular institutions and practices rather than an overarching theory of society

**Thomas theorem** The proposition that the way people interpret a situation has real consequences for how they act.

**Total institutions** Institutions like prisons, nursing homes, or the military that control every aspect of their members' lives.

**Traditional authority** A form of persuasive power in which people follow a leader's orders because of the weight of tradition or custom.

**Traditional values** Widely held social beliefs that emphasize the importance of traditional religion, family, national pride, and obedience to authority.

**Transgender** A term for people assigned male at birth who do not identify as men and people who are assigned female at birth who do not identify as women.

**Transnational community** A community that reaches beyond national boundaries.

**Transnational family** A household that is maintaining strong family bonds and simultaneous connections to multiple countries.

**Treadmill of production** A social process in which the continuous quest for economic growth encourages businesses to pursue strategies that cause large and unsustainable environmental damage.

**Triad** A group of three people with three relationships.

**Underclass** A social group described by William Julius Wilson that experiences long-term unemployment and social isolation, and often lives in impoverished urban neighborhoods.

**Upper-middle class** A social class group at the top of the middle-class system with good job security and high-paying salaries of over $100,000 per year.

**Urbanization** A social process in which the population shifts from the country into cities, and where most people start to live in urban rather than rural areas.

**Utopia** An image of an imaginary, perfect world in which there is no conflict, hunger, or unhappiness.

**Validity** The result of using data to accurately measure the phenomenon under study.

**Values** General social ideas about what is right and wrong, good and bad, desirable and undesirable, important or unimportant.

**Variable** A quantity that changes, or varies, in a research population.

**Vertical occupational segregation** A pattern in occupations where men tend to hold higher, better-paid positions than women within the same occupation.

**Vertical social mobility** Social mobility up or down in the socioeconomic stratification system.

**Violent crime** Defined by the Uniform Crime Reporting Program as homicide, aggravated assault, rape, and robbery.

**Warehousing theory** A theory that focuses on the ways that postsecondary education acts as a holding place that protects people from unstable labor market conditions.

**Wealth** The stock of valuable assets including physical and intellectual property, art, jewelry, and other valuable goods.

**White-collar crime** Financially motivated nonviolent crime, usually committed by business professionals in the course of doing their jobs.

**Worker productivity** The amount that a worker can produce or accomplish within a given quantity of labor output.

**Working poor** People and families in poverty despite having at least one person who works for a wage.

**Workplace sexual harassment** Unwelcome and offensive conduct that is based on gender that has become a condition of employment, or conduct that creates an intimidating, hostile, or abusive work environment.

**World society** The view that there is a common global culture consisting of shared norms about progress, science, democracy, human rights, and environmental protection.

**World systems theory** A way to think about global stratification that emphasizes the relative positions of countries in the world economy as crucial determinants of inequality.

**Xenophobia** Fear and hatred of strangers who have a different cultural background.

**Zone of permitted variation** A social space around a boundary where rules can be contested.

# References

AAPI. 2022, June. "State of Asian Americans, Native Hawaiians, and Pacific Islanders in the United States." https://aapidata.com/wp-content/uploads/2022/06/State-AANHPIs-National-June2022.pdf.

Abbasi, Daniel. 2006. *Americans and Climate Change: Closing the Gap between Science and Action*. New Haven, CT: Yale School of Forestry and Environmental Studies. https://climatecommunication.yale.edu/publications/americans-and-climate-change/.

Abbott, Andrew. 2001. *Chaos of the Disciplines*. Chicago: University of Chicago Press.

Abelman, Nancy, and Jiyeon Kang. 2014. "Memoir/Manuals of South Korean Pre-College Study Abroad: Defending Mothers and Humanizing Children." *Global Networks* 14: 1–22.

Acker, J. 1973. "Women and Social Stratification: A Case of Intellectual Sexism." *American Journal of Sociology* 78(4): 936–945.

Acosta, Pablo, Pablo Fajnzylber, and J. Lopez. 2008. "How Important Are Remittances in Latin America?" In *Remittances and Development: Lessons from Latin America*, ed. P. Fajnzylber and J. Lopez (pp. 21–50). Washington, DC: The World Bank.

Adler, N. E., and D. H. Rehkopf. 2008. "US Disparities in Health: Descriptions, Causes, and Mechanisms." *Annual Review of Public Health* 29: 235–253.

Adler, Patricia, and Peter Adler. 1998. *Peer Power: Preadolescent Culture and Identity*. New Brunswick, NJ: Rutgers University Press.

Adler, Patricia, Steven Kless, and Peter Adler. 1992. "Socialization to Gender Roles: Popularity among Elementary School Boys and Girls." *Sociology of Education* 65: 169–187.

Adorno, Theodor W., Else Frenkel-Brunswik, Daniel J. Levinson, and R. Nevitt Sanford. 1950. *The Authoritarian Personality*. New York: Harper & Brothers.

Ajunwa, I., K. Crawford, and J. Schultz. 2017. "Limitless Worker Surveillance." *California Law Review*: 735–776.

Alarcón, R. 1999. "Recruitment Processes Among Foreign-Born Engineers and Scientists in Silicon Valley." *American Behavioral Scientist* 42(9): 1381–1397.

Alba, R., B. Beck, and D. Basaran Sahin. 2018. "The Rise of Mixed Parentage: A Sociological and Demographic Phenomenon to be Reckoned With." *The Annals of the American Academy of Political and Social Science*, 677(1): 26–38

Alba, Richard D. 1976. "Social Assimilation Among American Catholic National-Origin Groups." *American Sociological Review* 41(6): 1030–1046.

Alba, Richard D. 1990. *Ethnic Identity: The Transformation of White America*. New Haven, CT: Yale University Press.

Alba, Richard, and Victor Nee. 2003. *Remaking the American Mainstream: Assimilation and Contemporary Immigration*. Cambridge, MA: Harvard University Press.

Alberta, Tim. 2017, September/October. "Is The Electoral College Doomed?" *Politico*. https://www.politico.com/magazine/story/2017/09/05/electoral-college-national-popular-vote-compact-215541.

Alémán, J., and D. Woods. 2016. "Value Orientations from the World Values Survey: How Comparable Are They Cross-Nationally?" *Comparative Political Studies* 49: 1039–1067.

Alexander, Jeffrey C. 1987. *Twenty Lectures: Sociological Theory since World War II*. New York: Columbia University Press.

Alexander, Jeffrey C. 2003. *The Meanings of Social Life: A Cultural Sociology*. New York: Oxford University Press.

Alexander, Jeffrey C. 2006. *The Civil Sphere*. New York: Oxford University Press.

Alexander, Jeffrey C. 2011. *Performative Revolution in Egypt: An Essay in Cultural Power*. London: Bloomsbury Academic.

Alexander, Robert, 2019. *Representation and the Electoral College*. New York: Oxford University Press.

Alex-Assensoh, Yvette, and Lawrence Hanks, eds. 2000. *Black and Multiracial Politics in America*. New York: NYU Press.

Alfonso, M. 2006. "The Impact of Community College Attendance on Baccalaureate Attainment." *Res High Educ* 47: 873–903. https://doi.org/10.1007/s11162-006-9019-2.

Alfonso, Y. N., J. P. Leider, B. Resnick, J. M. McCullough, and D. Bishai. 2021. "US Public Health Neglected: Flat or Declining Spending Left States Ill Equipped to Respond to COVID-19: Study Examines US Public Health Spending." *Health Affairs* 40(4): 664–671.

Alinsky, Saul. [1971] 2010. *Rules for Radicals*. New York: Random House.

Alkon, Cynthia. 2014. "The U.S. Supreme Court's Failure to Fix Plea Bargaining: The Impact of Lafler and Frye." *Hastings Constitutional Law Quarterly* 41(3): 561–622.

Allen, Joseph, and Claudia Allen. 2009. *Escaping the Endless Adolescence*. New York: Ballantine Books.

Almeida, I. L. L., J. F. Rego, A. C. G. Teixeira, and M. R. Moreira. 2021, October 4. "Social Isolation and Its Impact on Child and Adolescent Development: A Systematic Review." *Revista Paulista de Pediatria* 40. doi: 10.1590/1984-0462/2022/40/2020385.

Almond, Gabriel, R. Scott Appleby, and Emmanuel Sivan. 2003. *Strong Religion: The Rise of Fundamentalisms around the World*. Chicago: University of Chicago Press.

Aloe, Carli, Martin Kulldorff, and Barry R. Bloom. 2017. "Geospatial Analysis of Nonmedical Vaccine Exemptions and Pertussis Outbreaks in the United States." *Proceedings of the National Academy of Sciences of the United States of America* 114(27): 7101–7105.

Alschuler, A. 1975. The Defense Attorney's Role in Plea Bargaining. *The Yale Law Journal* 84(6):1179–1314. doi:10.2307/795498.

Alschuler, Albert. 1968. "The Prosecutor's Role in Plea Bargaining." *The University of Chicago Law Review* 36(1): 50–112. doi:10.2307/1598832.

Amar, Akhil Reed. 2007. "Some Thoughts on the Electoral College: Past, Present, and Future." *Faculty Scholarship Series. Paper* 790. http://digitalcommons.law.yale.edu/fss_papers/790.

Amato, Paul R. 2010. "Research on Divorce: Continuing Trends and New Developments." *Journal of Marriage and Family* 72: 650–666. https://doi.org/10.1111/j.1741-3737.2010.00723.x.

Amato, Paul, Laura Loomis, and Alan Booth. 1995. "Parental Divorce, Marital Conflict, and Offspring Well-Being During Early Adulthood." *Social Forces* 73: 895–815.

American Association of Public Opinion Researchers. 2015. "AAPOR Statement on 'Push Polls.'" https://www.aapor.org/Standards-Ethics/Resources/AAPOR-Statements-on-Push-Polls.aspx.

American Civil Liberties Union. 2020. "Racial Profiling." https://www.aclu.org/issues/racial-justice/race-and-criminal-justice/racial-profiling

American Immigration Council. 2021. "How the United States Immigration System Works." Fact Sheet. https://www.americanimmigrationcouncil.org/research/how-united-states-immigration-system-works

American Psychological Association. 2017a. "Answers to Your Questions about Individuals with Intersex Conditions." http://www.apa.org/topics/lgbt/intersex.aspx.

American Psychological Association. 2017b. "Transgender People, Gender Identity and Gender Expression." http://www.apa.org/topics/lgbt/transgender.aspx.

American Sociological Association. 2017, July 13. "Love, Money and HIV: Becoming a Modern African Woman in the Age of AIDS." https://www.asanet.org/news-events/asa-news/love-money-and-hiv-becoming-modern-african-woman-age-aids.

Anderson, Benedict. 2006. *Imagined Communities: Reflections on the Origin and Spread of Nationalism*. New York: Verso.

Anderson, C. A., and B. J. Bushman. 2018. "Media Violence and the General Aggression Model." *Journal of Social Issues* 74: 386–313. doi:10.1111/josi.12275.

Anderson, Elijah. 1999. *The Code of the Street: Decency, Violence and the Moral Life of the Inner City*. New York: W.W. Norton and Company.

Anderson, James. 2015. *Criminological Theories*. Burlington, MA: Jones and Bartlett.

Anderson, James. 2007. *Daily Life during the French Revolution*. Westport, CT: Greenwood Press.

Anderson, Lydia, Chanell Washington, Rose M. Kreider, and Thomas Gryn. 2023. *Share of One-Person Households More Than Tripled from 1940 to 2020*. American Counts. US Census.

Anderson, Monica. 2015, April 9. "A Rising Share of the US Black Population Is Foreign Born." *Pew Research Center Social and Demographic Trends*. http://www.pewsocialtrends.org/2015/04/09/a-rising-share-of-the-u-s-black-population-is-foreign-born/.

Anderson, Perry. 1974. *Lineages of the Absolutist State*. London: Verso.

Anderson, Tom. 2015, March 12. "'Boomerang Kids' Are Ruining Their Parents Retirement." *CNBC*. http://www.cnbc.com/2015/03/12/saving-for-retirement-boomerang-kids-are-ruining-their-parents-retirement.html.

Andres, Lesley. 2022. "Higher Education and the Marriage Market." *Canadian Journal of Higher Education | Revue canadienne d'enseignement supérieur* 52(1): 51–69.

Anning, W. D., and L. Carlson. 2021. "Trends in Cohabitation Prior to Marriage. Family Profiles, FP-21-04." Bowling Green State University, National Center for Family & Marriage Research. https://doi.org/10.25035/ncfmr/fp-21-04.

Anyon, Jean. 2006. "Social Class, School Knowledge, and the Hidden Curriculum: Retheorizing Reproduction." In *Ideology, Curriculum, and the New Sociology of Education*, ed. L. Weis, C. McCarthy and G. Dimitriadis (pp. 37–46). New York: Taylor and Francis.

Aoki, Deb. 2023, April 21. "Are Sales of Manga Evening Out?" *Publishers Weekly*. https://www.publishersweekly.com/pw/by-topic/industry-news/comics/article/92089-will-sales-of-manga-ever-even-out.html#:~:text=Still%2C%20manga%20is%20a%20dominant,annual%20report%20for%20the%20Beat.

Appadurai, Arjun. 1996. *Modernity at Large: Cultural Dimensions of Globalization*. Minneapolis: University of Minnesota Press.

Appiah, Kwame Anthony, and Amy Gutmann. 1998. *Color Conscious: The Political Morality of Race*. Princeton, NJ: Princeton University Press.

Apted, Michael. 2009. "Interview with Michael Apted." *Ethnography* 10: 321–325.

Aragao, Carolina, Kim Parker, Shannon Greenwood, Chris Baranavski, and John Mandapat. 2023, September 14. "*The Modern American Family: Key Trends in Marriage and Family Life*." Pew Research Center. https://www.pewresearch.org/social-trends/2023/09/14/the-modern-american-family/.

Ariens, Chris. 2014, October 30. "Weather Channel Distances Itself from Founder's Climate Change Comments," Adweek. http://www.adweek.com/tvnewser/weather-channel-distances-itself-from-founders-climate-change-comments/245200.

Armstrong, Elizabeth, and Laura Hamilton. 2013. *Paying for the Party: How College Maintains Inequality*. Cambridge, MA: Harvard University Press.

Arrighi, Giovanni. 1994. *The Long Twentieth Century*. London: Verso.

Arsenault, Mark. 2012, May 11. "Beverly Mother Gets Jail for Permitting Teenage Drinking." *Boston Globe*. http://www.bostonglobe.com/metro/2012/05/11/salem-woman-gets-six-months-jail-six-months-house-arrest-for-providing-alcohol-daughter-party/2InVsVtiBXkHVK0dd4zKVM/story.html.

Arum, Richard, and Michael Hout. 1998. "The Early Returns: The Transition from School to Work in the United States." In *From School to Work: A Comparative Study of Educational Qualifications and Occupational Destination*, ed. Yossi Shavit and Walter Muller (pp 471–510). Oxford, England: Clarendon Press.

Asante-Muhammad, Dedrick, and Natalie Gerber. 2018, January 8. "African Immigrants: Immigrating into a Racial Wealth Divide." *Huffington Post*. https://www.huffpost.com/entry/african-immigrants-immigrating-into-a-racial-wealth_b_5a539aa9e4b0cd114bdb353c.

Assari, Shervi. 2017, March 8. "Why Do Women Live Longer Than Men?" *The Conversation*. https://theconversation.com/if-men-are-favored-in-our-society-why-do-they-die-younger-than-women-71527.

Associated Press. 2020. "Explaining AP style on Black and white." https://apnews.com/article/archive-race-and-ethnicity-9105661462

Attia, Peter, 2023. *Outlive: The Science and Art of Longevity*. New York: Harmony Books.

Au, Wayne. 2008. "Devising Inequality: A Bernsteinian Analysis of High-Stakes Testing and Social Reproduction in Education." *British Journal of Sociology of Education* 29(6): 639–651.

Auster, C. J., and C. S. Mansbach. 2012. "The Gender Marketing of Toys: An Analysis of Color and Type of Toy on the Disney Store Website." *Sex Roles* 67, 375–388. https://doi.org/10.1007/s11199-012-0177-8.

Austin, Joe. 2001. *Taking the Train: How Graffiti Art Became an Urban Crisis in New York City*. New York: Columbia University Press.

Avanesian, Garen, Suguru Mizunoya, and Diogo Amaro. 2021. "How Many Students Could Continue Learning During COVID-19-Caused School Closures? Introducing a New Reachability Indicator for Measuring Equity of Remote Learning." *International Journal of Educational Development* 84: 102421.

Avert. 2024. "What Is HIV Stigma and Discrimination?" Be in the KNOW. https://www.beintheknow.org/living-hiv/health-and-wellbeing/hiv-stigma.

Avvisati, F. 2020. "Where Did Reading Proficiency Improve over Time?" *PISA in Focus* 103. https://doi.org/10.1787/e54d62dc-en.

Ayres, Ian, and Peter Siegelman. 1995. "Race and Gender Discrimination in Bargaining for a New Car." *American Economic Review* 85: 304–321.

Ayres-Brown, A. 2014, April 21. "McDonald's Gave Me the 'Girl's Toy' with My Happy Meal. So I Went to the CEO." *Slate*. https://slate.com/human-interest/2014/04/mcdonald-s-and-me-my-fight-to-end-gendered-happy-meal-toys.html.

Back, Les, Andy Bennett, Laura Desfor Edles, Margaret Gibson, David Inglis, Ronald Jacobs, and Ian Woodward. 2012. *Cultural Sociology: An Introduction*. Hoboken, NJ: Wiley-Blackwell.

Bagdikian, Ben. 2004. *The New Media Monopoly*, 20th ed. New York: Beacon Press.

Bai, X., T. McPhearson, H. Cleugh, H. Nagendra, X. Tong, T. Zhu, and Y. G. Zhu. 2017. "Linking Urbanization and the Environment: Conceptual and Empirical Advances." *Annual Review of Environment and Resources* 42: 215–240.

Baierl, Edgar. 2004. "Why Is Life Expectancy Longer for Women Than It Is for Men?" *Scientific American* 291(6): 120.

Bail, Christopher A. 2014. "The Cultural Environment: Measuring Culture with Big Data." *Theory and Society* 43: 465–482.

Bail, Christopher. 2008. "The Configuration of Symbolic Boundaries against Immigrants in Europe." *American Sociological Review* 73: 37–59.

Baiocchi, Gianpaolo. 2012. "The Power of Ambiguity: How Participatory Budgeting Travels 8(2): 1–12.8: Article 8.

Baker, D. P., and G. K. LeTendre. 2005. *National Differences, Global Similarities: World Culture and the Future of Schooling*. Stanford, CA: Stanford University Press.

Baker, C. Edwin. 2006. *Media Concentration and Democracy: Why Ownership Matters*. Cambridge: Cambridge University Press.

Baker, Houston, Jr. 1987. *Modernism and the Harlem Renaissance*. Chicago: University of Chicago Press.

Bakshy, E., S. Messing, and L. A. Adamic. 2015. "Exposure to Ideologically Diverse News and Opinion on Facebook." *Science* 348(6239): 1130–1132.

Baltzell, Digby E. 1958. *The Philadelphia Gentleman. The Making of a National Upper Class*. New York: Free Press.

Bandarage, Asoka. 2015, March 3. "Proselytism or a Global Ethic?" *Huffington Post*. https://www.huffingtonpost.com/asoka-bandarage/proselytism-or-a-global-e_b_6779640.html.

Banerjee, A., E. Duflo, M. Ghatak, and J. Lafortune. 2013. "Marry for What? Caste and Mate Selection in Modern India." *American Economic Journal: Microeconomics* 5(2), 33–72.

Bank, Andre, Christiane Froehlich, and Andrea Schneiker. 2016. "The Political Dynamics of Human Mobility: Migration out of, as and into Violence" *Global Policy* 8. https://onlinelibrary.wiley.com/doi/full/10.1111/1758-5899.12384.

Banks, Ann. 2008, January 14. "Dirty Tricks, South Carolina, and John McCain." *The Nation*. https://www.thenation.com/article/dirty-tricks-south-carolina-and-john-mccain/.

Banks, James. 2010. "Regulating Hate Speech Online." *International Review of Law, Computers and Technology* 24(3): 233–239.

Bapna, Manish, and John Talbert. 2011, April 5. "Q&A: What Is a 'Green Economy?'" World Resources Institute. https://www.wri.org/blog/2011/04/qa-what-green-economy-0.

Barker, Martin, and Julian Petley, eds. 2001. *Ill Effects: The Media/Violence Debates*, 2nd ed. New York: Routledge.

Batalova, Jeanne. 2024, March 13. "Frequently Requested Statistics on Immigrants and Immigration in the United States.: *Migration Information Source*. Migration Policy Institute.

Bauman, Zygmunt. 2000. *Liquid Modernity*. Malden, MA: Polity Press.

Bauman, Zygmunt. 2002. *Society Under Siege*. Cambridge: Polity Press.

Bauman, Zygmunt. 2003. *Wasted Lives: Modernity and Its Outcasts*. Malden, MA: Polity Press.

Bauman, Zygmunt. 2004. *Wasted Lives: Modernity and Its Outcasts*. Indianapolis, IN: Wiley.

Baumeister, Roy, Katherine Vohs, Jennifer Aaker, and Emily Garbinsky. 2013. "Some Key Differences between a Happy Life and a Meaningful Life." *The Journal of Positive Psychology* 8: 505–516.

Baumgartner, Frank R., Jeffrey M. Berry, Marie Hojnacki, Beth L. Leech, and David C. Kimball. 2009. *Lobbying and Policy Change: Who Wins, Who Loses, and Why*. Chicago: University of Chicago Press.

Beal, Becky. 1995. "Disqualifying the Official: An Exploration of Social Resistance through the Subculture of Skateboarding." *Sociology of Sport Journal* 12: 252–267.

Beck, Ulrich. 2005. *Power in the Global Age: A New Global Political Economy*. Indianapolis, IN: Wiley.

Beck, Ulrich. 2006. *Cosmopolitan Vision*. Malden, MA: Polity.

Becker, Howard, S. 1963. *Outsiders. Studies in the Sociology of Deviance*. New York: Free Press.

Bedeley, R., D. Carbaugh, H. Chughtai, J. George, J. Gogan, S. Gordon, and A. Young. 2019. "Giving Voice to the Voiceless: The Use of Digital Technologies by Marginalized Groups." *Communications of the AIS*. https://aisel.aisnet.org/cais/vol45/iss1/2/.

Behal, M., and P. Soni. 2018. "Media Use and Materialism: A Comparative Study of Impact of Television Exposure and Internet Indulgence on Young Adults." *Management and Labour Studies* 43(4): 247–262. https://doi.org/10.1177/0258042X18791613.

Beisel, Nicola. 1998. *Imperiled Innocents: Anthony Comstock and Family Reproduction in Victorian America*. Princeton, NJ: Princeton University Press.

Bekhuis, Hidde, Marcel Lubbers, and Ultee Wout. 2014. "A Macro-sociological Study into the Changes in the Popularity of Domestic, European, and American Pop Music in Western Countries." *European Sociological Review* 30(2): 80–193.

Bell, Daniel A. 2015. *The China Model: Political Meritocracy and the Limits of Democracy*. Princeton, NJ: Princeton University Press.

Bell, Daniel. 1973. *The Coming of Post-industrial Society. A Venture in Social Forecasting*. New York: Basic Books.

Bell, Ruth, and Clifford Russell. 2002. "Environmental Policy for Developing Countries." *Issues in Science and Technology* 18. http://issues.org/18-3/greenspan/.

Bem, S. L. 1974. "The Measurement of Psychological Androgyny." *Journal of Consulting and Clinical Psychology* 42: 155–162.

Benavot, Aaron, Yun-Kyun Cha, David Kamens, John W. Meyer, and Suk-Ying Wong. 1991. "Knowledge for the Masses: World Models and National Curricula: 1920–1987." *American Sociological Review* 56: 85–100.

Bendell, Jem, ed. 2009. *The Corporate Responsibility Movement*. Greenleaf Publishing, Sheffield.

Bendix, Reinhard. 1964. *Nation-Building and Citizenship: Studies of Our Changing Social Order*. New York: Wiley.

Bennett, Tony, Mike Savage, Elizabeth Bortolaia Silva, Alan Warde, Modesto Gayo-Cal, and David Wright. 2009. *Culture, Class, Distinction*. New York: Routledge.

Bennett, W. Lance and Robert M. Entman. 2001. *Mediated Politics: Communication in the Future of Democracy*. Cambridge: Cambridge University Press.

Bennett, W. Lance, Regina G. Lawrence, and Steven Livingston. 2008. *When the Press Fails: Political Power and the News Media from Iraq to Katrina*. Chicago: University of Chicago Press.

Benson, Rodney, and Daniel C. Hallin. 2007. "How States, Markets and Globalization Shape the News: The French and US National Press, 1965–97." *European Journal of Communication* 22(1): 27–48. http://ejc.sagepub.com/content/22/1/27.

Benson, Rodney. 2009. "What Makes News More Multiperspectival? A Field Analysis." *Poetics* 37(5–6): 402–418.

Benson, Rodney. 2010. "Futures of the News." In *New Media, Old News: Journalism and Democracy in the Digital Age*, ed. N. Fenton. Thousand Oaks, CA: SAGE Publications.

Berg, Justin. 2012. "Opposition to Pro-immigrant Public Policy: Symbolic Racism and Group Threat." *Sociological Inquiry* 83: 1–31.

Berger, Peter, ed. 1999. *The Desecularization of the World*. Washington, DC: Eerdmans.

Berger, Peter. 1967. *The Sacred Canopy: Elements of a Sociological Theory of Religion*. New York: Penguin.

Berk, Ronald. 2005. "Survey of 12 Strategies to Measure Teaching Effectiveness," *International Journal of Teaching and Learning in Higher Education* 17: 48–62.

Berk, Sarah Fenstermaker. 1985. *The Gender Factory: The Apportionment of Work in American Households*. New York: Plenum.

Berman, Eli. 2009. *Radical, Religious, and Violent: The New Economics of Terrorism*. Cambridge, MA: MIT Press.

Berman, Elizabeth. 2012. *Creating the Market University: How Academic Science Became an Economic Engine*. Princeton, NJ: Princeton University Press.

Bernstein, Mary, and Renate Reimann. 2001. *Queer Families, Queer Politics*. New York: Columbia University Press.

Bertrand, Marianne, Claudia Goldin, and Lawrence F. Katz. 2010. "Dynamics of the Gender Gap for Young Professionals in the Financial and Corporate Sectors." *American Economic Journal: Applied Economics* 2 (3): 228–255.

Bertrand, Natasha. 2015. "'Fifty Shades of Grey' Started Out as 'Twilight' Fan Fiction before Becoming an International Phenomenon." *Business Insider*. http://www.businessinsider.com/fifty-shades-of-grey-started-out-as-twilight-fan-fiction-2015-2.

Berwick, Carly. 2015, November 3. "The Great German School Turnaround." *The Atlantic*. https://www.theatlantic.com/education/archive/2015/11/great-german-scool-turnaround/413806/.

Bhambra, Gurminder K. 2009. "Postcolonial Europe : Or, Understanding Europe in Times of the Post-Colonial." In *The SAGE Handbook of European Studies*, ed. C. Rumford (pp. 69–86). Los Angeles: SAGE.

Bhattarai, Abha, and Federica Cocco. 2024, May 27. What Does It Take to Buy a House? Increasingly, Mom and Dad. *Washington Post*. https://www.washingtonpost.com/business/2024/05/19/home-buyers-parents-help-housing-affordability/.

Bhutta, Neil, Andrew C. Chang, Lisa J. Dettling, and Joanne W. Hsu with assistance from Julia Hewitt. 2020, September 28. "Disparities in Wealth by Race and Ethnicity in the 2019 Survey of Consumer Finances." Federal Reserve Bank.,. https://www.federalreserve.gov/econres/notes/feds-notes/disparities-in-wealth-by-race-and-ethnicity-in-the-2019-survey-of-consumer-finances-20200928.htm.

Bhutta, Neil, Jesse Bricker, Andrew C. Chang, Lisa J. Dettling, Sarena Goodman, Joanne W. Hsu, Kevin B. Moore, Sarah Reber, Alice Henriques Volz, and Richard A. Windle, Kathy Bi, Jacqueline Blair, Julia Hewitt, and Dalton Ruh. 2020. Changes in U.S. Family Finances from 2016 to 2019: Evidence from the Survey of Consumer Finances Changes in U.S. Family Finances from 2016 to 2019: Evidence from the Survey of Consumer Finances. *Federal Reserve Bulletin* 106(5): 1–42. https://www.federalreserve.gov/publications/files/scf20.pdf Accessed January 5, 2021.

Bianchi, S., L. Subaiya, and J. Kahn. 1999. "The Gender Gap in the Economic Well-Being of Nonresident Fathers and Custodial Mothers." *Demography* 36: 195–203.

Bianchi, Suzanne M., Liana C. Sayer, Melissa A. Milkie, and John P. Robinson. 2012. "Housework: Who Did, Does or Will Do It, and How Much Does It Matter?, *Social Forces* 91(1): 55–63.

Bianchi, Tiago. 2023, September 20. "Advertising Revenue of Google from 2001 to 2022." *Statista*. https://www.statista.com/statistics/266249/advertising-revenue-of-google/#:~:text=In%202022%2C%20Google's%20ad%20revenue,and%20apps)%20to%20web%20users.

Bibbins-Domingo, K., and A. Fernandez. 2007. "BiDil for Heart Failure in Black Patients: Implications of the U.S. Food and Drug Administration Approval." *Annals of Internal Medicine* 146(1): 52–56.

Biblarz, Timothy J., and Evren Savci. 2010. "Lesbian, Gay, Bisexual, and Transgender Families." *Journal of Marriage and Family* 72(3): 480–497. http://www.jstor.org/stable/40732492.

Bidadanure, J. 2019. "The Political Theory of Universal Basic Income." *Annual Review of Political Science* 22(1): 481–501.

Bidwell, Allie. 2014, February 5. "STEM Job Market Much Larger Than Previously Reported." U.S. News & World Report. https://www.usnews.com/news/stem-solutions/articles/2014/02/05/report-stem-job-market-much-larger-than-previously-reported.

Birchall, Elaine, and Suzanne Cronkwright. 2020, April 7. "Dealing with Hoarding Disorder during a Pandemic. Are there positives we can take away from current times?" *Psychology Today*. https://www.psychologytoday.com/us/blog/conquer-the-clutter/202004/dealing-hoarding-disorder-during-pandemic

Bittman, M., P. England, L. Sayer, N. Folbre, and G. Matheson. 2003. "When Does Gender Trump Money? Bargaining and Time in Household Work." *American Journal of Sociology* 109: 186–214.

Black Lives Matter. https://blacklivesmatter.com/about/ Accessed November 30, 2020.

Black, Sandra E., and Paul J. Devereux. 2011. "Recent Developments in Intergenerational Mobility." In *Handbook of Labor Economics*, Vol. 4B, eds. Orley Ashenfelter and David Card (pp. 1487–1541). Amsterdam: North Holland.

Black, Sandra, Paul Devereux, and Kjell Salvanes. 2005. "The More the Merrier? The Effects of Family Size and Birth Order on Children's Education." *The Quarterly Journal of Economics* 120(2): 669–700.

Blau, Francine D., and Lawrence M. Kahn. 2017. "The Gender Wage Gap: Extent, Trends, and Explanations." *Journal of Economic Literature* 55(3), 789–865.

Blau, Peter, and Otis Dudley Duncan 1967. *The American Occupational Structure*. New York: Wiley.

Bloemraad, I., and M. Wright. 2014. "'Utter Failure' or Unity out of Diversity? Debating and Evaluating Policies of Multiculturalism." *International Migration Review* 48(S1): S292–S334.

Blossfeld, Hans-Peter. 1986. "Career Opportunities in the Federal Republic of Germany: A Dynamic Approach to the Study of Life Course, Cohort, and Period Effects." *European Sociological Review* 2: 208–225.

Blum, Ben. 2018. "The Lifespan of a Lie." *Medium*. https://medium.com/s/trustissues/the-lifespan-of-a-lie-d869212b1f62.

Blumberg, Rae, ed. 1991. *Gender, Family, and Economy: The Triple Overlap*. Newbury Park, CA: SAGE.

Blumer, Herbert. 1968. *Symbolic Interactionism: Perspective and Method*. Berkeley, CA: University of California Press.

Blundell, R., M. Costa Dias, J. Cribb, R. Joyce, T. Waters, T. Wernham, and X. Xu. 2022. "Inequality and the COVID-19 Crisis in the United Kingdom." *Annual Review of Economics* 14: 607–636.

Bobo, Lawrence, and Camille L. Zubrinsky. 1996. "Attitudes on Residential Integration: Perceived Status Differences, Mere In-Group Preference, or Racial Prejudice?" *Social Forces* 74(3): 883–909. doi:10.2307/2580385.

Bockerman, Petri, and Pekka Ilmakunnas. 2012. "The Job Satisfaction–Productivity Nexus: A Study Using Matched Survey and Register Data." *Industrial & Labor Relations Review* 65: 244–262.

Boczkowski, Pablo. 2010. *News at Work: Imitation in an Age of Information Abundance*. Chicago: University of Chicago Press.

Boli, John, Francisco Ramirez, and John Meyer. 1985. "Explaining the Origins and Expansion of Mass Education." *Comparative Education Review* 29: 145–170.

Bond, Paul. 2016, February 29. "Leslie Moonves on Donald Trump: 'It May Not Be Good for America, but It's Damn Good for CBS.'" *Hollywood Reporter*.

Bonilla-Silva, Eduardo [2003] 2018. *Racism without Racists: Color-Blind Racism and the Persistence of Inequality in America*. Lanham, MD: Rowman and Littlefield.

Bonin, H., and N. Valério. 2016. *Colonial and Imperial Banking History*. London and New York: Taylor & Francis Group.

Bookman, Sonia. 2016. "Cultural Sociology: Brands." In *Sage Handbook of Cultural Sociology*, ed. D. Inglis and A. Almila (pp. 578–589). Thousand Oaks, CA: Sage.

Boorstin, Daniel J. 1961. *The Image: A Guide to Pseudo-events in America*. New York: Vintage.

Borkum, Jared. 2016, June 9. "Local Content Quotas on TV Are Global—They Just Don't Work Everywhere." The Conversation. https://theconversation.com/local-content-quotas-on-tv-are-global-they-just-dont-work-everywhere-60656.

Borowczyk-Martins, D., and E. Lalé. 2020. "The Ins and Outs of Involuntary Part-Time Employment." *Labour Economics* 67: 101940.

Bourdieu, Pierre, and Jean Claude Passeron. 1979. *The Inheritors: French Students and Their Relation to Culture*. Chicago: University of Chicago Press.

Bourdieu, Pierre, and Jean Claude Passeron. 1990. *Reproduction in Education, Society and Culture*. Newbury Park, CA: SAGE.

Bourdieu, Pierre. 1984. *Distinction: A Social Critique of the Judgement of Taste*. Cambridge, MA: Harvard University Press.

Bourdieu, Pierre. 1986. "The forms of capital." In *Handbook of Theory and Research for the Sociology of Education*, ed. J. Richardson (pp. 241–258). Westport, CT: Greenwood.

Bourdieu, Pierre. 1998. *The State Nobility: Elite Schools in the Field of Power*. Stanford, CA: Stanford University Press.

Bourdieu, Pierre. 2000. *The Weight of the World. Social Suffering in Contemporary Society*. Stanford, CA: Stanford University Press.

Bourdieu, Pierre. 2010. *Sociology Is a Martial Art: Political Writings by Pierre Bourdieu*. New York: New Press.

Bowles, Samuel, Herbert Gintis, and Melissa Groves, eds. 2008. *Unequal Chances: Family Background and Economic Success*. Princeton, NJ: Princeton University Press.

Bowman, Karlyn. 2017, January 13. "Interracial Marriage: Changing Laws, Minds, and Hearts," *Forbes*. https://www.forbes.com/sites/bowmanmarsico/2017/01/13/interracial-marriage-changing-laws-minds-and-hearts/#ecd5ee67c597.

boyd, dana. 2018. "Media Manipulation, Strategic Amplification, and Responsible Journalism." Presentation at the Online News Association conference, Austin, Texas.

Bozdag, E., and J. Van Den Hoven. 2015. "Breaking the Filter Bubble: Democracy and Design." *Ethics and Information Technology* 17: 249–265.

Bozick, Robert. 2009. "Job Opportunities, Economic Resources, and the Postsecondary Destinations of American Youth." *Demography* 46: 493–512.

Brake, Mike. 2013. *The Sociology of Youth Culture and Youth Subcultures: Sex and Drugs and Rock "n" Roll*. New York: Routledge.

Brattain, Michelle. 2007, December. "Race, Racism, and Antiracism: UNESCO and the Politics of Presenting Science to the Postwar Public." *The American Historical Review* 112(5): 1386–1413. https://doi.org/10.1086/ahr.112.5.1386.

Breen, Richard, and Jan O. Jonsson. 2005. "Inequality of Opportunity in Comparative Perspective: Recent Research on Educational Attainment and Social Mobility." *Annual Review of Sociology* 31: 223–243.

Brenan, Megan. 2019. "Women Still Handle Main Household Tasks in U.S." Gallup *Politics*. https://news.gallup.com/poll/283979/women-handle-main-household-tasks.aspx#:~:text=Although%20mothers%20are%20more%20likely,parent's%20employment%20situation%20and%20earnings.

Brenan, Megan. 2020. *Women Still Handle Main Household Tasks in U.S*. Gallup Politics.

Brenner, Philip. 2016. "Cross-National Trends in Religious Service Attendance," *Public Opinion Quarterly* 80: 563–583.

Brooks, Arthur. 2003. "Religious Faith and Charitable Giving." *Policy Review* 121: 39–48.

Brooks, Clem. 2014. "Introduction: Voting Behavior and Elections in Context." *The Sociological Quarterly* 55: 587–595.

Brooks, Roy L. 1994. "Critical Race Theory: A Proposed Structure and Application to Federal Pleading." *Harvard BlackLetter Law Journal* 11: 85–113.

Brown, B. B., and J. Larson. 2009. "Peer Relationships in Adolescence." In *Handbook of Adolescent Psychology*, ed. R. M. Lerner and L. Steinberg (pp. 74–103). Hoboken, NJ: John Wiley and Sons.

Brown, Sarah. 2023, April 11. "*Report Sums Up Bolsonaro's Destruction Legacy and Amazon's Next Critical Steps*." *Mongabay*. https://news.mongabay.com/2023/04/report-sums-up-bolsonaros-destruction-legacy-and-amazons-next-critical-steps/.

Brown, Simon. 2015. "Crowdsourcing Social Research." Technology Research Stream. Social Science Matrix. University of California, Berkeley. http://matrix.berkeley.edu/research/crowdsourcing-social-research.

Brubaker, Rogers. 1992. *Citizenship and Nationhood in France and Germany*. Cambridge, MA: Harvard University Press.

Bruce, Steve, and David Voas. 2023. "Secularization Vindicated." *Religions* 14(3): 301. https://doi.org/10.3390/rel14030301.

Brulle, Robert. 2010. "From Environmental Campaigns to Advancing the Public Dialog: Environmental Communication for Civic Engagement." *Environmental Communication* 4: 82–98.

Bryc, Katarzyna, Eric Y. Durand, J. Michael Macpherson, David Reich, and Joanna L. Mountain. 2015. "The Genetic Ancestry of African Americans, Latinos, and European Americans across the United States." *The American Journal of Human Genetics* 96(1): 37–53.

Buchanan, Larry, Quoctrung Bui, and Jugal Patel. 2020, July 3. "Black Lives Matter May Be the Largest Movement in US History." *New York Time*. https://www.nytimes.com/interactive/2020/07/03/us/george-floyd-protests-crowd-size.html.

Buckles, Kasey, and Elizabeth Munnich. 2012, Summer. "Birth Spacing and Sibling Outcomes." *Journal of Human Resources* 47(3): 613–642.

Budig, Michelle, and Paula England. 2001. "The Wage Penalty for Motherhood," *American Sociological Review* 66: 204–225.

Budiman, Abby, and Neil Ruiz. 2021, April 29. "*Key Facts About Asian Americans, a Diverse and Growing Population*." Pew Research Center. https://www.pewresearch.org/short-reads/2021/04/29/key-facts-about-asian-americans/.

Budman, Matthew, Blythe Hurley, Narita Gangopadhyay, and Anya Tharakan. 2020. "Talent and Workforce Effects in the Age of AI." *Deloitte Insights*. https://www2.deloitte.com/content/dam/insights/us/articles/6546_talent-and-workforce-effects-in-the-age-of-ai/DI_Talent-and-workforce-effects-in-the-age-of-AI.pdf.

Bunker, S. G., and P. Ciccantell. 2004. *Globalization and the Race for Resources*. Baltimore, MD: Johns Hopkins University Press.

Burawoy, Michael. 1998. "The Extended Case Method." *Sociological Theory* 16: 4–33.

Burawoy, Michael. 2005. "2004 American Sociological Association Presidential Address: For Public Sociology." *British Journal of Sociology* 56: 259–294.

Burdick, Kailee, Areeba Kara, Patricia Ebright, and Julie Meek. 2017. "Bedside Interprofessional Rounding. The View from the Patient's Side of the Bed." *Journal of Patient Experience* 4(1): 22–27.

Bureau of Labor Statistics, U.S. Department of Labor. 2020, September 1. "Employment by Major Occupational Group.",https://www.bls.gov/emp/tables/emp-by-major-occupational-group.htm.

Bureau of Labor Statistics, U.S. Department of Labor. 2021, April. "April 2021, Report 1092." *Women in the Labor Force: A Databook*. https://fraser.stlouisfed.org/title/307#624705.

Burgason, K. A., O. Sefiha, and L. Briggs. 2019. "Cheating Is in the Eye of the Beholder: An Evolving Understanding of Academic Misconduct." *Innovative Higher Education* 44: 203–218. https://doi.org/10.1007/s10755-019-9457-3.

Burning Glass. 2014, February. "Real-Time Insight into the Market for Entry-Level STEM Jobs." https://www.voced.edu.au/content/ngv%3A84336.

Burrows, Dan. 2023, February 27. "The 30 Best Stocks of the Past 30 Years." *Kiplinger Personal Finance*. https://www.kiplinger.com/investing/stocks/603777/30-best-stocks-of-the-past-30-years.

Burt, Martha, Laudan Aron, Edgar Lee, and Jesse Valente. 2001. *Helping America's Homeless: Emergency Shelter or Affordable Housing?* Washington, DC: Urban Institute Press.

Buscho, Ann Gold. 2019, December 18. "Understanding the Effects of High-Conflict Divorce on Kids." *Psychology Today*. https://www.psychologytoday.com/ca/blog/better-divorce/201912/understanding-the-effects-high-conflict-divorce-kids.

Butler, J. 2006. *Gender Trouble: Feminism and the Subversion of Identity*. New York: Routledge.

Cahalan, Margaret W., Laura W. Perna, Marisha Addison, Chelsea Murray, Pooja R. Patel, and Nathan Jiang. 2020. *Indicators of Higher Education Equity in the United States: 2020 Historical Trend Report*. Washington, DC: The Pell Institute for the Study of Opportunity in Higher Education, Council for Opportunity in Education (COE), and Alliance for Higher Education and Democracy of the University of Pennsylvania (PennAHEAD). http://pellinstitute.org/downloads/publications-Indicators_of_Higher_Education_Equity_in_the_US_2020_Historical_Trend_Report.pdf.

Caiola, C., S. Docherty, M. Relf, and J. Barroso. 2014. "Using an Intersectional Approach To Study the Impact of Social Determinants of Health for African-American Mothers Living with HIV." *Advances in Nursing Science* 37(4): 287–298.

Calhoun, Craig. 1988. "Populist Politics, Communications Media and Large-Scale Societal Integration." *Sociological Theory* 6(2): 219–241. https://doi.org/10.2307/202117.

Calhoun, Craig. 1992. "The Infrastructure of Modernity: Indirect Social Relationships, Information Technology, and Social Integration." *Social Change and Modernity*: 205–236.

Camacho, Keith L. 2016. "Filipinos, Pacific Islanders, and the American Empire." In *The Oxford Handbook of Asian American History*, eds. David K. Yoo and Eiichiro Azuma (pp. 13–29). New York: Oxford University Press. http://www.oxfordhandbooks.com/view/10.1093/oxfordhb/9780199860463.001.0001/oxfordhb-9780199860463-e-8.

Campbell, Don. 1997. *The Mozart Effect: Tapping the Power of Music to Heal the Body, Strengthen the Mind, and Unlock the Creative Spirit*. New York: Avon Books.

Campbell, Don. 2000. *Mozart Effect for Children: Awakening Your Child's Mind, Health & Creativity with Music*. New York: William Morrow.

Cara Brennan Allamano. 2020. *Paid Paternity Leave Should Be the Norm in the US*. World Economic Forum Blog.

Carleton, Cheryl. 2014, February 13. "Why We Pay Teachers, Secretaries, and Home Health Aides So Little." *Business Insider*. https://www.businessinsider.com/low-pay-caring-industry-2014-2.

Carney, Stephen, Jeremy Rappleye, and Iveta Silova. 2012. "Between Faith and Science: World Culture Theory and Comparative Education." *Comparative Education Review* 56: 336–393.

Carrington, Daisy. 2013, June 3. "Iran Tightens Grip on Cyberspace with 'Halal Internet.'" CNN. http://www.cnn.com/2013/06/03/world/meast/iran-internet-restrictions-halal-internet/index.html.

Carson, E. Ann, and Daniela Golinelli. 2013, December. "Prisoners in 2012." Bureau of Justice Statistics. http://www.bjs.gov/content/pub/pdf/p12tar9112.pdf.

Carver, Lisa F., Afshin Vafaei, Ricardo Guerra, Aline Freire, and Susan P. Phillips. 2013. "Gender Differences: Examination of the 12-item Bem Sex Role Inventory (BSRI-12) in an Older Brazilian Population." *Plos ONE* 8: e76356. https://journals.plos.org/plosone/article?id=10.1371/journal.pone.0076356.

Casanova, Jose, 1994. *Public Religions in the Modern World*. Chicago: University of Chicago Press.

Cashin, S. 2005. *The Failures of Integration: How Race and Class Are Undermining the American Dream*. New York: Public Affairs.

Casserley, Meghan. 2012, December 10. "The 10 Skills That will Get You Hired in 2013." *Forbes*. https://www.forbes.com/sites/meghancasserly/2012/12/10/the-10-skills-that-will-get-you-a-job-in-2013/.

Castells, Manuel. 1999. *The Information Age*. New York: Blackwell Press.

Cavanagh, S. E., and P. Fomby. 2019. "Family Instability in the Lives of American Children." *Annual Review of Sociology* 45: 493–513. https://doi.org/10.1146/annurev-soc-073018-022633.

Center for Constitutional Rights. 2009. "Racial Disparity in NYPD Stops-and-Frisks: The Center for Constitutional Rights Preliminary Report on UF-250 Data from 2005 through June 2008." https://ccrjustice.org/sites/default/files/assets/Report-CCR-NYPD-Stop-and-Frisk_3.pdf.

Center for Responsive Politics. n.d. "Lobbying Database." https://www.opensecrets.org/lobby.

Centers for Disease Control and Prevention. 2013, December. "U.S. Public Study Health Service Syphilis Study at Tuskegee." http://www.cdc.gov/tuskegee/index.html.

Centers for Disease Control. 2019a. "Measles Cases and Outbreaks." https://www.cdc.gov/measles/cases-outbreaks.html.

Centers for Disease Control. 2019b. "Pertussis (Whooping Cough). Surveillance and Reporting" Trends. https://www.cdc.gov/pertussis/php/surveillance/index.html.

Chahal, K. 2016. "Hate in a Digital World." In *Supporting Victims of Hate Crime* (pp. 19–28). Bristol, UK: Policy Press.

Chahal, Sunil. 2023. "Navigating Financial Evolution: Business Process Optimization and Digital Transformation in the Finance Sector." *International Journal of Finance* 8(5): 67–81.

Champagne, Duane. 2008. "From First Nations to Self-Government: A Political Legacy of Indigenous Nations in the United States." Special Issue on Indigenous Peoples: Struggles Against Globalization and Domination, eds. James V. Fenelon and Salvador J. Murguia. *American Behavioral Scientist* 51(13): 1672–1693.

Chandralal, Lalith, and Fredy-Roberto Valenzuela, 2013. "Exploring Memorable Tourism Experiences: Antecedents and Behavioral Outcomes." *Journal of Economics, Business and Management* 1: 177–181.

Chase-Dunn, Christopher, Yukio Kawano, and Benjamin Brewer. 2000. "Trade Globalization since 1795: Waves of Integration in the World-System." *American Sociological Review* 65: 77–95.

Chatterjee, Rhitu. 2018, February 21. "A New Survey Finds 81 Percent of Women Have Experienced Sexual Harassment." *The Two-Way*. National Public Radio. https://www.npr.org/sections/thetwo-way/2018/02/21/587671849/a-new-survey-finds-eighty-percent-of-women-have-experienced-sexual-harassment.

Chaves, Mark, and Alison J. Eagle. 2016. "Congregations and Social Services: An Update from the Third Wave of the National Congregations Study." *Religions* 7: 55.

Chaves, Mark. 1994. "Secularization as Declining Religious Authority." *Social Forces* 72(3): 749–774. doi:10.2307/2579779.

Chaves, Mark. 2017. *American Religion: Contemporary Trends*. Princeton, NJ: Princeton University Press.

Chen, Feinian. 2009. "Family Division in China's Transitional Economy." *Population Studies* 63: 53–69.

Cheng, Simon, and Brian Powell. 2015. "Measurement, Methods, and Divergent Patterns: Reassessing the Effects of Same-Sex Parents." *Social Science Research* 52: 615–626.

Cherlin, Andrew, and Frank F. Furstenberg, Jr. 1988. "The Changing European Family: Lessons for the American Reader." *Journal of Family Issues* 9(3): 291–297. doi:10.1177/019251388009003001.

Chetty, Raj, John N. Friedman, Emmanuel Saez, Nicholas Turner, and Danny Yagan. 2017. "Mobility Report Cards: The Role of Colleges in Intergenerational Mobility." National Bureau Of Economic Research. Working Paper 23618 http://www.nber.org/papers/w23618

Childs, Dennis. 2015. *Slaves of the State: Black Incarceration from the Chain Gang to the Penitentiary*. Minneapolis: University of Minnesota Press.

Childs, Erica. 2009. *Fade to Black and White: Interracial Images in Popular Culture*. Lanham, MD: Rowman and Littlefield.

Childs, Erica. 2005. *Navigating Interracial Borders: Black–White Couples and their Social Worlds*. New Brunswick, NJ: Rutgers University Press.

Chin, Christine B. N. 2013. *Cosmopolitan Sex Workers: Women and Migration in a Global City*. New York: Oxford University Press.

Chin, J., M. S. Senter, and R. Spalter-Roth. 2011. "Love to Teach, but Hate Assessment?" *Teaching Sociology* 39(2): 120–126. https://doi.org/10.1177/0092055X11401562.

Chomsky, Noam. 2006. *Language and Mind*. New York: Cambridge University Press.

Choo, Hae Yeon, and Myra Marx Ferree. 2010. "Practicing Intersectionality in Sociological Research: A Critical Analysis of Inclusions, Interactions, and Institutions in the Study of Inequalities." *Sociological Theory* 28(3): 129–149.

Chou, Rosalind S., and Joe R. Feagin. 2008. *Myth of the Model Minority: Asian Americans Facing Racism*, 2nd ed. Boulder, CO: Paradigm Publishers.

Chugh, Abhinav. 2021, November 29. "What Is 'The Great Resignation'? An Expert Explains." *World Economic Forum*. https://www.weforum.org/agenda/2021/11/what-is-the-great-resignation-and-what-can-we-learn-from-it/.

Chung, Angie. 2007. *Legacies of Struggle: Conflict and Cooperation in Korean-American Politics*. Stanford, CA: Stanford University Press.

Cimpian, Joseph, Take Kim, and Zachary McDermott, 2020. "Understanding Persistent Gender Gaps in STEM." *Science* 368, 4697: 1317–1319. DOI: 10.1126/science.aba7377.

Cislak, A., M. Formanowicz, and T. Saguy. 2018. Bias against Research on Gender Bias. *Scientometrics* 115, 189–200.

Cislak, A., M. Formanowicz, and T. Saguy. 2018. "Bias against Research on Gender Bias." *Scientometrics* 115: 189–200.

Clark, Barry. 2016. *Political Economy: A Comparative Approach*, 3rd ed. New York: Praeger.

Clark, R., and R. Filinson. 2011. "Kicking and Screaming: How One Truculent Sociology Department Made Peace with Mandatory Assessment." *Teaching Sociology* 39(2): 127–137. https://doi.org/10.1177/0092055X11400439.

Clarke, Matt. 2013, January. "Dramatic Increase in Percentage of Criminal Cases Being Plea Bargained." *Prison News*, p. 20. https://www.prisonlegalnews.org/news/2013/jan/15/dramatic-increase-in-percentage-of-criminal-cases-being-plea-bargained.

Clear, Todd. 1994. *Harm in American Penology: Offenders, Victims, and Their Communities*. Albany, NY: State University of New York Press.

Cohen, Cathy J., and Sarah J. Jackson. 2016. "Ask a Feminist: A Conversation with Cathy Cohen on Black Lives Matter, Feminism, and Contemporary Activism." *Signs* 41(4): 775–792. http://signsjournal.org/ask-a-feminist-cohen-jackson.

Cohen, Philip. 2014. *The Family: Diversity, Inequality, and Social Change*. New York: W. W. Norton.

Cohen, Raina. 2016, September 7. "What Programming's Past Reveals about Today's Gender-Pay Gap." *Atlantic*.

Cohen, Stanley. 2002. *Folk Devils and Moral Panics: The Creation of the Mods and Rockers*. New York: Routledge.

Colburn, Gregg, and Clayton Page Aldern. 2022. *Homelessness Is a Housing Problem: How Structural Factors Explain U.S. Patterns*. Berkeley, CA: University of California Press.

Coleman, M., M. A. Fine, L. H. Ganong, K. J. M. Downs, and N. Pauk. 2001. "When You're Not the Brady Bunch: Identifying Perceived Conflicts and Resolution Strategies in Stepfamilies." *Personal Relationships* 8: 55–73.

Colley, A., G. Mulhern, J. Maltby, and A. M. Wood. 2009. "The Short Form BSRI: Instrumentality, Expressiveness and Gender Associations among a United Kingdom Sample." *Personality and Individual Differences* 46: 384–387.

Collins, Patricia Hill. 1990. "Black Feminist Thought in the Matrix of Domination." In *Black Feminist Thought: Knowledge, Consciousness, and the Politics of Empowerment* (pp. 221–238). Boston: Unwin Hyman.

Collins, Randall. 2011. "Credential Inflation and the Future of Universities." *Italian Journal of Sociology of Education* 2: 228–251.

Colomer, Josep. 2016, December 11. "The Electoral College Is a Medieval Relic. Only the US Still Has One." *Washington Post*. https://www.washingtonpost.com/news/monkey-cage/wp/2016/12/11/the-electoral-college-is-a-medieval-relic-only-the-u-s-still-has-one/?noredirect=on&utm_term=.14d6f2affdb5.

Conk, M. A. 1978. "Occupational Classification in the United States Census: 1870–1940." *The Journal of Interdisciplinary History* 9(1): 111–130.

Conk, M. A. 1989. "Accuracy and Efficiency and Bias: The Interpretation of Women's Work in the U.S. Census of Occupations, 1890–1940." *Historical Methods* 14(2), 65–72.

Conley, Dalton. 2005. *The Pecking Order: Which Siblings Succeed and Why*. New York: Pantheon Books.

Conley, Dalton. 2001. "Capital for College: Parental Assets and Postsecondary Schooling." *Sociology of Education* 74: 59–72.

Connell, R. W. 1987. *Gender and Power: Society, the Person and Sexual Politics*. Stanford, CA: Stanford University Press.

Connell, Raewyn. 1995. *Masculinities*. Berkeley: University of California Press.

Conrad, Peter, and Joseph W. Schneider. 1992. *Deviance and Medicalization: From Badness to Sickness*. Philadelphia: Temple University Press.

Conrad, Peter. 1975. "The Discovery of Hyperkinesis: Notes on the Medicalization of Deviant Behavior." *Social Problems* 23(1): 12–21.

Conrad, Peter. 2006. "Introduction to Expanded Edition." *Identifying Hyperactive Children: The Medicalization of Deviant Behavior, Expanded ed.* Aldershot, UK: Ashgate.

Conrad, Peter. 2007. *The Medicalization of Society: On the Transformation of Human Conditions into Treatable Disorders*. Baltimore: Johns Hopkins University Press.

Cook, John, Naomi Oreskes, Peter T. Doran, William R. L. Anderegg, Bart Verheggen, Ed W. Maibach, J. Stuart Carlton, Stephan Lewandowsky, Andrew G. Skuce, Sarah A Green, Dana Nuccitelli, Peter Jacobs, Mark Richardson, Bärbel Winkler, Rob Painting, and Ken Rice. 2016, April 13. "Consensus on Consensus:

A Synthesis of Consensus Estimates on Human-Caused Global Warming." *Environmental Research Letters* 11(4): 1–7. doi:10.1088/1748-9326/11/4/048002.

Cooley, Charles Horton. [1922] 2012. *Human Nature and the Social Order.* Lenox, MA: HardPress Publishing.

Copeland, Larry. 2014, October 8. "Life Expectancy in the USA Hits a Record High." *USA Today.* https://www.usatoday.com/story/news/nation/2014/10/08/us-life-expectancy-hits-record-high/16874039/.

Copen, C. E., K. Daniels, and W. D. Mosher. 2013. "First Premarital Cohabitation in the United States: 2006–2010 National Survey of Family Growth (National Health Statistics Reports, No. 64)." Hyattsville, MD: National Center for Health Statistics.

Cornwell, Erin, and Linda Waite. 2009. "Social Disconnectedness, Perceived Isolation, and Health among Adults." *Journal of Health and Social Behavior* 50: 31–48.

Corsaro, William. 2005. *The Sociology of Childhood*, 2nd ed. Newbury Park, CA: Pine Forge Press.

Costa, Daniel, and Ron Hira 2023, April 11. "Tech and Outsourcing Companies Continue to Exploit the H-1B Visa Program at a Time of Mass Layoffs." Economic Policy Institute Working Economics Blog.

Council, Stephen. 2023, July 24. "Google Software Engineer Got $605,000 Bonus, Plus More from Massive Salary Leak." *SFGate.* https://www.sfgate.com/tech/article/google-employee-pay-2022-leak-18257972.php.

Craig, S. L., and L. McInroy. 2014. "You Can Form a Part of Yourself Online: The Influence of New Media on Identity Development and Coming Out for LGBTQ Youth." *Journal of Gay & Lesbian Mental Health* 18(1): 95–109.

Crank, John. 2004. *Understanding Police Culture*, 2nd ed. New York: Routledge.

Credit Suisse. 2020. *The Global Wealth Report 2020.* https://www.credit-suisse.com/media/assets/corporate/docs/about-us/research/publications/global-wealth-report-2020-en.pdf

Credit Suisse. 2023. *The Global Wealth Report 2023.* https://www.ubs.com/global/en/family-office-uhnw/reports/global-wealth-report-2023/_jcr_content/pagehead/link2.0466322293.file/PS9jb250ZW50L2RhbS9hc3NldHMvd20vZ2xvYmFsL2ltZy9nbG9iYWwtZmFtaWx5LW9mZmljZS9kb2NzL2tiZ2JoYzEzZWFsdGgtcmVwb3J0LTIwMjMtZW4ucGRm/global-wealth-report-2023-en.pdf

Crenshaw, Kimberlé, Neil Gotanda, Garry Peller, and Kendall Thomas. 1996. *Critical Race Theory: The Key Writings That Formed the Movement.* New York: New Press.

Crenshaw, Kimberlé. 1989. "Demarginalizing the Intersection of Race and Sex: A Black Feminist Critique of Antidiscrimination Doctrine, Feminist Theory and Antiracist Politics," *University of Chicago Legal Forum* 1989(1), Article 8.

Crenshaw, Kimberlé. 2016. "The Urgency of Intersectionality." TEDWomen 2016. https://www.ted.com/talks/kimberle_crenshaw_the_urgency_of_intersectionality.

Crimmins, Eileen M., Mark D. Hayward, and Teresa E. Seeman. 2004. "Race/Ethnicity, Socioeconomic Status, and Health in Critical Perspectives on Racial and Ethnic Differences in Health in Late Life." In *Panel on Race, Ethnicity, and Health in Later Life,* ed. N. B. Anderson, R. A. Bulatao, and B. Cohen (pp. 310–352). Washington, DC: National Academies Press.

Crockett, Jason L., Albert S. Fu, Joleen L. Greenwood, and Mauricia A. John. 2018. "Integrated Sociology Program Assessment: Inclusion of a Senior Portfolio Graduation Requirement." *Teaching Sociology* 46(1): 34–43. https://doi.org/10.1177/0092055X17726833.

Crowder, Kyle, and Liam Downey. 2010. "Inter-Neighborhood Migration, Race, and Environmental Hazards: Modeling Micro-Level Processes of Environmental Inequality." *American Journal of Sociology* 115: 1110–1149.

Csizmadia, Annamaria, and Annabelle L. Atkin. 2022. "Supporting Children and Youth in Multiracial Families in the United States: Racial-Ethnic Socialization and Familial Support of Multiracial Experiences." *Journal of Child and Family Studies* 31(3): 664–674.

Cuadra, M., Baruch, R., Lamas, A., Morales, M. E., Arredondo, A., and Ortega, D. 2024. "Normalizing Intersex Children through Genital Surgery: The Medical Perspective and the Experience Reported by Intersex Adults." *Sexualities* 27(3): 533–552.

Culver, Stephen. 2010. "Course Grades, Quality of Student Engagement, and Students' Evaluation of Instructor." *International Journal of Teaching and Learning in Higher Education* 22: 331–336.

Cunningham-Parmeter, K. 2016. "From Amazon to Uber: Defining Employment in the Modern Economy." *Boston University Law Review* 96: 1673–1728.

Curry, Jennifer, Christopher Belser, and Ian Binns. 2013. "Integrating Postsecondary College and Career Options in the Middle Level Curriculum," *Middle School Journal* 44: 26–32.

Cyphers, Luke, and Ethan Trex. 2011, September 19. "The History of the National Anthem in Sports." *ESPN The Magazine*. http://espn.go.com/espn/story/_/id/6957582.

Damian, Rodica, and Brent Roberts. 2015. "Settling the Debate on Birth Order and Personality," *PNAS* 112(46): 14119–14120.

Danchin, P. G. 2008. "The Emergence and Structure of Religious Freedom in International Law Reconsidered." *Journal of Law and Religion* 23(2): 455–534.

Danielian, Lucig, and Stephen Reese. 1989. "A Closer Look at Intermedia Influences On Agenda Setting: The Cocaine Issue of 1986." In *Communication Campaigns about Drugs: Government, Media, and the Public* (pp. 47–66). Hillsdale, NJ: Erlbaum.

David, C. C., M. R. S. San Pascual, and M. E. S. Torres. 2019. "Reliance on Facebook for News and Its Influence on Political Engagement." *PLOS ONE* 14(3): e0212263. https://doi.org/10.1371/journal.pone.0212263.

Davidson, Adam. 2014, June 20. "It's Official: The Boomerang Kids Won't Leave." *New York Times*. https://www.nytimes.com/2014/06/22/magazine/its-official-the-boomerang-kids-wont-leave.html?_r=1.

Davis, Angela. 2001. *The Prison Industrial Complex* (audio CD). Chico, CA: AK Press.

Davis, David Brion. 2001. "Impact of the French and Haitian Revolutions." In *The Impact of the Haitian Revolution in the Atlantic World*, ed. D. Geggus (pp. 3–9). Columbia, SC: University of South Carolina Press.

Davis, Kingsley, and Wilbur E. Moore. 1945. "Some Principles of Stratification." *American Sociological Review* 10: 242–249.

Davoli, Maddalena, and Horst Entorf. 2018. "The PISA Shock, Socioeconomic Inequality, and School Reforms in Germany." IZA Policy Paper, No. 140, Institute of Labor Economics (IZA), Bonn.

Dayan, Daniel, and Elihu Katz. 1992. *Media Events: The Live Broadcasting of History*. Cambridge, MA: Harvard University Press.

De Graaf, N. D., P. De Graaf, and G. Kraaykamp. 2000. "Parental Cultural Capital and Educational Attainment in the Netherlands: A Refinement of the Cultural Capital Perspective." *Sociology of Education* 73: 92–111.

De La Rey, C. 2005. "Gender, Women and Leadership." *Agenda: Empowering Women for Gender Equity* 65: 4–11. http://www.jstor.org/stable/4066646.

De Nardi, M., E. French, J. Jones, and J. McCauley. 2016. "Medical Spending of the US Elderly." *Fiscal Studies* 37: 717–747.

de Vaus, D., M. Gray, L. Qu, and D. Stanton. 2017. "The Economic Consequences of Divorce in Six OECD Countries." *Australian Journal of Social Issues* 52: 180–199. doi: 10.1002/ajs4.13.

Dedehayir, O., and Steinert, M. 2016. "The Hype Cycle Model: A Review and Future Directions." *Technological Forecasting and Social Change* 108: 28–41.

Deegan, Mary Jo. 1990. "Review of The Chicago School: A Liberal Critique of Capitalism; Myths of the Chicago School of Sociology." *British Journal of Sociology* 41: 587–590.

Deegan, Mary Jo. 2007. "The Chicago School of Ethnography." In *Handbook of Ethnography* (pp. 11–25). Thousand Oaks, CA: SAGE.

Delmas, Magali, Jinghui Lim, and Nicholas Nairn-Birch. 2015. "Corporate Environmental Performance and Lobbying." *Academy of Management Discoveries* 2: 175–197.

Delmas, Magali. 2016, October 19. "Research: Who's Lobbying Congress on Climate Change." *Harvard Business Review*. https://hbr.org/2016/10/research-whos-lobbying-congress-on-climate-change.

Demarinis, S. 2020. "Loneliness at Epidemic Levels in America." *Explore* 16(5):278–279. https://www.sciencedirect.com/science/article/pii/S1550830720302159?via%3Dihub.

Demby, Gene. 2016, March 2. "Combing through 41 Million Tweets to Show How #BlackLivesMatter Exploded." *NPR Code Switch*. http://www.npr.org/sections/codeswitch/2016/03/02/468704888/combing-through-41-million-tweets-to-show-how-blacklivesmatter-explode.

Demerath, N. Jay III, and Yonghe Yang. 1997. "What American Culture War? A View from the Trenches as Opposed to the Command Posts and the Press Corps." In *Cultural Wars in American Politics* (pp. 17–38). Hawthorne, NY: Aldine de Gruyter.

Demleitner, N. V. 2022. "Criminal Disenfranchisement in State Constitutions: A Marker of Exclusion, Punitiveness, and Fragile Citizenship." *Lewis & Clark Law Review* 26: 531.

Derrick, J. L., S. Gabriel, and B. Tippin. 2008. Parasocial Relationships and Self-Discrepancies: Faux Relationships Have Benefits for Low Self-Esteem Individuals." *Personal Relationships* 15(2): 261–280.

Devers, Lindsay. 2011. "Plea and Charge Bargaining. Research Summary." Bureau of Justice Assistance, US Department of Justice. https://www.bja.gov/Publications/PleaBargainingResearchSummary.pdf.

Dewan, Shaila, and Robert Gebeloff. 2012, May 21. "More Men Enter Fields Dominated by Women." *New York Times*. https://www.nytimes.com/2012/05/21/business/increasingly-men-seek-success-in-jobs-dominated-by-women.html.

Dhaouadi, Mahmoud. 1990. "Ibn Khaldun: The Founding Father of Eastern Sociology." *International Sociology* 5: 319–335.

Diamond, Anna. 2016, November 17. "South Korea's Testing Fixation." *The Atlantic*. https://www.theatlantic.com/education/archive/2016/11/south-korean-seniors-have-been-preparing-for-today-since-kindergarten/508031/.

Diamond, Edwin, Martha Mckay, and Robert Silverman. 1993. "Pop Goes Politics: New Media, Interactive Formats, and the 1992 Presidential Campaign." *American Behavioral Scientist* 37(2): 257–261.

DiMaggio, Paul. 1982. "Cultural Capital and School Success: The Impact of Status Culture Participation on the Grades of US High School Students." *American Sociological Review* 47: 189–201.

Dimock, Michael, and Richard Wike. 2020, November 13. "America Is Exceptional in the Nature of Its Political Divide." *Fact Tank News in the Numbers*.,. https://www.pewresearch.org/fact-tank/2020/11/13/america-is-exceptional-in-the-nature-of-its-political-divide/.

Dobrow, S. R., Y. Ganzach, and Y. Liu. 2018. "Time and Job Satisfaction: A Longitudinal Study of the Differential Roles of Age and Tenure." *Journal of Management* 44(7): 2558–2579.

Doherty, Brian, and Timothy Doyle. 2006. "Beyond Borders: Transnational Politics, Social Movements, and Modern Environmentalisms." *Environmental Politics* 15: 697–612.

Domhoff, G. W. 2017. *Studying The Power Elite: Fifty Years of Who Rules America?* New York: Routledge.

Domhoff, G. William. 2013. *Who Rules America? The Triumph of the Corporate Rich*, 7th ed. New York: McGraw-Hill.

Donohue, J. M., and E. Miller. 2020. "COVID-19 and School Closures." *JAMA* 324(9):845–847. doi:10.1001/jama.2020.13092.

Dordick, Gwendolyn. 1997. *Something Left to Lose: Personal Relations and Survival among New York's Homeless*. Philadelphia: Temple University Press.

Dorn, Emma, Bryan Hancock, Jimmy Sarakatsannis, and Ellen Viruleg. 2020. "COVID-19 and Student Learning in the United States: The Hurt Could Last a Lifetime." *McKinsey & Company* 1: 1–9. https://www.childrensinstitute.net/sites/default/files/documents/COVID-19-and-student-learning-in-the-United-States_FINAL.pdf.

Doyle, Aaron, Randy Lippert, and David Lyon. 2012. *Eyes Everywhere: The Global Growth of Camera Surveillance*. New York: Routledge.

Drescher, J. 2015. "Out of DSM: Depathologizing Homosexuality." *Behavioral Sciences* 5(4), 565–575. http://doi.org/10.3390/bs5040565.

Drori, G. S., J. W. Meyer, F. O. Ramirez, and E. Schofer. 2003. *Science in the Modern World Polity*. Stanford, CA: Stanford University Press.

Drye, Willie. 2017, November 30. "2017 Hurricane Season Was the Most Expensive in US History." *National Geographic*. https://news.nationalgeographic.com/2017/11/2017-hurricane-season-most-expensive-us-history-spd/.

Du Bois, W. E. B. [1899] 1967. *The Philadelphia Negro: A Social Study*. New York: Schocken Books.

Du Bois, W. E. B. [1903] 1994. *The Souls of Black Folk*. New York: Dover Publications.

Du Bois, W. E. B. 1903. "The Talented Tenth." In *The Negro Problem: A Series of Articles by Representative American Negroes of Today*, ed. Booker T. Washington (pp. 31–75). New York: James Pott & Co.

Du Bois, W. E. B. 1935. *Black Reconstruction in America 1860–1880*. New York: Simon & Schuster.

Du Bois, W. E. B. 1947. *The World and Africa: An Inquiry into the Part Which Africa Has Played in World History*. New York: Viking.

Dunatchik, A., K. Gerson, J. Glass, J. A. Jacobs, and H. Stritzel. 2021. "Gender, Parenting, and The Rise of Remote Work During the Pandemic: Implications for Domestic Inequality in the United States." *Gender & Society* 35(2): 194–205. https://doi.org/10.1177/08912432211001301.

Duneier, Mitchell. 2000. *Sidewalk*. New York: Farrar, Straus and Giroux.

Dunlap, Riley E., and Aaron M. McCright. 2015. "Challenging Climate Change: The Denial Countermovement." In *Climate Change and Society: Sociological Perspectives (Report of the ASA Task Force on Sociology and Global Climate Change)*, eds. R. E. Dunlap and R. J. Brulle (pp. 300–332). New York: Oxford University Press.

Dunlap, Riley E., and Richard York. 2008. "The Globalization of Environmental Concern and the Limits of the PostMaterialist Explanation: Evidence from Four Cross-National Surveys." *Sociological Quarterly* 49: 529–563.

Durkheim, Émile. [1893] 2014. *The Division of Labour in Society*. New York: Free Press.

Durkheim, Émile. [1895] 2014. *The Rules of Sociological Method*. New York: Free Press.

Durkheim, Émile. 1961. *Moral Education*. New York: Free Press.

Durkheim, Émile. 2008. *The Elementary Forms of Religious Life*. Oxford, UK: Oxford University Press.

Durose, Matthew R., Erica L. Smith, and Patrick A. Langan. 2005. "*Contacts between Police and the Public, 2005.*" U.S. Department of Justice, Office of Justice Programs, Bureau of Justice Statistics Special Report. http://www.bjs.gov/content/pub/pdf/cpp05.pdf.

Duru, O. K., N. T. Harawa, D. Kermah, and K. C. Norris. 2012. "Allostatic Load Burden and Racial Disparities in Mortality." *Journal of the National Medical Association* 104(1–2): 89–95.

Duvall, Steven. 2021. "A Research Note: Number of Adults Who Homeschool Children Growing Rapidly." *Journal of School Choice* 15(2): 215–224. doi: 10.1080/15582159.2021.1912563.

Dyrbye, L. N., M. R. Thomas, and T. D. Shanafelt. 2005. "Medical Student Distress: Causes, Consequences, and Proposed Solutions." *Mayo Clinical Proceedings* 80: 1613–1622.

Dyrbye, L. N., C. P. West, D. Satele, S. Boone., L. Tan, J. Sloan, and T. D. Shanafelt. 2014. "Burnout Among U.S. Medical Students, Residents, and Early Career Physicians Relative to the General U.S. Population." *Academic Medicine* 89(3): 443–451. doi: 10.1097/ACM.0000000000000134.

Eagly, A. H., and B. T. Johnson. 1990. "Gender and Leadership Style: A Meta-analysis." *Psychological Bulletin* 108(2), 233–256. http://dx.doi.org/10.1037/0033-2909.108.2.233.

Ebadi, A., and A. Schiffauerova. 2015. "How to Receive More Funding for Your Research? Get Connected to the Right People!" *PLoS ONE* 10(7): e0133061. https://doi.org/10.1371/journal.pone.0133061.

Ecklund, Elaine, David Johnson, Christopher Scheitle, Kirstin Matthews, and Steven Lewis. 2016. "Religion among Scientists in Comparative Context: A New Study of Scientists in Eight Regions." *Socius* 2: 1–9. doi:10.1177/2378023116664353.

Edin, Kathryn, and Maria Kefalas. 2005. *Promises I Can Keep: Why Poor Women Put Motherhood before Marriage*. Berkeley: University of California Press.doi: 10.1080/10911350802427480.

Edin, Kathryn, Maria Kefalas, and Frank Furstenberg. 2011. *Promises I Can Keep: Why Poor Women Put Motherhood before Marriage*. University of California Press; Revised edition.

Edmonds-Poli, Emily, and David Shirk. 2012. *Contemporary Mexican Politics*. Lanham, MD: Rowman and Littlefield.

Einarsen, Stale, Helge Hoel, Dieter Zapf, and Cary Cooper, eds. 2003. *Bullying and Emotional Abuse in the Workplace: International Perspectives in Research and Practice*. New York: Taylor and Francis.

Elder, Glenn. 1998. *Children of the Great Depression*. Boulder, CO: Westview Press.

Eliasoph, Nina, and Jade Lo. 2012. "Broadening Cultural Sociology's Scope: Meaning-Making in Mundane Organizational Life." In *The Oxford Handbook of Cultural Sociology*, eds. Jeffrey Alexander, Philip Smith, and Ronald Jacobs (pp. 763–787). New York: Oxford University Press.

Elliott, Annabel Fenwick. 2014, July 8. "'Do You Wanna Be White?' Korean Skincare Brand Sparks Backlash by Posing Controversial Question on a Billboard in New York." *Daily Mail*. https://www.dailymail.co.uk/femail/article-2684956/Do-wanna-white-Korean-skincare-brand-sparks-backlash-posing-controversial-question-billboard-New-York.html.

Elliott, Larry. 2024. "World's Billionaires Should Pay Minimum 2% Wealth Tax, Say G20 Ministers," *The Guardian, April* 25, 2024.

Ellison, Christopher G., and Marc A. Musick. 1993. "Southern Intolerance: A Fundamentalist Effect?" *Social Forces* 72: 379–398.

Emerson, Michael, and David Hartman. 2006. "The Rise of Religious Fundamentalism," *Annual Review of Sociology* 32: 127–144.

Emery, Robert. 2009, March 18. "Joint Physical Custody." *Psychology Today*. https://www.psychologytoday.com/blog/divorced-children/200905/joint-physical-custody.

England, P. 2010. "The Gender Revolution: Uneven and Stalled." *Gender & Society* 24(2), 149–166.

Enss, C. 2005. *Hearts West: True Stories of Mail-Order Brides on the Frontier*, 1st ed. Guilford, CT: TwoDot Globe Pequot Press.

Environmental Protection Agency. 2016. "Climate Change Indicators: Global Greenhouse Gas Emissions." https://

www.epa.gov/climate-indicators/climate-change-indicators-global-greenhouse-gas-emissions.

Epstein, Cynthia Fuchs, and William Josiah Goode. 1971. *The Other Half: Roads to Women's Equality*. Upper Saddle River, NJ: Prentice-Hall.

Epstein, David. 2019. *Range: Why Generalists Triumph in a Specialized World*. New York: Riverhead Books.

Epstein, Nancy E. 2014. "Multidisciplinary In-Hospital Teams Improve Patient Outcomes: A Review." *Surgical Neurology International* 5(Suppl 7): S295–S303.

Equal Employment Opportunity Commission. 2024. "Harassment." https://www.eeoc.gov/laws/types/harassment.cfm.

*Equaldex*. 2024, July 10. "Legal Recognition of Non-Binary Gender." https://www.equaldex.com/issue/non-binary-gender-recognition.

Ericson, Richard V., and Kevin D. Haggerty. 2006. *The New Politics of Surveillance and Visibility*. Toronto: University of Toronto Press.

Eshbaugh-Soha, Matthew, and Jeffrey S. Peake. 2011. *Breaking through the Noise: Presidential Leadership, Public Opinion, and the News Media*. Stanford, CA: Stanford University Press.

Esposito, John, Darrell Fasching, and Todd Lewis. 2014. *World Religions Today*, 5th ed. New York: Oxford University Press.

Evans, John. 2011. "Epistemological and Moral Conflict between Religion and Science." *Journal for the Scientific Study of Religion* 50: 707–727. doi:10.1111/j.1468-5906.2011.01603.x.

Evjemo, L. D., T. Gjerstad, E. I. Grøtli, et al. 2020. "Trends in Smart Manufacturing: Role of Humans and Industrial Robots in Smart Factories." *Curr Robot Rep* 1: 35–41. https://doi.org/10.1007/s43154-020-00006-5.

Eyal, Gil. 2010. *The Autism Matrix*. Cambridge, MA: Polity.

Eyal, Gil. 2013. "For a Sociology of Expertise: The Social Origins of the Autism Epidemic." *American Journal of Sociology* 118(4): 863–907. doi:10.1086/668448.

Eyerman, Ron, and Andrew Jamison. 1998. *Music and Social Movements: Mobilizing Traditions in the Twentieth Century*. Cambridge, UK: Cambridge University Press.

Fahmy, Dalia. 2018, April 25. "Key Findings about Americans' Belief in God." Pew Research Center. https://www.pewresearch.org/short-reads/2018/04/25/key-findings-about-americans-belief-in-god/.

Faist, Thomas, and Eyüp Özveren. 2004. *Transnational Social Spaces: Agents, Networks, and Institutions*. Burlington, VT: Ashgate.

Faist, Thomas. 2000. "Transnationalization in International Migration: Implications for the Study of Citizenship and Culture." *Ethnic and Racial Studies* 23: 189–222.

Faludi, Susan. 2006. *Backlash: The Undeclared War against American Women*. New York: Three Rivers Press.

Fan, Victoria Y., Dean T Jamison, and Lawrence H Summers. 2018. "Pandemic Risk: How Large Are the Expected Losses?" *Bulletin of the World Health Organization* 96: 129–134.

Fanelli, D., and W. Glänzel. 2013. "Bibliometric Evidence for a Hierarchy of the Sciences." *PLoS ONE* 8(6): 49–50. https://journals.plos.org/plosone/article?id=10.1371/journal.pone.0066938.

Fang, Marina. 2013, August 5. "Public Schools Slash Arts Education and Turn to Private Funding." https://thinkprogress.org/public-schools-slash-arts-education-and-turn-to-private-funding-f16ff3b0bda5/#.6avz40f22.

Far, Tara Sephehri. 2023, June 26. "Unveiling Resistance: The Struggle for Women's Rights in Iran." *Human Rights Watch*. Accessed at https://www.hrw.org/news/2023/06/26/unveiling-resistance-struggle-womens-rights-iran.

Faragher, E. B., M. Cass, and C. L. Cooper. 2005. "The Relationship between Job Satisfaction and Health: A Meta-analysis." *Occupational and Environmental Medicine* 62: 105112.

Faris, R., and D. Felmlee. 2014. "Casualties of Social Combat: School Networks of Peer Victimization and Their Consequences." *American Sociological Review* 79(2): 228–257. https://doi.org/10.1177/0003122414524573.

Farrell, Justin. 2015. *The Battle for Yellowstone: Morality and the Sacred Roots of Environmental Conflict*. Princeton, NJ: Princeton University Press.

Fawaz, Leila. 2014. *A Land of Aching Hearts: The Middle East in the Great War*. Cambridge, MA: Harvard University Press.

Fazio, Marie. 2020. "Georgia Businessman Charged With Hoarding Face Masks and Price Gouging." New York: New York Times Company.

Feagin, J. R., and M. P. Sikes. 1994. *Living with Racism: The Black Middle-Class Experience*. Boston: Beacon.

Feathers, Todd. 2021, April 15. "Big Tech is Pushing States to Pass Privacy Laws, and Yes, You Should Be Suspicious." *The Markup*. https://themarkup.org/privacy/2021/04/15/big-tech-is-pushing-states-to-pass-privacy-laws-and-yes-you-should-be-suspicious.

Federal Interagency Forum on Child and Family Statistics. 2023. *America's Children: Key National Indicators of Well-Being, 2023*. Washington, DC: U.S. Government Printing Office.

Feldscher, Karen. 2017, July 11. "Increase in Pertussis Outbreaks Linked with Vaccine Exemptions, Waning Immunity." *Harvard T. H Chan School of Public Health News*. https://www.hsph.harvard.edu/news/features/increase-in-pertussis-outbreaks-linked-with-vaccine-exemptions-waning-immunity/.

Ferguson, Priscilla Parkhurst. 2014. *Word of Mouth: What We Talk about When We Talk about Food*. Berkeley, CA: University of California Press.

Fetner, T. 2016. "U.S. Attitudes Toward Lesbian and Gay People are Better than Ever." *Contexts* 15(2): 20–27.

Fingerhut, Hannah. 2016, May 12. "Support Steady for Same-Sex Marriage and Acceptance of Homosexuality." Pew Research Center.https://www.pewresearch.org/short-reads/2016/05/12/support-steady-for-same-sex-marriage-and-acceptance-of-homosexuality/

Finke, Roger, and Rodney Stark. 1998. "Religious Choice and Competition." *American Sociological Review* 63(5): 761–766. http://www.jstor.org/stable/2657339.

Finlayson, G. 2017. "Food Addiction and Obesity: Unnecessary Medicalization of Hedonic Overeating." *Nature Reviews Endocrinology* 13: 493–498.

Finley, Ashley. 2021. "How College Contributes to Workforce Success: Employer Views on What Matters Most." Association of American Colleges and Universities. https://files.eric.ed.gov/fulltext/ED616977.pdf.

Firebaugh, Glenn, and Laura Tach. 2012. "Income, Age, and Happiness in America." In *Trends in the United States, 1972–2006: Evidence from the General Social Survey*, ed. P. Marsden (pp. 267–287). Princeton, NJ: Princeton University Press.

Fischer, Claude S. 1975. "Toward a Subcultural Theory of Urbanism." *American Journal of Sociology* 80(6): 1319–1341.

Fisher, E., and Y. Mehozay. 2019. "How Algorithms See Their Audience: Media Epistemes and the Changing Conception of the Individual." *Media, Culture & Society* 41(8): 1176–1191.

Fisher, George. 2003. *Plea Bargaining's Triumph: A History of Plea Bargaining in America*. Stanford, CA: Stanford University Press.

Fitsilis, F. 2019. *Imposing Regulation on Advanced Algorithms*. Cham: Springer.

Flanagan, S., and A. R. Lee. 2003. "The New Politics, Culture Wars, and the Authoritarian-Libertarian Value Change in Advanced Industrial Democracies." *Comparative Political Studies* 26: 235–270.

Fletcher, P. 2016, November 30. "Native Advertising Will Provide a Quarter of News Media Revenue by 2018." *Forbes*. https://www.forbes.com/sites/paulfletcher/2016/11/30/native-advertising-will-provide-a-quarter-of-news-media-revenue-by-2018/#75950afa2d0c.

Flook, Lisa, Rena Repetti, and Jodie Ullman. 2005. "Classroom Social Experiences and Predictors of Academic Performance." *Developmental Psychology* 41: 319327.

Foley, Kristie, David Altman, Robert Durant, and Mark Wolfson. 2004. "Adults Approval and Adolescent Alcohol Use." *Journal of Adolescent Health* 35: 17–26.

Foner, Nancy, and Joanna Dreby. 2011. "Relations between the Generations in Immigrant Families." *Annual Review of Sociology* 37: 545–564.

Fong, Clara, Kelly Percival, and Thomas Wolf. 2023, March 7. "The Impact of Reforming Census Questions about Race and Ethnicity." Brennan Center for Justice.

Fontenot, Kayla, Jessica Semega, and Melissa Kollar. 2018, September. "Income and Poverty in the United States: 2017." Current Population Reports. https://www.census.gov/content/dam/Census/library/publications/2018/.../p60-263.pdf.

Food and Drug Administration. 2016, October 26. "Collection of Race and Ethnicity Data in Clinical Trials Guidance for Industry and Food and Drug Administration Staff." https://www.fda.gov/regulatory-information/search-fda-guidance-documents/collection-race-and-ethnicity-data-clinical-trials.

*Forbes*. 2019. "Largest Public Companies, 2019 rankings." *Forbes*. https://www.forbes.com/sites/sarahhansen/2019/05/15/americas-largest-public-companies-2019/

Ford, Steve. 2009, November 10. "US Nurses and Doctors at Loggerheads." *Nursing Times*. https://www.nursingtimes.net/news/hospital/us-nurses-and-doctors-at-loggerheads/5008121.article.

Forret, Monica L., and Thomas W. Dougherty. 2004. "Networking Behaviors and Career Outcomes: Differences for Men and Women." *Journal of Organizational Behavior* 25(3): 419–437.

Foucault, Michel. [1963] 1973. *The Birth of the Clinic*. London: Tavistock.

Foucault, Michel. [1977] 1995. *Discipline and Punish: The Birth of the Prison*. New York: Vintage Books.

Foucault, Michel. 1965. *Madness and Civilization*. New York: Bantam Books.

Foucault, Michel. 1988. *Madness and Civilization: A History of Insanity in the Age of Reason*. New York: Knopf Doubleday.

Fox, Jonathan. 2019. "A World Survey of Secular-Religious Competition: State Religious Policy from 1990 to 2014." *Religion, State & Society* 47(1): 10–29. doi: 10.1080/09637494.2018.1532750

Frank, D. J., and J. W. Meyer. 2007. "University Expansion and the Knowledge Society." *Theory & Society* 36: 287–311.

Frank, Thomas. 2004. *What's the Matter with Kansas? How Conservatives Won the Heart of America*. New York: Metropolitan Books.

Frankel, Fred. 1996. *Good Friends Are Hard to Find*. New York: Perspective Publishing.

Frankfurt, Harry. 1987. "Equality as a Moral Ideal." *Ethics* 98: 21–43.

Fraser, Nancy, and Rahael Jaeggi. 2018. *Capitalism: A Conversation in Critical Theory*. New York, Cambridge, MA: Polity.

Fraser, Nancy. 2013. *Fortunes of Feminism: From State-Managed Capitalism to Neoliberal Crisis*. New York: Verso.

Freeman, Gary P. 1995. "Modes of Immigration Politics in Liberal Democratic States." *The International Migration Review* 29(4): 881–902.

Freese, Jeremy, 2008. "Genetics and the Social Science Explanation of Individual Outcomes." *American Journal of Sociology* 114: S1–S35.

Freidson, Eliot. [1970] 1988. *Profession of Medicine: A Study of the Sociology of Applied Knowledge*. Chicago: University of Chicago Press.

Frey, C. B., and M. A. Osborne. 2017. "The Future of Employment: How Susceptible Are Jobs to Computerisation?" *Technological Forecasting and Social Change* 114: 254–280.

Frey, William H. 2018, December 17. "Black–White Segregation Edges Downward since 2000, Census Shows." Brookings Institution. https://www.brookings.edu/blog/the-avenue/2018/12/17/black-white-segregation-edges-downward-since-2000-census-shows/.

Frey, William H., and Zachary Zimmer. 1998, September. "Defining the City and Levels of Urbanization." PSC Research Report No. 98-423.

Fried, J. M., M. Vermillion, N. H. Parker, and S. Uijtdehaage. 2012. "Eradicating Medical Student Mistreatment: A Longitudinal Study of One Institution's Efforts." *Academic Medicine: Journal of the Association of American Medical Colleges* 87: 1191–1198.

Fried, SueEllen. 1998. *Bullies and Victims: Helping Your Children through the Schoolyard Battlefield*. Lanham, MD: M. Evans and Company.

Friedan, Betty. [1963] 2001. *The Feminine Mystique*. New York: W.W. Norton.

Friedland, Roger. 2001. "Religious Nationalism and the Problem of Collective Representation." *Annual Review of Sociology* 27: 125–152. http://www.jstor.org/stable/2678617.

Friedman, Lisa. 2020, April 7. "New Research Links Air Pollution to Higher Coronavirus Death Rates." *New York Times*. https://www.nytimes.com/2020/04/07/climate/air-pollution-coronavirus-covid.html.

Friedman, Thomas. 2005. *The World is Flat: A Brief History of the Twenty-First Century*. New York: Farrar, Strauss and Giroux.

Friedmann, Alex. 2012, January. "The Societal Impact of the Prison Industrial Complex, or Incarceration for Fun and Profit—Mostly Profit." *Prison Legal News* 23(1): 20–23.

Friedrich, Johannes, and Thomas Demassa. 2014, May 21. "The History of Carbon Dioxide Emissions." *World Resources Institute*. https://www.wri.org/insights/history-carbon-dioxide-emissions

Frueh, Sarah. 2020, July 9. "COVID-19 and Black Communities." The National Academies of Sciences, Engineering, Medicine. https://www.nationalacademies.org/news/2020/07/covid-19-and-black-communities.

Fulcher, Megan, Erin L. Sutfin and Charlotte J. Patterson. 2008. "Individual Differences in Gender Development: Associations with Parental Sexual Orientation, Attitudes, and Division of Labor." *Sex Roles* 58(5–6): 330–341.

Funes, Yessenia. 2019, September 3. "California Is Blaming Prison Reform for Incarcerated Fire Fighting Labor Shortage." *Gizmodo*. https://earther.gizmodo.com/california-is-blaming-prison-reform-for-incarcerated-fi-1837612038.

Funk, Cary, Kim Parker, and Haley Nolan. 2021, April 1. "*STEM Jobs See Uneven Progress in Increasing Gender, Racial, and Ethnic Diversity*." Pew Research Center. https://www.pewresearch.org/science/wp-content/uploads/sites/16/2021/03/PS_2021.04.01_diversity-in-STEM_REPORT.pdf.

Furuta, J. 2017. "Rationalization and Student/School Personhood in U.S. College Admissions: The Rise of Test-Optional Policies, 1987 to 2015." *Sociology of Education* 90(3): 236–54. https://doi.org/10.1177/0038040717713583.

Gabriel, R. 2016. "A Middle Ground? Residential Mobility and Attainment of Mixed-Race Couples" *Demography* 53: 165188.

Gac, Scott. 2007. *Singing for Freedom: The Hutchinson Family Singers and the Nineteenth-Century Culture of Reform*. New Haven, CT: Yale University Press.

Gallup. 2024, August. "LGBTQ+ rights." https://news.gallup.com/poll/1651/gay-lesbian-rights.aspx.

Gans, Herbert J. 1979. *Deciding What's News: A Study of CBS Evening News, NBC Nightly News, Newsweek, and Time*. Evanston, IL: Northwestern University Press.

Ganzeboom, Harry, Donald Treiman, and Wout Ultee. 1991. "Comparative Intergenerational Stratification Research: Three Generations and Beyond." *Annual Review of Sociology* 17: 277–302.

Gao, Helen. 2012, March 28. "How China's New Love Affair with US Private Schools Is Changing Them Both." *The Atlantic*. http://www.theatlantic.com/international/archive/2012/03/how-chinas-new-love-affair-with-us-private-schools-is-changing-them-both/255154/.

Gardner, W. L., and M. L. Knowles. 2008. "Love Makes You Real: Favorite Television Characters Are Perceived as 'Real' in a Social Facilitation Paradigm." *Social Cognition* 26(2): 156–168.

Garfinkel, Harold. 1967. *Studies in Ethnomethodology*. Englewood Cliffs, NJ: Prentice-Hall.

Garland, David. 2010. *Peculiar Institution: America's Death Penalty in an Age of Abolition*. Cambridge, MA: Harvard University Press.

Gates, Warren E. 1967. "The Spread of Ibn Khaldûn's Ideas on Climate and Culture." *Journal of the History of Ideas* 28: 415–422.

Gatrell Peter. 2013. *The Making of the Modern Refugee*. Oxford, UK: Oxford University Press

Gatta, Mary L., and Patricia A. Roos. 2005. "Rethinking Occupational Integration." *Sociological Forum* 20(3): 369–402.

Gausvik, C., A. Lautar, L. Miller, H. Pallerla, and J. Schlaudecker. 2015. "Structured Nursing Communication on Interdisciplinary Acute Care Teams Improves Perceptions of Safety, Efficiency, Understanding of Care Plan and Teamwork As Well As Job Satisfaction." *Journal of Multidisciplinary Healthcare* 14(8): 33–37.

Gelfand, M. J., J. L. Raver, L. H. Nishii, L. M. Leslie, J. Lun, B. C. Lim, L. Duan, A. Almaliach, S. Ang, J. Arnadottir, Z. Aycan, K. Boehnke, P. Boski, R. Cabecinhas, D. Chan, J. Chhokar, A. D'Amato, M. Ferrer, I.C. Fischlmayr, R. Fischer, M. Fülöp, J. Georgas, E.S. Kashima, Y. Kashima, K. Kim, A. Lempereur, P. Marquez, R. Othman, B. Overlaet, P. Panagiotopoulou, K. Peltzer, L.R. Perez-Florizno, L. Ponomarenko, A. Realo, V. Schei, M. Schmitt, P. B. Smith, N. Soomro, E. Szabo, N. Taveesin, M. Toyama, E. Van de Vliert, N. Vohra, C. Ward, and S. Yamaguchi. 2011. "Differences between Tight and Loose Cultures: A 33-Nation Study." *Science* 332(6033): 1100–1104. doi: 10.1126/science.1197754.

Geronimus, A. T., M. Hicken, D. Keene, and J. Bound. 2006. "'Weathering' and Age Patterns of Allostatic Load Scores among Blacks and Whites in the United States." *American Journal of Public Health* 96(5): 826–833.

Gersema, Emily. 2020. "Election 2020 Chatter on Twitter Busy with Bots and Conspiracy Theorists." *USC News*. https://news.usc.edu/177963/election-2020-twitter-social-media-bots-foreign-interference-usc-study/.

Gerstel, Naomi. 1987. "Divorce and Stigma." *Social Problems* 34: 172–186.

Gerstmann, Evan, and Matthew Streb. 2004. "Putting an End to Push Polling: Why It Should Be Banned and Why the First Amendment Lets Congress Ban It." *Election Law Journal* 3: 37–46.

Ghilarducci, Teresa. 2008. *When I'm Sixty-Four: The Plot against Pensions and the Plan to Save Them*. Princeton, NJ: Princeton University Press.

Gibson-Davis, C. M., K. Edin, and S. McLanahan. 2005. "High Hopes but Even Higher Expectations: The Retreat from Marriage among Low-Income Couples." *Journal of Marriage and Family* 67: 1301–1312.

Giddens, A. 1992. *The Transformation of Intimacy: Sexuality, Love and Eroticism in Modern Society*. Cambridge, MA: Polity.

Giddens, Anthony, and Simon Griffiths. 2006. *Sociology*. New York: Polity.

Giddens, Anthony. 1990. *Consequences of Modernity*. Stanford, CA: Stanford University Press.

Giddens, Anthony. 1991. *Modernity and Self-Identity: Self and Society in the Late Modern Age*. Stanford, CA: Stanford University Press.

Giddens, Anthony. 2009. *The Politics of Climate Change*. Cambridge, MA: Polity.

Gieryn, Thomas. 1999. *Cultural Boundaries of Science*. Chicago: University of Chicago Press.

Gilbert, Sophie. 2017, October 16. "The Movement of #MeToo." *The Atlantic*. https://www.theatlantic.com/entertainment/archive/2017/10/the-movement-of-metoo/542979/.

Gilliam, F. D., and S. Iyengar. 2000. "Prime Suspects: The Influence of Local Television News on the Viewing Public." *American Journal of Political Science* 44: 560–573.

Giridharadas, Anand. 2018. *Winners Take All: The Elite Charade of Changing the World*. New York: Knopf.

Giroux, Henry, and David Purpel, eds. 1983. *The Hidden Curriculum and Moral Education: Deception or Discovery*. San Pablo, CA: McCutchan Publishers.

Gitlin, Todd. 1995. *The Twilight of Common Dreams: Why America Is Wracked by Culture Wars*. New York: Henry Holt & Co.

Gitlin, Todd. 2001. *Media, Unlimited. How The Torrent of Images and Sounds Overwhelms Our Lives*. New York: Metropolitan Books.

Gittleman, Maury. 2022, July. "The 'Great Resignation' in Perspective." *Monthly Labor Review*, U.S. Bureau of Labor Statistics. https://doi.org/10.21916/mlr.2022.20.

Glaser, Barney G. 1978. *Theoretical Sensitivity: Advances in the Methodology of Grounded Theory*. Mill Valley, CA: The Sociology Press.

Glick, Jennifer. 2010. "Connecting Complex Processes: A Decade of Research on Immigrant Families." *Journal of Marriage and Family* 72: 498–515.

Global Services in Education. 2023, March 21. "Opting Out of Korea's Cutthroat Educational System: The Role of International Schools." Korea: The Rise of Foreign International Schools (gsineducation.com).

Glynn, Sarah, Jane Farrell, and Nancy Wu. 2013, May 7. "The Importance of Preschool and Childcare for Working Mothers." Report. Center for American Progress. https://www.americanprogress.org/issues/education-k-12/reports/2013/05/08/62519/the-importance-of-preschool-and-child-care-for-working-mothers/.

Go, J., 2017. Decolonizing Sociology: Epistemic Inequality and Sociological Thought. *Social Problems*, 64(2), 194–199.

Go, J. 2023. Thinking against Empire: Anticolonial Thought as Social Theory. *The British Journal of Sociology* 74: 279–293.

Go, Julian. 2016. *Postcolonial Thought and Social Theory*. New York NY: Oxford University Press.

Goel, Vindu. 2014, June 29. "Facebook Tinkers with Users' Emotions in News Feed Experiment, Stirring Outcry." *New York Times*. https://www.nytimes.com/2014/06/30/technology/facebook-tinkers-with-users-emotions-in-news-feed-experiment-stirring-outcry.html.

Goffman, Erving. 1959. *The Presentation of Self in Everyday Life*. New York: Anchor.

Goffman, Erving. 1963. *Stigma: Notes on the Management of Spoiled Identity*. Englewood Cliffs, NJ: Prentice-Hall.

Goldberg, Carey. 2016, April 11. "'Genetic Superheroes': Rare Exceptions Resist Mutations Thought to Be Disease Destiny." *WBUR Radio Boston*. http://www.wbur.org/commonhealth/2016/04/11/genetic-superheroes.

Goldin, Claudia, and Maria Shim. 2004. "Making a Name: Women's Surnames at Marriage and Beyond." *Journal of Economic Perspectives* 18: 143–160.

Goldthorpe, John, and Clive Payne. 1986. "Trends in Intergenerational Class Mobility in England and Wales, 1972–1983." *Sociology* 20: 1–24.

Golebiewski, Michael, and danah boyd. 2019. *Data Voids: Where Missing Data Can Easily Be Exploited*. Research Report, Data and Society. https://datasociety.net/wp-content/uploads/2019/11/Data-Voids-2.0-Final.pdf.

Goodenough, Ward. 1970. *Description and Comparison in Cultural Anthropology*. Chicago: Aldine.

Gordon, Raymond G., ed. 2005. *Ethnologue: Languages of the World*, 15th ed. Dallas: SIL International.

Gorski, P. S., and A. Altınordu. 2008. "After Secularization?" *Annual Review of Sociology* 34(1): 55–85.

Gottschalk, Marie. 2007. "Dollars, Sense, and Penal Reform: Social Movements and the Future of the Carceral State." *Social Research* 74(2): 669–694.

Gottshalk, Marie. 2007. "Dollars, Sense, and Penal Reform: Social Movements and the Future of the Carceral State," *Social Research* 74(2): 669–694.

Gowan, Teresa. 2010. *Hobos, Hustlers, and Backsliders: Homeless in San Francisco*. Minneapolis: University of Minnesota Press.

Graber, Doris. 1980. *Crime News and the Public*. New York: Praeger.

Grady, Constance. 2023, February 3. "The Mounting, Undeniable MeToo Backlash." *Vox*. https://www.vox.com/culture/23581859/me-too-backlash-susan-faludi-weinstein-roe-dobbs-depp-heard.

Graf, Nikki, Anna Brown, and Eileen Patten. 2019, March 22. "The Narrowing, but Persistent, Gender Gap in Pay." Pew Research Center. https://www.pewresearch.org/short-reads/2023/03/01/gender-pay-gap-facts/.

Graffam, J., A. J. Shinkfield, and L. Hardcastle. 2008. "The Perceived Employability of Ex-Prisoners and Offenders." *International Journal of Offender Therapy and Comparative Criminology* 52(6): 673–685. https://doi.org/10.1177/0306624X07307783.

Gramlich, John. 2017, March 1. "Most Violent and Property Crimes in the U.S. Go Unsolved." Pew Research Center. https://www.pewresearch.org/short-reads/2017/03/01/most-violent-and-property-crimes-in-the-u-s-go-unsolved/.

Gramlich, John. 2020, November 20. "*What the Data Says (and Doesn't Say) about Crime in the United States.*" Pew Research Center. https://www.pewresearch.org/short-reads/2020/11/20/facts-about-crime-in-the-u-s/.

Gramsci, Antonio. 1971. *Prison Notebooks*. New York: International Publishers.

Grand View Research. 2019. *Skin Lightening Products Market Size, Share & Trends Analysis Report by Product (Cream, Cleanser, Mask), by Nature (Synthetic, Natural, Organic), by Region, and Segment Forecasts, 2019–2025*. Report ID: GVR-3-68038-541-0. https://www.grandviewresearch.com/industry-analysis/skin-lightening-products-market.

Granovetter, Mark S. 1973. "The Strength of Weak Ties." *American Journal of Sociology* 78(6): 1360380. http://www.jstor.org/stable/2776392.

Granovetter, Mark S. 1995. *Getting a Job: A Study of Contacts and Careers*. Chicago: University of Chicago Press.

Grant, Adam. 2014. *Give and Take: Why Helping Others Drives Our Success*. New York: Penguin.

Grasgruber, P., J. Cacek, T. Kalina, and M. Sebera. 2014. "The Role of Nutrition and Genetics as Key Determinants of the Positive Height Trend." *Economics and Human Biology* 15: 81–100.

Grattet, Ryken, and Valerie Jenness. 2001. "Examining the Boundaries of Hate Crime Law: Disabilities and the Dilemma of Difference." *Criminology* 91: 653–698.

Gray, M. L. 2009. "Negotiating Identities/Queering Desires: Coming Out Online and the Remediation of the Coming-Out Story." *Journal of Computer-Mediated Communication* 14(4): 1162–1189.

Greely, Henry T., Barbara Sahakian, John Harris, Ronald C. Kessler, Michael S. Gazzaniga, Phillip Campbell, and Martha J. Farah. 2008, December 11. "Toward Responsible Use of Cognitive Enhancing Drugs by the Healthy." *Nature* 456 (7223): 702–705.

Greenberg, Alissa. 2020, July 14. "How the Stress of Racism Can Harm Your Health—And What That Has to Do with Covid-19." *NOVA PBS*. https://www.pbs.org/wgbh/nova/article/racism-stress-covid-allostatic-load/.

Greenwood, Jeremy, Nezih Guner, Georgi Kocharkov, and Cezar Santos. 2014, May, revised. "Marry Your Like: Assortative Mating and Income Inequality." *American Economic Review (Papers and Proceedings)* 104(5): 348–353.

Gregoire, Carolyn. 2015, May 15. "How Being an Oldest, Middle, or Youngest Child Shapes Your Personality." *Huffington Post*. http://www.huffingtonpost.com/2015/05/13/birth-order-personality_n_7206252.html.

Greguletz, E., M.-R. Diehl, and K. Kreutzer. 2019. Why Women Build Less Effective Networks Than Men: The Role of Structural Exclusion and Personal Hesitation. *Human Relations* 72(7): 1234–1261. https://doi.org/10.1177/0018726718804303.

Groves, Robert. 2011, August 12. "Women at Work." Census Blog. https://www.census.gov/newsroom/blogs/director/2011/08/women-at-work.html.

Grusky, David B. 2001. "The Past, Present, and Future of Social Inequality." In *Social Stratification: Class, Race, and Gender in Sociological Perspective* (Second Edition), ed. David B. Grusky (pp. 3–51). Boulder, CO: Westview Press.

Grusky, David, and Tamar Kricheli-Katz, eds. 2012. *The New Gilded Age*. Stanford, CA: Stanford University Press.

Grusky, David. 1994. "The Contours of Social Stratification." In *Social Stratification: Class, Race, and Gender in Sociological Perspective*, ed. D. Grusky (pp. 3–35). Boulder, CO: Westview Press.

Gudykunst, William B. 2004. *Bridging Differences: Effective Intergroup Communication*, 4th ed. Newbury Park, CA: SAGE.

Guhin, J., J. M. Calarco, and C. Miller-Idriss. 2021. "Whatever Happened to Socialization?" *Annual Review of Sociology* 47: 109–129.

Guibemau, M., 2020. Marx and Durkheim on Nationalism. In *Rethinking Nationalism and Ethnicity* (pp. 73–90). Routledge.

Gupta, Alinda. 2023, October 26. "What Are AI Doom Scenarios, and How Likely Are They to Happen?" *Jumpstart*. https://www.jumpstartmag.com/what-are-ai-doom-scenarios-and-how-likely-are-they-to-happen/#:~:text=A%20few%20experts%20have%20equated,to%20the%20destruction%20of%20humanity.

Gusfield, Joseph. 1963. *Symbolic Crusade: Status Politics and the American Temperance Movement*. Urbana: University of Illinois Press.

Habermas, Jürgen. 1975. *Legitimation Crisis*. Boston: Beacon Press.

Habermas, Jürgen. 1989. *The Structural Transformation of the Public Sphere: An Inquiry into a Category of Bourgeois Society*. Cambridge: Polity Press.

Habermas, Jürgen. 1996. *Between Facts and Norms: Contributions to a Discourse Theory of Law and Democracy*. Boston: Polity Press.

Habermas, J. 1998. *Between Facts and Norms: Contributions to a Discourse Theory of Law and Democracy*. Cambridge, MA: MIT Press.

Habermas, Jürgen. 2008. "Notes on Post-secular Society." *New Perspectives Quarterly* 25(4): 17–29.

Haddad, L. 1977. "A Fourteenth-Century Theory of Economic Growth and Development." *Kyklos* 30: 195–213.

Hagan, John, and R. Dinovitzer. 1999. "Collateral Consequences of Imprisonment for Children, Communities and Prisoners." In *Crime and Justice: Prisons*, Vol. 26, ed. M. Tonry and J. Petersilia (pp. 121–162). Chicago: University of Chicago Press.

Haggerty, B. B., H. Du, D. P. Kennedy, T. N. Bradbury, and B. R. Karney. 2023. "Stability and Change in Newlyweds' Social Networks over the First Years of Marriage." *Journal of Family Psychology* 37(1): 20–30. https://doi.org/10.1037/fam0001016.

Hall, John R., Laura Grindstaff, and Ming-cheng Miriam Lo. 2010. *Handbook of Cultural Sociology*. New York: Routledge.

Hall, P., and D. Ellis. 2023. "A Systematic Review of Socio-Technical Gender Bias in AI Algorithms." *Online Information Review* 47(7): 1264–1279. https://doi.org/10.1108/OIR-08-2021-0452.

Hall, Stuart, Chas Critcher, Tony Jefferson, John Clarke, and Brian Roberts. 1978. *Policing the Crisis: "Mugging," the State and Law and Order*. London: Macmillan.

Hall, Stuart. 1973. *Encoding and Decoding in the Television Discourse*. Birmingham, UK: University of Birmingham.

Hallin, Daniel C., and Paolo Mancini. 2004. *Comparing Media Systems: Three Models of Media and Politics*. Cambridge, MA: Cambridge University Press.

Halperin, David M. 1997. *Saint Foucault: Towards a Gay Hagiography*. Oxford, UK: Oxford University Press.

Hamermesh, D. S., and A. Parker. 2005. "Beauty in the Classroom: Instructors' Pulchritude and Putative Pedagogical Productivity." *Economics of Education Review* 24(4), 369–376.

Hamidi, S., and R. Ewing. 2014. "A Longitudinal Study of Changes in Urban Sprawl between 2000 and 2010 in the United States." *Landscape and Urban Planning* 128: 72–82.

Hamidi, S., R. Ewing, I. Preuss, and A. Dodds. 2015. "Measuring Sprawl and Its Impacts: An Update." *Journal of Planning Education and Research* 35(1): 35–50.

Hamilton, J. T. 2004. *All the News That's Fit to Sell: How the Market Transforms Information into News*. Princeton, NJ: Princeton University Press.

Hamilton, Vivian. 2006. *Principles of U.S. Family Law*, 75 *Fordham Law Review* 31(1): 31–73. https://ir.lawnet.fordham.edu/flr/vol75/iss1/2.

Hampton, Keith, Inyoung Shin, and Weixu Lu, 2017. "Social Media and Political Discussion: When Online Presence Silences Offline Conversation." *Information, Communication and Society* 20: 1090–1107.

Hankivsky, Olena. 2014. *Intersectionality 101*. The Institute for Intersectionality Research & Policy, SFU.

Harcourt, Bernard E. 2012. *The Illusion of Free Markets: Punishment and the Myth of Natural Order*. Cambridge, MA: Havard University Press.

Hardy, Bradley, and Trevon Logan. 2020, February 2018. "Race and the Lack of Intergenerational Economic Mobility in the United States." Washington Center for Equitable Growth. https://equitablegrowth.org/race-and-the-lack-of-intergenerational-economic-mobility-in-the-united-states/.

Hari, A. 2017. "Who Gets to 'Work Hard, Play Hard'? Gendering the Work–Life Balance Rhetoric in Canadian Tech Companies." *Gender, Work & Organization* 24(2), 99–114.

Harper, Christopher, and T. Alan Lacey. 2016, July 28. "Get a STEM Job with Less Than a Four-Year Degree." US Department of Labor Blog. https://blog.dol.gov/2016/07/28/get-a-stem-job-with-less-than-a-4-year-degree/.

Harrell, Erika. 2019, January. "Victims of Identity Theft, 2016." *Bureau of Justice Statistics*, NCJ 251147. https://www.bjs.gov/content/pub/pdf/vit16.pdf.

Harris, David. 1999. "The Stories, the Statistics, and the Law: Why 'Drivin While Black' Matters," *Minnesota Law Review* 84: 265–326.

Harrison, R. J. 2002. "Inadequacies of Multiple-Response Race Data in the Federal Statistical System." In *The New Race Question: How the Census Counts Multiracial Individuals*, eds. J. Perlmann and M.C. Waters (pp. 137–160). New York: Russell Sage Foundation.

Hartley, John. 1999. *Uses of Television*. London, UK: Routledge.

Hartmann, Tilo. 2017. "Parasocial Interaction, Parasocial Relationships, and Well-Being." In *The Routledge Handbook of Media Use and Well-Being*, ed. L. Reinecke and M. Oliver (pp. 131–144). New York: Routledge.

Hartmans, Avery, and Nathan McAlone. 2016, August 1. "The Story of How Travis Kalanick Built Uber into the Most Feared and Valuable Startup in the World." *Business Insider*. http://www.businessinsider.com/ubers-history.

Haskins, Ron. 2008. "Education and Economic Mobility." Economic Mobility Project, Pew Charitable Trusts. https://www.brookings.edu/wp-content/uploads/2016/07/02_economic_mobility_sawhill_ch8.pdf.

Hausladen, Gary J. 2000. "The Evolution of the Place-Based Police Procedural." In *Places for Dead Bodies* (pp. 11–32). Austin: University of Texas Press. http://www.jstor.org/stable/10.7560/731271.6.

Haveman, Robert, and Timothy Smeeding. 2006. "The Role of Higher Education in Social Mobility." *The Future of Children* 16: 125–150.

Hawkins, Tyleah. 2012, December 28. "Will Less Art and Music in the Classroom Really Help Students Soar Academically?" *Washington Post*. https://www.washingtonpost.com/blogs/therootdc/post/will-less-art-and-music-in-the-classroom-really-help-students-soar-academically/2012/12/28/e18a2da0-4e02-11e2-839d-d54cc6e49b63_blog.html?utm_term=.d08ea6922669.

Hayden, Dolores. 2004. *A Field Guide to Sprawl*. New York: W.W. Norton.

Hazir, Irmak Karademir. 2018. "Cultural Omnivorousness." *Oxford Bibliographies*. http://www.oxfordbibliographies.com/view/document/obo-9780199756384/obo-9781997563840134.xml.

He, Wan, Daniel Goodkind, and Paul Kowal. 2016. *U.S. Census Bureau, International Population Reports, P95/16–1, An Aging World: 2015*. Washington, DC: US Government Publishing Office. https://www.census.gov/content/dam/Census/library/publications/2016/demo/p95-16-1.pdf.

Health Resources and Services Administration. 2018. "Organ Donation Statistics." U.S. Government Information on Organ Donation and Transplantation. Department of Health and Human Services. Web. https://www.organdonor.gov/statistics-stories/statistics.html.

Healthcare.gov, 2024. "Federal Poverty Level." https://www.healthcare.gov/glossary/federal-poverty-level-fpl/.

Heath, L., and K. Gilbert. 1996. "Mass Media and the Fear of Crime." *American Behavioral Scientist* 39(4): 379–386.

Hebdige, Dick. 1979. *Subculture: The Meaning of Style*. New York: Routledge.

Heelas, Paul. 1996. *The New Age Movement*. Malden, MA: Blackwell.

Hegewisch, Ariane, and Asha DuMonthier. 2015. "The Gender Wage Gap by Occupation 2015 and by Race and Ethnicity." Institute for Women's Policy Research. http://www.iwpr.org/publications/pubs/the-gender-wage-gap-by-occupation-2015-and-by-race-and-ethnicity/.

Held, David. 1999. *Global Transformations: Politics, Economics and Culture*. Stanford, CA: Stanford University Press.

Helland, M. S., T. von Soest, K. Gustavson, E. Røysamb, and K. S. Mathiesen. 2014. "Long Shadows: A Prospective Study of Predictors of Relationship Dissolution over 17 Child-Rearing Years." *BMC Psychology* 2: 40.

Herbst, Susan. 1995. *Numbered Voices: How Opinion Polling Has Shaped American Politics*. Chicago: University of Chicago Press.

Herman, M., and M. Campbell. 2012. "I Wouldn't, but You Can: Attitudes toward Interracial Relationships." *Social Science Research* 41(2): 343–358.

Hern, Alex. 2020, January 3. "Technology in 2050: Will It Save Humanity—Or Destroy Us?" *The Guardian*. https://www.theguardian.com/technology/2020/jan/03/technology-2050-save-humanity-or-destroy-us.

Hernandez, M., D. R. Avery, S. D. Volpone, and C. R. Kaiser. 2019. "Bargaining while Black: The Role of Race in Salary Negotiations." *Journal of Applied Psychology* 104(4): 581–592. https://doi.org/10.1037/apl0000363.

Herold, Benjamin. 2016, February 5. "Technology in Education: An Overview." *Education Week*. https://www.edweek.org/ew/issues/technology-in-education/.

Hesmondhalgh, David. 2019. *The Cultural Industries*, 4th ed. London: Sage.

Hickel, Jason. 2016, April 8. "Global Inequality May Be Much Worse Than We Think." *The Guardian*. https://www.theguardian.com/global-development-professionals-network/2016/apr/08/global-inequality-may-be-much-worse-than-we-think.

High Fliers Research Limited. 2016. *The Graduate Market in 2016*. London: High Fliers Research Limited. https://www.highfliers.co.uk/download/2016/graduate_market/GMReport16.pdf.

Hill, Catherine, Christianne Corbett, and Andresse St. Rose, 2010. *Why So Few? Women in Science, Technology, Engineering, and Mathematics*. Washington, DC: American Association of University Women.

Hill, Christopher. [1972] 1984. *The World Turned Upside Down: Radical Ideas during the English Revolution*. London: Penguin.

Hill, Michael R. 2002. *Harriet Martineau: Theoretical and Methodological Perspectives*. New York: Routledge.

Hirsch, A. R. 1983. *Making the Second Ghetto: Race and Housing in Chicago, 1940–1960*. Cambridge, UK: Cambridge University Press.

Hirschi, Travis. 1969. *Causes of Delinquency*. Los Angeles, CA: University of California Press.

Ho, Karen. 2009. *Liquidated: An Ethnography of Wall Street*. Durham, NC: Duke University Press.

Hoang, Kimberly Kay. 2015. *Dealing in Desire: Asian Ascendancy, Western Decline, and the Hidden Currencies of Global Sex Work*. Oakland: University of California Press.

Hobbs, Tawnell D., and Lee Hawkins. 2020, June 5. "The Results Are in for Remote Learning: It Didn't Work." *Wall Street Journal*. https://www.wsj.com/articles/schools-coronavirus-remote-learning-lockdown-tech-11591375078

Hochschild, Arlie. 2012. *The Second Shift*. NY: Penguin.

Hochschild, Arlie. 2018. *Strangers in Their Own Land. Anger and Mourning on the American Right*. New York: New Press.

Hochschild, J., and V. Weaver. 2010. "There's No One as Irish as Barack O'Bama: The Politics and Policy of Multiracialism in the United States." *Perspectives on Politics* 8: 737–760.

Hodson, Randy, Vincent Rosigno, and Steven Lopez. 2006. "Chaos and the Abuse of Power: Workplace Bullying in Organizational and Interactional Context." *Work and Occupations* 33: 382–416.

Hollister, Sean. 2014, February 26. "Welcome to Googletown. Here's how a city becomes company property The Verge. https://www.theverge.com/2014/2/26/5444030/company-town-how-google-is-taking-over-mountain-view.

Holzer, Harry. 1996. *What Employers Want: Job Prospects for Less-Educated Workers*. New York: Russell Sage Foundation.

Homans, Charles. 2010, January/February. "Hot Air: Why Don't TV Weathermen Believe in Climate Change?" *Columbia Journalism Review*. https://sciencepolicy.colorado.edu/students/envs_4800/homans_2010.pdf.

hooks, bell. 2000. *Feminist Theory: From Margin to Center*. Boston: South End Press.

Hoornweg, Daniel, and Perinaz Bhada-Tata. 2012. "What a Waste: A Global Review of Solid Waste Management." Urban Development Series; Knowledge Papers No. 15. Washington, DC: World Bank. https://openknowledge.worldbank.org/handle/10986/17388.

Horowitz, Juliana Menasce. 2022, April 8. "More Than Half of Americans in Their 40s Are 'Sandwiched' between an Aging Parent and Their Own Children." Pew Research Center.

Horton, D., and R. Wohl. 1956. "Mass Communication and Para-Social Interaction: Observations on Intimacy at a Distance." *Psychiatry* 19: 215–229.

Hourigan, Kristen Lee. 2021. "Girls Try, Boys Aim High: Exposing Difference in Implied Ability, Activity, and Agency of Girls Versus Boys in Language on McDonald's Happy Meal Boxes." *Sex Roles* 84: 377–391.

Hourihan, Matt, and Allessandra Zimmermann. 2022, May 10. "*US R&D and Innovation in a Global Context: 2022 Data Update*." American Association for the Advancement of Science. https://www.aaas.org/sites/default/files/2022-05/AAAS%20Global%20R%26D%20Update%20May%202022.pdf.

Hout, M., and A. M. Greeley. 1998. "What Church Officials' Reports Don't Show: Another Look at Church Attendance Data." *American Sociological Review* 63(1): 113–119.

Hout, Michael, and Claude S. Fischer. 2002. "Why More Americans Have No Religious Preference: Politics and Generations." *American Sociological Review* 67(2):165–190.

Hsu, Francis. 1981. *Americans and Chinese: Passages to Differences*. Honolulu: University of Hawaii Press.

Hsu, Jeremy. 2024, January 4. "There's a 5% Chance of AI Causing Humans to Go Extinct, Say Scientists." *New Scientist*. https://www.newscientist.com/article/2410839-theres-a-5-chance-of-ai-causing-humans-to-go-extinct-say-scientists/#:~:text=Almost%2058%20per%20cent%20of,extremely%20bad%20AI%2Drelated%20outcomes.

Hu, Winnie. 2010, September 30. "Making Math as Easy as 1, Pause, 2, Pause. . . ." *New York Times* https://www.nytimes.com/2010/10/01/education/01math.html.

Hudak, J. 2014. *Presidential Pork: White House Influence over the Distribution of Federal Grants*. Washington, DC: Brookings Institution Press.

Hudson, David, and Lata Nott. 2017, March. "Hate Speech and Campus Speech Codes." Newseum Institute. http://www.newseuminstitute.org/first-amendment-center/topics/freedom-of-speech-2/free-speech-on-public-college-campuses-overview/hate-speech-campus-speech-codes/.

Hudson, Lisa, Danielle Battle, Talia Kaatz, Stephen Bahr, Sandy Eyster, and L. Jane Hall, 2023. "2019 Homeschooling and Full-Time Virtual Education Rates." Institute of Education Sciences Stats in Brief, September 2023. https://nces.ed.gov/pubs2023/2023101.pdf.

*Huffington Post*. 2012, March 19. "Sofia Vergara: Is She taking The Latino Stereotype Too Far?" https://www.huffpost.com/entry/sofia-vergara-is-she-taking-the-latino-stereotype-too-far_n_1363193.

Hulac, Benjamin. 2016, September 9. "Clean Energy Firms Lobby Congress as Much as Dirty Firms Do." *Scientific American*. https://www.scientificamerican.com/article/clean-energy-firms-lobby-congess-as-much-as-dirty-firms-do/.

Hunt, K., and M. Gruszczynski. 2021. "The Influence of New and Traditional Media Coverage on Public Attention to Social Movements: The Case of The Dakota Access Pipeline Protests." *Information, Communication & Society* 24(7): 1024–1040.

Hunter, James Davison, and Alan Wolfe. 2006. *Is There a Culture War?: A Dialogue on Values and American Public Life*. Washington, DC: Brookings Institution Press.

Hunter, James Davison. 1991. *Culture Wars: The Struggle to Define America*. New York: Basic Books.

Iannaccone, Laurence. 1997. "Toward an Economic Theory of 'Fundamentalism.'" *Journal of Institutional and Theoretical Economics* 153: 100–116.

Ibarra, H. 1993. "Personal Networks of Women and Minorities in Management: A Conceptual Framework." *The Academy of Management Review* 18(1), 56–87. http://www.jstor.org/stable/258823.

IBIS World. 2024, May 18. "Greeting Cards and Other Publishing in the US." IBIS World Industry Statistics. https://www.ibisworld.com/industry-statistics/market-size/greeting-cards-other-publishing-united-states/#:~:text=The%20market%20size%2C%20measured%20by,pages%20of%20data%20and%20analysis.

IEA. 2024. "Renewables 2024." https://www.iea.org/reports/renewables-2024.

Igielnik, Ruth. 2020, May 15. "Majority of Americans Who Lost a Job or Wages Due to COVID-19 Concerned States Will Reopen Too Quickly." Pew Research Center. https://www.pewresearch.org/short-reads/2020/05/15/majority-of-americans-who-lost-a-job-or-wages-due-to-covid-19-concerned-states-will-reopen-too-quickly/.

Ignatiev, Noel. 2008. *How the Irish Became White*. New York: Routledge.

Inglehart, Ronald, and Christian Welzel. 2005. *Modernization, Cultural Change, and Democracy: The Human Development Sequence*. Cambridge, UK: Cambridge University Press.

Inglehart, Ronald, Roberto Foa, Christopher Peterson, and Christian Welzel. 2008. "Development, Freedom, and Rising Happiness: A Global Perspective (1981–2007)." *Perspectives on Psychological Science* 3: 264–285.

Ingraham, Christopher. 2014, December 22. "A Lot Of Southern Whites Are a Little Bit Black." *Washington Post*. https://www.washingtonpost.com/news/wonk/wp/2014/12/22/a-lot-of-southern-whites-are-a-little-bit-black/.

International Labour Organization. 2014. *Profits and Poverty: The Economics of Forced Labour*. https://www.ilo.org/wcmsp5/groups/public/—ed_norm/—declaration/documents/publication/wcms_243391.pdf

International Labour Organization. 2017. *Labour Force Participation Rate—ILO Modelled Estimates, July 2018*. http://www.ilo.org/ilostat/faces/oracle/webcenter/portalapp/pagehierarchy/Page3.jspx?MBI_ID=15&_afrLoop=1079054415126282&_afrWindowMode=0&_afrWindowId=npx41s27r_1#!%40%40%3F_afrWindowId%3Dnpx41s27r_1%26_afrLoop%3D1079054415126282%26MBI_ID%3D15%26_afrWindowMode%3D0%26_adf.ctrl-state%3Dnpx41s27r_33.

International Labour Organization. 2020. *Policy Brief: The COVID-19 response: Getting gender equality right for a better future for women at work*. https://www.ilo.org/wcmsp5/groups/public/---dgreports/---gender/documents/publication/wcms_744685.pdf.

Irfan, Umair. 2019, November 18. "Brazil's Amazon Rainforest Destruction Is at Its Highest Rate in More Than a Decade New Satellite Measurements Show an Alarming Spike in Deforestation This Year." *Vox*. https://www.vox.com/science-and-health/2019/11/18/20970604/amazon-rainforest-2019-brazil-burningdeforestation-bolsonaro.

Isaac, Mike, Michael J. De La Merced and Andrew Ross Sorkin. 2019, May 17. "How Enthusiasm for Uber Evaporated before I.P.O." *New York Times*. https://www.nytimes.com/2019/05/15/technology/uber-ipo-price.html.

Ishizuka, P. 2018. "The Economic Foundations of Cohabiting Couples' Union Transitions." *Demography* 55(2): 535–557.

Ising, M., and F. Holsboer. 2006. "Genetics of Stress Response and Stress-Related Disorders." *Dialogues in Clinical Neuroscience* 8: 433–444.

Jaarsma, Pier, and Stellan Welin. 2012. "Autism as a Natural Human Variation: Reflections on the Claims of the Neurodiversity Movement." *Health Care Analysis* 20(1): 20–30.

Jackson, K. T. 1985. *Crabgrass Frontier: The Suburbanization of the United States*. New York: Oxford University Press.

Jackson, Philip W. 1968. *Life in Classrooms*. New York: Holt, Rinehart and Winston.

Jacobs, Julia. 2020, June 12. "First Black 'Bachelor,' Matt James, Cast by ABC." *New York Times*,. https://www.nytimes.com/2020/06/12/arts/television/matt-james-black-bachelor.html.

Jacobs, Ronald N., and Daniel J. Glass. 2001. "Media Publicity and the Voluntary Sector: The Case of Nonprofit Organizations in New York City." *Voluntas: International Journal of Voluntary and Nonprofit Organizations* 13(3): 235–252.

Jacobs, Ronald N., and Eleanor Townsley. 2011. *The Space of Opinion: Intellectuals, Media and the Public Sphere*. New York: Oxford University Press.

Jacobs, Ronald N., and Eleanor Townsley. 2014. "The Hermeneutics of Hannity: Format Innovation in the Space of Opinion after September 11." *Cultural Sociology* 8(3):1–18.

Jacobson, Thomas. 2017. "Trending Theory of the Public Sphere." *Annals of the International Communication Association* 41(1): 70–82. doi:10.1080/23808985.2017.1288070.

Jamie Ducharme. 2024, April 10. Why So Many Women Are Waiting Longer to Have Kids. *Time Magazine*. https://time.com/6965267/women-having-kids-later/ Accessed June 3, 2024.

Jamieson, Kathleen Hall. 2020. *Cyberwar. How Russian Hackers and Trolls Helped Elect a President: What We Don't, Can't, and Do Know*. New York: Oxford University Press.

Jamison, Anne. 2013. *Fic: Why Fanfiction Is Taking over the World*. Dallas, TX: SmartPop.

Jencks, Christopher. 1995. *The Homeless*. Cambridge, MA: Harvard University Press.

Jennings, Jennifer, and Heeju Sohn. 2014. "Measure for Measure: How Proficiency-Based Accountability Systems Affect Inequality in Academic Achievement." *Sociology of Education* 87(2): 125–141.

Jerolmack, Colin, and Shamus Khan. 2014. "Talk Is Cheap: Ethnography and the Attitudinal Fallacy." *Sociological Methods & Research* 43: 178–209.

Jerrim, John, and Lindsey Macmillan. 2015, December. "Income Inequality, Intergenerational Mobility, and the Great Gatsby Curve: Is Education the Key?" *Social Forces* 94(2): 505–533. https://doi.org/10.1093/sf/sov075.

John W. Mohr, Christopher A. Bail, Margaret Frye, Jennifer C. Lena, Omar Lizardo, Terence E. McDonnell, Ann Mische, Iddo Tavory, and Frederick F. Wherry. 2020. *Measuring Culture* New York: Columbia University Press.

Johns Hopkins University Coronavirus Resource Center. 2020. "COVID-19 Data in Motion." https://coronavirus.jhu.edu/.

Johnson, Arianna 2023, March 31. "Which Jobs Will AI Replace? These 4 Industries Will Be Heavily Impacted." *Forbes*. https://www.forbes.com/sites/ariannajohnson/2023/03/30/which-jobs-will-ai-replace-these-4-industries-will-be-heavily-impacted/?sh=9d9b105957f8.

Johnson, Stephanie, Jessica Kirk, and Ksenia Keplinger. 2016, October 4. "Why We Fail to Report Sexual Harassment." *Harvard Business Review*. https://hbr.org/2016/10/why-we-fail-to-report-sexual-harassment.

Johnson, Suzanne, and Elizabeth O'Connor. 2002. *The Gay Baby Boom: The Psychology of Gay Parenthood*. New York: NYU Press.

Joint Commission. 2008, July 9. "Behaviors That Undermine a Culture of Safety." *Sentinel Event Alert* 40. http://www.jointcommission.org/sentinel_event_alert_issue_40_behaviors_that_undermine_a_culture_of_safety/.

Jones, Megan A. 2002. "Deafness as Culture: A Psychosocial Perspective." *Disability Studies Quarterly* 22(2): 51–60.

Joppke, Christian. 2004. "The Retreat of Multiculturalism in the Liberal State: Theory and Policy." *British Journal of Sociology* 55: 237–257.

Joppke. Christian. 2015. *The Secular State Under Siege: Religion and Politics in Europe and America*. Cambridge: Polity.

Jordan, Lucy, and Elspeth Graham. 2015. "Early Childhood Socialization and Wellbeing." In *Routledge Handbook of Families in Asia*, ed. S. Quah (pp. 175–190). New York: Routledge.

Jorgenson, A. K. 2016. "Environment, Development, and Ecologically Unequal Exchange." *Sustainability* 8(3): 227.

Jorgenson, A., and B. Clark. 2009. "Ecologically Unequal Exchange in Comparative Perspective: A Brief Introduction." *International Journal of Comparative Sociology* 50:211–214.

Jost, Timothy. 2017, December 20. "The Tax Bill and The Individual Mandate: What Happened, and What Does It Mean?" Health Affairs Blog. https://www.healthaffairs.org/do/10.1377/hauthor20091027.990764/full/.

Juergensmeyer, Mark. 2003. *Terror in the Mind of God: The Global Rise of Religious Violence*. Berkeley: University of California Press.

Julian, Tiffany, and Robert Kominski. 2011. *Education and Synthetic Work-Life Earnings Estimates*. Washington, DC: US Department of Commerce, Economics and Statistics Administration, Census Bureau.

Juster R. P., B. S. McEwen, and S. J. Lupien. 2010. "Allostatic Load Biomarkers of Chronic Stress and Impact on Health and Cognition." *Neuroscience and Biobehavioral Reviews* 35(1): 2–16. doi:10.1016/j.neubiorev.2009.10.002.

Kaczmarek, E. 2022. "Promoting Diseases to Promote Drugs: The Role of the Pharmaceutical Industry in Fostering Good and Bad Medicalization." *British Journal of Clinical Pharmacology* 88(1): 34–39. doi:10.1111/bcp.14835.

Kahn, Johnathan. 2007. "Race in a Bottle." *Scientific American* 297(2): 40–45.

Kahn, Jonathan. 2013. *Race in a Bottle: The Story of BiDil and Racialized Medicine in a Post-Genomic Age*. New York: Columbia University Press.

Kaiser Family Foundation. 2019. "Health Insurance Coverage of the Total Population." State Health Facts. https://www.kff.org/other/state-indicator/total-population/?dataView=0&currentTimeframe=0&selectedDistributions=employer&sortModel=%7B%22colId%22:%22Location%22,%22sort%22:%22asc%22%7D

Kalleberg, A. L., P. V. Marsden, J. Reynolds, and D. Knoke. 2006. "Beyond Profit? Sectoral Differences in High-Performance Work Practices." *Work and Occupations* 33(3): 271–302.

Kalleberg, Arne. 2013. *Good Jobs, Bad Jobs*. NY: Russell Sage Foundation.

Kalleberg, Arne. 1977. "Work Values and Job Rewards: A Theory of Job Satisfaction." *American Sociological Review* 42: 124–143.

Kane, J., and A. D. Wall. 2005. *National Public Survey on White-Collar Crime*. Fairmont, VA: National White-Collar Crime Center.

Kanter, R. M. 1977. *Men and Women of the Corporation*. New York: Basic Books.

Kaplan, Dana, 2003. *American Reform Judaism: An Introduction*. New Brunswick, NJ: Rutgers University Press.

Karabel, Jerome. 2005. *The Chosen: The Hidden History of Admission and Exclusion at Harvard, Yale, and Princeton*. New York: Houghton Mifflin.

Karen, David. 2005. "No Child Left Behind? Sociology Ignored!" *Sociology of Education* 78(2): 165–169.

Kate H. Choi. 2021, March 11. "Family Relations after Interracial Marriage." *Psychology Today*. https://www.psychologytoday.com/us/blog/social-fabric/202103/family-relations-after-interracial-marriage#:~:text=Despite%20more%20favorable%20attitudes%20towards,friends%20before%20and%20after%20marriage.

Katz, V. S., A. B. Jordan, and K. Ognyanova. 2021. "Digital Inequality, Faculty Communication, and Remote Learning Experiences During the COVID-19 Pandemic: A Survey of U.S. Undergraduates." *PLoS ONE* 16(2): e0246641. https://doi.org/10.1371/journal.pone.0246641.

Kearney, Melissa, and Benjamin Harris. 2013. *A Dozen Facts about America's Struggling Lower-Middle Class*. Hamilton Project Policy Paper, Brookings Institution. https://www.brookings.edu/research/a-dozen-facts-about-americas-struggling-lower-middle-class/.

Keisler-Starkey, Katherine, and Lisa Bunch. 2022, September 13. "Health Insurance Coverage in the United States: 2021." U.S. Census Bureau. https://

www.census.gov/library/publications/2022/demo/p60-278.html#:~:text=Of%20the%20subtypes%20of%20health%20insurance%20coverage%2C%20employerbased,percent%29%2C%20and%20VA%20and%20CHAMPVA%20coverage%20%281.0%20percent%29.

Keller, Amy. 2016, April 26. "How to Talk to Doctors." Daily Nurse. https://dailynurse.com/how-to-talk-to-doctors/.

Kelling, Georle L., and James Q. Wilson. 1982, March. "Broken Windows: The Police and Neighborhood Safety." *The Atlantic* 248. https://www.theatlantic.com/magazine/archive/1982/03/broken-windows/304465/.

Kennedy, Randall. 1997. *Race, Crime and the Law*. New York: Pantheon Books, Random House.

Khaldûn, Ibn. 2004. *The Muqaddimah: An Introduction to History*. Princeton, NJ: Princeton University Press.

Khan, Shamus. 2012. *Privilege: The Making of an Adolescent Elite at St. Paul's School*. Princeton, NJ: Princeton University Press.

Khosrokhavar, Farhad. 2008. *Inside Jihadism*. New York: Routledge.

Kidd, Dustin. 2014. *Pop Culture Freaks: Identity, Mass Media, and Society*. Boulder, CO: Westview Press.

Kidd, Dustin. 2010. *Legislating Creativity: The Intersections of Art and Politics*. New York: Routledge.

Killewald, Alexandra, Angela Lee, and Paula England. 2023. "Wealth and Divorce." *Demography* 60(1): 147–171. https://www.jstor.org/stable/48711996.

Kim, Kyounghee. 2009. "Change and Challenge of Korean Family in the Era of Globalization: Centering Transnational Families." *Journal of Ritsumeikan Social Sciences and Humanities* 1: 167–181.

Kim, S., J. Urpelainen, and J. Yang. 2016. "Electric Utilities and American Climate Policy: Lobbying by Expected Winners and Losers." *Journal of Public Policy* 36(2): 251–275.

Kimmel, Michael. 2010. *Misframing Men: Essays on the Politics of Contemporary Masculinities*. New Brunswick, NJ: Rutgers University Press.

King, Mary C. 1992. "The Evolution of Occupational Segregation by Race and Gender, 1940–1988." *Monthly Labor Review* 115(4): 30–36.

King, Ryan S., and Marc Mauer. 2002, February. *State Sentencing and Corrections Policy in an Era of Fiscal Restraint*. Washington, DC: The Sentencing Project.

Kirby, Dianne. 2020. "The Rise of Religious Fundamentalism." In *Understanding Global Politics*, ed. K. Larres and R. Wittlinger. New York: Routledge.

Klass, Perri. 2017, April 10. "Rude Doctors, Rude Nurses, Rude Patients." *New York Times*. https://www.nytimes.com/2017/04/10/well/family/rude-doctors-rude-nurses-rude-patients.html.

Klinenberg, E., M. Araos, and L. Koslov. 2020. "Sociology and the Climate Crisis." *Annual Review of Sociology* 46: 649–669.

Klinenberg, Eric. 2012. *Going Solo: The Extraordinary Rise and Surprising Appeal of Living Alone*. NY: Penguin.

Kluegel, James. 1990. "Trends in Whites' Explanations of the Black-White Gap in Socioeconomic Status, 1977–1989. *American Sociological Review* 55(4): 512–525.

Kochhar, Rakesh, and Stella Sechopoulos, 2022, April 20. "How the American Middle Class Has Changed in the Past Five Decades." Pew Research Center. https://www.pewresearch.org/short-reads/2022/04/20/how-the-american-middle-class-has-changed-in-the-past-five-decades/.

Kochhar, Rakesh. 2023, March 1. "The Enduring Grip of the Gender Pay Gap." Pew Research Center. https://www.pewresearch.org/social-trends/2023/03/01/the-enduring-grip-of-the-gender-pay-gap/#:~:text=not%20entirely%20clear.,Gender%20pay%20gap%20differs%20widely%20by%20race%20and%20ethnicity,the%20earnings%20of%20White%20men.&text=In%202022%2C%20Blac.

Kochhar, Rakesh. 2023, July 26. "Which US Workers Are More Exposed to AI in Their Jobs?" Pew Research Center. https://www.pewresearch.org/social-trends/2023/07/26/which-u-s-workers-are-more-exposed-to-ai-on-their-jobs/.

Koffler, Jacobs. 2015, June 29. "Here Are Places Women Can't Take Their Husband's Name When They Get Married." *Time*. http://time.com/3940094/maiden-married-names-countries/.

Koontz, Stephanie. 2016. *The Way We Never Were: American Families and the Nostalgia Trap*, Revised and Updated edition. New York: Basic Books.

Kopelman, Richard, Rita Fossen, Eletherios Paraskevas, Leanna Lawter, and David Prottas. 2009. "The Bride Is Keeping Her Name: A 35-Year Retrospective Analysis of Trends and Correlates." *Social Behavior and Personality* 37(5): 687–700.

Koutsouris, George, Anna Mountford-Zimdars, and Kristi Dingwall. 2021. "The 'Ideal' Higher Education Student: Understanding the Hidden Curriculum to Enable Institutional Change." *Research in Post Compulsory Education* 26(2): 131–147, doi: 10.1080/13596748.2021.1909921.

Kovacs, B., N. Caplan, S. Grob, and M. King. 2021. Social Networks and Loneliness During the COVID-19 Pandemic. *Socius* 7. https://doi.org/10.1177/2378023120985254.

Kovács, Z., G. Harangozó, C. Szigeti, K. Koppány, A. C. Kondor, and B. Szabó. 2020. Measuring the Impacts of Suburbanization with Ecological Footprint Calculations. *Cities* 101: 102715.

Kovalik, Dan. 2021. *Cancel This Book: The Progressive Case Against Cancel Culture*. New York: Hot Books.

Kramer, Stephanie. 2019, December 12. "US has World's Highest Rate of Children Living in Single-Parent Households." Pew Research Center. https://www.pewresearch.org/short-reads/2019/12/12/u-s-children-more-likely-than-children-in-other-countries-to-live-with-just-one-parent/.

Krauss, Lawrence. 2010, August 1. "Faith and Foolishness: When Religious Beliefs Become Dangerous." *Scientific American*. https://www.scientificamerican.com/article/faith-and-foolishness/.

Kretchmer, Harry. 2020, June 23. "Chart of the Day: Renewables are Increasingly Cheaper than Coal." World Economic Forum. https://www.weforum.org/agenda/2020/06/renewable-energy-cheaper-coal/.

Krislov, Marvin. 2013, December 5. "The Enduring Relevance of a Liberal Arts Education." The Hechinger Report. http://hechingerreport.org/the-enduring-relevance-of-a-liberal-arts-education/.

Krogstad, Jens, Jeffrey Passel, Mohamad Moslimani, and Luis Noe-Bustamante. 2023, September 22. "Key Facts About US Latinos for National Hispanic Heritage Month." Pew Research Center. https://www.pewresearch.org/short-reads/2023/09/22/key-facts-about-us-latinos-for-national-hispanic-heritage-month/#:~:text=The%20roughly%2037.4%20million%20people,on%20the%20island%20in%202022.

Kuisel, Richard. 1996. *Seducing the French: The Dilemma of Americanization*. Berkeley: University of California Press.

Kuo, Hsiang-Hui Daphne, Hyunjoon Park, Taissa S. Hauser, Robert M. Hauser, and Nadine F. Marks. 2019. "Surveys of the Life Course and Aging: Some Comparisons." Working Paper No. 2001-06. Center for Demography and Ecology, University of Wisconsin, Madison. https://cde.wisc.edu/wp-2001-06/.

Kutateladze, Besiki, Whitney Tymas, and Mary Crowley. 2014. "Race and Prosecution in Manhattan." Research Summary. Vera Institute of Justice. Prosecution and Racial Justice Program. https://www.vera.org/publications/race-and-prosecution-in-manhattan.

Lachmann, Richard. 2003. "Elite Self-Interest and Economic Decline in Early Modern Europe." *American Sociological Review* 68: 346–372.

LaFontana, Kathryn, and Antonius Cillessen. 2010. "Developmental Changes in the Priority of Perceived Status in Childhood and Adolescence." *Social Development* 19(1): 130–147.

Landivar, Liana. 2013. "*Disparities in STEM Employment by Sex, Race, and Hispanic Origin.*" American Community Survey Reports, September 2013. Washington, DC: US Census Bureau.

Landivar, Liana Christin, Leah Ruppanner, and William J. Scarborough. 2021, Aptil 1. "Are States Created Equal? Moving to a State with More Expensive Childcare Reduces Mothers' Odds of Employment." *Demography* 58 (2): 451–470. doi: https://doi.org/10.1215/00703370-8997420.

Lane, Christopher. 2007. *Shyness: How Normal Behavior Became a Sickness*. Princeton, NJ: Princeton University Press.

Lang, Hannah, Elizabeth Howcroft, and Tom Wilson. 2023, November 3. "The Crypto Market Bears the Scars of FTX's Collapse." *Reuters*. https://www.reuters.com/technology/crypto-market-still-bears-scars-ftxs-collapse-2023-10-03/.

Lansford, Jennifer E. 2009. "Parental Divorce and Children's Adjustment." *Perspectives on Psychological Science* 4(2): 140–152. http://www.jstor.org/stable/40212308.

Lareau, Annette. 2011. *Unequal Childhoods: Race, Class, and Family Life. Second Edition. A Decade Later*. Berkeley, CA: University of California Press.

Lareau, Annette, Elliot B. Weininger, and Amanda Barrett Cox, 2018. "Parental Challenges to Organizational Authority in an Elite School District: The Role of Cultural, Social, and Symbolic Capital." *Teachers College Record* 120 (January): 1–46.

Larson, Reed, and Maryse Richards. 1991. "Daily Companionship in Late Childhood and Early Adolescence: Changing Developmental Contexts." *Child Development* 62: 284–300.

Laughlin, Linda, and Cheridan Christnacht. 2017, October 3. "Women in Manufacturing." U.S. Census Bureau. https://www.census.gov/newsroom/blogs/random-samplings/2017/10/women-manufacturing.html.

Laurent, Eloi. 2015, March. "Social Ecology: Exploring the Missing Link in Sustainable Development." Working Paper, OFCE-Sciences-Po, Stanford

University. https://www.ofce.sciences-po.fr/pdf/dtravail/WP2015-07.pdf.

Laursen, B., and R. Veenstra. 2021. "Toward Understanding the Functions of Peer Influence: A Summary and Synthesis of Recent Empirical Research." *Journal of Research on Adolescence* 31: 889–907. https://doi.org/10.1111/jora.12606.

Lavery, James V., Rachael M. Porter, and David G. Addiss. 2023. "Cascading Failures in COVID-19 Vaccine Equity." *Science* 380(6644): 460–462.

Lazoritz, Stephen. 2008. "Don't Tolerate Disruptive Physician Behavior." *American Nurse Today* 3(3). https://www.americannursetoday.com/dont-tolerate-disruptive-physician-behavior/.

Le, Tianhao Le, Yuan Wang, Lang Liu, Jiani Yang, Yuk L. Yung, Guohui Li, and John H. Seinfeld. 2020. "Unexpected Air Pollution with Marked Emission Reductions During the COVID-19 Outbreak in China. *Science* 369:702–706. doi:10.1126/science.abb7431.

Lea, John, and Jock Young. 1984. *What Is to Be Done about Law and Order?* New York: Penguin.

Leasca, Stacey. 2017, July 17. "These Are the Highest Paying Jobs in the Gig Economy." *Forbes*. https://www.forbes.com/sites/sleasca/2017/07/17/highest-paying-jobs-gig-economy-lyft-taskrabbit-airbnb/#6abf5d127b64.

Lee, D., and S. McLanahan. 2015. "Family Structure Transitions and Child Development: Instability, Selection, and Population Heterogeneity." *American Sociological Review* 80: 738–763.

Lee, Dohoon, and Sara McLanahan. 2015. "Family Structure Transitions and Child Development: Instability, Selection, and Population Heterogeneity." *American Sociological Review* 80(4): 738–763.

Lee, R., Y. Qian., and C. Wu. 2022. "Coethnic Concentration and Asians' Perceived Discrimination across US Counties during COVID-19." *Socius* 8: 23780231221124580.

Legatum. 2023. "The 2023 Legatum Prosperity Index." https://www.prosperity.com/download_file/view_inline/4789.

Lele, Uma, and Steven W. Stone. 1989. *Population Pressure, the Environment and Agricultural Intensification: Variations on the Boserup Hypothesis*. Managing Agricultural Development in Africa (MADIA) discussion paper no. 4. Washington, DC: The World Bank. http://documents.worldbank.org/curated/en/809971468739234405/Population-pressure-the-environment-and-agricultural-intensification-variations-on-the-Boserup-hypothesis.

Lemert, Charles C. 2008. *Social Things: An Introduction to the Sociological Life*. Lanham, MD: Rowman & Littlefield.

Lemert, Edwin. 1967. *Human Deviance, Social Problems and Social Control*. Englewood Cliffs, NJ: Prentice-Hall.

Lengermann, Patricia M., and Jill Niebrugge-Brantley. 1998. *The Women Founders: Sociology and Social Theory, 1830–1930 : A Text/Reader*. Boston: McGraw-Hill.

Lenhart, Amanda. 2015, April 9. "Teens Social Media and Technology Overview 2015." Pew Research Center. http://www.pewinternet.org/2015/04/09/teens-social-media-technology-2015/.

Leong, Lisa. 2021, September 27. "Here Comes the Great Resignation: Why Millions of Employees Could Quit Their Jobs Post-Pandemic." ABC News Australia. https://www.abc.net.au/news/2021-09-24/the-great-resignation-post-pandemic-work-life-balance/100478866.

Leopold, Thomas. 2018. "Gender Differences in the Consequences of Divorce: A Study of Multiple Outcomes." *Demography* 55(3): 769–797. http://www.jstor.org/stable/45048008.

Leszczensky, L., and S. Pink. 2019. "What Drives Ethnic Homophily? A Relational Approach on How Ethnic Identification Moderates Preferences for Same-Ethnic Friends." *American Sociological Review* 84(3): 394–419. https://doi.org/10.1177/0003122419846849.

Levanon, Asaf, Paula England, and Paul Allison. 2009. "Occupational Feminization and Pay: Assessing Causal Dynamics Using 1950–2000 US Census Data." *Social Forces* 88(2): 865–891.

Levin, D. 2020, October 12. "No Home, No Wi-Fi: Pandemic Adds to Strain on Poor College Students." *New York Times*. https://www.nytimes.com/2020/10/12/us/covid-poor-college-students.html.

Levitt, Peggy, and Deepak Lamba-Nieves. 2011. "Social Remittances Revisited." *Journal of Ethnic and Migration Studies* 37(1): 1–22.

Levitt, Peggy, and Nina Glick Schiller. 2004. "Conceptualizing Simultaneity: A Trans-national Social Field Perspective on Society." *International Migration Review* 38(3): 1002–1039.

Levitt, Peggy. 2001. *The Transnational Villagers*. Stanford: University of California Press.

Levitt, Steven. 2004. "Understanding Why Crime Fell in the 1990s: Four Factors That Explain the Decline and Six That Do Not." *Journal of Economic Perspectives* 18: 163–190.

Lewallen, J., and E. Behm-Morawitz. 2016. "Pinterest or Thinterest?: Social Comparison and Body Image on Social Media." *Social Media + Society* 2(1): 2056305116640559.

Lewis, C. E., and M. A. Lewis. 1984. "Peer Pressure and Risk-Taking Behaviors in Children." *American Journal of Public Health* 74: 580–594.

Liberman, A. M., D. S. Kirk, and K. Kim. 2014. "Labeling Effects of First Juvenile Arrests: Secondary Deviance and Secondary Sanctioning." *Criminology* 52: 345–370. https://doi.org/10.1111/1745-9125.12039.

Lieberson, Stanley. 1980. *A Piece of the Pie: Blacks and White Immigrants Since 1880*. Berkeley: University of California Press.

Liebman, Charles S. 1973. *The Ambivalent American Jew*. Philadelphia: Jewish Publication Society.

Lienesch, Michael. 1993. *Redeeming America: Piety and Politics in the New Christian Right*. Chapel Hill: University of North Carolina Press.

Lin, Alex. 2015. "Citizenship Education in American Schools and Its Role in Developing Civic Engagement: A Review of the Research." *Educational Review* 67(1): 35–63. doi: 10.1080/00131911.2013.813440.

Ling, T., J. Phillips, and S. Weihrich. 2012. "Online Evaluations vs In-Class Paper Teaching Evaluations: A Paired Comparison." *Journal of the Academy of Business Education* 12: 150–161.

Link, Bruce, Jo Phelan, Ann Stueve, Robert Moore, and Ezra Susser. 1995. "Lifetime and Five-Year Prevalence of Homelessness in the United States: New Evidence on an Old Debate." *American Journal of Orthopsychiatry* 65: 347–354.

Lipka, Michael, and Conrad Hackett. 2017, April 6. "Why Muslims Are the World's Fastest-Growing Religious Group." Pew Research Center. http://www.pewresearch.org/fact-tank/2017/04/06/why-muslims-are-the-worlds-fastest-growing-religious-group/.

Lipsitz, Keena. 2009. "The Consequences of Battleground and 'Spectator' State Residency for Political Participation." *Political Behavior* 31: 187–209.

Lischer, Sarah. 2014. "Conflict and Conflict Induced Displacement." In *Oxford Handbook of Refugee and Forced Migration Studies*, ed. E. Qasmiyeh, G. Loescher, K. Long, and N. Sigona (pp. 317–329). New York: Oxford University Press.

Livingston, Gretchen, and Anna Brown. 2017, May. "Intermarriage in the U.S. 50 Years after Loving v. Virginia." Pew Research Center. https://www.pewresearch.org/social-trends/2017/05/18/intermarriage-in-the-u-s-50-years-after-loving-v-virginia/.

Livingston, Gretchen. 2017, June 16. "The Rise of Multiracial and Multiethnic Babies in the US." Pew Research Center. https://www.pewresearch.org/short-reads/2017/06/06/the-rise-of-multiracial-and-multiethnic-babies-in-the-u-s/.

Livingston, Gretchen. 2017, June 6. "The Rise of Multiracial and Multiethnic Babies in the U.S." Pew Research Center. https://www.pewresearch.org/short-reads/2017/06/06/the-rise-of-multiracial-and-multiethnic-babies-in-the-u-s/

Livingston, Gretchen. 2018, April 8. "About One-Third of U.S. Children Are Living with an Unmarried Parent." Pew Research Center. https://www.pewresearch.org/short-reads/2018/04/27/about-one-third-of-u-s-children-are-living-with-an-unmarried-parent/.

Lochner, Lance. 2011. "Nonproduction Benefits of Education: Crime, Health, and Good Citizenship." In *Handbook of the Economics of Education*, Vol. 4, eds. Eric A. Hanushek, Stephen Machin, and Ludger Woessmann (pp. 183–282). Amsterdam: North Holland.

Lockwood, Matthew. 2018. "Right-Wing Populism and the Climate Change Agenda: Exploring the Linkages." *Environmental Politics* 4: 712–732.

Loft, Phili. 2023. "Iran Protests 2022: Human Rights and International Response." House of Commons Library Research Briefing, May. Accessed at https://researchbriefings.files.parliament.uk/documents/CBP-9679/CBP-9679.pdf.

Logan, J. G., and D. J. Barksdale. 2008. "Allostasis and Allostatic Load: Expanding the Discourse on Stress and Cardiovascular Disease." *Journal of Clinical Nursing* 17(7B): 2018.

Lorenz, Taylor, Kellen Browning, and Sheera Frenkel. 2020, June 21. "Tik Tok Teens and K-Pop Stans Say They Sank Trump Rally." *New York Times*. https://www.nytimes.com/2020/06/21/style/tiktok-trump-rally-tulsa.html.

Lotz, Roy. 1991. *Crime and the American Press*. New York: Praeger.

Lowi, Theodore J. 1986. *The Personal President: Power Invested, Promise Unfulfilled*. Ithaca, NY: Cornell University Press.

Lutfey, K., and J. T. Mortimer. 2003. "Development and Socialization through the Adult Life Course." In *Handbook of Social Psychology* (pp. 183–202). Boston, MA: Springer US.

Luthar, Suniya, and Lucia Ciciolla. 2015. "Who Mothers Mommy? Factors That Contribute to Mothers' Well-Being. *Developmental Psychology*, 51(12): 1812–1823.

Lyonette, Clare, and Rosemary Crompton. 2015. "Sharing the Load? Partners' Relative Earnings and the Division of Domestic Labour." *Work, Employment and Society* 29: 23–40.

Maani, N., and S. Galea. 2020. "COVID-19 and Underinvestment in the Public Health Infrastructure of the United States." *The Milbank Quarterly* 98(2): 250.

Madden, Mary, Amanda Lenhart, Sandra Cortesi, Urs Gasser, Maeve Duggan, Aaron Smith, and Meredith Beaton. 2013, May 21. "Teens, Social Media, and Privacy." Pew Research Center, Internet Science and Tech. http://www.pewinternet.org/2013/05/21/teens-social-media-and-privacy/.

Madhani, Aamer, Darlene Superville, and Matthew Lee. 2023, August 18. "*US, Japan and South Korea agree to expand security ties at summit amid China, North Korea worries*." Associated Press. https://apnews.com/article/camp-david-summit-biden-south-korea-japan-0bc36bb3705a3dc1b69dc8cd47b35dd3.

Magill, Katie. 2023, July 6. "Jobs of the Future, Now Hiring: AI Job Titles and What They Do." *Data Space*. https://dataspace.com/talent-acquisition/ai-job-titles/.

Mahnken, Kevin. 2017, January 29. "An Arts Education Crisis? How Potential Federal Cuts Could Decimate School Arts Programs." *The 74*. https://www.the74million.org/article/potential-federal-cuts-may-decimate-school-arts-programs/.

Mann, Michael. 1993. *The Sources of Social Power: The Rise of Classes and Nation-States, 1760–1914*. Cambridge, UK: Cambridge University Press.

Mannheim, Karl. 1952. "The Problem of Generations." In *Essays on the Sociology of Knowledge: Collected Works*, Volume 5, ed. Paul Kecskemeti (pp. 276–322). New York: Routledge.

Manokha, Ivan. 2020. "The Implications of Digital Employee Monitoring and People Analytics for Power Relations in the Workplace." *Surveillance & Society* 18(4): 540–554.

Manyika, James, Susan Lund, Jacques Bughin, Kelsey Robinson, Jan Mischke, and Deepa Mahajan. 2016, October. "Independent Work: Choice, Necessity, and the Gig Economy." McKinsey Global Institute. https://www.mckinsey.com/global-themes/employment-and-growth/Independent-work-Choice-necessity-and-the-gig-economy.

Manza, Jeff, and Chris Uggen. 2006. *Locked Out: Felon Disenfranchisement and American Democracy*. New York: Oxford University Press.

Marcotte, D. E., T. Bailey, C. Borkoski, and G. S. Kienzl. 2005. "The Returns of a Community College Education: Evidence from the National Education Longitudinal Survey." *Educational Evaluation and Policy Analysis* 27(2), 157–175. https://doi.org/10.3102/01623737027002157.

Mare, Robert D. 1981. "Change and Stability in Educational Stratification." *American Sociological Review* 46(1): 72–87.

Margalit, Avishai. 1996. *The Decent Society*. Cambridge, MA: Havard University Press.

Martin, E. 1990. "Science and Women's Bodies." In *Body/Politics: Women and the Discourses of Science*, eds. Mary Jacobus, Evelyn Fox Keller, and Sally Shuttleworth, eds. (pp. 69–82). New York and London: Routledge.

Martin, Wednesday. 2013, January 23. "Banning the 'Blended' Family: Why Step-Families Will Never Be the Same as First Families." *Telegraph*. http://www.telegraph.co.uk/women/mother-tongue/9820359/Banning-the-blended-family-why-step-families-will-never-be-the-same-as-first-families.html.

Martineau, Harriet. 1837. *Society in America*. London: Saunders and Otley.

Martineau, Harriet. 1838. *How to Observe: Morals and Manners*. Whitefish, MT: Kessinger Publishing.

Marwell, Gerald, and Pamela Oliver. 1993. *The Critical Mass in Collective Action. A Micro-Social Theory*. Cambridge: Cambridge University Press.

Marx, Karl, and Friedrich Engels. 1848. *The Communist Manifesto*. New York: Penguin.

Mason, Mary Ann, Sydney Harrison-Jay, Gloria Messick Svare, and Nicholas H. Wolfinger. 2002. "Stepparents: De Facto Parents or Legal Strangers?" *Journal of Family Issues* 23(4): 507–522.

Massey, Douglas S. 1999. "International Migration at the Dawn of the Twenty-First Century: The Role of the State." *Population and Development Review* 25(2): 303–322.

Massey, Douglas S., and Nancy A. Denton. 1993. *American Apartheid: Segregation and the Making of the Underclass*. Cambridge, MA: Harvard University Press.

Massey, Douglas. 1995. "The New Immigration and Ethnicity in the United States." *Population and Development Review* 21: 631–652.

Mast, Jason L. 2012. *The Performative Presidency. Crisis and Resurrection during the Clinton Years.* Cambridge: Cambridge University Press.

Matheson, T. J. 1992. "Marcuse, Ellul, and the Science-Fiction Film: Negative Responses to Technology." *Science Fiction Studies*: 326–339.

Mathews, Carol. 2020, November 17. "Hoarding, Stockpiling, Panic Buying: What's Normal Behavior in an Abnormal Time?" *The Conversation.* https://theconversation.com/hoarding-stockpiling-panic-buying-whats-normal-behavior-in-an-abnormal-time-149422.

Matthews, T. J., and B. E. Hamilton. 2014. "First Births to Older Women Continue to Rise." *NCHS Data Brief* 152: 1–8.

Matthews, Jennifer. 2009. *Chicle: The Chewing Gum of the Americas, From the Ancient Maya to William Wrigley.* Tuscon, Arizona: University of Arizona Press.

Mayer, Susan E. 2001. "How Did the Increase in Economic Inequality between 1970 and 1990 Affect Children's Educational Attainment?" *American Journal of Sociology* 107:1–32.

Mayol-Garcia, Yeris, Benjamin Gurrentz, and Rose M. Kreider. 2021, April. "Number, Timing, and Duration of Marriages and Divorces: 2016." Current Population Reports, U.S. Census Bureau Report Number P70-167.

McAdam, Doug. 1982. *Political Process and the Development of Black Insurgency, 1930–1970.* Chicago: University of Chicago Press.

McCarthy, John D., and Mayer N. Zald. 1977. "Resource Mobilization and Social Movements: A Partial Theory." *American Journal of Sociology* 82(6): 1212–1241.

McCurry, Justin. 2020, June 24. "How U.S. K-Pop Fans Became a Political Force to be Reckoned With." *The Guardian.* https://www.theguardian.com/music/2020/jun/24/how-us-k-pop-fans-became-a-political-force-to-be-reckoned-with-blm-donald-trump#:~:text=Those%20hoping%20to%20hold%20back,memes%20of%20their%20favourite%20artists%2C.

McErlean, K. 2021, September 22. "The Growth of Education Differentials in Marital Dissolution in the – United States." *Demographic Research* 45: 841–856. doi:10.4054/demres.2021.45.26.

McGann, James G. 2019. "2018 Global Go To Think Tank Index Report." Think Tanks and Civil Societies Program, University of Pennsylvania. https://repository.upenn.edu/think_tanks/16.

McGregor, Jena. 2017, September 1. "Job Satisfaction Is Up, but Well Below All-Time Highs." *Washington Post.* https://www.washingtonpost.com/news/on-leadership/wp/2017/09/01/job-satisfaction-is-up-but-still-well-below-one-time-highs/?utm_term=.eb466e925414.

McIntosh, Kriston, Emily Moss, Ryan Nunn, and Jay Shambaugh. 2020, February 27. "Examining the Black–White Wealth Gap." Brookings Institution. https://www.brookings.edu/blog/up-front/2020/02/27/examining-the-black-white-wealth-gap/.

McKay, Ramah. 2003, May 1. "Family Reunification." Migration Policy Institute. https://www.migrationpolicy.org/article/family-reunification.

McKendrick, Joe, 2023, August 13. "Time to Redesign Your Career for the Age of Artificial Intelligence." *Forbes.* https://www.forbes.com/sites/joemckendrick/2023/08/13/time-to-redesign-your-career-for-the-age-of-artificial-intelligence/?sh=1da7e5381a24.

McKinlay, J. B. and L. D. Marceau. 2002. "The End of the Golden Age of Doctoring." *International Journal of Health Services* 32(2): 379–416.

McKinlay, J. B., and L. D. Marceau. 2008. "When There Is No Doctor: Reasons for the Disappearance of Primary Care Physicians in the US during the Early 21st Century." *Social Science & Medicine* 67(10): 1481–1491.

McLanahan, S., L. Tach, and D. Schneider. 2013. "The Causal Effects of Father Absence." *Annual Review of Sociology* 39: 399–427.

McNicholas, Celine, and Margaret Poydack. 2020, June 22. "Workers Are Striking during the Coronavirus." Economic Policy Institute Working Economics Blog. https://www.epi.org/blog/thousands-of-workers-have-gone-on-strike-during-the-coronavirus-labor-law-must-be-reformed-to-strengthen-this-fundamental-right/.

Mead, George Herbert. 1967. *Mind, Self, and Society from the Standpoint of a Social Behaviorist.* Chicago: University of Chicago Press.

Mead, M. 1928. *Coming of Age in Samoa.* New York: William Morrow.

Means, B., and J. Neisler. 2021. "Teaching and Learning in the Time of COVID: The Student Perspective." *Online Learning* 25(1): 8–27. https://doi.org/10.24059/olj.v25i1.2496.

Medhora, S. 2015, January 8. "ACT Moves to Expunge Historic Convictions of Homosexuality." *The Guardian.*

https://www.theguardian.com/world/2015/jan/09/act-moves-expunge-historic-convictions-homosexuality.

Medvetz, Thomas. 2012. *Think Tanks in America*. Chicago: University of Chicago Press.

Melucci, Alberto, John Keane, and Paul Mier. 1989. *Nomads of the Present: Social Movements and Individual Needs in Contemporary Society*. Philadelphia: Temple University Press.

Menjivar, C. 2000. *Fragmented Ties: Salvadoran Immigrant Networks in America*. Berkeley: University of California Press.

Menjivar, Cecilia. 1997. "Immigrant Kinship Networks and the Impact of the Receiving Context: Salvadorans in San Francisco in the Early 1990s." *Social Problems* 44: 104–123.

Merten, Paxtyn, 2024, July 30. "Here's How the Average Childbirth Age Has Changed over Time." Northwell Health. Retrieved from https://www.northwell.edu/news/the-latest/geriatric-pregnancy-increases-complication-rate#:~:text=Those%20giving%20birth%20in%202022,Center%20for%20Health%20Statistics%20data.

Merton, Robert K. 1988. "The Matthew Effect in Science, II: Cumulative Advantage and the Symbolism of Intellectual Property." *Isis* 79(4): 606–623. http://www.jstor.org/stable/234750.

Merton, Robert. [1942] 1973. *The Sociology of Science: Theoretical and Empirical Investigations*. Chicago: University of Chicago Press.

Merton, Robert. 1968. "The Matthew Effect in Science." *Science* 159: 56–63.

Merton, Robert. 1968. *Social Theory and Social Structure*. New York: Free Press.

Messner, Steven F., and Richard Rosenfeld. 2007. *Crime and the American Dream*. Belmont, CA: Wadsworth.

Messner, Steven F., Sandro Galea, Kenneth J. Tardiff, Melissa Tracy, Angela Bucciarelli, Tinka Markham Piper, Victoria Frye, and David Vlahov. 2007. "Policing, Drugs, and the Homicide Decline in New York City in the 1990s." *Criminology* 45(2): 385–413.

Metz, C. 2015. "Why WhatsApp Only Needs 50 Engineers for Its 900 Million Users." https://www.wired.com/2015/09/whatsapp-serves-900-million-users-50-engineers/.

Meyer, John W. 2010. "World Society, Institutional Theories, and the Actor." *Annual Review of Sociology* 36: 1–20.

Meyer, John W., Francisco O. Ramirez, and Yasemin N. Soysal. 1992. "World Expansion of Mass Education, 1870–1970." *Sociology of Education* 65(2): 128–149.

Meyer, John W., John Boli, George M. Thomas, and Francisco O. Ramirez. 1997. "World Society and the Nation-State." *American Journal of Sociology* 103(1): 144–181.

Meyers, Seth. 2022, December 9. "5 Principles to Manage the Complex Bind of Step-Parenting." *Psychology Today*.

Milanovic, Branco. 2010. *The Haves and the Have-Nots: A Brief and Idiosyncratic History of Global Inequality*. New York: Basic Books.

Milanovic, Branco. 2016. *Global Inequality: A New Approach for the Age of Globalization*. Cambridge, MA: Harvard University Press.

Miles, A. 2015. "The (Re) Genesis of Values: Examining the Importance of Values for Action." *American Sociological Review* 80(4): 680–704.

Miller, Claire Cain. 2016, March 18. "As Women Take Over a Male-Dominated Field, the Pay Drops." *New York Times*. https://www.nytimes.com/2016/03/20/upshot/as-women-take-over-a-male-dominated-field-the-pay-drops.html.

Miller, Marc. 2016, August 17. "To Get A Job, Use Your Weak Ties." *Forbes*. https://www.forbes.com/sites/nextavenue/2016/08/17/to-get-a-job-use-your-weak-ties/#2ea3dd846b87.

Miller, Peter, and Nikolas Rose. 1997. "Mobilising the Consumer: Assembling the Subject of Consumption." *Theory, Culture & Society* 14(1): 1–36.

Mills, C. Wright. 2000. *The Sociological Imagination*. New York: Oxford University Press.

Minkin Rachel, Kim Parker, Juliana Menasce Horowitz, and Carolina Aragão. 2024. "Parents, Young Adult Children and the Transition to Adulthood." Pew Research Center. https://www.pewresearch.org/social-trends/2024/01/25/parents-young-adult-children-and-the-transition-to-adulthood/.

Minkoff, D. 2016. "The Payoffs of Organizational Membership for Political Activism in Established Democracies." *American Journal of Sociology* 122(2): 425–468.

Minkoff, Debra C. 1997. "Producing Social Capital: National Social Movements and Civil Society." *American Behavioral Scientist*, 40(5): 606–619.

Misachi, John. 2017, April 25. "The Nations of Europe by the Average Age at First Marriage." World Atlas.

https://www.worldatlas.com/articles/the-nations-of-europe-by-the-average-age-at-first-marriage.html.

Mishel, L., E. Gould, J. and Bivens. 2015. "Wage Stagnation in Nine Charts." *Economic Policy Institute* 6: 2–13.

Misner, Ivan, Hazel M. Walker, and Frank J. De Raffelle Jr. 2012. *Business Networking and Sex: Not What You Think*. Irvine, CA: Entrepreneur Press.

Mohanty, C. T. 1984. "Under Western Eyes: Feminist Scholarship and Colonial Discourses." *boundary 2*, 12(3): 333–358.

Mojola, Sanyu A. 2014. *Love, Money and HIV: Becoming a Modern African Woman in the Age of AIDS*. Berkeley: University of California Press.

Mol, Arthur, and Gert Spaargaren. 2000. "Ecological Modernisation Theory in Debate: A Review." In *Ecological Modernisation around the World*, eds. A. Mol and D. Sonnenfeld (pp. 17–49). London: Frank Cass Publishers.

Molina-Guzmán, Isabel. 2010. *Dangerous Curves: Latina Bodies in the Media*. New York: New York University Press.

Molla, Rani, and Peter Kafka. 2019, April 3. "Here's Who Owns Everything in Big Media Today. It Probably Won't Look Like This for Long." *Recode*. https://www.recode.net/2018/1/23/16905844/media-landscape-verizon-amazon-comcast-disney-fox-relationships-chart.

Molotch, Harvey. 2005. *Where Stuff Comes From: How Toasters, Toilets, Cars, Computers and Many Other Things Come to Be as They Are*. New York: Routledge.

Moore, L., and A. Diez-Roux. 2006. "Associations of Neighborhood Characteristics with the Location and Type of Food Stores." *American Journal of Public Health* 96: 325–331.

Moore, Randy, and William McComas, 2016. *The Scopes Monkey Trial*. Charleston, SC: Arcadia Publishing.

Mora, G. Christina. 2015. *Making Hispanics: How Activists, Bureaucrats, and Media Constructed a New American*. Chicago: University of Chicago Press.

Morgan, Michael, Jorgen Elbe, and Javier Curiel. 2009. "Has the Experience Economy Arrived? The Views of Destination Managers in Three Visitor Dependent Areas." *International Journal of Tourism Research* 11: 201–216.

Morgan, Rachel E., and Alexandra Thompson. 2022. "The Nation's Two Crime Measures, 2011–2020." Statistical Brief. Us Department of Justice, Office of Justice Programs, Bureau of Justice Statistics. NCJ 303385.

Morgan, Stephen, and Youn-Mi Kim. 2006. "Inequality of Conditions and Intergenerational Mobility: Changing Patterns of Educational Attainment in the United States." In *Mobility and Inequality: Frontiers of Research From Sociology and Economics*, eds. S. Morgan, D. Grusky, and G. Fields (pp. 165–194). Stanford, CA: Stanford University Press.

Morran, C. 2014, April 21. "McDonald's Trying to Stop Differentiating between 'Girls' and 'Boys' Toys in Happy Meals." *The Consumerist* (archives). Yonkers, NY: Consumer Reports https://consumerist.com/2014/04/21/mcdonalds-trying-to-stop-differentiating-between-girls-and-boys-toys-in-happy-meals/.

Morrione, Thomas J. 1988. "Herbert G. Blumer (1900–1987): "A Legacy of Concepts, Criticisms, and Contributions." *Symbolic Interaction* 11: 1–12.

Morris, Aldon. 2015. *The Scholar Denied: W. E. B. Du Bois and the Birth of Modern Sociology*. Los Angeles: University of California Press.

Morris, Carolyn. 2021, November 22. "How Much Are People Making from the Sharing Economy?" Earnest Blog. https://www.earnest.com/blog/sharing-economy-income-data/.

Mosca, Gaetano. 1939. *The Ruling Class*. New York: McGraw-Hill.

Moss, Geoffrey, Keith McIntish, and Ewa Prasiuk. 2023. *Barista in the City: Subcultural Lives, Paid Employment and the Urban Context*. New York: Taylor and Francis.

Moss-Racusin, C. A., J. F. Dovidio, V. L. Brescoll, M. J. Graham, and J. Handelsman. 2012. "Science Faculty's Subtle Gender Biases Favor Male Students." *Proceedings of the National Academy of Sciences* 109(41): 16474–16479.

Movement Advancement Project. 2024. "Bans on Transgender People Using Public Bathrooms and Facilities According to Their Gender Identity." Equality Maps. https://www.lgbtmap.org/equality-maps/nondiscrimination/bathroom_bans.

Moynihan, Ray. 2003. "The Making of a Disease: Female Sexual Dysfunction." *British Medical Journal* 326(45). https://www.bmj.com/content/326/7379/45?ijkey=1100a4d8cd38ed943debc246da5f84e93b5c71b2&keytype2=tf_ipsecsha.

Mrkonjic, Elma. 2022. "27 Alarming Sexual Harassment in the Workplace Statistics." *GoRemotely*.

https://goremotely.net/blog/sexual-harassment-in-the-workplace-statistics.

Mukerji, Chandra, and Michael Schudson, eds. 1991. *Rethinking Popular Culture: Contemporary Perspectives in Cultural Studies*. Berkeley, CA: University of California Press.

Muller, Christopher, Robert Sampson, and Alix Winter. 2018. "Environmental Inequality: The Social Causes and Consequences of Lead Exposure." *Annual Review of Sociology* 44: 263–282.

Mullings, L., and A. J. Schulz. 2006. "Intersectionality and Health: An Introduction." In *Gender, Race, Class & Health: Intersectional Approaches*, eds. A. J. Schulz and L. Mullings (pp. 3–17). San Francisco: Jossey-Bass.

Mundy, Liza. 2017. *Code Girls: The Untold Story of the American Women Code Breakers of World War II*. New York: Hachette Books.

Muro, Mark. 2020, March 3. "No Matter Which Way You Look at It, Tech Jobs Are Still Concentrating in Just a Few Cities." Brooking Institute. https://www.brookings.edu/research/tech-is-stillconcentrating/.

Murrell, Nathaniel Samuel. 1998. *Chanting Down Babylon: The Rastafari Reader*. Philadelphia: Temple University Press.

Murthy, Vivek. 2023. "Our Epidemic of Loneliness and Isolation." *The U.S. Surgeon General's Advisory on the Healing Effects of Social Connection and Community*. Washington, DC: Health and Human Services.

Murthy, Vivek. 2023, May 23. "Surgeon General Issues New Advisory About Effects Social Media Use Has on Youth Mental Health." U.S. Department of Health and Human Services. https://www.hhs.gov/about/news/2023/05/23/surgeon-general-issues-new-advisory-about-effects-social-media-use-has-youth-mental-health.html.

Musick, Kelly and Meier, Ann. 2010. "Are Both Parents Always Better Than One? Parental Conflict and Young Adult Well-Being." *Social Science Research* 39: 814–30.

Musick, Kelly, Jennie E. Brand, and Dwight Davis. 2012. "Variation in the Relationship Between Education and Marriage: Marriage Market Mismatch?" *Journal of Marriage and Family* 74(1): 53–69.

NACE. 2023, March. "Executive Summary: 2023 Internship and Co-op Report." National Association of Colleges and Employers. https://www.naceweb.org/uploadedFiles/files/2023/publication/executive-summary/2023-nace-internship-and-co-op-report-executive-summary.pdf.

Nahin, Richard L., Patricia M. Barnes, and Barbara J. Stussman. 2016. "*Expenditures on Complementary Health Approaches: United States, 2012*." National Health Statistics Reports 95. Hyattsville, MD: National Center for Health Statistics.

Nam, H. H., K. Sawyer, and H. K. Style. 2022. "Understanding Anti-Asian Sentiment and Political Behavior in the Wake of COVID-19." *Politics, Groups, and Identities* 12(2): 395–414. https://doi.org/10.1080/21565503.2022.2137051.

Namie, Gary. 2017. "2017 WBI US Workplace Bullying Survey." https://workplacebullying.org/wbi-research/.

Nanos, Janelle. 2016, June 22. "Millennials' Strange Love Affair with Greeting Cards." *Boston Globe*. https://www.bostonglobe.com/business/2016/06/21/stationery/cB8ULjVpWBDiJfrlJGpzxH/story.html.

Naples, N. A. 2004. "From the SWS President: Queer Parenting in the New Millennium." *Gender and Society* 18(6), 679–684. http://www.jstor.org/stable/4149389.

National Academies of Sciences, Engineering, and Medicine. 2017. *Community Violence as a Population Health Issue: Proceedings of a Workshop*. Washington, DC: The National Academies Press. doi: https://doi.org/10.17226/23661.

National Association of Colleges and Employers. 2024. *Job Outlook 2024*.

National Endowment for the Arts. 2012. *How the United States Funds the Arts*, 3rd edition. NEA Office of research and Analysis. https://www.arts.gov/impact/research/publications/how-united-states-funds-arts.

National Endowment for the Arts. 2015. "A Decade of Arts Engagement: Findings from the Survey of Public Participation in the Arts, 2002–2012." NEA Research Report #58. Office of Research and Analysis. https://www.arts.gov/sites/default/files/2012-sppa-feb2015.pdf.

National Institute of Environmental Health Sciences. 2019. "Health and Education. Women's Health." https://www.niehs.nih.gov/health/topics/population/whealth/index.cfm.

National Institutes of Health. 2017. "Genomic Medicine for Patients and the Public. Frequently Asked Questions about Genetic Testing." https://www.genome.gov/19516567/faq-about-genetic-testing/.

NCES. 2023. "Fast Facts." National Center for Education Statistics. https://nces.ed.gov/fastfacts/index.asp?faq=FFOption4#faqFFOption4.

Nebehay, Stephanie. 2020, April 7. "Nurses Must be Protected from Abuse During Coronavirus Pandemic: WHO, Nursing Groups." *Reuters*. https://www.reuters.com/article/us-health-coronavirus-nurses/nurses-must-be-protected-from-abuse-during-coronavirus-pandemic-who-nursing-groups-idUSKBN21O317/.

Neckerman, Kathryn, and Florencia Torche. 2007. "Inequality: Causes and Consequences," *Annual Review of Sociology* 33: 335–357.

Newport, Frank. 2013, July 25. "In US, 87% Approve of Black-White Marriage, vs. 4% in 1958." Gallup. http://www.gallup.com/poll/163697/approve-marriage-blacks-whites.aspx.

Ng, Pak Tee. 2017, September 20. "The Education Paradoxes of Singapore." *International Herald News*. Web. https://internationalednews.com/2017/09/20/the-education-paradoxes-of-singapore/.

Nguyen, A. 2021. "The Constant Boss: Work under Digital Surveillance." *Data and Society*. https://datasociety.net/wp-content/uploads/2021/05/The_Constant_Boss.pdf.

Nicas, Jack. 2020a, March 14. "He Has 17,700 Bottles of Hand Sanitizer and Nowhere to Sell Them." *New York Times*. https://www.nytimes.com/2020/03/14/technology/coronavirus-purell-wipes-amazon-sellers.html.

Nicas, Jack. 2020b, March 15. "The Man with 17,700 Bottles of Hand Sanitizer Just Donated Them." *New York Times*. https://www.nytimes.com/2020/03/15/technology/matt-colvin-hand-sanitizer-donation.html.

Nielsen. 2016, April 26. "Nearly 75% Of Global Consumers List Brand Origin as Key Purchase Driver." https://www.prnewswire.com/news-releases/nielsen-nearly-75-of-global-consumers-list-brand-origin-as-key-purchase-driver-300257709.html

NitroMed. 2007, July 30. "BiDil Maker NitroMed Responds to 'Race In A Bottle.'" *Scientific American*. https://www.scientificamerican.com/article/bidil-maker-nitromed-responds-to-race-in-a-bottle/.

Noam, E. 2009. *Media Ownership and Concentration in America*. New York: Oxford University Press.

Noam, Eli M. 2016. *Who Owns the World's Media? Media Concentration and Ownership around the World*. Oxford, UK: Oxford University Press.

Norris, P. 2023. "Cancel Culture: Myth or Reality?" *Political studies* 71(1): 145–174.

North, Douglass C. 1961. *The Economic Growth of the United States, 1790–1860*. Englewood Cliffs: Prentice-Hall.

Nyenyembe, J. 2017. "Stewards of God's Mercy: Vocation and Priestly Ministry in Africa." *Journal of Global Catholicism* 1(2):74–95.

O'Barr, W. M. 2012. "Sexuality, Race, and Ethnicity in Advertising." *Advertising & Society Review* 13(3). https://muse.jhu.edu/article/491084.

Office for Human Research Protections. United States. 1978. *The Belmont Report: Ethical Principles and Guidelines for the Protection of Human Subjects of Research*. Bethesda, Md.: The Commission. https://www.hhs.gov/ohrp/regulations-and-policy/belmont-report/read-the-belmont-report/index.html.

Okamoto, Dina, and Kim Ebert. 2016. "Group Boundaries, Immigrant Inclusion, and the Politics of Immigrant-Native Relations." *American Behavioral Scientist* 60: 224–250.

Okoro, Catherine A., NaTasha D. Hollis, Alissa C. Cyrus, and Shannon Griffin-Blake. 2018. "Prevalence of Disabilities and Health Care Access by Disability Status and Type Among Adults—United States, 2016." *Morbidity and Mortality Weekly Report* 67(32): 882–887. doi:http://dx.doi.org/10.15585/mmwr.mm6732a3.

Oliphant, Baxter J. 2023, April 7. "Top Tax Frustrations for Americans: The Feeling that Some Corporations, Wealth People Don't Pay Fair Share." Pew Research Center. https://www.pewresearch.org/short-reads/2023/04/07/top-tax-frustrations-for-americans-the-feeling-that-some-corporations-wealthy-people-dont-pay-fair-share/.

Oliver, Melvin L., and Thomas M. Shapiro. 2006. *Black Wealth/White Wealth. A New Perspective on Racial Inequality*. New York: Routledge.

Olson, Mancur. 1971. *The Logic of Collective Action: Public Goods and the Theory of Groups*. Cambridge MA: Harvard University Press.

Olzak, Susan. 1994. *The Dynamics of Ethnic Competition and Conflict*. Stanford, CA: Stanford University Press.

Omi, Michael, and Howard Winant. 1994. *Racial Formation in the United States: From the 1960s to the 1990s*. New York: Routledge.

Omohundro, Stephen M. 2008. "The Basic AI Drives." In *Artificial General Intelligence 2008: Proceedings of the First AGI Conference*, ed. Pei Wang, Ben Goertzel, and

Stan Franklin (pp. 483–492). Frontiers in Artificial Intelligence and Applications 171. Amsterdam: IOS.

Onwuachi-Willig, Angela, and Jacob Willig-Onwuachi. 2009. "A House Divided: The Invisibility of the Multiracial Family." *Harvard Civil Rights–Civil Liberties Law Review* 44: 231–253.

Open Doors. 2022, November 14. "Open Doors 2022: Report on International Educational Exchange." Institute of International Education. https://opendoorsdata.org/annual-release/international-students/.

Open Secrets. 2023. Lobbying Data Summary. https://www.opensecrets.org/federal-lobbying.

Organ Procurement and Transplantation Network. n.d. "*How Organ Allocation Works*." Washington, DC: US Department of Health and Human Services. https://optn.transplant.hrsa.gov/learn/about-transplantation/how-organ-allocation-works/.

Organisation for Economic Co-operation and Development. 2012. *Redefining "Urban": A New Way to Measure Metropolitan Areas*. Paris: OECD Publishing. https://doi.org/10.1787/9789264174108-en.

Organisation for Economic Co-operation and Development. 2013a. *OECD Skills Outlook 2013: First Results from the Survey of Adult Skills*. Paris: OECD Publishing. http://dx.doi.org/10.1787/9789264204256-en.

Organisation for Economic Co-operation and Development. 2018. "Marriage and Divorce Rates." *OECD Family Database*. OECD, Social Policy Division, Directorate of Employment, Labour and Social Affairs. Web. http://www.oecd.org/els/family/database.htm.

Organisation for Economic Co-operation and Development. 2017. *Health at a Glance 2017: OECD Indicators*. Paris: OECD Publishing. https://doi.org/10.1787/health_glance-2017-en.

Ortiz-Ospina, Esteban, and Max Roser. 2024. "Marriages and Divorces" *Our World in Data*. https://ourworldindata.org/marriages-and-divorces.

Ostrower, Francie. 2004. *Partnerships between Large and Small Cultural Organizations: A Strategy for Building Arts Participation*. Washington, DC: Urban Institute.

Otterman, Sharon. 2011, March 29. "In City Schools, Tech Spending to Rise Despite Cuts," *New York Times*. https://www.nytimes.com/2011/03/30/nyregion/30schools.html.

Otto, Amy. 2014, April 23. "Feminists Fighting McDonald's Are Learning the Wrong Lessons." *The Federalist*. FDRLST Media. Web. https://thefederalist.com/2014/04/23/feminists-fighting-mcdonalds-are-learning-the-wrong-lessons/.

Outram, Simon. 2010. "The Use of Methylphenidate among Students: The Future of Enhancement?" *Journal of Medical Ethics* 36(4): 198–202.

Overton, Mark. 1996. *Agricultural Revolution in England: The Transformation of the Agrarian Economy 1500–1850*. Cambridge: Cambridge University Press.

Owens, Ernest. 2023. *The Case for Cancel Culture: How This Democratic Tool Works to Liberate Us All*. New York: St. Martin's Press.

Pager, D. 2007a. "The Use of Field Experiments for Studies of Employment Discrimination: Contributions, Critiques, and Directions for the Future." *Annual American Academy of Political and Social Sciences* 609: 104–133.

Pager, Devah. 2007b. *Marked: Race, Crime, and Finding Work in an Era of Mass Incarceration*. Chicago: University of Chicago Press.

Pager, D., and H. Shepherd. 2008. "The Sociology of Discrimination: Racial Discrimination in Employment, Housing, Credit, and Consumer Markets." *Annual Review of Sociology* 34: 181–209.

Pager, Devah, Bruce Western, and Bart Bonikowski. 2009. "Discrimination in a Low-Wage Labor Market: A Field Experiment." *American Sociological Review* 74: 777–799.

Pager, Devah. 2003. "The Mark of a Criminal Record." *American Journal of Sociology* 108: 937–975.

Paino, M., C. Blankenship, L. Grauerholz, and J. Chin. 2012. "The Scholarship of Teaching and Learning in Teaching Sociology: 1973–2009." *Teaching Sociology* 40(2): 93–106. https://doi.org/10.1177/0092055X12437971.

Panofsky, A. 2014. *Misbehaving Science: Controversy and the Development of Behavior Genetics*. Chicago: University of Chicago Press.

Parente, V., L. Hale, and T. Palermo. 2013. "Association between Breast Cancer and Allostatic Load by Race: National Health and Nutrition Examination Survey 1999–2008." *Psychooncology* 22(3): 621–628. doi:10.1002/pon.3044.

Pariser, E. 2011. *The Filter Bubble: What the Internet Is Hiding from You*. New York: Penguin Press.

Parker, Kim, and Juliana Horowitz. 2022, March 9. "Majority of Workers Who Quit a Job in 2021 Cite

Low Pay, No Opportunities for Advancement, Feeling Disrespected." Pew Research Center. https://www.pewresearch.org/short-reads/2022/03/09/majority-of-workers-who-quit-a-job-in-2021-cite-low-pay-no-opportunities-for-advancement-feeling-disrespected/.

Parker, Kim, and Rachel Minkin. 2023, September 14. "The Future of the Family." Pew Research Center. https://www.pewresearch.org/social-trends/2023/09/14/the-future-of-the-family/.

Parker, Kim, and Renee Stepler. 2017. "As U.S. Marriage Rate Hovers at 50%, Education Gap in Marital Status Widens." Pew Research Center. https://www.pewresearch.org/short-reads/2017/09/14/as-u-s-marriage-rate-hovers-at-50-education-gap-in-marital-status-widens/.

Parker, Kim, Nikki Graf, and Ruth Igielnik. 2019, January 17. "Generation Z Looks a Lot Like Millennials on Key Social and Political Issues." Pew Research Center. https://www.pewresearch.org/social-trends/2019/01/17/generation-z-looks-a-lot-like-millennials-on-key-social-and-political-issues/.

Parker, Kim, Rachel Minkin, and Jesse Bennett. 2020, September 24. "Economic Fallout from COVID-19 Continues to Hit Lower-Income Americans the Hardest." Pew Research Center. https://www.pewresearch.org/social-trends/2020/09/24/economic-fallout-from-covid-19-continues-to-hit-lower-income-americans-the-hardest/#one-third-of-adults-who-said-they-were-laid-off-because-of-the-coronavirus-outbreak-are-back-in-their-old-jobs.

Parolin, Gianluca. 2009. *Citizenship in the Arab World*. Amsterdam: Amsterdam University Press.

Parr, Chris. 2013, May 10. "Not Staying the Course." *Inside Higher Ed.* http://www.insidehighered.com/news/2013/05/10/new-study-low-mooc-completion-rates.

Parrado, Emilio and William Kandel. 2008. "New Hispanic Migrant Destinations: A Tale of Two Industries." In *New Faces in New Places: The Changing Geography of American Immigration*, ed. D. Massey (pp. 99–123). Russell Sage Foundation.

Parsons, Talcott. 1943. "The Kinship System of the Contemporary United States." *American Anthropologist* 45: 22–38.

Parsons, Talcott. 1959. "The School Classroom as a Social System: Some of Its Functions in American Society." *Harvard Educational Review* 29(4): 297–318.

Parsons, Talcott, and Neil Joseph Smelser. 1956. *Economy and Society: A Study in the Integration of Economic and Social Theory*. New York: Free Press.

Parsons, Talcott, and Robert Bales. 1955. *Family, Socialization and Interaction Process*. Glencoe, IL: Free Press.

Pascoe, C. J. 2011. *Dude, You're a Fag: Masculinity and Sexuality in High School*. Berkeley: University of California Press.

Pastor, Manuel. 2015, Winter. "How Immigrant Activists Changed LA." *Dissent*. https://www.dissentmagazine.org/article/how-immigrant-activists-changed-los-angeles.

Pasura, Dominic. 2016. "Transnational Religious Practices and Negotiation of Difference among Zimbabwean Catholics." In *Migration, Transnationalism, and Catholicism: Global Perspectives*, ed. D. Pasura and M. Erdai (pp. 121–144). London: Palgrave Macmillan.

Patten, Eileen. 2013, August 28. "The Black–White and Urban–Rural Divides in Perceptions of Racial Fairness." Pew Research Center. https://www.pewresearch.org/short-reads/2013/08/28/the-black-white-and-urban-rural-divides-in-perceptions-of-racial-fairness/.

Patterson, Orlando. 1982. *Slavery and Social Death*. Cambridge, MA: Harvard University Press.

Pattison, Mark. 2015, June 3. "Africa's Catholic Population Has Grown by 238 Percent Since 1980." *Catholic Herald*. https://catholicherald.co.uk/africas-catholic-population-has-grown-by-238-per-cent-since-1980/#:~:text=The%20Catholic%20population%20in%20Africa%20has%20grown,percent%2C%20and%20of%20parishes%2C%20up%20112%20percent.&text=This%20would%20result%20in%20a%20Catholic%20population%20of%20460%2C350%2C000%20in%20Africa%2C%E2%80%9D%20the%20study%20said.

Payne, Brian. 2011. *White Collar Crime*. New York: Sage Publications.

Pebley, A. R. 1998. "Demography and the Environment." *Demography* 35: 377–389.

Pedulla, David S., and Sarah Thébaud. 2015. "Can We Finish the Revolution? Gender, Work-Family Ideals, and Institutional Constraint." *American Sociological Review* 80(1): 116–139.

Pelaez, Vicky. 2008, March 10. "The Prison Industry in the United States: Big Business or a New Form of Slavery?" *El Diaro-La Prensa*, New York and Global

Research. https://www.globalresearch.ca/the-prison-industry-in-the-united-states-big-business-or-a-new-form-of-slavery/8289.

Pellow, D. N., H. and Nyseth Brehm. 2013. "An Environmental Sociology for the Twenty-First Century." *Annual Review of Sociology* 39 229–250.

Pepin, J. R., and P. N. Cohen. 2024. "Growing Uncertainty in Marriage Expectations among U.S Youth." *Socius* 10. https://doi.org/10.1177/23780231241241035.

Perc, M. 2014. The Matthew Effect in Empirical Data. *Journal of The Royal Society Interface* 11(98): 20140378.

Perlin, Ross. 2012. *Intern Nation: How to Earn Nothing and Learn Little in the Brave New Economy*. New York: Penguin.

Perlmann, Joel, and Mary C. Waters, eds. 2002. *The New Race Question: How the Census Counts Multiracial Individuals*. New York: Russell Sage Foundation.

Peterson, Richard A. 1992. "Understanding Audience Segmentation: From Elite and Mass to Omnivore and Univore." *Poetics* 21: 243–258.

Peterson, Richard. 1996. "A Re-evaluation of the Economic Consequences of Divorce." *American Sociological Review* 61: 528–536.

Pew Research Center. 2010a. "How the Great Recession Has Changed Life in America." https://www.pewresearch.org/social-trends/2010/06/30/how-the-great-recession-has-changed-life-in-america/.

Pew Research Center. 2010b. "The Decline of Marriage and Rise of New Families." https://www.pewresearch.org/social-trends/2010/11/18/the-decline-of-marriage-and-rise-of-new-families/.

Pew Research Center. 2011, January 13. "A Portrait of Stepfamilies." https://www.pewresearch.org/social-trends/2011/01/13/a-portrait-of-stepfamilies/

Pew Research Center. 2012, December 18. "The Global Religious Landscape." https://www.pewresearch.org/religion/2012/12/18/global-religious-landscape-exec/.

Pew Research Center. 2015, December 17. "Parenting in America: Outlook, Worries, Aspirations Are Strongly Linked to Financial Situation." https://www.pewresearch.org/wp-content/uploads/sites/20/2015/12/2015-12-17_parenting-in-america_FINAL.pdf.

Pew Research Center. 2015a, June 10. "What Census Calls Us: A Historical Timeline." /https://www.pewresearch.org/social-trends/feature/what-census-calls-us/.

Pew Research Center. 2015b, June 11. "Multiracial in America: Proud, Diverse, and Growing in Numbers." https://www.pewresearch.org/social-trends/2015/06/11/multiracial-in-america/#fnref-20523-7.

Pew Research Center. 2017, September 8. "Indians in the U.S. Fact Sheet." https://www.pewresearch.org/social-trends/fact-sheet/asian-americans-indians-in-the-u-s/.

Pew Research Center. Oct. 3, 2017. "Many Countries Favor Specific Religions, Officially or Unofficially." https://www.pewresearch.org/wp-content/uploads/sites/20/2017/09/FULL-REPORT-FOR-WEB.pdf.

Pew Research Center. 2018, May 31. "Media Use among US Teens." From "Teens, Social Media and Technology 2018." https://www.pewresearch.org/internet/2018/05/31/teens-social-media-technology-2018/.

Pew Research Center. 2019, December 12. "Religion and Living Arrangements Around the World." https://www.pewresearch.org/religion/2019/12/12/religion-and-living-arrangements-around-the-world/.

Pew Research Center. 2024, January. "Parents, Young Adult Children and the Transition to Adulthood." https://www.pewresearch.org/wp-content/uploads/sites/20/2024/01/ST_2024.01.25_Parents-Young-Adults_Report.pdf.

Phelan, Jo, Bruce Link, Robert Moore, and Anne Stueve. 1997. "The Stigma of Homelessness: The Impact of the Label 'Homeless' on Attitudes about the Poor." *Social Psychology Quarterly* 60: 323–337.

Phillips, Kevin. 2002. *Wealth and Democracy: A Political History of the American Rich*. New York: Broadway Books.

Phuyal, Sudip, Diwakar Bista, and Rabindra Bista. 2020. "Challenges, Opportunities and Future Directions of Smart Manufacturing: A State of Art Review." *Sustainable Futures* 2. https://doi.org/10.1016/j.sftr.2020.100023.

Pierret, Janine. 2003. "The Illness Experience: State of Knowledge and Perspectives for Research." *Sociology of Health and Illness* 25(3): 4–22.

Piketty, Thomas. 2014. *Capital in the Twenty First Century*. New York: Belknap.

Pine, B. Joseph II, and James H. Gillmore. 1999. *Experience Economy*. Cambridge, MA: Harvard Business School Press.

Pinon, Natasha. 2023, August 1. "So Long, Prompt Engineers." *CFO Brew*. https://www.cfobrew.com/stories/2023/08/01/so-long-prompt-engineers.

Pinsker, Joe. 2015, February 26. "White Privilege, Quantified." *The Atlantic*. http://www

.theatlantic.com/business/archive/2015/02/white-privilege-quantified/386102/.

Piore, Michael J. 1979. *Birds of Passage: Migrant Labor and Industrial Societies*. New York: Cambridge University Press.

Piper, Rob. 2023. "The Institutional Drivers Contributing to Billionaire Wealth at the Sector Level." *Class, Race and Corporate Power*: Vol. 11: Iss. 1, Article 3. doi: 10.25148/CRCP.11.1.010593.

Piven, Frances Fox, and Richard Cloward. 1978. *Poor People's Movements: Why They Succeed, How They Fail*. New York: Vintage Books.

Plumer, Bradford. 2006, May 22. "The Origins of Anti-Litter Campaigns." *Mother Jones*. https://www.motherjones.com/politics/2006/05/origins-anti-litter-campaigns/.

Pollack, Craig Evan, Catherine Cubbin, Ayesha Sania, Mark Hayward, Donna Vallone, Brian Flaherty, and Paula A. Braveman. 2013. "Do Wealth Disparities Contribute to Health Disparities within Racial/ethnic Groups?" *Journal of Epidemiology and Community Health (1979–)* 67(5): 439–445. http://www.jstor.org/stable/43281547.

Polletta, Francesca, and James M. Jasper. 2001. "Collective Identity and Social Movements." *Annual Review of Sociology* 27: 283–305.

Polletta, Francesca. 1998. "'It Was Like a Fever . . .' Narrative and Identity in Social Protest." *Social Problems* 45(2): 137–159.

PON Staff. 2020, November 19. "Counteracting Negotiation Biases Like Race and Gender in the Workplace." Daily Blog, Program on Negotiation, Harvard Law School. https://www.pon.harvard.edu/daily/leadership-skills-daily/counteracting-racial-and-gender-bias-in-job-negotiations-nb/.

Popper, Karl. 2005. *The Logic of Scientific Discovery*. New York: Routledge.

Porter, M. E., and M. R. Kramer. 2006. "Strategy & Society: The Link between Competitive Advantage and Corporate Social Responsibility." *Harvard Business Review* 84: 78–92.

Portes, Alejandro, and Robert D. Manning. 1986. "The Immigrant Enclave: Theory and Empirical Examples." In *Competitive Ethnic Relations*, eds. J. Nagel and S. Olzak (pp. 47–64). Orlando, FL: Academic Press.

Portes, Alejandro. 1995. "Children of Immigrants: Segmented Assimilation and its Determinants." In *The Economic Sociology of Immigration*, ed. A. Portes (pp. 248–280). New York: Russell Sage Foundation.

Possamai, Adam. 2019. *In Search of New Age Spiritualities*. New York: Routledge.

Powers, William. 2016, February 23. "Who's Influencing Election 2016?" *Medium*. https://medium.com/@socialmachines/who-s-influencing-election-2016-8bed68ddecc3.

Prince, Martin J., Fan Wu, Yanfei Guo, Luis M. Gutierrez Robledo, Martin O'Donnell, Richard Sullivan, and Salim Yusuf. 2014. "The Burden of Disease in Older People and Implications for Health Policy and Practice." *Lancet* 385(9967): 549–562.

Prison Policy Initiative. 2020, November 24. "Responses to the COVID-19 Pandemic." https://www.prisonpolicy.org/virus/virusresponse.html.

Prouty, Robert W., Gary Smith, and K. Charlie Lakin. 2007. *Residential Services for Persons with Developmental Disabilities: Status and Trends through 2006*. Minneapolis: University of Minnesota, Research and Training Center on Community Living.

Przeworski, Adam. 2016. "Democracy: A Never-Ending Quest." *Annual Review of Political Science* 19: 1–12.

Pugh, Allison. 2009. *Longing and Belonging*. Oakland: University of California Press.

Putnam, Robert. 2000. *Bowling Alone*. New York: Simon & Schuster.

PWC. 2023. "Tech Workers Love Their Jobs. They're Also Leaving." PWC Leadership Agenda. https://www.pwc.com/gx/en/issues/c-suite-insights/the-leadership-agenda/technology-job-market-employee-trends.html.

Quah, John. 2010. *Public Administration, Singapore Style*. Bingley, West Yorkshire, England: Emerald Group Publishing.

Querolo, Nic, and Leslie Patton. 2020, October 27. "Food-Stockpiling Is Back, with 3,400% Pantry Surge." *Bloomberg*. https://www.bloomberg.com/news/articles/2020-10-27/second-food-stockpiling-wave-is-here-with-3-400-pantry-surge.

Quillian, Lincoln. 1995. "Prejudice as a Response to Perceived Group Threat: Population Composition and Anti-immigrant and Racial Prejudice in Europe." *American Sociological Review* 60: 586–611.

Quillian, Lincoln, Anthony Heath, Devah Pager, Arnfinn H. Midtbøen, Fenella Fleischmann, and Ole Hexel. 2019. "Do Some Countries Discriminate More than Others? Evidence from 97 Field Experiments of Racial Discrimination in Hiring." *Sociological Science* 6(18): 467–496. http://dx.doi.org/10.15195/v6.a18d.

Quillian, Lincoln, Devah Pager, Ole Hexel, and Arnfinn H. Midtbøen. 2017. Meta-Analysis of Field Experiments Shows No Change in Racial Discrimination in Hiring Over Time. *Proceedings of the National Academy of Sciences*. 114(41): 10870–10875. https://doi.org/10.1073/pnas.1706255114.

Rauscher, Frances H., Gordon L. Shaw, and Catherine N. Ky. 1993. "Music and Spatial Task Performance." *Nature* 365: 611.

Rauscher, Frances H., Gordon L. Shaw, Linda J. Levine, Catherine N. Ky, and Eric L. Wright. 1994. "Music and Spatial Task Performance: A Causal Relationship." Paper presented at the 102nd Annual Convention of the American Psychological Association, Los Angeles.

Ray, R. S., and P. M. Ong. 2020. "Unequal Access to Remote Work During the Covid-19 Pandemic." UCLA Center for Neighborhood Knowledge. https://drive.google.com/file/d/1kW_o6fZ2dLQM9ar9Yx6m0F44CHpj3YDO/view.

Reed, Bronwen. 2015, June 16. "'Wild Geese Families': Stress, Loneliness, for South Korean Families Heading Overseas to Gain Edge in 'Brutal' Education System." *ABC News*. http://www.abc.net.au/news/2015-06-16/thousands-of-south-korea-families-apart-for-australian-education/6547604.

Reer, F., W. Y. Tang, and T. Quandt. 2019. "Psychosocial Well-Being and Social Media Engagement: The Mediating Roles of Social Comparison Orientation and Fear of Missing Out." *New Media & Society* 21(7): 1486–1505.

Reeves, Richard. 2014, August 20. "Saving Horatio Alger: Equality, Opportunity, and the American Dream." Washington DC: Brookings Institution Press. http://csweb.brookings.edu/content/research/essays/2014/saving-horatio-alger.html#.

Reiner, R., S. Livingstone, and J. Allen. 2003. "From Law and Order to Lynch Mobs: Crime News Since the Second World War." In *Criminal Visions: Media Representations of Crime and Justice*, ed. P. Mason (pp. 13–32). Devon, UK: Willan Publishing.

Reuter, Peter H. 2009. *Assessing the Operation of the Global Drug Market. Report 1.* RAND Corporation. https://www.rand.org/pubs/technical_reports/TR705.html.

Reuters Staff. 2009, June 3. "Singapore Bureaucracy Best in Asia, India Worst—Survey." *Reuters*. https://www.reuters.com/article/idINIndia-40062020090603.

Reuters. 2024, February 1. "Amazon Fund for Rainforest Received $640 Million in New Pledges in 2023." *Reuters*. https://www.reuters.com/sustainability/climate-energy/amazon-fund-rainforest-received-640-mln-new-pledges-2023-2024-02-01/.

Revers, Matthias. 2014. "Journalistic Professionalism as Performance and Boundary Work: Source Relations at the State House." *Journalism* 15(1): 37–52.

Reynolds, L. 2021. "First Divorce Rate in the U.S., 2019." Family Profiles, FP-21-10. Bowling Green, OH: National Center for Family and Marriage Research. https://doi.org/10.25035/ncfmr/fp-21-10.

Reynolds, L. 2021. "The U.S. Remarriage Rate, 2019: Trends and Geographic Variation by Gender." Family Profiles, FP-21-18. Bowling Green, OH: National Center for Family & Marriage Research. https://doi.org/10.25035/ncfmr/fp-21-18

Ricapito, Maria. 2020. "Season's (and Other . . .) Greetings." *Marie Claire*. https://www.marieclaire.com/culture/a34212191/greeting-cards-millennials-gen-z/.

Rideout, V., A. Peebles, S. Mann, and M. B. Robb. 2022. *Common Sense Census: Media Use by Tweens and Teens, 2021*. San Francisco, CA: Common Sense.

Rigaud, K. K., A. De Sherbinin, B. Jones, J. Bergmann, V. Clement, K. Ober, et al. 2018. *Preparing for Internal Climate Migration*. Washington, DC: The World Bank. https://doi.org/10.7916/D8Z33FNS.

Rincón, Lina. 2015. "Between Nations and the World: Negotiating Legal and Social Citizenship in the Migration Process." Unpublished PhD dissertation, State University of New York at Albany.

Riordan, Bruce. 2018, September 26. "The Evolution of the Police Procedural. 50 Years and 2 Golden Ages of Cops on Screen." *CrimeReads*. https://crimereads.com/the-evolution-of-the-police-procedural/.

Rivera, Lauren. 2015. *Pedigree: How Elite Students Get Elite Jobs*. Princeton, NJ: Princeton University Press.

Roberts, Dorothy. 2012. *Fatal Invention: How Science, Politics, and Big Business Re-create Race in the Twenty-first Century*. New York: New Press.

Robins, Alexandra. 2015a. *The Nurses: A Year of Secrets, Drama, and Miracles with the Heroes of the Hospital*. New York: Workman.

Robins, Alexandra. 2015b, April 27. "Mean Girls of the ER: The Alarming Nurse Culture of Bullying and Hazing." *Marie Claire*. https://www.marieclaire.com/culture/news/a14211/mean-girls-of-the-er/.

Robinson, A., A. Bonnette, K. Howard, N. Ceballos, S. Dailey, Y. Lu, and T. Grimes. 2019. "Social Comparisons, Social Media Addiction, and Social Interaction: An Examination of Specific Social Media Behaviors Related to Major Depressive Disorder in a Millennial

Population." *Journal of Applied Biobehavioral Research* 24(1): e12158.

Robinson, Laura, Sheila Cotten, Hiroshi Ono, Anabel Quaan-Haase, Gustavo Mesch, Wenhong Chen, Jeremy Schulz, Timothy Hale, and Michael Stern, 2015. "Digital Inequalities and Why They Matter," *Information, Communication and Society* 5: 569–582.

Rodriguez, Clara E. 2004. *Heroes, Lovers, and Others: The Story of Latinos in Hollywood*. Washington, DC: Smithsonian Books.

Roedifer, Henry, Adam Putnam, and Megan Smith. 2011. "The Benefits of Testing and Their Applications to Educational Practice." *Psychology of Learning and Motivation* 55: 1–36.

Rogers, Everett M., and James W. Dearing. 2012. "Agenda-Setting Research: Where Has It Been, Where Is It Going?" *Communication Yearbook* 11 (pp. 555–594). New York: Routledge.

Rohlinger, D. A., and D. S. Meyer. 2022. "Protest During a Pandemic: How Covid-19 Affected Social Movements in the United States." *American Behavioral Scientist* 68(6). https://doi.org/10.1177/00027642221132179.

Roksa, Josipa. 2008. "Structuring Access to Higher Education: The Role of Differentiation and Privatization." *Research in Social Stratification and Mobility* 26:57–75.

Romalino, Carly. 2014, December 16. "Millennials Embrace Sending Christmas Cards." *South Jersey Courier-Post*. http://www.courierpostonline.com/story/news/local/south-jersey/2014/12/16/millennials-embrace-sending-christmas-cards/20517669/.

Romano, Aja. 2020, August 25. "Why We Can't Stop Fighting About Cancel Culture." *Vox*. https://www.vox.com/culture/2019/12/30/20879720/what-is-cancel-culture-explained-history-debate.

Roncarati, Jill S., Thomas H. Byrne, and D. Keith McInnes. 2021, November. "Invited Commentary: Data Sources for Estimating Numbers of People Experiencing Homelessness in the United States—Strengths and Limitations." *American Journal of Epidemiology* 190(11): 2437–2440. https://doi.org/10.1093/aje/kwab104.

Rootes, Christopher. 1999. "Environmental Movements: From the Local to the Global," *Environmental Politics* 8: 1–12.

Roscigno, Vincent, Sherry Mong, Reginald Byron, and Griff Tester. 2007. "Age Discrimination, Social Closure, and Employment." *Social Forces* 83: 313–344.

Rose, Nikolas. 2007a. *The Politics of Life Itself: Biomedicine, Power, and Subjectivity in the Twenty-First Century*. Princeton, NJ: Princeton University Press.

Rose, Nikolas. 2007b. "Beyond Medicalisation." *Lancet*, 369 (February 24): 700–702.

Rosenfeld, Richard. 2002. "Crime Decline in Context." *Contexts* 1(1): 25–34.

Rosenstein, A. H., and M. O'Daniel. 2008. "A Survey of the Impact of Disruptive Behavior and Communication Defects on Patient Safety." *The Joint Commission Journal on Quality and Patient Safety* 34(8): 464–471.

Roser, Max, and Esteban Ortiz-Ospina. 2018. "Literacy." *Our World in Data*. https://ourworldindata.org/literacy.

Roser, Max. 2015, December 4. "Democratisation." *Our World in Data*. https://ourworldindata.org/democracy.

Rossi, Peter H. 1989a. *Down and Out in America: The Origins of Homelessness*. Chicago: University of Chicago Press.

Rossi, Peter H. 1989b. *Homelessness in America: Selected Topics*. Amherst, MA: Social and Demographic Research Institute.

Rossiter, Margaret. 1993. "The Matthew Matilda Effect in Science." *Social Studies of Science* 23(2): 325–341. doi:10.1177/030631293023002004, ISSN 0306-3127.

Rothkopf, David. 2008. *Superclass: The Global Power Elite and the World They are Making*. New York: Farrar, Strauss and Giroux.

Rothwell, Jonathan. 2014, September 30. "How the War on Drugs Damages Black Social Mobility." Brookings Institution. http://www.brookings.edu/blogs/social-mobility-memos/posts/2014/09/30-war-on-drugs-black-social-mobility-rothwell.

Rouse, Cecilia. 1995. "Democratization or Diversion? The Effect of Community Colleges on Educational Attainment." *Journal of Business and Economic Statistics* 13: 217–224.

Rowley, Anthony. 2017, October 11. "Remittances Remain Crucial to Philippines Economy. Cash Sent Home from All over the World Was Worth US$26.9 Billion in 2016." *The National*. https://www.thenational.ae/business/remittances-remain-crucial-to-philippines-economy-1.666517.

Royal, James, and Mercedes Barba. 2024, February 1. "What Income and Wealth Put You in The Top 1%?" *Bankrate*. https://www.bankrate.com/investing/income-wealth-top-1-percent/.

Rubin, Kenneth, and Hildy Ross, eds. 1982. *Peer Relationships and Social Skills in Childhood*. New York: Springer.

Rudel, T. K., J. T. Roberts, and J. Carmin. 2011. "Political Economy of the Environment." *Annual Review of Sociology* 37: 221–238.

Ruggles, Steven. 2012. "The Future of Historical Family Demography." *Annual Review of Sociology* 38: 423–441.

Rumbaut, Rubén G., and Egon Bittner. 1979. "Changing Conceptions of the Police Role: A Sociological Review." *Crime and Justice* 1: 239–288.

Ryan, Tom. 2020, July 1. "Anti-Mask Shoppers Find Themselves Publicly Shamed." *Retail Wire*. https://retailwire.com/discussion/anti-mask-shoppers-find-themselves-publicly-shamed/.

Sabato, Larry. 1996. "When Push Comes to Poll." *Washington Monthly* 28(6): 26–31.

Sackmann, Rosemarie, Bernhard Peters, and Thomas Faist. 2003. *Identity and Integration: Migrants in Western Europe*. Aldershot, UK: Ashgate.

Sadker, Myra, and David Sadker. 1995. *Failing at Fairness: How America's Schools Cheat Girls*. New York: Scribner.

Saeji, C. 2020, June 24. "The K-Pop Revolution and What It Means for American Politics." *Washington Post*. https://www.washingtonpost.com/outlook/2020/06/24/what-is-k-pop-how-did-its-fans-humiliate-president-trump/.

Saenz, Rogelio. 2005, August. "The Changing Demographics of Roman Catholics." Population Reference Bureau.

Saez, Emmanuel, and Gabriel Zucman. 2020. "The Rise of Income and Wealth Inequality in America: Evidence from Distributional Macroeconomic Accounts." *The Journal of Economic Perspectives* 34(4): 3–26. doi:10.2307/26940888.

Sagioglou, C., and T. Greitemeyer. 2014. "Facebook's Emotional Consequences: Why Facebook Causes a Decrease in Mood and Why People Still Use It." *Computers in Human Behavior* 35: 359–363.

Saguy, Abigail C. 2014. *What's Wrong with Fat?* New York: Oxford University Press.

Sampson, R. J., S. W. Raudenbush, and F. Earls. 1997. "Neighborhoods and Violent Crime: A Multilevel Study of Collective Efficacy." *Science* 277: 918–924.

Sampson, Robert J., and John H. Laub. 1995. *Crime in the Making: Pathways and Turning Points through Life*. Cambridge, MA: Harvard University Press.

Sanders, Bernie. 2016. "Issues. Income and Wealth Inequality" (Campaign website). https://berniesanders.com/issues/income-and-wealth-inequality/.

Sanders, Bernie. 2023. *It's OK to Be Angry About Capitalism*. New York: Crown Books.

Sarche, Michelle, and Paul Spicer. 2008. "Poverty and Health Disparities for American Indian and Alaska Native Children: Current Knowledge and Future Prospects." *Annals of the New York Academy of Sciences* 1136: 126–136.

Sargen, Nick. 2023, November 8. "The US Equity Market's Dominance Is Tied to Tech and AI's Evolution." *Forbes*. https://www.forbes.com/sites/nicksargen/2023/11/08/the-us-equity-markets-dominance-is-tied-to-tech-and-ais-evolution/?sh=2e2e252b25ad.

Sassler, Sharon, and Anna Cunningham. "How Cohabitors View Childbearing." *Sociological Perspectives* 51(1): 3–28.

Satariano, Adam. 2018, May 24. "G.D.P.R., a New Privacy Law, Makes Europe World's Leading Tech Watchdog." *New York Times*. https://www.nytimes.com/2018/05/24/technology/europe-gdpr-privacy.html.

Satran, Joe. 2013, December 14. "The Secret History of the War on Public Drinking." *Huffington Post*. http://www.huffingtonpost.com/2013/12/14/public-drinking-laws_n_4312523.html.

Saussure, Ferdinand. 1998. *Course in General Linguistics*. London: Open Court Classics.

Savage, Maddy. 2021, August 5. "Birdnesting: The Divorce Trend Where Parents Rotate Homes." *BBC*. https://www.bbc.com/worklife/article/20210804-birdnesting-the-divorce-trend-in-which-parents-rotate-homes.

Savage, Mike. 2015. *Social Class in the 21st Century*. New York: Penguin.

Savitsky, D. 2012. "Is Plea Bargaining a Rational Choice? Plea Bargaining as an Engine of Racial Stratification and Overcrowding in the United States Prison System." *Rationality and Society* 24(2): 131–167. https://doi.org/10.1177/1043463112441351.

Schiller, Herbert. 1991. *Culture, Inc: The Corporate Takeover of Public Expression*. New York: Oxford University Press.

Schlossberg, Nancy. 2009. *Revitalizing Retirement: Reshaping Your Identity, Relationships, and*

*Purpose*. Washington, DC: American Psychological Association.

Schmid, H., and C. Klimmt. 2011. "A Magically Nice Guy: Parasocial Relationships with Harry Potter across Different Cultures." *International Communication Gazette* 73(3): 252–269.

Schmitt, Christopher. 1991, December 8. "Plea Bargaining Favors Whites, as Blacks, Hispanics Pay Price," *San Jose Mercury News*, p. 1A.

Schnaiberg, Allan. 1980. *The Environment: From Surplus to Scarcity*. New York: Oxford University Press.

Schneider, Barbara, Erin Grogan, and Adam Meier, 2011. "Improving Teacher Quality: A Sociological Presage." In *Frontiers in Sociology of Education*, ed. M. Hallinan (pp. 163–180). London: Springer.

Schneider, Joseph. 2015. "The Medicalization of Deviance: From Badness to Sickness." In *The Handbook of Deviance*, ed. Erich Goode (pp. 137–153). New York: Wiley-Blackwell.

Schofer, Evan, and John W. Meyer. 2005. "The Worldwide Expansion of Higher Education in the Twentieth Century." *American Sociological Review* 70(6): 898–920.

Schor, Juliet B. 2004. *Born to Buy: The Commercialized Child and the New Consumer Culture*. New York: Scribner.

Schor, Juliet. 2016. "Debating the Sharing Economy." *Journal of Self-Governance and Management Economics* 4(3): 7–22.

Schreuer, Milan. 2017, October 25. "A #MeToo Moment for the European Parliament." *New York Times*. https://www.nytimes.com/2017/10/25/world/europe/european-parliament-weinstein-harassment.html.

Schudson, Michael. 1978. *Discovering the News: A Social History of American Newspapers*. New York: Basic Books.

Schudson, Michael. 1978. *Discovering the News: A Social History of American Newspapers*. New York: Basic Books.

Schudson, Michael. 2011. *The Sociology of News*, 2nd ed. New York: W. W. Norton.

Schuster, J. Mark Davidson. 1991. *The Audience for American Art Museums*. Research Division Report #23. Washington, DC: National Endowment for the Arts. http://eric.ed.gov/?id=ED351242.

Schweitzer, Kate. 2019, December 27. "McDonald's Asked for My Kid's Gender When I Ordered a Happy Meal—and We Need to End This Now." Popsugar blog. https://www.popsugar.com/family/mcdonald-happy-meal-toys-show-gender-bias-46828615.

Schweizer, V. 2019. The Retreat from Remarriage, 1950–2017. Family Profiles, FP-19-17. Bowling Green State University, National Center for Family & Marriage Research. https://doi.org/10.25035/ncfmr/fp-19-17.

Schweizer, V. J. 2020. "Divorce: More than a Century of Change, 1900–2018." Family Profiles, FP-20-22. Bowling Green, OH: National Center for Family & Marriage Research. https://doi.org/10.25035/ncfmr/fp-20-22.

*Scientific American*. 2007, July 31. "Race-Based Medicine: A Recipe for Controversy." https://www.scientificamerican.com/article/race-based-medicine-a-recipe-for-controversy/.

Scott, James. 1985. *Weapons of the Weak: Everyday Forms of Peasant Resistance*. New Haven, CT: Yale University Press.

Scott, John. 2006. *Social Theory: Central Issues in Sociology*. Thousand Oaks, CA: SAGE.

Scully, Jackie Leach. 2004. "What Is a Disease?" *EMBO Reports* 5(7): 650–653. http://doi.org/10.1038/sj.embor.7400195.

Sebring, J. C. 2021. "Towards a Sociological Understanding of Medical Gaslighting in Western Health Care." *Sociology of Health & Illness* 43(9): 1951–1964.

Sedgewick, E. K. 2008. *Epistemology of the Closet* (updated with a new preface). Los Angeles: University of California Press.

Seeman, T. E., E. Crimmins, M. H. Huang, B. Singer, A. Bucur, T. Gruenewald, L. F. Berkman, and D. B. Reuben. 2004. "Cumulative Biological Risk and Socio-economic Differences in Mortality: MacArthur Studies of Successful Aging." *Social Science and Medicine* 58(10): 1985–1997.

Seidman, Steven. 2002. *Beyond the Closet: The Transformation of Gay and Lesbian Life*. New York: Routledge.

Seidman, Steven. 2013. *Contested Knowledge: Social Theory Today*, 5th ed. Hoboken, NJ: Wiley.

Seigel, Micol. 2017. "The Dilemma of 'Racial Profiling': An Abolitionist Police History." *Contemporary Justice Review* 20(4): 474–490. doi: 10.1080/10282580.2017.1383773.

Sellman, Julia. 2020, December 2020. "The Last Children of Down Syndrome." *The Atlantic*. 326(5): 42–55.

Semega, Jessica, Melissa Kollar, Emily A. Shrider, and John Creamer. 2020, September. *Income and Poverty in the United States: 2019*. REPORT NUMBER P60-270

Table B-2. Families and People in Poverty by Type of Family: 2018 and 2019. Source: U.S. Census Bureau, Current Population Survey, 2019 and 2020 Annual Social and Economic Supplements (CPS ASEC). https://www.census.gov/content/dam/Census/library/publications/2020/demo/p60-270.pdf.

Sengupta, Somini. 2018, September 10. "U.N. Chief Warns of a Dangerous Tipping Point on Climate Change." *New York Times*. https://www.nytimes.com/2018/09/10/climate/united-nations-climate-change.html.

Sennett, Richard. 1972. *The Hidden Injuries of Class*. New York: Knopf.

Sennett, Richard. 2005, September 13. *The Culture of the New Capitalism*. New Haven, CT: Yale University Press.

Senter, Mary S., Roberta Spalter-Roth, and Nicole Van Vooren. 2015. "Jobs, Careers and Sociological Skills: The Early Job Experiences of Sociology Majors." Washington, DC: The American Sociological Association. http://www.asanet.org/research-and-publications/research-sociology/research-briefs/jobs-careers-sociological-skills-early-employment-experiences-2012-sociology-majors.

Serhan, D. 2020. "Transitioning from Face-To-Face to Remote Learning: Students' Attitudes and Perceptions of Using Zoom During COVID-19 Pandemic." *International Journal of Technology in Education and Science (IJTES)* 4(4): 335–342.

Shafer, Emily. 2006. "Are Men or Women More Reluctant to Marry in Couples Sharing a Non-Marital Birth?" *Gender Issues* 23(2): 20–43.

Shakespeare, Tom, and Nicholas Watson. 2001. "The Social Model of Disability: An Outdated Ideology?" In *Research in Social Science and Disability*, Vol. 2, eds. Sharon N. Barnartt and Barbara Altman eds. (pp. 9–28). Amsterdam and New York: JAI.

Shannon Schumacher, Shannon, Liz Hamel, Samantha Artiga, Drishti Pillai, Ashley Kirzinger, Audrey Kearney, Marley Presiado, Ana Gonzalez-Barrera, and Mollyann Brodie. 2023. *Understanding the U.S. Immigrant Experience: The 2023 KFF/LA Times Survey of Immigrants*. https://www.kff.org/racial-equity-and-health-policy/poll-finding/kff-la-times-survey-of-immigrants/.

Shapin, Steven, 1995. "Here and Everywhere: Sociology of Scientific Knowledge." *Annual Review of Sociology* 21: 289–321.

Shapiro, Thomas. 2005. *The Hidden Costs of Being African-American: How Wealth Perpetuates Inequality*. New York: Oxford University Press.

Shibutani, Tamotsu. 1988. "Herbert Blumer's Contribution to Twentieth-Century Sociology." *Symbolic Interactionism* 11(1): 23–31.

Shin, Laura. 2015, March 26. "The Racial Wealth Gap: Why a Typical White Household Has 16 Times the Wealth of a Black One." *Forbes*. http://www.forbes.com/sites/laurashin/2015/03/26/the-racial-wealth-gap-why-a-typical-white-household-has-16-times-the-wealth-of-a-black-one/#36a044b66c5b.

Shlay, Anne B., and Peter H. Rossi. 1992. "Social Science Research and Contemporary Studies of Homelessness." *Annual Review of Sociology* 18: 129–160.

Shorrocks, A. 2009. "On the Measurement of Unemployment." *The Journal of Economic Inequality*, 7, 311–327.

Short, Kevin. 2014, October 21. "Next Time Someone Says 'White Privilege Isn't Real,' Show Them This." *Huffington Post*. http://www.huffingtonpost.com/2014/10/21/upward-mobility-race_n_6016154.html.

Shrader, Brad, Jeffrey Kaufmann, and Sue Pickard Ravenscroft. 2006, June 15. "Why Do Some Students Cheat? They Rationalize It, ISU Research Finds." https://www.news.iastate.edu/news/2006/jun/rationalizing.shtml.

Shrider, Emily, and John Creamer. 2023, September. "*Poverty in the United States: 2022*." Current Population Reports, U.S. Census Bureau. https://www.census.gov/content/dam/Census/library/publications/2023/demo/p60-280.pdf.

Shrider, Emily. 2024, September. "Poverty in the United States: 2023." Current Population Reports, U.S. Census Bureau. https://www2.census.gov/library/publications/2024/demo/p60-283.pdf.

Shrum, Wesley, Meil Creek, and Suadra Hunter. 1988. "Friendship in School: Gender and Racial Homophily." *Sociology of Education* 61: 227–239.

Shrum, Wesley. 1996. *Fringe and Fortune: The Role of Critics in High and Popular Art*. Princeton, NJ: Princeton University Press.

Shuey, K. M., and A. E. Willson. 2008. "Cumulative Disadvantage and Black–White Disparities in Life-Course Health Trajectories." *Research on Aging* 30(2): 200–225.

Shumow, Lee B., and Jennifer A. Schmidt. 2013. *Enhancing Adolescents' Motivation for Science: Research-Based Strategies for Teaching Male and Female Students*. Thousand Oaks, CA: Corwin.

Shumway, D. 2003. *Modern Love. Romance, Intimacy, and the Marriage Crisis*. New York: NYU Press.

Siders, A. R. 2019. "Social Justice Implications of US Managed Retreat Buyout Programs." *Climate Change* 152(2): 239–257.

Sidibé, Michel. 2012, July 5. "Giving Power to Couples to End the AIDS Epidemic." *Huffington Post*. https://www.huffpost.com/entry/hiv-aids_b_1477206.

Siegel, Robert, and Michele Norris. 2007, June 11. "Loving Decision: 40 Years of Legal Interracial Unions." *NPR*. http://www.npr.org/templates/transcript/transcript.php?storyId=10889047.

Sikora, A. G., and M. Mulvihill. 2002. "Trends in Mortality Due to Legal Intervention in the United States, 1979 through 1997." *American Journal of Public Health* 92(5): 841–843.

Silverman, Rachel Emma, and Michelle Higgins. 2003, September 17. "When the Kids Get the House in a Divorce." *Wall Street Journal*. https://www.wsj.com/articles/SB106374829921566600.

Simko, C. 2011. *The Politics of Consolation: Memory and The Meaning of September 11*. New York: Oxford University Press.

Skelton, George. 2015, March 26. "Attitudes Shift on Illegal Immigration, but Unity Eludes Other Issues." *Los Angeles Times*. http://www.latimes.com/local/politics/la-me-cap-california-poll-20150326-column.html.

Skocpol, Theda. 1996. "The Politics of American Social Policy, Past and Future." In *Individual and Social Responsibility: Child Care, Education, Medical Care, and Long-Term Care in America*, ed. V. Fuchs (pp. 309–334). University of Chicago Press.

Slavin, Stuart J., and John T. Chibnall. 2017. "Mistreatment of Medical Students in the Third Year May Not Be the Problem." *Medical Teacher* 39(8): 891–893.

Smedley, Audrey. 1993. *Race in North America: Origin and Evolution of a Worldview*. Boulder, CO: Westview Press.

Smelser, Neil J. 1963. *The Sociology of Economic Life*. Englewood Cliffs, NJ: Prentice-Hall.

Smith, Anthony D. 2004. *Chosen Peoples: Sacred Sources of National Identity*. New York: Oxford University Press.

Smith, Brad, and Harry Shum. 2018. "The Future Computed: Artificial Intelligence and the Future of Society." Microsoft. https://news.microsoft.com/cloudforgood/_media/downloads/the-future-computed-english.pdf

Smith, C., and Castañeda-Tinoco, E. 2019. "Improving Homeless Point-In-Time Counts: Uncovering the Marginally Housed." *Social Currents* 6(2): 91–104. https://doi.org/10.1177/2329496518812451.

Smith, Christian, ed., 1996. *Disruptive Religion: The Force of Faith in Social Movement Activism*. New York: Routledge.

Smith, Lawrence, Lisa Best, D. Alan Stubbs, John Johnston, and Andrea Archibald. 2000. "Scientific Graphs and the Hierarchy of the Sciences." *Social Studies of Science* 30: 73–94.

Smith, N. 2023. "Salaries Soar in Chase." *Engineering & Technology* 18(1): 24–27. doi: 10.1049/et.2023.0107.

Smith, Philip, and Alexander Riley. 2008. *Cultural Theory: An Introduction*. Malden, MA: Wiley-Blackwell.

Smith, Philip, Timothy L. Phillips, and Ryan D. King. 2010. *Incivility: The Rude Stranger in Everyday Life*. New York: Cambridge University Press.

Smith, Philip. 2008. *Punishment and Culture*. Chicago: University of Chicago Press.

Smock, Pamela. 2000. "Cohabitation in the United States: An Appraisal of Research Themes, Findings, and Implications." *Annual Review of Sociology* 26: 1–20.

Snow, Anita, and Hannah Fingerhut. 2019, October 21. "AP-NORC Poll: Americans Agree on Many Aspects of US Identity." Associated Press,. https://apnews.com/article/466e86ac67ef4c609b6ee28e5eb151d9.

Snow, Charles Percy. [1959] 2001. *The Two Cultures*. London: Cambridge University Press.

Snow, David A., and Leon Anderson. 1993. *Down on Their Luck: A Study of Homeless Street People*. Oakland: University of California Press.

Snyder, Gregory. 2009. *Graffiti Lives: Beyond the Tag in New York's Urban Underground*. New York: NYU Press.

Sobieraj, Sarah. 2011. *Soundbitten: The Perils of Media-Centered Political Activism*. New York: NYU Press.

Sobieraj, Sarah. 2020. *Credible Threat: Attacks against Women Online and the Future of Democracy*. New York: Oxford University Press.

Soper, Taylor. 2013, May 22. "Report: Teens Leave Facebook for Twitter, Because They Want Less Drama." *Geekwire*. http://www.geekwire.com/2013/pew-report-teens-facebook-twitter-instagram/.

Sorensen, Aage, and Arne Kalleberg. 1981. "An Outline of a Theory of the Matching of Persons to Jobs." In *Sociological Perspectives on Labor Markets*, ed. I. Berg (pp. 49–74). New York: Academic Press.

Sorkin, Andrew Ross, Jason Karaian, Michael de la Merced, Lauren Hirsch, and Ephrat Livni. 2020,

November 6. "The Media's Complicated Relationship with Trump." *New York Times*. https://www.nytimes.com/2020/11/06/business/dealbook/media-trump-bump.html.

Southern Poverty Law Center. 2004, December 21. "Wal-Mart Drops Protocols, but Controversy Lives On." *Intelligence Report*. https://www.splcenter.org/fighting-hate/intelligence-report/2004/wal-mart-drops-protocols-controversy-lives.

Soysal, Yasemin, and David Strang. 1989. "Construction of the First Mass Education Systems in Nineteenth-Century Europe." *Sociology of Education* 62: 277–288.

Spalter-Roth, Roberta, and William Eskine. 2006. "'What Can I Do with a Bachelor's Degree in Sociology?' A National Survey of Seniors." Washington, DC: American Sociological Association. http://www.asanet.org/galleries/research/ASAchartBook_0117w1.pdf.

Spierenberg, Pieter. 1984. *The Spectacle of Suffering*. New York: Cambridge University Press.

Spradlin, J. Isaac. 2009, April 27. "The Evolution of Interns." *Forbes*. https://www.forbes.com/2009/04/27/intern-history-apprenticeship-leadership-careers-jobs.html#32c6b3a746b7.

Stacey, Judith, and Barrie Thorne. 1985. "The Missing Feminist Revolution in Sociology." *Social Problems* 32: 301–316.

Staggenborg, Suzanne. 2010. *Social Movements*. New York: Oxford University Press.

Stainback, Kevin, and Donald Tomaskovic-Devey. 2009. "Intersections of Power and Privilege: Long-Term Trends in Managerial Representation." *American Sociological Review* 74: 800–820.

Starr, Paul. [1982] 2017. *The Social Transformation of American Medicine: The Rise of a Sovereign Profession and the Making of a Vast Industry*. New York: Basic Books.

Statista. 2023, September 19. "Median Household Income in the United States in 2022, by Race and Ethnicity." *Statista Research Department*. https://www.statista.com/statistics/233324/median-household-income-in-the-united-states-by-race-or-ethnic-group/#:~:text=U.S.%20median%20household%20income%202022%2C%20by%20race%20and%20ethnicity&text=In%202022%2C%20the%20gross%20median,74%2C580%20U.S.%20dollars%20in%202022.

Statista. 2024. Instagram User Data. https://www.statista.com/statistics/325587/instagram-global-age-group/.

Steel, B. S., and R. L. Warner. 2018. "Job Satisfaction Among Early Labor Force Participants: Unexpected Outcomes in Public and Private Sector Comparisons." In *Public Service* (pp. 183–202). New York: Routledge.

Steel, J. 2023. "Free Speech, 'Cancel Culture' and the 'War on Woke.'" In *The Routledge Companion to Freedom of Expression and Censorship* (pp. 232–244). New York: Routledge.

Steffen, Will, Wendy Broadgate, Lisa Deutsch, Owen Gaffney, and Cornelia Ludwig. 2015. "The Trajectory of the Anthropocene: The Great Acceleration." *The Anthropocene Review* 2: 81–98. https://doi.org/10.1177%2F2053019614564785.

Steinmetz, G., ed. 2013. *Sociology and Empire: The Imperial Entanglements of a Discipline*. Durham, NC: Duke University Press.

Steinmetz, G. 2014. "The Sociology of Empires, Colonies, and Postcolonialism." *Annual Review of Sociology* 40: 77–103.

Stenmark, Mikael, 2015. "Relativism: A Pervasive Feature of the Contemporary Western World?" *Social Epistemology* 29: 31–43.

Stepler, Renee, and Anna Brown. 2016, April 19. "Statistical Portrait of Hispanics in the United States." Pew Research Center. https://www.pewresearch.org/hispanic/wp-content/uploads/sites/5/2016/09/PH_2016.09.08_Geography.pdf.

Steurer, M., and C. Bayr. 2020. "Measuring Urban Sprawl Using Land Use Data." *Land Use Policy* 97: 104799.

Stevens, Mitchell L., Elizabeth A. Armstrong, and Richard Arum. 2008. "Sieve, Incubator, Temple, Hub: Empirical and Theoretical Advances in the Sociology of Higher Education." *Annual Review of Sociology* 34: 127–151.

Stevens, Mitchell. 2001. *Kingdom of Children: Culture and Controversy in the Homeschooling Movement*. Princeton, NJ: Princeton University Press.

Stevens, Mitchell. 2007. *Creating a Class*. Cambridge, MA: Harvard University Press.

Stevenson, Betsy, and Justin Wolfers. 2007. "Marriage and Divorce: Changes and Their Driving Factors." NBER Working Paper 12944. http://www.nber.org/papers/w12944.pdf.

Stivers, Tanya, and Stefan Timmermans. 2020. "Medical Authority under Siege: How Clinicians Transform Patient Resistance into Acceptance." *Journal of Health and Social Behavior*, 61(1): 60–78.

Strauss, A., and B. Glaser. eds. 1975. *Chronic Illness and the Quality of Life*. St. Louis: Mosby.

Strauss, William, and Neil Howe, 2000. *Millennials Rising: The Next Great Generation.* New York: Vintage.

Streib, Jessi. 2017. "The Unbalanced Theoretical Toolkit: Problems and Partial Solutions to Studying Culture and Reproduction but Not Culture and Mobility." *American Journal of Cultural Sociology* 5(1–2): 127–153. https://doi.org/10.1057/s41290-016-0015-5.

Su, Dejun, and Lifeng Li. 2011. "Trends in the Use of Complementary and Alternative Medicine in the United States: 2002–2007." *Journal of Health Care for the Poor and Underserved* 22(1): 296–310.

Suarez-Orozco, C., and M. Suarez-Orozco. 2001. *Children of Immigration.* Cambridge, MA: Harvard University Press.

Sull, Donald, Charles Sull, and Ben Zweig. 2022, January 11. "Toxic Culture Is Driving the Great Resignation." *MIT Sloan Management Review.* https://sloanreview.mit.edu/article/toxic-culture-is-driving-the-great-resignation/.

Sullivan, Andrew. 2004. *Same-Sex Marriage: Pro and Con.* New York: Vintage.

Sullivan, Deborah A. 2001. *Cosmetic Surgery: The Cutting Edge of Medicine in America.* New Brunswick, NJ: Rutgers University Press.

Sundt, J. 2002. "Rehabilitation Model." In *Encyclopedia of Crime and Punishment*, ed. D. Levinson (pp. 1361–1367). Thousand Oaks, CA: SAGE.

Sutherland, Anna. 2014. "The Rise of Cohabitation." Institute for Family Studies Blog. https://ifstudies.org/blog/the-rise-of-cohabitation/.

Sweeney, Megan M. 2010. "Remarriage and Stepfamilies: Strategic Sites for Family Scholarship in the 21st Century." *Journal of Marriage and Family* 72(3): 667–684. http://www.jstor.org/stable/40732502.

Sweet, S., and M. Cardwell. 2016. "Editor's Comment: Considering Assessment." *Teaching Sociology* 44(3): 149–150. https://doi.org/10.1177/0092055X16650659.

Sweet, S., K. McElrath, and E. L. Kain. 2014. "The Coordinated Curriculum: How Institutional Theory Can Be Used to Catalyze Revision of the Sociology Major." *Teaching Sociology* 42(4): 287–297. https://doi.org/10.1177/0092055X14541551.

Swidler, Ann. 1986. "Culture in Action: Symbols and Strategies." *American Sociological Review* 51(2): 273–286.

Swire, Peter. 2015. "The USA FREEDOM Act, the President's Review Group and the Biggest Intelligence Reform in 40 Years." *Privacy Perspectives.* https://iapp.org/news/a/the-usa-freedom-act-the-presidents-review-group-and-the-biggest-intelligence-reform-in-40-years.

Syrda, J. 2023. "Gendered Housework: Spousal Relative Income, Parenthood and Traditional Gender Identity Norms." *Work, Employment and Society* 37(3): 794–813. https://doi.org/10.1177/09500170211069780.

Tach, L. M., and A. Eads. 2015. "Trends in the Economic Consequences of Marital and Cohabitation Dissolution in the United States. *Demography* 52: 401–432.

Tamim, Baba. 2023, February 26. "ChatGPT Shrinks Human Workforce in US Amid Tech Layoffs, Reveals Survey." *Interesting Engineering.* https://interestingengineering.com/culture/chatgpt-shrinking-human-workforce-america.

Tarrow, Sidney G. 1989. *Democracy and Disorder: Protest and Politics in Italy, 1965–1975.* Oxford, UK: Oxford University Press.

Tatum, Beverly. 1997. *"Why Are All the Black Kids Sitting Together in the Cafeteria?" and Other Conversations about Race.* New York: Basic Books.

Taylor, Charles. 2007. *A Secular Age.* Cambridge, MA: Harvard University Press.

Telep, Cody, and David Weisburd, 2012. "What Is Known about the Effectiveness of Police Practices in Reducing Crime and Disorder?" *Police Quarterly* 20: 1–27.

Telles, Edward E. 2002. "Racial Ambiguity among the Brazilian Population." *Ethnic and Racial Studies* 25(3): 415–441.

Telzer, E. H. 2010. "Expanding the Acculturation Gap-Distress Model: An Integrative Review of Research." *Human Development* 53(6): 313–340. https://www.jstor.org/stable/26764975

Tepper, Steven J. 2011. *Not Here, Not Now, Not That!* Chicago: University of Chicago Press.

Terpstra, Jan. 2011. "Two Theories on the Police—The Relevance of Max Weber and Emile Durkheim to the Study of the Police." *International Journal of Law Crime and Justice* 39(1): 1–11. https://doi.org/10.1016/j.ijlcj.2011.01.009.

Thoits, Peggy. 2010. "Stress and Health: Major Findings and Policy Implications." *Journal of Health and Social Behavior* 51: S41–S53.

Thomas, Kevin J. A. 2012. "Demographic Profile of Black Caribbean Immigrants in the United States." Washington DC: Migration Policy Institute.

Thompson, Caroline. 2017, May 4. "Fat-Positive Activists Explain What It's Really Like to Be Fat." *Vice.* https://www.vice.com/en_us/article/gvzx94/fat-positive-activists-explain-what-its-really-like-to-be-fat.

Thompson, John. 1991. *Ideology and Modern Culture: Critical Social Theory in the Era of Mass Communication.* Stanford, CA: Stanford University Press.

Thompson, Kenneth, 2012. "Globalization and Religion." In *The Oxford Handbook of Cultural Sociology*, eds. Jeffrey Alexander, Philip Smith, and Ronald Jacobs (pp. 471–486). New York: Oxford University Press.

Thornton, Claire. 2022, December 9. "Decades-Old US Poverty-Level Formula 'Makes No Sense' in 2022, Expert Say. Here's Why It's Still Used." *USA Today.* https://www.usatoday.com/story/news/nation/2022/12/09/why-federal-poverty-line-not-effective/10827076002/.

Tilcsik Andras. 2011. "Pride and Prejudice: Employment Discrimination against Openly Gay Men in the United States." *American Journal of Sociology* 117: 586–626.

Tilly, Charles, and Lesley J. Wood. 2012. *Social Movements 1768–2012.* New York: Routledge.

Tilly, Charles. 1999. *Durable Inequality.* Berkeley: University of California Press.

Tilly, Charles. 2004. *Social Movements, 1768–2004.* Boulder, CO: Paradigm.

Timmermans, Stefan. 2008. "Oh Look, There Is a Doctor after All: About the Resilience of Professional Medicine: A Commentary on McKinlay and Marceau's 'When There Is No Doctor.'" *Social Science & Medicine* 67(10): 1492–1496.

Tocqueville, Alexis de. [1835, 1840] 2003. *Democracy in America*, ed. L. Kramnick. London: Penguin Classics.

Tolnay, Stewart. 2003. "The African-American 'Great Migration' and Beyond." *Annual Review of Sociology* 29: 209–232.

Tomaskovic-Devey D., M. Thomas, and K. Johnson. 2005. "Race and the Accumulation of Human Capital across the Career: A Theoretical Model and Fixed-Effects Application." *American Journal of Sociology* 111: 58–89.

Tomaskovic-Devey, Donald, and Patricia Warren. 2009. "Explaining and Eliminating Racial Profiling." *Contexts* 8: 34–39.

Tonry, M. 2007. "Looking Back to See the Future of Punishment in America." *Social Research* 74(2): 353–378.

Tonry, Michael. 1995. *Malign Neglect.* New York: Oxford University Press.

Tonry, Michael. 2014. "Remodeling American Sentencing: A Ten-Step Blueprint for Moving Past Mass Incarceration." *Criminology and Public Policy* 13: 503–533.

Toosi, Negin R., Shira Mor, Zhaleh Semnani-Azad, Katherine W. Phillips, and Emily T. Amanatullah. 2019. "Who Can Lean In? The Intersecting Role of Race and Gender in Negotiations." *Psychology of Women Quarterly* 43(1): 7–21. https://doi.org/10.1177/0361684318800492.

Touraine, Alain. 1981. *The Voice and the Eye.* Cambridge: Cambridge University Press.

Touraine, Alain. 1971. *The Post-industrial Society: Tomorrow's Social History: Classes, Conflicts and Culture in the Programmed Society.* New York: Random House.

Treatment Advocacy Center. 2021. Office of Research and Public Affairs. Arlington VA. https://www.treatmentadvocacycenter.org/component/content/article/183-in-a-crisis/2614-understand-criminal-justice-involvement Accessed April 26, 2021.

Tresch, A. 2009. "Politicians in the Media: Determinants of Legislators' Presence and Prominence in Swiss Newspapers." *The International Journal of Press/Politics* 14(1): 67–90.

Tretina, Kat. 2022, October 13. "The Average Age of Retirement in the US." *Forbes Advisor.* https://www.forbes.com/advisor/retirement/average-retirement-age/.

Trottier, D. 2020. "Denunciation and Doxing: Towards a Conceptual Model of Digital Vigilantism." *Global Crime* 21(3–4): 196–212.

Tuchman, Gaye. 1978. *Making News: A Study in the Construction of Reality.* New York: Free Press.

Tukachinsky, Riva, Nathan Walter, and Camille J. Saucier. 2020, December. "Antecedents and Effects of Parasocial Relationships: A Meta-Analysis" *Journal of Communication* 70(6): 868–894. https://doi.org/10.1093/joc/jqaa034.

Tunstall, Jeremy. 2007. *The Media Were American: U.S. Mass Media in Decline.* New York: Oxford University Press.

Turkle, Sherry. 2011. *Alone Together: Why We Expect More From Technology and Less From Each Other.* New York: Basic Books.

Turkle, Sherry. 2015. *Reclaiming Conversation: The Power of Talk in a Digital Age.* New York: Penguin Press.

Turnbull, Sue. 2014. "The Roots of Crime." In *The TV Crime Drama* (pp. 20–43). Edinburgh: Edinburgh University Press. http://www.jstor.org/stable/10.3366/j.ctt1g0b60z.6.

Turow, Joseph. 1998. *Breaking Up America: Advertising and the New Media World.* Chicago: University of Chicago Press.

Twenge, J. M., J. Haidt, A. B. Blake, C. McAllister, H. Lemon, and A. Le Roy. 2021. "Worldwide Increases in Adolescent Loneliness." *Journal of Adolescence* 93: 257–269.

U.S. Census Bureau. 2023. "Decennial Censuses, 1890 to 1940, and Current Population Survey, March and Annual Social and Economic Supplements, 1947 to 2023." https://www.census.gov/data/tables/time-series/demo/families/marital.html.

U.S. Department of State. 2022, March 31. "X Gender Marker Available on U.S. Passports Starting April 11." U.S. Department of State Press Release. https://www.state.gov/x-gender-marker-available-on-u-s-passports-starting-april-11/#:~:text=After%20thoughtful%20consideration%20of%20the,individuals'%20privacy%20while%20advancing%20inclusion.

Uggen, Christopher, Jeff Manza, and Melissa Thompson. 2006. "Citizenship, Democracy, and the Civic Reintegration of Criminal Offenders." *The Annals of the American Academy of Political and Social Science* 605: 281–310.

UN Department of Economic and Social Affairs. 2019, September. "International Migration Stock 2019." https://www.un.org/en/development/desa/population/migration/publications/migrationreport/docs/MigrationStock2019_TenKeyFindings.pdf.

UNAIDS. 2017. "Make Some Noise for Zero Discrimination on 1 March 2017." http://www.unaids.org/sites/default/files/media_asset/2017-zero-discrimination-day_en.pdf.

UNESCO. 2017. *School Violence and Bullying: Global Status Report.* http://unesdoc.unesco.org/images/0024/002469/246970e.pdf.

Unger, Roberto. 1976. *Law in Modern Society.* New York: Free Press.

UNHCR. 2023. United Nations High Commission on Refugees Refugee Data Finder. https://www.unhcr.org/refugee-statistics/.

UNICEF. 2022, June. "Primary Education. UNICEF Data: Monitoring the Situation of Women and Children." https://data.unicef.org/topic/education/primary-education/#:~:text=Globally%2C%20the%20adjusted%20net%20attendance%20rate%20reached%2087,children%20was%20reduced%20by%20over%2035%20per%20cent.

United Nations Development Programme (UNDP). 2009. Human Development Report 2009: Overcoming barriers: Human mobility and development. New York.

United Nations, Department of Economic and Social Affairs, Population Division. 2016a. *The World's Cities in 2016—Data Booklet (ST/ESA/SER.A/392).* New York, NY: United Nations. https://www.un.org/en/development/desa/population/publications/databooklet/index.asp.

United Nations, Department of Economic and Social Affairs, Population Division. 2016b. International Migration Report 2015: Highlights (ST/ESA/SER.A/375).

United Nations, Department of Economic and Social Affairs, Population Division. 2019. "The Number of International Migrants Reaches 272 Million, Continuing an Upward Trend iIn All World Regions, Says UN." https://www.un.org/development/desa/en/news/population/international-migrant-stock-2019.html#:~:text=The%20number%20of%20international%20migrants%20globally%20reached%20an%20estimated%20272,by%20the%20United%20Nations%20today. Accessed November 29, 2020

United Nations. 2020. *World Drug Report 2020.* https://wdr.unodc.org/wdr2020/index.html.

United Nations. 2022. "World Population Prospects 2022." United Nations Department of Economic and Social Affairs. https://www.un.org/development/desa/pd/sites/www.un.org.development.desa.pd/files/wpp2022_summary_of_results.pdf.

Upchurch, D. M., B. W. Rainisch, and L. Chyu. 2015. "Greater Leisure Time Physical Activity Is Associated with Lower Allostatic Load in White, Black, and Mexican American Midlife Women: Findings from the National Health and Nutrition Examination Survey, 1999 through 2004." *Women's Health Issues* 25(6): 680–687. doi:10.1016/j.whi.2015.07.002.

US Census. 2022. "Historical Poverty Tables: People and Families—1959 to 2019. Table 2. Poverty Status of People by Family Relationship, Race, and Hispanic Origin." https://www2.census.gov/programs-surveys/cps/tables/time-series/historical-poverty-people/hstpov2.xlsx.

US Census. 2024. "Poverty Thresholds by Size of Family and Number of Children. Data." https://www.census.gov/data/tables/time-series/demo/income-poverty/historical-poverty-thresholds.html.

US Centers for Disease Control and Prevention and National Cancer Institute. 2019. "Cancer Statistics Data Visualizations Tool, based on November 2018 submission data (1999-2016)." U.S. Cancer Statistics

Working Group. U.S. Department of Health and Human Services. www.cdc.gov/cancer/dataviz.

US Congress, Office of Technology Assessment. 1992, February. "Testing in American Schools: Asking the Right Questions, OTA-SET-519." Washington, DC: US Government Printing Office.

US Department of Health and Human Services. 2016. "Physicians and Hospitals in U.S. Health Systems, 2016." Data Infographics. Agency for Health Research and Quality. https://www.ahrq.gov/sites/default/files/wysiwyg/data/infographics/physicians-hospitals.pdf.

US Department of State. About Human trafficking. https://www.state.gov/humantrafficking-about-human-trafficking/.

US National Libraries of Medicine. 2022, June 23. "Can the Results of Direct-to-Consumer Genetic Testing Affect My Ability to Get Insurance?" *MedlinePlus* https://medlineplus.gov/genetics/understanding/dtcgenetictesting/dtcinsurancerisk/#:~:text=This%20means%20that%20health%20insurance,you%20to%20pay%20higher%20premiums.&text=GINA%20does%20not%20apply%20to,care%20insurance%2C%20or%20life%20insurance.

US National Library of Medicine. 2020. "Can the Results of Direct-to-Consumer Genetic Testing Affect My Ability to Get Insurance?" *MedLinePlus*. https://medlineplus.gov/genetics/understanding/dtcgenetictesting/dtcinsurancerisk/#:~:text=This%20means%20that%20health%20insurance,you%20to%20pay%20higher%20premiums.&text=GINA%20does%20not%20apply%20to,care%20insurance%2C%20or%20life%20insurance.

Vaillant, George. 2012. *Triumphs of Experience: The Men of the Harvard Grant Study*. Cambridge, MA: Belknap Press.

Vaisey, S. 2009. "Motivation and Justification: A Dual-Process Model of Culture in Action." *American Journal of Sociology* 114(6): 1675–1715.

Valdivia, Angharad N. 2010. *Latina/os and the Media*. Cambridge, UK: Polity.

van Emmerik, Hetty I., M. C. Euwema, M. Geschiere, and M. F. A. G. Schouten. 2006. "Networking Your Way through the Organization." *Women in Management Review* 21(1): 54–66.

Varanasi, Lakshmi, Sarah Jackson, Britney Nguyen, and Sindu Sundar. 2023, July 26. "The Rise and Fall of FTX's Sam Bankman-Fried, the Onetime Crypto Billionaire Prosecutors Now Want Jailed after They Say He Interfered with Witnesses in His Criminal Case." *Business Insider*. https://www.businessinsider.com/ftx-crypto-king-sam-bankman-fried-rise-and-fall-2022-11.

Vasilogambros, Matt. 2016, April 7. "Cuba, the Brand." *The Atlantic*. https://www.theatlantic.com/business/archive/2016/04/little-havana-miami/477204/.

Vaughan, Diane. 1990. *Uncoupling: Turning Points in Intimate Relationships*. New York: Vintage.

Venn, C. 2009. "Neoliberal Political Economy, Biopolitics and Colonialism: A Transcolonial Genealogy of Inequality." *Theory, Culture & Society* 26(6), 206–233.

Venter, Zander S., Kristin Aunan, Sourangsu Chowdhury, and Jos Lelieveld. 2020. "COVID-19 Lockdowns Cause Global Air Pollution Declines." *PNAS* 117(32): 18984–18990. https://doi.org/10.1073/pnas.2006853117.

Vercayie, Diemer, and Marc Herremans. 2015. "Citizen Science and Smartphones Take Roadkill Monitoring to the Next Level." *Nature Conservation* 11: 29–40. doi:10.3897/natureconservation.11.4439.

Verhoeven, Beatrice, and Rasha Ali. 2016, June 7. "'The Bachelorette' So White: Inside the Show's Diversity Deficit." *The Wrap*. https://www.thewrap.com/bachelorette-so-white-abc-dating-show-diversity-woes-continue-jojo-fletcher/.

Vigdor, Neil. 2020a, April 27. "2 Sought $4 Million for Face Masks that Didn't Exist, US Says." *New York Times*. https://www.nytimes.com/2020/04/27/us/california-coronavirus-ppe-face-mask-scam.html.

Vigdor, Neil. 2020b, April 22. "Tennessee Brothers Who Hoarded Hand Sanitizer Settle to Avoid Price Gouging Fine." *New York Times*. https://www.nytimes.com/2020/04/22/us/hand-sanitizer-matt-colvin-noah-coronavirus.html.

Vigdor, Neil. 2020a, April 27. "2 Sought $4 Million for Face Masks That Didn't Exist, U.S. Says." *New York Times*. https://www.nytimes.com/2020/04/27/us/california-coronavirus-ppe-face-mask-scam.html.

Vigdor, Neil. 2020b, June 22. "Tennessee Brothers Who Hoarded Hand Sanitizer Settle to Avoid Price-Gouging Fine." *New York Times* https://www.nytimes.com/2020/04/22/us/hand-sanitizer-matt-colvin-noah-coronavirus.html.

Villada, C., V. Hidalgo, M. Almela, and A. Salvador. 2016. "Individual Differences in the Psychobiological Response to Psychosocial Stress (Trier Social Stress

Test): The Relevance of Trait Anxiety and Coping Styles. *Stress Health.* 32(2): 90–99. doi: 10.1002/smi.2582. Epub 2014 Jun 11. PMID: 24916722.

Voas, David, and Mark Chaves. 2016. "Is the United States a Counterexample to the Secularization Thesis?" *American Journal of Sociology* 121: 1517–1556.

Vogel, E. A., J. P. Rose, L. R. Roberts, and K. Eckles. 2014. "Social Comparison, Social Media, and Self-Esteem." *Psychology of Popular Media Culture* 3(4): 206.

Vogels, Emily, Monica Anderson, Margaret Porteus, Chris Baranavski, Sara Atske, Colleen McClain, Brooke Auxier, Andrew Perrin, and Meera Ramshankar. 2021, May 19. "Americans and 'Cancel Culture': Where Some See Calls for Accountability, Others See Censorship, Punishment." Pew Research Center. https://www.pewresearch.org/internet/2021/05/19/americans-and-cancel-culture-where-some-see-calls-for-accountability-others-see-censorship-punishment/

Voss, Kim, and Irene Bloemraad, eds. 2011. *Rallying for Immigrant Rights: The Fight for Inclusion in 21st Century America.* Berkeley: University of California Press.

Waddington, P. A. J., 2002. *Policing Citizens: Police, Power, and the State.* New York: Routledge.

Wagner, Kurt, Mark Bergen, and Sarah Frier. 2020, November 3. "Big Tech Draws Record Revenue and Harsh Criticism with US Election Ads." *Japan Times.* https://www.japantimes.co.jp/news/2020/11/03/business/big-tech-record-revenue-us-election-ads/.

Wakefield, Melanie A., Barbara Loken, and Robert C. Hornik. 2010. "Use of Mass Media Campaigns to Change Health Behaviour." *Lancet* 376(9748): 1261–1271.

Wallerstein, Immanuel Maurice. 2004. *World-Systems Analysis: An Introduction.* Durham, NC: Duke University Press.

Wallerstein, Immanuel. 1976. "From Feudalism to Capitalism: Transition or Transitions?" *Social Forces* 55: 273–283.

Wallerstein, Judith. 1991. "The Long-Term Effects of Divorce on Children: A Review." *Journal of the American Academy of Child and Adolescent Psychiatry* 30: 349–360.

Wall-Parker, A. 2019. "Measuring White Collar Crime." In *The Handbook of White-Collar Crime*, ed. M. L. Rorie. https://doi.org/10.1002/9781118775004.ch3

Wallsten, Kevin. 2015. "Non-Elite Twitter Sources Rarely Cited in Coverage." *Newspaper Research Journal* 36(1): 24–41. doi:10.1177/0739532915580311.

Wang, Wendy. 2012, February 16. "The Rise of Intermarriage." Pew Research Center. https://www.pewresearch.org/social-trends/2012/02/16/the-rise-of-intermarriage/.

Waters, Mary. 1990. *Ethnic Options: Choosing Identities in America.* Berkeley: University of California Press.

Waters, Mary. 2001. *Black Identities: West Indian Immigrant Dreams and American Realities.* Cambridge, MA: Harvard University Press.

Watkins-Hayes, Celeste, 2019. *Remaking a Life: How Women Living With HIV/AIDS Confront Inequality.* Berkeley, CA: University of California Press.

Watson, Carol, Jenna Plump, and James Durham. 2022. "Gender Bias in the Middle Level Classroom: The Intersection of Observation, Teacher Self-Perceptions, and Student Perceptions." *Journal of Research in Education* 31(1):124–150. https://eric.ed.gov/?q=Gender+Bias+in+the+Middle+Level+Classroom%3a+T&id=EJ1368436

Webber, Craig. 2021. "Rediscovering the Relative Deprivation and Crime Debate: Tracking Its Fortunes from Left Realism to the Precariat." *Critical Criminology* 30: 321–347. doi:10.1007/s10612-021-09554-4.

Weber, Max. 1969. *The City.* New York: Free Press.

Weber, Max. [1905] 2011. *The Protestant Ethic and the Spirit of Capitalism.* New York: Oxford University Press.

Weber, Max. 1946. *From Max Weber: Essays in Sociology.* New York: Oxford University Press.

Webley, K. 2010, April 30. "A Brief History of the Happy Meal." *Time.* http://content.time.com/time/nation/article/0,8599,1986073,00.html.

Weidner, D. 2014. "The Rhetoric of Secularization." *New German Critique* 41(1): 1–31.

Weil, Patrick. 2001. "Access to Citizenship: A Comparison of Twenty Five Nationality Laws." In *Citizenship Today: Global Perspectives and Practices*, eds. T. Alexander Aleinikoff and Douglas Klusmeyer (pp. 17–35). Carnegie Endowment for International Peace, Washington DC.

Weiss, A., and S. M. Chermak. 1998. "The News Value of African American Victims: An Examination of the Media's Presentation of Homicide." *Journal of Crime and Justice* 21: 71–88.

Weiss, Rick, and Justin Gillis. 2000, June 27. "Teams Finish Mapping Human DNA." *Washington Post.*

https://www.washingtonpost.com/archive/politics/2000/06/27/teams-finish-mapping-human-dna/3af9bfcf-e7b6-4ac1-bcdb-f4fc117c19bd/?utm_term=.b3e595005bb8.

Weller, Jennifer, Matt Boyd, and David Cumin. 2014. "Teams, Tribes and Patient Safety: Overcoming Barriers to Effective Teamwork in Healthcare." *Postgraduate Medical Journal* 90(1061): 149–154.

Welsh, Brandon C., and David P. Farrington. 2009, October. "Public Area CCTV and Crime Prevention: An Updated Systematic Review and Meta-Analysis." *Justice Quarterly* 26(4): 716–745.

Welzel, Christian, and Ronald Inglehart. 2009. "Political Culture, Mass Beliefs and Value Change." In *Democratization* (pp. 126–144). Oxford, UK: Oxford University Press.

Western, Bruce, and Becky Petit. 2005. "Black–White Earnings Inequality, Employment Rates, and Incarceration." *American Journal of Sociology* 111: 553–578.

Western, Bruce, and Sara McLanahan. 2000. "Fathers behind Bars: The Impact of Incarceration on Family Research." *Contemporary Perspectives in Family Research* 2: 309–324.

Western, Bruce. 2006. *Punishment and Inequality in America*. New York: Russell Sage Foundation.

Western, Bruce. 2018. *Homeward: Life in the Year After Prison*. New York: Russell Sage Foundation.

Wilkinson, Richard, and Kate Pickett. 2009. *The Spirit Level: Why Greater Equality Makes Societies Stronger*. London: Bloomsbury Press.

Williams, C. L. 1992. "The Glass Escalator: Hidden Advantages for Men in the "Female" Professions." *Social Problems* 39(3): 253–267.

Williams, C. L. 2013. "The Glass Escalator, Revisited. Gender Inequality in Neoliberal Times." *Gender and Society* 27(5): 609–629.

Williams, Fiona. 2018. "A Global Crisis in Care?" *Global Dialogue* 8(2). http://globaldialogue.isa-sociology.org/a-global-crisis-in-care/.

Williams, Johnny E. 2016. *Decoding Racial Ideology in Genomics: Why We Pretend Race Exists in America*. Lanham, MD: Lexington Books.

Williams, Raymond. 1983. *Culture and Society: 1780–1950*. New York: Columbia University Press.

Willis, Paul. 1977. *Learning to Labor*. New York: Columbia University Press.

Wilmoth, Janet. 2004. "Questions and Comments about National, Externally Graded Assessment Exams: A Response to Wagenaar." *Teaching Sociology* 32(2): 241–243.

Wilson, James Q. 1968. *Varieties of Police Behavior*. Cambridge, MA: Harvard University Press.

Wilson, William J. 1987. *The Truly Disadvantaged: The Inner City, the Underclass, and Public Policy*. Chicago: University of Chicago Press.

Wingfield, Adia Harvey. 2009. "Racializing the Glass Escalator: Reconsidering Men's Experiences with Women's Work." *Gender and Society* 23(1): 5–26.

Wogan, J. B. 2016, June. "Who's an Employee? The Uber-Important Question of Today's Economy." *Governing*. http://www.governing.com/topics/mgmt/gov-uber-employee-lawsuits-sharing-economy.html.

Wolf, Michael, Bruce Friedman and Daniel Sutherland. 1998. *Religion in the Workplace*. Chicago, IL: American Bar Association.

Wolfe, Michelle, Bryan D. Jones, and Frank R. Baumgartner. 2013. "A Failure to Communicate: Agenda Setting in Media and Policy Studies." *Political Communication* 30(2): 175–192. doi:10.1080/10584609.2012.737419.

Wolfson, Evan. 2004. *Why Marriage Matters: America, Equality, and Gay People's Right to Marry*. New York: Simon & Schuster.

Wood, Molly. 2014, July 28. "OKCupid Plays with Love in User Experiments." *New York Times*. https://www.nytimes.com/2014/07/29/technology/okcupid-publishes-findings-of-user-experiments.html.

Woodhouse, Kellie. 2015, May 22. "Doing Their Fair Share." *Slate*. http://www.slate.com/articles/life/inside_higher_ed/2015/05/wealthy_universities_like_harvard_leave_low_income_students_behind_despite.html.

Woodward, Ian. 2012. "Consumption as Cultural Interpretation: Taste, Performativity and Navigating The Forest Of Objects." In *The Oxford Handbook of Cultural Sociology*, eds. Jeffrey Alexander, Philip Smith, and Ronald Jacobs (pp. 671–697). New York: Oxford University Press.

Wooley, Samuel, and Philip Howard. 2019. "Introduction: Computational Propaganda Worldwide." In *Computational Propaganda: Political Parties, Politicians, and Political Manipulation on Social Media*, ed. S. Wooley and P. Howard (pp. 3–20). New York: Oxford University Press.

World Bank. 2018. *Piecing Together the Poverty Puzzle. Poverty and Shared Prosperity*. Washington, DC: The World Bank.

World Bank. 2020. *Reversals of Fortune. Poverty and Shared Prosperity Report 2020*. https://openknowl

edge.worldbank.org/bitstream/handle/10986/34496/9781464816024.pdf.

World Bank. 2022, May 12. "Remittances to Reach $630 Billion in 2022 with Record Flows into Ukraine." https://www.worldbank.org/en/news/press-release/2022/05/11/remittances-to-reach-630-billion-in-2022-with-record-flows-into-ukraine.

World Drug Report 2020 (United Nations publication, Sales No. E.20.XI.6). https://wdr.unodc.org/wdr2020/index2020.html.

World Economic Forum. 2018. "Global Risks Report 2018," 13th ed. http://reports.weforum.org/global-risks-2018/.

World Health Organization. 1946. "Constitution of the World Health Organization as adopted by the International Health Conference, New York, 19–22 June 1946." Quoted in Grad, Frank P. 2002. "The Preamble of the Constitution of the World Health Organization." *Bulletin of the World Health Organization*. 80(12): 982.

World Health Organization. 2020. *World Health Statistics 2020*. https://iris.who.int/bitstream/handle/10665/332070/9789240005105-eng.pdf.

World Health Organization. 2004. *A Glossary of Terms for Community Health Care and Services for Older Persons (WHO Centre for Health Development Ageing and Health Technical Report Vol. 5)*. https://iris.who.int/handle/10665/68896 Accessed October 24, 2024.

Wu, Xiaoxu, Yongmei Lu, Sen Zhou, Lifan Chen, and Bing Xu. 2016. "Impact of Climate Change on Human Infectious Diseases: Empirical Evidence and Human Adaptation." *Environment International* 86: 14–23.

Wuthnow, Robert. 1989. *The Struggle for America's Soul: Evangelicals, Liberals, and Secularism*. Grand Rapids, MI: Wm. B. Eerdmans Publishing Co.

Wuthnow, Robert. 1997. *The Crisis in the Churches: Spiritual Malaise, Fiscal Woe*. New York: Oxford University Press.

Wyatt, Ian, and Daniel Hecker. 2006. "Occupational Changes during the Twentieth Century." *Monthly Labor Review* 129(3): 35–57.

Wyatt, Ronald M. 2013, October 2. "Revisiting Disruptive and Inappropriate Behavior: Five Years after Standards Introduced." Center for Transforming Healthcare Leaders. https://www.jointcommission.org/jc_physician_blog/revisiting_disruptive_and_inappropriate_behavior/.

Yale Climate Connections. 2010, January 19. "San Diego TV Meteorologist John Coleman Arouses Scripps Ire with 'Other Side' Special." https://yaleclimateconnections.org/2010/01/coleman-arouses-scripps-ire/.

Yancy, C. W. 2020. "COVID-19 and African Americans." *JAMA* 323(19): 1891–1892. doi:10.1001/jama.2020.6548.

Yancy, Clyde W. 2007, July 30. "The Association of Black Cardiologists Responds to "Race in a Bottle. A Misguided Passion." *Scientific American*. https://www.scientificamerican.com/article/the-association-of-black-cardiologists-responds-to-article/.

Yang, Guobin. 2011. *The Power of the Internet in China: Citizen Activism Online*. New York: Columbia University Press.

Yanich, Danilo. 2001. "Location, Location, Location: Urban and Suburban Crime on Local TV News." *Journal of Urban Affairs* 23: 3–4, 221–241. Doi:10.1111/0735-2166.00086.

Yavorsky, Jill, and Janette Dill. 2020, January 7. "Unemployment Pushes More Men to Take on Female-Dominated Jobs." *The Conversation*.

Yosso, Tara J. 2005. "Whose Culture Has Capital? A Critical Race Theory Discussion of Community Cultural Wealth." *Race Ethnicity and Education* 8(1): 69–91.doi:10.1080/1361332052000341006.

Yu, Wei-Hsin, and Janet Chen-Lan Kuo. 2024. "Research Note: New Evidence on the Motherhood Wage Penalty." *Demography* 61(2): 231–250.

Yuan, S., and C. Lou. 2020. "How Social Media Influencers Foster Relationships with Followers: The Roles of Source Credibility and Fairness in Parasocial Relationship and Product Interest. *Journal of Interactive Advertising* 20(2): 133–147.

Zarulli, Virginia, Julia A. Barthold Jones, Anna Oksuzyan, Rune Lindahl-Jacobsen, Kaare-Christensen, and James W. Vaupel. 2018. "Women Live Longer Than Men Even During Severe Famines and Epidemics." *Proceedings of the National Academy of Sciences of the United States of America* 115(4): 832–840.

Zaveri, Miri. 2020, June 8. "BTS Fans Say They've Raised $1 Million for Black Lives Matter Groups." *New York Times*. https://www.nytimes.com/2020/06/08/arts/music/bts-donate-black-lives-matter.html.

Zetter, Roger, and James Morrissey, 2014. "The Environment-Mobility Nexus: Reconceptualizing the Links Between Environmental Stress, (Im)Mobility, and Power." In *Oxford Handbook of Refugee and Forced Migration Studies*, ed. E. Qasmiyeh, G. Loescher, K. Long, and N. Sigona (pp. 342–354). New York: Oxford University Press.

Zhao, Y. V., and J. L. Gibson. 2022. "Evidence for Protective Effects of Peer Play in the Early Years: Better Peer Play Ability at Age 3 Years Predicts Lower Risks of Externalising and Internalising Problems at Age 7 Years in a Longitudinal Cohort Analysis." *Child Psychiatry and Human Development* https://doi.org/10.1007/s10578-022-01368-x.

Zhou, M. 1998. "'Parachute Kids' in Southern California: The Educational Experience of Chinese Children in Transnational Families." *Education Policy* 12: 682–702.

Zhou, M., and C. Bankston. 1998. *Growing Up American: How Vietnamese Children Adapt to Life in the United States*. New York: Russell Sage Foundation.

Zhou, Min, 1997. "Segmented Assimilation: Issues, Controversies, and Recent Research on the New Second Generation." *International Migration Review* 31(4): 825–858.

Zimbardo, Philip. 2007. *The Lucifer Effect: Understanding How Good People Turn Evil*. New York: Random House.

Zimmerman, Frederick J., Dimitri A. Christakis, and Andrew N. Meltzoff. 2007. "Associations between Media Viewing and Language Development in Children under Age 2 Years." *Journal of Pediatrics* 151: 364–368.

Zipperer, B., C. McNicholas, M. Poydock, D. Schneider, and K. Harknett. 2022. "National Survey of Gig Workers Paints a Picture of Poor Working Conditions, Low Pay." *El Trimestre Económico* 89(356), 1199–1214.

Zong, Jie, Jeanne Batalova, and Jeffrey Hallock. 2018, February 8. "Frequently Requested Statistics on Immigrants and Immigration in the United States." Migration Policy Institute. https://www.migrationpolicy.org/article/frequently-requested-statistics-immigrants-and-immigration-united-states.

Zou, M. 2015. "Gender, Work Orientations and Job Satisfaction." *Work, Employment and Society* 29(1): 3–22. doi: https://doi.org/10.1177/0950017014559267.

Zuckerman, Harriet. 1977. *Scientific Elite: Nobel Laureates in the United States*. New York: Free Press.

Zweigenhaft, Richard, and G. William Domhoff. 2006. *Diversity in the Power Elite*. Lanham, MA: Rowman and Littlefield.

# Credits

## CHAPTER 1
**2** Orange Pics BV/Alamy Stock Photo; **8** Dmitry Molchanov/Shutterstock; **9** AP Photo/Craig Ruttle; **13** dpa picture alliance/Alamy Stock Photo; **14** AP Photo/Marcio Jose Sanchez; **18** Valerie Plesch/Bloomberg via Getty Images; **19** Caio Pederneiras/Shutterstock; **21** AP Photo/Mark Lennihan

## CHAPTER 2
**26** baipooh/Shutterstock; **29** Data Courtesy Department of Labor Logo United States Department of Labor; **30** Courtesy of Nik Mills; **32** Universal History Archive/UIG/Shutterstock; **32** Cci/Shutterstock; **33** Gianni Dagli Orti/Shutterstock; **33** Historia/Shutterstock; **34** Historia/Shutterstock; **34** Historia/Shutterstock; **35** Keystone Press/Alamy Stock Photo; **35** Ian Dagnall Computing/Alamy Stock Photo; **36** Charles Wenzelberg/Shutterstock; **37** vkilikov/Shutterstock; **38** Historia/Shutterstock; **38** GBM Historical Images/Shutterstock; **41** Kristina Bumphrey/Starpix/Shutterstock; **42** Everett Collection Inc/Alamy Stock Photo; **43** A Katz/Shutterstock; **43** Peter Klaunzer/EPA/Shutterstock; **47** Png Studio Photography/Shutterstock; **48** Georg Berg/Alamy Stock Photo; **49** Monkey Business Images/Shutterstock; **53** US Census; USDA; **58** Kiselev Andrey Valerevich/Shutterstock; **59** Zoom Historical/Alamy Stock Photo

## CHAPTER 3
**68** MediaPunch Inc/Alamy Stock Photo; **76** mama_mia/Shutterstock; **78** White House Photo/Alamy Stock Photo; **79** Andrey_Popov/Shutterstock; **81** elbud/Shutterstock; **82** Igor Golovniov/Shutterstock; **83** A_Lesik/Shutterstock; **84** Retro AdArchives/Alamy Stock Photo; **86** a katz/Shutterstock; **87** Bubbers BB/Shutterstock; **90** pio3/Shutterstock; **91** AP Photo/Ryan Sun; **92** Gregory Reed/Shutterstock; **93** Efired/Shutterstock; **95** Anna K Majer/Shutterstock; **97** Juanjo Martin/EPA/Shutterstock; **99** Anton_Ivanov/Shutterstock

## CHAPTER 4
**104** RESERVATION DOGS © 2023 FX Networks, LLC.; **108** Emese/Shutterstock; **109** ANURAK PONGPATIMET Shutterstock; **111** Monkey Business Images/Shutterstock; **111** polya_olya/Shutterstock; **113** alicephoto/Shutterstock; **114** Monkey Business Images/Shutterstock; **115** John Keith/Shutterstock; **118** AP Photo/Saurabh Das; **119** bbernard/Shutterstock; **122** Sergei Bachlakov/Shutterstock; **123** FiledIMAGE/Shutterstock; **124** Eric. E. Castro/Wikimedia Commons (CC BY 2.0); **126** Eddie Gerald/Alamy Stock Photo; **127** MOLPIX/Shutterstock; **128** Kelleher Photography/Shutterstock

## CHAPTER 5
**136** corgarashu/Shutterstock; **140** AP Photo/Charles Dharapak; **142** Kevin McGovern/Shutterstock; **143** Arnie Sachs/Shutterstock; **144** © EQRoy/Shutterstock; **145** Eye Ubiquitous/Alamy Stock Photo; **146** 4kclips/Shutterstock; **147** Richard Levine/Alamy Stock Photo; **158** AP Photo/Frank Augstein; **161** Newsmakers/getty Images

## CHAPTER 6
**172** Gino Santa Maria/Shutterstock; **176** Nathan Laine/Bloomberg via Getty Images; **180** Tom Wurl/Shutterstock; **182** Helioscribe/Shutterstock; **183** Viktor Gladkov/Shutterstock; **184** B.Zhou/Shutterstock; **185** Courtesy of Emmanuel Saez; **188** zstock/Shutterstock; **197** futurewalk/Shutterstock; **198** Right Coast Images/Shutterstock; **201** Jim West/Alamy Stock Photo; **203** John Fleenor/© ABC/Getty Images

## CHAPTER 7
**208** Darleine Heitman/Shutterstock; **223** Everett Collection/Shutterstock; **232** Kristi Blokhin/Shutterstock; **233** karenfoleyphotography/Shutterstock; **235** Robert P. Alvarez/Shutterstock; **243** Felix Mizioznikov/Shutterstock; **243** © Kit/Shutterstock; **246** Joseph Sohm/Shutterstock; **247** mikeledray/Shutterstock, matt gush/Shutterstock; **249** Kathy Hutchins/Shutterstock

## CHAPTER 8

**258** Katrina Elena/Shutterstock; **258** BearFotos/Shutterstock; **259** rSnapshotPhotos/Shutterstock; **262** Mangostar/Shutterstock; **266** Data courtesy of Gallup; **267** Powerful Design/Shutterstock; **271** B Greenwood/Daily Mail/Shutterstock; **273** Tyler Olson/Shutterstock; **274** Alesia Verem/Shutterstock; **275** AP Photo/Rich Pedroncelli; **275** Nine African-American women posed, standing, full length, with Nannie Burroughs holding banner reading, "Banner State Woman's National Baptist Convention." [Between 1905 and 1915] Photograph. https://www.loc.gov/item/93505051/; **276** mark reinstein/Shutterstock; **277** AP Photo/Kathy Willens; **279** GrAl/Shutterstock; **280** Koca Vehbi/Shutterstock; **280** © Chris Barham/Daily Mail/Shutterstock; **280** Anindito Mukherjee/EPA/Shutterstock; **282** AS project/Shutterstock; **284** Juan Camilo Bernal/Shutterstock; **286** boys: AP Photo/Eric Risberg, girls: AP Photo/Jeff Chiu

## CHAPTER 9

**294** Chris Bull/Alamy Stock Photo; **297** © Antonio Calanni/AP; **298** Dobo Kristian/Shutterstock; **299** szefei/Shutterstock; **301** Mariia Boiko/Shutterstock; **304** Monkey Business Images/Shutterstock; **304** Oksana Kuzmina/Shutterstock; **306** 20TH CENTURY FOX TV/Album/Alamy Stock Photo; **306** Moviestore/Shutterstock; **306** Abc-Tv/Kobal/Shutterstock; **307** Monkey Business Images/Shutterstock; **309** OurWorldInData.org/democracy | CC BY; **309** Source: NCFMR analyses of U.S. Census Bureau, American Community Survey, 1-yr. est., 2019; **311** "The Modern American Family Key trends in marriage and family life." Pew Research Center, Washington, D.C. (September 14, 2023) https://www.pewresearch.org/social-trends/2023/09/14/the-modern-american-family/; **312** "The Modern American Family Key trends in marriage and family life." Pew Research Center, Washington, D.C. (September 14, 2023) https://www.pewresearch.org/social-trends/2023/09/14/the-modern-american-family/; **315** Aleutie/Shutterstock; **317** Stacy Arezou Mehrfar/The New York Times/Redux; **322** AP Photo; **323** Dmytro Zinkevych/Shutterstock

## CHAPTER 10

**328** RNL/Shutterstock; **333** Tupungato/Shutterstock; **335** Album/Alamy Stock Photo; **338** ChameleonsEye/Shutterstock; **338** WH_Pics/Shutterstock; **338** Africa Studio/Shutterstock; **340** Leonard Zhukovsky/Shutterstock; **341** Data courtesy of PEW Research Center; **342** nicolasdecorte/Shutterstock; **343** Michael715/Shutterstock; **344** Mohamed Reedi/Shutterstock; **346** Pikoso.kz/Shutterstock; **347** 501room/Shutterstock; **349** Data courtesy of PEW Research Center; **351** Shutterstock; **355** Richard Thornton/Shutterstock; **356** Sheila Fitzgerald/Shutterstock; **358** Levent Konuk/Shutterstock; **360** Pictorial Press Ltd/Alamy Stock Photo; **362** JW Company/Shutterstock; **363** iQoncept/Shutterstock; **365** illustratorkris/Shutterstock; **366** Everett Collection/Shutterstock

## CHAPTER 11

**372** runzelkorn/Shutterstock; **375** mofaez/Shutterstock; **376** Miaron Billy/Shutterstock; **378** stock_photo_world/Shutterstock; **379** Jim Smeal/Shutterstock; **381** Hadrian/Shutterstock; **382** pbk-pg/Shutterstock; **383** Svetlana Miljkovic/wikimedia Commons; **386** Ken Wolter/Shutterstock; **392** stock_photo_world/Shutterstock; **393** Phil's Mommy/Shutterstock; **397** ImageFlow/Shutterstock; **401** lev radin/Shutterstock; **402** fizkes/Shutterstock; **404** Amanda Schwab/Starpix/Shutterstock; **406** MikeDotta/Shutterstock

## CHAPTER 12

**412** Photo by FOX via Getty Images; **414** fizkes/Shutterstock; **416** "Kaiser Family Foundation analysis of March 2015 Current Population Survey, Annual Social and Economic Supplement"; **420** meunierd/Shutterstock; **424** Master1305/Shutterstock; **426** Source: avert.org. Adapted from United Nations Development Programme; **427** Photo by Matt Sayles/Invision for Weight Watchers/AP Images; **433** from National Library of Medicine; **433** From National Library of Medicine; **435** BoxerX/Shutterstock; **436** Gorodenkoff/Shutterstock; **438** RGB Ventures/SuperStock/Alamy Stock Photo; **439** Roberto Galan/Shutterstock; **442** Khairil Azhar Junos/Shutterstock; **442** Khairil Azhar Junos/Shutterstock; **443** Reprinted from Bryc, Katarzyna, Eric Y. Durand J. Michael Macpherson, David Reich and Joanna L. Mountain. 2015. "The Genetic Ancestry of African Americans, Latinos, and European Americans across the United States." *The American Journal of Human Genetics* 96(1):37–53, with permission from Elsevier

## CHAPTER 13

**448** American Photo Archive/Alamy Stock Photo; **455** Idealink Photography/Alamy Stock Photo; **456** mark reinstein/Shutterstock; **457** OurWorldInData.org/democracy | CC BY; **458** The British Ministry of Defence/UPI/Shutterstock; **459** Joseph Sohm/Shutterstock; **460** Courtesy of Dr. Michael P. McDonald and US Elections Project; **469** Everett Collection Historical/Alamy Stock Photo; **471** G. Ronald Lopez/Alamy Stock Photo; **472** Tor Eigeland/Alamy Stock Photo; **475** nisargmediaproductions/Shutterstock; **476** ChameleonsEye/Shutterstock; **477** NurPhoto SRL/Alamy Stock Photo; **480** Andre Pain/EPA/Shutterstock; **480** Olivier Hoslet/EPA/Shutterstock; **481** Kim Kelley-Wagner/Shutterstock

## CHAPTER 14

**488** AdriaVidal/Shutterstock; **492** RGR Collection/Alamy Stock Photo; **493** Grenar/Shutterstock; **494** Courtesy of HBO; **495** Frederic Legrand - COMEO/Shutterstock; **497** JHVEPhoto/Shutterstock; **502** KIMMO BRANDT/EPA-EFE/Shutterstock; **507** Skorzewiak/Shutterstock; **510** Yonhap/EPA-EFE/Shutterstock; **512** Ringo Chiu/Shutterstock; **514** iQoncept/Shutterstock; **515** Lev Radin/Pacific Press/Shutterstock; **516** John Nacion/Shutterstock

## CHAPTER 15

**524** SvetlanaSF/Shutterstock; **530** rblfmr/Shutterstock; **531** AP Photo/Pat Sullivan; **539** REUTERS/Alamy Stock Photo; **541** ANP/Alamy Stock Photo; **544** REUTERS/Alamy Stock Photo; **548** National Park Service via AP; **549** Frank Castoral/NY Daily News via Getty Images; **550** PMGphotog/Shutterstock; **552** Ashley Cooper pics/Alamy Stock Photo

# Index

Note: Page references followed by a *t* indicate table; *f* indicate figure; italicized references indicate illustrations or photos.

ability, 425–26, 428
abortion, 276
Abraham, 342
Abramson, Corey, 420
absolute mobility, 193
absolute monarchies, 454
Abu Ghraib prison, 124
achieved status, 116
Acker, Joan, 262–63
ACLU. *See* American Civil Liberties Union
active audiences, 83–84
ACT UP, 478
acute diseases, 423
ADA. *See* Americans with Disabilities Act (1990)
Adams, John Quincy, 482
Adams, Thomas, 139
Adler, Patricia, 395
Adler, Pete, 395
adult socialization, 112–16
*The Adventures of Ozzie and Harriet* (television show), 305, *306*
advertising
  culture jamming and, *84*, 97
  jobs in, 95
  media shaped by, 504, 506
  multiculturalism and, 238, 281
  parasocial relationships and, 512
  political, 450, 507
  race and, 279, 281
  romance and, 279
Aerie, 427
Affordable Care Act (2010), 441
Africa
  Catholicism in, 345
  Christianity and, 344, 351, 353
  climate change impacts in, 529
  colonialism and, 190, 233, 464, 466
  fertility rates in, 435
  life expectancies in, 415
  migration from, 221, 240
  poverty in, 189
African American people, 220–22
African National Congress, 180
Afrikaaner National Party, 179–80
agenda-setting, 503–4
agents of socialization, 109–12
AI. *See* artificial intelligence
AI chatbots, 489–90, 500
AIDS, 422–23, 425, 437, 478
Airbnb, 406
air pollution
  COVID-19 and, 530–31
  industrialization and, 536
  urbanization and suburbanization and, 534–35
Alameda Research, 516–17
Alexander, Jeffrey, 491, 494
algorithms, 506, 508
alienation, 34–35
Alinsky, Saul, 479
allostatic load, 417–18
*Alone Together* (Turkle), 513
Alphabet, 497
AMA. *See* American Medical Association
Amazon, 498, 508
Amazon Fund, 554–55
Amazon rainforest, 553–55
American Academy of Pediatrics, 58
American Association for Public Opinion Research, 459
American Association of Retired Persons, 460
American Association of University Professors, 389
American Civil Liberties Union (ACLU), 151, 322, 366–67
American Civil War, 155
American dream, 79, *79*
American Medical Association (AMA), 429–30, 460
American National Election Studies, 337
American Psychiatric Association, 428
American Revolution, 32, 466
American Samoa, 226
Americans with Disabilities Act (1990) (ADA), 428
"America the Beautiful" (song), 100
Amini, Mahsa, 121
Amnesty International, 124
Ancestry.com, 297, 442–43
androcentrism, 264
Angelou, Maya, 301
anomie, 36, 38
Anthropocene, 527
anti-environmental movements, 543, 550
Anti-Graffiti Task Force, 144
anti-immigrant movements, 246–48
antimiscegenation laws, 320
anti-Semitism, 82, 342–43
antivaccination movement, 433
apartheid system, 179–80
Apple, 128, 407, 495–96, 505
applied research, 57
Arbery, Ahmaud, 231

# 636 INDEX

Aristotle, 304
  geocentric universe, 331, 332f
  on inequality, 175
Armenians, 233
Army Help the Planet, 510
artificial intelligence (AI), 491–92
  doomsday scenarios for, 493–94
  job titles and, 500–501
  work and, 400
Arts & Culture Trust, 96
Aryan Brotherhood, 145
ascribed status, 116
ascriptiveness, 178, 181
Asia
  climate change impacts in, 529
  colonialism and, 464, 466
  migration from, 240
  poverty in, 189
Asian American people, 226–27
assessment
  in education, 387–94
  self, 107
assimilation, 236
Association of Black Cardiologists, 418
Association of Boarding Schools, 191
Association of Trial Lawyers of America, 460
astronomy, 331, 334
ATM skimming, 156
attention-deficit/hyperactivity disorder, 428
attorneys, 151
at-will employment laws, 399
authority, 453
automation, 400, 500
Ayres-Brown, Antonia, 285–87

*Baby Einstein* (video), 58
Baby Einstein Company, 58
*The Bachelor* (television show), 202–4
Bacon, Francis, 335
badminton, 118
Bagdikian, Ben, 505
Baha'i, 351
Balfour Declaration, 346
Baltzell, E Digby, 220

Bankman-Fried, Sam, 516–18
Barry, Halle, 237
basic research, 57
battleground states, 483
Bauman, Zygmunt, 6, 41, 463
Baylor Religion Survey, 337
Beck, Ulrich, 463, 527
Becker, Howard, 148
beliefs
  culture and, 70
  defining, 44, 70
  importance of, 363–65
  knowledge and, 363
Bell, Daniel, 469
Bell, Jocelyn, 360
Ben Ali, Zine al-Abidine, 455
Bennis, Walter, 499
Bentham, Jeremy, 160
Berger, Peter, 339, 350
Bernstein, Herman, 82
Bertelsmann, 505
Bevin, Matt, 407
*Beyond the Closet* (Seidman), 283
Bezos, Jeff, 495, 501
Biden, Joe, 3, 77–78, *78*, 84, 441, 450, 552
BiDil, 418–19
Big Bang, 333
big data, 56–57
Biles, Simone, 3–4, *13*, 13–14
biodiversity, 527
biomedical institutions, 413
biomedical research, 431, 434
  race and, 419
bird-nesting, 313
birth control, 275–76
birth order effects, 302
Bitcoin, 516
Black Lives Matter movement, 165, 209–10, 218, 229, 235, 514, 544
*Black Mirror* (television show), 494
Black people, 220–21
  discrimination against, 230–31
  ethnicity and, 214
  Great Migration and, 213
  policing and, 158–59
  politics and, 222–23
  prison rates and, 164–65
  violence against, 229, 234

*Black Reconstruction in America* (Du Bois), 37
Bland, Sandra, 231, 234–35
Blau, Peter, 194–95
blended families, 318–20
Blinken, Antony, 259
blockbusting, 230
blue-collar workers, 187
Blumer, Herbert, 39–40
BMI. *See* body mass index
Boas, Franz, 213
body mass index (BMI), 427
Boli, John, 376
Bolsonaro, Jair, 555
Bonhomme, I. F., *32*
boomerang kids, 314–15
Boric, Gabriel, 510
Bouazizi, Mohamed, 454
Bourdieu, Pierre, 6–7, 96, 98, 196
Brazil, 553–55
Break Free campaign, 547
Brigham Young University, 336, 338
broken windows theory, 157–58
Brown, Michael, 235
*Brown v. Board of Education*, 384
Bryan, William Jennings, 365–66
BTS, 509–10
BTS Army, 509–10
Buddhism, 341f, 347
  fundamentalism in, 355
Buffett, Warren, 495
bullying
  in health care settings, 436
  school and, 394–96
  in workplace, 400
bureaucracy, 34–35, 126–29, 182
  upper class jobs and, 186
Bureau of Indian Affairs, 217
Bureau of Labor Statistics, 300, 470
Burke, Tarana, 401
Burnett, Demi, 202
Bush, George W., 482
Butler, John, 366
Butler, Judith, 42, *43*, 283
Butler Act (Tennessee), 365–66

Cameron, David, 237
Camp, Garrett, 405
campus speech codes, 389–90

Canada
  immigration to, 240, 242, 245
  multiculturalism policy, 236
  wildfires in, 525
cancel culture, 514–15
canon
  defining, 33–34
  European, 33–36
capitalism, 33, 35, 466
  crisis of care and, 438
  defining, 467
  environment and, 536–37
  transition to, 467–69
capital punishment, 165
carbon dioxide ($CO_2$), 537, 553
career planning, social mobility and, 197
care facilities, 434
care work, 434–40
Caribbean
  colonialism and, 464
  migration from, 221
  slave trade and, 465
Carnegie Steel Company, 200
Casanova, Jose, 354
case study research, 53
casinos, 219
caste systems, 178–79
categorical inequality, 176
categorical variables, 51
Catholic Surfing Ministries, 352
causation, 53–54
cause, 53–54
*Causes of Delinquency* (Hirschi), 140, 142
CBS Television, 449
CDC. *See* Centers for Disease Control and Prevention
celebrities, 186
Center for Responsive Politics, 461
Centers for Disease Control and Prevention (CDC), 431
charismatic authority, 453
charity, 340
Charles III (King), *458*
Charter Communications, 505
ChatGPT, 489–90
Chauvin, Derek, 209–10
Chavez, Cesar, 478
chewing gum, 139

Chicago, homeless population of, 10
*Chicago Hope* (television show), 413
Chicago School, 38–39
chicle, 139
Chiclets, 139
childcare, 381–82
childhood poverty, 310
childhood vaccinations, 432–33
children
  joint custody of, 313
  living arrangements of, 310*f*
  single-parent families and, 309–11
  step-parents and, 320
*Children of the Great Depression* (Elder), 117
Chin, Kimberly, 281
China, 179, 352
  elite US schools and wealthy students from, 191
  renewable energy and, 543
Chinese Exclusion Act (1882), 226
Christianity, 339–40, 341*f*, 343–44
  evolution and, 365–66
  fundamentalism in, 354–55
  Roman Empire and spread of, 352
  secularization and, 348
chronic disease, 424
chronic stress, 418
Chuck D, 92
cisgender, 257
citizen science, 48
citizenship
  education and, 376
  laws about, 245–46
civil disobedience, 547
civil law, 150
civil liberties, 276
civil rights, 266, 479, 539
Civil Rights Act (1968), 155
Civil Rights Movement, 7, 480
  music and, 92
  political opportunity structure and, 479
Civil War (United States), 155, 220, 222
class
  health inequality and, 416

  income inequality and, 399
  inequality and, 178
  status groups and, 181
  systems of, 180–81
classical sociology, 31–33
classification systems, 71
class size, 392
Cleveland, Grover, 482
climate, 527
climate change, 329, 526
  culture, media, and socialization and, 540–41
  defining, 527
  denial and expertise about, 538
  free-rider problem and, 551–52
  geography of risks, 529
  immigration and, 241
  risk society and, 527–31
Clinton, Hillary, 482
cliques, 394–96
CNN, 502
$CO_2$. *See* carbon dioxide
Coalition for Evidence-Based Policy, 336
Coca-Cola, 87
code-switching, 119
coercive power, 452–53
cognitive load, 73
cohabitation, 311–12
Cohen, Bernard, 322
Cohen, Philip, 297
Cohen, Stanley, 141
Cold War, 469
  racism and, 479
Coleman, John, 329
collective representations, 36, 38
colleges, 385–86
  campus speech codes, 389–90
  as marriage markets, 396
Collins, Patricia Hill, 6–7
Collins, Randall, 379
Colombia, 225
colonialism, 32–33, *33*, 38, 190, 464, 466
  Christianity and, 344
  genocide and, 233
Colvin, Matt, 141
Colvin, Noah, 141
Combinations of Workmen Act (1825) (United Kingdom), 200

Comcast, 450, 505
coming-of-age stories, 105
commercial culture, 93, *93*, 94
Commission on Filipinos Overseas, 438
Committee on Civil Rights, 479
commodity, 93
common sense, 27
   gender binary and, 258
   hegemony and, 265
Common Sense Media, 111
*Communist Manifesto* (Marx and Engels), 34
community colleges, 386
comparative-historical, 55
comparative strategies, 178
complementary and alternative medicine, 413–14
computer engineers, 225
Comstock laws, 275
Comte, Auguste, 30, 37
concentrated disadvantage, 528–29, 531
concerted cultivation, 115
confirmation bias, 10, 47
conflict, 16–17, 56
   Amazon rainforest and, 555
   *The Bachelor* and, 203
   defining, 17
   Electoral College and, 483
   elite, 182
   family names and, 324
   feminist politics and, 277
   genetic testing and, 443
   medical settings and, 436
   parenting styles and, 308
   police procedurals and, 166
   race and, 42
   racial, 232–34
   racial and ethnic identity and, 249
   between science and humanities, 407
   social, 201–2
   workers' strikes and, 200–201
   Yellowstone National Park and, 548
conflict theory, 39–40
Confucius, 303
Conk, Margaret, 263

*The Connecticut Mirror* (newspaper), 159
Connell, R. W., 265
Conrad, Peter, 149, 428–29
conscious rap, 92
consensus theory, 39–40
constitutional monarchies, 456–57
contentious politics, 201
contingency, 21, 82, 100, 131
   AI and, 493–94
   Amazon rainforest and, 554
   *The Bachelor* and, 204
   co-parenting strategies and, 313
   defining, 20
   Electoral College and, 482
   family names and, 324
   FTX and, 518
   genetic testing and, 443
   indoor cycling and, 404–5
   Native American casinos, 219
   organ transplants and, 439
   police procedurals and, 167
   racial and ethnic identity and, 248
   science and humanities and, 408
   Scopes Monkey Trial and, 367
   in social interactions, 287
   Social Security and, 199
contingent workers, 498
continuous variables, 50
contraception, 276
controlled experiment, 45
conurbation, 534
convenience, paradox of, 492, 494
convenience sample, 52
Cooley, Charles Horton, 39, 107
co-parenting strategies, 313
core nations, 192
corporate social responsibility, 543, 546
correctional treatment specialists, 151
correlation, 53–54
cosmology, 331
   religious, 332–34
   scientific, 333–36
Coulter, Ann, 389
countermovements, 481, 550
*Cours de Philosophie Positive* (Comte), 37

COVID-19 pandemic, 31, 59–60, 315, 417, 450
   air pollution and, 530–31
   Chinese students in United States and, 191
   crisis of care and, 437
   digital learning and, 387
   disruptive behavior in medical settings during, 436
   economic impacts of, 189
   erosion of trust and, 528
   gender and family roles and, 304–5
   Generation Z and, 112
   global impacts of, 19, 43
   global stratification and, 189
   green recovery proposals after, 546
   health insurance and, 441
   hoarding during, 141
   homeschooling and, 384
   loneliness and, 515
   lower-middle class during, 188
   luxury yachts during, 183
   media consumption during, 112
   norms and, 75
   parenting and, 115
   patterns in economic impact of, 264
   philanthropy changes from, 98
   prejudice from, 227
   prison conditions and, 165
   public health and, 431–33
   racial differences in, 416, 418
   remote learning during, 194
   schools during, 384
   social interactions during, 120, 130
   social policies during, 200
   structural mobility and, 198
   work impacts of, 399
cram schools, 316
creative industries, 95
credential inflation, 379
credentialism, 379–80
Crenshaw, Kimberlé Williams, *41*, 42, 271
Crick, Francis, 360

# INDEX

crime, 138, 150–51, 160
  categories of, 152–56
  deviance and, 146–47
  policing, 156–59
  rates of, 152, 153t, 154–55, 164
  relative deprivation and, 176
crime stories, 166–67
crime syndicates, 145
criminal defense attorneys, 151
criminal justice field, 151
criminal justice system, 150
  rehabilitation and, 163–64
criminal recidivism, 162–63
*The Crisis* (publication), 223
crisis of care, 437–38
crisis of knowing, 363–65
critical literacy
  AI and, 501
  research methods and, 47–49
critical questions, 28–30
critical race theory, 42
crowdsourcing data, 48
cryptocurrencies, 516–18
crystallization, 181
  degree of, 178
  media and, 202–4
Cullors, Patrisse, 235
cultural capital, 96, 98, 380
  family and, 196
cultural critics, 84–85
cultural gatekeepers, 94
cultural hierarchies, 81, 83
cultural imperialism, 87–88
cultural norms
  heteronormativity and, 282
  world society and, 88
cultural performance, 479–80
cultural pluralism, 237
cultural power, 77–86
cultural relativism, 85
cultural turn, 43
cultural variation, 146
culture
  beliefs and, 70
  commercial, 93, *93*, 94
  defining, 70–72
  development of, 71
  dominant, 89, 91
  environment and, 540–41
  global, 86–89

  high, 96, 98, *99*
  ideal, 72–76
  language and, 71–74, 540
  material, 72, 76
  organizational, 128
  popular, 93
  power and, 77–86
  social mobility and, 196
  types of, 86–99
culture jamming, *84*, 97
culture war, 75, 86
curative medical care, 434
Current Population Survey, 10
cybercrime, 156

D'Adamo, Peter J., 442
Dahrendorf, Ralf, 39, 178
Dakota Access pipeline, 218, 544–45
Darrow, Clarence, 365
Darwin, Charles, 334–35
data
  analyzing, 54
  big, 56–57
  publicly available sources, 55–56
data protection laws, 508
Davis, David Brion, 465
Davis, Kingsley, 176
Davis-Moore theory, 176–77
deafness, 426
decarceration movement, 165
Declaration of Independence (United States), 454
Declaration of the Rights of Man and the Citizen (France), 454, 465
decoding, 84
*Decoding Racial Ideology in Genomics* (Williams, J.), 419
Deepwater Horizon oil spill, 547
deforestation, 527, 553–55
degree of crystallization, 178
degree of inequality, 178
deinstitutionalization, 438, 440
deliberation, 456
delinquency, 48
democracy
  Electoral College and, 482–83
  politics and, 454–61
  social capital and, 481

Democratic Party, 173–74, 479
democratic republics, 456–57
demographic transition, 532
demography
  Catholicism in Africa and, 345
  environmental risks and, 532–33
  health, 415
  marketing and, 281
  urban sprawl measurement and, 535
denominations, 344
Department of Health and Human Services, 434
Department of Housing and Urban Development, 227
Department of Justice, 159
  Civil Rights Division, 200
Department of Labor, 29
dependent variable, 51
*The Descent of Man* (Darwin), 334
Desmond, Matthew, 57
development
  of culture, 71
  stages of, 108–9
deviance, 138–39, 141
  cultural variation and, 146
  everyday, 146
  medicalization of, 149–50
  power to call things, 146–47
  reasons for existence of, 140, 142–45
  social change and, 142–43
  social construction of, 145–50
  socialization and, 146–47
  social stigma and, 148–49
  wastefulness, 547, 549–50
*Deviance and Medicalization* (Conrad and Schneider), 149
deviant subcultures, 143, 145
*Diagnostic and Statistical Manual of Mental Disorders* (DSM), 150, 428
  gender dysphoria in, 282
Dickens, Charles, 399
digital age
  schools in, 386–87
  social interaction in, 120–22
digital learning, 387
digital surveillance, 499, 501
disability, 425–26, 428

discourses, 80
discrimination, 227
   consequences of, 231–32
   employment, 232
   racial, 229–31
disease, 423
   inequality and, 176
disenchantment, 35
Disney, 505
disruption, 113–14
disruptive behavior, in medical settings, 436
division, politics of, 459
division of labor, 32, 35–36
   gender and, 267–72
   household, 272, 318–19
*The Division of Labor in Society* (Durkheim), 35, 150
divorce, 11, 113–14, 307–9, 309f, 318
DIY culture, 94
*Dobbs v. Jackson*, 266
Doctors Without Borders, 88
dominant culture, 89, 91
Don't Make a Wave Committee, 476
Dornan, Jamie, 97
Dove, 427
draft riots, 229
dramaturgical theory, 119–20
drug cartels, 157
drug trade, 157
DSM. *See Diagnostic and Statistical Manual of Mental Disorders*
Du Bois, W. E. B., 5, 7, 37–38, *38*, 211, 213, 222–23
Duncan, Otis Dudley, 194–95
Duneier, Mitchell, 59
Durkheim, Émile, 5, 31, 33, *35*, 35–37, 39
   on civil and criminal cases, 150
   on deviance, 143
   on moral education, 377
   on public shaming, 514
   on punishment, 161
   on religion, 338–39
   on social cosmology, 331
dyad, 122

Earth Day, 547
Eastern Orthodox Church, 343
echo chambers, 506, 508
ecological modernization, 546
economy
   COVID-19 impacts on, 189
   defining, 466
   environment and, 542–46
   globalization and, 471–72
   green, 545–46
   historical changes in, 466–72
   immigration and, 241
   political, 462
   politics and, 461–66
education. *See also* learning; schools
   accountability and, 390
   assessment in, 387–94
   campus speech codes, 389–90
   childcare and employment and, 381–82
   citizenship, 376
   cram schools, 316
   credentialism and, 379–80
   cultural capital and, 380
   earnings and, 29
   experience and process of, 382–96
   in Germany, 375
   as human right, 376
   inequality and, 380
   making friends and building networks and, 394–96
   middle class and, 187
   modern economy needs from, 407–8
   moral, 377
   national and international differences in performance in, 391, 394
   privilege and, 380–81
   public health, 431–32
   purposes of, 375–82
   remote learning, 194
   Singapore math, 393–94
   socialization and, 110–11, 376–77
   social mobility and, 193–94
   in South Korea, 316–17
   standardized tests and drive for assessments in, 388, 390–91
   teaching and learning, 387–94
   work and, 374, 377–79
effective altruism, 517
ego, 108–9
Egypt, 480, *480*
Einstein, Albert, 142
Elder, Glen, 117
Electoral College, 482–83
Electronic Frontier Foundation, 507
Electronic Privacy Information Center, 507
*The Elementary Forms of the Religious Life* (Durkheim), 331, 338
elites, 181
   conflict among, 182
   WASPs and, 220
Ellison, Larry, 495
Emancipation Proclamation, 480
Emerson, Michael, 354
empirical evidence, 44
employer-based health insurance, 441
employment discrimination, 232
encoding, 84
*The End Game* (Abramson), 420
Engels, Friedrich, 34
England, Paula, 271
English Civil War, 454
environment
   capitalism and, 536–37
   controlling narrative about, 538–42
   crisis in, 526
   culture, media, and socialization and, 540–41
   distribution of risks, 528–31
   economy and, 542–46
   free-rider problem and, 551–52
   health and, 417–18
   human impact on, 527
   industrialization and, 536–37
   politics and, 542–46
   science and religion and, 541–42
   structural factors contributing to risks, 531–37
*The Environment* (Schnaiberg), 537

# INDEX

environmentalism, 330, 547, 549–50
epidemic, 431
epidemiology, 431
epigenetics, 417
epistemic privilege, 421
epistemology, 363
Epstein, Steven, 56
Equaldex, 259
Equal Justice Initiative, 151
Equal Protection Clause, 323
ethics
　defining, 45
　social research and, 45–46
ethnic cleansing, 233
ethnic groups
　in Singapore, 127
　in United States, 214–27
ethnicity, 210, 248–49
　defining, 214
　multiethnic identities, 237, 239
　race and, 214
　symbolic, 214
ethnocentrism, 85
ethnography, 55
European Union, 401
　data privacy and, 508
everyday deviance, 146
evolution, 334–35
　debating, 365–67
experience
　of education, 382–96
　of illness, 422–23
experience economy, 404
experiments, 55
　social, by Facebook, 46
　Stanford Prison Experiment, 124
extended family, 305–7
*Exxon Valdez* (ship), 547

Facebook, 69, 130, 499, 505–7
　political advertising on, 450
　social effects of, 515
　social experiments by, 46
Fair Housing Act (1968), 230
fair play, 118
"Faith and Foolishness" (Krauss), 356
false consciousness, 34

falsifiability, 44
family
　in advertising, 279
　blended, 318–20
　challenging forms of, 318–23
　changes in, 305–17
　cultural capital and, 196
　defining, 296–97
　extended, 305–7
　immigration and, 242
　industrialization and, 307
　inequality and, 299–301
　intimacy and social support and, 298–99
　kinship and society and, 297–98
　lesbian and gay, 321, 323
　multiracial, 320–21
　names, 324
　nuclear, 305–7
　parenting styles and, 115
　single-parent, 309–11
　as social institution, 301, 303–5
　socialization and, 109–10, 115, 195, 299
　social mobility and, 195–96
　therapists for, 300, 313
　traditional, 305–7
　transnational, 315–17
family roles, 304–5
fanfiction, 97
Fanon, Frantz, 42, *42*
farming, 467
fat acceptance movement, 427
*Fatal Intervention* (Roberts), 419
FBI, 143
　crime statistics from, 152, 153*t*, 154, 167
Federal Trade Commission, 58
*The Feminine Mystique* (Friedan), 318
femininity, 261
feminism, 41
　backlash against, 481
　challenges to family, 318–19
　politics and, 277
　second wave of, 276
Ferguson, Priscilla Parkhurst, 71
fertility rates, 435
feudalism, 467

field experiment, 55
Fifteenth Amendment (United States), 458
*Fifty Shades of Grey* (James), 97, *97*
filter bubbles, 122, 506, 508–9
fine particulate matter (PM 2.5), 530
Fischer, Claude, 143
Fleming, Alexander, 362
Flint, Michigan, 538–39
Floyd, George, 209–10, 229, 231, 235, 475, 514
Flywheel, 405
focus groups, 54
Foley, James, 97
folkways, 76
Food and Drug Administration, 418
*Forbes* list of wealth Americans, 495
Ford, Henry, 82
Foucault, Michel, 80–81, 160
Foxwoods Casino, 219
France, 454
　religion in, 352–53
Francis (Pope), 345
*Frankenstein* (Shelley), 492
Franklin, Rosalind, 360, *360*
Fraser, Nancy, 438
free-rider problem, 478, 551–52
free speech, 389–90
French Revolution, 32, 352, 465–66
Freud, Sigmund, 39, 108–9
Friedan, Betty, 318–19
Friedman, Thomas, 31
friendships
　parenting styles and, 308
　school and, 394–96
FTX, 516–18
Fukushima nuclear accident, 547
functional equilibrium, 39
fundamental sciences, 30

Galileo Galilei, 334–35
game stage, 108
Gans, Herbert, 214
Garfinkel, Harold, 83
Garner, Eric, 231, 235
Garza, Alicia, 235
Gates, Bill, 29, 407

# INDEX

Gatta, Mary L., 273
gay liberation, 283
gay rights movement, 276, 283
GDP. *See* gross domestic product
GDPR. *See* General Data Protection Regulation
gender
  cues, 258
  defining, 256–57
  division of labor and, 267–72
  income inequality and, 399
  job satisfaction and, 402
  legal, 259
  McDonald's and intersections of, 285–87
  occupational segregation and, 270–72
  performance, 258
  power and, 264–78
  scripts, 257, 260
  separate spheres and, 268–70
  socialization, 258
  social research bias and, 262–63
  stereotypes, 260–61, 261*t*
gender binary, 256–57
gender dysphoria, 282
gender equality movements, 319
gender identity, 283–84
gender-nonconforming people, 282
gender norms
  workplace sexual harassment and, 274
gender order, 265
gender roles, 304–5
  cohabitation and, 312
genealogy, 297
General Data Protection Regulation (GDPR), 508
generalized other, 108
generalizing, 54
General Motors, 271–72, 538
General Social Survey, 337
generation, 112
Generation Z, 112
Genetic Information Nondiscrimination Act (GINA), 422
genetics, 416–17
genetic testing, 442–43
genocide, 232–33, 343

*The GenoType Diet* (D'Adamo), 442
gentrification, 230–31
geocentric universe, 331, 332*f*
geolocation, 499
geopolitics, 464, 466
German Sociological Association, 5
Germany, 233
  education in, 375
Gerson, Kathleen, 272
*Getting a Job* (Granovetter), 129
Giddens, Anthony, 279, 539–40
Giddens Paradox, 539
gig economy, 406, 498
GINA. *See* Genetic Information Nondiscrimination Act
Glasgow Climate Pact, 552
global
  Amazon rainforest and, 554
  *The Bachelor* and, 203
  bureaucracy in Singapore, 127–28
  computer engineers, 225
  as context, 43–44
  Electoral College and, 483
  family names and, 324
  fandoms and, 509–10
  FTX and, 517
  genetic testing and, 443
  Greenpeace and, 476
  income inequality, 189
  McDonald's as, 287
  poverty, 189–90
  power elite, 463
  racial and ethnic identity and, 249
  science and humanities and, 408
  Scopes Monkey Trial and, 367
  sex work and, 280–81
  transboundary water pollution and, 552–53
global capitalism, 536–37
global culture, 86–89
global drug trade, 157
*A Global Green New Deal* (UNEP), 545
globalization, 32–33, 43–44
  culture and, 86–89
  defining, 19
  economy and, 471–72
  work and, 400

global population growth, 532–33
Global South, 281
  care work and, 438
  environmental risks and, 529
  poverty in, 189
  remittances and, 244
global stratification, 189–92
global warming, 329
Go, Julian, 465
Goedsche, Herman, 82
Goffman, Erving, 12, 40, 119–20
*Going Solo* (Klinenberg), 318
Goldberg, Johnny, 404–5
Goldilocks effect, 121
*Good Jobs, Bad Jobs* (Kalleberg), 471
Google, 128, 215, 497–98, 505
graduate programs, 378
graffiti, 144
Gramsci, Antonio, 453
Grandmaster Flash, 92
Granovetter, Mark, 129
Graves, Philip, 82
Gray, Freddie, 235
*Gray's Anatomy* (television show), 413
Great Depression, 117, 199
Great Migration, 213, 221
Great Pacific Garbage Patch, 552
Great Railroad Strike of 1877, 200
Great Recession of 2008, 198
great resignation, 402–3
green economy, 545–46
greenhouse gases, 526–27, 543
Green Party, 547
Greenpeace, 88, 476, 549, 554
greeting cards, 295
gross domestic product (GDP), 495
group life, 122–25, 127
  bureaucracy in, 126, 128–29
  social networks in, 129–30
groups
  in- and out-, 125
  primary and secondary, 123, 125
  reference, 125
  size, 122–23
Grusky, David, 178
*The Guardian* (newspaper), 491
guidance counselors, 197
Guterres, António, 60
gut reactions, 73

H-1B visas, 227, 240–42
Haggerty, Kristian, 202
Haiti, 465–66
Hall, Stuart, 83
Hallmark, 295
Halperin, David, 283
Hamilton, Alexander, 462
Happy Meal, 285–87
*Hard Times* (Dickens), 399
Harris, Kamala, 237
Harris, Patricia, 285
Hart-Celler Act (1965), 242
Hartman, David, 354
hate crime, 155, 155*t*
Hate Crimes Sentencing Enhancement Act, 155
Hate Crimes Statistics Act, 155
hate groups, 145
Hawaii, 226
Hayes, Rutherford B., 482
HBO, 4
health, 414–15, 420
　defining, 421–22
　environment and, 417–18
　genetics and, 416–17
　inequality and, 176
　intersectional perspective on, 419, 421
　mental, 4, 428
　multilevel approach to, 421
　race-based medicine, 418–19
　worksites and, 417
health behaviors, 413
health care system, 434
　access to, 440–41
　crisis of care and, 437–38
　disruptive behavior in, 436
　national, 440–41
health demography, 415
health insurance, 441
heart disease, 418–19
heatwaves, 526
hegemonic masculinity, 265, 274
hegemony, 265, 453, 464
heresy, 334
heteronormativity, 277, 281–83
heterosexism, 42
heterosexuality, 277–78
Hewish, Anthony, 360

hidden curriculum, 110, 377
Higgins, Ben, 203
high culture, 96, 98, *99*
*hijab*, 121
Hinduism, 339, 341*f*, 346–47
　fundamentalism in, 354
hip-hop music, 92
hiring
　bureaucracy and, 182
　elite jobs and, 397–98
　racial discrimination in, 13, 231
　social mobility and, 197
Hirschi, Travis, 140, 142
Hispanic or Latino people, 223–26
Hitler, Adolf, 342–43
HIV, 422–23, 425, 426*f*, 437
hoarding, 141–42
Hochschild, Arlie, 79, 272
Holocaust, 343
homeless population, 9, 9–10
homeschooling, 383–84
homophobia, 42
homosexuality, 282
　depathologizing of, 422
　families and, 321, 323
　medicalization of deviance and, 149–50
　stigma and, 149
horizontal mobility, 193
horizontal occupational segregation, 270
Horton, Donald, 511
hospitals, 434
house meetings, 478
*How to Observe Morals and Manners* (Martineau), 37
human rights, 282, 353
　education as, 376
Human Rights Campaign, 480–81
Hurricane Harvey, 525
Hurricane Katrina, 529
Hurricane Maria, 525
hurricanes, 525–26
Hutchinson Family Singers, 92
Hutus, 233
Huxley, Thomas, 335
hype cycle, 517–18

hyperkinesis, 428
hypothesis, 53–54

Ibn Khaldun, 37
id, 108–9
ideal culture, 72–76
identity claims, 474
identity theft, 156
ideology, 78–79
　deviance and, 147
IGRA. *See* Indian Gaming Regulatory Act
"I Have a Dream" (King), 480
illness
　defining, 421–22
　experience of, 422–23
　labeling and stigma and, 425
　multilevel approach to, 421
　stigma and, 425, 426*f*
immigrant enclaves, 243–44
immigration, 239
　care work and, 438
　causes of, 241–42
　communities and, 242–45
　laws about, 226, 245–46
　movements against, 246–48
　politics of, 245–48
　remittances and, 244–45, 315, 438
　transnational families and, 315–17
　trends in, 240–41
Immigration Act (1965), 226
Immigration and Nationality Act, 315
imperialism, cultural, 87–88
incarceration, 162–65, 164*t*
*Inclusion* (Epstein), 56
income, 185
income inequality, 176, 399
　global, 189
independent contractors, 405–6, 498
independent variables, 51
in-depth interviews, 54
India, 179
　poverty in, 189
Indian Gaming Regulatory Act (IGRA), 219
indirect research techniques, 73
indoor cycling, 404–5

industrialization
  environment and, 536–37
  family and, 307
  internal migration and, 240
Industrial Revolution, 31–32, 32–33, 468, 499, 527, 531, 536–37
  air pollution and, 530
  urbanization and, 533
inequality, 18–19, 37, 98, 100, 174
  *The Bachelor* and, 202
  categorical, 176
  causes of, 175
  in class systems, 181
  colonialism and, 190
  defining, 18, 175–77
  degree of, 178
  divorce and, 308
  education and, 380
  Electoral College and, 482
  environmental movements and, 550
  environmental risk and, 529, 531
  family and, 299–301
  family names and, 324
  Flint, Michigan water contamination, 538–39
  FTX and, 517
  genetic testing and, 443
  Google and, 497–98
  health, 415–16
  income, 176, 399
  intersectionality and, 277
  marketing to super-rich and, 183
  marriage and, 303
  measuring, 178
  old age and, 420
  party systems and, 182, 184
  pink-collar jobs and, 273
  police procedurals and, 166
  punishment and plea-bargaining and, 163
  racial and ethnic identity and, 249
  science and humanities and, 408
  science and Matthew effect and, 359–60
  Scopes Monkey Trial and, 366
  social change and, 198–202
  South Africa apartheid system and, 179–80
  stratification and, 177
  technology and, 496, 498
  in United States, 184–85
  in workplace, 399–400
informed consent, 45
in-group, 125, 181
inherited wealth, 186
*Inherit the Wind* (film), 367
Instagram, 69, 94
institutionalized reflexivity, 424
institutionalized sexism, 270
institutional level of analysis, 11, 15–16
institutional principles, 22
institutional reflexivity, 49, 58
institutional review board, 45
institutions
  defining, 15
  elements of religious, 338–40
  marriage and family as, 301, 303–5
  public schools as, 383
  religion as, 336–47
  science as, 356–61
  total, 112
integrated medical care, 434
intelligence tests, 388
interactional norms, 22
interest groups, 460–61
intergenerational mobility, 193
internal migration, 240
international trade, 464, 466
internships, 373–74
interracial marriage, 230, 320, 322
intersecting identities, 248–49
intersectional health perspective, 419, 421
intersectionality, 42, 271, 277
intersex, 257, 259, 282
intimacy
  family and, 298–99
  mediated relationships and, 512–13
  parasocial relationships and, 511
  romance and, 279
IQ tests, 213
Iran, *480*
  gender norms in, 121

Irish Americans, 229
Islam, 340, 341*f*, 344, 346, 352
  fundamentalism in, 354–55
Islamic Revolution (1979) (Iran), 121
*It's OK to be Angry About Capitalism* (Sanders), 173
Ivy League universities, 197, 397

Jackson, Philip W., 377
James, E. L., 97
James, Matt, 203
Japan
  life expectancy in, 415
  mask-wearing in, 138–39
Jefferson, Thomas, 462, 482
Jeter, Derek, 237
Jim Crow laws, 221, 234
jobs
  AI and titles for, 500–501
  in creative industries, 95
  education and, 407–8
  elite, 397–98
  green economy, 545–46
  inequality and, 176–77
  marginalized groups and, 177
  sociology of satisfaction with, 400, 402–4
  STEM and non-STEM salaries, 496
  technology and, 499–501
  weak ties and getting, 129
Jobs, Steve, 29, 407–8
job training, 376
Johnny G Spinner bikes, 404–5
Johns Hopkins University, 385
Johnson, Dakota, 97
Johnson, Dwayne, "The Rock," 131–32
Johnson, Jeh, 389
Johnson, Rocky, 131
Joint Commission, 436
Joly, Maurice, 82
*Journal of Adolescent Health*, 137
Judaism, 338–40, 341*f*, 342–43, 350
  fundamentalism in, 355
  Nazi genocide against, 233
Judge, Mike, 399
JustBeInc., 401

# INDEX

Kaepernick, Colin, 99
Kahn, Jonathan, 419
Kalanick, Travis, 405
Kalleberg, Arne, 400, 471
Karen, David, 390
Kast, José Antonio, 510
Kay, Herma Hill, 307
"Keep America Beautiful" campaign, 543
Kelling, George, 157
Kennedy, John F., 229
Kennedy, Randall, 159
Kennedy, Robert F., 322
Kenya, 437
King, Martin Luther, Jr., 143, *143*, 479–80
kinship systems, 297
Kirk, Charlie, 3
Kishida, Fumio, 77, *78*, 84
Klinenberg, Eric, 318
knowledge
  belief and, *363*
  crisis of knowing, 363–65
  cultural power and, 80–81
  everyday, 10–11
  science and religion and, 331–36
  scientific, 363
  social research and contributing to, 47
Knowles-Carter, Beyoncé, 324
Knowles-Carter, Shawn, 324
Koreatown, *243*, 244
K-pop, 509–10
Krauss, Lawrence, 356
Ku Klux Klan, 145, 155
Kweli, Talib, *92*
Kyoto Protocol, 551

labeling, illness and, 425
labeling theory, 148
*Laboratory Life* (Latour and Woolgar), 361
labor strikes, 200–201
land-use density, 536
language
  anti-immigrant movements and, 247
  culture and, 71–72, 540
  defining, 73–74
  ethnicity and, 214
  gender identity and, 284
  globalization and, 88
  ideal culture and, 73–74
  manga and, 90
  multiculturalism and, 236, 238
  race and, 212–13
  in Singapore, 127
Lareau, Annette, 15, 115
Latin America
  climate change impacts in, 529
  migration from, 240
Latino people, 223–26
Latour, Bruno, 361
laws, 150
  immigration, 226
learning, 387–91, 394
  measuring outcomes of, 392–93
legal gender, 259
Lemert, Charles, 27
lesbian and gay families, 321, 323
Levellers, 454
levels of analysis, 11–16
liberation theology, 350
Liebman, Charles, 343
life expectancy, 415, 418
*Life in Classrooms* (Jackson), 377
*Life on the Screen* (Turkle), 120
Linde, Andrei, 333
Lindsay, Rachel, 203
linear variables, 50
literacy, 377
  critical, 47–49, 501
  defining, 375–76
  scientific, 356
Little Havana (Miami neighborhood), 243, *243*
lobbyists, 460–61
local
  Amazon rainforest and, 554
  *The Bachelor* and, 203
  bureaucracy in Singapore, 127–28
  computer engineers, 225
  defining, 19
  Electoral College and, 483
  family names and, 324
  FTX and, 517
  genetic testing and, 442–43
  global fandoms and, 509–10
  Greenpeace and, 476
  racial and ethnic identity and, 249
  science and humanities and, 408
  Scopes Monkey Trial and, 367
  sex work and, 280–81
  transboundary water pollution and, 552–53
location tracking, 507
logic, 44
London Olympics of 2012, 118
loneliness, 513, 515
looking-glass self, 107
loose societies, 146
*Love, Money, and HIV* (Mojola), 437
Loving, Mildred, 322
Loving, Richard, 322
*Loving v. Virginia*, 322
low-carbon projects, 545
lower-middle class, 187–88
Lula da Silva, Luiz Inácio, 510
Lyft, 406

Machung, Anne, 272
macrosociology, 11, 14–15
Madd Dogg Athletics, 404–5
Madoff, Bernard, 156
mafia, 145
majority groups, 228–29
major religions, 340–47, 341*f*
*Making Hispanics* (Mora), 224
male breadwinner, 268
Mamas Day, 295
Manchester General Strike, *34*
manga, 90
Mann, Horace, 384
Mannheim, Karl, 112
March on Washington, 479
Marcuse, Herbert, 492
marginalization, 426*f*
marginalized groups
  jobs and, 177
  Latinos as, 224
  voice and engagement among, 508–9
marginal productivity theory, 177
marketing
  multicultural, 238
  to super-rich, 183

marriage, 11–12
  blended families and, 319–20
  changes in, 305–17
  delay and decline of, 311–12, 312f, 314
  interracial, 230, 320, 322
  legal biases in favor of, 303
  rates of, 309f
  remarriage, 318
  same-sex, 266, 321, 323
  as social institution, 301, 303–5
  therapists for, 300
marriage markets, 396
Mars, Bruno, 237
Martin, Emily, 263
Martin, Trayvon, 210, 235
Martineau, Harriet, 37, *38*
Marx, Karl, 33–36, *34*
  on class systems, 180
  ideology theory of, 78
  on inequality, 175, 178
  political economy and, 462
  on religion as ideology, 348
  socialism and, 468
  social movements and, 468, 473
  on technology, 491
masculinity, 261
  hegemonic, 265, 274
Mashantucket Pequot tribe, 219
Massachusetts, 137
mass education, 376–77
mass incarceration, 165
mass media campaigns, public health education and, 432
mass production, 468
material culture, 72, 76
*The Matrix* (film), 494
Matthew effect, 359
Matthew Matilda effect, 360
McAdam, Doug, 479
MCAT. *See* Medical College Admission Test
McCain, John, 459
McDonald's, 87, *87*, 554
  gender intersections at, 285–87
Mead, George Herbert, 39, 108–9
meaning
  outside of work, 403–4
  symbolic, 71

means of symbolic production, 80
measles, 432–33
measurement
  of inequality, 178
  of learning outcomes and teaching effectiveness, 392–93
  levels of, 50t
  of media engagement, 506
  race, in official government data, 216–17
  reliability and validity of, 52–53
  of religious commitment, 337
  of status attainment and social mobility, 194–95
  of stratification, 178
  of unemployment rate, 470
  variables for, 50–51
*Measuring Culture*, 72
mechanical solidarity, 35–36
media, 490
  advertising shaping, 504, 506
  agenda-setting and, 503–4
  crystallization and, 202–4
  deviance and, 147
  economic dimensions of, 495–501
  economic distortions and, 504–5
  elite sources and, 502
  environment and, 540–41
  filter bubbles, algorithms, and social polarization and, 506, 508
  measuring engagement with, 506
  old age and, 114
  ownership of, 504–5
  politics and, 502–9
  socialization and, 111–12
  social relationships and, 511–16
  voice and engagement among marginalized groups, 508–9
media concentration, 505
mediated relationships
  benefits of, 511–13
  social harms of, 513, 515–16
medical authority, 429–30
Medical College Admission Test (MCAT), 435
medical dramas, 413

medical gaslighting, 424
medical institutions, 433–40
medicalization, 428–29
  of deviance, 149–50
medical professions, 429–30
medical research, 56
medical risk, 422
medical settings, disruptive behavior in, 436
medicine
  defining, 430
  race-based, 418–19
  sociology and, 435
men
  in pink-collar jobs, 273
  social networks and, 262
Mencken, H. L., 366–67
Mendes, Chico, 555
mental health, 428
  deinstitutionalization and, 438, 440
  inequality and, 176
  sports and, 4
meritocracy, 182, 184
Merton, Robert, 41, 358–60
"The Message" (song), 92
Mestral, George de, 362
Meta, 215, 508
ME TOO Congress Act, 401
#MeToo movement, 274, *279*, 401, 514
Mexican Americans, 223–24
Mexican-American War (1848), 223
Meyer, John, 88, 376
Michigan Civil Rights Commission, 539
microsociology, 11–14
Microsoft, 407, 490, 496
middle class, 186–88
*Mighty Atom* (Tezuka), 90
migrants
  care work and, 438
  internal, 240
  remittances from, 315, 438
Milano, Alyssa, 401
Mills, C. Wright, 6–7, 29, *30*, 39, 462
Ministry of Culture, 96
*Minority Report* (film), 494

ModCloth, 427
*Modern Family* (television show), 248–49, 305, *306*
Mojola, Sanyu, 437
monotheism, 332
Moonves, Les, 449
Moore, Wilbert E., 176
Mora, Christina, 224
moral crusaders, 141
moral education, 377
moral indifference, 128
morality
 measuring, 337
 punishment as display of, 161–62
 superego and, 108
moral order, 265
moral panic, 141–42, 146
mores, 76
Mormon Church, 336–37
Mountain View, California, 497–98
Mozart effect, 58
*Mulan* (film), 255–56, 279
multiculturalism, 85–86, 236–37
 in workplace, 238–39
multiculturalism policy of Canada, 236
multicultural marketing, 281
multiethnic identities, 237, 239
multilevel approach to health and illness, 421
multilineal, 298
multinational corporations, 43
multiracial families, 320–21
multiracial identities, 237, 239
Murthy, Vivek, 515–16
music, 69–71, 93–94, 96
 social protest and, 92
*Music and Social Movements*, 92
Musk, Elon, 495, 501
mutual funds, 495
Myanmar, 233

Nabisco, 3
Nakamoto, Satoshi, 516
Nasmyth, James, *33*
national anthem, protesting, 99
National Association of Realtors, 299
National Association to Advance Fat Acceptance, 427
National Center for Education Statistics, 384
National Center for Health Statistics, 414, 427
National Criminal Victimization Survey (NCVS), 154
National Defense Education Act (1958), 366
National Endowment for the Arts (NEA), 96
National Governors Association, 407
national health care systems, 440–41
National Incident-Based Reporting System (NIBRS), 154
National Institute of Environmental Health Sciences (NIEHS), 417
National Institutes of Health (NIH), 427, 431
National Organization for Women, 319
National Organ Transplant Act, 439
National Park Service, 548
National Popular Vote Interstate Compact, 483
National Probation Act (1925), 162
National Rifle Association, 460
national solidarity, 100
*A Nation at Risk* report, 390
Native American people, 105, 217–18
 casinos and, 219
 Dakota Access pipeline and, 544
 health care and, 441
 official government data and, 216
nature and nurture, 106–7
Nawaat (blogging group), 455
Nazis, 213, 342–43
 concentration camps, 46
 propaganda by, 82
NCVS. *See* National Criminal Victimization Survey
NEA. *See* National Endowment for the Arts
*The Negro Problem*, 37
Nelson, Alondra, 57, *59*
neoliberalism, 464
Netflix, 505–6
the Netherlands, multiculturalism and, 236
network centrality, 130
networking, 396
net worth, 185
neurodiversity, 428
New Age spirituality, 351
*New Atlantis* (Bacon), 335
News Corporation, 505
New York City
 graffiti in, 144
 homeless population of, *9*
 policing policies in, 158–59
*New York Times* (newspaper), 141, 450, 502, 509
NIBRS. *See* National Incident-Based Reporting System
NIEHS. *See* National Institute of Environmental Health Sciences
NIH. *See* National Institutes of Health
Nineteenth Amendment (United States), 458
nitrogen dioxide, 530
NitroMed, 418
Nivea, 238
No Child Left Behind Act, 390
"No Child Left Behind? Sociology Ignored!" (Karen), 390
no-fault divorce, 307–8
nominal variables, 51
nonbinary, 257–59
nongovernmental organizations, 88
normalization, 109
norms, 75
 cultural, 88
 heteronormativity, 277, 281–83
 world society and, 88
nuclear family, 305–7
Nuremberg Code, 46
nursing, *273*

Obama, Barack, 139, *139*, 237, 407, 544
*Obergefell v. Hodges*, 266
occupational segregation, 270–72
Occupy Wall Street, 202

ocean acidification, 526–27
Office for Human Research Protections, 46
Office of Science and Technology Policy, 57, 59
*Office Space* (film), 399
official sources, 502
OKCupid, 46
old age, 114, 116
   inequality and, 420
Olympic badminton controversy of 2012, 118
Omohundro, Stephen, 493
on-call workers, 498
*One-Dimensional Man* (Marcuse), 492
*On the Origin of Species* (Darwin), 334
OpenAI, 489–90
opera, 98
operationalization, 52
opinions
   defining, 44
   public, 457–58
OPTN. *See* Organ Procurement and Transplantation Network
Oracle, 495
ordinal variables, 51
organic solidarity, 35–36
Organisation for Economic Co-operation and Development, 535
organizational culture, 128
organizational routines, 22
organizational structure, 127
Organ Procurement and Transplantation Network (OPTN), 439
organ transplants, 439
Osaka, Naomi, 4
osteoporosis, 421
Ottoman Empire, 233, 346, 352
out-group, 125
overeating, 429
Oxfam, 88

PACs. *See* political action committees
Paine, Thomas, 199
paired concepts, 16–21
   artificial intelligence and doomsday scenarios, 493–94
   bird-nesting and co-parenting, 313
   Black politics, 222–23
   BTS Army, 509–10
   bureaucracy in Singapore, 127–28
   creation of Social Security, 199
   Dakota Access pipeline protests, 544–45
   disruptive behavior in medical settings, 436
   elite students and elite jobs, 397–98
   fandoms and elections, 509–10
   feminist politics, 277
   Flint, Michigan, water issues, 538–39
   forgotten founders in sociology, 37–39
   global and local, 19
   Google employees, 497–98
   Greenpeace, 476
   Haiti and French Revolution, 465–66
   identity and US Senators, 456
   indoor cycling industry, 404–5
   inequality and old age, 420
   inequality and privilege, 18–19
   invention of Velcro, 362
   Irish Americans and whiteness, 229
   Latino computer engineers, 225
   legal biases and marriage, 303
   marketing to super-rich, 183
   men in pink-collar work, 273
   museums and opera, 98
   Native American casinos, 219
   organ transplant lists, 439
   parenting styles, 308
   politics of medical research, 56
   power and resistance, 17–18
   privacy, 507–8
   punishment and plea-bargaining, 163
   religious proselytizing, 353
   science and Matthew effect, 359–60
   sex work, 280–81
   society and illness, 437
   solidarity and conflict, 16–17
   Stonewall, 284
   structure and contingency, 20
   transboundary water pollution, 552–53
   Tunisia protests, 454–55
   workers' strikes, 200–201
   Yellowstone, 548
Palestine, 346
palliative care, 434
pandemic, 431
Panopticon, 160
paradox of convenience, 492, 494
Paramount, 505
parasocial relationships, 511–12
parenthood
   co-parenting strategies, 313
   delaying, 314
   gay and lesbian families and, 323
   nuclear and traditional families, 305–7
   single-parent families, 309–11
parenting styles, 115, 308
Paris Agreement, 551–52, 555
Pariser, Eli, 509
Parks, Rosa, 479
parliamentary systems, 457
parole, 162
   federal sentencing and, 164
parole officers, 151
Parsons, Talcott, 31, 39, 296–97
   on moral education, 377
   on sick role, 423
participant-observation, 55
party systems, 182, 184
patriarchy, 264
   challenging, 275–78
patrilineal, 298
peasants, 467–68
*Pedigree* (Rivera), 397
peer groups
   old age and, 116
   parenting styles and, 115
   resocialization and, 113
   socialization and, 110–11
peer pressure, 110
peer review, 45
penicillin, 362
Pentecostalism, 350–51

performance
  gender, 258
  social self and, 119–20
peripheral nations, 192
persuasive power, 452–53
Phelps, Michael, 4
*The Philadelphia Negro* (Du Bois), 37
the Philippines, 438
pink-collar jobs, 270, 273
PISA. *See* Programme for International Student Assessment
play stage, 108
plea-bargaining, 163
PM 2.5. *See* fine particulate matter
polarization
  political, 75
  social, 121–22, 506, 508
police, 151, 156
  broken-windows theory and, 157–58
  discretion in work of, 158
police procedural stories, 166–67
policing, 156–59
political action committees (PACs), 461
political advertising, 450, 507
political economy, 462
political opportunity structure, 478–79
political power, 454
politics
  Black people and, 222–23
  contentious, 201
  defining, 452
  democracy and, 454–61
  of division, 459
  economy and, 461–66
  environment and, 542–46
  feminism and, 277
  geopolitics, 464, 466
  of immigration, 245–48
  media and, 502–9
  religion and, 352–55
  sociology and, 475
  as struggle for influence, 451–54
  symbolic, 479
*The Politics of Climate Change* (Giddens), 539
poll taxes, 458

pollution, 32
  air, 530–31, 534–36
  water, 534, 536, 552–53
polytheism, 332
popular culture, 93
popular sovereignty, 454
population growth, 532–33
post-colonial theory, 42
*Postcolonial Thought and Social Theory* (Go), 465
post-industrialism, 469, 471, 499, 514
Postmates, 406
post-secular society, 364–65
poverty, 8, 10
  allostatic load and, 418
  childhood, 310
  environmental hazard exposure and, 528–29
  global, 189–90
  single-parent families and, 310
  in United States, 188–89
power, 18, 131
  Amazon rainforest and, 554
  *The Bachelor* and, 203
  coercive, 452–53
  culture and, 77–86
  Dakota Access pipeline protests, 544–45
  defining, 17, 451–52
  Electoral College and, 482
  family names and, 324
  FTX and, 518
  gender and, 264–78
  genetic testing and, 442
  persuasive, 452
  police procedurals and, 166
  political, 454
  privacy and, 507–8
  racial and ethnic identity and, 248
  science and humanities and, 407
  science and religion and, 334–35
  state, 452
  types of, 452–53
  in workplace, 399–400
*The Power Elite* (Mills), 462–64
precarious housing, 10
*The Presentation of Self in Everyday Life* (Goffman), 40
presidential systems, 457

preventive medical care, 434
price-gouging, 141–42
primary deviance, 148
primary groups, 123, 125
primary school, 384–85
primogeniture, 301
Prison Activist Resource Center, 151
prison-industrial complex, 165
prison population rates, 164
prison sentences, 164–65
privacy, 507–8
private schools, 383–84
privilege, 18, 37, 60, 98
  *The Bachelor* and, 202
  defining, 19
  education and, 380–81
  Electoral College and, 482
  environmental movements and, 550
  family names and, 324
  Flint, Michigan water contamination, 538–39
  FTX and, 517
  genetic testing and, 443
  Google and, 497–98
  intersectionality and, 277
  Irish Americans becoming white, 229
  of majority groups, 228–29
  marketing to super-rich and, 183
  marriage and, 303
  old age and, 420
  pink-collar jobs and, 273
  police procedurals and, 166
  punishment and plea-bargaining and, 163
  racial, 277
  racial and ethnic identity and, 249
  science and humanities and, 407
  science and Matthew effect and, 359–60
  Scopes Monkey Trial and, 366
  white, 228
  in workplace, 399–400
probation officers, 151
profane objects, 338–39
professionalization, 429–30
program claims, 474

Programme for International Student Assessment (PISA), 391, 393
prompt engineer, 500–501
propaganda, 82
property crime, 152
props, 12
prosecuting attorneys, 151
proselytizing, 346, 353
*The Protestant Establishment* (Baltzell), 220
Protestantism, 348–49
Protestant Reformation, 343–44
*The Protocols of the Elders of Zion*, 82
Provo, Utah, 336, 338
pseudoscience, 361
public bathrooms, 267
Public Enemy, 92
Public Facilities Privacy & Security Act (2016) (North Carolina), 267
public health, 431–33
public health education, 431–32
public health policy, 432–33
public opinion, 457–58
public religion, 353–54
*Public Religion in the Modern World* (Casanova), 354
public safety campaigns, 81
public schools, 383–84
public shaming, 514
public sociology, 57
public spaces
  multiracial families and, 321
  sexual exclusion in, 272, 274–75
  subcultures and, 91
public sphere, 502
Puerto Rico, 225
Pullman Company, 201
punishment, 160, 163–65
  as morality display, 161–62
  treatment and, 162
push polls, 459
Putnam, Robert, 481

qualitative methods, 51
quantitative methods, 49–50
queer identities, 283–84
queer theory, 42–43
quest culture, 351

race, 229
  advertising and, 279, 281
  allostatic load and, 418
  biology and, 211–12
  biomedical research and, 419
  changing understandings over time of, 212–13
  conflict and, 42
  COVID-19 pandemic and, 416, 418
  defining, 210
  ethnicity and, 214
  health inequality and, 416
  income inequality and, 399
  interracial marriage, 320, 322
  language and, 212–13
  multiracial families, 320–21
  official government data and, 216–17
  policing and, 158–59
  single-parent families and, 310
  social construction of, 42, 211–14
  stereotypes and, 212
  in United States, 214–27
*Race, Crime, and the Law* (Kennedy), 159
race-based medicine, 418–19
*Race in a Bottle* (Kahn), 419
race riots, 221
racial bias, 231
  measuring teaching effectiveness and, 392
  policing and, 158–59
racial conflict, 232–34
racial determinism, 212–13
racial discrimination, 229–31
  in hiring, 13
racial integration
  multiracial families and, 321
  of sports, 14–15
Racial Integrity Act (Virginia), 322
racial privilege, 277
racial profiling, 158, 234
racial segregation, 229–31
racial steering, 230
racial violence, 234
racism, 479
Ramirez, Francisco, 376
random sample, 52

rationalization, 34–35
rational-legal authority, 453
reactivity, 55, 57
Reagan, Ronald, 8, 390
*Reclaiming Conversation and the Power of Talk in a Digital Age* (Turkle), 513
Red Crescent, 88
Red Cross, 88
redlining, 230
Red Power Movement, 218
Red Summer, 234
Reeves, Keanu, 237
reference groups, 125
reflection, 107
reflexivity, 29
  institutionalized, 424
Reform Party, 449
rehabilitation, 81, 162–64
relative deprivation, 176
relative mobility, 193
relativism, 364
reliability, 52
religion
  declining importance of, 348–49
  defining, 338
  elements of institutions, 338–40
  environment and, 541–42
  major, 340–47, 341*f*
  measuring commitment to, 337
  new forms, 350–52
  persistence of, 350–52
  politics and, 352–55
  public, 353–54
  sacred texts in, 333
  science coexistence with, 364–65
  as social institution, 336–47
  as way of knowing about world, 331–36
religious cosmologies, 332–34
religious fundamentalism, 354–55
religious proselytizing, 353
*Remaking a Life* (Watkins-Hayes), 422–23
remarriage, 318
remittances, 244–45, 315, 438
remote learning, 194
renewable energy, 543

representation
  mechanisms of, 458–61
  systems of, 456–58
representative, 53
reproductive labor, 434
*#Republic* (Sunstein), 121
Republican Party, 449
research methods, 10
  birth order effects and, 302
  critical literacy and, 47–49
  defining and measuring race and, 216–17
  indirect, 73
  measuring learning outcomes and teaching effectiveness, 392–93
  measuring religious commitment, 337
  measuring status attainment and social mobility, 194–95
  qualitative, 51
  quantitative, 49–50
  race-based medicine, 418–19
  sociological, 49–51
  urban sprawl measurement, 535–36
research population, 52
*Reservation Dogs* (television series), 105
*The Resident* (television show), 413
residential density, 536
residential segregation, 230
resistance, 18, 131
  Amazon rainforest and, 554
  *The Bachelor* and, 203
  to cultural power, 83–86
  Dakota Access pipeline protests, 544–45
  defining, 17
  Electoral College and, 483
  family names and, 324
  genetic testing and, 442
  police procedurals and, 166
  privacy and, 507–8
  racial and ethnic identity and, 248
  science and religion and, 334–35
resocialization, 113
resource mobilization theory, 476
retirement, 114, 116

Reuter, Peter, 157
Rice, Anne, 97
Rice, Tamir, 235
rigidity, 178
risk society, 527–31
ritual, 339
Rivera, Lauren, 397
Roberts, Dorothy, 419
Robin Hood Foundation, 9
*Roe v. Wade*, 266, 276
Rohingya Muslims, 233
role, 116
  defining, 119
  sex, 261*t*
  sick, 423–24
role conflict, 119
role strain, 119
Roman Catholic Church, 334–35, 343, 350
  in Africa, 345
romance, marketing of, 278–79, 281
Roman Empire, 343, 352
Roos, Patricia A., 273
Rosenfeld, Richard, 152
Ross, Fred, 478
Rothkopf, David, 463
Rousseau, Jean-Jacques, 175
Russia, 233
Rwanda, 233

*The Sacred Canopy* (Berger), 339
sacred objects, 338–39
sacred texts, 333
Saguy, Abigail C., 427
Said, Edward, 42, *43*
Saint-Domingue, 465
same-sex marriage, 266–67, 321, 323
Samoa, 131–32
sample, 52
Sampson, Robert, 48
sanctions, 76
Sanders, Bernie, 173–74
sandwich parents, 314–15
Sanger, Margaret, 275
Santa Anna, Antonio López de, 139
satisfaction
  job, 400, 402–4
  outside of work, 403–4

Saweetie, 237
#SayHerName, 234
Schiller, Herbert, 88
Schnaiberg, Allan, 537
Schneider, Joseph, 149
schools
  as childcare, 381–82
  colleges and universities, 385–86
  during COVID-19 pandemic, 384
  digital age and, 386–87
  elite students and jobs and, 397–98
  making friends and building networks in, 394–96
  national and international differences in performance in, 391, 394
  pecking orders in, 395–96
  primary and secondary, 384–85
  public and private, 383–84
  socialization and, 110–11
  social networks and, 396
  types of, 382–87
Schwartz, Pepper, 57
Schwinn, 404
science
  environment and, 541–42
  normative structure of, 359
  religion coexistence with, 364–65
  as social institution, 356–61
  sociology of, 358–61
  understandings of race and, 212–13
  as way of knowing about world, 331–36
science, technology, engineering, and mathematics (STEM)
  jobs in, 496
  social mobility and careers in, 197
  women's careers in, 357–58
science and technology studies, 361
*Scientific American* (magazine), 356, 419, 509
scientific cosmologies, 333–36
scientific knowledge, 363
scientific literacy, 356

# INDEX

Scopes Monkey Trial, 365–67
Scott, Rick, 407
scripts, 40
   gender, 257, 260
   sex, 260
sea levels, 526
secondary deviance, 148
secondary groups, 123, 125
secondary school, 384–85
second shift, 272
second wave of feminism, 276
sects, 343–44
secularism, 348–49
secularization thesis, 348–49
secular-rational values, 74
Sedgwick, Eve, 283
Seeger, Pete, 92
segregation, 227
   racial, 229–31
   residential, 230
Seidman, Steven, 42, 283
selection effect, 56–57
self
   looking-glass, 107
   social, 39, 107–9
*Self* (magazine), 248
self-assessment, 107
self-concept, 39
self-control, 80–81
self-expression values, 74
self-help, 81
selfhood, 106
semi-peripheral nations, 192
Sentencing Project, 151
separate spheres, 267–70
*Seven Up!* (film), 117
sex
   defining, 256
   roles, 261*t*
sexism, 262–64
   institutionalized, 270
sex scripts, 260
sexual harassment, 401
   in workplace, 272, 274–75, 400
sexuality
   cohabitation and, 312
   fluidity of, 283
   marketing of romance and, 278–79, 281
   social construction of, 278

sex work, 278, 280–81
sharing economy, 406
Shelley, Mary, 492
Shia Islam, 344
shyness, 429
sick role, 423–24
Silicon Valley, 128
Simmel, Georg, 122
*The Simpsons* (television show), 305, 306
Singapore, 127–28
   gum-chewing and, 139
   math education and, 393–94
single-parent families, 309–11, 310*f*
skepticism, 363
Skinner, B. F., 335
slash fanfiction, 97
Slatery, Herbert H., III, 141
slavery, 220–21, 465
   caste systems and, 179
Small, Albion, 5
smart manufacturing, 499
Smith, Adam, 334, 377–78, 491
   on inequality, 176
Smith, Al, 229
Snow, C. P., 407
snowball sample, 53
social anxiety disorder, 429
social capital, 130, 481
social change, 39, 472–81
   deviance and, 142–43
   inequality and, 198–202
social classes, 178
social conflict, 201–2
social control theory, 140
social criticism
   in music, 92
   school policy and, 384
   subcultures and, 91
social distancing, 60, 75
social eugenics, 275
social facts, 31
social host law (Massachusetts), 137
social interaction
   in digital age, 120–22
   norms and, 75
   parenting styles and, 115
   as performance, 119–20
   roles and, 119
   self shaped by, 107

socialism, 468–69
Socialist Labor Party, 469
socialization, 71
   adult, 112–16
   agents of, 109–12
   defining, 106
   deviance and, 146–47
   divorce, unemployment, and disruption and, 113–14
   education and, 376–77
   environment and, 540–41
   family and, 109–10, 115, 195, 299
   gender, 258
   life-course research on, 117
   media and, 111–12
   nature and nurture, 106–7
   peer groups and, 110–11
   retirement and old age, 114, 116
   school and peer groups, 110–11
   workplace and, 113
social media
   agenda-setting and, 503
   cancel culture and, 514–15
   deviance and, 147
   Goldilocks effect and, 121
   hate and intolerance on, 513
   LGBTQ youth and, 512
   polarization and, 121–22
Social Media Addiction Scale, 516
social mobility
   career planning and, 197
   culture and, 196
   defining, 192
   education and, 193–94
   family background and, 195–96
   measuring, 194–95
   social factors associated with, 193–96
   structural, 196, 198
   types of, 192–93
social movements, 472–74
   agenda-setting and, 503
   environmentalism, 546–47, 549
   formation and mobilization of, 475, 477–78
   getting noticed, 478–80
   success of, 480–81
social network, 129–30
   schools and, 396
   women and men and, 262

social polarization, 121–22, 506, 508
social policy, 199–200
social protest, music and, 92
social relationships
  inequality and, 175
  media and technology and, 511–16
social research
  defining, 44–45
  ethics and, 45–46
  gender bias in, 262–63
  goals of, 47
  human subject protection in, 46
  purpose and process, 44–59
social rules, 40
social science, 30
social scripts, 22
Social Security Act (1935), 199
social self, 39, 107–9
  performance and, 119–20
social solidarity, 481
social stigma, deviance and, 148–49
social structures, 40
  challenging, 21
  defining, 20
social support, 298–99
*The Social Transformation of American Medicine* (Starr), 429
social trust, in doctors, 430
society
  technology and, 491–94
  tight and loose, 146
  world, 88
*Society in America* (Martineau), 37
socioeconomic status, 184
sociological imagination
  critical questions and, 28–30
  defining, 7
  uses of, 22
sociological research methods, 49–51
sociology
  in America, 38–41
  Chicago School, 38–39
  classical, 31–33
  common sense difference from, 27
  contemporary, 44

  in criminal justice field, 151
  defining, 5
  discipline of, 8–10
  European canon, 33–36
  everyday knowledge and, 10–11
  forgotten founders in, 37
  as fundamental science, 30
  of health and illness, 415
  of job satisfaction, 400, 402–4
  majors in, 6
  medicine and, 435
  politics and, 475
  public, 57
  reasons for, 21–22
  of science, 358–61
  theory and contexts, 30–44
*Sociology of Education* (journal), 390
sodomy laws, 282
soft news, 504
solar power, 543
solidarity, 16, 36, 37, 56
  Amazon rainforest and, 555
  *The Bachelor* and, 202
  defining, 17
  Electoral College and, 483
  family names and, 324
  feminist politics and, 277
  genetic testing and, 443
  levels of, 60
  mechanical, 35–36
  medical settings and, 436
  national, 100
  organic, 35–36
  parenting styles and, 308
  police procedurals and, 166
  racial and ethnic identity and, 249
  between science and humanities, 407
  social, 481
  workers' strikes and, 200–201
  Yellowstone National Park and, 548
Soul Cycle, 404, 405
*The Souls of Black Folk* (Du Bois), 37
South Africa, 179–80
Southern Poverty Law Center, 82
South Korea, education in, 316–17
Soviet Union, 352, 469, 479
SpaceX, 495

Spanish-American War, 226
speech codes, 389–90
Speedwatch, 48
spinning, 404–5
sports
  mental health and, 4
  racial integration of, 14–15
Spotify, 506
standardized tests, 388, 390–91
standing claims, 474
Standing Rock Sioux Reservation, 218, 544
Stanford Prison Experiment, 124
Starr, Paul, 429
"Star-Spangled Banner" (song), 99–100
*Star Trek*, 97
state atheism, 352
*The State of Tennessee v. John Thomas Scopes*, 365–67
state power, 452
status, 116, 119
  measuring attainment of, 194–95
  systems of, 181–82
status group, 181
STEM. *See* science, technology, engineering, and mathematics
step-parents, 320
stereotypes, 79–80
  ethnocentrism and, 85
  gender, 260–61, 261*t*
  HIV-AIDS and, 425
  race and, 212
stigma
  deviance and, 148–49
  illness and, 425, 426*f*
  size and, 427
  social media and, 512
stigmatized out-groups, 125
stocks, 495–96
Stonewall Uprising, 284
stratification
  caste systems, 178–79
  class systems, 180–81
  comparative strategies and, 178
  defining, 177
  global, 189–92
  inequality and, 177
  measuring, 178

stratification (*continued*)
   types of, 177–84
   in United States, 184–89
straw polls, 458
street population, 9–10
strikes, 200–201
Strong Families Network, 295
structural mobility, 196, 198
structural strain theory, 475
structure, 20–21, 100, 131
   AI and, 493–94
   Amazon rainforest and, 554
   *The Bachelor* and, 204
   co-parenting strategies and, 313
   Electoral College and, 482
   environmental risk factors, 531–37
   family names and, 324
   gender conformance and, 287
   genetic testing and, 443
   indoor cycling and, 404–5
   Native American casinos, 219
   organizational, 127
   organ transplants and, 439
   police procedurals and, 167
   racial and ethnic identity and, 248
   science and humanities and, 408
   Scopes Monkey Trial and, 367
   Social Security and, 199
student ratings, 392
subcultures, 89, 91
   deviant, 143, 145
   graffiti, 144
suburbs, 534
Sunni Islam, 344
Sunstein, Cass, 121–22
*Superclass* (Rothkopf), 463
superego, 108–9
super-PACs, 461
surveillance, 81, *81*, 160
   digital, 499, 501
Survey of Chicago Catholics, 337
surveys, 54
survival values, 74
sustainability, 546–52
Sweden, life expectancy in, 415
symbolic ethnicity, 214
symbolic interactionism, 39–40
symbolic meaning, 71

symbolic politics, 479
symbolic production, 80

Taft-Hartley Act (1947), 201
Tahrir Square protests, 480, *480*
"The Talented Tenth" (Du Bois), 37
TaskRabbit, 406
Tatum, Beverly, 111
Tax Cuts and Jobs Act (2017), 441
Taylor, Breonna, 229, 231, 234
teaching, 387–94
   measuring effectiveness of, 392–93
   to tests, 391
technology, 490
   critical perspective on, 494
   economic dimensions of, 495–501
   frameworks for understanding, 491–92
   inequality and, 496, 498
   jobs and, 499–501
   paradox of convenience and, 492, 494
   privacy and, 507–8
   social relationships and, 511–16
   society and, 491–94
   voice and engagement among marginalized groups and, 508–9
temporary workers, 498
Tesla, 495
Tezuka, Osamu, 90
Thatcher, Margaret, 5
theodicy, 339
theoretical sample, 53
theory
   about difference, 41–42
   importance of, 31
   of the middle range, 41
   sociology history and, 30–44
therapists
   family, 300, 313
   marriage, 300
thinking relationally, 16–21
think tanks, 461
Thirteenth Amendment (United States), 221
Thomas theorem, 43, 211
Thunberg, Greta, 540–41, 547

tight societies, 146
TikTok, 94, 508, 510
Tilden, Samuel, 482
Tilly, Charles, 176, 201, 473
Time Warner, 505
Tokyo Olympics of 2021, 3–4
Tometi, Opal, 235
total institutions, 112
"tough on crime" policies, 164
Touraine, Alain, 469
trade
   drug, 157
   international, 464, 466
   slave, 465
traditional authority, 453
traditional family, 305–7
traditional values, 74
Trans-Amazonian highway, 553–54
transboundary water pollution, 552–53
transgender, 257, 267
transnational families, 315–17
travel marketing, 183
treadmill of production, 537
treatment, punishment and, 162
Treatment Advocacy Center, 440
triad, 123
triads (crime syndicates), 145
*The Truly Disadvantaged* (Wilson), 7–8
Trump, Donald, 79, 142, 449–50, 482, 510, 543–44, 552
   immigration and, 247
Tufecki, Zeynep, 509
Tunisia, 454–55
Turkle, Sherry, 120–21, 513
Tuskegee Institute, 46
Tutsis, 233
Twenty-fourth Amendment (United States), 458
23andMe, 442–43
Twitter (X), 69, 401, 503
   cancel culture and, 514
"The Two Cultures" (Snow), 407
Tyson, Neil deGrasse, 334

Uber, 405
Uberization, 400, 405–6
UCR. *See* Uniform Crime Reports

# INDEX

UCR Summary Reporting Program, 154
unemployment, 113–14
  educational attainment and, 29
  great resignation and, 403
  measuring rate of, 470
UNEP. *See* United Nations Environment Programme
*Unequal Childhoods* (Lareau), 15
*The Unfinished Revolution* (Gerson), 272
unhoused people, 9, 9–10
UN Human Rights Council, 121
Uniform Crime Reports (UCR), 152–54
United Farm Workers, 478
United Kingdom, multiculturalism and, 236–37
United Nations, 88, 233
  Declaration of Human Rights, 353
  Framework Convention on Climate Change, 551
  Senate, 456
  social policies and, 200
  South Africa and, 180
United Nations Educational, Scientific, and Cultural Organization, 211
United Nations Environment Programme (UNEP), 545
United States, 454, 479
  anti-immigrant movements in, 247
  Electoral College, 482–83
  health care system in, 434, 441
  immigration policy in, 240–42, 315
  inequality in, 184–85
  interracial marriage in, 320
  middle class in, 186–88
  poor in, 188–89
  prison population rate, 164
  racial and ethnic groups in, 214–27
  rates of immigration to, 240
  social policies and, 199–200
  stratification in, 184–89
  upper class in, 185–86

wealthy Chinese students in, 191
universalism, 359
universities, 385–86
  campus speech codes, 389–90
  as marriage markets, 396
University of Bologna, 385
*Up* (film series), 117
upper class, 185–86
upper-middle class, 186
urbanization, 32, 533–35
  internal migration and, 240
urban sprawl measurement, 535–36
US Census Bureau, 29, 441
  childhood poverty data from, 310
  defining and measuring race, 216
  family definition by, 296
  on median household income, 186
  on poverty levels, 188
  on racial and ethnic groups, 214–15, 215*t*
US Citizenship and Immigration Service (USCIS), 240–41
US Constitution
  Electoral College and, 482
  Equal Protection Clause, 323
  Fifteenth Amendment to, 458
  on Native American tribes, 219
  Nineteenth Amendment to, 458
  Thirteenth Amendment, 221
  Twenty-fourth Amendment to, 458
utopia, 335
Uyghurs, 233

vaccines, 432–33
Vaisey, Stephen, 72
validity, 52
values
  culture and, 72
  defining, 74
  globalization and, 88
  ideal culture and, 73–76
  shared, 77
  subcultures and, 91
  world culture and, 88–89

*Vampire Chronicles* series, 97
vandalism, 144
Velcro, 362
Venter, Craig, 211
Vergara, Sofía, 248–49
vertical occupational segregation, 271
vertical social mobility, 192
Viacom, 505
Viagra, 422
Violence Against Women Act, 155
violent crime
  against Black people, 221
  rates of, 152, 153*t*, 154, 164
Virginia, mask-wearing in, 138
Visa, 3
vocational schools, 378
Voltaire, 348
Vonn, Lindsay, 4
voting, 458, 460
  Electoral College and, 482–83
Voting Rights Act (1965), 266

Wagner Act (1935), 201
*Walden Two* (Skinner), 335–36
WalkScore, 536
The Walt Disney Company, 505
warehousing theory, 381
Warsaw Pact, 469
Washington, Booker T., 222–23
WASPs. *See* white Anglo-Saxon Protestants
wastefulness, as deviance, 547, 549–50
water pollution
  industrialization and, 536
  transboundary, 552–53
  urbanization and suburbanization and, 534
Waters, Mary, 244
Watkins-Hayes, Celeste, 422–23
Watson, James, 360
weak ties, 129
wealth, 185, 495–96
  inherited, 186
*The Wealth of Nations* (Smith), 334, 377–78
The Weather Channel, 329
weather extremes, 526

Weber, Max, 5, 33–36, *35*, 39, 331, 339
  on bureaucracy, 126
  on class systems, 181
  on credentialism, 379
  political economy and, 462
  on power, 451–53
Weinstein, Harvey, 401
"We Shall Overcome" (song), 92
Western, Bruce, 165
*Westworld* (television show), 494
WhatsApp, 499
*What's Wrong with Fat?* (Saguy), 427
White, Shad, 407
white Anglo-Saxon Protestants (WASPs), 220, 229
white-collar crime, 155–56
white-collar workers, 187
#WhiteLives Matter, 509–10
white people, 219–20, 229
white privilege, 228
WHO. *See* World Health Organization
whooping cough, 432–33
"Why Are All the Black Kids Sitting Together in the Cafeteria?" and Other Conversations about Race (Tatum), 111
Wikipedia, 509
Wilberforce, Samuel, 335
wildfires, 525
"wild geese" families, 316–17
Williams, Johnny, 419
Williams, Raymond, 70
Wilson, James Q., 157
Wilson, William Julius, 7–8
*Wired* (magazine), 509
Wohl, Richard, 511
wolves, 548
women
  care work and, 434

  social networks and, 262
  STEM careers, 357–58
  voting and, 275
"Women and Social Stratification" (Acker), 262–63
women's movement, 275–78
Women's Rights Convention, 275
Woods, Tyler, 237
Woodstock Music Festival, 92
Woolgar, Steve, 361
*Word of Mouth* (Ferguson), 71
work, 398
  artificial intelligence and, 400
  care, 434–40
  education and, 374, 377–79
  globalization and, 400
  independent contractors, 405–6
  inequality and, 176–77
worker productivity, 499
workers' strikes, 200–201
working poor, 189
workism, 403
workplace
  bullying in, 400
  COVID-19 pandemic impacts on, 399
  digital surveillance in, 499, 501
  health and, 417
  multiculturalism in, 238–39
  power, privilege, and inequality in, 399–400
  sexual exclusion in, 272, 274–75
  sexual harassment in, 272, 274–75, 400
  socialization and, 113
*The World and Africa* (Du Bois), 38
World Bank, 127, 200
World Christian Fundamentals Association, 366

World Economic Forum, 500
World Health Organization (WHO), 415–16, 421, 423, 431, 434, 440
*The World is Flat* (Friedman), 31
world society, 88
world systems theory, 190
World Union of Progressive Judaism, 350
World Wildlife Fund, 549
World Wrestling Federation (WWF), 131
Wrigley, William, 139
Wuhan, China, 530
WWF. *See* World Wrestling Federation

X. *See* Twitter
xenophobia, 85
Xi Jinping, 191

yakuza, 145
Yale Program on Climate Change Communication, 330, 364
Yellowstone National Park, 548
Yoon Suk Yeol, 77, *78*, 84
YouTube, 94
Yuan Dynasty, 179

zero-tolerance policies, 158
Zimbardo, Philip, 124
Zimmerman, George, 210, 235
Zionism, 343
zone of permitted variation, 140
Zoom, 387
Zoungrana, Paul, 345
Zuckerberg, Mark, 29, 501
Zuckerman, Harriet, 359–60